# CONTRACT LAW IN IRELAND

## FOURTH EDITION

### BY

**ROBERT CLARK**
B.A., LL.M., Ph.D.
Barrister-at-Law (King's Inns)
Statutory Lecturer in Law, Faculty of Law
University College, Dublin

ROUND HALL SWEET & MAXWELL
DUBLIN 1998

Published in 1998 by
Round Hall Sweet & Maxwell
Brehon House, 4 Upper Ormond Quay,
Dublin 7.
Typeset by
Carrigboy Typesetting Services, Durrus, County Cork.
Printed by
ColourBooks, Dublin.

ISBN 1–899738–91–6 (Hardback)
ISBN 1–899738–83–5 (Paperback)

A catalogue record for this book
is available from the British Library.

To Alice

# Preface

My objective in writing and updating the various texts that now find shape in the form of the fourth edition of *Contract Law in Ireland* is to provide readers with an accurate and yet accessible guide to Irish contract law. While Irish case law is not voluminous and the Oireachtas does not intervene in private law areas in any systematic way, some Irish case law provides a quite different slant on common law and equitable concepts. The case law on unconscionable bargains and undue influence is the most obvious instance of this, for it is clear that Irish judges were and are more interventionary than their English counterparts. More recent instances can be found in the tangled jurisprudence over "subject to contract" and the strangely enduring, but somewhat elliptical, references in Irish case law to duties of good faith in contract. However, although in the main Irish contract law is still heavily influenced by the judicial utterances of the English, there are a significant number of other influences which are reshaping Irish contract law. The Constitution and constitutional imperatives are controlling the way in which statutory powers are exercised via contract, the legitimate expectation doctrine is strong in Irish law, and the impact of E.U. legislation, particularly the Unfair Contract Terms Directive, are the most prominent factors in assisting in the creation of a distinct Irish jurisprudence.

In the fourth edition, a number of significant English and Commonwealth developments are collected and put into an Irish context. *Barclays Bank v. O'Brien* and the aftermath, the decision in *Pan Atlantic*, which has a particular resonance with some of the Irish cases decided in the 1980s and the important decisions of the House of Lords in *Malik v. BCCI* and *Ruxley Engineering*, spring readily to mind. Notable Irish decisions, particularly on part performance, illegal contracts and restitution, are also addressed. The Oireachtas has been relatively active since 1992 and these developments, particularly on consumer credit and unfair contract terms are noted.

I would like to thank the staff of Round Hall Sweet & Maxwell for all the assistance given to me in producing this edition of the book. They have been enthusiastic, courteous and most helpful. My colleague Tony Kerr continues to assist in tracking down unreported judgments. My students are also to be thanked for allowing me to air my thoughts and prejudices before an invited yet captive audience. All errors and omissions are mine but I do not accept any liability for any shortcoming contained in this text. The law is stated as of June 30, 1998.

ROBERT CLARK
MOUNT MERRION
*August 1998*

# Table of Contents

Contents

# Table of Cases

# Table of Statutes

### 3. Acts of the Oireachtas

# Table of European Material

# Table of Constitutional Provisions

# Part 1

# Formation of a Binding Contract

# 1 The Rules of Offer and Acceptance

## Introduction

The primary characteristic of a binding contract is one of bargain. Generally, the common law rules on the enforceability of promises entitle members of society to expect that a promise will be enforced by the courts or made the subject of monetary compensation because the promise was made in the context of an exchange relationship. In other words, the common law does not normally make a promise binding as a contract simply because the promise was made. By the same token once a promise is made in return for another promise or some requested action it is generally unnecessary for the promise to be made or evidenced in writing.

There are of course several circumstances in which the bargain model is not truly applicable. In many instances the contract is not the result of a negotiated bargain, as in the case of public utility companies such as the electricity and communications industries where the terms of supply are fixed either by legislation or standard contracts which leave little or no room for variation. The bargain model is also incapable of explaining several situations where the courts have upheld a contract while at the same time finding it difficult or even unnecessary to locate a true exchange between the parties. In general however, the common law recognises enforceable contractual arrangements are in place even when the agreement is purely verbal and the terms of the contract have not been reduced into writing. A striking illustration of this kind of agreement is provided by the recent case of *Pernod Ricard & Comrie plc v. FII Fyffes plc*.[1] The defendants were the registered owners of shares in Irish Distillers plc. The plaintiffs placed a general offer to purchase the shares owned or controlled by the defendants, this agreement being verbally negotiated over a two-day period, the parties eventually reaching agreement on price and the method of payment and shaking hands on the deal. Costello J. rejected submissions that the agreement was conditional on a written contract being executed, observing:

> "It is true that no written form of irrevocable undertaking had been produced for the defendant's inspection at that time [of agreement] and that it was understood that one would be executed [the following day]. But the contract which the parties had entered into was not required by law to be in writing and the execution of a written document was not made a condition precedent to the defendant's liability under the agreement; it was merely a means of implementing a concluded bargain."

---

[1]  Unreported, High Court, October 21, 1988.

3

The Supreme Court[2] upheld Costello J. and decreed specific performance of a multi-million pound take-over transaction even though no contemporaneous document evidencing the agreement existed.

In some circumstances, however, there are formal statutory requirements which must be complied with if a contract is to be enforceable and it is increasingly common to require written documents if consumer transactions are to be enforced. In general however, the common law system utilises a minimal number of formal devices.

## Prima Facie Rules of Interpretation

As a result it has become necessary to create rules on the formation of contracts that enable judges to view everyday incidents and actions as having legal consequences. The rules of offer and acceptance for example are designed to determine whether the parties have reached agreement on the subject matter, price, and other material terms, or whether the parties remain locked in negotiation, still edging their way towards agreement.

Many contractual relationships are forged almost instantaneously. By stepping on a bus or buying a newspaper or a lottery ticket[3] for example we enter into a contract, and in this context it seems artificial to isolate these transactions into separate stages. Lord Wilberforce remarked during a complex dispute where it seemed obvious to him that a bargain should be enforced that the only problem was to make the facts amenable to the rules on formation.

> "It is only the precise analysis of this complex of relations into the classical offer and acceptance with identifiable consideration that seems to present difficulty, but this same difficulty exists in many situations of daily life, *e.g.* sales at auction, supermarket purchases; boarding an omnibus; purchasing a train ticket, tenders for the supply of goods; offers of rewards; acceptance by post. . . . These are all examples which show that English law, having committed itself to a rather technical and schematic doctrine of contract, in application takes a practical approach, often at the cost of forcing the facts to fit uneasily into the marked slots of offer, acceptance and consideration."[4]

This observation can also be applied to the rules of offer and acceptance applied by the Irish courts for they are in substance the same.

---

[2] Unreported, Supreme Court, November 11, 1988.
[3] *Carroll v. An Post National Lottery Company* [1996] 1 I.R. 443.
[4] *The Eurymedon* [1974] 1 All E.R. 1015 at 1020.

# Offer

An offer may be defined as a clear and unambiguous statement of the terms upon which the offeror is willing to contract, should the person or persons to whom the offer is addressed decide to accept. It is important to distinguish an offer from a statement made without intending that a contract result if the person to whom it is made indicates his assent to those terms. Such statements are often called "an invitation to treat". In such a case the courts often view the response itself to be an offer which can in turn be accepted or rejected. The distinction is not always easy to draw but litigation has produced a series of prima facie rules which are approximate guides to the student.

## *(1) Auction sales*

Under section 58(2) of the Sale of Goods Act 1893 a sale by auction is complete when the auctioneer announces its completion, normally by the fall of the hammer. It is clear then that it is the bidder who makes the offer and that the offer is accepted or rejected by the auctioneer. The auctioneer who announces that a sale will take place at a certain time does not make an offer to sell goods which will be accepted by arriving at the saleroom. The auctioneer then cannot be liable in contract if the sale does not take place: see *Harris v. Nickerson*.[5] On the other hand an announcement by an auctioneer that a sale will take place "without reserve" may give rise to liability if bidding commences but the auctioneer refuses to sell to the highest bidder.

By announcing that he will sell to the highest bidder the auctioneer is said to make an offer which is accepted by attending the sale and bidding, although the person making the highest bid at the time of refusal to sell is thought to be the only person entitled to recover damages: see *Tully v. Irish Land Commission*.[6] Therefore the statement that goods will be sold "without reserve" has two consequences; it invites persons to make offers to purchase the property or the goods in question and it constitutes an offer made by the auctioneer for which he will be liable in damages should he refuse to knock down the goods after bidding has started. Of course if the auctioneer has been authorised to sell "without reserve" and the refusal to sell is the result of the owner's change of mind the auctioneer should be indemnified by the owner for any damages he has had to pay.

On the measure of damages that may be recovered, the leading English case of *Warlow v. Harrison*[7] indicates that the correct approach to be adopted is to measure the difference between the highest bona fide bid, made presumably by the plaintiffs, and the price at which the hammer falls. This will not, however, always be possible (for example, where the goods are withdrawn) and other

---

5  (1873) L.R. 8 Q.B. 286.
6  (1961) 97 I.L.T.R. 174.
7  (1859) 1 E. & E. 309.

cases, such as the leading Australian case of *Ulbrick v. Laidlaw*,[8] lend support for the view that damages will tend to be nominal. Another approach would require the court to speculate on the full market value of the property in question and award the difference between this figure and the plaintiff's bid.

## (2) Display of goods

In the case of *Minister for Industry and Commerce v. Pim*[9] a coat was displayed in a shop window with a notice declaring the cash price and indicating that credit terms were available. It was an offence to offer for sale goods on credit terms without specifically setting out those terms and the shopkeeper was prosecuted. The prosecution failed. It was held that to display goods with a price tag is not to offer them for sale. This display constitutes an invitation to treat, an action tantamount to inviting offers from members of the public. This rule is said to protect shopkeepers who would otherwise be obliged to sell goods to anyone who saw them in the window and came into the shop demanding that they can be purchased. If this represented the law a shopkeeper who had already sold the goods to another person would be obliged to sell them a second time, making him liable in contract or tort to the first buyer.

On the other hand, if I camp outside a department store for three days waiting for the January sale to commence in the hope of purchasing a furniture suite displayed in the window with a sale tag of £5 attached, it would be monstrous if the salesman could lawfully refuse to sell it to me when the sale began. Remember that these are only prima facie rules and in such a case the display would be regarded as an offer. See the American case of *Lefkowitz v. Gt. Minneapolis Surplus Store*.[10] In the leading English case of *Pharmaceutical Society v. Boots Cash Chemists*[11] the Court of Appeal held that when a shopper takes goods from a shelf he does not accept an offer made by the storekeeper when he displays the goods. The acts of appropriation and approaching the cash desk constitute an offer by the prospective purchaser which is accepted by the cashier.

Many of these cases are not contract cases at all but are criminal prosecutions for misleading advertising. Some statutes make it an offence to "expose for the purpose of sale" which would catch acts of display: see *Minister for Industry and Commerce v. Pim* itself. Section 1 of the Registration of Potato Growers and Potato Packers Act 1984 defines sell so as to include "agree to sell, expose for sale, invite an offer to buy and offer to sell."

## (3) Advertisements

In most cases an advertisement is considered to be an invitation to treat, so if an advertisement for goods appears in a newspaper a person writing to order

---

[8] [1924] V.L.R. 247.
[9] [1966] I.R. 154.
[10] 86 N.W. 2d 689 (1957).
[11] [1953] 1 Q.B. 401.

those goods cannot sue in contract if the vendor replies that he is out of stock and cannot meet the order. The rationale behind this rule is the same as that mentioned in relation to display of goods cases. In the English case of *C.A. Norgren Co. v. Technomarketing*[12] Walton J. refused to make out a committal order against one of the defendants for allegedly breaching an undertaking given to the High Court that the defendants would not "make, offer for sale, sell or distribute" items that were the subject of copyright. The defendants had distributed a price list and brochure which included an item covered by the undertaking. Walton J. upheld the contention of the defendant that, in general terms, the distribution of advertising material constituted an invitation to treat and was not an offer.

Consumer protection legislation in Ireland however would make a person who invites offers by way of false or misleading statements as to price guilty of a criminal offence; see section 7 of the Consumer Information Act 1978 which amends the provisions of the Merchandise Marks Acts 1887–1970. Specific legislation is in force[13] which requires the supplier of credit facilities in respect of goods, services, accommodation, or facilities of any description, to provide information on the annual percentage rate of charge applicable to the goods, etc., in question.

An advertisement will, however, be considered to be an offer if the court is convinced that it is seriously intended to be binding should persons come forward prepared to act on it. Such contracts are known as *unilateral* contracts. In normal cases where a contract exists both parties are bound. These contracts are called *bilateral contracts*. On the other hand, an advertisement may bind the party issuing the advertisement without creating any concurrent obligation upon any other person. The leading English case of *Carlill v. Carbolic Smoke Ball*[14] is an example of a unilateral contract in which an advertisement was declared to be an offer. The defendants manufactured a proprietary medicine that was advertised to be so efficient that should anyone catch influenza after purchasing and using it they would be entitled to £100. As a mark of the manufacturers sincerity, the advertisement continued, £1,000 was deposited with a bank to meet any claims. Mrs. Carlill read the advertisement, used the medicine but caught influenza nevertheless. The advertisement was held to be an offer and Mrs. Carlill entitled to £100.

An interesting if somewhat inconclusive illustration of this analysis can be found in the case of *Kennedy v. London Express Newspapers*.[15] Readers of the Daily Express were invited to become registered readers of the newspaper and induced to do so by an offer of free accident insurance for the year 1929. The plaintiff's wife was registered in 1929 and the offer was renewed for the year 1930, by advertisement in the newspaper, registration not being needed if the reader was registered during 1929. The plaintiff's wife died in an accident

---

[12] *The Times*, March 3, 1983.
[13] Consumer Credit Act 1995, s.31.
[14] [1893] 1 Q.B. 256.
[15] [1931] I.R. 532; *Lowden v. Accident Insurance Co.* (1904) 43 I.L.T.R. 277.

during 1930 and the plaintiff sought to recover the insurance payable under an alleged contract but the defendant claimed that one of the conditions had not been met by the deceased, that is, taking the newspaper on a daily basis. The defendants conceded that their advertisements constituted an offer to Mrs. Kennedy, which in order to be validly accepted, required Mrs. Kennedy to register and take the newspaper on a daily basis. Kennedy C.J. held that the contract had been formed in Ireland, the valid act of acceptance being the placing of an order with a local newsagent.

Two further cases, possessing superficially similar facts but differing conclusions, are instructive. In the first case, *Wilson v. Belfast Corporation*,[16] an unauthorised newspaper report which indicated that the Council would pay half wages to any employee who enlisted during the Great War was held incapable of being an offer. An advertisement in similar terms, posted by the employer on his own premises, was held in *Billings v. Arnott*[17] to be an offer which was accepted by an employee when he enlisted. The defendants argued that when their representative attempted to dissuade the employee from enlisting this was not sufficient to constitute a retraction of the offer. The important point to note about *Wilson v. Belfast Corporation* is that the newspaper report was not intended to be the medium by which the local authority intended to communicate with its employees and, as such, it would be premature to characterize a preliminary initiative of this kind as an offer. In the case of *Tansey v. The College of Occupational Therapists Ltd.*,[18] the plaintiff unsuccessfully attempted to build a contract between herself and the defendant by utilizing the *Carlill* decision. Ms. Tansey had enrolled as a student at St. Joseph's College, Dun Laoghaire, in the hope that she would successfully complete a course of study which would result in the award of a Diploma by the defendant, a professional body that set an examination for students and recognised, *inter alia*, St. Joseph's College as a competent institution to educate students. Ms. Tansey, upon enrolment, was given a handbook which stated that students would have a right to sit two repeat examinations if unsuccessful. There were disputed facts about whether the handbook had been amended by an erratum slip but the repeat rule was revised so as to give one repeat examination only. The plaintiff claimed that the defendant had a contractual relationship with the plaintiff, concluded via the agency of St. Joseph's College, after the plaintiff had offered to enrol as a student in the college. The plaintiff contended that her offer was accepted by the defendant when their agents handed her a copy of the defendant's manual, the contract being concluded on the terms of the (unamended) manual. Murphy J. rejected this submission, holding that *Carlill* did not assist the plaintiff because she was not aware of any offer made by the defendant when she enrolled in the college in respect of multiple rights of examination re-sits. The manual, as such, was intended to convey information and not to constitute an offer to

---

[16] (1921) 55 I.L.T.R. 205.
[17] (1945) 80 I.L.T.R. 50.
[18] Unreported, High Court, August 27, 1986.

contract. In contrast, a majority of the English Court of Appeal, in *Bowerman v. Association of British Travel Agents Ltd*.[19] held that a notice displayed on the premises of ABTA holiday tour operators could constitute an offer made by ABTA, so that when a specific ABTA member became insolvent ABTA were held bound by a statement in the notice that clients would be completely reimbursed for wasted expenditure. Acceptance of the offer was constituted by booking a holiday through an ABTA member. While the notice was held to be a mixture of "information, promise, disclaimer and reassurance", the majority of the Court of Appeal held that on this point the specific promise was clear enough so as to come within the *Carbolic Smoke Ball* case. Hirst L.J. dissented, viewing the entire notice as descriptive rather than contractual in character.

### (4) Tenders

When a manufacturer or a local authority issues advertisements soliciting tenders, whether it be to supply goods or build a school for example, the advertisement is an invitation to treat. The tender setting out the terms upon which the supplier or builder is prepared to contract constitutes an offer. There is no obligation upon the offeree to accept any of the tenders unless he has promised in the statement inviting tenders to accept the lowest figure. In these instances the situation is amenable to the collateral contract analysis that is found in auction sales "without reserve", and, as the "sealed bid" case of *Harvela Investments Ltd. v. Royal Trust Co. of Canada and Outerbridge*[20] illustrates, there can be a substantial remedy in appropriate circumstances. Here, the first defendant invited the plaintiff and the second defendant to submit sealed bids to purchase shares which the first defendant held as trustee, offering to accept the highest bid. The second defendant made a bid which was lower than that of the plaintiff but he added a referential clause, *i.e.* he agreed to pay $101,000 more than any higher bid submitted, if any. The first defendant accepted the referential bid. In the House of Lords the plaintiff was able to overturn the sale. The first defendant, in promising to sell to the highest bidder, was not simply issuing an invitation to tender – an invitation to negotiate. As Lord Diplock said, the statement was a unilateral or "if" contract issued to the two potential bidders. There was thus an obligation to sell to the highest bona fide bidder. In these circumstances the referential bid was not acceptable because the unilateral contract was to invite fixed bids rather than "auction-type" bids.

In some instances the bidder does not, however, have all the advantages of a unilateral offeror, who is normally free to retract his bid at any time prior to acceptance. In many tender documents there may be a clause which forbids retraction by the bidder at any time after it has been delivered, or opened, as the case may be. These clauses have been held effective in the Supreme Court of Canada.[21] However, these decisions are exceptional and in most instances the

---

[19] *The Times*, November 24, 1995.
[20] [1986] A.C. 207.
[21] *R., in Right of Ontario v. Ron Engineering & Construction* (1981) 119 D.L.R. (3d) 267; *Calgary v. Northern Construction* [1988] 2 W.W.R. 193.

intending contractor will be free to disregard a tender altogether. The recent Canadian case of *Yorkton Flying Services Ltd. v. Saskatchewan*[22] indicates that while there may be circumstances where a trade custom may create a right for the most competitive tenderer to obtain the contract, a so called "privilege" clause, giving the offeree the right not to award the contract to the lowest tenderer, will prevail. However, if there is a previous relationship between the contractor and the employer and invitations to tender are invited, a general invitation of this kind may oblige the employer to consider a particular tender if the invitation is specific and others are considered, as a matter of contract not mere expectation.[23]

### (5) Agreement on price in sale of land cases

While it is sometimes said that there is no difference in approach to be adopted in various kinds of negotiation, some judges do qualify this to a limited extent: see *Bigg v. Boyd-Gibbins Ltd.*[24] Practical considerations may come into the equation. Given that contracts for the sale of land are often negotiated over a prolonged period of time and given that conveyancing practice is often complicated and protracted it is sometimes stated that there is a presumption against mere agreement on price constituting a binding contract. *Harvey v. Facey*[25] is the case most often cited in this respect. The appellants telegraphed "will you sell us Bumper Hall Pen Telegram lowest cash price." The respondents telegramed "Lowest cash price for Bumper Hall Pen £900." The appellants replied that they would pay that price. The appellants action failed. The Privy Council held that the respondents telegram was only a statement of the price they would be prepared to accept should they decide later to sell. If the correspondence is clear and unequivocal, however, there is no reason why the courts will not hold an agreement to have been made although enforceability will depend on compliance with the Statute of Frauds (Ireland) 1695.

The action in *Harvey v. Facey* failed because there was no indication that the sellers wanted to assent to a sale of their property. The negotiations were still in their early stages. In the leading Irish case of *Boyers & Co. v. Duke*[26] the plaintiff wrote asking for the lowest quotation the defendants could make for 3,000 yards of canvas. The defendants wrote that the lowest price was $4^5/8$ d. per yard. The plaintiffs replied that they would accept this "offer". The defendants then realised that they had underestimated the price and refused to make up the fabric at the price quoted. Lord O'Brien C.J., following *Harvey v. Facey*, said of the plaintiffs' second letter that "it is not the acceptance of an offer because the letter to which it was a reply was a quotation and not an offer." It should be noted that the purported letter of acceptance itself recog-

---

[22] [1995] 9 W.W.R. 184.
[23] *Blackpool and Fylde Aero Club v. Blackpool Borough Council* [1990] 3 All E.R. 25; see Adams and Brownsword (1991) 54 M.L.R. 281.
[24] [1971] 2 All E.R. 183.
[25] [1893] A.C. 552.
[26] [1905] 2 I.R. 617.

nised that no binding contract was concluded by it because the plaintiffs gave the names of referees who would vouch for their commercial reliability.

## Acceptance

Acceptance may be defined as a final and unequivocal expression of agreement to the terms of an offer. To acknowledge that an offer has been received is not to accept the offer. In one English case an offer to build a freight terminal was made by tender. The offeror who quoted two prices, in the alternative, was told that his offer had been accepted. The "acceptor," however, did not indicate which price he was prepared to accept. It was held that the acceptance was invalid: see *Lind v. Mersey Docks & Harbour Board*.[27]

Acceptance is divided into two constituent parts.

### (1) The fact of acceptance

It is particularly obvious that acceptance may take place by performing a stipulated or requested action if the offer is a unilateral contract. So in *Billings v. Arnott*[28] the offer to pay half of any employee's wages who joined the defence forces was accepted by Billings when he performed the action requested. In commercial life offers are often accepted, not by stating "I agree" or "I accept" but by performance. An offeror who posts a letter asking for goods to be supplied will often find his offer has been accepted when the delivery van arrives to transfer the goods themselves. As a general rule acceptance may often take place by the offeree acting in response to the offer in the manner stipulated. See the English case of *Howard Marine Dredging v. A. Ogden*[29] and the older Irish case of *Saunders v. Cramer*.[30] In these circumstances a distinction must be drawn between acceptances which take place in the context of a unilateral offer, as distinct from an offer which is bilateral in form – that is, where the offeror is requesting a promise or undertaking as distinct from the thing itself. The leading Irish case is *Brennan v. Lockyer*.[31] An offer was posted in which the applicant requested certain benefits be made available to him by his trade union through enrolment. The union sent a certificate of enrolment which was posted in London and which arrived in Dublin, the certificate recording the fact of enrolment in London. The question arose whether the contract was completed in London, when the certificate was despatched, or in Dublin, when it was communicated to the union member. A distinction was drawn between an acceptance in relation to an offer asking for information and an offer that requests an act be done. When the acceptance consists of a

---

27 [1972] 2 Lloyd's Rep. 234.
28 (1945) 80 I.L.T.R. 50.
29 [1978] 2 W.L.R. 515.
30 (1842) 5 I.Eq.R. 12.
31 [1932] I.R. 100; *Clarke v. Gardiner* (1861) 12 I.C.L.R. 472.

promise this must be validly communicated, but if the offeror requests action, such as the posting of goods, no further communication is necessary.

Where the offer takes place within a bilateral contract framework, the courts are less willing to dispense with the communication of acceptance requirement, because absence of a final communication is often indicative of the parties still being locked in negotiation. In *Anglia Television & Others v. Cayton & Another*[32] it was held that before an offer could be accepted by conduct there must be some unequivocal offer which exists in a form capable of being accepted. There must also be subsequent conduct by way of acceptance which is exclusively applicable to the offer. The litigation involved a dispute between Anglia Television and other television companies who had allegedly interfered in contractual arrangements to allow Anglia Television to show the Bruno v. Tyson fight in 1989. The action failed because documents that were alleged to record the terms of the contract were inconsistent with the alleged contract. The court held that the subsequent conduct in question, namely, accepting fee payments were just as consistent with one-off payments for other bouts as an alleged contract to screen the fight.

Where, however, subsequent conduct can be added so as to show prejudicial reliance by the alleged offeree this will raise the likelihood that a contract by conduct will be imputed, as in the older Irish case of *McEvoy v. Moore*.[33] Ultimately the issue is whether the offeree intended to accept the offer. In the case of *Parkgrange Investments Ltd. v. Shandon Park Mills Ltd.*[34] Carroll J. held that there was no contract, despite the fact that the offeree signed a draft agreement. Carroll J. accepted the offeree's evidence that he signed the document as a preparatory measure, intending to use the document to obtain a capital gains tax clearance certificate if the offeree should at a later date resolve to accept the offer.

In some cases the courts have held that a contract exists because the parties have conducted themselves so as to indicate that they believed a contract existed. Where *animus contrahendi* is present the difficulty of accommodating the conventional rules on offer and acceptance will not always prove insurmountable. In *Wettern Electric Ltd. v. Welsh Development Agency*[35] the plaintiffs failed to reply to the defendants letter containing an offer and prescribed form of acceptance but instead began to perform under the terms of the offer. The court held that, by their conduct, the plaintiffs were offering to contract on the terms of the earlier letter written by the defendants. The defendants in turn, by their acquiescence, were held to have accepted this offer. While this conclusion is difficult to reconcile with the rule which allows an offeree the power to decide whether to decline or accept an offer – or indeed ignore it altogether – the result was a just one on the facts of the case.

---

[32] *The Independent*, February 14, 1989.
[33] (1902) 36 I.L.T.R. 99.
[34] Unreported, High Court, May 2, 1991.
[35] [1983] Q.B. 796.

Sometimes the form of the offer may, by implication, be prescribed by the terms of the invitation to treat. In *Harvela Investments Ltd. v. Royal Trust Co. of Canada and Outerbridge*[36] the vendors of shares invited bids from a small group of interested parties, promising to sell to the highest bidder. The bids, to be made by way of sealed offers, would all be opened together, at which time the highest bidder would be known. The second defendant made a fixed bid and a referential bid; *i.e.* agreed to pay either a fixed amount but, in the event that this bid was "topped" by another bidder, he agreed to pay $101,000 more than the highest rival bid. The House of Lords held that the vendor could not accept the referential bid and that the highest bona fide bidder was entitled to receive the shares.

**Counter-offers.** If a valid acceptance exists then the acceptor must be prepared to accept the terms proposed. As Murphy J. said in *Tansey v. The College of Occupational Therapists Ltd.*[37]:

> "it is difficult to conceive of an acceptance which would itself prescribe conditions. Ordinarily a communication in the course of negotiations leading to a contract which contains conditions not previously agreed by the party to whom the communication is addressed will fall to be treated as a new or counter-offer rather than an acceptance."

If the response by the offeree is not a clear and unconditional acceptance of the offer, the response itself may be described as a counter-offer which in turn may be accepted or ignored by the person to whom it is addressed. In *Swan v. Miller*[38] the defendants offered to sell their interest in a lease for £4,750 plus ground rent of £50. The plaintiffs replied that they would pay £4,450. This response to the defendants' offer was a counter-offer and as such was not itself capable of producing a binding contract.

The rules on counter-offers have another consequence. If an offer is met with a counter-offer then this response has the same effect as a rejection of the first offer. If the counter-offer is in turn refused the initial offer cannot now be accepted. If A offers to sell iron to B for £100 and B replies with an offer to purchase for £90 which A refuses, B cannot now hold A to his offer to sell for £100. The case of *Wheeler v. Jeffrey*[39] provides an excellent illustration of this. The parties were negotiating a contract under which the plaintiffs were to act as agent to sell the defendants goods. During correspondence no mention of a commencement date was made. On June 10, the plaintiffs wrote "we agree to carry on your agency as from 1st July next." On June 12, the defendants wrote their acceptance. The issue was whether a contract was formed on June 10, or 12. The Court of Appeal, reversing the Kings Bench Decision held the contract

---

[36] [1986] A.C. 207.
[37] Unreported, High Court, August 27, 1986.
[38] [1919] 1 I.R. 151.
[39] [1921] 2 I.R. 395.

formed on June 12. As Lord Chancellor Campbell pointed out, the mention of a commencement date added a new term to the negotiations. But for this the letter of June 10 would have been an acceptance, the law implying commencement within a reasonable time. It was possible for the defendants to reply that July 1 was not acceptable and had they done so there would have been no contract, in the absence of some later agreement.

However, the courts are quite sensitive to commercial practice and, rather than oblige the parties to recommence negotiations whenever a somewhat ambiguous response is made by an offeree, the courts do at least strive to keep the offer open if the offeree's response can be characterised as one in which the offeree seeks clarification or additional information from the offeror, although the boundary between a request for additional terms and an implied or express counter-offer is at times difficult to draw. If the offeree, however, is presented with a written offer and the offeree adds in additional material which has been negotiated, but omitted from the document, and the offeree then signs that document, as requested, the case of *Lynch v. The Governors, etc. of St. Vincents Hospital*[40] is authority for the proposition that this is a valid acceptance. If, however, the offeree adds new terms which have not been settled by antecedent negotiations then the leading case of *Gt. Northern Railway Co. v. Witham*[41] is still operative and the offeree's response will be a counter-offer.

Of course it becomes particularly difficult to tell when an offer or counter-offer has been made when negotiations consist of each party sending printed forms back and forth. This problem has been discussed by the English Court of Appeal in *Butler Machine Tool Co. v. Ex-Cell-O Corp.*[42] The sellers of a machine tool quoted a price of £75,000, the offer including a price variation clause under the terms of which the price would rise if costs rose for the sellers before delivery, which was to take place 10 months later. The buyers responded by placing an order on the foot of their own documentation which did not permit a price variation. The sellers did not reject this but returned a portion of the buyers' printed form acknowledging the contract took place on the buyers' conditions. The Court of Appeal held for the buyers; the sellers quotation was held to be an offer. The buyers' response was a counter-offer which was accepted by returning the slip. The fact that the sellers included a covering letter which reasserted their own terms of contract applied was ignored.

In a most helpful judgment in *Butler Machine Tool Co. v. Ex-Cell-O Corp.*, Lord Denning M.R. stressed that there are no hard and fast results in "battle of the forms" cases. In *Chichester Joinery v. John Mowlem*[43] the *Butler* case was distinguished. Mowlem was the successful main contractor for a construction project. The plaintiff, Chichester Joinery, tendered for sub-contracting work and their tender followed upon a written statement, dated March 14, by

---

[40] Unreported, High Court, July 31, 1987.
[41] (1873) L.R. 9 C.P. 16.
[42] [1979] 1 W.L.R. 401; *Buchanan v. Brook Walker & Co.* [1988] N.I. 116.
[43] (1987) 42 Build.L.R. 100; *Percy Trentham v. Archital Luxfer Ltd.* [1993] 1 Lloyd's Rep. 25.

Mowlem, which stated their requirements. Mowlem added that acceptance by Chichester Joinery of the proposed contract would be on Mowlem's terms and conditions as set out on the form and that any delivery made would constitute an acceptance of the order. Chichester Joinery responded by agreeing to the contract, in writing dated April 30, "subject to the conditions overleaf." It was held that at this point there was no contract – the Chichester Joinery letter was a counter-offer which destroyed the offer of March 14. However, when Chichester Joinery later delivered goods that were in accordance with the needs of Mowlem and Mowlem accepted the goods, the last act, the acceptance of the goods, was held to be an acceptance of the printed terms of Chichester Joinery, despite the earlier, inconclusive, "battle of the forms."

It is widely felt that the counter-offer rules are likely to result in a holding that no contract exists at all. Other solutions have been suggested; the United States Uniform Commercial Code, section 2–207 provides that an acceptance is effective even if it contains additional or different terms to those offered or agreed upon unless acceptance is expressly made conditional on assent to those new terms. The section goes on to specify that, as between merchants, new terms become part of the contract unless, *inter alia*, these terms materially alter the original offer. For an analysis of British legislation that also attempts to deal with the counter-offer in the context of international sales see the discussion in the *Butler Machine Tool* case. It is doubtful whether this kind of solution is really much of an improvement. There are problems of definition involved here that seem to be as difficult as the counter-offer rule itself. In any event the fact that the counter-offer rules are surmounted where necessary – see *Butler Machine Tool Co. v. Ex-Cell-O Corp.* itself – and the possibility that a contract will result from the conduct of the parties makes a finding that no contract exists rather unlikely. Even if this does happen relief by way of restitution is available.

### (2) Communication of acceptance

Once it is established that the offeree intends to accept the offer he generally has to go further and communicate his acceptance to the offeror.[44] The offeror may stipulate that it will be enough to communicate acceptance to an agent or he may dispense with, or "waive," the need for communication. This is impliedly the case when the offer is an offer to enter into a unilateral contract. Mrs. Carlill did not have to inform the Carbolic Smoke Ball Company that she intended to purchase and use their medicine; the employee in *Billings v. Arnott*[45] did not have to inform his employer that he intended to enlist. In these cases the act of acceptance and performance are one and the same.

It should be noted that the offeror can only waive the need for acceptance to be communicated to him; he cannot oblige the offeree to respond to the offer by stipulating that failure to communicate rejection of the offer shall be

---

[44] *Embourg Ltd. v. Tyler Group* [1996] 3 I.R. 480.
[45] (1945) 80 I.L.T.R. 50.

deemed consent. This is illustrated by the facts of *Russell & Baird v. Hoban*.[46] The defendant in Castlebar negotiated with the plaintiffs to purchase oatmeal. He asked the plaintiff's manager if they could supply a fixed amount. The plaintiff's manager, on his return to Dublin sent a note indicating that they could supply that amount. The note provided that "if this sale note be retained beyond three days after this date, it will be held to have been accepted by the buyer." The Court of Appeal held that there was no contract. Ronan L.J. observed "[n]o man can impose such conditions upon another. The document is conclusive evidence against the parties who sent it, that it was an offer which required acceptance." Because the defendant decided not to respond there was no contract.

So the practice of inertia-selling, that is, posting unsolicited goods to members of the public and obliging them to return them within a certain period of time, or, in default, pay the price, is both a dubious commercial practice and is outside established principles of law. In the Republic, section 47 of the Sale of Goods and Supply of Services Act 1980 deems such a delivery a gift in certain cases and the 1997 E.U. Distance Selling Directive (see Chapter 8) makes such practices unlawful also.

For acceptance to be effective the general rule that the offeror is bound when he (or his agent for the purpose of receipt of acceptance) learns from the offeree of his acceptance. At that moment a contract springs into existence. This general rule was once illustrated by Lord Denning by two hypothetical examples. A is in communication with B, both parties standing on opposite banks of a river. A shouts an offer to B; B shouts his reply but this is drowned out either by an airplane flying overhead or by the sound of rushing water. B must repeat his reply before any contract can result. The second example extends this rule into modern means of communication. A telephones an offer to B, B replies but the line goes dead. If B intends to accept he must repeat his words of acceptance, the contract being concluded when A hears them. The point is not as metaphysical as it sounds because important jurisdictional questions may depend on where a contract is concluded. In the leading English case of *Entores Ltd. v. Miles Far East Corporation*[47] an offer sent by telex from the plaintiffs' offices in London to the defendants in Amsterdam was accepted by telex. The only problem concerned where the contract came into existence. The Court of Appeal held the contract was concluded in London when notice of acceptance was received there.

In *Brinkibon Ltd. v. Stahag Stahl und Stahlwarenhandelgesellschaft GmbH*[48] the House of Lords approved the *Entores* decision while at the same time indicating that the general rule will not prove dispositive in all cases where actual communication by telex is not instantaneous. If the general rule should prove inconvenient or inappropriate, as where the telex is sent by or to an agent

---

[46] [1922] 2 I.R. 159.
[47] [1955] 2 Q.B. 327. For an Irish case which appears to apply this case see the Supreme Court's judgment in *Unidare plc and Unidare Cable Ltd. v. James Scott Ltd.*, unreported, Supreme Court, May 8, 1991.
[48] [1983] 2 A.C. 34.

with limited authority, or where the telex arrives outside office hours, for example, then it seems likely that the general rule will not be automatically applicable. Lord Wilberforce said of these and other problematic situations "[n]o universal rule can cover all such cases; they must be resolved by reference to the intentions of the parties, by sound business practice and in some cases by a judgment where the risks should lie."

In practical terms the use of new information technology in the ordering and distribution of goods and services will no doubt raise the applicability of this general rule. Many companies and groups of companies active in manufacturing and assembly industries utilise computer networks which automatically review and order goods for the workplace when stocks fall to a predetermined level. The rules governing Electronic Data Exchange and contract formation are under review by various international agencies[49] and the rather flexible approach taken in *Brinkibon* may still prove to be serviceable in this context also.

**Acceptance by post.**   The general rule, which determines that a contract comes into being when the offeror learns of acceptance, does not apply where the parties intend that acceptance is to be communicated by post, neither party stipulating that acceptance is only to be valid when the offeror receives notification thereof. The so-called "postal rule" indicates that a contract is concluded when the offeree posts the letter of acceptance. This rule, which was established in England as early as 1818[50] has not found universal acceptance; German law for example, holds acceptance to be effective when brought to the place of business of the offeror. The Irish courts, however, have followed the English rule. In *Sanderson v. Cunningham*[51] the plaintiff, through a Dublin insurance broker, sent in a proposal for an insurance policy. This constitutes an offer by the prospective insured. The defendant company in London decided to issue a policy which they posted to the plaintiff's agent. The plaintiff read the policy and indicated his assent by signing it. The plaintiff, who wished to sue the defendants in Ireland, could only commence proceedings if the contract was concluded in Ireland. The claim failed. The Court of Appeal in Ireland held that the contract was concluded by posting it in London.

Not all the cases in which the issue of formation of a contract by the use of the postal services possess a transnational dimension. The case of *Dooley v. Egan*[52] may be prosaic but it illustrates the rule admirably. The defendants, based in Cork, sent a postcard to the plaintiff to inquire whether the plaintiff could supply them with a medical cabinet. By letter posted in Dublin the plaintiff on June 22 stated that they could supply an enclosed list of goods at

---

49  See Schauss, in *Telebanking, Teleshopping and The Law* (ed. Poullet & Vandenberghe, Kluwer, 1988), pp. 69–95. Kelleher and Murray, *Information Technology Law in Ireland* (1997), Chap. 27.
50  *Adams v. Lindsell* (1818) 1 B. & Ald. 681; *Winfield* (1939) 55 L.Q.R. 499.
51  [1919] 2 I.R. 234. Contrast *O'Leary v. Law Integrity Ins.* [1912] 1 I.R. 479. An attempt to similarly displace the postal rule failed in *Kelly v. Cruise Catering Ltd.* [1994] 2 I.L.R.M. 394.
52  (1938) 72 I.L.T.R. 155.

fixed prices, the "quotation" being for immediate acceptance only. The defendants on June 24 replied by ordering two medical cabinets not one. The plaintiff on June 26 replied with their own letter in which the plaintiff agreed to supply two medical cabinets. The issue was whether the contract was formed in Dublin or Cork. Meredith J. held that the letter of the plaintiff of June 22 was an offer, notwithstanding the nomenclature of "quotation". The reply of the defendant, posted in Cork, was not an acceptance, but a counter-offer which was accepted in Dublin on June 26 when the plaintiff posted the letter of acceptance. The contract was formed in Dublin.

The postal rule has been heavily criticised as leading to injustice. The well known English case of *Household Fire Insurance v. Grant*[53] illustrates this point graphically. Grant issued an offer to take an insurance policy. The company posted an acceptance. The letter never arrived. Grant was held liable to pay the premiums. The rule has been said to rest upon the unsatisfactory theory that a letter handed to the postal authorities amounts to communication to an agent. This of course ignores the fact that the "agent" is unaware of what the letter contains. Even if the postal agency knows that the letter contains a reply to an offer, the agency presumably has not opened the letter to discover its contents.

In truth the rule is one of convenience. It is said to be convenient for two reasons. The now obsolete practice of recording the date of issue of letters in office ledgers indicated to the nineteenth century judges that a letter had at least been posted. The fact of posting was easier to verify than the non-arrival of the letter. Secondly, the postal rule, while it seems to unduly favour the offeree, is rational enough for if another rule applied the offeree could not rely on his act of acceptance. He would have to contact the offeror to ensure that his letter had actually arrived before he could safely assume that a contract had resulted, and act accordingly. Indeed, it has been argued that the rule does not in fact unduly favour the offeree. In *Household Fire Insurance v. Grant* it was pointed out that the offeror can stipulate for receipt of the acceptance, thereby protecting himself from the perils of an inefficient postal service. This was successfully achieved by the defendant in *Holwell Securities v. Hughes*,[54] when the contract provided that if the plaintiff wished to exercise an option to purchase a house owned by the defendant this had to be done "by notice in writing" within six months. Shortly before the time elapsed the plaintiff posted a letter which did not arrive. The English Court of Appeal held that while the parties intended the postal service to be the means of communication the words of the agreement indicated that the defendant was only bound when the letter arrived. The postal rule was displaced and it mattered not that the defendant had been told by his own solicitor who had received a copy of the letter of acceptance that the plaintiff was about to exercise the option. Lawton L.J. in the English Court of

---

[53] (1879) L.R. 4 Ex. 216.
[54] [1974] 1 W.L.R. 155: see, however, *Hippodrome Night Club v. Sean Quinn Properties*, unreported, High Court, December 13, 1989 (notice in right of pre-emption cases).

Appeal stated that not only will the rule not apply where the offeror specifies that acceptance must reach him "It probably does not operate if its application would produce manifest inconvenience and absurdity." The implications of this dictum have yet to be explored.

In essence the postal rule will be quite easily displaced if the language of the offer is incompatible with that rule. In *Nunin Holdings Property v. Tullamarine Estates Property*[55] the plaintiff was held by the terms of his offer, namely that he would be bound "upon receipt by us of an identical contract". The posting of that identical contract did not conclude the matter so when the defendants, in the period between posting and delivery, telephoned to revoke their posted acceptance that revocation was held effective.

The courts may decide not to apply the postal rule for reasons other than a desire to avoid injustice between the parties. In *Apicella v. Scala*,[56] the plaintiffs in England sued the defendant who had purchased Irish sweepstake tickets as part of an alleged partnership arrangement. One of the tickets drew first prize. Meredith J. considered whether the worldwide distribution of tickets could be considered an offer, accepted when the counterfoils are posted back to the organisers of the sweepstake. The learned judge concluded that:

> "The ticket is not an offer. It, with the attached counterfoil, is more like a proposal form, and an offer is first made by forwarding the counterfoil with the price of the ticket, the ticket being retained by the purchaser. If the offer is accepted the price of the ticket is retained and an official receipt is forwarded, the contract is thus concluded."[57]

In rejecting the postal rule in this context, Meredith J. was concerned to permit the organizers the freedom to regulate the number of tickets included in the draw, and more importantly, to ensure that the organizers did not envisage breaches of the domestic law of other states in which lotteries are illegal. "If the transmission of the counterfoils was illegal in a particular country, and if the encouragement of breaches of the law of that country were resented, the Management Committee might decide to refuse all counterfoils transmitted from that country." In short, the postal rule will not be allowed to operate so as to breach principles of international law such as the rule relating to comity of nations: contrast the approach taken in *Stanhope v. Hospitals Trust (No. 2)*.[58]

The old Irish case of *Clarke v. Gardiner*[59] decides that where a letter of offer arrives from an offeror and the offeree validly accepts by despatching the goods by courier, the offeror cannot validly withdraw the offer before the goods arrive, the Court of Common Pleas holding that if a letter of acceptance

---

[55] [1994] 1 V.R. 74; *Elizabeth City Centre Property v. Corralyn Property* (1994) 63 S.A.S.R. 235.

[56] (1931) 66 I.L.T.R. 33.

[57] *Ibid.* at 40.

[58] [1936] Ir.Jur.Rep. 25.

[59] (1861) 12 I.C.L.R. 472.

cannot be retracted before it arrives then conduct amounting to acceptance cannot be treated any differently. However, Christian J. stated *obiter* that if the act of acceptance is countermanded (*e.g.* by the offeree repossessing goods before they are delivered to the offeror and before the offeror learns that the offeree intended to accept) he was of the view that there would be no contract.

No modern Irish court has considered whether a letter of acceptance which has been posted can be rendered ineffective if the offeree changes his mind before the letter arrives. If this issue arises in the near future Lawton L.J.'s dictum in *Holwell Securities v. Hughes* may help allow the offeree to retract for unless there is proof of loss to the offeror no hardship would be produced by such a result.[60] *Nunin Holdings Property v. Tullamarine Estates Property*[61] holds that revocation can be effective in these circumstances but in that case the postal rule itself was displaced by the terms of the offer.

In cases where there is a prescribed method of acceptance, whether it be the post, hand-delivery, or a facsimile machine, to give but three examples, the question of whether another method may be utilized may arise. It is reasonably clear that where some other method is used but the acceptance is not as expeditious as the stipulated method and it arrives after arrival via the stipulated method could have been anticipated, then the offeror is not bound and can ignore the purported acceptance, although there is no clear case law on this point. But if the method used is more expeditious (*e.g.* the offeror requests a reply by motor cycle courier and it is instantly faxed instead) it would be necessary for the offeror to have insisted upon the stated method only, in the clearest terms, for the acceptance to be defeated. In *Staunton v. The Minister for Health*[62] a method of acceptance was stated to have been laid down by the offeror, that is signature of a contract document. It was held that a verbal acceptance was adequate. The Northern Ireland case of *Walker v. Glass*[63] more directly addresses this question for, in considering whether a purported acceptance which was not in precise compliance with the offer, Lord Lowry said that the essential test was whether the method used was as beneficial to the offeror as the method stated.

A further problem that may arise from time to time is whether an offer may be accepted by an offeree who is unaware of the existence of the offer. The situation that is likely to produce this set of circumstances is encapsulated in the reward cases – instances where a felon is captured but the person who is responsible for effecting this (an informant for example) is unaware of the existence of a reward offer.[64] Oblique Irish authority against the existence of such a contract is provided by Kenny J. in *Tully v. Irish Land Commission*[65]

---

[60] See Fried, *Contract as Promise* (Harvard, Cambridge Mass., 1981), pp. 52–53.
[61] [1994] 1 V.R. 74.
[62] Unreported, High Court, February 21, 1986.
[63] [1979] N.I. 129.
[64] *R. v. Clarke* (1927) 40 C.L.R. 227.
[65] (1961) 97 I.L.T.R. 174.

and, more recently, by Murphy J. in *Tansey v. College of Occupational Therapists Ltd.*[66]

## Termination of an Offer

An offer may be incapable of producing a contract for a variety of reasons.

### *(1) Revocation*

It is established that an offer can be revoked or withdrawn at any time before it is validly accepted. In cases where the offer is to enter into a bilateral contract, that is, a contract to which both parties are bound, it should be remembered that acceptance has two elements; (a) the intention to accept and (b) communication of acceptance. In the case of *The Navan Union v. McLoughlin*[67] the defendant submitted a tender to the plaintiffs, a poor law authority. The guardians met amongst themselves and agreed to accept the defendant's tender but before acceptance was communicated to McLoughlin he revoked his offer. Because the plaintiffs had not validly accepted the defendant's offer he was held to be entitled to withdraw it.

For revocation to be effective the offeror need only show that at the time of purported acceptance the offeree knows that the subject matter is no longer available to the offeree. This follows from the much criticised English case of *Dickinson v. Dodds.*[68] Dodds offered to sell his house to Dickinson for an agreed sum. The offer was to remain open "until Friday, June 12th 9.00 a.m." On the Thursday, Dickinson was told that the house may have been sold to a third party. This information was communicated to Dickinson by a man called Barry who had not been authorised by Dodds to communicate this information to Dickinson. Dickinson handed a letter of acceptance to Dodds before the deadline set. The Court of Appeal held that because Dickinson had notice of the sale, even if the informant was not the offeror or an agent, the offer then became incapable of acceptance. Dickinson could not obtain the property or damages.

It seems that Dickinson intended to purchase before he learnt of the intervening sale. Had he given even a nominal consideration then the promise to keep the offer open until Friday would have been binding. In the United States a promise to keep an offer open is described as a "firm offer" and it cannot be revoked. The English Law Commission in a 1975 Working Paper suggested that the law be changed to make a promise such as that made by Dodds binding if it is deliberately meant and made in the course of business.[69]

It should also be noted that a letter of revocation does not become effective by posting it. In other words, the postal rule does not apply to letters revoking

---

[66] Unreported, High Court, August 27, 1986.
[67] (1855) 4 I.C.L.R. 451.
[68] (1876) 2 Ch.D. 463.
[69] Working Paper No. 60. This has not been acted upon.

an offer. That letter only becomes effective when it arrives. This is established by the English case of *Byrne v. Van Tienhoven*.[70]

The important decision of Lord Lowry C.J. in the Northern Ireland case of *Walker v. Glass*[71] provides an excellent analysis of the basic rules on offer and acceptance. Walker wished to purchase an estate owned by Glass and to this end persuaded Glass to consider selling it to him. The parties contracted solicitors to draw up a form of offer in which Glass offered to sell the estate for £400,000, a deposit of £40,000 being payable. The offer was declared to be open for acceptance until March 13, 1979. Acceptance was prescribed; Walker had to sign a form of acceptance and forward the deposit before that date. On March 1, Walker notified Glass of his intention to buy but failed to forward the deposit until March 12. In the meantime Glass had "revoked" the offer. Walker's action for specific performance failed. Despite the statement to the contrary in the offer, revocation could be effective at any time before acceptance. Walker argued that the offer had been effectively accepted on March 1. By communicating acceptance before purported withdrawal on March 2, this effectively "froze" the transaction which was concluded on payment of the deposit. Lord Lowry C.J. refused to accept this theory. He noted that the prescribed mode of acceptance had to be satisfied. Payment of the deposit was not a neutral act, as counsel for Walker contended, because the failure to proceed would result in any deposit paid being forfeited by the seller.

If the offer is an offer to enter into a unilateral contract then difficulties may arise in regard to revocation. If, as we said earlier, acceptance and performance are one act and if revocation is possible before it is accepted then it should follow that an offer of this nature can be revoked any time until completion, even if the offeree has started to accept by performance. If I offer a man £20 to walk from Cork to Dublin, can I revoke the offer when I see him on the outskirts of Kildare Town?

An affirmative answer would be clearly unjust but finding a jurisprudential basis for denying the offeror the right to revoke is difficult. If the offeror revokes before the offeree starts to perform no injustice results. However, the English Court of Appeal, in dealing with the more difficult problem of revocation after performance has commenced, has decided that an offer to enter into a unilateral contract is subject to an implied obligation "that [the offeror] would not render the performance by [the offeree] of the acts necessary for acceptance impossible . . . and . . . that the [offeror] could not withdraw . . . once [the offeree] . . . embarked on those acts" *per* Buckley L.J. in *Daulia Ltd. v. Four Millbank Nominees*.[72]

Although conclusive English authority on this point is of fairly recent origin the Australian courts, since the 1860 case of *Abbott v. Lance*,[73] have held the offer irrevocable once performance has commenced. The High Court of

---

[70]  (1880) 5 C.P.D. 344.
[71]  [1979] N.I. 129.
[72]  [1978] Ch. 231 at 245.
[73]  (1860) Legges N.S.W.R. 1283.

Australia in a decision in 1987 has confirmed this rule: *Pavey and Matthews Pty. Ltd. v. Paul.*[74] There is some slight Irish authority for the point for the Supreme Court followed *Offord v. Davies,*[75] a leading early English authority, in *O'Connor v. Sorahan*[76] but the point remains open in Irish law.

## (2) *Rejection of the offer*

Clearly his refusal to accept the offer will make it impossible for the offeree, in the absence of a fresh offer, to change his mind and later accept. As we have seen, if a counter-offer is made by the offeree in response to an offer this has the effect of destroying the first offer. Such drastic consequences have been criticised and the courts often give the offeree's response a neutral effect by charac-terising it as a request for information – which does not destroy the offer – rather than a counter-offer. If this is the case then the offer can be validly accepted. The court may also describe the added term as of importance to the offeree only which he can also waive; see the decision of the House of Lords in the Irish case of *Maconchy v. Trawer.*[77]

## (3) *Lapse of time*

If the offeree does not respond quickly to the offer he may find his tardiness will prevent him from being able to accept the offer. The offeror may expressly stipulate that the offer is for immediate acceptance only as was the case in *Dooley v. Egan.*[78] If the offeror is silent on the method of communicating accep-tance the courts may hold that the medium of communication used indicates that acceptance take place immediately. An offer posted by airmail or sent by telegram from Australia to Dublin could not be validly accepted by sending a reply by surface mail. In all other cases acceptance must take place within a reasonable time. The commodity in question will be an important factor here because acceptance of an offer to purchase perishable goods or a commodity that fluctuates wildly in price such as oil or shares may have to take place earlier than a similar offer to purchase land. In *Commane v. Walsh*[79] O'Hanlon J. stated that an offer was open for acceptance until it was withdrawn or until it would be unreasonable to hold the offeror to it any longer because of the length of time which had elapsed without acceptance. After citing the leading case of *Ramsgate Hotel Co. v. Montefiore*[80] O'Hanlon J. held that the casual approach of the parties in relation to closing a contract for the sale of land, allied to an understanding that the transaction would be attended with a considerable

---

[74] (1987) 162 C.L.R. 221; *Lyndel Nominees Pty. Ltd. v. Mobil Oil Australia Ltd.* (1997) 37 I.P.R. 599.
[75] (1862) 12 C.B.(N.S.) 748.
[76] [1933] I.R. 591 at 599–560, *per* Kennedy C.J.
[77] [1894] 2 I.R. 663.
[78] (1938) 72 I.L.T.R. 155.
[79] Unreported, High Court, May 3, 1983.
[80] (1866) L.R. 1 Ex. 109; *Dencio v. Zivanovic* (1991) 105 F.L.R. 117.

amount of delay, meant that an offer to transfer part of the property in a separate transaction could still be accepted four months after it had been made.

However, the courts will require compelling evidence before holding that the offeror was prepared to indulge the offeree, even in land transactions. The words of Carroll J. in *Parkgrange Investments Ltd. v. Shandon Park Mills Ltd.*[81] are cautionary indeed:

> "a purchaser who does not accept a contract as proferred runs the risk that his counter offer will not be accepted. A purchaser who ignores a time limit for accepting an offer runs the risk that it will lapse."

### (4) Death

With the exception of *Re Whelan*[82] there are no Irish cases which discuss whether an offeror's death before acceptance can make it impossible to accept the offer, so as to hold the estate of the deceased liable. Even the English cases are unclear on this question. Death may of course terminate a contractual obligation through the doctrine of frustration but we will deal with this later.

## Ambiguous, Illusory and Uncertain Contract Terms

If the parties have concluded negotiations then they will consider agreement to have been reached. It often becomes apparent later that the parties have not reached agreement on every important issue or it may be that the contract document is unclear on certain matters. It is suggested that there are several distinct problems here.

A contract term may be ambiguous, that is, capable of being interpreted in two or more ways. The courts do not readily hold that the doubts surrounding the negotiations must lead to the contract being deprived of all effect. In *E.S.B. v. Newman*[83] the plaintiffs supplied electricity to a Mrs. Waddington at four different premises in Dublin. The defendant who had agreed to indemnify Mrs. Waddington, was sued by the plaintiffs for the total sum due on all four "accounts." The defendant pleaded that the contract of indemnity applied only to one of the four premises. Judge Davitt held that the word "accounts" was ambiguous because it could apply either to all four premises or the periodic accounts submitted in relation to one of them. Judge Davitt refused to hold that no contract existed; he instead admitted parol evidence to show that the indemnity was intended only to apply to one of the premises.

Just as a contract term may be capable of more than one meaning so too can a contract term be devoid of any meaning. This kind of term is called an illusory promise. Here words are used which show that the "promisor" has

---

[81] Unreported, High Court, May 2, 1991.
[82] [1897] 1 I.R. 575.
[83] (1933) 67 I.L.T.R. 124.

attempted to give himself a discretion to perform by qualifying his promise so much that it has no promissory content at all. This often happens with a clause excluding or limiting liability for goods sold or services to be conferred. In the leading Australian case of *MacRobertson Miller Airlines v. Commissioners of State Taxation*[84] an airline company promised to fly a passenger from X to Y but reserved for itself the power to cancel any flight, ticket or booking. This promise was held by the High Court of Australia to be illusory. The airline had given itself a discretion to perform or decline to do so. Promises "to deliver goods if I feel like it" or to supply "all the petrol you may require if I am not liable for non delivery" are also illusory. In *Provincial Bank of Ireland v. Donnell*[85] a guarantor's promise to provide security for her husband's bank account in consideration of "advances . . . that might hereafter be made" was held illusory. The bank retained an absolute discretion on whether future advances would be made or not. On the other hand, in the case of *O'Mullane v. Riordan*[86] a purchaser of land agreed to pay £1,500 an acre or such larger sum as the purchaser later stipulated. McWilliam J. held that this promise was not illusory. The purchaser was obliged to pay a minimum of £1,500 per acre even though this sum could be varied upwards by the purchaser at his discretion. Similarly, in *Rooney v. Byrne*[87] a promise to purchase a house "subject to the getting an advance on the property" was held not to give the promisor an election whether to apply for the loan or advance. O'Byrne J. held the promisor was obliged to make reasonable efforts to secure an advance on reasonable terms.

In many contractual arrangements the parties seek to build into the agreement some degree of flexibility so that the agreement can be adjusted if certain contingencies occur. Obvious instances of this kind arise when one party is obliged to make periodic monetary payments over a prolonged period of time. The contract may be drafted in a way that allows the payee to adjust payments due if interest rates, taxation rates or other costs rise. Is such an agreement void for uncertainty? The English Court of Appeal, in *Lombard Tricity Finance Ltd. v. Paton*[88] held that a credit agreement which allowed the credit supplier to vary the interest rate payable, on notification to the borrower, was lawful as being an express term which was drafted in plain terms. Clauses of this kind are in common use in Irish commercial contracts. Leasing contracts for example often contain clauses giving the lessor of movables the right to adjust rental rates if there should be adverse movements in relation to interest rates, capital allowances and other factors.

If a promise lacks any substance the courts may do one of two things; the court can look to see if the promisee subsequently performs and permit him to recover the remuneration promised. So, if I ask someone to deliver a ton of coal indicating that in return "I may pay you £50" the supplier who delivers

---

[84] (1975) 133 C.L.R. 125.
[85] (1932) 67 I.L.T.R. 142.
[86] Unreported, High Court, April 20, 1978.
[87] [1933] I.R. 609.
[88] [1989] 1 All E.R. 918. See now S.I. No. 27 of 1995.

coal will be entitled to recover the sum in question. This is necessary to prevent unjust enrichment. Secondly, the court may delete or sever the illusory promise from the contract and enforce the rest of it. In *Mackey v. Wilde and Longin*[89] the Supreme Court however refused to sever a vague promise that the plaintiff would agree with the defendant that only 25 annual fishing permits and "a few" day tickets would be issued. The vagueness of the " a few" day tickets was held fatal to the entire agreement although the Supreme Court declined to explain why severance was an inappropriate response to this situation.

A vague or uncertain contract can exist in a variety of forms. In *Central Meat Products v. Carney*[90] an action was brought to prevent the sale of cattle by the defendants to third parties, the plaintiff claiming that he had concluded an agreement with the defendant which provided that all the cattle the defendant acquired for canning purposes would be sold to the plaintiff. Overend J. held that there was no agreement capable of being enforced. There was no clear acceptance, nor was there agreement on important issues including price variation clauses and insurance arrangements.

In cases where the contractual arrangement seems to lack clarity on the meaning to be attached to essential terms, or in cases where the contract is silent altogether, there are a number of devices and techniques that can be used by the courts to ascertain the intention of the parties, in the objective sense. In cases where the clause is part of a contract which in previous years has been adequately performed, a vague clause which relates to future supplies may provide appropriate points of clarification. So, in *Hillas & Co. Ltd. v. Arcos Ltd.*[91] a contractual option for the sale of timber, being described as "100,000 standards" was given greater precision by reference to the fuller description of the goods found in the contract relating to the previous growing season. However, if there is no previous course of dealing between the parties, or the clause in question purports to refer to a set of criteria or situation which is not uniform within the industry, or has not been delimited or defined by a course of dealing between the parties, then the clause may be incapable of being given any meaning: *Scammell v. Ouston*.[92] Additionally, the courts may opt to fill in gaps by reference to the standard of reasonableness. This is quite common in cases where the contract is silent altogether and the contract does not purport to provide machinery which will somehow produce a result (*e.g.* an arbitration clause). The general power of the courts to imply terms so as to give the contract the efficacy, it must be assumed the parties intended, does not subvert the general principle of private autonomy.

A most important decision of the English Court of Appeal stresses a fundamental distinction to be drawn between terms which are essential and terms which are non-essential. While this dichotomy is not new, the Court, in

---

[89] Unreported, Supreme Court, December 17, 1997.
[90] (1944) 10 Ir.Jur.Rep.34.
[91] (1932) Com.Cas. 23.
[92] [1941] A.C. 251.

*Pagnan Sp.A. v. Feed Products Ltd.*,[93] built upon it to stress the difference between instances where the parties have reached agreement on essential terms, and the evidence suggests that the parties intended and believe they have made a binding contract, and instances where the parties have not reached agreement on terms which they do not regard as essential to a binding agreement. In this latter situation there can be no enforceable contract. However, in the Court of Appeal the situation before the court was said to be a somewhat intermediate one: the parties had intended to continue to negotiate on some inessential or incidental matters. The issue before the court was whether their intention was that until these matters were resolved there was no binding contract. Each case depends on its facts, objectively ascertained. In some instances it may be clear that the parties may intend not to be bound unless this incidental matter is agreed, as in *Love and Stewart v. Instone*.[94] In other cases it may be evident that the parties may intend to be bound forthwith, notwithstanding the need to agree further terms or carry out some formality such as executing a formal document. Where this does not happen it is only because the outstanding matter not agreed upon results in an uncertain or unworkable contract. So, in *Pagan Sp.A. v. Feed Products Ltd.* the agreement on parties, price, identity and quality of goods and terms of shipment were held to constitute a binding contract, notwithstanding the existence of later negotiations and subsequent failure to agree on loading rate, demurrage and despatch and carrying charges. Each case is said to depend and turn on their own facts.[95] Even employment contracts to work on a casual or required basis may appear to contain enough promissory content to give rise to legally enforceable mutual obligations: *Carmichael v. National Power plc*.[96]

To similar effect is the decision of Carroll J. in *Parkgrange Investments Ltd. v. Shandon Park Mills Ltd.*[97] The failure of a contract for the sale of an interest in land to record an undertaking by the vendor to exercise best efforts to arrange the transfer of a policy of insurance to the purchaser did not undermine the validity of the contract: "the agreement about insurance was peripheral."

### Agreements to agree in the future

The decision of the Court of Appeal in *Pagnan Sp.A. v. Feed Products Ltd.*[98] re-emphasises the importance of interpreting contracts in their entirety and the fact that the process of interpretation is intended to give effect to the intentions of the parties. As such, reasonable persons are taken to have intended their agreements to have reasonable effect. While it is possible for the parties to stipulate that until every detail is negotiated the agreement is unenforceable,

---

[93] [1987] 2 Lloyd's Rep. 601.
[94] [1917] 33 T.L.R. 475.
[95] *Granit SA. v. Benship International* [1994] 1 Lloyd's Rep. 526; *The Gladys* (No. 2) [1994] 2 Lloyd's Rep. 402.
[96] *The Times*, April 2, 1998.
[97] Unreported, High Court, May 2, 1991.
[98] [1987] 2 Lloyd's Rep. 601.

the courts are now less willing to hold that the failure to agree an outstanding matter will result in the contract being void for uncertainty. Certainly, the following words of Lord Dunedin in *May & Butcher v. The King*[99] are no longer to be taken literally:

> "to be a good contract there must be a concluded bargain, and a concluded contract is one which settles everything that is necessary to be settled and leaves nothing to be settled by agreement between the parties."[100]

In sale of goods cases, if the parties fail to agree on a price and they have not covenanted that they will negotiate on price at some future date, section 8(2) of the Sale of Goods Act 1893 intervenes to require the payment of a reasonable price. However, if the agreement is executory, that is, it must be performed at some future date, there may be considerable difficulty in enforcing such an undertaking. If the contract is outside the Act, a building contract or sale of land for instance, failure to agree on a price may be fatal as was the case in *Courtney & Fairbairn v. Tolaini Brothers (Hotels)*,[101] an English Court of Appeal decision. In this case a builder provided finance to a developer in return for a promise that he would be awarded the construction contract itself, on the basis that the developer's quantity surveyor would negotiate a fair and reasonable contract sum. The plaintiff argued that while he had not entered into a binding contract to build the defendant had broken a contract to negotiate. The theory that someone can "contract to make a contract" was rejected by the Court of Appeal, primarily because the damages to be awarded are too uncertain. Who can tell if the negotiations will be successful? The *Tolaini Brothers* case was recently followed in the British Columbia case of *Maunpar Enterprises Ltd. v. Canada*[102] when a mining renewal clause allowing renewal "for a further five year period subject to satisfactory performance and renegotiation of the royalty rate and annual surface rental" was held to be a bare agreement to negotiate and void for uncertainty. In this decision the British Columbia Court refused to imply a duty to negotiate in good faith in order to repair the deficiencies in the wording of the clause. In *Walford v. Miles*[103] the House of Lords have reaffirmed the view that there cannot be a contract requiring the parties to negotiate in good faith because the right of each party to withdraw at any time from the negotiations is simply incompatible with such a contract; Lord Ackner observed that it was quite impractical to expect the courts to police such an inherently vague agreement of the kind contended for. Lord Ackner, however, did indicate that a contract to use best endeavours may be enforceable and it has been held that if an enforceable contract exists but other covenants which lack precision are identified, the *Courtney & Fairbairn* case does not prevent a court from

---

[99] [1934] 2 K.B. 17n.
[100] *Ibid.*
[101] [1975] 1 All E.R. 716.
[102] (1997) 33 B.C.L.R. (3d) 203.
[103] [1992] 2 A.C. 128; *Arnold v. Northern Bank* [1995] N.I.J.B. 55.

implying a further term that the parties will negotiate in good faith about future terms to be inserted into a written agreement: see *Donwin Productions v. E.M.I. Films*.[104]

Nevertheless the view that "a contract to contract" may exist finds tentative support in Ireland in the case of *Guardians of Kells Union v. Smith*.[105] The Guardian of a poor law district advertised by tender for the supply of meat, the advertisement providing that a formal contract would be signed on a fixed day. The defendant was told that he had been the successful offeror but he refused to sign the formal contract. It was held that while no contract to supply meat existed because no formal contract had been concluded the defendant had broken a contract to enter into this formal contract and he was liable. Damages were nominal. It can be argued that this "contract to contract" is designed to show that parties are obliged to negotiate in good faith: *culpa in contrahendo*,[106] as long as there is an obligation which can be given some meaning within the context of the relationship between the parties. In *Lambert v. HTV Cymru*[107] the assignee of copyright in cartoon characters was contracted to "use all reasonable endeavours" to obtain future book rights for the assignor in subsequent dealings in the characters. It was held that this clause was not void for uncertainty. Another way of trying to compel another person to conclude a deal is found in so called lock-out agreements, that is, on agreement whereby one party agrees not to negotiate with others in relation to a proposed transaction. While these agreements are invalid if no fixed limit is set by the contract, these agreements have been held to be legally effective in other circumstances.[108]

One way of avoiding the consequences of *Courtney & Fairbairn*, and other situations in which the parties fail to reach complete agreement, is for them to create some method or machinery for resolving any disagreement. However, a general arbitration clause may be allowed to function once a contract has come into existence, but according to *May & Butcher v. The King*,[109] a general clause cannot repair a failure to agree on price when the contract contemplated that price would be a matter of mutual agreement as between the parties. Section 8(1) of the Sale of Goods Act 1893 suggests a similar solution in cases where the parties to a contract for the sale of goods intended to reach agreement.

Notwithstanding *May & Butcher v. The King*, many more English cases demonstrate a greater judicial willingness to find that the parties have created an enforceable contract (see, for example *Beer v. Bowden*[110]) or, alternatively, have done enough to allow the courts to effectively repair any defects that the

---

[104] *The Times*, March 9, 1984. See also *Renard v. Minister of Public Works* (1992) 33 Con. L.R. 72 at 112–3; *Philips v. BSB* [1995] E.M.L.R. 472.

[105] (1917) 52 I.L.T.R. 65.

[106] Kessler and Fine (1964) 77 Harv.L.R. 401; *Walford v. Miles* [1992] 2 A.C. 128 indicates this is not part of English law.

[107] *The Times*, March 17, 1998.

[108] *Walford v. Miles* [1992] 2 A.C. 128; *Pitt v. PHH Asset Management Ltd.* [1993] 4 All E.R. 961.

[109] [1934] 2 K.B. 17n.

[110] [1981] 1 W.L.R. 522.

agreement itself contains. The leading case is *Sudbrooke Trading Estate v. Eggleton.*[111] Under the terms of a lease the lessees were entitled to exercise an option to purchase the reversion at a valuation to be agreed by two valuers. The valuers were to be nominated one, by the lessor, the other by the lessee. In default of agreement by the valuers the price was to be settled by an umpire appointed by the valuers. The lessor refused to appoint his valuer and therefore claimed the contract was unenforceable, citing authorities for the proposition that where an agreement is incomplete because something further has to be done, the court is powerless. The House of Lords, however, by a majority of four to one resisted this contention on the ground that some decisions show that when a contract is agreed at a "fair valuation" there is an enforceable contract. Their Lordships described the machinery for valuation in the present case as a non-essential term and interpreted the clause so that the price would be a fair price. Specific performance of the agreement was decreed. In the case of *Voest Alpine Intertrading v. Chevron Int. Oil Co.*[112] Hirst J. went further and held that where an arbitration clause is found in the contract, and the contract has been carried into effect, the court may itself rule on what is a reasonable price for the commodity in question. However, it remains a question of interpretation whether the parties have intended the valuation to be at a fair and reasonable price. Should the arbitrator be named, or the criteria be a subjective valuation, it may not be possible to operate the *Sudbrooke* analysis, helpful though it may be. This point is made eloquently by the decision in *Lonergan v. McCartney.*[113] Here, an option clause in respect of the purchase of "premises" was held void for uncertainty; the valuer could not be sure whether the valuation process was to be the full value of the premises, or the landlord's interest. Other factors influencing "value" such as renewal rights under statute and the possible relevance of the tenants improvements made the clause unworkable in the view of Gibson L.J.. However, Carswell L.J. in the later case of *North Down Hotels Ltd. v. Province-Wide Filling Stations Ltd.*[114] was able to distinguish *Lonergan v. McCartney* on the ground that Carswell L.J. was being invited to repair defective valuing machinery in respect of the reversionary interest in property and while such a process would not be easy, the issue of fixing a value was something that a competent professional would be able to resolve on objective grounds.

Murphy J. in *Bula Ltd. & Others v. Tara Mines Ltd. & Others*[115] has mapped out the option that faces a court in the Republic of Ireland in relation to this issue. The dispute related to the enforceability of a co-operation clause in a mining lease, the lease containing a general arbitration clause. Murphy J. summarised the issue thus:

---

[111]  [1982] 3 W.L.R. 315; *The Didymi* [1988] 2 Lloyd's Rep. 108.
[112]  [1987] 2 Lloyd's Rep. 547.
[113]  [1983] N.I. 129.
[114]  [1993] N.I. 261.
[115]  [1987] I.R. 95.

"It was contended by the defendants that this clause was void for uncertainty. It was said that it was no more than an agreement to agree and that such a concept is a contradiction in terms. But the defendants went even further, relying on the decision of Lord Denning M.R. and the Court of Appeal in *Courtney & Fairbairn Ltd. v. Tolaini Brothers (Hotels) Ltd.* [1975] 1 W.L.R. 297. They contended that the law does not recognise a contract to negotiate and adopted the language of Lloyd J. in *The "Scraptrade"* [1981] 2 Lloyd's Rep. 425 at p. 432 in the following terms:

'. . . for an agreement to seek a mutually acceptable conclusion is like an agreement to agree, or an agreement to negotiate. It is a thing writ in water. It confers no rights or obligations of any kind; see *Courtney Faibairn Ltd. v. Tolaini Bros. (Hotels) Ltd.* [1975] 1 W L.R. 297.'

Moreover, the defendants in this regard can find further support from the decision in the *Cadbury Ireland Ltd.* Case [1982] I.L.R.M. 77 where Barrington J. found a particular clause in issue as being unenforceable because at best it involved a "commitment to enter into honest negotiations" – see page 85.

Notwithstanding the impressive arguments adduced by the defendants in this regard it does seem to me that consideration must still be given to the observations (albeit *obiter*) of Lord Wright in *Hillas & Co. Ltd. v. Arcos Ltd.* (1932) 147 L.T. 503 at p. 515 when he said:

'There is then no bargain except to negotiate, and negotiations may be fruitless and end without any contract ensuing; yet even then, in strict theory, there is a contract (if there is good consideration) to negotiate, though in the event of repudiation by one party the damages may be nominal, unless a jury think that the opportunity to negotiate was of some appreciable value to the injured party.'

This is of course the view which the Court of Appeal rejected in the *Courtney & Fairbairn Ltd.* Case [1975] 1 W.L.R. 297 but it does offer the bones of an argument which, as I understand it, the plaintiffs seek to couple with the arbitration clause in the present case. As I understand it it is their argument that the facts are such that reasonable negotiation would necessarily produce a viable solution and that the arbitration clause is capable of procuring reasonableness in the negotiations if duly held."[116]

The trend before the English courts is to interpret agreements so as to produce a positive rather than a negative interpretation, a point emphasised by Ralph Gibson L.J. in *Corson v. Rhuddlan B.C.*[117] Nevertheless, even when the more liberal approach outlined by the House of Lords in *Sudbrooke*, and subsequently adopted by the Privy Council in the New Zealand case of *Money v. Ven-Lu-Ree*

---

[116] [1987] I.R. 95 at 102.
[117] [1989] 59 P. & C.R. 185.

*Ltd.*[118] is adopted, there will still be instances where a contract cannot be pieced together. Many illustrations can be found in sale of land transactions. Failure to agree on the period for which a lease is to run will be fatal (*Lindsay v. Lynch*[119]) as will failure to reach agreement on the commencement of the lease.[120] When the agreement is executory there is less likelihood of the agreement being carried into effect because there is less incentive for the courts to try and salvage an agreement than in cases where the agreement has been acted upon: see Denning M.R. in *Sykes (Wessex) Ltd. v. Fine Fare Ltd.*[121] Some judges support a radical approach to defeating issues of uncertainty of terms when the purported contract is set out in documentary form. Even if a chain of correspondence does not cumulatively create a clear offer and acceptance there is some support for the view that the courts may be driven to conclude that if there exists agreement on essential terms a contract should result, at least in cases where the parties have actually completed their intended project.[122]

Even if the agreement is void for uncertainty there is the possibility that any work done, on request, by one party for another, will have to be paid for on the basis of *quantum meruit*. In England this is recognised by *British Steel Corporation v. Cleveland Bridge and Engineering Co. Ltd.*[123] and the Irish case of *Folens v. Minister for Education*[124] provides clear support in Ireland for this basic principle of quasi-contract, or restitution.

## "Subject to Contract"

Where two persons seemingly conclude negotiations for the sale of land either or both of them may wish to protect themselves by stipulating that in certain instances the agreement will not be binding. The owner may want to reserve for himself the right to accept a better offer for example; the purchaser on the other hand may want to ensure that he has the money to pay for the property and permit himself to withdraw without being liable for breach of contract. Each could stipulate that agreement is conditional on such and such an eventuality. In *O'Mullane v. Riordan*[125] the purchaser agreed to buy subject to planning permission being obtained. In such cases until planning permission is given the contract is said to exist but it is unenforceable. If planning permission is not given the purchaser is not bound to purchase but he can waive this term

---

[118] [1989] 3 N.Z.L.R. 129.

[119] (1804) 2 Sch. & Lef. 1.

[120] *Kearns v. Manning* [1935] I.R. 869. Failure to agree on payment of a deposit, when clearly an important matter, will also be fatal: *Boyle and Boyle v. Lee and Goyns* [1992] I.L.R.M. 65.

[121] [1967] 1 Lloyd's Rep. 53.

[122] *Clarke v. Dunraven* [1897] A.C. 59; *Gibson v. Manchester City Council* [1979] 1 All E.R. 972, as discussed in *Marist Bros. Community v. Harvey Shire* (1994) 14 W.A.R. 69. See also *Regalian Properties plc v. London Dockland Development Corp.* [1995] 1 All E.R. 1005.

[123] [1984] 1 All E.R. 504.

[124] [1984] I.L.R.M. 265; contrast *Malcolm v. University of Oxford* [1994] E.M.L.R. 17.

[125] Unreported, High Court, April 20, 1978.

(if property values have risen he may do this) at which point the contract becomes enforceable.[126]

Instead of inserting a specific stipulation into the contract, lawyers, estate agents and others may use the expression, "subject to contract." This formula has been interpreted to mean that until the formal contract is signed by both parties (the normal Irish practice), or until contracts are exchanged (the conventional practice in England), no contract of sale exists.[127] The English authorities are summarised by Lord Denning in the leading case thus: "[t]he effect of the words 'subject to contract' is that the matter remains in negotiation until a formal contract is executed."[128]

The Irish courts have also ruled that if the phrase is used by the parties during negotiations then there is no contract until exchange of contracts or signature by both parties takes place. The leading Irish case is *Thompson v. The King*.[129] After a series of offers, rejections and counter-offers, the plaintiff received a telegram from the defendant stating "will accept subject contract . . . £24,200 for Waterford factory." Three days later the plaintiff responded by telegram "we accept your offer . . . at £24,200." The negotiations then broke down and the plaintiff sought specific performance of the contract, which the plaintiff contended, had been formed following this exchange of telegrams. After considering the effect of the words "subject contract" the Kings Bench Divisional Court held that there was no concluded contract. The words used and surrounding circumstances deferred the contractual obligation until a formal contract was settled, accepted and executed (*per* Gibson J.). This was not a case where the parties intended there and then to be bound, the further contract only being a matter of form which did not pre-empt a finding of contractual intention.

While the "subject to contract" usage generally developed to protect purchasers from entering into "open," legally binding contracts, *Thompson v. The King* illustrates the point that the usage can be utilised by either party. It follows, therefore, that if a property owner offers to sell "subject to contract," "acceptance" by the offeree will simply mark a step in the march towards a binding contract. If the offeree on the other hand introduces the term "subject to contract" his response is not a counter-offer requiring the offeror to respond, but of course the point is of little importance given that either party can refuse to proceed.

There are important differences between the Irish and English cases on the question of "subject to contract" agreements. First, suppose the words are added by the solicitor for the purchaser in a letter "confirming" that agreement has been reached "subject to contract." Suppose also neither the vendor nor the purchaser used the words when they were discussing details of the sale. Under

---

[126] *Malone v. Elf Investments*, unreported, High Court, December 7, 1979.
[127] For an interesting discussion on conveyancing practice on the question of closure of a contract see the Supreme Court decision in *Embourg Ltd. v. Tyler Group* [1996] 3 I.R. 480.
[128] *Tiverton Estates Ltd. v. Wearwell* [1975] Ch. 146.
[129] [1920] 2 I.R. 365.

English law the "subject to contract" letter cannot satisfy the statute requiring a memorandum in writing evidencing the agreement. The Irish courts in contrast, have permitted the vendor to introduce parol evidence to show that oral agreement was reached. The letter containing the "subject to contract" phrase will not be allowed to operate because it was added after the oral agreement had been struck. This important difference between the English and Irish position was established by *O'Flaherty v. Arvan Property*[130] and *Casey v. Irish Intercontinental Bank*.[131] In the *O'Flaherty* case the purchasers of property were handed a receipt for the deposit which contained all the material terms adding "subject to contract." The plaintiffs successfully argued that at the time of negotiation nothing was said about the sale being "subject to contract." McWilliam J. ordered that the sale be completed. This decision meant that Irish solicitors, auctioneers and others cannot rely on this phrase to protect their clients if they attempt to add the "subject to contract" formula after oral negotiations between the principals have ended, the principals themselves failing to use the phrase. Secondly, there is Irish authority for the view that the phrase "subject to contract" may be ignored if, within the context of the contract in question, it is a meaningless phrase. The decision of the Supreme Court in *Kelly v. Park Hall Schools*[132] proved to be a controversial one and it may rest on its own particular facts. Nevertheless, the Supreme Court in that case were prepared to scrutinise the negotiations to see if all the terms have been settled and, if so, "subject to contract" added in any letter will be treated as if it were an ambiguous or meaningless phrase. In the Supreme Court case of *McCarthy v. O'Neill*,[133] Henchy J. said "subject to contract" normally means that "a full contract," has yet to be agreed, which, in the authors view, is a mistaken interpretation of the older cases.

There are several subsequent High Court cases which reassert the orthodox view, namely that "subject to contract" agreements cannot be enforced simply by admitting parol testimony about the circumstances surrounding the bargain. The *Tiverton* case has been followed by Keane J. in *Mulhall v. Haren*[134] and in *Dorene Ltd. v. Suedes (Ireland) Ltd.*[135] Costello J. held that a "subject to contract" acceptance meant that the parties were still in negotiation " . . . there was no legally binding agreement." Indeed, in the Circuit Court case of *Cunningham v. Maher*,[136] Judge Sheridan, after describing the "quite bewildering number of recent Irish cases touching upon the question arising out of oral agreements made subject to contract" held that, faced with a set of irreconcilable authorities he preferred to follow *Tiverton* and *Mulhall v. Haren*.

---

[130] Unreported, High Court, November 3, 1976. While the Supreme Court overruled McWilliam J. in a judgment delivered on July 21, 1977 this point was not at issue.

[131] [1979] I.R. 364; for an interesting follow up case see *Park Hall School Ltd. v. Overend* [1987] I.R. 1.

[132] [1979] I.R. 340.

[133] [1981] I.L.R.M. 443.

[134] [1981] I.R. 364.

[135] [1981] I.R. 312.

[136] Unreported, Circuit Court, March 1983.

The Supreme Court, in *Boyle and Boyle v. Lee and Goyns*[137] has reconsidered *Kelly v. Park Hall School* and *Casey v. Irish Intercontinental Bank*. The soundness of both cases was doubted by Finlay C.J., Hederman J. concurring, and by McCarthy J. These judges observed that, insofar as *Kelly* contemplated the introduction of parol evidence to gainsay the "subject to contract" correspondence, it should not be followed, and similar observations were made about the decision in *Casey*. O'Flaherty J. observed that both *Kelly* and *Casey* turned on their own special facts.[138] Thus, it seems, the Supreme Court, having approved of both *Tiverton* and Keane J.'s masterly review of the law in *Mulhall v. Haren*, have brought Irish law back into the fold of orthodoxy.

Only in the most exceptional cases will "subject to contract" be ignored. If the words appear by mistake (*Michael Richards Properties v. Corporation of Wardens of St. Saviours, Southwark*[139]) and do not reflect the intention of the parties (see *Guardian Builders Ltd. v. Patrick Kelly*[140]) they will be ignored. If, on the true construction of the contract, the words were not intended to render the agreement still under negotiation a binding contract will be upheld, as in the recent English case of *Alpenstowe Ltd. v. Regalian Properties Ltd.*[141] In that case the "subject to contract" formula was held irreconcilable with an express obligation to close the sale within a stipulated period. One problem that may arise because of the considerable delay that can occur before completion of a real property transaction arose in *Tevanon v. Norman Brett (Builders) Ltd.*[142] Suppose the parties reach an agreement which is labelled "subject to contract." Some time later the agreement is replaced by another, which is not stated to be "subject to contract". The general position will be that the two agreements will generally be governed by the "subject to contract" stipulation unless the later agreement is expressly or impliedly nullified.

### *Where "subject to contract" is not used in negotiations*

The "subject to contract" usage is simply a convenient and shorthand method of indicating that the agreement is not to have legal effect until signature of the contract (or an exchange of contracts) takes place. There are other ways of negating contractual effect. In *Brien v. Swainson*[143] the cases were said by Chatterton V.C. to divide into two classes:

> "First, where there is a complete agreement signed by the parties containing their actual contract. If there be a concluded agreement, it will be specifically enforced, though by its terms it contemplates some more

---

[137] [1992] I.L.R.M. 65.
[138] Egan J. did not consider the "subject to contract" issue in detail, but the learned judge approved of both *Tiverton* and *Mulhall v. Haren*.
[139] [1975] 3 All E.R. 416.
[140] Unreported, High Court, March 31, 1981.
[141] [1985] 1 W.L.R. 721.
[142] (1972) 223 E.G. 1945; *Sherbroke v. Dipple* (1980) 225 E.G. 1203.
[143] (1877) 1 L.R.(Ir.) 135.

formal contract being entered into. The other class is where the terms are to a greater or less extent contained in a duly signed writing, but expressed in that writing to be liable to be modified or added to, by a future contract then in the contemplation of the parties."[144]

If the "subject to contract" formula is not used the correspondence may make it quite clear that only upon exchange of contracts in some form will a contract come into existence: see *Kelly v. Irish Landscape Nursery*.[145] The courts will honour such an intent. The exact meaning of such a conditional statement is a matter of interpretation. In the case of *Irish Mainport Holdings Ltd. v. Crosshaven Sailing Centre Ltd.*[146] the words "my Board have agreed in principle," were held not to prevent a concluded agreement coming into existence. Keane J. held these words could not be equated with the words "subject to contract."

The contrasting decision of Keane J. in *Silver Wraith Ltd. v. Siviere Eireann cpt*[147] provides a most useful illustration of this process of interpretation. The defendants wrote, "the following terms are acceptable subject to full lease being agreed." The letter went on to set out the terms. In considering whether this constituted evidence of a concluded agreement between the parties, Keane J. noted that the question was what the phrase used suggested in relation to the contracting state of mind of the parties. Keane J. noted that here the phrase made the existence of a full lease a condition of the agreement. The defendants were lay persons, not qualified lawyers, and they could not be expected to be legally bound to a complex lease transaction of the kind anticipated, without resorting to legal advice and assistance.

## Gazumping – Recent Developments

Conveyancing practice in both England and Ireland can leave the purchaser at the mercy of the vendor in a rising market. The long interval which can sometimes occur between a subject to contract agreement being struck, and contracts being sent out (much less signed) may give rise to temptation for the vendor in the form of subsequent higher offers. A debate has opened in England about ways of reducing this temptation by making much of the preparatory conveyancing material available at the time the property is put up for sale, thus speeding up the process. Some commentators favour adoption of Scottish conveyancing practices where steps of this kind are the norm. In Ireland, particularly within the Dublin area, there is widespread concern about the re-emergence of gazumping, particularly in relation to a number of well

---

[144] (1877) 1 L.R. (Ir.) 135 at 139–140.
[145] [1981] I.L.R.M. 433.
[146] Unreported, High Court, October 14, 1980.
[147] Unreported, High Court, June 8, 1989.

publicised accounts in which first time buyers in particular have put "booking deposits" down for a house in a new development but have not signed a contract. When at a later stage the process has moved on to putting the arrangement on a contractual footing these purchasers have sometimes found the price has been raised by the developer – in one case from £69,000 to £89,000 within a 9 month period.[148] A Fine Gael Private Members' Bill, the Home Purchasers (Anti-Gazumping) Bill 1998,[149] seeks to address problems of this kind by making the payment of a booking deposit by the purchaser of residential property an event which triggers a number of legal obligations for a vendor. Delivery of a contract and supporting documents to the purchaser must take place within 14 days of payment, and for a further 14 days of receipt of those documents the vendor is precluded from selling the property to a third party. Should the purchaser sign the contract and return it along with a sum of money that brings the payments received by the vendor up to 10 per cent of the purchase price, this will conclude the contract of purchase, and only on default by the purchaser at the end of this 14 day grace period may the vendor sell the property to a third party. The booking deposit must however be returned. This proposal will address a specific problem but it does so through the criminal law and this is widely regarded as an unacceptable aspect of the legislative proposal. Nor does the proposal have much to do with subject to contract agreements where no deposit is paid, and some professional bodies such as the Irish Auctioneers and Valuers Institute have suggested[150] other solutions such as making the issue of a contract by a vendor legally binding if it is returned by a purchaser without significant alteration within two weeks. It is not clear to this writer how such a proposal would significantly improve matters, for the difficulty often arises simply because documents may issue from the vendor somewhat tardily, if at all. Conveyancing practice itself cannot always be adjusted to make up for the frailty of human nature.[151]

---

[148] See "Order Restrains Company from selling house" *Irish Times*, July 21, 1998.
[149] Hayes "The Home Purchasers (Anti-Gazumping) Bill 1998" (1998) 3(3) C.P.L.J. 48.
[150] "Auctioneers' body suggests law change" *Irish Times*, July 29, 1998.
[151] Wylie, *Conveyancing Law* (2nd ed., 1996), paras 6.04–6.05.

# 2 The Doctrine of Consideration

## Introduction

If it is clear that one party has made a promise to another person who in turn has assented to it, to the knowledge of the promisor, there is at first sight no reason why the Irish courts should refuse to enforce the promise. Yet this would make all promises enforceable and legal historians have pointed out that no legal system has enforced a promise simply upon proof that it was made.

The English common law recognised a promise to be enforceable if the promisee provided something in exchange for the promise – *a quid pro quo* – or if the promise was contained in a deed under seal. The first route to enforcement helps form the basis of the modern doctrine of consideration. The alternative, obtaining the assent of the promisor to a deed under seal, is not as difficult or technical as it sounds. Once the seal is affixed (and this is done by placing a red sticker on the paper or simply drawing a circle with L.S. stamped on it) the deed takes effect on delivery. In this context the word delivery is interpreted very liberally: see the leading Irish case of *Evans v. Gray*.[1] It seems that the promisor does not even have to sign the document. In *Drimmie v. Davies*[2] two partners exchanged promises and recorded these promises in a deed under seal. The Irish Court of Appeal held that adopting this form made it unnecessary to decide if consideration was present. Several Lords Justices stated *obiter* that consideration was also present. In normal business practice people do not execute deeds under seal so if a promise is enforceable the promise must show that he has provided consideration in exchange for the promise. It is through the doctrine of consideration that the common law identifies promises that are to be enforced simply because they have been made.

At the heart of the doctrine of consideration is the idea of mutuality of obligation but, as the authors of *Corbin on Contracts* declare, the notion of mutuality can be vague:

> "Mutuality of obligation should be used solely to express the idea that each party is under a legal duty to the other; each has made a promise and each is an obliger. This is the meaning with which the term is commonly used. There are cases, however, in which it is otherwise defined. In order to save the supposed requirement of 'mutuality' it is sometimes declared that it means nothing more than that there must be a sufficient consideration. Even though one of the parties has made no promise and is bound

---

[1]  (1882) 9 L.R. (Ir.) 539.
[2]  [1899] 1 I.R. 176, 186.

by no duty, the contract has sufficient mutuality if he has given an executed consideration."[3]

The consideration doctrine is at times ambiguous; in the above extract *Corbin* is contrasting the classical exchange model with situations where one person makes a promise – the unilateral contract – and, because it is foreseeable that the promisee will rely on the promise, that promise may itself be binding. This will be particularly so if the promise contains a request that the person or persons to whom the promise is addressed do some act stipulated by the promisor: *Carlill v. Carbolic Smoke Ball Co.*[4] But commercial convenience has also led the courts to hold that an implied request may be attributed to the promisor (or, to put it another way, the person addressed has impliedly promised to do or abstain from doing something) and in such cases the promise will be held binding upon proof that the promise caused the other party to provide an executed consideration: see *Commodity Broking Co. v. Meehan*[5] discussed below.

The common law and the insistence on utilising an external test of contractual intention, the doctrine of consideration, stands in marked contrast with the position of most other legal systems which do not require an additional substantive element before holding a promise to be enforceable. For many other legal systems the question whether a promise is enforceable is answered by the test of whether there was a deliberate and voluntary undertaking by the promisor. The law of Scotland for example adopts such a position but many promises must be formally reduced into writing, and in Scotland and elsewhere a written requirement is often insisted upon as a measure of the promisor's intention to be bound by the promise. Critics of the common law system point out that if other legal systems can function without the consideration requirement the common law should be revised. The attacks on the bargain model of consideration in particular come from a variety of philosophical positions and, as such, these commentators point out that the bargain model lacks historical legitimacy, is conceptually uncertain, and fails to explain a diverse body of case law that throws up exceptions and qualifications to the bargain model, exceptions that make the bargain a quite inaccurate means of explaining why and when a promise is enforceable as a contract.[6]

In general however the doctrine of consideration enables the courts to discriminate between promises that are enforceable as contracts and promises that may be binding through some other legal concept. For example, if I promise to give my car to X the promise alone cannot lead to X successfully suing for delivery. He has provided nothing for my promise. Suppose I deliver the car to X. My action will make it difficult if not impossible for me to recover the vehicle but it is the transfer of possession allied with my gratuitous promise

---

[3] s.152.

[4] [1893] 1 Q.B. 256.

[5] [1985] I.R. 12.

[6] *e.g.* Fried, *Contract as Promise* (Harvard, Cambridge Mass., 1981); Atiyah, *Essays on Contract* (Clarendon, Oxford, 1986); Wright, (1936) 49 Harv.L.R. 1225.

that makes it impossible to recover the vehicle. Even so, there is still no contract. I have made a promise but the promise is to be seen as a promise of a gift. Until delivery of the promised item the promisee has no right to performance, merely a hope or expectation which the courts will not, of itself, realise for the promisee. Suppose, however, I promise to give my car to the first person to pay or offer to pay £5 for it. Here the promise has an entirely different quality. My promise is allied to a request: I stipulate that in return for my promise I require something to be done in exchange. On performance of the act, or when performance is promised, a bargain springs into existence. The opening sentence to this book drew attention to bargain as the primary characteristic of a contract; it is through the doctrine of consideration that the distinctive features of the common law model of contract take shape. A striking illustration of the difference between motive and exchange is afforded by the recent English case of *Taylor v. Dickens*.[7] Here an elderly lady promised that she would leave her house to the plaintiff who was her part-time gardener. The plaintiff later indicated that he would not take payment for his gardening services. It was held that there was no contract, the court observing that there "was no offer, no acceptance, no exchange of promises, no mutually binding obligations".

The best definition of consideration is that of Sir Frederick Pollock who argued that consideration is the price a promisee pays in return for a promise.

> "An act or forbearance of the one party, or the promise thereof, is the price for which the promise of the other is bought, and the promise thus given for value is enforceable."

In commenting on this definition in a famous article,[8] Lord Wright indicated that this definition stresses that the act or forbearance must first be of value, something which in a materialistic sense can be given a price by the courts. The act or forbearance must also be purchased:

> "[I]t is done or suffered by the one party at the request of the other: it is a matter of mutuality, not a motive or emotion of affection, benevolence bounty or charity which from their nature must be personal to the promisor . . . the test of contractual intention is thus external, objective, realistic."[9]

Conventional case law affirms that the orthodox view of consideration retains its essential vitality. The courts will retain the power to rule that a promised exchange does not have value in the eyes of the law, as in the unusual case of

---

[7] *The Times*, November 24, 1997.

[8] Wright, (1936) 49 Harv. L.R. 1225.

[9] *Ibid.* at 1227. On the distinction between motive and promise see *Thomas v. Thomas* (1842) 2 Q.B. 851. In *Akazawa v. Firestone and Firestone* [1992] I.L.R.M. 31, Morris J. found that a promise was unenforceable for want of consideration: "it was a voluntary document given by Mr. Firestone in the hope of cementing business relationships": *Ibid.* at 48.

*O'Neill v. Murphy*[10] when it was held that parish building undertaken as part of an exchange in which the consideration moving from the parish was the saying of prayers for the benefit of the builder and his family, was held to be not a good and valuable consideration in the eyes of the law. Conventional case law in Ireland also requires the element of mutuality referred to by Lord Wright if a promise is to be contractually enforceable: it is not, as the law in Ireland currently stands, possible to enforce one promise as a contract simply by showing that but for the promise of another the promisee would have followed a course of conduct which would have been different to that followed as a result of the promise. This point can be made clear by a simple example.

I promise X that on her birthday next week I will give her my car. My promise is conditional on her reaching her next birthday. However, my failure to honour the promise will not be actionable because it is simply a promise to make a gift. Suppose X now informs me that she has given away her bicycle because she expected me to honour my promise. To be sure, "the price she has paid" for my promise is loss of her bicycle; she has not, however, provided consideration. My own promise caused this to occur but I did not request or stipulate that before X could acquire my car she had to transfer her bicycle. It may be that X will receive some limited compensation through the doctrine of estoppel but she cannot satisfy the needs of the conventional doctrine of consideration.

## Historical Antecedents

While it is clear that executory transactions in which each party assumes a duty to the other have been enforceable since the seventeenth century and the decision in *Slade's* case,[11] it is by no means established that the bargain model has long represented the basic or fundamental premise upon which enforceable contracts are formed. Simpson, in his analysis of the evolution of consideration,[12] advances the view that equitable and common law concepts of consideration were far from identical, and that the origins of consideration in *assumpsit* are traceable back to canon law or civil law. Atiyah argues strenuously that the bargain model was never representative of equitable practice and that equity generally recognised a promise to be enforceable when the promisee relied upon it. These views at least serve to point to the diversity of view, and uncertainty, that still surrounds the consideration doctrine. In any event, it is reasonably clear that since the eighteenth century the English and Irish courts have rejected the view that a gift made in consideration of natural love and affection, even within the context of a family unit, can be enforceable as a contract. A recent illustration of this is found in the case of *Re Wilson, Grove-White v. Wilson*,[13] where

---

[10] [1936] N.I. 16; *Allied Irish Banks plc v. Fagan and others*, unreported, High Court, November 10, 1995.
[11] (1602) 46. Rep. 91a.
[12] *A History of the Common Law Contract* (Clarendon, Oxford, 1975).
[13] [1933] I.R. 729.

Johnston J. held that an agreement for a valuable consideration cannot be sustained where a father makes over property to a son "for natural love and affection" and then gives an allowance to the son to assist in maintaining that property, following *Lee v. Matthews*[14] and disapproving *Price v. Jenkins*.[15]

The doctrine of consideration is foreign to many legal systems including that of Scotland which historically is closer to the Roman law tradition than that of the common law world. If a Scottish court is convinced that a promise is seriously meant then the fact that it was not given in the context of a bargain will not prevent enforcement of the promise. Lord Mansfield was undoubtedly the most influential figure in moulding modern English commercial law and his Scottish ancestry no doubt helps explain his attempts during the eighteenth century to uproot the doctrine of consideration. One attack mounted against the doctrine occurred in a series of cases in which Lord Mansfield argued that a promise to pay an antecedent debt, the debt itself being unenforceable, would be supported by moral consideration alone. If an infant, a discharged bankrupt and married woman promised to pay a debt incurred during infancy, bankruptcy of coverture respectively, this promise would be void. However, Lord Mansfield argued a subsequent promise would be enforceable for this promise, in his view, should be both morally and legally binding. The "moral consideration" theory was dismissed as alien to English law in *Eastwood v. Kenyon*.[16] It is also clear that the moral consideration theory at no time formed part of the jurisprudence developed by the Irish courts. In *Ferrar v. Costelloe*[17] the Irish Court of Exchequer held that a married woman who promised to be jointly and severally liable upon a bill of exchange signed with her husband could not be liable upon a new promise made after her husband died and the disability of coverture ended. Brady L.C. noted that *Eastwood v. Kenyon* went "a great way to overrule this doctrine of moral obligation." Richards C.B. in *Bradford v. Roulston*[18] also rejected the moral obligation theory.

The doctrine of consideration is not as irrational as many of its critics have argued. It is through the doctrine that the courts often satisfy themselves that a promise was in fact seriously meant. This has been described as "the deliberative function."[19] By adopting the form of an exchange of promises this ritual should indicate to a court that each intended to be bound. Whether other forms of ritual evidencing intent should be permitted this effect, such as recording a promise in writing, is another question. Several American jurisdictions enforce promises evidenced in this fashion and several commentators, including Lord Wright, have been attracted to such a reform.

---

[14]   (1880) 6 L.R. (Ir.) 530.
[15]   (1876) 5 Ch.D. 619.
[16]   (1840) 11 A. & E. 458.
[17]   (1841) 4 I.L.R. 425.
[18]   (1858) 8 I.R.C.L. 468.
[19]   Fuller (1941) 41 Col. L.Rev. 799.

## Adequacy and Sufficiency of Consideration

If the terms of the bargain are unduly favourable to one of the parties in the sense that the price paid by him is disproportionate to that which he obtains in return, the consideration may be said to be inadequate. Nevertheless, it is axiomatic that the courts will not investigate the adequacy of the consideration. If a landowner wishes to let his property for a handful of peppercorns or give an option to purchase his estate for one pound that is his affair. The attitude of the courts was neatly summed up by Manners L.C. in *Grogan v. Cooke*[20]: "If there be a fair and bona fide consideration the Court will not enter minutely into it, and see that it is full and ample." So if the bargain is an honest one it will be enforced, even if one party gets more from the bargain than the other. There is more recent authority on this question. In *Kennedy v. Kennedy*,[21] a case in which there was no allegation of improper pressure or disparity of intellect on either side, Ellis J. remarked that "once there is consideration its adequacy in this sort of case is irrelevant to its validity and enforceability." This basic rule of contract law was illustrated by the recent sale of Irish Steel Ltd. to a foreign consortium for a payment of one pound; the transaction involved a number of collateral undertakings that made the overall bargain a balanced one but the central issue, about the transfer of ownership in the assets of the company, is in point.[22]

Disparity of the exchange will, however, be an important factor in alerting the courts to the possibility of fraud or the existence of an unconscionable or improvident bargain, considered later in this book. Indeed, the enforceability in equity of a contract entered into with a person who is mentally incapable of looking after business affairs and is unable to understand the transaction will turn upon whether the transaction is "fair and bona fide." In the leading Irish case of *Hassard v. Smith*[23] Vice Chancellor Chatterton indicated that to satisfy this test the consideration paid must be an ample or fair price.

The operation of this procedure is well illustrated by the decision of Lynch J. in *Noonan (A Ward of Court) v. O'Connell*.[24] An application was brought to set aside the transfer of farmland owned by the plaintiff which was made at a time when the plaintiff was suffering from senile dementia, the defendant being a relative of the plaintiff. The transfer had been supervised by a solicitor and had been drafted so as to record the transaction as a sale of land for 50 pence. After finding that there was gross inequality in the position of plaintiff and defendant, and that the transaction had not been clearly explained to the plaintiff, the weaker party, Lynch J. dealt with the contention that the transaction was one of sale rather than a gift transfer: "On its face it is a purely voluntary transfer and of course the reference to fifty pence consideration is a complete

---

[20] (1812) 7 Ball & B. 234.

[21] Unreported, High Court, January 12, 1984.

[22] See the annotation to the Irish Steel Limited Act 1996, in *Irish Current Law Statutes Annotated* (Round Hall Sweet & Maxwell, 1996).

[23] (1872) 6 I.R. Eq. 429.

[24] Unreported, High Court, April 10, 1987.

anachronism and does not constitute any consideration." Had the transfer been freely agreed between parties standing on equal terms the form may have been recognised as a valid contract. Leases for peppercorn or nominal rents are still recognised as valid although even these transactions may be overturned if improvident or unconscionable.

Nevertheless, the provision of tokens or vouchers will not always constitute consideration. In the case of *Lipkin Gorman v. Karpale*[25] the House of Lords rejected the argument that when a casino provided a gambler with gaming chips, the provision of chips constituted a valuable consideration. The chips remained the property of the casino and were simply a convenient device to enable gaming to be conducted.

The leading English textbook writers, however, indicate that while consideration need not be adequate it must be sufficient. This means that before the consideration promised can support a counter promise it must not run foul of a series of rules designed to indicate when a promise will not suffice in law. These rules are often dictated by the needs of public policy. While the Irish courts have not as yet ruled conclusively on sufficiency the decision of the Northern Ireland Court of Appeal in *O'Neill v. Murphy*[26] provides a useful illustration of a case in which the alleged consideration was held to be insufficient. A builder executed work for the parish next to the one in which he resided; an allegation of undue influence on the part of the religious advisor of the builder was countered by an argument based on contract; the builder had agreed to do the work in consideration of prayers being said for his intentions. It was held that there was no consideration in law for the builder's work. Andrews L.J. said that "while it is clear that the courts will not interfere with the exercise of free will and judgement of the parties by enquiry into the adequacy of consideration, it is necessary that it should be sufficient in law. Thus, neither a mere voluntary courtesy nor some act already executed will suffice."

First, a promise in exchange for performing a duty already imposed by the general law, such as answering a subpoena, would not be enforceable. Public agencies and citizens should perform their public or statutory duties without hoping for or encouraging payment. The owner of a burning building who promises to pay £1,000 to a group of firemen if they save the premises could only be sued on this promise if the firemen's actions went beyond those required or expected of public service firemen.

The leading English case is the decision of the House of Lords in *Glasbrook Bros. Ltd. v. Glamorgan County Council.*[27] The appellants sought police protection of their coal mine and its equipment during the currency of a strike. In the view of the police authority the mine could be adequately protected by patrolling the mine and its environs. The appellants sought a standing guard and, as such, the police authority 'lent' constables for this purpose and imposed a charge. The

---

[25] [1991] 3 W.L.R. 10.
[26] [1936] N.I. 16.
[27] [1925] A.C. 270.

House of Lords held that the practice was both legal and done for a valuable consideration, although several members of the House indicated that if the measures taken were taken after the police authority had formed the view that these measures were necessary for the maintenance of property and keeping the peace then no charge could be levied. Here, however, no such opinion had been formed and the police officers had been billeted at the mine in order to meet the wishes of the appellants.

In the case of *Harris v. Sheffield United Football Club*,[28] however, the Court of Appeal had to consider whether a professional football club could be liable for the cost of the internal and external policing of their stadium by members of the South Yorkshire Police Force. The Club argued that these charges, in the unfortunately violent climate of the 1980s, were not recoverable because the prospects of crowd misbehaviour and the attendant risk to property and persons made the provision of policing services an essential part of the duty owed by the Police Authority to the public generally. The Court of Appeal rejected this view. Given the fact that the premises were, by and large private premises, the fact that the event, a football match, had been privately organised, and the strain that resulted on scarce resources (constables were often off-duty and were required at weekends) meant that these services were special police services and overtime payments and other expenses were recoverable from the Football Club.

The only Irish case in which this kind of argument has arisen is *McKerring v. The Minister for Agriculture*.[29] The case arose out of a dispute between the minister and the plaintiff farmer in respect of grant payments under the Tuberculosis and Brucellosis Eradication Scheme. The plaintiff had been disallowed payment because of non-compliance with the rules and one issue that arose was whether the scheme was a discretionary scheme or one in which payment was made under contract. Although the point was not a contentious one O'Hanlon J. wondered whether merely complying with the scheme as was required by statute could not constitute consideration moving from the plaintiff. O'Hanlon J. found that the plaintiff did provide consideration:

> "it appears to me that there is sufficient consideration involved in strict compliance with all the conditions, even though *some of them* may be a matter of legal obligation as well" (emphasis added).

Secondly, performance of a duty already owed *to the promisor* may constitute consideration although the limits of this doctrine have yet to be established. The older cases *Stilk v. Myrick*[30] and *Hartley v. Ponsonby*[31] suggest that only if the initial contract is discharged can a second promise be actionable by a party who in substance performs the duty owed under the first contract. The view is

---

[28] [1987] 2 All E.R. 836.

[29] [1989] I.L.R.M. 82: see also *Rooney v. Minister for Agriculture and Food and Others, Irish Times Law Report*, February 3, 1992.

[30] (1809) 2 Comp. 317.

[31] (1857) 7 E & B 872. See, however, *The Sansone* (1851) 3 Ir. Jur. Rep. (O.S.) 258.

supported in the Irish case of *Farrington v. Donoghue*.[32] More recently, however it has been suggested that generally a promise to perform an existing duty is sufficient consideration for a promise: see *Williams v. Williams*.[33] The case of *Williams v. Williams* concerned the enforceability of a promise made in a maintenance agreement whereby the husband promised to pay £1 10s. per week to his wife if she would maintain herself and for as long as she lived apart from him. The majority of the Court of Appeal were able to find a sufficient consideration to the husband from the fact that, during her "desertion" from him, he was no longer bound to maintain her and that she could have resumed cohabitation with him or sought maintenance if he refused to accept her offer to return. Denning L.J., while attracted to such sophistry, took a more forthright view, stating *obiter*:

> "I agree that in promising to maintain herself whilst she was in desertion, the wife was only promising to do that which she was already bound to do. Nevertheless, a promise to perform an existing duty is, I think, sufficient consideration to support or promise, so long as there is nothing in the transaction which is contrary to the public interest."[34]

These two lines of authority have been fully discussed in *North Ocean Shipping v. Hyundai*.[35] Mocatta J. suggested that if the duty owed arises under statute then performance of that duty will be consideration for a promise. The point can be illustrated from Irish statute law. Under the old Poor Laws (which have been supplanted by provisions in the Social Welfare (Consolidation) Act 1993 section 285) the mother of an illegitimate child had a statutory duty of support. Should the father promise to pay a fixed sum every week the mother would on this modern line of authority be able to recover, even though she owes a statutory duty to do that requested by the promisor. If, however, the duty owed springs from *contract* it cannot provide consideration for a promise. In the *North Ocean Shipping* case a shipbuilding company was promised an increase in the price payable for building the vessel. Mocatta J. held the promise enforceable because on the facts additional consideration was provided for the increased price but was clearly of the view that unless the additional element was present, the discharge of an existing contractual duty owed by the promisee is an insufficient consideration. O'Hanlon J. in *Kenny v. An Post*[36] has also reiterated the orthodox view said to be laid down in *Stilk v. Myrick*.[37]

---

[32] (1866) I.R. I.C.L. 675. However, see *Pordage v. Canter* (1854) 6 Ir. Jur. Rep. (O.S.) 246 where additional consideration provided by mother's promise to remain chaste.
[33] [1957] 1 W.L.R. 148.
[34] *Ibid.* at 150–151.
[35] [1978] 3 All E.R. 1170.
[36] [1988] J.I.S.L.L. 187.
[37] (1809) 2 Comp. 317.

This entire area of law has been thrown into confusion by the decision of the Court of Appeal in *Williams v. Roffey Brothers & Nicholls (Contractors) Ltd.*[38] The defendants were contractors who awarded a sub-contract for joinery work to the plaintiff. The contract and sub-contract involved the refurbishment of the roof and interior of some 27 flats and the price agreed involved a payment of £20,000 impliedly payable in stages as work progressed. After the roof and nine flats had been totally refurbished and the remaining 18 flats had been partially refurbished, the plaintiff approached the defendant seeking additional payments because the plaintiff had seriously underestimated the cost of carrying out the work and this, allied to his failure to properly supervise his workmen, made it difficult for him to complete for the agreed amount without facing financial difficulties. The plaintiff, having received interim payments totalling £16,200 and having brought his difficulties to the attention of the defendant, obtained a promise that upon completion of the work he would be paid a further £10,300. The plaintiff's representative persuaded the defendant that it was in their own interests that their subcontractor should not be held to perform for too low a price for, in Glidewell L.J.'s words, the main contractor "will never get the job finished without paying more money." In response to the plaintiff's action on the promise the defendant, relying on *Stilk v. Myrick*, argued that because the plaintiff was only promising to do that which he was bound to do for the defendant anyway, the promise to pay an additional amount was unenforceable for want of consideration.

Notwithstanding the decision in *Stilk v. Myrick*, and the reaffirmation of the proposition that "consideration" remains a fundamental requirement before a contract not under seal can be enforced, the Court of Appeal took, in the words of Russell L.J., a "pragmatic approach" to the relationship between the parties. Consideration could be found in the fact that a haphazard system of payment was replaced by a more structured payment system and the plaintiff had provided consideration by giving the defendant grounds for believing that the work would be completed without interruption by reason of insolvency or other difficulty, a very real benefit from promisor to promisee for the construction contract contained a penalty clause which would have operated against the defendant in the event of any delay. In the leading judgment Glidewell L.J. stated that the law supported the following propositions:

> "(i) if A has entered into a contract with B to do work for, or to supply goods or services to, B in return for payment by B and (ii) at some stage before A has completely performed his obligations under the contract B has reason to doubt whether A will, or will be able to, complete his side of the bargain and (iii) B thereupon promises A an additional payment in return for A's promise to perform his contractual obligations on time and (iv) as a result of giving his promise B obtains in practice a benefit, or obviates a disbenefit, and (v) B's promise is not given as a result of

---

[38] [1990] 1 All E.R. 512.

economic duress or fraud on the part of A, then (vi) the benefit to B is capable of being consideration for B's promise, so that the promise will be legally binding."[39]

The application of such a controversial and difficult proposition not only threatens to further undermine the bargain theory; it also makes the boundary between promissory estoppel and consideration even more difficult to draw. Perhaps a more rational response would have required the Court of Appeal to negative the consideration argument that the plaintiff successfully utilised, and to address the issues from a promissory estoppel perspective. The *Roffey Brothers* case has been held to apply only in cases where the promise by A consists of rendering services to B in return for B's promise of additional payment. The decision in *Re Selectmove*[40] makes it clear that *Roffey Brothers* does not change the rule that payment of part of a liquidated debt will not constitute consideration for a promise to forego the remainder of the amount due.

Thirdly, performance of a duty owed *to someone other than the promisor* may support a promise. Students will find the application of the old case of *Scotson v. Pegg*[41] by the Privy Council in 1974 in *The Eurymedon* case instructive. Simply put, if A owes a contractual duty to marry B and a third party (the father of B perhaps) promises to pay A £1,000 after the ceremony, A can enforce this promise. While it is no longer possible to sue in the Republic of Ireland for breach of promise to marry, the cause of action having been abolished by the Family Law Act 1981, *Saunders v. Cramer*[42] is an Irish authority in favour of this rule. Indeed, there are several mid-nineteenth century Irish cases which demonstrate that if a promise of this kind is evidenced in writing, so as to satisfy the requirements of section 2 of the Statute of Frauds 1695, the argument that the engaged couple could not provide consideration for a third party promise by marrying, was never raised.[43] Some explanation for this can be found in the leading English case of *Shadwell v. Shadwell*.[44] Here the plaintiff's uncle, upon learning of his nephew's engagement, wrote promising to assist the nephew upon commencement of his married life by providing him with £150 yearly until such time as the nephew's annual earnings at the Chancery bar reached 600 guineas. An action to enforce the promise against his uncle's executors was successful. One of the justifications advanced by Earle C.J. was the accrual of a benefit to the uncle in such a situation, saying that a marriage may be a matter of interest to a near relative. In his dissenting judgment Byles J. pointed out that there was no evidence to support the view that the

---

[39] [1990] 1 All E.R. 512 at 521–522.
[40] [1995] 2 All E.R. 531, followed by Keane J. in *Truck and Machinery Sales Ltd. v. Marubeni Komatsu Ltd.*, unreported, High Court, February 23, 1996 see also *Musumeci v. Winadell Pty Ltd.* (1994) 34 N.S.W.L.R. 723.
[41] (1861) 6 H. & N. 295.
[42] (1842) 5 I.Eq. R. 12.
[43] *O'Sullivan v. O'Callaghan* (1849) 2 Ir.Jur. 314; *Arthure v. Dillon* (1849) 2 Ir.Jur. 162.
[44] (1860) 9 C.B. (N.S.) 159.

marriage resulted in any personal benefit to the plaintiff's uncle, and it is submitted that this dissenting judgment provides a clearer analysis of the case, if we are concerned to retain the view that consideration must consist of some tangible exchange between the parties and is not to include cases of supposed psychological gratification.

## The Rule against Past Consideration

Because the common law recognises that contracts are enforced in order to carry into effect the expectations of the parties responsible for creating them, there are instances where a contract will be held to exist where neither party has attempted to perform their respective promises. If A agrees to purchase six tons of coal from B in six months time and to pay a price of £10 a ton, a contract exists as from the exchange of promises. The consideration provided is the promised act of each; in this bilateral contract the consideration is said to be executory. While neither party has performed as yet, both parties are said to have provided consideration by their exchange of promises. Should *one* party perform (for example, when A forwards the price of the coal to B) the consideration by A is executed and he can of course maintain an action against B in the event of delivery.

Professor Atiyah in his book, *Promises, Morals, and Law* has challenged the view that bilateral executory contracts, that is, cases in which the parties have simply exchanged promises without either party having acted to implement the exchange, often are not, and should not be, given the same weight and importance as executed or completed exchanges. This argument has been repudiated by the Court of Appeal in *Centrovincial Estates Plc. v. Merchant Investors Assurance Co. Ltd.*[45] The lessee of a building was informed by the lessor that following upon the operation of a rent review clause the rent due for the future would be reduced. The lessor asked the lessee to indicate acceptance of this offer which the lessee promptly did. The lessor then discovered that the rent review had been incorrectly carried out and he sought to retract the accepted offer by arguing that where an offer is accepted the offer can be withdrawn by the offeror if the offeree has not suffered a detriment, and in this case, neither side had acted upon the offer. The Court of Appeal, allowing the lessee's appeal, held the offer, once validly accepted, could not be withdrawn save in instances of operative mistake. In the Court of Appeal Slade L.J. pointed out that the offeree had given consideration when he gave the promise requested and that it was irrelevant whether or not the offeree had changed his position beyond giving the promise requested by him.

It is well established, however, that if a promise is made after some gratuitous act has been performed by the promisee the subsequent promise is not supported by consideration. The benefit conferred before the promise was made cannot

---

[45] [1983] Com. L.R. 158.

be said to have been made by reference to an antecedent promise. We have already seen that promises are not enforced because they satisfy a test of causation; if I promise to give my house to my brother because he paid my hospital bill during an earlier illness my promise was the result of a benefit already conferred. Nevertheless, it was not given in the context of an exchange of promises so no bargain or contract will result. Here the consideration is said to be past consideration which is no consideration at all.

The leading English case is *Roscorla v. Thomas.*[46] The plaintiff purchased a horse for £30 from Thomas who, following the sale, warranted the horse "free from vice." The horse bit and was therefore not as warranted. The action failed; the pleadings clearly indicated that the sale had been completed when the warranty was given. Roscorla then had provided no consideration; the promise to pay the purchase price was not given in exchange for the warranty sued upon. The courts however do not sit over the negotiations ready to record and examine the exchange of promises second by second. In *Smith v. Morrison*[47] the Irish Queens Bench Division distinguished *Roscorla v. Thomas*. It was pleaded that the sale of a horse took place contemporaneously with the giving of the warranty. It was held that if this be so the promise will not be held to have been given for a past consideration.

The wording of the promise will no doubt provide guidance on this; the past tense will indicate that the promised act has already been performed but parol evidence is admissible to show whether the consideration is past or not. In *Bewley v. Whiteford*[48] the Court of Exchequer indicated that if after hearing parol testimony the court is in doubt whether the consideration is wholly executed (past) or executory then an action on the promise will not succeed: see also *Gorrie v. Woodley.*[49] The leading modern English case is *Re McArdle.*[50] The plaintiffs were promised a sum of money "in consideration of your carrying out certain alterations and improvements" to property in which the promisors had an interest. Upon proof that the words indicated work that had already been done, rather than work that had yet to be completed, the action upon the promise failed. Another difficulty that a plaintiff may face is that promises given by members of a family may be held unenforceable for lack of legal intent – see Chapter 3.

The leading modern Irish case is *Provincial Bank of Ireland v. Donnell*[51] a decision of the Northern Ireland Court of Appeal. The bank sued the defendant on a deed (not under seal) in which she agreed to provide security for her husband's overdraft in consideration of "advances heretofore made or that might hereafter be made." The action failed. The consideration stated here was either past or illusory; the advances that had earlier been made were a past

---

[46] (1842) 3 Q.B. 234.
[47] (1846) 10 I.L.R.C.L. 213.
[48] (1832) Hayes 356.
[49] (1864) 17 I.C.L.R. 221.
[50] [1951] Ch. 669.
[51] (1932) 67 I.T.L.R. 142.

consideration while the advances that "might hereafter be made" gave the bank a total discretion whether they would provide advances or not. The promises then should have been recorded in a deed under seal in order to render them enforceable. There may be statutory provisions that authorise a different construction; see section 288 of the Companies Act 1963 and *Re Daniel Murphy Ltd.*[52]

A promise made after the promisee has conferred a benefit upon another person may be enforceable if the court is able to bring the case within the seventeenth century English case of *Lampleigh v. Braithwait.*[53] This case holds that while a past consideration will not of itself provide support for an implied promise to pay, it may support a subsequent express promise made by the beneficiary. The rule itself, which predates *Lampleigh v. Braithwait* was applied by the Court of Exchequer in *Bradford v. Roulston.*[54] Roulston was employed by Bradford to find a purchaser for Bradford's boat. A third party agreed to purchase the vessel but when the bill of sale was to be completed the purchaser did not have sufficient funds to pay the purchase price. Bradford was about to withdraw from the transaction when he was asked by Roulston to sign. Bradford signed the bill of sale. After the bill of sale was signed Roulston promised in writing that he would ensure payment of the balance the following day. Roulston was sued on this promise. The consideration provided, signature of the bill of sale by Bradford, was clearly past. Pigot C.B. stated in his speech, however, that "[w]here there is a past consideration, consisting of a previous act done at the request of the defendant, it will support a subsequent promise; the promise being treated as coupled with the previous request." The fact that the plaintiff was out of pocket was significant. In the majority of these cases existence of a benefit conferred upon the defendant tends to explain why the plaintiff succeeds. In this instant case, Bradford was held entitled to claim the sum promised because he had signed the bill of sale at Roulston's behest. What is important here is that when the requested act is provided, the parties must not have intended the act to be gratuitious. Evidence that the parties intended the promise to be compensable at some later date will be necessary. In fact in *Bradford v. Roulston* the defendant may well have uttered his promise to pay the plaintiff when the bill of sale was to be signed but the plaintiff chose to rely on the promise in the letter because had he relied exclusively on the earlier oral promise he may have encountered problems in relation to the Statute of Frauds (Ireland) 1695. In *Pao On v. Lau Yiu Long*[55] Lord Scarman summarised the exception to the rule against past consideration thus:

"The act must have been done at the promisor's request, the parties must have understood that the act was to be remunerated either by a payment

---

[52] [1964] I.R. 1.
[53] (1615) Hob. 105.
[54] (1858) 8 I.R.C.L. 468.
[55] [1979] 3 All E.R. 65.

or the conferment of some other benefit, and payment, or the conferment of a benefit, must have been legally enforceable had it been promised in advance."[56]

An illustration of this principle not being satisfied can be found in the old Irish case of *Morgan v. Rainsford*[57] decided in 1845. Specific performance of a promise was sought, the promise being "in consideration of the permanent improvements you have made and have promised to make." The action failed: the reference to past improvements was held back and the reference to future improvements was too vague. The failure to specify these improvements meant that that part of the alleged consideration was void for uncertainty. It may be difficult for the plaintiff to satisfy the second of Lord Scarman's three conditions if a family relationship or a close friendship subsists between the parties for the court may conclude that the plaintiff's conduct was motivated by factors other than the expectation of remuneration.[58]

## Consideration must Move from the Promisee

Where the contract is executory the bargain may remain to be performed yet the exchange of promises gives each party the right to seek and obtain performance or monetary compensation. If A promises to buy coal from B tomorrow, paying £100 for the goods, each is a promisor and each is a promisee. A has given his promise to pay £100 and has received B's promise to deliver and *vice versa*. The nineteenth century authorities indicate that consideration exists where the promisee, the party seeking enforcement, can point to performance of a detrimental act (or the promise thereof) on the part of the promisee: *Lowry v. Reid*.[59] Alternatively, if the promisor has received a requested benefit from the promisee consideration is present. The essential requirement is that the promisee must have provided the benefit or incurred the detriment, as the case may be.

Take the facts of *McCoubray v. Thompson*.[60] AG owned land, goods and chattels worth £196 which he intended to transfer to M and T, share and share alike. T wanted the land to himself and it was agreed that in consideration for AG transferring everything to T, T would pay M £98, half the value of the property. T defaulted and was sued by M. Clearly the defendant had made a promise; it was also addressed to both AG and M, so they constituted joint promisees. Applying the rule requiring consideration to move from the promisee however it is clear that M had no cause of action in contract. He had

---

[56] [1979] 3 All E.R. at 74.
[57] (1845) 8 Ir. E.R. 299.
[58] *Sim Tony v. Lim Ah Ghee* [1995] 4 L.R.C. 377.
[59] [1927] N.I. 142.
[60] (1868) 2 I.R.C.L. 226.

made no promise in return for T's own promise to pay £98; the sole consideration for T's promise moved from AG. Monaghan C.J. held that where three parties join in an allegedly tripartite contract such as this the plaintiff must be able to show that *he* has provided consideration in some sense.

In *Barry v. Barry*[61] a similar transaction was held to give a valid cause of action. Under the terms of his father's will the defendant was to receive the family farm if he promised to pay personally legacies to members of the family, including the plaintiff, a younger brother. If the defendant was unwilling to do this the legacy was to be payable from the land. The defendant promised to be personally liable to pay the legacies, whereupon the executors permitted him to use the farm. The promise was addressed to the executors and the plaintiff. When the defendant defaulted the plaintiff sued claiming the defendant was personally bound by his promise. The Court of Appeal held that consideration had moved from the promisee. The defendant by his promise led the plaintiff to give up any right to have the legacy realised out of the property; by forbearing to exercise rights over the estate at the implied request of the defendant the promisee had provided consideration. The difference between this case and *McCoubray v. Thompson* is that McCoubray had no rights at all, however ill-defined, over the property which he could give up or refrain from exercising, so consideration could not be provided from this source.

A distinction, however, is to be drawn between cases where the promisor makes a promise to two persons, in circumstances where both promisees are intended to benefit, either jointly or severally, but only one promisee will actually provide the necessary exchange. It is hardly surprising that the courts will not provide a promisor with a defence to an action on the promise in such circumstances, for the application of a strict consideration requirement here would prove commercially inconvenient in many everyday contexts. So, although the joint promisee should provide consideration before he can enforce this promise, it has been recognised that this may be inconvenient if a joint bank account is opened but one of the parties does not intend to provide consideration by paying funds into the account. Could a bank refuse to pay him funds held in the account on the grounds that it has no contract with this person because he has not provided consideration? It seems not. See the opinions of the members of the House of Lords in *McEvoy v. Belfast Banking Co. Ltd.*[62] and the controversial Australian case of *Coulls v. Bagot's Trustee*,[63] criticised by Coote.[64] Notwithstanding these criticisms by Professor Coote, Brennan J., in the High Court of Australia's decision in *Thomas v. Hollier*,[65] seemed prepared to apply this reasoning to the case at the bar but found that this doctrine was not satisfied by the facts of the case before him.

---

[61] (1891) 28 L.R. (Ir.) 45.
[62] [1935] A.C. 24.
[63] [1967] A.L.R. 385.
[64] [1978] C.L.J. 301.
[65] [1984] A.L.R. 39.

## Compromise of a Claim

It is well established that an undertaking not to continue civil litigation or an agreement to compromise a claim will provide consideration for the promise of another. Indeed, the courts view it as in the public interest to encourage out of court settlement of civil disputes. In *Taylor v. Smyth and Others*[66] Lardner J. said:

> "it is also well established that where proceedings between parties are settled by an agreement to compromise, the agreement to compromise constitutes a new and independent contract between the parties made for good consideration and the original rights of the parties and causes of action become superceded by the compromise agreement."[67]

A difficulty may arise however if the claim that one party agrees to give up subsequently turns out to have had little or no chance of success. The promisor who is sued upon this agreement to compromise may argue that the claim was so vacuous and of such doubtful validity that it cannot provide consideration for his own promise.

The courts, however, refuse to hold that because the earlier cause of action had no chance of success the compromise is invalid. It is the legitimacy of the compromise that must be assessed. If both parties, however, know that the initial claim was invalid then the compromise too will fail. This view was taken by Palles C.B. in *O'Donnell v. O'Sullivan*.[68] The parties agreed to compromise a claim for £137 by the defendant paying £75. During the trial it became clear that the original debt was a gambling debt, unenforceable at law. While this fact alone did not make the compromise invalid for want of consideration the fact that both parties knew this to be so did. The Chief Justice Baron declared "[i]t is settled law that unless there is a reasonable claim which is bona fide intended to be pursued the settlement of that claim cannot be good consideration for a compromise."

In general, the compromise must satisfy three conditions:

(1) the initial claim must have been reasonable and not vexatious or frivolous;

(2) the plaintiff must have had an honest belief in the chances of its success;

(3) the party contending that the compromise is valid must not have withheld or suppressed facts that would have shown the claim in a truer light.

The third condition is normally broken by a defendant who threatens an action while suppressing facts which clearly show that the claim would no

---

[66] [1990] I.L.R.M. 377.

[67] *Ibid.* at 389, citing, *inter alia Green v. Rozen* [1955] 2 All E.R. 797; *O'Mahony v. Gaffrey* [1986] I.R. 36.

[68] (1913) 47 I.L.T.R. 253.

doubt fail. In the case of *Leonard v. Leonard*[69] a claim was compromised between two half brothers who each claimed entitlement to an estate. The plaintiff agreed to compromise his claim because he had been advised that on the facts the claim was not certain to succeed. The defendant, however, had withheld information from the plaintiff which suggested that the claim would indeed succeed. The compromise was held invalid because the defendant had exploited the plaintiff's ignorance of all the facts.

Part of the reason why bona fide compromises of doubtful claims have been upheld can be attributed to the view that it is for the parties to make their own bargain. Indeed, there is a considerable body of support for the view that when the consideration requested by the promisor is the surrender or delivery of a document, the contractual compromise is valid, notwithstanding the fact that the document is worthless. As long as the transaction is an arm's length commercial transaction the instructive New Zealand case of *Veitch v. Sinclair*[70] supports the proposition, but if the surrender takes place in circumstances where the policy of the law is to protect one of the parties, the compromise may not be valid. So in *O'Reilly v. Connor; O'Reilly v. Allen*[71] the Court of Kings Bench refused to uphold the validity of a compromise in which the plaintiff accepted a compromise of an unenforceable claim against a borrower, the plaintiff alleging that the later compromise allowed him to sue on a promissory note. Barton J. distinguished this situation from the leading English case of *Haigh v. Brooks*[72] on the ground that this transaction was a loan transaction subject to strict statutory provisions to protect borrowers from oppressive practices.

Professor Kelly has convincingly argued that just as the surrender of a case of action may constitute a valuable consideration, so too may the surrender of a defence to an action.[73]

## Forbearance – Promise and Fact

A promise to abstain from doing something will in many cases be as valuable to the promisee as a positive action. Pollock's definition of consideration refers to forbearance *or the promise thereof* as capable of supporting another promise. In the American case of *Hamer v. Sidway*[74] an uncle promised his nephew $5,000 if he refrained from drinking, using tobacco, swearing or gambling until 21. The nephew met these conditions and was successful in an action for the promised sum. He had a legal privilege to do these things and the acts of forbearance, requested by his uncle, provided consideration for the promise.

---

[69]  (1812) 2 Ball & B. 171.
[70]  [1975] 1 N.Z.L.R. 264.
[71]  (1904) 38 I.L.T.R. 21.
[72]  (1839) 10 Ad & El. 309.
[73]  (1964) 27 M.L.R. 540.
[74]  (1891) 124 N.Y. 583.

The court was satisfied that the promise was seriously meant; it had been earnestly repeated before assembled members of the family.

Any expressly requested forbearance then will provide consideration. If I indicate I wish to leave my job and my employer promises me £1,000 if I remain in his employment for another six weeks this will be good consideration for although I will be performing the same tasks as before my forbearance will entitle me to claim the sum promised after performance.

The most common act of forbearance to come before the courts arises in cases where a promise is given in return for a promise not to enforce a legal remedy. In the leading English case of *Cook v. Wright*[75] parish trustees threatened the occupant of a house with proceedings unless he signed promissory notes. Under a local Act of Parliament rates could be levied on owners in order to maintain local services. An action on the notes succeeded because the trustees had provided consideration by refraining to take proceedings to recover the rates due. Incidentally, the claim by the defendant that he was not the owner and therefore not liable to pay the rate failed; as we have seen it was enough for the trustees to have a reasonable belief that proceedings would have been successful.

If the promise has to be recorded in writing so as to satisfy the Statute of Frauds the courts have held that the consideration should be stated in the alleged memorandum. It is sufficient if the consideration is stated, expressly or impliedly, on the memorandum itself. In *Hibernian Gas Company v. Parry*[76] a hotel business fell into receivership, one of the creditors being the plaintiff company. The plaintiffs were owed £32 for gas supplied. The receiver executed a document in favour of the company promising to pay all sums due six months hence. The consideration for this promise was not expressly stated on the memorandum (a contract of guarantee requiring a memorandum) but the Court of Exchequer unanimously held the receiver liable on his promise. Pennefather B. pointed out that the memorandum implicitly recorded two requested acts in the form of forbearance for the £32 due and continued supply of gas for the future. When the company agreed to these terms a contract was concluded, for as Brady C.B. observed, if the company sought to recover sums due before the six-month period elapsed the action would not have succeeded. Students should contrast the terms of the promise given here with that in the earlier English case of *Wood v. Benson*[77] where part of a similar guarantee was held to infringe the rule against past consideration.

The context within which the promise was made may assist the court in finding consideration for a seemingly gratuitous promise. In *Blandford & Houdret Ltd. v. Bray Travel Holdings Ltd. & Hopkins*[78] the plaintiff sought to recover on a guarantee, executed by the second defendant in favour of the plaintiff, in which the second defendant promised to pay debts of the first

---

[75] (1861) 1 B. & S. 559.
[76] (1841) 4 I.L.R. 453.
[77] (1831) 2 C. & J. 94.
[78] Unreported, High Court, November 11, 1983.

defendant already due to the plaintiff. While the instrument itself did not specify the consideration provided by the plaintiff – Gannon J. stated that on its face consideration was past – the facts revealed that the guarantee was given on the understanding that the plaintiff impliedly promised to forbear from exercising his right to withhold future services from the first defendant, something the plaintiff was entitled to do under the contract when payments were not made.

Many of the leading cases concern undertakings given by a debtor to a creditor whereby the debtor undertakes to provide security for the debt. The question often arises: what consideration moves from the creditor to the debtor in such a context? A not untypical case is provided by *Re Montgomery*[79] where a creditor was able to establish forbearance as consideration for promises by the defendant to meet trading debts incurred by the defendant's father while operating the family business. The role of forbearance as part of the doctine of consideration takes on a very controversial aspect when it is said that a promise may be supported simply upon proof that the promisor relied upon the promise. At this point the entire bargain theory of consideration begins to split at the seams. The leading English case of *Alliance Bank Ltd. v. Broom*[80] was applied by the House of Lords in *Fullerton v. Bank of Ireland.*[81] The bank wrote a letter to Colonel Stevenson, drawing his attention to the fact that his account was overdrawn. The client responded that he would provide title deeds to property as security. The Law Lords held that the consideration provided for this promise was the restraint and patience displayed by the bank in not immediately calling in the overdraft: "such forbearance in fact although there was no agreement by the bank to forbear suing Colonel Stevenson for any indefinite period was sufficient consideration to support his promise to give the security."[82]

In *The Commodity Broking Co. v. Meehan*[83] the defendant, sole beneficial owner of all shares in P. Ltd., ran up a large account with the plaintiffs in the name of the company. When the account reached an indebtedness of £36,000 the defendant was asked to give a personal guarantee; he refused but promised to pay off the debt at the rate of £1,000 per month. He failed to honour this promise and in reply to an action on the promise pleaded an absence of consideration. After reviewing the English authorities and in particular *Alliance Bank Ltd. v. Broom*[84] Barron J. held that it was not necessary to find that the parties had reached an actual agreement not to sue upon the debt. Barron J. stated "[t]he better view is that where a request express or implied to forbear from bringing proceedings induces such forbearance this amounts to good consideration." On the facts before him Barron J. found that there was no consideration. The plaintiff company had abstained from seeking a remedy

---

[79] (1876) 10 Ir.Rep.Eq. 479.
[80] (1864) 2 Dr. & Sm. 289.
[81] [1903] A.C. 309.
[82] *Ibid.* at 315.
[83] [1985] I.R. 12.
[84] Above, n.80.

from P. Ltd. because the company was insolvent and the exercise would have been pointless: see also Denning L.J. in *Combe v. Combe*.[85]

Some cases are even more difficult to reconcile with the orthodox doctrine of consideration. It has been convincingly argued by Professor Atiyah in his *Rise and Fall of Freedom of Contract*[86] that in certain types of transaction no exchange exists but, nevertheless, the courts have held a promise enforceable through the concept of contract, largely because the promisee has or may have relied upon the promise. This is particularly so, Atiyah points out, in relation to promises made to an engaged couple. The likelihood that these persons may rely on the promise – buy expensive furniture, rent or buy a house – in a way they would not have done if the promise had not been made explains the decision in many cases, amongst them *Shadwell v. Shadwell*[87] and the Irish case of *Saunders v. Cramer*.[88] In *Moore v. Kelly*,[89] Ronan L.J. remarked that the cases support the proposition that "If there is an honest family transaction a slight legal consideration is sufficient to take the case out of the category of voluntary deeds." So it is certainly arguable that in certain types of relationship the courts may impose qualitively different standards before the promise can be enforced, standards that may not be as exacting as in other areas of human or commercial relationships. Consideration may not be one doctrine but in fact several doctrines.

Atiyah has argued that in cases where a promise was made in order to induce the promisee into a course of action which causes the promisee to act, thereby incurring a liability that would not otherwise have arisen, the courts of equity, certainly by the beginning of the nineteenth century, regarded the promise as enforceable. Atiyah gives as an illustration the decision of Lord Eldon in *Crosbie v. McDougall*.[90] In the case of *Wilcocks v. Hennyngton*[91] Sugden L.C. approved *Crosbie v. McDougall* but on the facts before him was unable to find any altered change of position.

## Payment of an Existing Debt

The rule in *Pinnel's* case,[92] as laid down by the English Court of Common Pleas, dictates that if a liquidated sum is owed by A to B, a promise by B to take a lesser sum in full satisfaction of the larger debt will not bind B. After receipt he can immediately sue for the balance because the debtor has only performed part of a contractual duty already owed to the creditor. In other words, the creditor's promise is unenforceable for lack of consideration. In

---

85 [1951] 2 K.B. 215.
86 (Clarendon, Oxford, 1979) at pp. 457–458.
87 (1860) 9 C.B. (N.S.) 159.
88 (1842) 5 I.Eq.R. 12.
89 [1918] 1 I.R. 169.
90 (1806) 13 Ves. 148.
91 (1855) 5 I.Ch.R. 38.
92 (1602) 5 Co. Rep. 117a.

*O'Neill v. Murphy*[93] the rule in *Pinnel's* case was described by Andrews L.J. as a landmark "too firmly fixed in our law to be shaken."

The decision of the House of Lords in *Foakes v. Beer*[94] places the consideration doctrine at the forefront of promises to make, and also discharge, contracts. In this case Beer, a judgment creditor in the sum of £2,090, gave Foakes a promise that if he paid £500 and the balance by instalments, she would not "take any proceedings whatever on the judgment." Judgments carried interest and the issue arose whether her promise estopped Beer from seeking the interest. Interpreting the agreement as if it impliedly contained a promise to forego interest, the House of Lords held that the interest could be recovered because Beer's promise to forego interest was unsupported by consideration. The decision is a harsh and somewhat mechanical one and it fails to meet commercial expectations and commercial practice. As we shall see, the issue of reconciling this case with promissory estoppel remains problematical in English and Irish law.

Other jurisdictions, however, have been more forthright in addressing the venerable line of authority that starts with the dictum in *Pinnel's* case. In Canada, the New Brunswick Court of Appeal has held that the rule in *Pinnel's* case had to be qualified in the light of the need to produce a more reasoned result according with day to day business practice.[95] A bank agreed to accept $1,000 in full discharge of a judgment debt awarded against a debtor for $3,780, this agreement being confirmed in writing by the bank. At first instance the settlement was held not to be binding, following *Pinnel's* case. On appeal, consideration was held to be present. Angers J.A. declared:

> "it cannot be denied that a financial institution, of its own accord and knowing all the consequences of its action, entered into an agreement by which it agreed to waive the priority of a judgment in its favour in return for part payment of the debt due to it. This agreement constituted full satisfaction. The consideration for the Caisse Populaire was the immediate receipt of payment and the saving of time, effort and expense."[96]

However, in these islands, *Foakes v. Beer* has yet to be directly challenged and some courts[97] are constrained by the doctrine of *stare decisis* in finding ways around such an illogical proposition.

If, however, a new element is introduced into the relationship the promise will be binding; there will be both agreement (accord) and consideration (satisfaction) for the promise to release the debtor from his obligation to pay the larger debt. So, if instead of paying £10 I pay by giving an object, this new

---

[93] [1936] N.I. 16. See also *Ferguson v. Davies* [1997] 1 All E.R. 315.
[94] (1884) 9 App. Cas. 605. See also *Riordan v. Carroll* [1996] 2 I.L.R.M. 263.
[95] *Robichaud v. Caisse Populaire* (1990) 69 D.L.R. (4th) 589.
[96] *Ibid.* at 595.
[97] *Re Selectmove* [1995] 2 All E.R. 531.

element will suffice regardless of the worth of the object. It is established that payment by cheque is not a new element. Alternatively, payment of the lesser sum before the date due or in a different place to that previously agreed will suffice.

Although this rule was not applied by the House of Lords until 1884 it has been accepted and (reluctantly) acted upon by the courts for centuries. In *Drogheda Corporation v. Fairtlough*[98] premises were demised in 1820 for a period of 99 years to a local clergyman. The Corporation in 1837 passed a resolution agreeing to reduce the rent as a gesture to the tenant but before this could be done the clergyman died. The Corporation decided to carry out the resolution and in 1842 the old lease was surrendered and a new lease executed for the remainder of the 99-year period, rent reduced from £11 9s. 8d per annum to £5 6s. per annum. The rent was paid at the new rate until 1854 when the Corporation sued for the arrears of rent calculated at the original higher rate from 1842 until 1854. The action succeeded. Lefroy C.J. indicated that payment of a lesser sum under a parol agreement rather than one by deed cannot at common law be deemed any satisfaction of a larger, liquidated sum unless some collateral advantage, however small is given. In this case there was no collateral advantage. "What is the consideration which the corporation received for this agreement? They received a less rent; but upon the other hand the tenant was allowed to keep in his pocket the balance of the greater rent." This common law decision directly confronts the modern cases on promissory estoppel but before we turn to this difficult problem two exceptions to the rule that payment of a smaller sum is not sufficient consideration should be noted. These cases represent a significant exception to the rule that consideration must move from a promisee.

### (1) Compositions with creditors

Suppose X, a trader, has a large number of creditors but a small number of banknotes with which to pay them. He faces bankruptcy and the creditors run the risk of being paid little or nothing. It will be in the interest of all concerned for the creditors to agree to take less than that due. This agreement or composition is a valid way of ensuring that payment of the lesser sum will bind a creditor. So in *Morans v. Armstrong*[99] a partner in the plaintiff firm agreed to take 6s. 8d. in the pound on sums due the firm. When the money was tendered it was refused. An action to recover the original sum due failed.

### (2) Payment by a third party

In *Lawder v. Peyton*[100] the administrator of a creditor's estate sought execution over the property of the defendant who owed a debt of £534, £268 of which

---

[98]  (1858) 8 Ir.C.L.R. 98.
[99]  (1840) Arm. Mac. Og. 25.
[100]  (1877) 11 I.R.C.L. 41.

had been paid, not by the defendant but by a third party on the defendant's behalf. It was held that to permit recovery of the entire sum after payment would be a fraud upon the defendant. Although both this case and *Morans v. Armstrong*, above, seem based on the desire to prevent fraud it is doubtful whether it is the defendant who is defrauded. In these cases it seems more likely that the third parties involved are the sole victims. This alternative reasoning has been selected to justify similar rules developed by the English judges.[101]

## Promissory or Equitable Estoppel

The doctrine of estoppel is historically a common law doctrine. In the case of *Jorden v. Money*[102] the House of Lords declared the doctrine to apply only to cases where the statement made is one of existing fact. If therefore I say "X does not owe me £100" I will at common law be prevented or estopped from denying the truth of this promise. If, however, I say "you owe me £11 but pay me £6; I do not intend at any time to recover the balance", estoppel will not operate. My statement is one of intention, not fact. So, if we return to *Drogheda Corporation v. Fairtlough*, above, we can see that those facts fall into the second category. In the case of *Munster & Leinster Bank v. Croker*,[103] Black J. upheld the view that estoppel cannot operate on statements of intention. The really significant feature of *Jorden v. Money* is the extension of this distinction into cases where the power of a court of equity to prevent a promisor from going back on a promise is being invoked by the promisee. In *Jorden v. Money* the promisor led the promisee to believe that she would not seek to recover a debt, in consequence of which the promisee took on family commitments which he submitted he would not otherwise have done if the promisor had not given a voluntary undertaking not to seek to recover the debt in the future. The promisee sought a declaration that the debt was irrecoverable but failed on the ground that the doctrine of estoppel by representation only operated on statements of existing fact and not statements of law. In a vigorous dissenting judgment Lord St. Leonards argued that equitable case law would be operative in such a situation as the one before the House of Lords, but this approach did not find favour with the House.

Where the traditional, *i.e. Jorden v. Money*, approach is applied, the effect of the estoppel is exclusionary. The promisor is estopped from pleading or introducing facts which vary or contradict the representation already made. So while the estoppel can be used to provide the representee with a defence, or can be used in an ancillary way if the representee has an independent cause of action, it is rarely available to give the representee a cause of action, except in exceptional instances, such as giving a tenancy by estoppel: see *Ramsden v. Dyson*.[104]

---

[101] *Welby v. Drake* (1825) 1 C. & P. 557; *Cook v. Lister* (1863) 13 C.B. (N.S.) 543.
[102] (1845) 5 H.L.Cas. 185.
[103] [1940] I.R. 185.
[104] (1866) L.R. 1 H.L. 129.

There are nevertheless some excellent instances of an estoppel by representation being used to overcome some formidible obstacles to a plaintiff's success
in litigation. In *McNeill v. Miller*[105] the plaintiff left his motor car with the
defendants for repair. The plaintiff was told that the defendants had insurance
cover and, acting on this, the plaintiff did not obtain separate insurance. The
vehicle was destroyed by fire and the plaintiff sued on the misrepresentation of
fact, for it transpired that no cover was available. The defendants were held to
be estopped from denying that the motor car was insured for the plaintiff.
Wright J. observed that the general principle of estoppel applied notwithstanding the absence of a contract to insure.

Nevertheless it is clear that the line of equitable authority commencing with
*Hughes v. Metropolitan Railway Co.*[106] threatens this limited view of the estoppel
doctrine. In that case it was said by Lord Cairns L.C., an Irishman, that:

> "It is the first principle upon which all courts of equity proceed that if
> parties who have entered into definite and distinct terms involving
> certain legal results . . . afterwards by their own act . . . enter upon a
> course of negotiations which has the effect of leading one of the parties
> to suppose that the strict legal rights arising under the contract will not
> be enforced or will be kept in suspense . . . the person who otherwise
> might have these rights will not be allowed to enforce them where it
> would be inequitable, having regard to the dealings which have thus
> taken place between the parties."[107]

This line of authority, if carried to its logical conclusion, would mean that the
dicta in *Pinnel's* case[108] would be bad law and that all promises and not merely
those made in the context of a pre-existing contractual relationship are enforceable if the promise is seriously meant and the other party acts on it, even in a
way not stipulated or requested by the promisor. In short, the rule in *Drogheda
Corporation v. Fairtlough, Jorden v. Money*, and the entire bargain doctrine of
consideration would be swept aside. This movement towards making a non-
bargain promise enforceable began in earnest after the judgment in *Central
London Property Trust v. High Trees House.*[109] In that case Denning J. (as he
then was) stated *obiter* that he would apply Lord Cairn's principle to hold a
landlord estopped from going back on a promise to reduce the rent.

The facts of the *High Trees* case are instructive and straightforward. High
Trees House, a London block of flats, was the subject of a 99-year lease, the
rent being £2,500 per annum. After the outbreak of the Second World War it
became extremely difficult to let the flats so the lessee agreed to pay half the

---

[105]  [1907] 2 I.R. 328.
[106]  (1877) 2 App.Cas. 439.
[107]  *Ibid.* at 448.
[108]  (1602) 5 Co. Rep. 117a.
[109]  [1947] K.B. 130.

annual rent for as long as war conditions lasted. By the terms of the agreement the full rent would become payable when war conditions ended. By the beginning of 1945 the flats were all let and the receiver of the landlord company sought to recover rental arrears for the last half of 1945, effectively testing the basis for mounting a more extensive action. Denning J. held that while the terms of the agreement meant that the landlord was clearly entitled to succeed on this claim he stated *obiter* that the landlord could not succeed if he sought to resile from the agreement to take half the rental for the duration of the War. Relying on *Hughes v. Metropolitan Railway* and other cases[110] in which representations of future intention have been held to restrain a landlord from relying on strict legal rights against a tenant, Denning J. indicated that these cases were applicable to promises generally and that in his view the proper principle to apply is that "a promise intended to be binding, intended to be acted on, and in fact acted on, is binding so far as its terms properly apply". This principle is of great scope and has been cited with approval in several Irish cases. One of the most important decisions on the High Trees principle is that of Barron J. in *Kenny v. Kelly*.[111] The applicant sought, by way of judicial review a declaration that she was entitled to a place as an undergraduate Arts degree student at University College Dublin. As a transfering student from Trinity College Dublin, the applicant was of the belief that her application had been successfully processed by the defendant and that she had been given a right to defer taking up her place for one academic year. On the facts Barron J. found that such an assurance had been given and that she acted upon the assurance by making part payment of fees; citing Denning J. in *High Trees* Barron J. said that in that case "the essence of promissory estoppel was said to be a promise intended to be binding intended to be acted upon, and in fact acted upon".

Many judges and academic commentators have struggled to reconcile promissory estoppel with both consideration theory and accepted equitable principles. One school, for example, draws a distinction between promissory estoppel and proprietary estoppel, indicating that cases of promissory estoppel will sometimes afford a defence in a contractual context but that such an estoppel cannot create new rights or independent causes of action. Proprietary estoppel however may create new rights where it would be unjust or unconscionable for equity not to intervene, but this will only occur when the subject matter of the estoppel is real property. At the other extreme are commentators and judges who suggest a more universal approach is needed, the view being taken that illogical and fragmented categories should not be utilized just to preserve the bargain theory of consideration, for example.

---

[110] *Birmingham and District Land Co. v. London and North Western Rly* (1888) 40 Ch.D. 268.

[111] [1988] I.R.457; *Noonan v. O'Connell*, unreported, High Court, April 10, 1987.

*Orthodox views of equitable estoppel*

In later cases the English courts have attempted to limit the *High Trees* case to promises made, firstly, to suspend and not to give up altogether a legal right, the right to resile from the statement being available where reasonable notice is given: see *Ajayi v. R. T. Briscoe (Nigeria) Ltd.*[112] Secondly, the estoppel can only operate where a pre-existing legal relationship can be shown as between the parties: see *Combe v. Combe.*[113] A third limitation remains to be considered by the House of Lords. Is it necessary for the party pleading the estoppel to show that the promise caused the promisee to act to his or her detriment? Lord Denning has rejected this as an essential requirement, *e.g. Brikom Investments Ltd. v. Carr,*[114] but there are cases in which the courts have emphasised that if promissory estoppel is to apply there must be evidence that the promise has caused the person pleading estoppel to act in a certain way: see *The Scaptrade.*[115] Indeed in *McCambridge v. Winters,*[116] Murphy J. adopted as a correct statement of the law in Ireland a statement made by Diplock J. in *Lowe v. Lombank Ltd.*[117] in which Diplock J. held that for an estoppel to apply the representation made must be intended to be acted upon and in fact acted upon by the representee to his detriment: see also Costello J. in *Industrial Yarns Ltd. v. Greene.*[118] In *North Down Hotels Ltd. v. Province-Wide Filling Stations Ltd*[119] Carswell L.J. insisted that detriment was an essential requirement under *Hughes v. Metropolitan Railway.* The learned judge continued by holding that a tenant who was seeking to exercise an invalid option clause by appointing a valuer and preparing for an arbitration procedure did not thereby act to his detriment; the tenant "has not altered its position in doing so, merely incurred expenditure". With respect, this seems to be a very artificial view of what is needed to satisfy the detriment requirement and it may be better to regard the case as turning upon a finding that the *degree* of reliance was insufficient to make it inequitable to hold the landlord to honour his representation. A fourth limit holds that promissory estoppel cannot confer upon the party pleading estoppel a cause of action where none existed before: see Birkett L.J.'s "shield and sword" metaphor in *Combe v. Combe.*[120] In *Chartered Trust Ireland Ltd. v. Healy,*[121] Barron J. applied the shield and sword metaphor so as to deny a remedy in damages to the plaintiff who had purchased a motor vehicle in

---

[112] [1964] 1 W.L.R. 1326; *Offredy Developments Ltd. v. Steinback* (1971) 221 E.G. 963; *North Down Hotels Ltd. v. Province-Wide Filling Stations Ltd.* [1993] N.I. 261.
[113] [1951] 2 K.B. 215.
[114] [1979] Q.B. 467.
[115] [1983] 1 All E.R. 301.
[116] Unreported, High Court, August 28, 1984.
[117] [1960] 1 W.L.R. 196.
[118] [1948] I.L.R.M. 15; *Morrow v. Carty* [1957] N.I. 174.
[119] [1993] N.I. 261. It may be that detriment is an essential proof where promissory estoppel is pleaded but that it is not necessary in instances of proprietary estoppel when unconscionability is the central focus. Even this distinction is highly artificial.
[120] [1951] 2 K.B. 215.
[121] Unreported, High Court, December 10, 1985.

circumstances where the contract of sale itself was void. Because the contract was void the estoppel could not operate so as to confer a cause of action. However, the estoppel can be used to defeat a claim, or, in exceptional cases, may be used in an ancillary manner by a plaintiff who has been led to believe that a particular defence will not be asserted by the defendant. In this sense the estoppel operates in an exclusionary manner, as in *Traynor v. Fegan*[122] when the statements made by the defendant's solicitors in respect of whether service of proceedings would be accepted on behalf of the client were held to operate an estoppel, denying the defendant the right to plead non-compliance with the Statute of Limitations 1957; see also *Incorporated Food Products Ltd. (In Liquidation) v. Minister for Agriculture.*[123] In this writer's view the limitation seems a rather unsatisfactory one for if the whole basis of promissory estoppel is a desire to avoid the inequitable and unfair consequences that may follow from the non-observance of promises that are meant to be binding and acted upon, it seems vital that a flexible system of remedies, including damages, be available to the courts.

It is also clear from the cases that before an estoppel can operate there must be a clear and unambiguous statement of fact or intention; a vague statement cannot be used to justify imposing an estoppel upon the person making that vague or ambiguous statement: see *Woodhouse Ltd. v. Nigerian Produce Ltd.*[124] For this reason Ellis J. held in *Keegan & Roberts Ltd. v. Comhairle Chontae Átha Cliath*[125] that alleged assurances given could not create an estoppel.

The clearest and most rational statement on the application of promissory estoppel to contemporary commercial conditions is to be found in section 90(1) of the U.S. Restatement of Contracts (2nd).

> "A promise which the promisor should reasonably expect to induce action or forbearance on the part of the promisee and which does induce such action or forbearance is binding if injustice can be avoided only by enforcement of the promise. The remedy granted for breach may be limited as justice requires."

Section 90 does not dispense with the consideration doctrine. Contracts remain enforceable as contracts if consideration is present. Section 90 is often likely to be invoked in cases where a conditional contract exists and the promisee relies on assurances that are not actionable in contract but loss results from foreseeable reliance.[126] The flexibility of the remedy is an essential feature of section 90; normally the measure of damages will be gauged by reference to the losses incurred and not the benefit promised. In the U.S. case of *Grouse v.*

---

[122] [1985] I.R. 586.
[123] Unreported, High Court, June 6, 1984.
[124] [1972] A.C. 741; *North Down Hotels Ltd. v. Province-Wide Filling Stations Ltd.* [1993] N.I. 261.
[125] Unreported, High Court , March 12, 1981.
[126] *Hoffman v. Red Owl Stores Inc.* 133 N.W 2d. 267 (1965).

*Group Health Plan, Inc*[127] the plaintiff relied upon a promise of a job offer by giving notice to his employer and turning down another job offer. He was then injured when the offer was withdrawn following a reference given to the defendant. The loss suffered, rather than the benefit anticipated, was the basis of assessment in *Grouse*. While section 90 provides a very useful model for any future legislation, the Irish courts are meanwhile required to tease out the essential features of promissory estoppel, without the benefit of statutory guidance. In this context it is evident that the cases are not going to be consistent at such an early stage in the development of the concept.

The Australian courts have followed the general approach adopted by the English judiciary. Attempts have been made in the Australian courts to explore promissory estoppel and its relationship with older cases and in particular the link between promissory estoppel – which applies to promises of fact and future intention – and the older case of *Jorden v. Money*[128] in which the majority of the House of Lords limited estoppel to statements of fact. In *Reed v. Sheehan*[129] and in *Legione v. Hateley*[130] approval of the limited doctrine of promissory estoppel, enunciated in the Privy Council in *Ajayi v. R. T. Briscoe (Nigeria) Ltd.*[131] was given by the Federal Court of Australia and the High Court of Australia respectively. It is significant however that in *Legione v. Hateley* the members of the High Court of Australia refused to decide whether promissory estoppel should be limited to cases where there is a pre-existing legal relationship. The decision of the High Court of Australia in *Waltons Stores (Interstate) v. Maher*[132] unequivocally rules that promissory estoppel may be pleaded by a plaintiff when no pre-existing legal relationship exists and that the promissory estoppel principle may give a cause of action to the promisee. In this case negotiations for the sale of real property were at an advanced stage and prospective lessors undertook site clearance and construction work in the belief that a draft contract had been executed. The lessees were aware of the lessors' state of mind but withdrew from the transaction, some 40 per cent of the construction work stipulated in the lease having been completed. The lessors could not sue in contract but brought an action pleading promissory estoppel. The basic factor stressed by the members of the court was the unconscionable behaviour of the lessees in failing to disabuse the lessors of their mistaken belief and their willingness to allow the lessors to expend monies when the lessees knew there was a prospect of the lease not being signed. This case is of great importance, not least because several of the judges stressed that the basis of the decision was promissory estoppel rather than

---

[127] 306 N.W. 2d 114 (1981).

[128] (1845) 5 H.L.Cas. 185.

[129] [1982] F.L.R. 206.

[130] (1983) 57 A.L.J.R. 292.

[131] [1964] 1 W.L.R. 1326.

[132] (1988) 76 A.L.R. 513; *Austotel Ltd. v. Franklins Selfserve Pty.* (1989) 16 N.S.W.L.R. 582; *Commonwealth v. Verwayen* (1990) 64 A.L.J.R. 540; *Lyndel Nominees Pty Ltd. v. Mobil Oil Australia Ltd.* (1997) 37 I.P.R. 599.

proprietary estoppel and all members of the court were anxious to adopt a unitary view of the estoppel doctrine rather than the more fragmented perspective of some judges who emphasise the different nature of the various estoppels.

The case law in Ireland currently reveals that a more tentative position on promissory estoppel has been taken by Irish judges although some signs of a more ambitious approach are emerging. In *Folens v. The Minister for Education*,[133] McWilliam J. seemed prepared to allow the plaintiff to recover compensation for wasted pre-contractual expenditure, incurred at the behest of the defendant, but held that he was unable to do so because the *High Trees* principle required a definite commitment or representation be made, and, on the facts, no commitment or representation had been made. This is a somewhat oblique authority on this matter, however. The decision of Kenny J. in *Revenue Commissioners v. Moroney*[134] is of greater importance. The learned judge held that a father who had obtained his two son's signatures to a deed by promising them that at no time would they be expected to pay the consideration stated in the deed would be estopped, under *High Trees*, from reneging on his promise. Kenny J. not only implicitly rejected *Jorden v. Money*, for the father's promise referred to his future intention, Kenny J. also expressly rejected the view that estoppel only suspends a legal right and that for the estoppel to operate there must exist a legal relationship at the time the promise was made. In the Supreme Court the appeal was dismissed but the members of the Supreme Court used the parol evidence rule to explain the facts before them and declined to comment on *High Trees*.

In the present writer's view it is a mistake to see the *High Trees* case as presenting the courts with the problem of reconciling the authorities in such a way as to leave *Jorden v. Money* and the bargain theory of consideration intact. Lord Denning M.R. once wrote: "[w]e are approaching a state of affairs which Ames regarded as desirable, namely that any act done on the faith of a promise should be regarded as sufficient consideration to make it binding."[135] Some 28 years later Lord Denning viewed the cases on estoppel in his book, *The Discipline of Law*, as abolishing "the doctrine of consideration in all but a handful of cases."[136] While it is doubtful that the present English cases go so far the implications of equitable or promissory estoppel are profound; are we not in fact returning to Lord Mansfield's moral obligation theory? This is certainly the case if the courts favour the view that the estoppel will be upheld even in the absence of proof that the promisee has acted to his detriment; in such a situation the estoppel would be truly promissory. Some support for this view can be found in *Waltons Stores (Interstate) v. Maher*[137] when several members of the court indicated that a detrimental change of position is not needed to ground

---

133 [1984] I.L.R.M. 265. Contrast *McCarron v. McCarron*, unreported, Supreme Court, February 13, 1997, a proprietary estoppel case where expenditure of money and/or erection of buildings were held not to be sole criteria for establishing a proprietary estoppel.
134 [1972] I.R. 372.
135 (1951) 15 M.L.R. 1, pp. 9–10.
136 (London, 1979) p. 223.
137 (1988) 76 A.L.R. 513.

the estoppel, whether proprietory or promissory. Brennan J., for example, stated that the person pleading estoppel can successfully do so when that person "acts or abstains from acting in reliance on the assumption or expectation" created by the promisor. The emphasis on the unconscionable conduct of the promisor rather than the detrimental reliance of the promisee is a striking feature of this case. It is certainly true that emphasis is placed on the unconscionable consequences of the representation by many judges and that some progress could be made by adopting the term equitable estoppel as a unifying concept that, for example, sees detrimental reliance as an aspect of unconscionability.[138]

In Ireland, the development of the concept of promises being enforceable because of the legitimate expectation that the promise creates seems likely to deepen the conceptual confusion between promissory estoppel as a private law device, based perhaps on detrimental reliance as in section 90 of the U.S. Restatement 2nd., and the much looser and, frankly, unworkable concept of legitimate expectation, as a source of actionable right,[139] which stands apart from existing civil law concepts such as contract, unjust enrichment, actionable misrepresentation and promissory estoppel, to name but a few. In Ireland, severance of the link between legitimate expectation and injurious reliance seems to have already taken place.[140] We will examine legitimate expectation later in this chapter.

There must however be some doubt as to whether English law is about to undergo such a thorough revolution. There can be no doubt however that significant changes are in the wind. In *The Hannah Blummenthal*[141] Lord Diplock stated:

> "[t]he rule that neither party can rely on his own failure to communicate accurately to the other party his own real intention by what he wrote or said or did, as negativing the consensus ad idem, is an example of a general principle of English law that injurious reliance on what another person did may be a source of legal rights against him. I use the broader expression 'injurious reliance' in preference to 'estoppel' so as to embrace all circumstances in which A can say to B, 'you led me reasonably to believe that you were assuming particular legally enforceable obligations to me,' of which promissory or *High Trees* estoppel (see *Central London Property Trust Ltd. v. High Trees House Ltd.* (1946) [1956] 1 All E.R. 256, [1947] K.B. 130) affords another example, whereas 'estoppel,' in the strict sense of the term, is an exclusionary rule of evidence, though it may operate so as to affect substantive legal rights inter partes.[142]

Irish judges, however, are not it seems attracted to "injurious reliance" but there are a number of recent estoppel cases where broader approaches to the enforce-

---

138 Lunney [1992] *Conv.* 230; Halliwell [1994] *Legal Studies* 15.
139 The basis seems to be *Amalgamated Investment Property Co. v. Texas Commerce International Bank Ltd.* [1982] Q.B. 84.
140 *Webb v. Ireland* [1988] I.R. 353; *Duggan v. An Taoiseach* [1989] I.L.R.M. 710.
141 [1983] 1 All E.R. 34.
142 *Ibid.* at 49.

ment of non-contractual statements relating to land are evident. Some of these cases are instances which are traditionally to be regarded as proprietary estoppel cases. The decision of Costello J. in *In the matter of J.R.*[143] asserts that the distinction between promissory estoppel and proprietary estoppel remains valid. In the former case, Costello J. opined the estoppel will not result in the creation of a right or interest in land but, rather, the representee obtains a personal right which can operate against the representor. In cases of proprietary estoppel however the representation relates to the creation of rights in the representee and in equity a species of constructive trust is imposed to prevent the representor from relying on his legal rights when it is unconscionable so to do. While Costello J. relied upon statements in Snell's *Principles of Equity* and English case law to justify this distinction the underlying principles upon which the court intervenes under both these varieties of estoppel are fundamentally the same and it is not clear how such a distinction can be justified by reference to the consequences, or range of remedies, available to counterbalance the unfairness or unconscionability that the representor's statement or conduct has produced. The recent English case of *Taylor v. Dickens*[144] makes it clear that if there is no unconscionable aspect to the promisor seeking to resile from a promise then there can be no room for proprietary estoppel.[145] There a promise to leave property to the plaintiff in a will was held to have been validly countermanded by execution of a new later will because the promisor could not be understood to have promised that she would not change her mind.

In *Smith v. Ireland*,[146] Finlay P. endorsed the following statement of Lord Denning M.R. in *Crabb v. Arun District Council*[147] as a correct statement on the law relating to equitable estoppel:

> "Short of an actual promise, if he, by his words or conduct, so behaves as to lead another to believe that he will not insist on his legal rights knowing or intending that the other will act on that belief – and he does so act, that again will raise an equity in favour of the other, and it is for the court to say in what way the equity may be satisfied."[148]

While the Diplock and Denning statements take equitable estoppel beyond the limits placed by existing rules, there is a clear intimation in them that estoppel cannot be limited to being an exclusionary rule of evidence for much longer.

## Legitimate expectation

In order for promises to be enforceable in contract a litmus test of consideration is necessary. For a promise to be enforceable in equity the estoppel principle requires detrimental reliance and/or unconscionability to be shown,

---

[143] [1993] I.L.R.M. 657.
[144] *The Times*, November 24, 1997; *Gillet v. Holt, The Times*, June 18, 1998.
[145] See also *Smyth v. Halpin* [1997] 2 I.L.R.M. 38.
[146] [1983] I.L.R.M. 300.
[147] [1976] 1 Ch. 179.
[148] *Ibid.* at 188. See *In the matter of J.R.* (above) on flexibility of remedies.

although the precise scope of the broad equitable estoppel, and the specific varieties of the estoppels, await a definitive statement by the House of Lords, for example. In Ireland, as elsewhere, the possibility that decisions taken by public bodies may be the subject of judicial review has produced a further line of complication in the form of the concept of legitimate expectation. The principle emerged in English law through cases which indicated that a public body could in certain circumstances be bound to follow certain procedural steps (*e.g.* consult or negotiate) when that public body has either done so in the past or has indicated to the person in question that such a procedure would be followed in the instant case. The idea that such a benefit or advantage may be obtained via a "legitimate expectation", which may not be the same thing as something obtained via contract or a representation, was accepted by the House of Lords in *Council of Public Service Unions v. Minister for the Civil Service.*[149] The obligation to follow settled or agreed procedures has been accepted and extended by both the Irish and the U.K. courts. The leading Irish case is *Webb v. Ireland.*[150] Here the plaintiffs, the finders of the Derrynaflan Hoard, were told by the director of the National Museum that in response to their act of depositing the hoard with the National Museum the plaintiffs would be "honourably treated". The Supreme Court extended the notion so as to include the legitimate expectation that a financial payment would be made, observing that such a payment was an aspect of the plaintiffs being "honourably treated". In giving his judgment Finlay C.J. had this to say of the concept itself in *Webb v. Ireland*:

> "the doctrine of 'legitimate expectation' sometimes described as 'reason-able expectation' has not in those terms been the subject matter of any decision of our courts. However, the doctrine connoted by such expressions is but an aspect of the well recognised equitable concept of promissory estoppel . . . whereby a promise or representation as to intention may in certain circumstances be held binding on the representor or promisor."[151]

Later courts have continued to emphasise the links with promissory estoppel, the most striking example of which is probably the decision of O'Hanlon J. in *Association of General Practitioners v. Minister for Health*[152] in which O'Hanlon J. indicated that legitimate expectation cannot create a cause of action for the concept is only an aspect of promissory estoppel, citing *Combe v. Combe.*[153]

It must be said that it is only to be expected that concepts of this kind will be the subject of different judicial interpretations and that conflicting judgments will exist until the concept is bedded down. It is evident however that legitimate

---

[149] [1985] 1 A.C. 374.
[150] [1988] I.R. 353; [1988] I.L.R.M. 565.
[151] [1988] I.R. 353 at 384, citing Denning M.R. in the *Texas Commerce* case. See generally Delany (1990) 12 D.U.L.J. 1 on the early Irish case law.
[152] [1995] 2 I.L.R.M. 481; see also *Garda Representative Association v. Ireland* [1989] I.R. 193.
[153] [1951] 2 K.B. 215.

expectation is a feature of Irish public law. In the case of *Re La Lavia*[154] the Supreme Court reaffirmed the decision in *Webb v. Ireland* but found on the facts that no legitimate expectation arose. In this case the finders of three Spanish Armada wrecks claimed entitlement in law to monies for the discovery of that wreck site and artifacts. The Supreme Court distinguished *Webb* on the ground that in that case there was an express promise while in the instant case the applicants were maintaining title and negotiating with the state for a finder's reward, a somewhat contradictory position for them to maintain.

The possibility that a legitimate expectation may involve the acquisition of a tangible benefit in the form of a substantive right was affirmed by Hamilton P. in *Duggan v. An Taoiseach*.[155] Here civil servants were held to have a legitimate expectation that their work in the farm tax office would last until such time as the work of the office was terminated under statute. This expectation was frustrated by an unlawful government decision to terminate the work of that office and the applicants were held entitled to damages to vindicate the legitimate expectation in question. Whether this case is reliable given later decisions is open to question.

While most of the cases in which the legitimate expectation has been pleaded involve situations where a citizen is seeking to obtain some benefit or privilege such as a tax refund, a licence, or legal aid (and thus are not contract situations) the "legitimate expectation" has been used in order to forestall the exercise of contractual rights or discretions. In *Donegal County Council v. Porter and Others*[156] the blanket dismissal of part-time firemen by the County Council when they reached 55 years of age was held incompatible with a legitimate expectation that such employees could continue to work until 60 if they were fit enough. Flood J. said that fitness could have been assessed via a medical examination so there was no countervailing consideration that could have justified denial of such an expectation.[157] However, *Eogan v. University College Dublin*[158] indicates that if the employer is open and transparent about policies of this kind, and if the policy is rational and persons affected have the opportunity to comment on any scheme proposed, then any finding or arbitrary or oppressive conduct by a public body will not be sustainable by a court. Legitimate expectation has been pleaded in relation to the operations of professional or regulatory bodies such as the Medical Council[159] and the Law Society.[160] The universities[161] have also been considered to be within the scope

---

[154] [1996] 1 I.L.R.M. 194. See also *Duff v. Minister for Agriculture*, unreported, Supreme Court, March 4, 1997.

[155] [1989] I.L.R.M. 710. Contrast *Egan v. Minister for Defence*, unreported, High Court, November 24, 1988 and *White v. Glackin*, unreported, High Court, May 19, 1995.

[156] Unreported, High Court, July 12, 1993. See also *Navan Tanker Services v. Meath County Council*, unreported, High Court, December 13, 1996.

[157] Contrast *Egan v. Minister for Defence*, unreported, High Court, November 24, 1988.

[158] [1996] 2 I.L.R.M. 303.

[159] *Phillips v. Medical Council* [1991] 2 I.R. 115.

[160] *Abrahamson v. Law Society of Ireland* [1996] 2 I.R. 481. See also *Geoghegan v. Institute of Chartered Accountants in Ireland*, unreported, High Court, November 16, 1995.

[161] *Kenny v. Kelly* [1988] I.R. 457; *Eogan v. University College Dublin* [1996] 2 I.L.R.M. 303.

of judicial review via legitimate expectation and the courts have indicated that the concept of a public body is broadly judged. If the body makes the decision pursuant to a statute, if the decision maker is performing a duty relating to a matter of particular and immediate public concern, if the decision relates to an employment contract and the employee invokes statutory protection which are thus public rights, and finally, the decision maker depends on statute or legislative or governmental rights, and support for its continued exercise of powers, then such factors will influence the decision to trigger judicial review.[162]

### *The relationship between promissory estoppel and legitimate expectation*

Despite some observations to the effect that legitimate expectation is simply an aspect of promissory estoppel there are some signs that there are significant differences between these concepts. We have seen that while a legitimate expectation operates only *vis-à-vis* public bodies, the concept of a public body is broad indeed. Thus, sometimes estoppel and legitimate expectation are pleaded in the alternative, *e.g. Kenny v. Kelly*.[163]

While detrimental reliance appears to be an essential proof in cases of promissory estoppel this has been doubted in relation to legitimate expectation.[164] Orthodox estoppel theory also seems to require that a pre-existing legal relationship should subsist so that the estoppel may only operate within such a context, but no such prior relationship needs to exist between a citizen and a public body or a government department,[165] for example. It is also likely that legitimate expectation may operate by way of a practice or failure within the public body which may stop short of a promise or representation[166] and that while promissory estoppel may not be used to interfere with a minister's powers under statute, some Irish cases indicate that the legitimate expectation argument may prevail in such a context[167] although there are several cases which go against this argument[168] where the expectation in question is substantive rather than procedural. In *Galvin v. Chief Appeals Officer*[169] for example, Costello P. declined to allow the plaintiff to obtain a social welfare pension, despite procedural irregularities, because the plaintiff's contribution record meant that he was not legally entitled as a matter of substantive statutory entitlement.

---

[162] *per* Shanley J. in *Eogan v. University College Dublin* [1996] 2 I.L.R.M. 303 at 309.

[163] [1988] I.R. 457.

[164] *Attorney General of Hong Kong v. Ng Yeun Shiu* [1983] 2 A.C. 629; in *Abrahamson v. Law Society of Ireland* [1996] 2 I.R. 481 McCracken J. doubted whether reliance was an aspect of legitimate expectation.

[165] *Cosgrove v. Legal Aid Board*, unreported, High Court, October 17, 1990; *In Re La Lavia* [1996] 1 I.L.R.M. 194.

[166] *Ghneim v. Minister for Justice, The Irish Times,* September 2, 1989.

[167] *Conroy v. Garda Commissioner* [1989] I.R. 140.

[168] *Tara Prospecting Ltd. v. Minister for Energy* [1993] I.L.R.M. 771; *Abrahamson v. Law Society of Ireland* [1996] 2 I.L.R.M. 481; *Galvin v. Chief Appeals Officer*, unreported, High Court, June 27, 1997.

[169] Unreported, High Court, June 27, 1997.

# 3 Intention to Create Legal Relations

## Introduction

It is possible for the parties to negotiations to stipulate that, when the negotiating process is at an end, and the parties have apparently reached agreement on essential matters, any resultant agreement is not to be legally enforceable. This may be because each side wishes to reserve the right to reconsider his or her position; any agreement reached in such circumstances will be seen as some kind of half-way-house between preliminary, inchoate negotiations and a legally enforceable contract. The business usage that most clearly illustrates this is the "subject to contract" agreement in land transactions. O'Flaherty J. in *Boyle and Boyle v. Lee and Goyns*[1] has reminded us of the fact that "the historic purpose of the phrase 'subject to contract' was to keep negotiations in train and to allow either party to *resile* from the agreement made." A more general issue is whether it can be said that there is a specific requirement that enforceability of a contract will depend in part upon proof that a legally enforceable agreement was intended.

It is thus established that negotiations which meet the requirements of offer, acceptance and consideration may fail to be enforceable at common law as a contract because it is said that there was an absence of legal intent. This view has been challenged by several commentators who point out that it is only through the application of the doctrine that the common law distinguishes enforceable promises from non-enforceable promises. The need to show legal intent is said to be an interloper, of foreign extraction, which may be a legitimate requirement in civil law jurisdictions where no doctrine of consideration exists, but it is quite superfluous to the needs of the common law.

Professor Williston put forward this argument very strongly:

> "[t]he views of parties as to what are the requirements of a contract, as to what mutual assent means, or consideration, or what contracts are enforceable without a writing, and what are not, are wholly immaterial . . . [in this context] the law not the parties fixes the requirements of a legal obligation."[2]

It is evident that Williston's views are shared by many scholars,[3] who point out that an additional test of legal intent, based on the desires and beliefs of the parties, objectively determined, seems to be largely unnecessary, given that the

---

[1] [1992] I.L.R.M. 65.
[2] *Williston on Contracts* (1957), s.3, pp. 20–21.
[3] *e.g.* Hepple (1970) 28 C.L.J. 123; Unger (1956) 19 M.L.R. 96.

bargain theory of consideration is the common law test of contractual intention. Nevertheless, it is clear that under the private autonomy principle the parties are free to enter into arrangements and yet declare that these arrangements are not to be the subject of enforceable contractual rights. Furthermore, the courts, by using ordinary rules of construction, are free to conclude that some exchanges are not intended to be legally enforceable, even if there is a certainty and a finality about the negotiations. Sometimes legal intent questions overlap with the more common and fundamental problem of uncertainty of terms and it must be conceded that, at times, consideration[4] and uncertainty of terms[5] problems are not clearly distinguished by the judges.

Even though many of the legal intent cases can be argued away on alternative grounds there are several which can only be explained on the basis of lack of intent. No matter what objections may be levied against the legal intent requirement it has now taken root in English and Irish law.

## Family Arrangements

In *Mackay v. Jones*[6] the plaintiff's uncle promised that if the plaintiff, then a boy of 14 came to live with him and looked after the farm he would, on death, convey it to the boy by will. On the death of the promisor the property was bequeathed to a third party. Judge Deale in the Circuit Court refused to characterise the promise as absolutely binding; it was said to be an agreement to work in the expectation that the legacy would be given. This case can only be explained as one where the court refused to find that the promisor intended his promise to be binding.

The leading case on family arrangements in English law is that of *Balfour v. Balfour*.[7] In that case, Atkin L.J. stated *obiter* that contracts between husband and wife are not intended to be attended by legal consequences. In *Courtney v. Courtney*[8] an agreement made between a husband and wife who had decided to solve their matrimonial differences by living apart was upheld as legally binding. Although *Balfour v. Balfour* was distinguished in *Courtney* as applicable only to executory contracts it is established that where the parties have not been living together amicably any agreement made between them falls outside *Balfour v. Balfour*, otherwise separation agreements would not be enforceable. It has been suggested that if the parties in *Balfour v. Balfour* had done anything to indicate that they intended the promise to be legally enforceable, by getting a solicitor to draw up an agreement, for example, the presumption against enforcing an arrangement between husband and wife would be inapplicable. Note that in *Courtney v. Courtney* the promises were made with the sanction of

---

4 *e.g. Balfour v. Balfour* [1919] 2 K.B. 571.
5 *Carthy v. O'Neill* [1981] I.L.R.M. 443.
6 (1959) 93 I.L.T.R. 117; *Baldwin v. Lett*, unreported, High Court, February 1, 1971.
7 [1919] 2 K.B. 571.
8 (1923) 57 I.L.T.R. 42: see *Pettitt v. Pettitt* [1970] A.C. 777.

the local priest and this seems to have indicated to the court that the arrangement was seriously meant. See also *Hamer v. Sidway*[9] where the fact that a promise was repeated before others at a family gathering was another indication of legal intent.

The decision of the Supreme Court in *Rogers v. Smith*[10] illustrates that when a family arrangement is made the terms agreed are often ambiguous. Members of a family do not always haggle and bargain with the intensity of dealers at a horse fair. In *Rogers v. Smith* a mother promised her son that the cost of supporting her would be recoverable from her estate following her death. The Supreme Court refused to hold this promise was seriously intended. It was made in the most general terms; the "promisee" also gave evidence that if the promise had not been made he would have supported the "promisor" anyway.

In contrast, however, the case of *Hynes v. Hynes*[11] illustrates that an agreement between two brothers will be enforced, notwithstanding a plea that the blood relationship between the parties, and other circumstances, would indicate an absence of legal intent. In this case an agreement between the plaintiff and defendant, transferring a business owned and run by the plaintiff to the defendant, was held enforceable; the case is consistent with the English case of *Jones v. Padavatton*[12] in which Salmon L.J. indicated that the test for determining the enforceability of a family arrangement was objective; would a reasonable person, when the court looks at this agreement and its surrounding circumstances, have intended to create a legally binding agreement?

The factors that will influence a court when a plea of lack of intent is raised within a family context are numerous. The degree of closeness within the family relationship may be extremely relevant. Husband-and-wife and parent-and-child arrangements will be obviously very compelling relationships if in the individual case there is the degree of love and affection present that, in an ideal world, one would expect to see in every such relationship; parents are, however, no more immune from falling out with their children than a wife may be with her husband, and vice versa. Another factor that has proved influential, even where the blood or marriage link has not been very strong[13] (*e.g.* uncle and nephew), is the extent to which the promisee has acted in reliance. Moving from one continent to another,[14] or from one end of the country to the other,[15] or disposing of property as a result of a promise,[16] may indicate a degree of seriousness and deliberateness of purpose. Conversely, if the course of action taken was not momentous or prejudicial, or if the promisee would have acted in a similar way even without the promise sought to be enforced,[17] an absence

---

[9]  (1891) 124 N.Y. 583.
[10]  Unreported, Supreme Court, July 16, 1970.
[11]  Unreported, High Court, December 21, 1984.
[12]  [1969] 1 W.L.R. 328.
[13]  *Parker v. Clark* [1960] 1 All E.R. 93.
[14]  *Jones v. Padavatton* [1969] 1 W.L.R. 388.
[15]  *Parker v. Clark* [1960] 1 All E.R. 93.
[16]  *Ibid.*
[17]  *Rogers v. Smith*, unreported, Supreme Court, July 16, 1970.

of legal intent may be inferred. If the promise is vague or hastily made a plea of absence of legal intent may be more readily inferred than in cases where the promise is specific and reduced into writing. These factors are approximate guides only, however.

## Commercial Agreements

If the parties are commercial organisations or business persons then it is to be presumed that the contract will be attended by legal intent. The leading English case on honour clauses, *Rose and Frank Co. v. Crompton*[18] would no doubt be followed in Ireland. Readers should note that on the facts of *Rogers v. Smith*[19] it might have been possible to characterise the contract as a commercial one between the plaintiff and his father; this would have pointed towards enforcement. In *Apicella v. Scala*[20] an arrangement between plaintiff and defendant designed to enable all parties to take a share in sweepstake tickets to be purchased by the defendant was described as "a conditional or revocable decision"; even though Meredith J. would have found consideration to be present the absence of any intention to conclude a bargain was fatal to the plaintiff's action in contract.

In more recent times the courts have been prepared to uphold as contracts arrangements to purchase lottery tickets, or participate in gambling transactions, on the ground that the arrangement before the court has been specific and deliberately entered into with a view to sharing both the risks and the profits, if any. The leading English case is *Simpkins v. Pays.*[21] Readers of a newspaper were invited to take part in a competition, paying a fee of about five pence for each attempt. The defendant was the owner of a residence which she shared with her grandaughter and a paying boarder, the plaintiff. These three persons regularly competed but there were no specific agreed rules on completion of the entry and payment of postage and the entry fee. Each selected an entry each week and on one occasion the defendant's grandaughter won £750. The plaintiff successfully brought an action to recover £250. Sellers J. said that the issue of who actually paid the entry fee was not the central issue but rather the question of whether this was a syndicate in which risks and profits were to be shared. It may have been a very loose syndicate but it was seriously intended so to be. Sellers J. rejected the argument that because the arrangement involved a grandaughter and grandmother it was not supported by legal intent. In Ireland, there have been several cases in which injunctive relief has been obtained to prevent the National Lottery from paying the entire amount of winnings on a lottery ticket to the holder of the ticket on the basis, *inter alia,* that the ticket

---

[18] [1923] 2 K.B. 261.
[19] Unreported, Supreme Court, July 16, 1970.
[20] (1931) 66 I.L.T.R. 33.
[21] [1955] 1 W.L.R. 975.

has been purchased as part of a structured pooling arrangement between persons. Each case, however, must be judged on its own facts, but it can hardly be doubted that pooling arrangements of this kind should really be regarded as *prima facie* contractual, given the potential for great financial enrichment for the participants.

If the court establishes that, on its true construction, an alleged agreement was not intended to have legal consequences as a contract then it may be that what would otherwise appear to be a commercial contract will be denied the status of an enforceable contract. In *Cadbury Ireland Ltd. v. Kerry Co-operative Creameries Ltd.*[22] an agreement under which the defendant had effectively promised to continue to supply milk to the plaintiff company, when the defendant acquired a small creamery that had previously supplied milk to the plaintiffs, was held not capable of enforcement. Despite the presumption and despite the apparent solemnity with which the clause was drafted and inserted into the agreement a closer scrutiny of the circumstances of the case convinced Barrington J. that this agreement was non-contractual. The clause itself was unspecific; the parties themselves had not relied upon it to determine their rights and obligations after the agreement was signed, choosing instead to negotiate subsequent contracts for the supply of milk. The agreement was a statement in which all involved had evinced an intention to subsequently draw up clear and binding agreements and, in the absence of any later agreements, this provision itself lacked any real status in a legal sense. A similar situation is provided by *Cunard Steamship Co. v. The Revenue Commissioners*[23] where a booking arrangement was denied the status of a contract because it was intended that a subsequent contract would be made. These cases are very exceptional ones and it is true to say that, generally, a plea of absence of legal intent will be given short shrift; witness Barron J.'s decision in *The Commodity Broking Co. v. Meehan.*[24] In *Bowerman v. Association of British Travel Agents Ltd.*[25] the majority of the Court of Appeal held that a notice produced by the defendant and displayed in premises run by members of the Association was to be given legal effect. Hobhouse L.J. in particular remarked that the defendants had intended to publish the notice and reasonable persons reading it would regard the notice as having legal consequences. The fact that the defendants privately did not intend to expose themselves to legal liability was held to be irrelevant in such a context.

In recent years the issue of legal intent has proved to be most likely to arise in cases involving "letters of comfort". This expression as a term of art is applied to an undertaking given by a government, or a state agency, or by a company, in respect of some related or subsidiary body, and which sets out a particular set of circumstances, or gives an assurance that the government, state

---

22 [1982] I.L.R.M. 77.
23 [1931] I.R. 287.
24 [1985] I.R. 12.
25 *The Times*, November 24, 1995.

agency or company intends to maintain or adopt a position in relation to that related or subsidiary body. However, if the assurance leads the party to whom it is given to adopt a certain course of action, trade with or supply credit to the subsidiary body for example, is the assurance to be seen as promissory or a declaration of intent that is not actionable? The leading English case is *Kleinwort Benson Ltd. v. Malaysia Mining Corporation Bhd.*[26] The defendant owned a subsidiary company that traded in tin on the London Metal Exchange. The defendant sought a credit facility for the subsidiary, giving an undertaking that "it is our policy to ensure that the business [of the subsidiary] is at all times in a position to meet its liabilities to you." The assurance had been given after the defendant had refused to give a formal guarantee on behalf of the subsidiary. When the tin market collapsed the plaintiff sued on the assurance, the subsidiary having gone into liquidation. Hirst J., relying upon the concept of legal intent and the presumption that commercial undertakings are enforceable, held that the letter of comfort was actionable. The Court of Appeal overruled Hirst J., declaring that the undertaking itself was a statement of existing fact and that as it was not a misrepresentation of existing fact it was not actionable. The undertaking was drafted in a way that segregated it from other promissory undertakings, and, although the arguments of counsel had changed somewhat since the first instance hearing before Hirst J., the Court of Appeal held that Hirst J. had been incorrect in viewing the promise as governed by the *Edwards v. Skyways*[27] presumption: indeed, their Lordships viewed the case as depending on whether there was any promise at all in respect of future policy changes.

There is a considerable degree of uncertainty surrounding letters of comfort. If the letter can be viewed as merely an acceptance of an offer, then any cautionary or ambivalent language will not prevent a court from holding that there is legal intent, as in *Wilson Smithett & Cape (Sugar) Ltd. v. Bangladesh Sugar and Food Industries Corporation.*[28] The document, however, must be interpreted in its entirety. In the Victorian case of *Commonwealth Bank of Australia v. T.L.I. Management Property Ltd.*[29] a letter of comfort given by a company to confirm that it would take over another company, subject to shareholders' permission, was held not to constitute an undertaking, but rather, was merely a non-binding expression of intention. Had the words "we agree", "we promise" or "we undertake" been used then a contrary decision may well have resulted. The ad hoc nature of the cases has been criticised by one Australian judge, on the ground that considerable uncertainty is engendered by the notion that some business transactions, even though no honour clause is attached thereto, may "reside in a twilight zone of merely honourable engagement."[30] However, in

---

[26] [1989] 1 All E.R. 785; *Chemco Leasing S.p.a. v. Rediffusion* [1987] 1 F.T.L.R. 201.

[27] [1964] 1 W.L.R. 349.

[28] [1986] 1 Lloyd's Rep. 378.

[29] [1990] V.L.R. 510.

[30] Rogers C.J. in *Banque Brussels Lambert v. Australian National Industries Ltd.* (1989) 21 N.S.W.L.R. 502; see Tyree (1989) 2 J.C.L. 279.

*Australia European Finance Corp. v. Sheahan*[31] Rodgers C.J. was himself criticised for subjecting the clauses in *Banque Brussels Lambert* to the kind of minute textual analysis that he himself had complained about when he was reviewing earlier cases, including *Commonweatlh Bank of Australia v. TLI Management Property Ltd.* However, in *Australia European Finance Corp. v. Sheahan* the clauses under review were clearly tentative and non-promissory in tone and it was not necessary for Matheson J. in that case to really distinguish the lines of authority.

The latest English case, however, helps to point up a regrettable trend in finding lack of contractual intent from circumstances surrounding the contract. In *Orion Insurance plc. v. Shere Drake Insurance Ltd.*[32] the plaintiffs were held to have proved, on the balance of probabilities, that an agreement entered into in 1975 by two insurance companies and signed by both parties, was not intended to have legal consequences. The agreement was in the nature of an estimate of future liabilities and was made in circumstances where future events could make the calculations entirely inappropriate. Despite the fact of the agreement and signature of a document containing these terms by both parties, Hirst J. found the agreement was in the nature of a "gentleman's agreement". Hirst J. stressed that the onus was a heavy one, and that the degree of probability varied, depending on the nature of the context and the allegation of lack of intent. It is doubtful whether the courts are acting wisely in reaching decisions of this kind and it is preferable for the courts to insist on express disclaimers, by way of honour clauses, before decisions of the kind reached in *Orion Insurance* become more frequent.

## Collective Agreements

Two issues should be kept apart. First of all, collective agreements may be a valid source of contractual terms if they are subsequently incorporated into individual contracts of employment: see *N.C.B. v. Galley.*[33] So in the Employment Appeals Tribunal case of *Lynch & O'Brien v. Goodbody Ltd.*[34] the appellants had been dismissed according to the terms of an agreement struck between union and management governing procedures for dismissal. Applying the dictum in the leading English case of *Blackman v. P.O.*[35] it was held that the appellants were dismissed by reason of the union/management agreement and not because of redundancy. More recently, the English E.A.T. has held that while the terms of a redundancy clause found in a collective agreement may be binding in honour only, if those terms find their way into the

---

[31]  (1993) 60 S.A.S.R. 187.
[32]  [1990] 1 Lloyd's Rep. 465.
[33]  [1958] 1 W.L.R. 16; *Molloy v. IMPACT and another*, unreported, High Court, June 15, 1995.
[34]  M24/1978.
[35]  [1974] I.C.R. 151.

individual contract of employment they become binding: see *Marley v. Forward Trust Group*,[36] applying *Robertson v. B.G.C.*[37]

This line of case law, however, is not to be taken too far. In *Kenny & Others v. AN Post*[38] a group of postal sorters claimed that a work practice giving the plaintiffs a casual break at a fixed time, during which they would be paid, was a contractual entitlement. The practice had been developed following the act of a supervisor which had not been authorised by the higher echelons of management. O'Hanlon J. held that the supervisor had no authority to bind the defendant employer but implicitly drew a distinction between ad hoc variations in work practices and more formal collective agreements on terms and conditions. In respect of the former O'Hanlon J. said "where a particular change in the terms of employment is intended to be regarded as binding contractually the parties should take some positive steps to achieve this object."

The second issue is whether breach of a disputes procedure by unions or management will be a breach of contract rendering the party in breach liable in the ordinary courts. Following the decision in *Ford v. A.E.U.W.*[39] the common law position in England is often said to be that a collective agreement between trade unions and employers or employers organisations is not enforceable in the courts. In *Ford*, however, it was held that this particular agreement was not intended to have legally enforceable consequences[40]: Otto Kahn Freund argued that a collective agreement resembles an industrial "peace treaty" rather than a contract. The view that collective agreements are not enforceable at common law is of fairly recent origin; Kahn Freund himself argued[41] that in general such agreements are contractually enforceable: contrast his later views, cited in *Ford v. A.E.U.W.*

Irish case law provides support for the views that at common law the collective agreement may be enforceable in the ordinary courts: see *McLoughlin v. G.S. Ry. Co.*[42] In *Ardmore Studios v. Lynch*[43] the plaintiffs, who owned a film studio, entered into an agreement with a trade union that electricians would be drawn only from a "seniority list" of union electricians. The plaintiffs hired electricians not on the list. The plaintiffs sought an injunction to restrain the defendants from picketing their premises. The company argued that the agreement had been terminated before the electricians who had been the cause of the dispute had been hired. Budd J. gave the plaintiffs an interlocutory injunction, refusing to decide whether the agreement was binding. McLoughlin J. at trial of the action declared *obiter* that in his view the agreement was not binding *because of uncertainty of terms*. In other words, had the agreement been clear and specific the collective agreement would have possessed contractual effect.

---

[36] [1986] I.C.R. 891.
[37] [1983] I.C.R. 351.
[38] [1988] J.I.S.L. 187.
[39] [1969] 1W.L.R. 339.
[40] Hepple, (1970) 28 C.L.J. 122.
[41] (1940) 4 M.L.R. 225 and (1943) 6 M.L.R. 112. See generally Wedderburn, *The Worker and the Law* (3rd ed., 1986).
[42] [1944] I.R. 479.
[43] [1965] I.R. 1.

In Ireland the Supreme Court have unanimously endorsed the view that collective agreements can be binding in the ordinary courts. In *Goulding Chemicals Ltd. v. Bolger*[44] trade union members refused to accept the terms of a redundancy scheme agreed between their employer and the unions. Picketing commenced in breach of the redundancy agreement. While the Supreme Court advanced the view that unauthorised industrial action by the union members did not involve a breach of contract on their part (there being no evidence that the agreement was incorporated into their contract), the agreement did bind the unions and union officials. O'Higgins C.J. said that in this situation *Edwards v. Skyways*[45] indicated that the agreement was binding; Kenny J. went so far as to state that *Ford* was wrongly decided in the light of *Edwards v. Skyways*. Kenny J. approved Megaw J.'s dictum in *Edwards* that the onus of showing absence of legal intent is a heavy one. While the Supreme Court's observations on the point were delivered *obiter*, *Ford* is clearly not good law in Ireland if it is held to be authority for the proposition that all collective agreements are unenforceable. Nevertheless the *Report of the Commission of Inquiry on Industrial Relations* found that both sides of industry were generally against legal enforcement of collective agreements and recommended that it would not be advisable to make collective agreements legally binding by statute.[46]

In general, collective agreements are (often deliberately) loosely drafted and ambiguous in their terms, so in practice the agreement may fail to satisfy the requirements as to certainty of terms. But in some situations, and in particular where the law of mistake is pertinent, a plea of absence of legal intent may be defeated. This point has in a sense been made already: issues of legal intent are resolved by reference to objective factors; what the parties said, did and wrote may overcome an objection that the defendant did not intend to be bound. In *O'Rourke & Others v. Talbot Ireland Ltd.*[47] a "guarantee" that there would be no redundancies amongst foremen in the defendant's works was given to an ad hoc negotiating committee, in writing, by the management. In response to a claim for damages for breach of the agreement the employer claimed the statement was not intended to be binding. While this may have been the case the plaintiffs, to the knowledge of the defendant's negotiating representatives, believed they had been given a legally enforceable "guarantee" and for this reason Barrington J. held that the objective test of intention had been met and that the presumption had not been rebutted.

This case does not run contrary to the *Ford* case in England – Barrington J. referred to the fact that the plaintiffs had negotiated for themselves and not through union representatives. Indeed the case provides some degree of support for the essentially pragmatic line taken in *Ford* for, speaking of the productivity agreements negotiated by the union and employer in *O'Rourke & Others v. Talbot Ireland Ltd.*, Barrington J. found that these agreements were

---

44  [1977] I.R. 211.
45  [1964] 1 W.L.R. 349.
46  (1981) (Pl. 114) para. 764.
47  [1984] I.L.R.M. 587.

not intended to be binding. The experience in England suggests that certain types of obligation – normally relating to pay, health and safety, hours of work – are likely to be legally enforceable but that other terms – creche facilities and productivity agreements – are unlikely to be given legal effect. Nevertheless in Ireland the Industrial Relations Act 1946 for the first time made provision for a method of enforcing all the terms in certain kinds of collective agreements. Agreements relating to wages and conditions of employment, defined as an "employment agreement", could be registered and enforced by the Labour Court under the terms of section 32 of the 1946 Act. If the agreement was vague and ambiguous the registrar refused to register it. The agreement could be varied or cancelled with the consent of all parties to the registered employment agreement. Some 60 agreements[48] were registered with the Labour Court but were not strictly observed. The conditions relating to pay and other contractual terms were rarely updated when improvements were negotiated and the principle reason why the agreements were registered at all was to make the disputes procedures contained therein legally binding. *The Report of the Commission of Inquiry on Industrial Relations* noted that these provisions are not particularly useful but no real changes (or even outright repeal) were recommended.[49] The essentially pragmatic nature of the industrial relations agreement is highlighted by the controversy surrounding the TEAM Aer Lingus letters of comfort which were negotiated by Aer Lingus, the TEAM unions and ICTU in 1990. This agreement, which all sides recognise as legally binding, gives TEAM workers contractual rights to sue Aer Lingus should Aer Lingus seek to change conditions of employment or transfer TEAM employees without their consent.[50] These contractual terms, set out in a "letter of comfort" are currently part of the items for negotiation between TEAM workers and Aer Lingus in relation to plans to restructure and sell off the TEAM maintenance division of Aer Lingus, and attempts to buy out these letters of comfort are, at the time of writing,[51] at an advanced stage. The majority of TEAM workers have accepted offers to purchase these comfort letters, allowing Aer Lingus to run down aircraft maintenance, the majority of aircraft maintenance workers transfering to a Danish company that will acquire TEAM from Aer Lingus. The *O'Rourke* case is an essential plank in the TEAM workers' view that they possess a contractual right. Sections 51–55 of the Labour Relations Act 1990 makes a number of adjustments to the legislation in force in relation to registered employment agreements.

---

[48] In 1986.

[49] (Pl. 114) para. 770.

[50] The text of the agreement is found on the Business This Week page of the *Irish Times*, November 28, 1997.

[51] See "TEAM Workers have one week to accept" *Irish Times*, July 21, 1998.

# 4 Formal and Evidentiary Requirements

## Introduction

In this Chapter we will consider those contracts which can only be enforced if the contract itself is reduced into written form or if the contract (which may have been struck orally) is evidenced in writing.

There are a diverse number of specific statutory provisions which may require a contract to be set out in writing before that contract can be enforced by way of an action. For example, contracts which seek to create a trust in consideration of marriage must be evidenced by a writing signed by the person entitled to declare a trust.[1] Provisions of this kind may be seen as anachronistic and it is noteworthy that in the case of the example just given the law in Northern Ireland no longer requires an agreement of this kind to be reduced into writing. There is, however, a trend towards reassessing the utility of formal requirements because of the fact that procedural methods, that is, an insistence that before certain contracts or obligations are enforceable there should be clear written evidence of assent and voluntariness on the part of all persons privy to the agreement, provide a most useful function when there is a risk of extreme prejudice to one party if the contract should be freely enforceable. Irish statute law has been reinvigorated recently by consumer protection measures which give the Irish consumer some redress against prejudicial or unfair contracts by the expedient of requiring certain kinds of agreement to be set out in writing, and in some cases, giving one of the parties a right to cancel contracts.

## Contracts that must be Evidenced in Writing

Section 2 of the Statute of Frauds (Ir.) 1695[2] provides in part:

> "no action shall be brought . . . whereby to charge the defendant upon any special promise to answer for the debt, default or miscarriage of another person, or to charge any person upon any agreement made upon consideration of marriage, or upon any contract or (*sic*) sale of lands, tenements or hereditaments or any interest in or concerning them, or upon any agreement that is not to be formed within the space of one year from the making thereof, unless the agreement upon which such action shall be brought, or some memorandum or note thereof, shall be in writing, and signed by the party to be charged therewith, or some other person thereunto by him lawfully authorised."

---

[1]  ss.2 and 4 of the Statute of Frauds (Ir.) 1695.
[2]  7 Will. 3, c. 12 based upon the provisions of s.4 of the 1677 English Act (29 C. II, c. 3).

## (1) Contracts to pay for the debt, etc., of another

Before such a contract falls within the Statute of Frauds it is essential to show that the contract is one of guarantee and not one of indemnity. The classical example of a contract of guarantee arises where A asks B to supply goods to C, a trader, adding that if C does not pay up then B, the supplier, can turn to A for payment. In such a case it can be seen that both C and A are liable to pay; C is described as the principal debtor, A the guarantor. A's promise is said to be a collateral promise, the consideration for it being B's act of supplying goods to the principal debtor; see the decision of the Court of Common Pleas in *Bull v. Collier*[3] and that of the Court of Exchequer in *Fennel v. Mulcahy.*[4] At times, however, it is difficult to decide whether the promise made is a personal promise which is enforceable because it has induced forbearance amounting to consideration, or because the promisee can produce a memorandum. Sometimes the distinction is not clearly brought out in litigation. In the 1908 case of *Dunville & Co. v. Quinn*[5] a solicitor acting for the vendor of a hotel wrote to a creditor of the vendor who was pressing for payment of a debt "I will pay you the amount of your account out of the proceeds of sale." This induced forbearance on the part of the creditor but when the proceeds were disbursed to other creditors, to the exclusion of the promisee, the creditor successfully brought an action against the solicitor who was held personally liable on this undertaking.

In the case of the *Maria D.*[6] the House of Lords considered whether the alleged guarantor could adduce evidence to show that the guarantee was signed in some capacity other than that of guarantor. In that case, the charterer of a vessel negotiated with the charterparty by way of an agent who affixed his name to the charter, the charter containing an undertaking by the agent that the agent would be liable for demurrage and freight. It was not clear whether this undertaking had been given by the agent personally or as guarantor of the principal. It was not disputed that there had been a previous oral agreement between the agents and the shipowners. In these circumstances the House of Lords held that signature by the agent was binding and it mattered not whether the agent signed as agent or in a personal capacity; see *Re Hoyle*[7] which was followed on this point. While the words debt or default refer to contractual liabilities which the main debtor owes to the creditor, the Statute of Frauds also extends into promises to answer for the "miscarriage" of another. Therefore, a promise to meet tortious obligations must be made in a written contract or evidenced in writing, as in *Kirkham v. Marter.*[8] Here the defendant orally promised to compensate the plaintiff, who had suffered loss as a result of the negligence of the defendant's son. The action failed for non-compliance with the Statute.

---

[3] (1842) 4 Ir.L.R. 107.
[4] (1845) 8 Ir.L.R. 434.
[5] (1908) 42 I.L.T.R. 49.
[6] [1991] 3 All E.R. 758.
[7] [1893] 1 Ch. 84.
[8] (1819) 2 B. & Ald. 613.

On the other hand, if the promise made envisages the promisor being solely liable to pay the debt then it is said to be an original promise and not a collateral one. This is a contract of indemnity and no memorandum is necessary here; the promisor can be liable on the oral promise. In *Barnett v. Hyndman*[9] the plaintiff held a bill of exchange which had been accepted by one Moore who was therefore liable on it. The bill had been dishonoured. The plaintiff was asked to relinquish his claim against Moore by the defendant who promised to give half the sum due and another note for the balance. The plaintiff agreed but payment was not made. The defendant was held liable on his promise; by dropping the claim against Moore the plaintiff provided consideration for the defendant's promise that he alone would meet the debt. It should be noted that the cause of action was the tort of deceit.

The Law Reform Committee of South Australia[10] has not been alone in regarding this indemnity/guarantee dichotomy as "a disgrace to the law and a trap for the unwary", for it is clear that this distinction between contracts of guarantee and contracts of indemnity is both difficult to apply and at times arbitrary in its consequences. However, when the choice has arisen between abolition of the writing requirement and retention, most jurisdictions have retained it. In some of the Canadian provinces, most notably British Columbia, the writing requirement has been extended into contracts of indemnity, thereby effecting a most welcome extension of requirements of form into contracts where the promisor may often act impulsively and without any obvious benefit accruing to the promisor personally.

The existing requirement in respect of contracts of guarantee has several exceptions. The first arises in cases where the law of agency recognises the status of a *del credere* agent, that is, an agent who gets a higher commission for ensuring that his principal is paid by the other contracting party. A second exception is also found in agency law. It is established that if the promise is made in the context of a larger contract (an agent's promise to pay sums due to his principal for example), because such a promise is given in the context of agency the Statute does not apply. Nor does the Statute of Frauds apply to cases where the liability arises on an implied promise or an account stated: see *Wilson v. Marshall*.[11] A further exception arises if the guarantor enjoys rights over property and makes a promise to a third party in order to free the property from an encumbrance.[12]

### (2) An agreement made in consideration of marriage

This provision does not require a contract of marriage to be evidenced in writing; the old practice of members of a family agreeing to transfer property or a sum of money to an engaged couple has to be evidenced in writing before

---

[9] (1840) 3 Ir.L.R. 109.
[10] 34th Report (1975).
[11] (1866) I.R. 2 C.L. 356.
[12] *Fitzgerald v. Dressler* (1859) 7 C.B.N.S. 374.

the promise can be enforced: see the judgment of Sugden L.C. in *Saunders v. Cramer*.[13] This part of the Statute is of little importance today and the English counterpart has been repealed. The Law Reform Commissions for Ontario, South Australia and Manitoba, amongst others, have recommended the repeal of this kind of provision from the law in force in those jurisdictions.

Despite the quaintness of this requirement there are isolated cases in which the defence may prevail. In *The Goods of Leslie Good, Deceased*[14] the applicant sought Letters of Administration over the estate of her deceased father in order to take an action against her stepmother so as to enforce an alleged contract between the deceased and the applicant's stepmother. The applicant claimed that, by agreement, the deceased and the applicant's stepmother had contracted that, upon their respective deaths, property would pass back to the children of each of the parties by their previous marriages and would not devolve under the intestacy provisions found in section 67(ii) of the Succession Act 1965. Hamilton P., relying on section 4 (*sic*) of the Statute of Frauds, noted that the applicant was seeking to enforce a verbal agreement made, *inter alia*, in consideration of marriage, and because the applicant did not suggest or claim that the agreement was in writing, nor evidenced by a memorandum, the application failed.

### (3) Contracts for the sale of lands or an interest therein

This very important part of section 2 has been considered by the Irish courts in a great many cases. Apart from contracts for the sale of freehold interests, contracts of assignment, leases and grants of incorporeal hereditaments, the sale of things attached to the land may also involve the sale of an interest in land and therefore fall within section 2. In *Mackey v. Wilde and Longin*[15] an alleged agreement in relation to the allocation of fishing rights over a river was clearly held to require the parties to comply with the Statute of Frauds. A conacre letting of land, that is, one under which certain grazing rights are transferred to another, does not create an interest in land and, as Wylie argues, should not be within the Statute.[16] If, however, the contract is for the sale of crops or the natural products of the land it is arguable whether, in each individual case, the contract is for the sale of goods or for the disposition of an interest in land.

However, it was held in *Scully v. Corboy*[17] that a letting of meadowing is a contract for the sale of goods under section 62 of the 1893 Act, and that payment on account is part payment within section 4. Wylie remarks of this part of section 2 that: "it is clear from the voluminous case law on the section that it applies to contracts for sale in the widest sense." Nevertheless there are inevitably going to be instances where the transaction will be marginal. One such example is found in *Guardian Builders Ltd. v. Sleecon Ltd. and Berville*

---

[13]  (1842) 5 I.Eq.R. 12.
[14]  Unreported, High Court, July 14, 1986.
[15]  Unreported, Supreme Court, December 17, 1997.
[16]  *Irish Conveyancing Law* (2nd ed., 1996), para. 6.09.
[17]  [1950] I.R. 140; *Dunne v. Ferguson* (1832) Hayes 521.

*Ltd.*[18] The plaintiff wished to purchase a building site but following advice on the best way of avoiding stamp duty and obtaining tax benefits, was advised to purchase the second defendant company, the owners of the site, and a wholly-owned subsidiary of the second defendant. In dealing with the question of whether the contract was a contract for the sale of shares or, in reality, a contract for the sale of land, Blayney J., *obiter*, indicated that on the facts of this case the transaction would not be within the Statute of Frauds. Where land is held by a corporate body the purchase of the shares of that body does not vest in the purchaser an actual interest in the land. Blayney J. distinguished the case at bar from *Boyce v. Greene*[19] on the ground that the property in that case was held by a partnership and the purchase of shares in the partnership vested in the purchaser an interest in land owned by the partnership.

### (4) Contracts not to be performed within one year

In order to eliminate the possibility of cases being decided on the strength of oral testimony which may be deficient simply because of the interval between formation of a bargain and the litigation, the Statute of Frauds required such contracts to be evidenced in writing. In *Tierney v. Marshall*[20] the plaintiff alleged that it had been agreed between himself and the defendant landlord that the rent payable by the plaintiff would not be paid over to the defendant but would be set off against sums due to the plaintiff as arrears of wages earned while in the defendant's employment. The plaintiff claimed that this oral agreement made the defendant's landlord's acts of distress unlawful. The rent payable was £17 per annum; sums due were in excess of £200. For the set-off to operate then the contract would run for 12 years before the arrears would be paid. It was the view of the court that the contract was intended to run for more than one year and because it was not evidenced in writing was unenforceable. Similarly, in *Naughton v. Limestone Land Co. Ltd.*[21] an oral contract of employment which was to run for four years was held unenforceable without a memorandum of agreement. In the case of *In the Goods of Leslie Good, Deceased,*[22] the facts of which are set out above in relation to contracts in contemplation of marriage, Hamilton P., alternatively, held that because either party could survive the making of the contract for more than one year, the contract was caught by this part of section 2 of the 1695 Act.

It is established, however, that if at the time the contract is struck the parties intend it to be performed within one year the Statute does not apply. If the contract is to be performed within one year by one of the parties, as would be the case if A promised to convey Whiteacre to B next week in return for B's promise to support A for life, the Statute does not apply: see *Murphy v.*

---

[18] Unreported, High Court, August 18, 1988.
[19] (1826) Batty 608.
[20] (1857) 7 I.C.L.R. 308.
[21] [1952] Ir.Jur.Rep. 19.
[22] Unreported, High Court, July 14, 1986.

*O'Sullivan.*[23] In the case of *Hynes v. Hynes*[24] a plea that a contract for the transfer of a business from one brother to another was unenforceable for want of a memorandum was rejected. Barrington J., looking at the situation prevailing at the time of agreement, held that there was no intention on either side that the agreement should not be completed within the space of one year; the intention was that the agreement would be implemented immediately and that completion take place as soon as possible. In such a case it is immaterial whether the agreement is, in fact, completed within one year or not. It does not suffice for there merely to exist the possibility that one party may perform within the one-year period: *Farrington v. Donoghue.*[25] In this case the contract will be unenforceable unless there is a memorandum. If the contract is terminable at will, *Dublin Corporation v. Blackrock Commissioners*[26] holds the contract is outside the Statute.

If, however, the employee performs his part of the bargain he may be entitled to reasonable remuneration by making a claim in *quantum meruit* as occurred in *Savage v. Canning.*[27] This case concerned an action to recover £500 due for work and labour carried out on the foot of a contract that could not be enforced because of non-compliance with the Statute of Frauds. An action in *quantum meruit* was permitted because the plaintiff had done every-thing necessary under the contract. The *quantum meruit* remedy should be noted because in cases of part performance the plea may not be available, even in cases of substantial or complete performance by the plaintiff of his obligations, unless a plea of specific performance would have been available to each contracting party, a proposition established by *Crowley v. O'Sullivan.*[28]

It is established in *Naughton v. Limestone Land Co.*[29] that the courts will not sever the contract and allow an action in contract to lie for the first year of the oral contract.

### (5) Contracts for the sale of goods in excess of £10

Section 13 of the 1695 Statute of Frauds declares that such contracts cannot be enforceable unless the buyer: (i) accepts and receives part of the goods sold; or (ii) he gives something in earnest to bind the bargain; or (iii) the buyer makes part payment. In all other cases a memorandum must exist. This section was substantially repeated by section 4 of the Sale of Goods Act 1893 and although the 1893 Act did not expressly repeal section 13 of the Irish Statute of Frauds the courts seem to have regarded the 1893 Act as effecting an implied repeal. Section 13 of the Statute of Frauds 1695 was eventually repealed by the Statute Law Revision (Pre-Union Irish Statutes) Act 1962, section 1 and Schedule.

---

23 (1866) 11 Ir.Jur.(N.S.) 111.
24 Unreported, High Court, December 21, 1984.
25 (1866) I.R. 1 C.L. 675.
26 (1882) 16 I.L.T.R. 111.
27 (1867) I.R. 1 C.L. 432.
28 [1900] 2 I.R. 478.
29 [1952] Ir.Jur.Rep. 19.

The three alternatives that present a means of enforcing the contract where no memorandum exists hinge upon the conduct of the buyer. "Acceptance and receipt" was considered in *Hopton v. McCarthy*.[30] A coachbuilder in Tipperary ordered materials from the plaintiff in England but he refused to proceed with the transaction when he learnt that the price payable was three times that indicated during negotiations. The seller sent the materials by rail. They were held in the carrier's warehouse awaiting collection by the defendant. The acceptance and receipt formula did not apply here because the defendant had not actually received them: delivery into the custody of a carrier was held not to satisfy this requirement because the carrier was not authorised to accept them for the defendant.

In most cases where the question of acceptance and receipt arises this will be a relatively easy requirement to satisfy; witness the decision of the Supreme Court in *Tradax (Ireland) Ltd. v. Irish Grain Board Ltd.*[31] affirming the decision of Gannon J. in which the learned judge held that, by accepting 1,871 tonnes of grain out of a total of 12,000 tonnes due under the contract, the defendant could not plead the absence of a memorandum under section 4 of the 1893 Act.

The buyer can also be held liable if at the time of the bargain something in earnest is given. This ancient and obscure provision would be satisfied if the buyer gave his business card, for example, as a gesture of his good faith. The modern practice, for example, in ordering goods by giving a credit card number over the telephone could conceivably be regarded as the giving of something in earnest, even if the credit card holder does not sign the transaction docket.

For part payment to have been made it is essential that the payment be tendered and accepted. To post a cheque which is immediately returned uncashed will not satisfy the part payment provision. It was argued in the case of *Kirwan v. Price*[32] that when the buyer offered the cash price payable for a horse which he had orally agreed to buy (the seller declining to proceed with the sale at the agreed price), this constituted "something given in earnest". The Circuit Court judge refused to accept the argument, indicating that while the distinction between part payment and tendering of something in earnest is not clear, acceptance by the seller is essential to both. If the contract is marginal in the sense that it may be either a contract for the sale of goods or an interest in land it seems that the party arguing for enforcement may stand a greater chance of success if he argues that it is a contract for the sale of goods. The decision in *Scully v. Corboy*[33] held a letting of meadowing to be a contract for the sale of goods and because there were acts of part payment the absence of a memorandum was not fatal under section 4. Had the court decided otherwise the action would have failed because payment of part of the price in a contract for the sale of an interest in land does not readily satisfy the doctrine of part

---

[30] (1882) 10 L.R.(Ir.) 266.
[31] [1984] I.R. 1.
[32] [1958] Ir.Jur.Rep. 56.
[33] [1950] I.R. 140.

performance: see *Clinan v. Cooke*.[34] We will consider this doctrine later in the section devoted to equitable routes to enforcement.

The retention of section 4 of the 1893 Act is anachronistic and provides a technical and unmeritorious defence to executory contracts, regardless of the transaction type or status of the buyer. It has been repealed in most other jurisdictions, including the United Kingdom in 1954.

## The Requirements of the 1695 Statute

### (1) The memorandum

It is not necessary for the memorandum to have been specifically drafted as a memorandum before the Statute of Frauds can be satisfied. Letters written by solicitors, estate agents and others setting out the terms of the agreement have been held to constitute a memorandum even though the solicitor did not intend the document to take on the character of such an instrument. Other instruments that have been held to suffice include auctioneer's sale books, cheques for a deposit, receipts, all of which were not intended to *evidence* the contract. Indeed, in *Tradax (Ireland) Ltd. v. Irish Grain Board Ltd.*[35] the Supreme Court upheld the decision of the judge at the first instance in which it was held that a letter written by the defendant's agent in which the agent repudiated the contract could constitute a memorandum of agreement because it set out all the material terms of the oral agreement.

The only compelling requirement is that the memorandum should have come into existence before the commencement of the action brought to enforce the contract in question. So, in one case,[36] an action was brought in the name of a plaintiff who sought specific performance against the defendant. The defendant filed a defence in which it was asserted that a contract existed but that a company other than the plaintiff was the purchaser. The plaintiff then sought to amend the writ and statement of claim so as to instate the company as plaintiff. Leave was granted. The defendant's pleadings were regarded as being a sufficient memorandum of the alleged agreement between the company and the defendant for, in essence, the amendment of the writ and statement of claim, constituted commencement of a new action.

Some memoranda actually pre-date the conclusion of the contract itself. There are several cases[37] which indicate that a letter of offer may be a valid memorandum even though the offer, *ipso facto*, does not acknowledge the existence of a contract. In *Boyle and Boyle v. Lee and Goyns*,[38] O'Flaherty J. defended this "anomalous" exception of a written offer being accepted orally

---

[34] (1802) 1 Sch. & Lef. 22.
[35] [1984] I.R. 1.
[36] *Farr, Smith & Co. v. Messers Ltd.* [1928] 1 K.B. 397.
[37] *e.g. Reuss v. Picksley* (1866) L.R. 1 Ex. 342.
[38] [1992] I.L.R.M. 65.

as turning on the fact that "once there is an oral acceptance of a written offer it is at that moment that a contract comes into existence and, therefore, the note or memorandum becomes relevant."

### *(2) Contents of the memorandum*

The memorandum must contain the names of both parties to the contract or describe them in such a way as to make it possible to identify them. This provision is, like other parts of the Statute, read liberally, the courts preferring to find a contract to be enforceable than unenforceable. In *Bacon & Co. v. Kavanagh*[39] the words "you" and "your employment" in a contract of guarantee were held to be sufficiently clear to identify the party charged after surrounding circumstances were adverted to. In *Guardian Builders Ltd. v. Patrick Kelly & Park Avenue Ltd.*,[40] Costello J. stated that the test was whether the parties can be readily identified. In that case the name of the plaintiff company was mis-stated and the reference to the buyer failed to refer to the corporation involved, referring only to the person of the first defendant. It was held nevertheless to be sufficient to enable the court to identify the parties. The words used may not be such as to identify one of the parties but if proof of identity from an external source is possible the memorandum may suffice. Thus, in *Rossiter v. Miller*[41] it was held that if an agent signs *qua* agent for "the owner," parol evidence to prove the identity of the owner will perfect the memorandum.

If all the essential matters have been agreed then the court will hold that there is an oral contract, and will then proceed to consider whether there is an adequate memorandum. It is of course essential that there be agreement on the property to be transferred and that this description finds its way into the memorandum. In some instances the memorandum may refer only to the seller's property but, if this can be readily identified, then the contract will be enforceable. Should the memorandum fail to refer to the entire property and omits to mention a small offshore island of little value, for example, then the defect may be waived at the option of the purchaser, as in *Barrett v. Costello*.[42]

It is also necessary for the contract to state the consideration. In *Lynch v. O'Meara*[43] Butler J. held that it is not necessary to add whether the mode of payment will be in cash or by cheque.[44] However, if the parties refer to the balance payable after the purchaser has paid a deposit, in a manner that makes the reference misstate the total consideration, the memorandum will be defective. In *Black v. Grealy*,[45] where just such a situation arose, Costello J. said:

---

[39] (1908) 42 I.L.T.R. 120.
[40] Unreported, High Court, March 31, 1981.
[41] (1878) 3 App.Cas. 1124.
[42] Unreported, High Court, July 13, 1973.
[43] Unreported, High Court, October 23, 1973.
[44] In *Aga Khan v. Firestone and Firestone* [1992] I.L.R.M. 31 Morris J. held that the allocation of relevant parts of consideration to components of the bargain is not necessary as an essential matter.
[45] Unreported, High Court, November 10, 1977.

"in the circumstances of the present case the document relied on does not omit the consideration – it contains a figure for the consideration for the sale which the evidence establishes is the balance of the purchase price . . . it is not apt to describe the resultant written document as a memorandum 'of' the parties' oral agreement (as it does not properly state the full consideration for the sale); rather, it is a memorandum which is 'in accordance with' one of the stipulations of the oral agreement – which is not the same thing."

The Supreme Court, in *Godley v. Power*,[46] affirmed the view that the memorandum must recite the property, the parties and the price. If these three material terms are set out then most contracts will be enforceable unless on the evidence it is clear that the parties intended additional provisions to be essential terms. Failure to add these material terms will result in the memorandum being defective.

Two distinct problems must be distinguished here. First of all, the parties may fail to agree on additional terms that the courts consider to be essential before a contract can be said to exist at all. Here the contract is void for uncertainty. This is to be contrasted with the case of an agreement struck on all essential terms, the parties failing to record these terms in the memorandum. Here the contract is unenforceable unless some other means of enforcement exists.

There may be circumstances in which both these defects coincide. In *Guardian Builders Ltd. v. Sleecon Ltd. and Berville Ltd.*[47] the plaintiff purchaser sought specific performance of an agreement to purchase land by way of a share purchase of the company owning the land. The plaintiff alleged that the oral agreement involved a covenant that there would be an indemnity for any tax losses that could not be transferred to the plaintiff upon acquisition and, further, the plaintiff sought specific performance of the alleged agreement and was not prepared to take the property unless the indemnity accompanied the property. Blayney J. held that the evidence did not establish any concluded oral agreement, much less an agreement upon an indemnity being available to the plaintiff from the defendants. Further, any such agreement would be unenforceable for the alleged memorandum omitted to mention the indemnity in question.

If the contract is for the sale or transfer of a leasehold interest in land it is well established that unless the parties agree on the date of commencement the contract is void: *Kerns v. Manning*.[48] If the contract is divisible then failure to agree may not always be fatal. In *Godley v. Power*[49] a contract to sell a leasehold interest in a pub with stock-in-trade was held not to be void because the parties had not agreed on the price of stock-in-trade. The majority of the Supreme Court held the contract for stock-in-trade to be a separate collateral contract.

On the other hand, a memorandum that fails to record all agreed terms is not defective for only essential terms need be included. The decisions of Lord

---

[46] (1961) 95 I.L.T.R. 135.
[47] Unreported, High Court, August 18, 1988.
[48] [1935] I.R. 869.
[49] (1961) 95 I.L.T.R. 135.

MacDermott in *Stinson v. Owens*[50] and Gannon J. in *Black v. Kavanagh*[51] show that only terms thought to be material by the parties are essential. The courts are prepared to indicate that unless there is clear evidence to the contrary, it is not essential for the memorandum to state whether a deposit is payable. Nor is the closing date normally a material term. It is also unnecessary to state the nature of the interest sold if on the evidence both parties know what this is. Another factor that may sometimes be a material term is whether the property, if rented out to a third party or owner-occupied, is to be given with vacant possession and when vacant possession is to be given. While this may normally be envisaged to be material, as in *Hawkins v. Price*,[52] there may be circumstances where it will not be so: *Doherty v. Gallagher*.[53] Certain apparent gaps in the memorandum may be repaired by judicial ingenuity. In some cases the courts will imply terms into both the contract and the memorandum. In *Kelly v. Park Hall School*[54] a failure to agree on the date for signing the contract was not fatal, the Supreme Court implying that this will take place within a reasonable time. Similarly in *Barrett v. Costello*[55] the failure of the parties to discuss a completion date was held to be no obstacle to enforcement, for completion will impliedly take place within a reasonable time.

The decision of Costello J., in *Guardian Builders Ltd. v. Patrick Kelly & Park Avenue Ltd.*[56] illustrates the extent to which the materiality of terms is a question of fact. If the parties discuss a variety of matters, the provision of roads, date for possession, for example, but no agreement has been made then the action cannot fail because of non-compliance with the Statute. It may be that the contract is void for uncertainty – no agreement has been reached – but this is a distinct matter. *Guardian Builders* also illustrates another point; if important matters have not in fact been discussed then they cannot possibly be material terms as long as the parties, price and property have been identified by the memorandum.

*(3) Signature*

The memorandum should be signed by the person to be charged or his agent. "Signature" has been interpreted very loosely and it has been held that a rubber stamp, typed words or an illiterate's mark may suffice. In the recent Supreme Court decision in *Casey v. Irish Intercontinental Bank*[57] a solicitor who instructed a secretary to type a letter setting out the material terms of the memorandum on headed notepaper was held to adopt the heading as his signature so even if he fails personally to sign the letter a signed memorandum will exist. On the

---

50 (1973) 24 N.I.L.Q. 218.
51 (1973) 108 I.L.T.R. 91.
52 [1947] Ch. 645.
53 Unreported, High Court, June 9, 1975.
54 [1979] I.R. 340.
55 Unreported, High Court, July 13, 1973.
56 Unreported, High Court, August 18, 1988.
57 [1979] I.R. 364.

other hand, the initials of a solicitor added as a reference were held not to constitute a signature in *Kelly v. Ross & Ross*.[58] It is established that if the "signature" is added as a point of information rather than a means of authenticating the document this will not be a valid signature for the purpose of the Statute: see *McQuaid v. Lynam*.[59] If initials are included at the foot of the page where the signature is normally to be found this may satisfy the Statute.

For a detailed account of the complex problem of the authority of an agent to bind his principal, students should examine Wylie, *Irish Conveyancing Law*.[60] In general terms, however, the capacity of professional persons to bind others who employ them to assist in obtaining a purchaser of real property is not in dispute; an auctioneer appointed for the purpose of finding a purchaser has the implied authority to write a letter setting out the terms of the oral agreement, particularly if the principal is aware that the agent intends to write such a letter and says nothing (*Guardian Builders Ltd. v. Patrick Kelly & Park Avenue Ltd.*[61]) and implied authority to execute a memorandum is also vested in a solicitor engaged to assist in the sale or purchase. Auctioneers expressly engaged to sell property by public auction similarly have implied authority to execute a memorandum. The authority of the auctioneer will ultimately turn on any express agreement between the parties, as in *Lynch v. Bulbulia*.[62] An estate agent, in contrast to an auctioneer, has no implied authority to accept an offer on behalf of the principal, nor has the estate agent any implied authority to execute a memorandum on behalf of the principal. No ostensible authority can arise in these circumstances either, according to a long line of cases that is exemplified by the decision of Hamilton J. in *Aherne v. Gilmore*.[63] However, in *Ballyowen Castle Homes Ltd. v. Collins*[64] the evidence persuaded Keane J. that the defendant vendor had not given her estate agent express or implied authority to accept an offer and that the defendant accepted the offer on her own behalf. The circumstances surrounding the transaction indicated that it was part of the estate agent's function to find a buyer at a satisfactory price and write letters confirming any agreement reached. Again, the facts of each case will determine the scope of the agent's authority.

### (4) Joinder of documents

It is established that a memorandum may be made up of two or more documents. If only one of the documents is signed however, difficulties will arise because it is said that signature must authenticate the entire memorandum. If at the time of signature the other document does not exist it is illogical to hold the

---

[58] Unreported, High Court, April 29, 1980.
[59] [1965] I.R. 564.
[60] (2nd ed., 1996), paras 6.34–6.47.
[61] Unreported, High Court, August 18, 1988.
[62] Unreported, High Court, July 25, 1980.
[63] Unreported, High Court, June 19, 1981.
[64] Unreported, High Court, June 26, 1986.

signature to refer to that document. The leading case on joinder of documents is *McQuaid v. Lynam.*[65]

The Irish courts have followed the English practice of requiring the signed document expressly or impliedly to refer to the other documents. In *Kelly v. Ross & Ross,*[66] McWilliam J. held that particulars and conditions of sale, drawings, solicitor's attendance dockets, an estate agent's day book and correspondence – a total of nine items in all – could not collectively or individually constitute one memorandum because the signed documents (which did not contain all material terms) did not refer to the other documents submitted in evidence.

### (5) "Subject to contract"

The English authorities show that if a document contains the hallowed phrase, "subject to contract", that document cannot constitute a memorandum because the memorandum must acknowledge that an oral contract exists. We saw at the end of Chapter 1 that "subject to contract" will normally be taken to mean that the parties are still negotiating and have yet to reach an agreement.

Although there is no statutory authority to support the position, some modern Irish cases indicate important differences in approach to the "subject to contract" formula. If oral negotiations have been concluded without the phrase being used a solicitor who adds the "subject to contract" formula in correspondence will not prevent a court from finding that an oral contract has been struck. Furthermore, the letter written will be held to constitute a memorandum even though the "subject to contract" phrase is thought to indicate that no contract exists. This unhappy conclusion is the result of the decision of the Supreme Court in *Kelly v. Park Hall Schools.*[67] The parties orally agreed to contract for the sale of land. The defendant's solicitor wrote "I confirm that we have agreed terms 'subject to contract' . . . ." The defendants refused to proceed and were held liable. The Supreme Court held that the letter acknowledged that an oral contract had been struck; this suggests that a memorandum cannot exist unless it acknowledges the existence of a contract. The Supreme Court, however, seems to have decided that over 100 years of conveyancing practice must be disregarded when the Court further held that in this context the words "subject to contract" were ambiguous and that they do not deny the existence of a contract; the words were seen as meaningless. This decision has been critically examined by Keane J. in *Mulhall v. Haren*[68] where the learned judge (who was incidentally the defendant's counsel in the *Park Hall Schools* case) went some way towards re-establishing orthodoxy by "distinguishing" *Park Hall* as depending on its own special facts. The *Park Hall* case makes it difficult for lawyers and auctioneers to know how they can protect their client

---

[65] [1965] I.R. 564; *Irvine v. Dare* (1849) 2 Ir.Jur.(o.s.) 205.
[66] Unreported, High Court, April 29, 1980.
[67] [1979] I.R. 340: see generally [1984] *Conveyancer* 173 at 254.
[68] [1981] I.R. 364.

and it makes it possible for oral testimony to override written documents, something the 1695 Statute was designed to prevent. In fact the *Park Hall Schools* case was described by Circuit Court Judge Sheridan in *Cunningham v. Maher*[69] as having been "distinguished out of existence" and the orthodox view, namely, that the memorandum must itself acknowledge the existence of a contract, has been re-emphasised in several recent Irish cases; see *Carthy v. O'Neill*,[70] *Barry v. Buckley*[71] and *Kelly v. Irish Landscape Nursery Ltd.*[72]

The Supreme Court, in *Boyle and Boyle v. Lee and Goyns*[73] has repudiated any tendency, inherent in the *Park Hall* case, to weaken the proposition that a memorandum of agreement must, directly or by implication, acknowledge the existence of a contract. O'Flaherty J. and Egan J. confined *Park Hall* to its own special facts. McCarthy J. was of the view that *Park Hall* and indeed *Casey v. Irish Intercontinental Bank* should not be followed. Finlay C.J., Hederman J. concurring, also agreed that *Casey v. Irish Intercontinental Bank*, like *Park Hall*, are not to be regarded as good law. All members of the Supreme Court approved of Keane J.'s approach to this problem in his judgment in *Mulhall v. Haren*.

*Non-Compliance – Common law consequences*

While the contract caught by the Statute will be unenforceable at common law for want of a memorandum, it is important to note that the Statute will not be interpreted so as to render the contract void. If, following an oral contract the purchaser has paid a deposit, then the vendor may retain the deposit and plead the oral agreement as a defence to an action for restitution.[74] Similarly in the case of *Re a Debtor (No. 517 of 1991)*[75] the applicant had agreed to guarantee the debts of a company. The creditor had orally agreed that monies advanced by the debtor to a third party should go towards the reduction of the debtor's liability on the guarantee. The creditor claimed this oral agreement was unenforceable. However, Ferris J. held that the oral agreement could nevertheless be utilised as a defence.

# Equitable means of enforcing the contract – Part Performance

The historical justification for the Statute of Frauds of the prevalence of fraudulent and perjured evidence being adduced before the common law courts and the jury, was never an attractive argument for the counts of equity. The weight of academic opinion tends towards the view that it was never the

---

[69] Unreported, Circuit Court, March, 1982.
[70] [1981] I.L.R.M. 443.
[71] [1981] I.R. 306.
[72] [1981] I.L.R.M. 433.
[73] [1992] I.L.R.M. 65.
[74] *Thomas v. Brown* (1876) 1 Q.B.D. 714.
[75] *The Times*, November 25, 1991.

intention of Parliament to inhibit equitable methods of enforcement of a contract. Corbin[76] states, quoting Thayer's *Preliminary Treatise on Evidence*:

> "the Statute of Frauds was passed as a limitation upon the power of juries at a time when the rules of evidence were not yet formulated and when the judges had less power than later to control the action of juries . . . This is no doubt one of the reasons why courts of equity felt less strongly the necessity of applying the Statute strictly and were much more ready to enforce parol contracts on grounds of part performance or mistake than were the common law judges."

However, not all judges favoured a very expansive role for equity and Lord Redesdale, for example, opined in *Lindsay v. Lynch*[77] that had equity not granted relief the practice of concluding parol agreements would have been eliminated and the more satisfactory practice of reducing the agreement into writing would have emerged. In any event, there is a considerable volume of case law which points to a number of methods of persuading a court, by way of equitable jurisdiction, to grant a remedy on the contract, notwithstanding non-compliance with the Statute of Frauds.

The doctrine of part performance is the most obvious route leading to enforcement of a contract which fails to satisfy the formal requirements of the Statute of Frauds. Although the precise basis of this equitable doctrine is disputed it seems that the acts of part performance raise an equity in favour of the plaintiff, an equity which the courts should enforce. This view was recently expressed by Lord Reid in *Steadman v. Steadman*[78] and it has the support of the two leading Irish cases, *Hope v. Lord Cloncurry*[79] and *Lowry v. Reid*.[80]

In *Lowry v. Reid* Andrews L.J. wrote:

> "the doctrine is a purely equitable one. Its underlying principle is that the court will not allow a Statute which was passed to prevent fraud to be made itself an instrument of fraud. In other words, the court disregards the absence of that formality which the Statute requires when insistence upon it would render it a means of effecting, instead of a means of averting, fraud. The question in each case is, whether the plaintiff has an equity arising from part performance which is so affixed upon the conscience of the defendant that it would amount to fraud on his part to take advantage of the fact that the contract is not in writing. The right to relief vests not so much on the contract as on what has been done in pursuance or in execution of it."[81]

---

76  *Contract* s.281; see also Costigan (1913) 26 Harv.L.R. 329.
77  (1804) 2 Sch. & Lef. 1 at 5.
78  [1976] A.C. 536.
79  (1874) I.R. 8 Eq. 555.
80  [1927] N.I. 142.
81  *Ibid.* at 154–155.

In an important article, Coughlan and Bently[82] have refined the argument found in *Lowry v. Reid* and have suggested that unconscionable conduct lies at the heart of the doctrine of part performance. This link between this ancient equitable doctrine and more recent phenomena such as proprietary estoppel is to be welcomed as marking a significant advance in understanding the judicial basis of many contemporary developments in equity.

A contrasting view of the rationale behind the part performance doctrine tends to focus on the evidentiary role of the writing requirement; the doctrine of part performance repairs the formal defect that arises where no memorandum exists and, for this reason, the evidence furnished by the acts of the parties should be unequivocal. In the opinion of Lord O'Hagan in *Maddison v. Alderson*,[83] the acts of part performance "must be sufficient of itself and without any other information or evidence, to satisfy a court, from the circumstances it has created and the relations it has formed; that they are only consistent with the assumption of the existence of a contract."

It is often also argued that the acts of part performance must, on the facts, be only compatible with a contract for the sale of land and such a title as that alleged. It is clear that if these strict standards were insisted upon the doctrine would be virtually impossible to satisfy and for this reason a practical compromise has been effected (see Lord Simon in *Steadman v. Steadman*) between these two theories. In recent times the courts have indicated that part performance will have been satisfied if, on the balance of probabilities, the acts of part performance have been carried out by the person alleging that the contract is not enforceable and that these acts of part performance are consistent with a contract for the sale of land: *Re Gonin*.[84] In the case of *Silver Wraith Ltd. v. Siuicre Éireann*[85] Keane J., *obiter*, indicated that the test to be applied is whether, as a matter of probability, the plaintiff can establish that the acts of part performance can be held unequivocally referable to the type of contract alleged. In *Mackey v. Wilde and Longin*[86] Barron J. addressed many of the central points that surround the scope of part performance. Barron J. cited with approval the words of Lord Simon of Glaisdale in *Steadman v. Steadman* and Andrews L.J. in *Lowry v. Reid,* and *Fry on Specific Performance.* The doctrine requires that the courts should investigate the acts of part performance to see if they refer to some contract; if those acts prove the existence of some contract and are consistent with the contract alleged then the acts of part performance should suffice. However, Barron J. stressed that "ultimately the court is seeking to ensure that a defendant is not, in relying upon the Statute, breaking faith with the plaintiff". Barron J. took the view that:

---

[82] (1988) 23 Ir. Jur. (N.S.) 38.
[83] (1883) 8 App.Cas. 467.
[84] [1977] 3 W.L.R. 379.
[85] Unreported, High Court, June 8, 1989.
[86] Unreported, Supreme Court, December 17, 1997.

"what is essential is that

(1) there was a concluded oral contract;
(2) that the plaintiff acted in such a way that showed an intention to perform that contract;
(3) that the defendant induced such acts or stood by while they were being performed; and
(4) it would be unconscionable and a breach of good faith to allow the defendant to rely upon the terms of the Statute of Frauds to prevent performance of the contract."

Barron J. also expressed the view that the court should take evidence of what was agreed and then look to the conduct of the parties to establish acts of part performance: classical formulations suggest that the sequence of events should be the first reference point, but Barron J. rejected this approach, opining that "it is more logical to find out what the parties agreed since, in the absence of a concluded agreement, there is no point in seeking to find acts of part performance". The judgment of Barron J., with which Hamilton C.J. and Barrington J. concurred, is of the first importance in presenting a contemporary foundation for resolving part performance disputes.

The most important effect of *Steadman v. Steadman* has been to compel the lower courts to revise the long established proposition which declares that payment of money can never, of itself, constitute an act of part performance: see *Clinan v. Cooke*.[87] In *Steadman v. Steadman*, the House of Lords indicated that if on the facts the payment is referable to a contract for the disposition of an interest in land and if the payee accepts the money, *e.g.* by cashing a cheque, then it may in these circumstances be inequitable to allow the payee to rely on non-compliance with the Statute: see *P. M. Howlin v. Thomas F. Power (Dublin) Ltd.*[88]; *Re Irish Commercial Society*.[89] For an illustration of the circumstances in which payment of money may satisfy the doctrine of part performance see the decision of Kilner Brown J. in *Cohen v. Nessdale Ltd.*[90] later affirmed by a unanimous Court of Appeal on another point.[91]

The classic act of part performance is entry into possession of the land with the agreement or acquiescence of the defendant: see *Kennedy v. Kennedy*.[92] In *Starling Securities v. Woods*[93] entry onto the site and demolition of derelict property was held to constitute part performance and in *W. P. McCarter & Co. v. Roughan*[94] the plaintiff purchaser's act of moving into possession, allied to incurring expenditure on the building, with the consent of the vendor, was held

---

[87] (1802) 1 Sch. & Lef. 22.
[88] Unreported, High Court, May 5, 1978; Tompkin (1978) 13 Ir.Jur. 343.
[89] Unreported, High Court, February 12, 1987.
[90] [1981] 3 All E.R. 118.
[91] [1982] 2 All E.R. 87.
[92] Unreported, High Court, January 12, 1984; *Rainsford v. Eager* (1853) 3 Ir.Jur. (O.S.) 240; *Steven's Hospital v. Dyas* (1864) 15 Ir.Ch.R. 405.
[93] Unreported, High Court, May 24, 1977.
[94] [1986] I.L.R.M. 447.

to constitute part performance. In the majority of cases the plaintiff will seek to adduce multiple acts of part performance, as in the case of *Howe v. Hall.*[95] Here the payment of an increased rent and the draining of agricultural land and planting of the land were held to be compelling and consistent acts of part performance: see also *Lanyon v. Martin.*[96] In a recent Supreme Court decision on part performance, *McCarron v. McCarron,*[97] the Court was persuaded by evidence pertaining to the relationship between the parties and the quality of the acts done by the plaintiff. The judgment of Murphy J. indicates that, despite the terse nature of the oral exchanges that were brought into evidence, the quality of the *res gestae* persuaded the Court that some bargain of the kind alleged was struck; such a paucity of evidence on the oral bargain could be explained away by cultural and sociological factors that would be unfamiliar to many in the Irish business community, for example. The acts of part performance consisted of work done around the farm rather than work done in relation to land and/or buildings.

## Other Equitable Devices

The precise limits of the doctrine of part performance remain unsettled in English law. There are suggestions in a handful of Irish cases that failure to satisfy the Statute and the doctrine of part performance may not always be fatal. Given that the 1695 Statute was designed to counteract conveyancing malpractices and other frauds it would be ironic if a person could shelter behind the strict letter of that Act and avoid liability for breach of contract. This irony has not escaped the judges. It has been said that the courts will not allow the Statute to be used as "an engine of fraud" and, while this helps explain the doctrine of part performance, the matter does not end there.

In *Doherty v. Gallagher*[98] the purchaser agreed to give the vendor a reasonable time to clear the land of his, the vendor's, cattle. This material term was not mentioned in the memorandum. Finlay P. awarded specific performance nevertheless, declaring that where there is a danger of encouraging fraud by a strict interpretation of the Statute this should be avoided if possible. Similarly, a trustee cannot plead the strict requirements of the Statute if to do so would permit him to commit a fraud: *McGillycuddy v. Joy.*[99] If there is a mistake in the memorandum in circumstances where rectification is not possible an oral agreement may be enforced regardless of the memorandum's deficiencies. In *Black v. Grealy*[100] Costello J. stressed that for the Statute to be held

---

[95] (1870) 4 I.Rep.Eq. 242.
[96] (1884) 13 L.R.Ir. 297.
[97] Unreported, Supreme Court, Feb 13, 1997.
[98] Unreported, High Court, June 9, 1975.
[99] [1959] I.R. 189; *Ballyowen Castle Homes v. Collins,* unreported, High Court, June 26, 1986; *Kavanagh v. Delicato,* unreported, High Court, December 20, 1996.
[100] Unreported, High Court, November 10, 1977.

inapplicable it must be proved that the defendant would thereby perpetrate a fraud. In that case, the defendant, Grealy, was responsible for the memorandum for it was prepared expressly in accordance with his wishes and for his benefit.

In *Black v. Grealy* Costello J., *obiter*, observed that a distinct plea of estoppel may also be utilised in appropriate cases, for the learned judge said:

> "there may well be cases (and this could be one of them) where a party, expressly agreeing to accept the adequacy of a memorandum of an oral agreement, is in subsequent proceedings estopped from alleging its inadequacy."

Indeed, there are instances of an estoppel being successfully utilised when the estoppel relates to whether or not a memorandum exists as a matter of fact. In *Thwaites v. Ryan*[101] Fullagar J. observed that the traditional view of estoppel prevented equitable estoppel from being utilised when the representation related to matters of intention.

*Black v. Grealy* also supports a further ground for avoiding the Statute. Several cases indicate that it is established that if a term orally agreed is inserted into a memorandum, the term being for the benefit of one party alone, and the term cannot be implemented, compliance with the term may be waived. In *Barrett v. Costello*[102] Kenny J. stressed that:

> "the note in writing for the purposes of the Statute of Frauds has to be of the contract sued on, not the contract made and the plaintiff may waive a term which is wholly in his favour and which is not referred to in the memorandum."

In *Healy v. Healy*[103] the plaintiff agreed to purchase land for £46,000. The memorandum inaccurately stated the consideration to be £40,000. The plaintiff was able to enforce the oral contract by unilaterally waiving the mistake in the memorandum and agreeing to pay the £46,000 orally agreed. Similarly, if the memorandum fails to record a material term it will be defective but enforceable through waiver; see the English case of *Martin v. Pyecroft*[104] which has been cited with approval in several Irish cases.

If the waiver is to be effective, however, the party who seeks to waive the omitted term must show that the oral term, whilst a material term, was inserted into the agreement for that person's benefit alone. So, in *Anom Engineering Ltd. v. Thornton*[105] specific performance of a contract for the sale of land was decreed in favour of the plaintiff purchaser because the omitted material term, which related to the plaintiff's right to obtain a water and sewage supply, was

---

[101] [1984] V.R. 85.
[102] Unreported, High Court, July 13, 1973.
[103] Unreported, High Court, December 3, 1973.
[104] (1852) 2 D.M. & G. 785.
[105] Unreported, High Court, February 1, 1983.

for the plaintiff's benefit alone. On the other hand, if the omitted term was part of the oral bargain and for the benefit of both parties, or solely for the benefit of the party resisting an action on the foot of the oral contract, waiver will not be possible: see *Tiernan Homes Ltd. v. Fagan*.[106]

## Possible Reform of the Statute of Frauds

There is no doubt that the 1695 Statute is in need of revision but there are situations in which section 2 remains a most useful hedge against improvident contracts. The present situation in which guarantees and not indemnities are within the Statute should be amended and indemnities added to the writing requirement. The repeal of the writing requirement in relation to contracts in consideration of marriage and contracts not to be performed within one year is overdue. In the United Kingdom the writing requirement in respect of contracts for the disposition of an interest in land has recently been revised by way of section 2 of the Law of Property (Miscellaneous Persons) Act 1989, discussed in *Record v. Bell*[107] and *Spiro v. Glencrown Properties Ltd.*[108] The net effect of this reform is to require all contracts to be made in writing, the contract to contain all express terms, and be signed by the parties thereto. In the present writer's view this is a very inflexible position, particularly in the light of the effective repeal of the part performance doctrine. Nevertheless O'Flaherty J. is in support of such a position, for in *Boyle and Boyle v. Lee and Goyns*[109] the learned judge observed:

> "The Statute of Frauds was enacted to prevent perjury and subornation of perjury as well as other fraudulent practices. In due course, equity made sure that the invocation of the Statute should not be used to bring about fraud and, thus, was developed the doctrine of part performance. However, it seems to me that equity has now done its work and the Statute should be looked at again because what it is now necessary to prevent is the burgeoning of actions based on subtleties and niceties to get around the clear wording of the statute. For my part, I would advocate that the Statute should be amended so as to provide that all contracts for the sale of land should be in writing. This is because life has not got any less complicated over the intervening centuries; nowadays, as this very case illustrates, there are often planning aspects to a sale; there is finance to be arranged; there is the tax end of matters to be sorted out (in this case there was the question of certain furnishings being part of the sale and no apportionment had been made in relation to them); family law

---

[106] Unreported, Supreme Court, July 23, 1981.
[107] [1991] 4 All E.R. 471.
[108] [1991] 1 All E.R. 600.
[109] [1992] I.L.R.M. 65.

legislation may often have some relevance, and, further, there is the fact that the boundaries of negligence in relation to people involved in the buying and selling of property have been widened over the last number of decades. In these circumstances, I would rather the occasional gazumper go unbound than that people should be involved in needless uncertainty leading often to long drawn out litigation."[110]

An inflexible requirement of this kind can only operate within the grounds of justice if some equitable remedy is available to the courts. In this regard section 139 of the U.S. Restatement (2nd) Contracts may be a useful addition to Irish law, either in tandem with the existing law or as part of a broader reform, as section 139 provides:

> "§139. Enforcement by Virtue of Action in Reliance
> (1) A promise which the promisor should reasonably expect to induce action or forbearance on the part of the promisee or a third person and which does induce the action or forbearance is enforceable notwithstanding the Statute of Frauds if injustice can be avoided only by enforcement of the promise. The remedy granted for breach is to be limited as justice requires.
> (2) In determining whether injustice can be avoided only by enforcement of the promise, the following circumstances are significant:
>     (a) the availability and adequacy of other remedies, particularly cancellation and restitution;
>     (b) the definite and substantial character of the action or forbearance in relation to the remedy sought;
>     (c) the extent to which the action or forbearance corroborates evidence of the making and terms of the promise, or the making and terms are otherwise established by clear and convincing evidence;
>     (d) the reasonableness of the action or forbearance;
>     (e) the extent to which the action or forbearance was foreseeable by the promisor."

## Corporations

At common law a contract was enforceable against or by a corporation only if the contract was executed under the common seal. The rule was never absolute, however. In *Donovan v. South Dublin Guardians*[111] it was held that if work was ordered, carried out and accepted by a statutory corporation, the work

---

[110] [1992] I.L.R.M. 65 at 89. One commentator is of the view that the writing requirement should be abolished altogether: see Bridge (1986) 64 Can.Bar.Rev. 58.
[111] (1904) N.I.J.R. 106.

being within the scope of its objects, the absence of a contract under seal was no defence if the Corporation was sued; similarly if it was the Corporation that was endeavouring to sue upon the contract.[112] Certain contracts require special procedures to be adopted; under the Public Health (Ireland) Act 1878, s.201(1), contracts whose value exceeds £50 must be in writing and sealed by the health authorities with their common seal; see also the Dublin Fever Hospital Act 1936, s.37(2).

In other cases the position of a company is assimilated to that of a living person by section 38 of the Companies Act 1963.

## Contracts that are Unenforceable or Void unless Recorded in Writing

As a result of the Consumer Credit Act 1995 there are significant changes to the law governing credit agreements. The new law now regulates credit agreements and makes significant changes to moneylending agreements and hire-purchase agreements. We will begin to summarise the law by looking at the old and the new law relating to hire-purchase agreements.

### *Hire-Purchase – the old law*

Under the Hire-Purchase Acts 1946–80 contracts which failed to meet the terms set out in section 3 of the 1946 Act were generally held to be unenforceable by the owner: section 3(2) has been discussed by Carroll J. in *Henry Forde & Son Finance Ltd. v. John Ford & General Accident Fire and Life Assurance Co.*[113] Strictly speaking, non-compliance with the Hire-Purchase Acts did not make the contract of hire-purchase void but unenforceable and the fact that most lending institutions used standard documents which comply with the statutory requirements in terms of format, made the most likely cause for default non-signature of the document. However, there was no statutory power given to the court to ignore the non-signature, even if the court could be persuaded that the hirer was not prejudiced, whereas non-compliance with other requirements could be ignored in cases of non-prejudice to the consumer: see the proviso to section 3(2). In the *Ford* case Carroll J. said:

> "the legislature considered it was essential for the enforcement of a hire purchase agreement that a note or memorandum should be signed by the hirer and by or on behalf of all other parties to the agreement."

---

[112] (1882) 16 I.L.T.R. 111.
[113] Unreported, High Court, June 13, 1986.

*Hire-Purchase – the new law*

A hire-purchase agreement[114] when the hirer is a consumer, where made after May 13, 1996, is regulated by the Consumer Credit Act 1995. Sections 58 to 62 of that Act set out information requirements that must be made to the hirer in the form of statements concerning hire purchase price, cash price, the amount of each installment, number of installments, names and addresses of the parties, and costs and penalties. A waivable 10-day cooling off period must be stated in the agreement. The hirer must sign the agreement. If the agreement is not signed by the hirer and a copy given to the hirer or delivered to the hirer the agreement is not enforceable. Other failures to satisfy the Act may lead a court to declare the agreement to be valid notwithstanding, if the failure was not deliberate, did not prejudice the hirer and it would be just and equitable for the court to make the agreement enforceable.

The Consumer Credit Act 1995 also regulates credit agreements made by a consumer. Similar obligations to those noted above in relation to information requirements, signature and form of agreement are imposed upon the creditor in sections 29–39. Consumer hire agreements are also regulated in the Act in this way (sections 84–91).

## Contracts Negotiated Away from Business Premises

The prospect of consumers being pressured into agreeing to purchase goods and services by way of high pressure and other unscrupulous sales techniques has long been of concern to the courts and Parliament, and the unconscionable bargain doctrine and various measures of statutory protection have been utilised to protect the public. A most significant measure of consumer protection is to be found in a recent statutory instrument, the European Communities (Cancellation of Contracts Negotiated Away from Business Premises) Regulations 1989.[115] In essence, a contract negotiated away from the business premises of a trader must provide a right to cancel the contract within a minimum period of seven days from the making of the contract. To this end the trader must provide a written notice of the cancellation right, as prescribed by the Regulations. Upon exercise of the right the contract is void. Failure to provide the cancellation notice makes the contract void also.

## Regulatory Powers under the Moneylenders Acts

Until recently it was a statutory requirement that moneylending contracts within the Moneylenders Acts 1900 to 1933 were to be recorded in writing.[116] While

---

[114] See Bird, *Consumer Credit Law* (Round Hall Sweet & Maxwell, 1998).

[115] S.I. 1989 No. 224, implementing Council Directive 85/577/EEC of December 20, 1985 to protect the consumer in respect of contracts negotiated away from business premises [1985] O.J. L372/31.

[116] *Handelman v. Davis* (1937) 71 I.L.T.R. 268.

the 1900 to 1933 legislation has been repealed by the Consumer Credit Act 1995, agreements made before May 13, 1996 are regulated by the old law. The 1995 Act sets out obligations in respect of records of agreement and repayment books. Non-compliance by a moneylender is normally addressed via the criminal law: Consumer Credit Act 1995, section 12.[117]

## Regulatory Powers under the Sale of Goods and Supply of Services Act 1980

Section 54 provides:

> "The Minister may by order provide, in relation to goods or services of a class described in the order, that a contract (being a contract for the sale of goods, an agreement for the letting of goods, otherwise than in a hire-purchase agreement, or a contract for the supply of a service) shall, where the buyer, hirer or recipient of the service deals as consumer, be in writing and any contract of such class which is not in writing shall not be enforceable against the buyer or hirer or recipient of the service."

This useful method of controlling high pressure sales techniques in which the consumer is unaware of the finer details of the suppliers' conditions of supply is rather vague. Does the consumer have to sign the contract? The section does not expressly state this. To-date, no orders have been made but work is in progress on preparing legislative controls on the, to-date, entirely unregulated area of leasing contracts: see the facts of *O'Callaghan v. Hamilton Leasing (Ireland) Ltd.*[118]

---

[117] See Bird, *Consumer Credit Law*, (Round Hall Sweet & Maxwell, 1998), Chap. 9.
[118] [1984] I.L.R.M. 146. The law relating to finance leasing is considered by the author in *Pacta Leasing 1991 Report – Ireland*, pp. 90–144 (Pacta Sophia-Antipolis, 1992).

# Part 2

# Construction of a Contract

# 5 Express Terms

## Introduction

Even if both parties to a dispute agree that a contract has been concluded the court will still have to determine what obligations each party has consented to. The statements made by each of them will be of paramount importance in limiting the scope of the bargain. Not every statement made will form part of the contract, however. A variety of reasons why this must be so will be evident to the reader. First, the statement may be made during preliminary negotiations when each party may be seeking to establish the best bargain possible, and if every statement made were contractual, the contract would probably contain inconsistent and contradictory terms on essential matters. Secondly, the parties may also not intend certain statements to be contractual; for example, laudatory claims about the goods may be an effective part of sales hype and uttered in circumstances where no reasonable person could believe the statement was seriously meant and intended to be relied upon. Sales "puffs" of this kind are at times difficult to disentangle from claims by the seller about the efficacy of goods, and the more specific the assertion, the more likely it is that the statement will be given contractual status. A third reason why a statement may be denied contractual effect can be said to be the result of a process of interpretation. The contract itself may contain other terms that are incompatible with the term alleged. The most obvious example of such a term is an exclusion clause, considered later in Chapter 7.

## The Basic Distinction

A distinction must be drawn between representations that do not have contractual effect and those that do. The former are called "mere representations" while the latter are often described as "warranties". In this context the word warranty is used in the neutral sense of "contractual" term rather than as a technical expression denoting a term, breach of which gives rise to a remedy in damages.[1]

The evolution of the law on warranties and mere representations is closely linked with the law of evidence and now outdated rules of pleading. A person who claimed that he had contracted because the other party represented a state of affairs existed which subsequently turned out to be untrue could recover only if the word "warrant" or similar phrases had been used. The courts moved

---

[1]  Sale of Goods Act 1893, s.11.

towards protecting a purchaser by discarding such a rule; as Lefroy B. remarked in the 1843 case of *Scales v. Scanlan*:

> "To make a warranty it is not necessary that the word 'warrant' or 'warranty' should be used. There was a time in the law when it was otherwise . . . but it has been long since well settled, that words of affirmation, affirming a matter of fact, on the faith of which the party contracts, are as competent to make a warranty as any strict technical term."[2]

Nevertheless, if a person simply affirms his belief to be "such and such" in circumstances that make it apparent that he does not take any responsibility for the accuracy of it then such a statement may be held to be an affirmation rather than a warranty. To state that a car is believed to be a 1948 model when it is in fact a 1939 model may be held to be a non-contractual affirmation or representation if the seller advises the buyer to verify this statement. Indeed, the seller may not be liable in contract if the purchaser is a motor dealer who had the resources available to check the year of manufacture and the seller is an individual lacking any professional skill, honestly believing the car to be as stated: see *Oscar Chess Ltd. v. Williams*.[3] In the recent case of *Hummingbird Motors v. Hobbs*[4] Hobbs sold a motor vehicle to Hummingbird Motors for £2,700. Hobbs had purchased the vehicle at a car auction for £2,275, the odometer reading 34,900 miles. When completing the transaction Hobbs signed the plaintiff's standard form which contained a declaration that the odometer reading was correct to the best of the seller's knowledge and belief. In fact the vehicle had done 80,000 miles. The Court of Appeal held that there was no warranty by Hobbs for there was no reasonable basis for Hummingbird Motors to believe that the seller here was making a contractual promise. Of course, if the sale was by Hobbs in circumstances where the history of the vehicle could have been known to Hobbs – he was selling as the first and only registered owner of the vehicle for example – a warranty could be inferred. On the whole the Irish courts have been less troubled by the affirmation/warranty dichotomy than their English brethren. In *McGuiness v. Hunter*[5] the defendant, who owned a horse told the plaintiff, a prospective purchaser, that "the horse is all right and I know nothing wrong about him." The plaintiff purchased the horse which soon afterwards died. Counsel for the plaintiff conceded that the words "is all right" amounted to a promissory statement and that if they had not been uttered the remainder of the statement would only amount to an affirmation. The statement was held to be a warranty. In *Schawel v. Reade*[6] the owner of a horse informed the plaintiff's agent, who was about to inspect the

---

2 (1843) 6 I.L.R.C.L. 432 at 457.
3 [1957] 1 W.L.R. 370.
4 [1986] R.T.R. 276.
5 (1853) 6 Ir. Jur. (O.S.) 103; *Murphy v. Hennessey* (1897) 3 I.L.T. 404.
6 [1913] 2 I.R. 81; contrast *Routledge v. McKay* [1954] 1 W.L.R. 615.

animal, that "you need not look for anything; the horse is perfectly sound. If there was anything the matter with the horse I should tell you." The agent broke off his inspection, the horse was purchased and later turned out to suffer from an eye defect that made it unsuitable for the purchaser's purpose. The Court of Appeal in Ireland held the statement to be merely an affirmation; the House of Lords unanimously reversed this decision. Had *McGuiness v. Hunter* been cited before the Irish Court of Appeal (which it was not), it is suggested that the purchaser would have there succeeded; the statement in *Schawel v. Reade* seems to be a more obvious warranty than the words uttered in *McGuinness v. Hunter*.

The courts often ask whether the representee acted on the faith of the truth of the statement rather than whether the representor intended the statement to be a warranty, the latter being a metaphysical test at the best of times. The modern law is admirably summarised by Kenny J. in *Bank of Ireland v. Smith*.[7] After discussing the older English case law he said: "The modern cases, however, show a welcome tendency to regard a representation made in connection with a sale as being a warranty unless the person who made it can show that he was innocent of fault in connection with it." Indeed, in the 1886 case of *Cobden v. Bagnell*[8] a father who stated an honest belief that his daughter was entitled to an estate under a complicated settlement was held not liable because the statement was found to be a reasonable but mistaken interpretation of the effect of the instrument. The test is not entirely new it seems.

## The Parol Evidence Rule

This controversial rule of evidence is designed to deal with problems that arise from attempts to introduce testimony about the terms agreed upon where the parties have subsequently executed a written document setting out their contract. The rule was stated in absolute terms by Lord Morris in *Bank of Australasia v. Palmer*[9]: "parol testimony cannot be received to contradict, vary, add to or subtract from the terms of a written contract or the terms in which the parties have deliberately agreed to record any part of their contract." At first blush the rule is a harsh one for it would exclude all parol evidence which was not incorporated into the written document. It is apparent that the rule is capable of causing injustice. The rule was designed to prevent litigation from being protracted, the theory being that if parol testimony was excluded and the attention of the jury (whose task was to decide issues of fact, including contract terms) focused on the written document alone then civil trials would be shorter and less expensive. One sixteenth century English judge observed that it was "better to suffer mischief to one man than an inconvenience to many."[10]

---

7 [1966] I.R. 161; *John O'Donoghue & Co. v. Collins*, unreported, High Court, March 10, 1972.
8 (1886) 19 L.R. (Ir.) 150.
9 [1897] A.C. 540.
10 See *Waberley v. Cockerel* (1542) 1 Oy. 51a.

Nevertheless, it is doubtful if litigation was shortened by the rule; indeed, the fact that the court heard the evidence and then decided whether to rule it admissible means that the rule often had the contrary effect. In any event, the decline of the institution of the jury in civil cases renders the rule out of date. It is nevertheless recited by the judges and relied upon by them even today. In *Macklin & McDonald v. Greacen & Co.*[11] the Supreme Court held that a contract, expressed to be one of sale of the licence of licensed premises, could not be varied by reference to parol evidence, for the contract had been reduced into writing and as such, the contract was unenforceable for the licence was inalienable from the premises in question. In the absence of a claim for rectification of the contract, in which case parol evidence would be admissible, the parol evidence rule was imposed with full force by the Supreme Court. The English Law Commission, in a important review of the operation of the parol evidence rule,[12] concluded that, despite calls for the abolition of the rule, it was a convenient procedural device, if properly understood by the judiciary. In the view of the Law Commission, abolition of the rule was unnecessary and undesirable. The rule however has never been applied absolutely and we shall now consider the many exceptions to it.

### (1) To establish the limits of the contract

The parol evidence rule can only apply if an attempt is made to seek to add to, vary or contradict a contract. The rule is not infringed if the party seeking to introduce parol testimony is trying to show that there was no contract at all (see *Pym v. Campbell*[13]) or show that there were two distinct contracts, one written and the other oral. This may prove a useful technique. In *Carrigy v. Brock*[14] a deed of assignment failed to mention that Brock was to pay a sum of money to Carrigy. This promise had been recorded in a memorandum of agreement. When Carrigy sought to recover, the defendant pleaded the parol evidence rule. The defence failed for, as Pigot C.B. said, the plaintiff was trying to recover on a separate contract – it would now be called a collateral contract – and was not trying to establish that this promise contained in the memorandum should vary the deed of assignment. Pigot C.B. called the defendant's attempt to invoke the parol evidence rule "a solecism of language".

A more recent illustration is afforded by the decision of the Court of Appeal in *Haryanto v. E.D. & F. Man Sugar Ltd.*[15] The defendant sought to argue that documents which set out contractual terms were not actionable because the documents merely set out the terms that would bind the parties should they, at a later date, conclude a contract. In the light of evidence that a contract was intended, the court ruled that documents that look like contracts are intended to be contracts. In cases of this kind the rule is essentially a convenient but

---

[11] [1983] I.R. 61.
[12] Law Com. No. 154.
[13] (1856) 6 El. & Bl. 370.
[14] (1871) I.R. 5 C.L. 501.
[15] [1986] 2 Lloyd's Rep. 44.

misleading rationalisation of the decision. The court does hear the evidence, *de bene esse*, but rejects it in the light of the balance of probability and contradictory evidence that a contract, in particular terms, was intended.

### (2) To explain the circumstances surrounding an agreement

In *Harries v. Hardy*[16] a ship-repairer brought an action against B and C, who, along with A, were the registered owners of the vessel under bills of sale. The action, brought to recover the cost of repairs carried out on the vessel failed because B and C were able to introduce parol evidence to show that the bills of sale were executed as mortgages. B and C were not liable as they were mortgagees, not owners. Similarly, in *Revenue Commissioners v. Moroney*,[17] the Supreme Court admitted parol evidence to show that an apparent sale was in fact intended to be a transfer by way of gift. In *The Ulster Bank v. Synnott*[18] the defendant deposited stock certificates with his bank as security "against acceptances made" on the defendant's account. Because the phrase "against acceptances made" could refer to either acceptances which have been heretofore made, or acceptances made during the currency of the security, parol evidence was admissible to determine whether the parties intended to cover future as well as past acceptances. The circumstances indicated that future acceptances would also be covered by the security in question. In *Grahame v. Grahame*[19] parol evidence was held to be admissible to show why a guarantee was executed; the purpose of admitting parol testimony was explained in this case as putting the court as nearly as possible in the position of the parties when entering into the agreement. More recently, in *Cuffe v. CIÉ and An Post*[20] the Supreme Court took cognisance of the intended purpose behind a contractual risk allocation clause, holding that in the light of the limited purpose of that clause there was no room for viewing the clause as having a wider import, especially when that construction would have been particularly onerous and inconsistent with the limited purpose behind the agreement itself.

A more controversial application of this exception can be found in some of the "subject to contract" cases. There are decisions which hold that parol evidence is admissible to explain that an alleged oral agreement was struck by the parties in circumstances where neither the offer nor the acceptance was "subject to contract". The Supreme Court in *Casey v. Irish Intercontinental Bank*[21] held that parol evidence, when accepted by the courts, will indicate that a later "subject to contract" memorandum will be regarded as an authorised variation of the oral agreement. It is submitted that the position thus adopted is

---

[16] (1851) 3 Ir. Jur. (O.S.) 290.
[17] [1972] I.R. 372.
[18] (1871) 5 I.R. Eq. 595.
[19] (1887) 19 L.R. (Ir.) 249.
[20] Unreported, Supreme Court, October 22, 1996; See also *Bank of Ireland v. McCabe and McCabe*, unreported, High Court, March 30, 1993 where Flood J. concluded that the evidence admitted did not alter the prima facie meaning of the document.
[21] [1979] I.R. 364.

both incompatible with earlier cases, which do not envisage such a departure from the rule, and undesirable in policy terms, for the memorandum necessary for the purposes of the Statute of Frauds is surely the best evidence available of what was agreed. In *Boyle and Boyle v. Lee and Goyns*[22] a majority of the Supreme Court were of the view that *Casey* should not be followed by any future court. O'Flaherty J. and Egan J. confined the decision in *Casey* to its own facts and thus effectively distinguished it out of existence.

### (3) To explain the subject matter of the contract

In *Chambers v. Kelly*[23] a contract was concluded for the sale of "all the oaks now growing on your lands called Greenmount near Enniscorthy, together with all other trees growing through the oak plantations and mixed with the said oak." The plaintiff vendor successfully contended that the parties had designated part of the plaintiff's land to be the oak plantation so that the felling of oak trees on other parts of the plaintiff's land constituted a breach of contract. A literal interpretation of the written document would produce a different result. Furthermore, the words "all other trees" were limited to larch trees, this being part of the oral contract.

It is said that parol evidence is only admissible if the contract itself is ambiguous. This view was categorically rejected by Chatterton V.-C. in *The Ulster Bank v. Synott*[24] but it was applied in the Circuit Court case of *Oates v. Romano*.[25] A hairdresser, employed by the plaintiff, agreed not to serve in "a like business" when he left the plaintiff's employment. The plaintiff attempted to adduce parol evidence that "like business" meant a specific type of hair-dressing establishment catering for the needs of the more affluent sector of Dublin society. The clause was not intended to prevent the defendant from working as a hairdresser in all salons. The Circuit Court judge held the rule to be that parol evidence was not admissible if the contract was on its face unam-biguous. This case must be regarded as wrongly decided. On the other hand, the court will understandably be reluctant to adduce parol evidence if this serves to render the terms of an otherwise unambiguous contract uncertain. In *Kinlen v. Ennis U.D.C.*[26] the House of Lords refused to allow a tender to be admitted in evidence when the contract itself was at variance with a tender. Lord Buckmaster pointed out that preliminary documents and discussions which are intended to be gathered up in the contract are inadmissible unless the contract is ambiguous. There are obvious dangers in admitting into evidence a tender which is itself ambiguous but in exceptional cases the tender has been admitted in the interpretation or construction of a contract that is itself unclear. In *H.A. O'Neill Ltd. v. John Sisk & Son Ltd.*[27] one price variation clause

---

[22] [1992] I.L.R.M. 65.
[23] (1873) 7 I.R.C.L. 231.
[24] (1871) 5 I.R. Eq. 595.
[25] (1950) 84 I.L.T.R. 161.
[26] [1916] 2 I.R. 299.
[27] Unreported, Supreme Court, July 30, 1984.

forming part of the conditions of tender was admitted to vary the standard form price clause in the contract document because there was a sufficient cross reference in the conditions of tender to a subsequent contract document. In the leading English case *Prenn v. Simmonds*[28] Lord Wilberforce stressed that the courts no longer interpret a contract by reference to internal linguistic considerations, isolated from the matrix of facts in which the clauses of the agreement are set. In cases where the words are plain and unambiguous and those words produce a logical result, the courts are not to introduce parol evidence of context: *Marathon Petroleum (Ireland) Ltd v. Bord Gáis Éireann.*[29] In cases where there may be inconsistency as between clauses in an agreement it is likely that during trial of an action the court "may well . . . think it proper to admit evidence of the factual matrix", to use Lord Wilberforce's words, in which the agreement was set, and which may assist the court in arriving at a construction of the clause.[30] Lord Hoffman, in *Investors Compensation Scheme Ltd v. West Bromwich Building Society*[31] has emphasised that the courts are to assimilate the way that commercial documents are to be interpreted by the judges to the common sense principles by which any serious utterance would be interpreted in everyday life. This means that, except for rules which exclude from the consideration of the courts any statements about subjective belief or intention, and the inadmissibility of preliminary negotiations or post contractual conduct,[32] there are very few *a priori* rules of interpretation which are exclusionary in nature and that issues of this kind are broadly matters of impression for the judge. The general view on reading clauses *contra proferens*, for example, seems to be that this approach only operates in relation to one-sided or exempting provisions.[33]

## (4) Mistake

If the contract document contains a mistake it is clearly possible to adduce parol testimony if the remedy sought is rectification: see *Macklin & McDonald v. Greacen & Co.*[34]

## (5) The consideration

If a contract is silent on the consideration to be provided parol evidence will be admissible to prove the price payable: see *Jeffcott v. North British Oil Co.,*[35] as well as to help the court decide whether the price has in fact been paid:

---

[28] [1971] 1 WLR 138; *Reardon Smith Line Ltd. v. Yngvar Hansen-Tangen* [1976] 1 W.L.R. 989.
[29] Unreported, Supreme Court, July 31, 1976.
[30] *LAC Minerals Ltd. v. Chevron Mineral Corp. of Ireland and Ivernia West plc,* unreported, High Court, August 6, 1993, *per* Keane J.
[31] [1998] 1 All E.R. 98.
[32] *Re Wogans Ltd.,* unreported, Supreme Court, April 10, 1991; *Scottish Power plc v. Britoil (Exploration) Ltd., The Times,* December 2, 1997.
[33] *Kramer v. Arnold,* unreported, Supreme Court, April 24, 1997.
[34] [1983] I.R. 61.
[35] (1873) I.R. 8 C.L. 17.

*Revenue Commissioners v. Moroney.*[36] If one party has waived the right to payment of part of the price, or indeed any other term, evidence of this will also be admissible according to *Greenham v. Gray.*[37]

Parol evidence can be admitted to show that the consideration stated in a memorandum, which apparently satisfies the Statute of Frauds, is accurate. So in *Black v. Grealy*[38] evidence was admissible to show that a memorandum which stated the consideration to be £40,000 was inaccurate, the court holding that parol evidence established that the price agreed was £46,000, the figure of £40,000 being the balance due after a deposit of £6,000 was paid.

## (6) Custom

If the parties to a contract recognise that a particular trade custom exists then the parties will be permitted to adduce parol testimony to bring this custom to the attention of the court. In *Wilson Strain Ltd. v. Pinkerton*[39] a bread roundsman who sold bread on credit terms was able to adduce evidence to show that it was an almost universal practice in the bakery industry in Belfast for the employer to take over outstanding debts when a roundsman left employment, rather than hold the roundsman personally liable. Clearly the unreasonableness of the view that the employee was himself liable influenced the court. If, however, the contract itself clearly provides another rule then the custom cannot be admissible: see *Malcolmson v. Morton.*[40] Should the contract be silent the position will be otherwise. In *Page v. Myer*[41] a custom peculiar to the grain trade was held admissible because the express terms of the contract did not cover the point in question. In exceptional cases it is not necessary for both parties to know of the existence of the custom or trade practice: see *King v. Hinde.*[42]

## (7) Where the written document is not the entire contract

Wedderburn, in an important article[43] argued that the parol evidence rule is little more than "a self-evident tautology". If the contract document is intended to be the entire contract parol evidence will not be admissible. If, however, the written document is not intended to be the entire contract but is to be supplemented by parol evidence then parol evidence will be admissible. The rule then, provides us with a presumption – a document that looks like a contract will be presumed to be the entire contract unless evidence to the contrary is forthcoming. The validity of this observation is graphically illustrated by the

---

[36] [1972] I.R. 372.

[37] (1855) I.C.L.R. 50. In *Boyle and Boyle v. Lee and Goyns* [1992] I.L.R.M. 65, Finlay C.J. left open the question of whether *Casey v. Irish Intercontinental Bank* [1979] I.R. 364 can still be an authority on waiver of rights and admissibility of evidence.

[38] Unreported, High Court, November 10, 1977.

[39] (1897) 3 I.L.T.R. 86. Contrast *Joynson v. Hunt & Son* (1905) 21 T.L.R. 692.

[40] (1847) 11 Ir. L.R. 230.

[41] (1861) 6 Ir. Jur. Rep. (N.S.) 27.

[42] (1883) 12 L.R. (Ir.) 113.

[43] (1959) 17 C.L.J. 58.

judgment of Wilson J. in *Howden v. Ulster Bank*.[44] The plaintiffs ordered a ship to be built by a Larne shipyard which went bankrupt shortly before the vessel was completed. The plaintiffs sued to recover damages for wrongful detention of the vessel by the trustee in bankruptcy who claimed that the ship formed part of the assets of the bankrupt. The issue turned on whether property in the vessel remained with the defendants or whether it passed to the plaintiffs on payment of the price by instalments. A memorandum of agreement indicated that title remained in the defendants but Wilson J. found for the plaintiffs after hearing oral testimony: "parol evidence of a verbal transaction is not excluded by the fact that a writing was made concerning or relating to it unless such writing was in fact the transaction itself and not merely a note or memorandum of it or a portion of the transaction." In *Clayton Love v. B + I Transport*,[45] Davitt P. held that parol evidence of the terms of a telephone conversation between the parties could be added to a written contract so as to form one contract, partly written and partly oral. Although the Supreme Court reversed Davitt P.'s judgment on another issue this view of the limits of the parol evidence rule was undisturbed.

If there is a contradiction between a written contract and an oral promise the courts will not enforce the oral promise, choosing instead the terms of the written document if they have been expressly drafted by one of the parties and agreed to. If, however, the written term is on a printed, standard form document the English case of *Evans v. Merzario*[46] suggests that the oral promise is to be given preference. It is hoped that this view will prevail in Ireland.

It should be noted that although the exceptions to the rule are so numerous and well established that it is doubtful whether any real injustice is caused by the rule, if it is applied properly, cases like *Oates v. Romano* (discussed above) show that judges who do not properly understand the role of the rule *as a presumption* may fall into error. The English Law Commission concluded that on balance legislative amendments or outright repeal of the parol evidence rule would be likely to cause greater confusion than enlightenment and that clarifying the law and re-education of the legal profession "is a more satisfactory means of achieving justice than any attempt to legislate."[47]

# Collateral Contracts

The partly written, partly oral contract seems to take effect as one contract. Nevertheless, certain judges take the view that the strict terms of the parol evidence rule can be evaded by holding that *two* contracts may come into existence. Indeed, one leading Irish judge, Murphy J. in *Cotter v. Minister for*

---

[44] [1924] I.R. 117.
[45] (1970) 104 I.L.T.R. 157.
[46] [1976] 1 W.L.R. 1078.
[47] Law Com. No. 154, para. 3.7.

*Agriculture*[48] observed that where a collateral agreement is established "it is hardly an exception at all" to the parol evidence rule. The facts of *Webster v. Higgin*[49] are instructive. The plaintiff inspected a vehicle owned by the defendants and was told by one of their employees, "if you buy the Hillman we will guarantee that it's in good condition and that you will have no trouble with it." An exclusion clause attempted to nullify this promise by excluding all warranties. Lord Greene M.R. held that this promise was a *collateral* warranty which was not covered by the exclusion clause in the contract document. This approach was recently approved by O'Hanlon J. in *Fitzpatrick v. Harty & Ballsbridge International Bloodstock Sales Ltd.*[50] The case concerned an action for the price of a horse purchased by the first defendant at a sale. The condition of sale limited the buyer's right to claim damage or rescind the contract should the horse turn out to be unsound. The defendant refused to pay the price when a veterinary surgeon found the horse to be unsound. O'Hanlon J. held that the conditions of sale applied "unless there were some collateral contract made outside the terms of the conditions of sale." While the issue of whether an employee has the status to give a warranty may arise and may turn upon each individual case there is a general inclination towards holding that employees at the time of sale do have the authority to give express warranties: see *Rooney v. Fielden*[51] when Palles C.B. held an employee had the authority to warrant the condition of a cow to be sold.

Consideration must exist before this second or collateral contract can be enforced. In *Webster v. Higgin* consideration is provided by entering the main contract of purchase. Similarly, a landlord who promises to repair drains if the promisee signs a lease which is silent on this obligation to repair will be liable on this collateral contract. By signing the lease the promisee provides consideration for his prospective landlord's promise.[52]

In most cases it makes no difference if the promise is enforced either as a collateral warranty, *i.e.* it forms part of one contract, or if it takes effect as a separate or collateral contract. There are nevertheless circumstances in which it is prudent to plead a separate contract, particularly if the main contract contains an exclusion clause or jurisdiction clause. In *Michelstown Co-operative Society Ltd. v. Société des Produits Nestlé SA*[53] the Supreme Court, reversing Egan J., found that the first defendant company could, acting with two related companies, enter into a collateral contract with the plaintiff company. The case involved a written licensing agreement whereby the plaintiff would manufacture yoghurt under the *Chambourcy* trademark owned by the first defendant. This written agreement, governed by Swiss law, was not actionable in the Irish courts. However, evidence was adduced to show that there was an arguable case that

---

[48] Unreported, High Court, November 15, 1991.
[49] [1948] 2 All E.R. 127.
[50] Unreported, High Court, February 25, 1983.
[51] (1899) 33 I.L.T.R. 100.
[52] *De Lasalle v. Guildford* [1901] 2 K.B. 215; *Record v. Bell* [1991] 4 All E.R. 471.
[53] [1989] I.L.R.M. 582.

the plaintiff had entered into an oral collateral contract under the terms of which the plaintiff would be supplied with yoghurt from a U.K. company until such time as the plaintiffs completed their own production unit, and that the plaintiff would be given exclusive distributorship rights in the yoghurt so supplied. This separate collateral contract could be the subject of an action before the Irish courts, notwithstanding the fact that the main licensing contract was governed by Swiss law.

The collateral contract device may prove useful in overcoming what would otherwise prove insurmountable hurdles. Take a case where the plaintiff is unable to show that consideration has moved from him, the promisee. There is clear English authority to support the proposition that if the manufacturer of goods gives a warranty to X that the goods manufactured are suitable for a particular purpose and X induces Y to purchase and use those goods, then X may sue the manufacturer if the use occasions loss to X: see *Shanklin Pier Ltd. v. Detel Products.*[54] In *McCullough Sales Ltd. v. Chetham Timber Co. Ltd.*[55] McCullough's sold building materials to Chetham, who, in turn complained that these materials were unfit for their purpose. Doyle J., finding for Chetham, stated *obiter* that it was possible that McCullough's may have a cause of action against the manufacturers of the building materials if the manufacturer made representations to McCullough's which caused McCullough's in turn to represent or warrant the goods to Chetham. Doyle J., citing *Shanklin Pier*, stated that this case "followed a venerable line of authority" and the learned judge clearly approved of this principle.

Should a contract for the sale of land be unenforceable because the memorandum is defective, it may be possible to remedy the situation by holding that there are in fact two contracts. In *Godley v. Power*[56] the Supreme Court held that a contract for sale of a public house plus stock in trade was in fact two contracts. The memorandum setting out the terms of the sale of the premises did not recite the terms of the contract for sale of stock in trade. By holding that the stock was the subject of a collateral contract which, by definition, did not have to be included in the memorandum, the sale of the pub was enforceable. A similar problem may arise if a contract is void for illegality; English case law suggests that, notwithstanding this, a separate collateral contract will be valid.[57]

The most important use to which the collateral contract – described by Roskill L.J. as "a lawyer's device" – can be put is to avoid the common law rule that a mere representation cannot lead to an award of damages. In order to avoid this rule it is increasingly common to plead that the statement made is independent or collateral to the main contract. While this practice may not now be as important, given the limited statutory reform effected in the Republic by the Sale of Goods and Supply of Services Act 1980, the collateral contract remains a useful part of a contract lawyers armoury.

---

[54] [1951] 2 K.B. 854.
[55] Unreported, High Court, February 1, 1983.
[56] (1961) 95 I.L.T.R. 135; contrast *Aga Khan v. Firestone and Firestone* [1992] I.L.R.M. 31.
[57] *Strongman (1945) Ltd. v. Sincock* [1955] 2 Q.B. 525.

# 6 Implied Terms

## Introduction

Contractual obligations may arise as a result of circumstances other than express agreement between the parties. In general, it is accepted that terms may be implied through the operation of certain common law doctrines, custom and practice, the operation of statute law rather than judicial intervention, and the 1937 Constitution.

## Implied Terms at Common Law

We have already seen that not everything stated, before or at the time of agreement, will necessarily form part of the contract. In this Chapter we will consider the converse proposition: can the courts hold the bargain to include terms or obligations not expressly stated? The question is a difficult one to answer. While it is clear that additional terms may be read into the contract the circumstances in which the implication may be made are not the subject of universal agreement amongst the judiciary. Traditionally, the courts do not relish implying terms into a bargain because this results in a modification of the contract as struck by the parties. The courts shelter behind the maxim that "it is for the parties to strike a bargain; the judiciary serve merely to enforce it." On the other hand, some judges take the view that it is in the interests of justice for the courts to take a more active role. Lord Denning M.R. supported this view of the judifical function and he argued that the courts may imply a term into a bargain simply because it is reasonable so to do. The House of Lords have rejected this view as "undesirable and way beyond sound authority": *per* Lord Wilberforce in *Liverpool City Council v. Irwin.*[1]

Similar statements can be found in the Irish Reports. In *Tradax (Ireland) Ltd. v. Irish Grain Board Ltd.*,[2] O'Higgins C.J. said that the power to imply terms "must, however, be exercised with care. The courts have no role in acting as contract makers, or as counsellors, to advise or direct which agreement ought to have been made by two people, whether businessmen or not, who chose to enter into contractual relations with each other." In the same case McCarthy J. said "[i]t is not the function of a court to write a contract for parties who have met upon commercially equal terms; if such parties want to enter into unreasonable, unfair or even disastrous contracts, that is their business, not the business of the Courts."

---

[1] [1977] A.C. 239. On leading English cases such as *Scally v. Southern Health and Social Services Board* [1991] 3 W.L.R. 778 see Phang [1998] J.B.L. 1.
[2] [1984] I.R. 1.

Nevertheless, if the courts start from the premise that the parties are reasonable persons who wish to act reasonably and facilitate the commercial interests of the other party, a considerable amount can be inserted into the agreement by way of implied terms. What is important, however, is the test used by the judge in the case at bar.

In recent years the Supreme Court has had occasion to discuss the juridical basis upon which implied terms are inserted into a contract by the judiciary. In *Sweeney v. Duggan*[3] Murphy J. observed:

> "There are at least two situations where the courts will, independently of statutory requirement, imply a term which has not been expressly agreed by the parties to a contract. The first of these situations was identified in the well-known *Moorcock* case (1889) 14 PD 64 where a term not expressly agreed upon by the parties was inferred on the basis of the presumed intention of the parties. The basis for such a presumption was explained by MacKinnon LJ in *Shirlaw v. Southern Foundries (1926) Ltd.* [1939] 2 KB 206 at p. 227 in an expression, equally memorable, in the following terms:
>
>> '*Prima facie* that which in any contract is left to be implied and need not be expressed is something so obvious that it goes without saying; so that, if while the parties were making their bargain, an officious bystander were to suggest some express provision for it in their agreement, they would testily suppress him with a common, "Oh, of course".'
>
> In addition there are a variety of cases in which a contractual term has been implied on the basis, not of the intention of the parties to the contract but deriving from the nature of the contract itself. Indeed in analysing the different types of case in which a term will be implied Lord Wilberforce in *Liverpool City Council v. Irwin* [1977] AC 239 preferred to describe the different categories which he identified as no more than shades on a continuous spectrum."

### *(1) The officious bystander test – obligations tacitly assumed*

It is clear that if a term is so obvious that it goes without saying that the bargain is subject to this unstated term then it will be included in the contract. This proposition is most clearly stated in the judgment of MacKinnon L.J. in *Shirlaw v. Southern Foundries (1926) Ltd.*[4] quoted immediately above. This test is extremely narrow. The court must find that *both* parties had the term contended for in mind when they contracted. The facts of *Kavanagh v. Gilbert*[5] may make this test clearer. The plaintiff sued an auctioneer who had agreed to

---

[3] [1997] 2 I.L.R.M. 211 at 218.
[4] [1939] 2 K.B. 206 at 227.
[5] (1875) I.R. 9 C.L. 136.

sell the plaintiff's farm by auction. A bid was accepted by the auctioneer but no binding contract was concluded because the auctioneer failed to draft a memorandum of agreement. While the contract was silent on this point an officious bystander who interjected: "surely the auctioneer will have to fill out a memorandum after the sale" would incur the wrath of both parties in the manner predicted by McKinnon L.J. It was held that there was an implied obligation placed on the auctioneer that he would use care and skill in concluding a binding contract.

In the Northern Ireland case of *Extrudakerb (Maltby Engineering) Ltd. v. Whitemountain Quarries Ltd.*[6] the failure by the parties to a building sub-contract to make express reference to an arbitration clause when agreeing to be bound by standard industrial conditions was held not to be fatal to the contractor's contention that the arbitration clause was part of the contract. Carswell L.J. observed that if the officious bystander had asked the parties whether they considered the arbitration clause would apply in the event of the dispute, the answer would have been clear that the question would have been answered in the affirmative: both were experienced and knowledgeable persons who were aware of the standard terms used in their industry. On the other hand, if the response of one of the parties at least would have been one of bemuse-ment because the term in question would have been unknown to that person the contention will fail. If the court concludes that one of the parties would have rejected the term contended for then no implication will be made. So, the Supreme Court in *Carna Foods Ltd. v. Eagle Star Insurance Co.*[7] declined to impose on an insurer an obligation to disclose reasons for a refusal to renew a policy because if this had arisen as an issue at formation the insurer would have declined to contract at all. In *Sweeney v. Duggan*[8] an employer was held not to be under a similar implied duty to inform employees about the employer's insurance cover for his workers, for the reason that the contract worked effectively and that if such a term was under discussion prior to agreement it would have either been rejected or only agreed upon after much negotiation. If the term contended for is inconsistent with a statutory provision and cannot therefore be lawfully conceded then the term will not be implied: *Sullivan v. Southern Health Board.*[9]

The English case of *The Moorcock*[10] is also said to be a case supporting the view that only if the court draws the conclusion that each party intended such and such a term to form part of their bargain can a term be implied. Bowen L.J. in giving judgment in that case, however, stated that "[t]he law is raising an implication from the presumed intention of the parties with the object of giving the transaction such efficacy as both parties must have intended that at all events it should have." This test is extremely ambiguous. It is a wider test than

---

6  *The Times*, July 10, 1996.
7  [1997] 2 I.L.R.M. 499.
8  [1997] 2 I.L.R.M. 211.
9  Unreported, Supreme Court, July 30, 1997.
10  (1889) 14 P.D. 64.

the officious bystander test for it is doubtful whether the facts of *The Moorcock* would fall within MacKinnon L.J.'s test. At its widest *The Moorcock* has been used to support the view that a reasonable term may be implied in the contract. Many judges have said that Bowen L.J. did not mean to go that far. Nevertheless *The Moorcock* was applied by a majority of the Irish Court of Appeal in the 1904 case of *Butler v. McAlpine*.[11] The facts of this case, which superficially at least resemble those of *The Moorcock* itself, involved a contract under which a wharfowner was to allow a shipowner to unload a cargo at his wharf. The vessel was damaged when, at low tide, it came to rest on a sack of concrete that had previously fallen onto the riverbed. The Court of Appeal by a majority held there was an implied duty upon the wharfowner to take reasonable care that the berth was reasonably safe for the barge to lie in. While the members of the Court of Appeal refused to be drawn upon the question of how far Bowen L.J.'s test is to apply, there have been several later cases, including decisions of the Supreme Court in which Bowen L.J.'s speech has been approved.

In agency contracts, the law relating to implied terms has often supplemented the express contractual terms: *The Moorcock* was considered in this context by the Supreme Court in *Ward v. Spivack Ltd.*[12] which held that sales agents could not obtain the benefit of commission after the termination of a contract on the basis of an implied term. Maguire C.J. held that it is not for the courts to use the implied term as a means of making a new contract for the parties.

In commercial contracts the courts often present the test in *The Moorcock* in a different way: is it necessary to imply this term into the contract so as to give the contract the business efficacy both parties must have intended it to have? This business efficacy test has been considered in several Irish cases. In *O'Toole v. Palmer*,[13] Palmer, an auctioneer, agreed with O'Toole that if O'Toole was able to find a purchaser willing to buy Vesey's land, then Palmer would agree to share the 5 per cent commission fee so long as the fee was paid by the purchaser. O'Toole introduced a client of his to Palmer and the sale was completed. The purchaser, however, did not agree to pay the commission and Palmer closed the sale without the commission having been paid. O'Toole sued Palmer claiming that by closing the sale without obtaining the agreement of the purchaser to pay a commission Palmer had broken an implied term that he would not prevent the plaintiff from earning his remuneration. Gavan Duffy J. dismissed the action: "I do not think there is any necessity to imply a term for the purpose of giving the contract a business efficacy. Here the terms are clearly expressed in writing and the plaintiff has undertaken an ordinary business risk." Similarly in *Tradax (Ireland) Ltd. v. Irish Grain Board Ltd.*[14] a majority of the Supreme Court held that an obligation could not be imposed by way of an officious bystander test upon the defendants to open a letter of

---

11  [1904] 2 I.R. 445.
12  [1957] I.R. 40.
13  (1945) Ir.Jur.Rep. 59.
14  [1984] I.R. 1.

credit. Despite the considerable volume of evidence which supported the view that in the industry in question this practice was normally to be expected, O'Higgins C.J., who gave the leading judgment, found that the officious bystander test was not satisfied because, on the facts, there was no evidence that the parties intended that this be done.

In *Murphy Buckley & Keogh v. Pye (Ireland)*[15] the defendants engaged the plaintiffs to sell a factory in Dundrum on a sole agency basis. The defendants later sold the premises to a purchaser not introduced by the plaintiffs. The plaintiffs were unable to claim that the contract impliedly prevented the defendants from finding a purchaser; not only was such a term inconsistent with the presumed intent of the parties, the contract expressly provided that the auctioneer's fee was only payable on completion of a transaction involving a purchaser introduced by the plaintiffs. The auctioneers were only entitled to recover advertising expenses. In his carefully structured judgment Henchy J. stressed that these sole agency cases depend very much upon their own facts, an observation that is graphically illustrated in *G.F. Galvin (Estates) Ltd. v. Hedigan.*[16] An estate agent claimed he was entitled to a fee for land sold by the defendant. The defendant had engaged the agent to lobby councillors to faci-litate the rezoning of farmland to an industrial user and had promised to pay a fee upon the successful conclusion of this process. Costello J. held that the case was distinguishable from *Murphy Buckley & Keogh v. Pye (Ireland)* because here the agent undertook to find a seller and carry on other activities and, in these circumstances, some obligation requiring the landowner to compensate the agent, should the landowner sell the land himself, was to be implied. On the facts however, the landowner was not liable in contract because the "business efficacy" and "officious bystander" tests only required this implied term to be imposed for a limited time and the sale was effected after the time elapsed.

The business efficacy test will not be utilised to undo an agreement which is enforceable as it stands. In *Aga Khan v. Firestone and Firestone*[17] it was submitted that the court should imply into a contract for the sale of lands, the contract being enforceable under the Statute of Frauds, a term that it was only to be carried into force when a formal contract had been executed. Morris J. observed that the essence of *The Moorcock* was a desire to prevent the failure of the contract. The term sought to be introduced would have the contrary effect and Morris J. refused to imply it.

## (2) Terms implied by law

Even though the courts have not carved out for themselves a sweeping power to insert terms into a bargain simply because the judge feels it reasonable so to do, there are well established instances of legal duties being imposed upon contracting parties when it is clear that the parties themselves have not antici-

---

[15] [1971] I.R. 57.
[16] [1985] I.L.R.M. 295.
[17] [1992] I.L.R.M. 31.

pated the dispute. In other words, a term will be implied at law because it is felt necessary to do so. In the English case of *Tournier v. National Provincial & Union Bank of England*,[18] Atkin L.J. stated that in appropriate cases the court may, as a matter of law, impose implied obligations upon a party to a contract. This statement was applied by the Northern Ireland Court of Appeal in *Potter v. Carlisle & Cliftonville Golf Club Ltd.*[19] A golfer who was struck in the eye by a ball hit by another golfer was held unable to recover damages against the defendant. By paying his green fee and walking onto the first tee the plaintiff was held to have impliedly contracted to take the course as he found it, provided it was free from unusual dangers or traps, and also to accept the risks of the game as between himself and the defendant club.

These duties often arise as incidents of well recognised legal relationships. In *Sweeney v. Duggan*[20] Murphy J. explained that whether an implied term is inserted into a contract as a matter of law, or presumed intention, there are common features:

> "Whether a term is implied pursuant to the presumed intention of the parties or as a legal incident of a definable category of contract it must be not merely reasonable but also necessary. Clearly it cannot be implied if it is inconsistent with the express wording of the contract and further-more it may be difficult to infer a term where it cannot be formulated with reasonable precision."

In essence, cases where presumed intention is not the basis for the implication of a term turn upon the existence of a defined relationship and a test of necessity. Should the evidence indicate that a term was missing because of the complexity of the issue then there can be no room for a term under either category: see *Ali v. Christien Salvesen Food Services Ltd.*[21] A landlord, for example, owes an implied duty to allow the tenant quiet possession of the demised premises. So, if a landlord fails to keep parts of a building well maintained, causing a nuisance to spread to property leased to tenants, the tenants have a cause of action even in the absence of an express covenant requiring the landlord to repair and maintain the exterior of the building: see *Byrne v. Martina Investments Ltd.*[22] A particular difficulty arises where a contract for the sale of a house or for the lease of unfurnished premises is silent upon the condition of the property. The English common law rule provided that if a house was sold or let unfurnished and it turned out to be defective the purchaser could not recover on an implied warranty. It has been the view of

---

[18] [1924] 1 K.B. 461.
[19] [1939] N.I. 114.
[20] [1997] 2 I.L.R.M.; *Glenavon Football and Athletic Club Ltd. v. Lowry, Irish Times Law Report*, September 7, 1992.
[21] *The Times*, October 29, 1996.
[22] [1984] 3 J.I.S.L.L. 116.

many judges and commentators that Davitt P. in *Brown v. Norton*[23] held this rule applicable in Ireland too. A close reading of the case discloses that Davitt P. held that on the sale of a house there is no *rule of law* that the premises will be fit for the purpose of occupation but there may still be room for an implied term. The Supreme Court held in *Siney v. Dublin Corporation*[24] that when the Corporation let a new unfinished flat to the plaintiff they were liable in contract when it transpired that the flat was badly ventilated, causing damp which damaged the plaintiff's belongings. The Supreme Court pointed out that the case depended upon the specific fact that the Dublin Corporation were under a statutory obligation under the Housing Act 1966 as a housing authority, (which would not operate in private sector letting contracts). In *Coleman & Coleman v. Dundalk U.D.C.*[25] the Supreme Court extended *Siney* by holding that a statutory housing authority cannot evade the obligation to ensure that the house was fit for human habitation by executing a lease rather than a tenancy agreement. *Siney* has been applied by a unanimous Supreme Court in *Burke and Others v. Corporation of Dublin.*[26] The defendant was sued in its capacity as a Housing Authority for the City of Dublin under which it provided housing to the various plaintiffs. The heating system provided solid fuel central heating and was found to be inefficient and unhealthy, causing physical damage to the personal belongings of one plaintiff and inducing bronchitis in another. There is a further significant extension of *Siney* in this case. One of the plaintiffs, while initially a tenant, had purchased the house from the Housing Authority and was therefore the owner of the fee simple at the time when proceedings commenced. However, the Supreme Court affirmed the view of Blayney J. at first instance where the learned judge had held that, because the sale and transfer of ownership had taken place under the Housing Act 1966, the implied duty could still arise. The Supreme Court, however, declined to decide on the position of a purchaser who, unlike the plaintiff in question, was not a tenant but nevertheless purchased property from a statutory Housing Authority. While the courts are constrained by authority to uphold the application of the *caveat emptor* principle in landlord and tenant contracts, there are other decisions which indicate that the immunity of the landlord will be narrowly interpreted. In England the decision in *Wettern Electric v. Welsh Development Agency*[27] illustrates that the old common law immunity from liability will not be extended into commercial property lettings. These developments may not only be considered to display the reluctance of the courts to allow the landlord to exploit the old common law immunity, these cases may foreshow the overruling of the older case law.

---

[23] [1954] I.R. 34.
[24] [1980] I.R. 400.
[25] Unreported, Supreme Court, July 17, 1985.
[26] [1991] I.R. 341.
[27] [1983] Q.B. 796.

If the vendor of property is also in the process of building the house there will be an implied term that the house will be built in an efficient manner and that it will be inhabitable: see *Morris v. Redmond and Wright*.[28] In the Northern Ireland case of *McGeary v. Campbell*[29] this implied term was extended to apply to work completed before and after the contract of purchase is concluded: see also *Corrigan v. Crofton & Crofton*[30] where the defendant builder conceded that, following *Brown v. Norton*, they were bound by an implied term that the work be carried out in a good and workman-like manner and with sound and suitable materials. In general, however, the vendor of a house is not to be taken to impliedly warrant the fitness of a house. In *Curling v. Walsh*,[31] Hamilton P. rejected the view that upon the sale of a house the vendor is taken to impliedly warrant that the premises are in a good and habitable state of repair and free from any structural defect.

Lord Wilberforce has pointed out that terms implied without reference to the intention of the parties are implied in order to make the existing contractual relationship work efficiently. The test then is necessity, not reasonableness. A contract to let premises in a multi-storey apartment building will not be effective unless the tenant can gain access to the apartment. The letting contract will include an obligation at law obliging the lessor to do everything reasonable to maintain and repair the stairways, lifts and escalators not included in the lease: see *Liverpool City Council v. Irwin*.[32]

Contracts of employment also contain terms that are imposed by operation of law. The duty of an employer to provide a safe system of work arises almost without question in many personal injury actions: *McCann v. Brinks Allied Ltd*.[33] There is considerable litigation on establishing the precise scope of contractual rights on other matters, particularly termination of a contract. In the case of *Royal Trust Company of Canada (Ireland) Ltd. and Another v. Kelly and Others*,[34] Barron J. stated that the basic rule in relation to contracts of employment is that "it is an implied term of every contract of employment other than for a fixed period that it can be terminated upon reasonable notice." In *Carvill v. Irish Industrial Bank*[35] the plaintiff served as managing director of the defendant company. By resolution of the board the plaintiff was discharged from his post and from the board of the company. He successfully contended that he had been discharged from a contract of employment in such a way as to breach the employer's obligation to give a reasonable period of notice. Given the position of the plaintiff, his length of service and other factors, a reasonable period of notice was calculated at one year. Similar obligations are imposed by

---

[28] (1935) 70 I.L.T.R. 8.
[29] [1975] N.I. 7.
[30] [1985] I.L.R.M. 189.
[31] Unreported, High Court, October 23, 1987.
[32] [1977] A.C. 239.
[33] [1997] 1 I.L.R.M. 461.
[34] Unreported, High Court, February 27, 1989.
[35] [1968] I.R. 325.

law on the employee. He has an obligation to faithfully serve his employer so if he "moonlights" by working for a rival concern he will break this implied term. In the Northern Ireland case of *A.F. Associates v. Ralston*[36] the defendants, prior to terminating their contracts of employment with the plaintiff company, started a business in direct competition with the plaintiff by canvassing clients of the plaintiff company. It was held that the defendants were in breach of an implied obligation not to use their employer's time in furthering their own interests. In the Tasmanian case of *Orr v. University of Tasmania*[37] a university professor who seduced a student was held to be in breach of the implied obligation to faithfully serve his employer and could be summarily dismissed. As we will see in a moment, there are also constitutional and statutory considerations which apply in employment contracts.

Perhaps the most interesting line of authority in the area of implied terms in contracts of employment is that which begins with the case of *Woods v. WM Car Services (Peterborough) Ltd.*[38] This case is authority for the proposition that employers will not, without reasonable cause, act in a manner calculated to destroy the relationship of confidence and trust between employer and employee. Such a broad duty to act in good faith has been utilised by the English Court of Appeal[39] and in the case of *Imperial Group Pension Trust Ltd. v. Imperial Tobacco Ltd.*[40] Browne-Wilkinson V.-C. held that this implied term could inhibit the right of a company to exercise control over a company pension fund by declining to agree to allow an increase in pensions payable out of the trust. So, if the company refused to allow such an increase because it wished to pressure employees into abandoning rights in the pension fund, such a collateral purpose would not be in accordance with a duty to act in good faith.

Contracts of agency are also terminable upon giving reasonable notice, according to *Ward v. Spivack Ltd.*[41] Sometimes, however, matters such as the method of termination and the effect of termination on related rights, such as future commission payments, are a fruitful source of litigation. For example, if the contract has been executed and partially performed, and the contract is silent on the method of termination then the courts will have to imply terms which will safeguard the legitimate interests of both parties. The leading authority here is the judgment of Finlay P. in *Irish Welding v. Philips Electrical (Ireland) Ltd.*[42] The defendants appointed the plaintiffs to be sole agents for the sale of electrodes manufactured by the defendants. The defendants supplied electrodes to another wholesaler whereupon the plaitiffs sought an injunction to restrain the defendants. The defendants denied that this agreement prevented them from supplying

---

[36] [1973] N.I. 229; *Cranleigh Precision Engineering v. Bryant* [1965] 1 W.L.R. 1293.
[37] [1956] Tas. S.R. 155.
[38] [1981] I.R.L.R. 347.
[39] *Lewis v. Motorworld Garages Ltd.* [1985] I.R.L.R. 465.
[40] [1991] 2 All E.R. 597; *Spring v. Guardian Assurance* [1994] 3 All E.R. 129.
[41] [1957] I.R. 40.
[42] Unreported, High Court, October 8, 1976; see also *McGahan v. Bioengineering Development*, unreported, High Court, February 17, 1995.

electrodes to third parties and they purported to immediately terminate the agreement. Finlay P. considered the question of whether and how the contract could be terminated. The plaintiffs argued it was not terminable at all. Finlay P. after referring to the complex chain of distributors built up by the plaintiffs said it was "quite unreal to suggest that it could possibly have been within the contemplation of either party that the other should be entitled to terminate the agreement instantly and without notice." Finlay P. held that the contract should be viewed as terminable after a reasonable period of time, in this case nine months: see also *Lennon v. Talbot Ireland Ltd.*[43]

Before the contract will be held to be terminable by giving reasonable notice the court will have to consider whether such a power is compatible with the intention of the parties. This is to be assessed by reference to the background against which the contract was formed and the intention of the parties, ascertained by reference to objective manifestations of intent. After all, it is possible for persons to contract and undertake to do things that are extremely burdensome, or indeed impossible, if this intention can be detected by the courts. In *Watford Borough Council v. Watford RDC*[44] the parties, in 1963, reached an agreement whereby each party would discharge statutory duties to provide burial grounds. The 1963 agreement, which resulted in cost sharing, proved to be quite onerous and the defendant, in 1984, purported to terminate the agreement, claiming that it was subject to an implied term that it could be ended by either party upon giving reasonable notice. This was rejected. There was no reason why a contract, entered into in order to meet a statutory obligation, could not run in perpetuity. There was no evidence to support the defendant's argument that the parties intended the agreement to be unilaterally terminable. A similar conclusion was reached, by a slightly different route, in *Harrods Ltd. v. Harrods Buenos Aires Ltd. and Another.*[45] The plaintiffs, by agreement between 1911 and 1914, established the first defendants with the object of allowing them to trade in South America. This intention was clear from the documents and surrounding circumstances and, further, was subject to an implied contract between the plaintiff and the first defendant which permitted the defendant to carry on business under the name "Harrods" anywhere in South America. That contact was irrevocable.

The fact that the parties have entered into an agreement under which they are subject to continuing and recurring obligations can be an appropriate basis upon which implied duties may be imposed. In *Royal Trust Company of Canada (Ireland) Ltd. and Another v. Kelly and Others*[46] the plaintiff had dismissed the staff of its Irish operation. As a financial institution the plaintiff had provided mortgage finance to these employees on preferential rates. The issue arose whether the termination of the contract of employment could take effect without

---

[43] Unreported, High Court, December 20, 1985; *O & E Telephones v. Alcatel Business Systems*, unreported, High Court, May 17, 1995.

[44] *The Times*, December 18, 1987.

[45] *The Times*, June 1, 1998.

[46] Unreported, High Court, February 27, 1989.

prejudice to the rights of the employees to preferential mortgage finance until the redemption of the loan. The defendants submitted that while the mortgage contract contained a term obliging the employee to repay the loan on cessation of employment, the mortgage should be subject to an implied term that cessation of employment should not be the result of the voluntary act of the plaintiff bank in closing its operations in Ireland. More specifically, it was submitted on behalf of the defendants that the loan contract contained an implied term whereby the plaintiff would not do anything to prevent the loan from being fully redeemed and closure of the Irish operation breached such a duty. Barron J. indicated that the cases

> "establish that a party to a contract cannot voluntarily create conditions which will prevent the performance of the contract. So where A contracts with B to catalogue his library, he cannot sell his books before B commences work. Where A agrees to assign a leasehold interest to B and to obtain the necessary consent of the lessor, he cannot refuse to seek such consent. The rule is analogous to the rule in property law that a grantor cannot derogate from his own grant."

While Barron J. felt unable to accept that any such implied term could be upheld, mainly because the contract of employment itself was terminable upon giving reasonable notice, there is a substantial body of case law which upholds the existence of this principle in contracts which are not real property transactions. In an English case a soccer club agreed to pay a transfer fee of £200,000 for a player, with an additional sum being payable if he scored 20 goals. The player was transferred to another club before he had a reasonable time to score the goals. This was held to breach an implied term: see *Bournemouth A.F.C. v. Manchester United.*[47]

As we have already seen, Browne-Wilkinson V.-C. in *Imperial Group Pension Trust Ltd. v. Imperial Tobacco Ltd.*[48] stressed that employment contracts contain an "implied obligation of good faith". While a general duty to perform a contract in good faith is traditionally alien to English and Irish law, such general duties are a feature of U.S. law and in many civil law jurisdictions some movement on this proposition can be anticipated at the level of general principle. Even some common law judges who are sympathetic to the good faith principle stress that not every contract is to be viewed in the same light.[49] There is some judicial support in Irish law for the view that where the parties to a contract go about performing and implementing the agreement there are implied obligations to do so in good faith. In *Rooney v. Byrne*[50] an implied obligation was

---

[47] *The Times*, May 22, 1980; *Fraser v. Thames Television* [1983] 2 W.L.R. 917.
[48] [1991] 2 All E.R. 597.
[49] See the Australian cases of *Service Station Associates Ltd. v. Berg Bennett Associates Property* (1993) 117 A.L.R. 393; *Renard Constructions v. Minister for Public Works* (1992) 33 Con. L.R. 72. See generally, Beatson and Friedmann, *Good Faith and Fault in Contract Law* (1995).
[50] [1933] I.R. 609.

imposed upon a buyer of property to secure finance. In *Fluid Power Technology Company v. Sperry (Ireland) Ltd.,*[51] Costello J. held that the express terms of a contract which gave the defendants a power to terminate a contract were subject to an implied obligation to exercise the power of termination in a bona fide manner, that is, for what the defendants honestly felt to be good cause. Through this approach the courts are able to limit the power of the contract draftsman to insert into a contract a discretionary or draconian provision. Only if the contract is unambiguous in its express terms will such implied obligations be excluded. However, if a contract contains express terms concerning the method of termination, the courts will hold that additional methods of termination cannot be implied. Although, the decision which supports this proposition is the employment contract case of *Grehan v. North Eastern Health Board,*[52] Costello J. clearly dealt with the implied term argument from first principles by holding that the business efficacy test was not satisfied by the implied term contended for.

While employment contracts and agency contracts[53] are instances where the relationship itself creates implied duties, there are other instances where implied obligations will arise, even if the contract is a one-off or isolated transaction. The provider of a service, whether it be the provision of false teeth, as in *Samuels v. Davis*[54] or information to subscribers to a wire service, as in *Allen v. Bushnell T.V. Co. and Broadcast News Ltd.*[55] must exercise reasonable care and skill in discharging the contract. In the leading case of *Norta Wallpapers (Ireland) Ltd. v. John Sisk & Son (Dublin) Ltd.*[56] the Supreme Court had to consider the liability of a contractor to the employer when defective materials are used by a sub-contractor. Henchy J. had this to say about the state of the law:

> "I conceive the law of the land to be that, unless the particular circumstances give reason for its exclusion, there is implied into the contract a term to the effect that the contractor will be liable to the employer for any loss or damage suffered by him as a result of the goods, materials or installations not being fit for the purpose for which they were supplied."[57]

## Terms Implied Under Statute

Several common law obligations have been codified into statutes which form part of a contractual relationship. The most important example of this is presented by the implied obligations arising under the Sale of Goods Act 1893

---

[51] Unreported, High Court, February 22, 1985.
[52] [1989] I.R. 422.
[53] *Wong Me Wan v. Kwan Kin Travel Services Ltd.* [1995] 4 All E.R. 745.
[54] [1943] K.B. 526.
[55] (1968) 1 D.L.R.(3d) 534.
[56] [1978] I.R. 114.
[57] *Ibid.* at 123.

and the Republic's Sale of Goods and Supply of Services Act 1980. Common law obligations requiring the seller of goods to supply goods which are of merchantable quality and which are fit for the purpose for which they are intended are part of the 1893 Act, s.14. These obligations could formerly be excluded if the parties so agreed but this is no longer possible in consumer sales after the 1980 Act. The important subject of statutory implied terms under the Sale of Goods Act 1893–1980 is considered in Chapters 8 and 9.

The employment contract provides another rich source of statutory implied terms. Wages are often pegged in a variety of industries by statutory bodies rather than by agreement between the parties, *e.g.* wages of agricultural labourers. The obligation on an employer to provide holiday pay stems from statute and not a contract expressly struck by the parties. There are important restrictions on the freedom of an employer to dismiss his employees without giving a minimum period of notice. An employee dismissed after 13 weeks of employment but before two years' service is entitled to one week's notice or wages in lieu thereof. This sliding scale progresses until workers who have served for more than 15 years are entitled to eight weeks' notice. These provisions, to be found in section 4 of the Minimum Notice and Terms of Employment Act 1973, cannot be excluded by agreement. They are a minimum requirement and can be expanded by agreement or by circumstances. The 1968 case of *Carvill v. Irish Industrial Bank* (see above page 127), would not be decided differently today. The most recent enhancement of workers' rights is found in the Terms of Employment (Information) Act 1994.

Statute also provides for implied terms to exist in landlord and tenant agreements. See, for example, the power of a housing authority to pass bye-laws under section 70 of the Housing Act 1966 to impose minimum standards for rented property within their functional area.

However, statutory authority for a particular practice, or the provision of a service, may preclude an argument based on implied contract. In *Monaghan Board of Health v. O'Neill*[58] the plaintiff provided hospital services for an elderly indigent person in pursuance of a statutory duty to maintain sick or feeble persons resident within its functional area. The plaintiff later sought to obtain a contribution from that person. It was held that the statutory obligation meant that there was no basis at common law for an implied term that money spent would be recoverable.

## Terms Implied Under the Constitution

Important differences between Irish contract law and English contract principles arise because of the operation of the 1937 Constitution which sets out certain fundamental freedoms, absent from the English common law. The

---

[58] (1934) 68 I.L.T.R. 239; *Gilheaney v. Revenue Commissioners*, unreported, High Court, October 4, 1995.

Constitution has proved important in employment law and its impact on principles of contract has, in this respect, proved substantial.

Article 40.6.1°iii and 40.6.2° have been interpreted as conferring upon citizens the right not only to form associations and unions but an implicit right not to join – a right of disassociation – see *Educational Company of Ireland Ltd. v. Fitzpatrick (No. 2)*.[59] The Supreme Court have ruled in *Meskell v. C.I.É.*[60] that this right of disassociation must be respected by an employer, even if the employer threatens to exercise his common law right of dismissal in a manner permissible at common law. Meskell was employed as a bus conductor. C.I.É. offered Meskell a new contract of employment which would oblige him to join and maintain membership of a trade union. Failure to assent would lead, after a reasonable period of notice, to termination of his employment. Meskell objected in principle and, following his refusal and dismissal, sued, alleging an actionable conspiracy by the unions and C.I.É. to infringe his Constitutional right of disassociation. Walsh J. in the leading judgment, held that the fact that a person seeks to exercise a common law right in such a way as to dissuade a citizen from exercising a constitutional right "must necessarily be regarded as an abuse of the common law right because it is an infringement, and an abuse, of the Constitution which is superior to the common law and which must prevail if there is a conflict between the two."[61] In other words, if a statutory provision can override a common law right (or even an express agreement) then a right implied under the Constitution must, *a fortiori*, take priority over this common law right. Damages will also be recoverable for infringement of this constitutional right even if no other cause of action would appear to exist; *per* Walsh J. in *Meskell v. C.I.É.*

Article 40.3 has been held to require that procedures and machinery established to reach decisions which effect the rights or liabilities of citizens must be fair. These procedures must allow a party to be heard if he is accused of breach of contract. In *Glover v. B.L.N.*[62] an employee was summarily dismissed for alleged misconduct. Clause 12(*c*) of the contract provided he could be so dismissed without compensation for serious misconduct. Walsh J. held that:

> "This procedure was a breach of the implied term of the contract that the procedure should be fair, as it cannot be disputed, in the light of so much authority on the point, that failure to allow a person to meet the charges against him and afford him an adequate opportunity of answering them is a violation of an obligation to proceed fairly."[63]

---

[59] [1961] I.R. 345. See Hogan and Morgan, *Administrative Law in Ireland* (Round Hall Sweet & Maxwell, 3rd ed., 1998), chaps 10 and 11.

[60] [1973] I.R. 121.

[61] *Ibid.* at 135.

[62] [1973] I.R. 388; *Mooney v. An Post*, unreported, Supreme Court, March 20, 1997.

[63] [1973] I.R. 388 at 425–426.

The obligation, which modifies the employer's common law right to dismiss an employee by reasonable notice does not extend to all employees but the applicability of this Constitutional obligation has been consistently stated by the Irish courts to depend on whether the employee enjoys the status of office-holder.[64] However, the Supreme Court, in *Gunn v. Bord an Choláiste Náisiúnta Ealaíne is Deartha*[65] held that termination of employment must take place in accordance with the principles of natural and constitutional justice and that these principles, when applicable, operate without regard to the status of the person who seeks to invoke them. Therefore, if a person is accused of wrongdoing, that person must be given details of the charge against him.[66] The procedures for investigation of these allegations must take place as soon as is reasonably practicable.[67] Sometimes constitutional rights and contractual rights may reinforce each other. The decision of the Supreme Court in *McAuley v. Commissioner of An Garda Síochána*[68] held that when a trainee garda was the subject of a disciplinary procedure, the requirements of the disciplinary code and his constitutional rights to constitutional justice had not been satisfied. In particular the plaintiff had not been provided with the evidence against him, nor was the decision to terminate his employment implemented in a lawful manner. In these circumstances the plaintiff was entitled to damages for breach of constitutional rights and breach of contract.

Apart from the obligation to give an employee the right to be heard – see *Allied Irish Banks v. Lupton*[69] – the Constitution and principles of natural justice also extend a right to be heard by an impartial tribunal. If the members of the disciplinary board are clearly not impartial then the rule *nemo iudex in causa sua* is infringed: see *National Engineering & Electrical Trade Union v. McConnell*.[70] However, a citizen cannot use the Constitution to frustrate an employer, for example, from investigating allegations of misconduct or dishonesty and the use of allegations of past misconduct may well be relevant in this regard: *Maher v. Irish Permanent plc*.[71]

While the provisions of Article 40.3 do not seem to do very much more than articulate the rules of natural justice that had already emerged in English administrative law there are important practical results which flow from the argument that the Constitution has integrated principles of natural justice into the scheme of human rights guaranteed by the Constitution. These issues are explored by Hogan.[72]

---

[64] *Garvey v. Ireland* (1979) 113 I.L.T.R. 61; *O'Reilly v. Minister for Industry and Commerce and Others* [1994] E.L.R. 48. The leading case is *Glover v. B.L.N.* [1973] I.R. 388.

[65] [1990] 2 I.R. 168.

[66] *N.E.E.T.U. v. McConnell* [1983] I.L.R.M. 422; *Gallagher v. Corrigan*, unreported, High Court, February 1, 1988.

[67] *Flynn v. An Post* [1987] I.R. 68.

[68] Unreported, Supreme Court, February 15, 1996.

[69] (1984) 3 J.I.S.L.L. 107.

[70] [1983] I.L.R.M. 422.

[71] Unreported, High Court, October 7, 1997.

[72] (1984) 19 Ir.Jur. 315.

There are other aspects to the Constitution that may in the future be developed. The equality provisions in the Constitution provide an example. While legislation limits the freedom of an employer to refuse to employ or dismiss an employee on the grounds of sex or marital status (Employment Equality Act 1977) or dismiss an employee on the grounds of pregnancy (Maternity Protection of Employees Act 1981), there are still cases where a refusal to contract with another person on the grounds of sex, age, race or creed may not infringe any legislative provision such as the Prohibition of Incitement to Hatred Act 1989. The Irish courts, however, have taken the view that the equality provisions in Article 40.1 do not interfere with the trading activities of citizens or the terms upon which those persons are employed: see *Murtagh Properties Ltd. v. Cleary*.[73] So in *Devaney v. Minister for Agriculture*[74] an attempt to challenge a contractual term, which required Department of Agriculture inspectors to provide their own transport, as unconstitutional because only persons who could afford to run a car would be eligible for appointment was rejected as incompatible with the pronouncement of Kenny J. in *Murtagh Properties v. Cleary* on the scope of Article 40.1:

> "this article is not a guarantee that all citizens shall be treated by the law as equal for all purposes but it means that they shall, as human persons be held equal before the law. It relates to their essential attributes as persons, those features which make them human beings. It has, in my opinion, nothing to do with their trading activities or with the conditions on which they are employed."[75]

Nevertheless Kenny J. did go on to consider whether Article 40.1 could be infringed if a trade union pressured (by mounting a picket) an employer into dismissing someone on the ground of sex and concluded that such pressure would breach a citizen's right to earn a livelihood. Whether pressure mounted by A against B, requiring B to discontinue providing C, a self employed female jobbing builder, with work, because A has a prejudice against women, would infringe the Consitution must be an open question.

The Supreme Court in *Tierney v. Amalgamated Society of Woodworkers*[76] held that the defendant union was free to decide whether it would permit the applicant to become a member of the trade union or not and that Article 40.6.1° (iii) extended to citizens a collective right to form unions and not an individual right which would require a union to accept a citizen's offer to become a member of that union. Even if the refusal prevented the applicant from taking up employment, thereby impeding the applicant from earning a livelihood – where a pre-entry closed shop operated – it seems that there is no remedy

---

[73] [1972] I.R. 330.
[74] Unreported, High Court, March 22, 1979.
[75] [1972] I.R. 330 at 335–336.
[76] [1959] I.R. 254; see, however, Finlay C.J. in *Burke and Others v. Mayor of Dublin* [1991] I.R. 341 on equality before the law.

unless perhaps the reason for refusal is itself discriminatory. In such a case the applicant may have a remedy. Under section 6 of the Employment Equality Act 1977, a trade union that discriminates, *inter alia*, in respect to applications for membership on the ground of sex or marital status should be in breach of the Act. Where the reason for refusal to obtain employment or union membership can be shown to be discriminatory on some other ground – colour, nationality, religious persuasion (or the lack of it) – the Constitution seems to afford no relief, save for the limited situation in Article 44.2.3°, that is if the State itself should prescribe that certain persons, on the ground of religion, be prevented, for example, from taking up employment in the Civil Service or in a State school.

These implied fundamental freedoms are not absolute, however. If the parties agree in circumstances where it is clear that each is in a position to freely negotiate and that each understands the bargain then it may be possible for a citizen to waive a constitutional right of disassociation or a guarantee as to fair procedures.[77] In certain cases a constitutional right may have to take its place within a hierarchy of constitutional rights. Further, a contract may have a significant role in determining such a hierarchy. In *Oblique Financial Services Ltd. v. The Promise Production Co.*[78] the various defendants, some of whom had covenanted to keep a secret while the others intended to publish the secret, could not assert an unlimited right to freedom to communicate information under article 40.3.1°. Such a right could be qualified by other legal constraints such as the duty to observe confidentiality, whether owed by the defendants in contract or as a matter of moral obligation.

## Custom

It is possible for terms to be implied into contracts because of the commercial or local backcloth against which a contract is to take effect. Customs within a trade or industry can become part of the contract; in *Taylor v. Hall*[79] an alleged custom in the building industry was rejected as inconsistent with the evidence adduced. In a leading early twentieth century Irish case the courts had to consider whether a particular practice in relation to the costs of unloading ships had become binding customs in the part in question.[80] The essential issues to be established are whether the practice can be shown to exist in the trade or locality, and that the parties have relied upon it. If these two points can be satisfied then the custom will generally be part of the contract unless it is excluded by an express term, or a term which is part of the contract and which is inconsistent with the custom in question.

---

[77] *Murphy v. Stewart* [1975] I.R. 97; Kerr and Whyte, *Irish Trade Union Law*, (1985) pp. 31–33.
[78] [1994] I.L.R.M. 74. See generally Lavery, *Commercial Secrets* (Round Hall Sweet & Maxwell, 1997).
[79] (1869) I.R. 5 C.L. 477.
[80] *Gallagher v. Clydesdale Shipowners Co.* [1908] 2 I.R. 482.

In the case of *O'Reilly v. Irish Press*[81] Maguire P. indicated that for a custom to be established there must be an element of notoriety or general acquiescence to it. The alleged custom was that chief sub-editors in a newspaper were entitled to six months notice:

> "a custom on usage of any kind is a difficult thing to establish. . . . I have to be satisfied that it is so notorious, well known and acquiesced in that in the absence of agreement in writing it is to be taken as one of the terms of the contract between the parties."

No such custom was established by the plaintiff in this case.

The difficulty of establishing, on the balance of probabilities, a trade custom is illustrated by *Eastwood and Others v. Ryder*.[82] It was alleged by the first plaintiff, a publisher, that there was an implied custom in the newspaper and periodical publishing industry that serialised extracts from a book, published in the plaintiff's magazine, would be true and not libellous. Michael Davies J. held that, after hearing expert testimony, this custom could not be established. The situation could be dealt with by way of an express indemnity but the contract between the defendant author and the first plaintiff did not deal with this kind of problem by way of an express indemnity, while the contract between the defendant and the second plaintiff, the book publisher, did contain such an indemnity. One further illustration is provded by *O'Connail v. The Gaelic Echo (1954) Ltd.*,[83] when a journalist recovered holiday pay on proof that it was a custom in Dublin that such payments were made to journalists. Similarly, local agricultural customs often become part of the agreement as an implied term. See for example the Ulster tenant's right of sale. Terms implied by way of custom are often found in landlord and tenant contracts and custom is a most fruitful basis for legislative action in this area of law. Many statutory obligations in landlord and tenant law are codifications of customary law.[84]

---

[81] (1937) I.L.T.R. 194.
[82] *The Times*, July 28, 1990.
[83] (1958) 92 I.L.T.R. 156.
[84] Wylie, *Irish Land Law* (3rd ed., 1996), para. 1.44.

# 7  The Exemption Clause

## Introduction

An exemption clause is a contractual term by which one party attempts to cut down either the scope of his contractual duties or regulate the other party's right to damages or other possible remedies for breach of contract. So in a *non-consumer* contract for the sale of goods any attempt by the seller to exclude implied obligations as to merchantability can be interpreted as effectively removing any obligation to supply merchantable goods; under the Sale of Goods Act 1893, as amended in the Republic by the Sale of Goods and Supply of Services Act 1980, such an attempt to eliminate this obligation must be shown to be fair and reasonable: see sections 14(2) and 55(4). One party may not attempt to eliminate the other's rights altogether but simply require any complaints about defective performance to be lodged within a set period, say within 14 days; failure to satisfy this term will result in loss of any cause of action. Alternatively, the seller may limit the damages recoverable to a fixed sum, *e.g.* £50. In *Leonard v. Gt. Northern Ry. Co.*[1] the plaintiff sent a consignment of turkeys by rail. On arrival, four were missing. Under the terms of the contract set out on the forwarding note the plaintiff was required to notify the carrier of loss within three days. The plaintiff failed to do this. The plaintiff's claim was dismissed because of failure to comply with the notice provision.

If the clause negatives a right to performance it is said to have *substantive* effect; if the clause regulates entitlement to damages it is *procedural*; only failure to satisfy the procedural steps laid down results in loss of the right to damages.[2]

## Substantive or Procedural?

It can sometimes prove difficult to decide whether the exemption clause has substantive or procedural effect. In *British Leyland Exports Ltd. v. Brittain Group Sales Ltd.*[3] a contract for the supply of motor vehicles to the defendants in kit form included a clause which provided that while the sellers would endeavour to meet orders placed they "shall not be liable for any failure, delay or error in delivery, or any consequential loss therefrom, however caused." O'Hanlon J. held that while this clause did not exclude the sellers' primary obligation to deliver complete and satisfactory kits, the clause did limit the

---

[1] (1912) 46 I.L.T.R. 220.
[2] The development of this analysis is generally attributed to Coote, *Exception Clauses* (1964).
[3] [1981] I.R. 35.

sellers' remedy by excluding the general secondary obligation to pay damages when defective kits were provided. With respect, this analysis seems to this writer to ignore the fact that the clause was in fact designed to limit the obligations on the sellers to meet orders where possible and effectively ensure that complete kits were provided. On this analysis there could be no room for a finding that the implied obligation excluded the claim for damages; the exclusion clause excluded the implied obligation and *ipso facto*, there was no contractual right which could bring the secondary obligation to pay damages into play. There are several English cases in which the courts have suggested that the effect of an exemption clause is to qualify or limit the scope of the contractual duties one party is to perform. In *Kenyon Son and Craven Ltd. v. Baxter Hoare & Co. Ltd.*[4] the defendant operated a warehouse and undertook to store peanuts owned by the plaintiff. This contract of bailment was concluded on the foot of the defendant's standard conditions of business. One of the clauses provided that the defendant was not to be liable for loss or damage to goods unless such loss or damage was due to wilful neglect or default. The peanuts were damaged by rats and although the defendant had been negligent they had not acted with wilful neglect or default. Donaldson J. held that the clause was effective. It provided the defendant with a complete answer to the action because the clause made it clear that the defendant was not undertaking to excuse reasonable care and skill. The clause also excluded the ordinary duty of a bailee for reward. This approach to the interpretation of the exemption clause is based on the assumption that the court should read the contract in its entirety and that a limitation of liability clause cannot merely limit liability but can also limit the duty undertaken by the person relying on the clause.

It must, however, be conceded that there are other views of the role of an exemption clause. Some judges hold that the clause merely operates as a defence to liability and that the approach to be adopted in the interpretation of an exemption clause is to leave the clause to one side and then interpret the contract so as to see what the parties have undertaken. The clause is then examined to see if it provides a defence to the plaintiff's action. The best example of such a process is the judgment of Denning L.J. in *Karsales (Harrow) Ltd. v. Wallis.*[5] This theoretical debate does have some important practical consequences, as we shall see.

The exemption clause possessing substantive effect is designed to allocate risk between contracting parties – should goods stored with a bailee under a bailment contract be destroyed while in his possession, the bailee may have anticipated this possibility and by contract transferred risk to the owner. In principle there is no reason why this should not be permitted where the bailee has not acted fraudulently or deliberately destroyed the goods. Difficulties arise when the party invoking the exemption clause is in a stronger bargaining

---

[4]  [1971] 2 All E.R. 708. On the meaning of wilful misconduct see *Laceys Footwear Ltd. v. Bowler, The Times,* May 12, 1997.
[5]  [1956] 1 W.L.R. 936.

position and has exploited this by including a draconian provision which, on its face, protects him in every situation. The courts and the legislature have dealt with such instances of abuse of freedom of contract in different ways. This Chapter is concerned with the judicial response to exemption clauses, and while the author concedes that no neat demarcation can exist here, the legislative method of countering abuse of superior bargaining power (and in particular the exemption clause) is considered in the next Chapter.

While most exemption clauses are written statements which are found either in the contract document itself, or in standard conditions of contract, there are instances where one party may verbally limit the scope of his contractual duty. In *Hughes v. J.J. Power Ltd. and Colliers Ltd.*[6] the plaintiff took a tractor engine to the second defendant, a motor engineer, in order to have the engine serviced. The work to be done was somewhat difficult due to certain defects in the engine and the second defendant indicated that he would do the work but that the work would be done at the owner's risk. Blayney J. held that the effect of this statement was that the second defendant would not be liable for any physical damage caused during the necessary work and that a term to this effect was imported into the contract. This case provides a neat illustration of the fact that clauses which exclude a particular duty are essentially concerned with risk transfer or risk allocation.

Before an exemption clause (also known as an exclusion or exculpatory clause) will be permitted to take effect, it must pass two tests. First of all, the provision upon which the party asserting it seeks to rely (the proferens) must be incorporated into the contract. Secondly, as a matter of construction, the clause must cover the events that have occured. We will deal with these issues separately.

## Incorporation

### (1) Basic rules

The Irish courts, like their English brethren, have struggled with the problem of incorporation because the tests advanced have varied from time to time. This is particularly so when it is clear that the party against whom the clause is asserted has not read the exempting provision. In one early Irish case the plaintiff was held bound by an exempting provision printed on a railway ticket which exempted the company from liability should passengers be injured. The plaintiff was bound because he was said to have had the means of discovering the clause, that is, constructive notice: *Johnson v. Gt. Southern & W. Ry.*[7] Three years later the English Court of Appeal decided the leading case of *Parker v. S.E. Railway.*[8] In cases where someone is given a ticket or document which

---

[6] Unreported, High Court, May 11, 1988.
[7] (1874) I.R. 9 C.L. 108.
[8] (1877) 2 C.P.D. 416.

140

sets out or refers to limiting conditions to be read elsewhere the proferens will be able to rely on the terms if he can show that the other party read them or that he, the proferens, did everything reasonable to bring the clause to the attention of the public. Several questions were set out in *Parker v. S.E. Railway* which the court should ask; these questions can be paraphrased in the following way:

(1) Did the party know of the conditions? If so he is bound.[9]

(2) Was notice given? If not the other party is not bound.[10]

(3) If notice was given but the other party did not know the notice contained writing he will not necessarily be bound.[11]

(4) If he did know there was writing on the document then the court must ask whether reasonable notice of the conditions has been given. If the other party knows the ticket contained not merely writing but conditions he will be bound even if he is unaware of the precise terms.[12]

The reasonableness test marks an improvement on the earlier *Johnson* case but there are still difficult issues of fact to be resolved. In the case of *Richardson Spence & Co. v. Rowntree*[13] the House of Lords applied the approach outlined earlier in *Parker*. The plaintiff was a passenger on a steamer travelling from Liverpool to Philadelphia. The plaintiff was given a folded ticket, no writing being visible in this form. The ticket when opened had a great many conditions, one of which limited liability for personal injury or loss of baggage to $100. The plaintiff never read the ticket. The plaintiff was injured whilst on the vessel. At first instance Bruce J. left three questions to the jury:

(1) Did the plaintiff know that there was writing on the ticket? This question was answered in the affirmative.

(2) Did the plaintiff know the writing contained conditions relative to the contract of carriage? This was answered in the negative.

(3) Did the defendants do what was reasonably sufficient to give the plaintiff notice of these conditions? This question was answered in the negative.

The High Court, Court of Appeal and House of Lords held that in the light of these findings the limitation clause was not available to the defendant. This decision was applied in *Ryan v. Great Southern & Western Ry.*[14] in 1898. The plaintiff's baggage had been lost by the defendant. The terms of the plaintiff's ticket referred to standard conditions which were available for inspection. Upon finding that the plaintiff was unaware that the ticket contained limiting

---

[9] (1877), 2 C.P.D. 416.
[10] *Roche v. Corke, Blackrock and Passage Railway* (1889) 24 L.R.(Ir.) 250.
[11] The inquiry then passes to examine whether reasonable notice was given.
[12] *Taggart v. Northern Counties Ry.* (1898) 32 I.L.T. 404.
[13] [1894] A.C. 297.
[14] 32 I.L.T.R. 108.

conditions of contract it was further held that insufficient notice had been given of the term. However, the case of *Taggart v. Northern Counties Ry.*,[15] also decided in 1898, illustrates the fact that if the plaintiff is found to know that the ticket or contract document contains contractual conditions, the plaintiff will be bound even if he is unaware of the precise terms of contract.

The Irish courts have not laid down exacting standards which a proferens must meet before the limiting term will be incorporated. In the case of *Early v. Gt. Southern Ry.*[16] the plaintiff was given an excursion ticket which on its face referred the passenger to the company's special conditions containing the limiting provisions. The plaintiff was injured. Notwithstanding the fact that the conditions were not available for inspection at this particular booking office the defendants were held entitled to rely on this clause. At times the judges display a quite unrealistic view of the problems confronting the person who contracts with a service provider, particularly when a monopoly is enjoyed by that provider. In *Shea v. Great Southern Ry.*[17] the plaintiff took a bicycle onto a crowded bus. The bus ticket referred to a notice excluding liability for theft. The plaintiff was held bound by the notice. Judge Davitt said that the plaintiff was "at liberty to get off the bus or remove his bicycle."

If the proferens wants to be sure that the clause will be incorporated into the contract he should obtain the signature of the other party to a contract document setting at the term: see *Duff v. Gt. Northern Railway.*[18] On signature the other party will be bound, even if the document is unread and the terms are set out in miniscule print. In the leading English case of *L'Estrange v. F. Graucob*[19] the Court of Appeal reaffirmed the statement made in the *Parker's* case about the effect of signature; only if the signature is obtained by fraud or misrepresentation will the contract be held not to include a limiting clause. While this proposition has never been overruled in England it must be considered as having been much qualified by the more recent English, Irish and Canadian cases, considered below.

### (2) The time at which notice was given

The general rule is that notice of a limiting clause, given after the contract is concluded, cannot bind the other party. In *Sproule v. Triumph Cycle Co.*[20] the plaintiff approached an agent of the defendants with a view to buying a motor cycle. He did not read a catalogue which attempted to limit the defendants' obligations to replacement of defective parts for three months after purchase. This "guarantee" was also set out on a card attached to the bike although this was not handed to the plaintiff and read by him until after the sale had been

---

[15] (1898) 32 I.L.T. 404.
[16] [1940] I.R. 414.
[17] [1944] Ir. Jur. Rep. 26.
[18] (1878) 4 L.R.(Ir.) 178.
[19] [1934] 2 K.B. 394.
[20] [1927] N.I. 83.

concluded. The plaintiff was held entitled to rely on section 14(1) of the 1893 Act. Moore C.J. held the guarantee ineffective because it was not read until after the contract had been concluded. It should be noted that when the case does not involve a railway ticket the onus on the proferens is greater when he alleges incorporation has occurred. In the leading English case of *Olley v. Marlborough Court Ltd.*[21] the defendant let a hotel room to a husband and wife. At the time of checking into the hotel, the defendants obtained payment in advance for a one-week stay. On arriving in the hotel room, the husband and wife for the first time were made aware in the form of a printed notice that the hotel proprietor sought to exclude liability for theft or loss of articles of property unless handed to the hotel management for safekeeping. The wife left the hotel room and left the key downstairs in reception. The key was taken by a thief who stole her furs. The defendant unsuccessfully pleaded the notice excluding liability. The majority of the Court of Appeal held that the notice was not part of the contract because the contract had been formed at the reception desk prior to entry into the room. In *Thornton v. Shoe Lane Parking Ltd.*[22] Denning M.R. used the same line of reasoning in the context of a contract whereby the plaintiff was permitted to use the defendants' multi-storey car park. Entry was effected by way of an automatic barrier, the barrier being operated through a ticket machine. While the ticket contained a notice that the ticket was issued subject to conditions displayed on the premises, actual notice of the terms could only be given to members of the public after entry into the building. Denning M.R. opined that the offer was made via the terms stated on the outside of the building and that the offer was accepted by approaching the barrier and taking the ticket: the contract was concluded on terms which did not include the terms found within the building. In contrast, however, in *Brady v. Aer Rianta,* the printed conditions were set out on the ticket and the terms were actually displayed on a notice board outside the entrance to the car parking area at Dublin Airport. Butler J. held that in these circumstances the contract was concluded before the plaintiff entered the parking area and the defendant had given reasonable notice of a limitation clause prior to the contract being formed. This reasoning has recently been followed in *O'Beirne v. Aer Rianta.*[23]

Two Irish cases that at first sight seem to be inconsistent with this reasoning are *Knox v. Gt. Northern Railway*[24] and *Slattery v. C.I.É.*[25] Both cases concerned contracts to transport a horse, the horse being injured as a result of the defendant's employee's negligence. In *Slattery v. C.I.É.* the plaintiff signed a consignment note which stated that delivery would take place at the owner's risk. This note was not signed until after the injury to the horse had occurred and after the journey had been completed: this was an oversight on the defendant's

---

[21] [1949] 1 K.B. 532; *Jayaar Impex Ltd. v. Toaken Group* [1996] 2 Lloyd's Rep. 437.
[22] [1971] 2 Q.B. 163.
[23] Judgment of Barrington J., delivered *ex tempore* on May 20, 1987. The earlier judgment of Butler J. in *Brady v. Aer Rianta* was delivered in 1974 but is undated.
[24] [1896] 2 I.R. 632.
[25] (1972) 106 I.L.T.R. 71.

part. The defendants were held to be entitled to rely on the document as setting out the terms of the agreement. It should be noted that in this case, as in *Knox*, the plaintiffs envisaged that the contract document had still to be completed; as Holmes J. said in *Knox*: "It is neither illegal, unreasonable nor unusual, for the terms of a contract to be reduced to writing after the performance of the services contracted for has been begun." If this was a case of the proferens attempting to add an exempting clause when a written or oral contract had already been completed, as occurred in *Olley v. Marlborough Court Ltd.*, such an attempt would no doubt fail in Ireland: *Moynihan v. Crowley & Warren & Co.*[26]

## (3) Incorporation – new wine in old bottles?

It is not too much of a generalisation to say that when the courts were faced with the problem of counteracting exemption clauses in circumstances where the agreement had not been freely negotiated or consented to, or where the result of allowing the exemption clause to operate was repugnant to the court's sense of justice and fair play, the most natural response was to require the clause itself to be couched in the clearest possible terms. At times this led to the most artificial distinctions imaginable; witness the attempt of counsel in *Ailsa Craig Fishing Co. Ltd. v. Malvern Fishing Co.*[27] to argue that the word "default" would allow the proferens to rely on an exemption clause if he attempted to discharge his contractual duty and failed, but that the clause would not be operative if there was a total failure to attempt performance. The House of Lords on several occasions has urged judges to resist "the temptation to resort to the device of ascribing to the words appearing in exemption clauses a tortured meaning": *per* Lord Diplock in *Ailsa Craig*, above. While the primary reason for this appeal to abandon the covert but unsatisfactory approach of giving plain words a strained and at times fanciful meaning is the fact that the legislators have intervened, another factor that must be considered is the greater awareness amongst the judiciary that the proferens was, under the old incorporation tests, given too much latitude. The proferens can no longer assume that the exemption clause will be readily admitted to the contract. The realisation that the rules on incorporation were framed during the heyday of freedom of contract and that these rules were often totally inappropriate, even at that time, has transformed the approach of the judges to questions of incorporation. As the judge in *Hollingworth v. Southern Ferries Ltd.*[28] put it:

> "Although the principles enunciated in *Parker* and reaffirmed subsequently have remained constant and do remain constant, the application

---

[26] [1958] Ir. Jur. Rep. 21.
[27] [1983] 1 W.L.R. 964. See also *Photo Production Ltd. v. Securicor Transport Ltd.* [1980] 2 W.L.R. 283; *George Mitchell (Chesterhall) Ltd. v. Finney Lock Seeds Ltd.* [1983] 2 A.C. 803; *Bovis Construction (Scotland) Ltd. v. Whatlings Construction Ltd.* (1995) 46 Con.L.R. 103.
[28] [1977] 2 Lloyd's, Rep. 70.

of those principles have altered considerably in recent years. There is increased consciousness of the need to protect consumers."[29]

Sometimes protection is afforded by adopting the view that before a particular clause can be incorporated the proferens must show that the other party should have normally encountered a clause of this type and scope. In *Thornton v. Shoe Lane Parking Ltd.*[30] a clause on a ticket issued from an automatic vending machine was denied effect by holding that it had not been incorporated into the contract. The ticket attempted to exclude liability, not simply for the theft of the car and/or its contents; but also for liability for personal injury to the consumer, even if caused by the negligence of company employees. Sufficient notice of this particular clause had not been given. Factors such as the size of the print, whether the clause was clearly set out, the kind of risk or liability it excluded or limited, were not generally relevant under the *Parker* tests and they were clearly irrelevant if the contract was signed. The decision of the Court of Appeal in *Interfoto Picture Library Ltd. v. Stiletto Visual Programmes Ltd.*,[31] while not ostensibly concerned with exemption clauses, promises to be seen as a landmark decision on the issue of incorporation of contractual terms, when not specifically drawn to the attention of the other party. The defendant, an advertising agency, obtained photographs from the plaintiff, a company that operated a photographic library. The photographs were to be used in preparing an advertising campaign, but the photographs were not actually used in the campaign. The parties had not dealt with each other before and the photographs were supplied on the foot of a delivery note which set out conditions of contract in some detail. These terms were probably not read. One of the terms provided that if not returned after 14 days a fee of £5.00 per day per photograph would be charged. By oversight the defendant held onto the transparancies for a further 14 days and was sent an invoice for the charges calculated under this condition: some £3,783.50. The defendant disputed the charge. The Court of Appeal held that the condition was not part of the contract because its existence had not been drawn to the attention of the defendant. Dillon L.J. said:

> "It is in my judgment a logical development of the common law into modern conditions that it should be held, as it was in *Thornton v. Shoe Lane Parking Ltd.*, that, if one condition in a set of printed conditions is particularly onerous or unusual, the party seeking to enforce it must show that that particular condition was fairly brought to the attention of the other party."[32]

---

[29] [1977] 2 Lloyd's Rep. 70 at 78, *per* Deputy Judge Ogden.
[30] [1971] 2 Q.B. 163.
[31] [1988] 1 All E.R. 348. See Bradgate (1997) 60 M.L.R. 582.
[32] [1988] 1 All E.R. 348 at 352.

This line of authority was endorsed by Costello J. in *Carroll v. An Post National Lottery Co.*[33] After finding that the plaintiff was aware that his lottery playslip contained conditions, even though the plaintiff did not read them, Costello J. considered that the defendant had to establish that where other contracting parties habitually did not read those conditions the party using such conditions "must show that it has been fairly and reasonably brought to the other party's attention." Costello J. stressed that this requirement was based on both contractual principles and the concept of fair dealing, as articulated by Bingham L.J. in the *Interfoto* case. Costello J. *obiter* concluded that on the facts before him, the particular clauses relied upon by the defendants were able to satisfy this reasonableness requirement.

No direct attack has been launched on the rule that signature of the contract, in the absence of fraud or misrepresentation, will incorporate the clause. This proposition, stated in *Parker* and reaffirmed in England in *L'Estrange v. F. Graucob*[34] and *Curtis v. Chemical Cleaning and Dyeing Co.*[35] has horrific results in cases where the proferens is allowed to utilise the signature rule in cases of personal injury or death, as the case of *Delaney v. Cascade River Holdings Ltd.*[36] illustrates. Cases such as *Crocker v. Sundance Northwest Resorts Ltd.,*[37] in which signature was held by the Supreme Court of Canada not to indicate assent to the terms proposed, are much to be preferred. Even in non-personal injury cases signature has been held to be inconclusive. For example, in two Canadian cases the consumer could not reasonably have expected this kind of clause to be included in the contract where the clause was tucked away in small print: see *Tilden Rent-A-Car Co. v. Glendenning*[38] followed in *Tilden Rent-A-Car Co. v. Chandra.*[39]

In Ireland there has not yet been any direct assault on the signature rule but in the case of *Regan v. The Irish Automobile Club Ltd. and Others*[40] Lynch J. noted that while the plaintiff had signed a release form which waived the liability of the defendant, it was also established by the evidence that the plaintiff was aware of the fact that she had signed a document that restricted her rights in the event of accidental injury. Also, in *O'Connor v. First National Building Society*[41] the plaintiff's signature on a house loan application form, which excluded the defendant from liability should the property be defective, was held to bind the plaintiff. It was significant, in Lynch J.'s view, that the exemption clause was prominently displayed just above the place of signature. These two cases provide evidence that the signature, *ipso facto*, will not

---

33 [1996] 1 I.R. 443.
34 [1934] 2 K.B. 394.
35 [1951] 1 K.B. 805.
36 [1983] 44 B.C.L.R. 24.
37 [1988] 1 S.C.R. 1186.
38 (1978) 83 D.L.R. (3d) 400.
39 (1984) 150 D.L.R. (3d) 685.
40 [1990] 1 I.R. 278.
41 [1991] I.L.R.M. 208; *Staunton v. Toyota (Ireland) and others* [1996] 1 I.L.R.M. 171.

necessarily incorporate the clause and in general this perspective is in line with the recent English and Canadian cases.

This approach is not confined to consumer transactions. In *Western Meats Ltd. v. National Ice and Cold Storage Co.*[42] a contract of bailment was allegedly concluded on the defendant's standard form conditions which provided, *inter alia*, that the company would not be answerable for any "delay, loss or damage caused by their own negligence or any cause whatsoever." The defendants negligently failed to label the plaintiff's goods so that when the plaintiff came to collect them they could not be easily retrieved, causing loss to the plaintiff's business. Barrington J. held that, while the parties were competent to agree on their own terms of contract "a businessman, offering a specialist service, but accepting no responsibility for it, must bring home clearly to the party dealing with him that he accepts no such responsibility." In commenting on this case in *Sugar Distributors Ltd. v. Monaghan Cash and Carry Ltd.,*[43] Carroll J. pointed out that the significant factors in the earlier case were that the service was a specialist one for which the specialist was taking no responsibility and that negotiations to commence the relationship between the parties did not involve mention of this sweeping clause set out on a receipt. In *Sugar Distributors* the reservation of title clause was a commonplace one couched in simple language and clearly visible on the face of the document. It was given effect.

### (4) *Incorporation by a course of dealing*

The rules on incorporation present difficult issues of fact for the courts because a litigant who argues that he did not read the document cannot prove this contention very easily, and vice versa. If the parties contract with each other frequently and on a regular basis, however, the court has to balance the obvious injustice of holding one party bound by a term which he did not read (much less assent to) against the expectations of the proferens. If the parties contract regularly and the proferens issues documents which transfer risk to the other party he is entitled to assume that there is assent to the terms offered. Thus, in *Spurling v. Bradshaw*[44] the owner of goods contracted to store his property with the defendant. These bailment contracts took place regularly. On each occasion the bailee handed over a document which limited the bailee's liability. The plaintiff at no time read the document or the conditions. This was not a ticket case – it was a contract freely negotiated. The English Court of Appeal held the plaintiff bound by this limiting clause: "by the course of business and conduct of the parties these conditions were part of the contract." If the clause in question is found in a particular trade or if it is commonly used in standard invoices, the term will be incorporated, even if it is utilised by a negligent defendant, certainly if there are as many as 11 previous instances of dealing between the parties: *Circle Freight International v. Medeast Gulf Exports.*[45]

---

42 [1982] I.L.R.M. 101.
43 [1982] I.L.R.M. 399.
44 [1956] 1 W.L.R. 461.
45 [1988] 2 Lloyd's Rep. 427.

For incorporation by a course of dealing to occur, the trade practice relied on by the proferens must be consistent. One or two isolated transactions do not constitute a course of dealing unless both parties are of similar bargaining strength and operate on terms which are acknowledged to be common within their industry: see *British Crane Hire Corporation v. Ipswich Plant Hire.*[46] The courts are less inclined to find a limiting clause has been incorporated if the transaction involves a large business and an individual consumer. In *Hollier v. Rambler Motors*[47] the owner of a motor vehicle had left his car to be repaired with the defendants on three or four occasions over a number of years. He had then been given a receipt containing a limiting clause. On the occasion in question he left his car with the defendants again but he was not given a receipt containing the clause. The Court of Appeal held that the three or four isolated transactions between consumer and proferens did not incorporate the limiting clause into their last contract. The plaintiff was able to recover for the loss of his car when the garage burnt down.

In *Miley v. R. & J. McKechnie Ltd.*[48] the plaintiff left a garment to be cleaned. The defendants' employee gave her a receipt, marked "important" which set out on the face "all orders accepted without guarantee" and directed the attention of holders to conditions printed on the back. Miss Miley had contracted with the defendants regularly and had always been given such a receipt. She claimed that she at no time read the conditions but did know that the writing contained conditions. Judge Shannon held that display of conditions and the invariable practice of handing a ticket were sufficient to exempt the defendants from liability. The fact that Miss Miley had not read the conditions and that the ticket was given after the contract was concluded was unimportant given the course of dealing between the parties. *Miley* would be decided differently under the 1980 Act; section 40 requires a limiting clause be specifically brought to the attention of the consumer although Costello J., in *Carroll v. An Post National Lottery Co.*, held that this provision can be satisfied even if the party relying on a printed condition does not expressly draw the consumer's attention to the clause at the time of agreement.

## Construction of the Exemption Clause

While it is no doubt paradoxical to adopt less than demanding rules on incorporation while at the same time requiring the proferens to draft the clause with great precision, Lord O'Hagan defended this position when he said in *McNally v. Lancs & York Railway*[49]:

---

[46] [1975] Q.B. 303.
[47] [1972] 2 Q.B. 71.
[48] (1949) 84 I.L.T.R. 89.
[49] (1880) 8 L.R. (Ir.) 81.

"There can be no hardship imposed by requiring companies to be clear and explicit in the framing of conditions designed for their own security. The humble and ignorant dealers who enter into transactions are at a disadvantage and at least they should be held strictly to the terms of the contracts deliberately prepared by their skilled advisors."[50]

In viewing an exemption clause restrictively the courts have developed several important rules or maxims of construction.

### *(1) The contra proferentem rule*

If the exempting provision is ambiguous and capable of more than one interpretation then the courts will read the clause against the party seeking to rely on it. This rule is of general application in some contractual settings and it has recently been discussed in the interpretation of an option agreement: *Kramer v. Arnold.*[51] The *contra proferentem* rule of interpretation however comes into its own in the context of exempting provisions in an agreement. In consumer transactions this will be an important rule, of benefit to the consumer, because it will generally be the seller who asserts that he is entitled to rely on the clause. In *Sproule v. Triumph Cycle Co.*[52] the seller of a motorbike tried to rely on a limiting clause excluding liability for breach of warranty. The purchaser argued that because section 14 of the Sale of Goods Act 1893 implies a condition, this word "warranty" should be given its narrower meaning under that Act. The point was not decided by the Court of Appeal for Northern Ireland although there are several clear illustrations of the rule in English case law. For example, in *Wallis, Son and Wells v. Pratt and Haynes*[53] a contract for the supply of "common English sanfoin" was formed, the seller contracting upon terms that he gave "no warranty, express or implied." A different variety of sanfoin was supplied so that the goods therefore failed to meet their description with a resulting breach of section 13 of the Sale of Goods Act 1893. The obligation in section 13 is an implied condition, and by giving the word warranty as it appeared in the contract a narrow interpretation, the exclusion clause was held inapplicable. In *Andrews v. Singer*[54] the contract was for the sale of a new Singer car. The vehicle delivered had 500 miles on the clock and could not be described as new. The contract purported to displace "any warranty (or condition) implied by common law statute or otherwise." The plaintiff successfully argued that the clause did not operate so as to displace express contractual obligations, only implied ones, and as the promise was to deliver a new car, this express term had not been complied with. Ultimately, the draftsman in *L'Estrange v. F. Graucob*[55]

---

[50] (1880) 8 L.R. (Ir.) 81 at 92.
[51] Unreported, Supreme Court, April 24, 1997.
[52] [1927] N.I. 83.
[53] [1910] 2 K.B. 1003.
[54] [1934] 1 K.B. 17.
[55] [1934] 2 K.B. 394.

managed to close these drafting errors and it was the fact that the judiciary became obliged to enforce unfair contracts that led to the development of the now largely discredited doctrine of fundamental breach of contract. The *contra proferentem* rule remains a useful but limited tool of interpretation.

The *contra proferentem* rule is only one of interpretation and can be overcome by intelligent drafting. A court may find that the proferens has employed a lawyer who has designed a clause so as to eliminate all liability for "breach of all conditions and warranties express or implied under statute or common law, and all collateral warranties." In such a case the usefulness of this rule comes to an end: see *Token Grass Products Ltd. v. Sexton & Co.*[56] In this case the defendant, who had supplied a grain dryer to the plaintiff, was held entitled to rely on printed conditions which excluded implied conditions under the 1893 Acts even after a *contra proferentem* interpretation of the clauses in question. As we shall see, there seems to be very little sympathy for treating limitation of damage clauses to a hostile interpretation, *contra proferentem*, although recent cases in England, Canada and Australia suggest that limitation of duty clauses are still to be read *contra proferentem*, as long as the interpretation placed upon the clause is not fanciful or disingenuous. For example, in the Manitoba case of *Caners v. Eli Lilley Canada*[57] "vague" instructions for the use of a weedkiller were held not to point to contributory negligence by the plaintiff, a farmer, who sued for damage done to his crops by use of the defendant's product.

### (2) The risk covered

Another approach advanced by the courts is to hold the words of an exempting clause inapplicable to certain eventualities. The words of the clause may not be viewed as excluding liability in several extreme cases. In *Ronan v. Midland Railway Co.*[58] the plaintiff agreed to ship his cattle with the defendants and he was given a receipt which said that the cattle were to travel "at owner's risk". The cattle were wilfully damaged and mutilated by the defendant's employees. The phrase "at owner's risk" was held not to exclude liability for deliberate acts of destruction. *Pearson v. Dublin Corporation*[59] was to similar effect, the House of Lords holding that a limiting clause cannot be allowed to exclude liability for a fraudulent misrepresentation made by the defendant to the plaintiff.

The courts are reluctant to permit a proferens to exclude liability for the negligence of himself or his agents or employees, but if the clause is specific enough then this will be permitted: see *Millar v. Midland Gt. W. Ry.*[60] If this happens the proferens will only be liable for wilful default. The judgment of Lord Morton in *Canada Steamship Lines v. The King*[61] provides the best

---

[56] Unreported, High Court, October 13, 1983.
[57] [1996] 5 W.W.R. 381.
[58] (1883) 14 L.R. (Ir.) 157.
[59] [1907] A.C. 351.
[60] (1905) 5 N.I.J.R. 202.
[61] [1952] A.C.192: *Spriggs v. Sotheby Parke Bernet & Co.* [1986] 1 Lloyd's Rep. 487; *Caledonia Ltd. v. Orbit Valve Co.* [1993] 2 Lloyd's Rep. 418.

summary of the rules a court should follow where a cause of action in negligence is at issue:

(1) If the clause expressly exempts the proferens from liability for his own negligence the clause must be given effect.

(2) If the clause does not expressly refer to negligence the question is whether the words, given their ordinary meaning, cover negligence. The *contra proferentem* rule comes into play here. Phrases that do exclude liability for negligence include "liability for all loss, *howsoever caused* is excluded" and "cars are driven at owner's sole risk" if the only liability possible is negligence: see *Rutter v. Palmer*.[62]

(3) If the ordinary words are wide enough to exclude liability for negligence the court has to consider whether some other basis of liability – statutory or contractual for example – can exist. If so, the proferens will be taken to have intended only to exclude liability for actions other than negligence. So in *White v. Warrick*[63] the hirer of a bicycle was injured when the saddle slipped while he was riding the machine. The limiting clause was held to exclude strict liability in contract while leaving the owner liable in negligence.

In contrast, however, stands the decision of Blayney J. in *Hughes v. J. J. Power Ltd. and Colliers Ltd.*[64] The plaintiff brought a damaged engine part to the premises of the second defendant in order to have the engine repaired. The process was a difficult one and the second defendant undertook the work at the plaintiff's risk. The work was carried out but damage resulted, and the issue was whether the second defendant was able to rely on the agreement that work would be undertaken at the plaintiff's risk. Blayney J. held that in this context the duty imposed by the contract upon the second defendant was the same as that in tort, that is, to exercise the ordinary skill of an ordinary competent person engaged in the particular trade in question. "There was, accordingly, only a single duty imposed on Colliers, though arising both in contract and tort, and there was nothing that the exclusion could apply to other than a failure to comply with that duty." Blayney J. distinguished *White v. Warrick* on the ground that, in the case before him "there were not two heads of liability, but one, breach of a single duty of care, since it was the same duty that arose both in contract and in tort."

At one time the view was expressed that if there could be only one basis of liability then a very general limiting clause must be read so as to exclude that cause of action; this view, attributed to Lord Greene in *Alderslade v. Hendon Laundry*,[65] has been rejected by members of the Court of Appeal in *Hollier v. Rambler Motors*[66] and *Gillespie v. Roy Bowles*.[67] These recent cases are in sympathy with the objective of protecting the consumer but at the risk of

---

[62] [1922] 2 K.B. 87.
[63] [1953] 1 W.L.R. 1285.
[64] Unreported, High Court, May 11, 1988.
[65] [1945] K.B. 189.
[66] [1972] 2 Q.B. 71.
[67] [1973] Q.B. 400.

putting a narrow and sometimes disingenuous interpretation on the meaning of the clause.

### (3) The main purpose rule

This important rule of construction is designed to cut down the effect of a limiting clause which would produce undesirable consequences if the clause was read literally. The courts look to circumstances surrounding the transaction and, aided by the sometimes dubious premise that both parties are acting as reasonable men, the judges cut down general words in a contract. So in *Glynn v. Margotson*[68] a general clause that gave the carrier of a cargo of fresh oranges the liberty to stay at any port in the Mediterranean, Black Sea or Adriatic was held not to exclude liability for damage to the cargo as a result of delay in proceeding directly from Malaga to Liverpool. The House of Lords presumed the main purpose of the contract was the safe transport of the goods. Lord Halsbury said: "looking at the whole instrument and seeing what one must regard as its main purpose one must reject words, indeed whole provisions, if they are inconsistent with what one assumes to be the main purpose of the contract." If the parties do intend to prevent the judges from imputing a main purpose they may do so but very clear evidence of intention and consent to such a term must be disclosed. Sometimes the main purpose, used to counteract the exemption clause, is identified from other express terms or from general contractual obligations. In *Sze Hai Tong Bank Ltd. v. Rambler Cycle Co.*[69] a carrier of goods claimed to be able to rely on an exemption clause which released the carrier from liability after discharge of the goods in port. After discharge of the goods, the carrier's agent released the goods without production of a bill of lading to the consignee. The consignee never paid for the goods and the plaintiff sued the carrier. The carrier sought to rely on the exception clause. The Privy Council held that the exception clause was subject to modification in order to give effect to the main object of the contract, which in this case included an obligation on the carrier to deliver the goods only to a person entitled to deliver, that is, a person who is able to produce the bill of lading.

While it may be that the main purpose rule of construction may seem of limited value if the courts first of all use the exemption clause in order to establish what the contract actually provided for – in this situation the express clause may lead us to conclude that the implied obligation is in fact excluded from the contract (see *British Leyland Exports Ltd. v. Brittain Group Sales Ltd.*[70]) – it can still prove useful. In *Sperry Rand Canada Ltd. v. Thomas Equipment,*[71] Thomas Equipment purchased transmission equipment to be fitted to loading equipment manufactured and sold by them. They relied on Sperry Rand to

---

[68] [1893] A.C. 351.
[69] [1959] A.C. 576; *Nissho Iwai Australia v. Malaysian International Shipping* (1989) 86 A.L.R. 375.
[70] [1981] I.R. 35.
[71] (1982) 135 D.L.R. (3d) 197.

select a suitable transmission system. The system selected and fitted turned out to be unsuitable as a system and Sperry Rand defended the action brought against them for breach of contract by relying on a clause in the contract. La Forest J.A., in the New Brunswick Court of Appeal, held the contractual conditions inapplicable. The main purpose of the contract was to provide a system that was satisfactory as a system. The clauses in the contract limited liability for failures and defects in relation to individual units and not the system as a whole.

### (4)  The type of clause involved

In *Ailsa Craig Fishing Co. v. Malvern Fishing Co.*[72] a distinction was drawn between a limitation clause (a clause limiting the remedy available to the injured party) and a clause of exemption (a clause which attempts to cut down the scope of the contractual duty). Because the former are usually clear and unambiguous in their terms it is less acceptable to give such a clause a secondary meaning than where the clause is an exemption clause. This approach has been followed in Canada in *Westcoast Transmission Co. Ltd. v. Cullen Detroit Diesel Allison Ltd.*[73] That case involved the supply of generators by a third party to the defendant for incorporation with motors to be supplied and used by the plaintiff. The defendant settled a claim brought by the plaintiff when the generators and thus the motors failed. The defendant sought an indemnity from the third party but the third party sought to rely on a clause which excluded "liability for consequential damages in case of failure to meet conditions of any guarantee." The British Columbia Court of Appeal held the clause to be effective, holding that a clause of this kind is to be treated with less hostility than a clause which entirely excludes statutory obligations *vis-à-vis* performance.

## The Core Obligation and Exclusion Clauses

Can a limiting clause be so widely drafted as to permit the proferens to avoid liability in cases which amount to non-performance of the promissory part of the contract? This proposition has troubled the English courts in particular for many years. The problem was identified in *L'Estrange v. F. Graucob*[74] when the plaintiff was held bound by her signature to a contract for the purchase of a cigarette vending machine. The exempting provisions of the contract protected the seller in the event of any breach of contract short of non-delivery of the machine and outright refusal to service it.

The problem raised by "catch-all" exemption clauses may be one of definition; can a contract exist if the limiting provisions are so sweeping as to empty the contract of all promissory content? An airline that promises, "we will fly

---

[72]  [1983] 1 W.L.R. 964.
[73]  (1990) 70 D.L.R. (4th) 503.
[74]  [1934] 2 K.B. 394.

you from A to B" and then conditions this promise by adding, "we will not be liable if we cancel all flights from A to B" is creating an illusory contract: *MacRobertson Miller Airlines v. Commissioners of State Taxation.*[75] The difficulty here stems from the fact that the passenger will generally not be aware of this qualifying term or be in a position to negotiate an improved contract – he will be told to take it or leave it.[76]

It may be that both parties are prepared to agree that the risk of non-performance is to be taken by the purchaser. If each is free to agree to such a contract then the courts should enforce the contract because the core obligation of the contract must be taken to involve this allocation of risk. Indeed, in two Irish cases, *Western Meats Ltd. v. National Ice and Cold Storage*[77] and *Token Grass Products v. Sexton & Co. Ltd.,*[78] Barrington J. and Doyle J. respectively pointed out that the intentions of the parties must be respected when they freely and voluntarily agree on the question of who is to bear a commercial risk. This point is well illustrated by two Irish cases decided in the 1940s. In *O'Connor v. McCowen & Sons Ltd.*[79] the defendants sold turnip seeds to the plaintiff. Prior to the sale the defendants stated that they had not obtained the seeds from their usual source and could not guarantee them. The seeds produced a plant that bore little resemblance to a turnip and was commercially worthless. The defendant argued that he was not liable because of his statement negativing a guarantee. Overend J. indicated that these words were not such as to amount to an agreement exempting the defendants from liability, following the leading English case of *Wallis Son and Wells v. Pratt & Haynes.*[80] Overend J. characterised this case as one where the purchaser was buying goods by description, the goods supplied not answering the description at all. If liability is to be excluded "the very clearest words must be used by the seller, such as: 'you may be purchasing seeds that are not turnip seeds at all.'" Overend J. continued by observing that the obligation in this case did not arise under the Sale of Goods Act: "the buyer, however, got something that was not turnip seed, and *quite apart from the Sale of Goods Act* he had a cause of action." In other words, the fact that a seller tries to exclude the terms implied under statute will not protect him in cases where he delivers goods different from those he contracted to sell. If, to use the facts of *O'Connor*, the purchaser is to take the risk of seeds not producing turnip plants at all he must be aware that this forms the basis of the contract. If the seeds sown had merely produced a poor crop of turnips then the seller may be protected, for this would not be the core obligation but a condition of warranty, then amendable to exclusion under section 55 of the 1893 Act. In *Wicklow Corn Co. Ltd. v. Edward Fitzgerald Ltd.,*[81] a

---

75 (1975) 133 G.L.R. 125.
76 *Shea v. Gt. S. Railway* [1944] Ir. Jur. Rep. 26.
77 [1982] I.L.R.M. 101.
78 Unreported, High Court, October 13, 1983.
79 (1943) 77 I.L.T.R. 64.
80 [1910] 2 K.B. 1003.
81 [1942] Ir. Jur. Rep. 48; *Sholedice v. Hurst Gunson Sope Tober Co.*, unreported, High Court, July 28, 1972.

Circuit Court case, Judge Davitt held a corn factor to be protected by a clause excluding section 14 of the 1893 Act when seed wheat sold produced a poor crop. Here the defect was held to be one of quality only rather than an extreme case where another substance is supplied. In cases where a different substance is supplied it is better to treat this as a case of non-performance, to which the exempting clause is inapplicable except where the evidence suggests that the core obligation was speculative; a *spes*. A contract to sell peas is not performed by supplying beans. A contract to sell a tractor is not performed by supplying three horses. The same point was made by Dodd J. in *Fogarty v. Dickson*[82] when he said "[i]f a man orders a golf cloth cap, the order is not fulfilled by sending him a stylish silk hat." See also the case of *American Can Co. v. Stewart*.[83] The solution is different, however, if the contract gives the supplier the freedom to supply goods that may not meet the description and if at the same time an exemption clause limits liability for the loss occasioned by the supply of these goods, as in *George Mitchell (Chesterhall) Ltd. v. Finney Lock Seeds Ltd.*[84] when the House of Lords held that a limitation clause was effective at common law when the supplier of seeds provided cabbage seeds of the "wrong" variety which produced a commercially useless crop due to climatic conditions and incorrect crop husbandry.

During the 1950s and 1960s the response of many members of the English judiciary to the problem of exemption clauses that had been imposed by one party on another, or had been included in a contract to which the other party had not freely consented, was to develop a rule of substantive law, expressed by Denning L.J. (as he then was), in the following terms: "[e]xempting clauses of this kind, no matter how widely they are expressed only avail the party when he is carrying out his contract in its essential respects." So the supply of a car that was totally incapable of propulsion could not be excused by a sweeping clause: see *Karsales (Harrow) v. Wallis*.[85] The supply of a tipping lorry that could not tip because of a defect in the hydraulic system was found to be fundamental breach: *Astley Industrial Trust v. Grimley*.[86] Theft by persons unknown of a carpet bailed for cleaning purposes too may constitute a fundamental breach of the cleaning contract, against which an exemption clause may not prevail: *Levison v. Patent Steam Carpet Cleaning Co.*[87] Cases that are decided by reference to such methods operate regardless of the intention of the parties and represent a belated, wrongheaded, but well intentioned effort to redress doctrinal difficulties and protect persons from sweeping or draconian exemption clauses.

This is the doctrine of fundamental breach of contract. The difficulty with this rule of law (as many critics have pointed out) is that it treats all exemption clauses and all parties as if they were alike; in fact there are cases where it may

---

[82]  (1913) 47 I.L.T.R. 281.
[83]  (1915) 50 I.L.T.R. 132.
[84]  [1983] 2 A.C. 803.
[85]  [1956] 1 W.L.R. 936.
[86]  [1963] 2 All E.R. 33.
[87]  [1978] Q.B. 69.

be reasonable to permit a limiting clause to operate so as to "shrink" the core obligation, thereby reallocating risk. The House of Lords in the *Suisse Atlantique*[88] case rejected this rule of substantive law, commenting *obiter* that the doctrine of fundamental breach was simply a rule of construction. In the later case of *Harbutt's Plasticine v. Wayne Tank Corp.*[89] the unsatisfactory nature of the fundamental breach doctrine was illustrated. The plaintiffs contracted with the defendants who were to install pipes into the plaintiffs' new factory where plasticine would be manufactured. Molten plasticine was to pass along the plastic pipes installed by the defendants, as per specification. Unfortunately the pipes were not strong enough for the task and the molten plasticine caused the pipes to melt, resulting in the total loss of the factory. The parties had agreed that for any loss caused by the defendants, damages payable would be limited to £15,000. Now this agreement was struck between two commercial concerns, both of whom had the right to consult lawyers. The agreement was obviously drafted by lawyers and the clause clearly covered the case. Insurance was to be arranged on the basis of this agreement but, because of the fundamental breach doctrine, reliance on the clause was denied to the defendants. The House of Lords in *Photo Production Ltd. v. Securicor Transport Ltd.*[90] have overruled *Harbutt's Plasticine* as being a doctrine of law of doubtful parentage.

The facts of *Photo Production Ltd. v. Securicor Transport Ltd.* concern a contract for the supply of security services in respect of the plaintiff's factory premises, the main dangers to the property being fire and theft. Under the contract the defendant agreed to provide services by patrolmen but standard conditions excluded liability for the acts or omissions of employees unless these could have been forseen and avoided by acts of due diligence by the employer, namely, the defendant. A patrolman started a fire which caused total destruction of the premises. It was not established that the patrolman intended to destroy the factory and there was no suggestion that the defendant had not exercised care in recruiting patrolmen in general, and this patrolman in particular. The court of first instance and the Court of Appeal held that the limiting clause could not be relied upon. In particular, Denning M.R. in the Court of Appeal considered whether the breach was fundamental and, after concluding that it was, held that the court could deprive the proferens of the exemption or limitation clause. The Court of Appeal's decision, in the view of the House of Lords, was insupportable, based as it was on *Harbutt's Plasticine*, a decision inconsistent with *Suisse Atlantique*. The issue for every court when interpreting an exception clause of any kind was said by Lord Wilberforce to rest entirely on principles of construction:

> "the question whether, and to what extent, an exclusion clause is to be applied to a fundamental breach, or a breach of a fundamental term, or

---

[88] *Suisse Atlantique Societe d'Armement Maritime SA v. NV. Rotterdamsche Kolen Centrale* [1967] 1 A.C. 361.
[89] [1970] 1 Q.B. 447.
[90] [1980] 2 W.L.R. 283.

indeed to any breach of contract, is a matter of construction of the contract . . . there are ample resources in the normal rules of contract law for dealing with these without the superimposition of a judicially invented rule of law."[91]

In the Commonwealth the *Photo Production* approach has been willingly followed by judges who are keen to reinstate an intelligible and coherent note into the common law. The Supreme Court of Canada in *Beaufort Realties (1964) Inc. v. Belcourt Construction (Ottawa) Ltd.*[92] adopted *Photo Production*. The High Court of Australia has also abandoned the fundamental breach as a rule of law approach, holding in the case of *Nissho Iwai Australia v. Malaysian International Shipping*[93] that a sweeping exception clause may operate even when defective performance of an obligation leads to the total loss, or self-induced frustration, of the contract in question.

## Fundamental Breach in Ireland

This recent line of development will no doubt cause the Irish Supreme Court to reconsider its own approach in the leading case of *Clayton Love v. B + I Transport.*[94] The parties contracted to transport deep frozen scampi from Dublin to Liverpool. The loading was conducted at atmospheric temperature and this led to the scampi deteriorating to the extent that it was condemned when it arrived in Liverpool. The plaintiffs sued but were met by two exemption clauses, one of which was drafted widely enough to protect the defendants from liability. The second clause obliged the plaintiffs to claim within three days, otherwise the claim would be absolutely barred. Davitt P. at first instance relied on the substantive rule of law and (now discredited) dicta in two English cases, *Spurling Ltd. v. Bradshaw*[95] and *Smeaton Hanscomb & Co. Ltd. v. Sassoon I. Setty*[96] and refused to apply the first limiting clause. It is symptomatic of the confusion and complexity of this doctrine that Davitt P. then shifted ground and applied the second clause by holding that "it was intended to, and does in fact cover the case of a clause arising from the breach of a fundamental term of the contract." This reasoning seems to be unsatisfactory because Davitt P. applied a rule of law to the first clause and a rule of interpretation to the other limiting clause. The Supreme Court eliminated this inconsistency by holding that the rule of law must apply to the second limiting clause, regardless of the intention of the proferens. A better approach to the problem in *Clayton Love* would have been to ask if the contract had been freely

---

[91] [1980] 2 W.L.R. 283 at 288–289.
[92] (1980) 116 D.L.R. (3d) 193.
[93] (1989) 86 A.L.R. 375.
[94] (1970) 104 I.L.T.R. 157.
[95] [1956] 1 W.L.R. 461.
[96] [1953] 1 W.L.R. 1468.

negotiated; did the shipper have a choice of terms upon which he could ship his goods (as in *Slattery v. C.I.É.*, discussed above at pages 143–144). Most importantly, did the shipper know and consent to loading of such delicate frozen goods at atmospheric temperatures and did he know of the existence of this sweeping clause? It is probable that the Supreme Court would have still found in favour of the plaintiffs but they would have addressed the issues of freedom of contract and consent, factors that were not always considered by pro-fundamental breach judges.

While one must doubt whether the doctrine of *stare decisis* would be satisfied should an Irish High Court judge follow a decision of the House of Lords instead of a decision of the Irish Supreme Court, there are two cases in which the reasoning in *Photo Production* has been cited with approval. In *Western Meats*[97] Barrington J. stated *obiter* that he would be prepared to follow *Photo Production*. Similarly, in *Fitzpatrick and Harty v. Ballsbridge International Bloodstock Sales*,[98] O'Hanlon J. stated that the exemption clause in that case would be with certain exemptions wide enough to exclude a claim for damages or rescission and that a fundamental breach of contract would not be sufficient to defeat the exclusion clause unless a collateral contract could be proved. The most recent discussion of *Clayton Love* occurred in the case of *Parkarran v. M & P Construction Ltd.*[99] but the court, somewhat diplomatically, refrained from commenting on just what *Clayton Love* was authority for! While this writer agrees that the reasoning of the House of Lords is to be preferred to "the rule of law" approach approved in *Clayton Love*, it is submitted that on this point (but not on other aspects of the *Photo Production* case: see O'Hanlon J. in *British Leyland Exports Ltd. v. Brittain Group Sales*) repudiation of *Clayton Love* must of course await a Supreme Court decision.

In the present uncertain climate it is hardly surprising to find that it remains a common practice for a litigant to plead that an exemption clause will be defeated by a finding of fundamental breach. The most recently reported case on this is *Regan v. The Irish Automobile Club Ltd. and Others*[100] the facts of which are that the plaintiff was injured while acting as a flag marshall for the Irish Automobile Club at a motor racing event in Phoenix Park, Dublin. She argued that the failure to provide safety barriers at the point where the accident occurred was a fundamental breach which disentitled the defendants from relying on an exemption clause that, on its construction, covered negligence of the defendants. While Lynch J. was able to avoid the fundamental breach plea by holding that there was insufficient evidence of a fundamental breach, the learned judge observed:

> "I am not to be taken as either accepting or rejecting the proposition that a fundamental breach of contract will necessarily have the results

---

[97] [1982] I.L.R.M. 101.
[98] Unreported, High Court., February 25, 1983.
[99] Unreported, High Court, November 11, 1995.
[100] [1990] I.R. 278.

submitted on behalf of the plaintiff, having regard to cases decided since the decision in *Clayton Love*."

To summarise: the exemption clause which attacks the core obligation does not attack mere conditions or warranties but the foundation of the contract. If this is the case then the courts should consider whether the parties are contracting in circumstances which show that risk is being freely and voluntarily redistributed by the contract. The courts will lean against enforcement of unconscionable bargains and illusory promises by using the rules and principles specifically developed to deal with such agreements, but, at the end of the day, it may be apparent that the parties have effectively contracted in such terms as to make it clear that one party has freely agreed to take the entire risk. In the 1894 case of *Devitt v. Glasgow, Dublin & Londonderry Steam Packet Company* a common carrier was held able to rely on his conditions of contract so as to avoid liability for the loss of part of a cargo he had contracted to transport from Dublin to Glasgow. Andrews J. stated:

> "The law imposes on carriers by sea the liability of common carriers, but the obligations thus implied are all the subject of contract, and if the parties think fit to contract themselves out of these obligations, they can, no matter how hard the result may be."[101]

## Refusal to Apply Exemption Clauses

An exemption clause will not be allowed to operate if someone assents to a clause, the terms of which are misrepresented by the proferens or his ostensible agent. It seems immaterial whether the misrepresentation is fraudulent or innocent. For an example where such an argument was raised see *Bolland v. Waterford, Limerick & Western Railway.*[102]

If an oral undertaking is given by the proferens the courts will regard the oral undertaking as taking priority over the printed terms in a standard form agreement: see *Evans v. Merzario.*[103] If, however, the oral undertaking is inconsistent with a document that was specifically drafted to record the agreement then it may be that the courts will feel compelled by the last vestiges of the parol evidence rule to give effect to the written terms.

An exemption clause which excludes "all warranties" may not be held applicable to "collateral warranties" unless "collateral warranties" are expressly negatived: see *Andrews v. Hopkinson*[104] and *Gallagher Ltd. v. British Road Services Ltd. and Another.*[105]

---

[101]  29 I.L.T.R. 30 at 32.
[102]  (1897) 31 I.L.T.R. 62.
[103]  [1976] 1 W.L.R. 1078.
[104]  [1957] 1 Q.B. 229
[105]  [1974] 2 Lloyd's Rep. 440.

Perhaps the most important basis upon which to justify a judicial refusal to apply an exemption clause is the equitable jurisdiction to provide relief against unconscionable bargains. While this doctrine is well established in the context of real property transactions and in several other contractual settings where the parties can be said to stand in a defined or fiduciary relationship to one another, there are only isolated instances where the doctrine has been considered relevant to exemption clauses. While Denning M.R. was prepared to canvass the adoption of such an expansion of the unconscionability doctrine in *Gillespie Bros. & Co. Ltd. v. Bowles (Roy) Ltd.,*[106] the courts have tended towards the view that interference with contractual allocations of risk should be seen as a matter for legislative interference only. However, the use of the concept of fair dealing in the context of incorporation rules by Costello J. in *Carroll v. An Post National Lottery Company* suggests that the day when an Irish court refuses to apply an exemption clause because the clause offends against this concept *as a matter of substantive result,* may not be far off. Indeed, in the Canadian case of *Atlas Supply Co. of Canada Ltd. v. Yarmouth Equipment Ltd*[107] a one-sided franchising agreement was set aside as unconscionable. The stronger party had managed to negative certain warranties that he had given by way of exclusion clauses. This decision has been criticised because of the commercial uncertainty it is said to engender.[108]

## Exemption Clauses and Third Parties

The principle known as privity of contract should, at first sight, provide a clear answer to the question of whether a third party can rely upon an exemption or limitation clause contained in a contract to which the third party is not privy. The answer should be in the negative, for it is axiomatic that only a party to a contract may enforce the contract or be the subject of obligations under it. Like most common law principles, however, the courts have tempered the doctrinal implications of the privity rule by reference to certain business realities and expectations. There are three areas of commercial activity where the privity rule has been drastically pruned back.

First, in contracts of carriage, whereby goods or persons are transported for reward, it frequently occurs that part of the contractual obligations due may be performed on behalf of the carrier by others. It was decided in *Adler v. Dickson*[109] that an exemption clause contained in a contract concluded between a shipping company and the plaintiff was not available to an employee of the shipping company when the plaintiff was injured by reason of the negligence of the employee on leaving the vessel in which he was sailing. The leading case is *Scruttons Ltd. v. Midland Silicones.*[110] The case concerned a contract of

---

[106]  [1973] Q.B. 400.
[107]  (1991) 103 N.S.R. (2nd) 1.
[108]  Da Re (1996) 27 C.B.L.J. 426.
[109]  [1955] 1 Q.B. 158.
[110]  [1962] A.C. 446.

carriage under which the carriers limited their liability for damage to goods transported by the carriers under the contract. The goods were damaged by stevedores engaged by the carrier, and the stevedores, in an action brought against them by the owners, unsuccessfully sought to rely on the exemption clause in the contract of carriage. This decision is doctrinally sound and, on construction of the clause, is defensible, as the protection of the limiting clause was only available to carriers and persons bound by the bill of lading, which did not include the stevedores. It is not, however, the last word on this question. The Privy Council has decided that if the exemption clause is properly worded, the third party provides consideration under a separate contract, and due performance is intended by both contracting parties to entitle the third party to avail of the clause, then the limitation clause can be relied upon: *The Eurymedon*.[111] The decision in the *Eurymedon* is a controversial one, although in some respects it merely re-instates the decision of the House of Lords in *Elder, Dempster & Co. v. Patterson Zochonis & Co.*[112] In this case, a unanimous House of Lords held that there were circumstances in which a third party could rely upon an exemption clause contained in a contract concluded between two other parties. More recent commonwealth cases affirm the view that if third parties are intended to be protected, this commercial expectation will be given effect, notwithstanding the doctrinal niceties of the traditional common law theory of privity of contract. In *Glebe Island Terminals Property Ltd. v. Continental Seagram Property Ltd*[113] an exemption clause was held to apply to exclude both the carrier and terminal operator who were each in fundamental breach in making unauthorised delivery to an unauthorised person. The consignee was held bound by a clause that expressly stated there would be no liability for a fundamental breach. However, in a later case a court in Victoria stressed the need for the clause to be drafted in clear language, especially in cases of fundamental breach, if clauses are not to be "read down" or denied effect by a court when the *proferens* is trying to exclude liability for the deliberate wrongs of his employees.[114]

Secondly, the courts have recently provided an exception to the privity rule in respect of certain types of construction contract. The cases which develop this exception have a basic set of facts which, boldly and directly, raise the privity doctrine. A construction contract is concluded between an employer and a main contractor. The contract provides that neither the main contractor nor the sub-contractor, nor their servants or agents, shall be liable in respect of defects in the construction work. In the first decision on this particular aspect of the problem, *Southern Water Authority v. Carey*,[115] the exclusion clause specifically referred to the defendant sub-contractor, and was concluded on the standard terms of the Institute of Mechanical Engineers/Institute of Electrical

---

[111] [1974] 1 All E.R. 1015.
[112] [1924] A.C. 522.
[113] (1993) 40 N.S.W.L.R. 206.
[114] *Kamil Export (Australia) Property Ltd. v. PPL Australia Property* [1996] 1 V.R. 538.
[115] [1985] 2 All E.R. 1077; *The Pioneer Container* [1994] 2 All E.R. 250.

Engineers Model Contract Form A, which stated that the main contractor contracted on his own behalf and as trustee for his sub-contractors, servants or agents. The Official Referee, Judge Smout held that in these circumstances the defendant could rely on the exclusion clause.

The decision of the Court of Appeal in *Norwich City Council v. Harvey*[116] represents a significant extension of the *Carey* case because the exemption clause in the contract between employer and main contractor clearly protected the main contractor but did not expressly refer to sub-contractors and failed to specify that the main contractor acted as agent or trustee of the sub-contractor for the purpose of the exemption clause. Notwithstanding lack of privity of contract, the fact that the sub-contractor had contracted on the basis that the exemption clause would be available to him meant that it would not be just and equitable to deprive the sub-contractor of protection under the exemption clause. Again, the practice in the industry, when the JCT Standard Form of Building Contract was used, as here, was to regard the employer as liable to bear the risk in question and for the employer to arrange insurance, regardless of the fact that the contract document itself did not reflect this reality.

Thirdly, the law of bailment provides a *sui generis* exception to the privity rule when a sub-bailee is sued in respect of loss of, or damage to, goods which have been bailed to the sub-bailee under a contract between bailee and sub-bailee. While in the case of *Morris v. Martin & Sons Ltd.*[117] Denning L.J. stated, *obiter*, that an appropriately worded clause could be effective, the issue has been directly confronted by Steyn J. in *Singer Co. (U.K.) and Another v. Tees and Hartlepool Port Authority*.[118] The plaintiff company, Singer, had engaged another company, Bachman (U.K.) Ltd., to arrange to load a drilling machine owned by Singer onto a vessel. Bachman (U.K.) Ltd., contracted as principals with the defendants in order to engage the defendants to load the machine. The machine was damaged by the defendants and when sued in negligence and bailment the defendants relied on standard conditions in the contract between themselves and Bachman (U.K.) Ltd. Steyn J. held that the defendants, as sub-bailees, could rely on the terms in the contract between themselves and the bailee, even against a bailor who is not contractually linked with the sub-bailee. The fact that the bailor authorised the bailee to contract with a sub-bailee meant that the bailor was bound by terms found in that contract. While Steyn J. refused to rule on the scope of this bailment principle, the case is a significant one.

---

[116] [1989] 1 All E.R. 1180.
[117] [1966] 1 Q.B. 716; *Spectra International plc v. Hayesoak* [1997] 1 Lloyd's Rep. 153.
[118] [1988] 2 Lloyd's Rep. 164.

# 8 Consumer Protection

## Introduction

In the previous chapter we considered the scope of the judicial power to control the use of exemption clauses. While no real dichotomy can be drawn between legislative and judicial attempts to control the possibilities of abuse of freedom of contract, when one party transfers a risk to another person through the medium of contract, the statutory provisions do provide a degree of protection for persons who do not contract "in the course of business". The need for greater legislative protection of the consumer than that afforded by the common law was recognised by Lord Reid in *Suisse Atlantique* when he considered the practical consequences of the substantive law doctrine of fundamental breach.

> "Exemption clauses differ greatly in many respects. Probably the most objectionable are found in the complex standard conditions which are now so common. In the ordinary way the customer has no time to read them, and if he did read them he would probably not understand them. And if he did understand and object to any of them, he would generally be told he could take it or leave it. And if he then went to another supplier the result would be the same. Freedom to contract must surely imply some choice or room for bargaining.
>
> At the other extreme is the case where parties are bargaining on terms of equality and a stringent exemption clause is accepted for a *quid pro quo* or other good reason. But this rule appears to treat all cases alike. There is no indication in the recent cases that the courts are to consider whether the exemption is fair in all the circumstances or is harsh and unconscionable or whether it was freely agreed by the customer. And it does not seem to me to be satisfactory that the decision must always go one way if, *e.g.* defects in a car or other goods are just sufficient to make the breach of contract a fundamental breach, but must always go the other way if the defects fall just short of that. This is a complex problem which intimately affects millions of people and it appears to me that its solution should be left to Parliament. If your Lordships reject this new rule there will certainly be a need for urgent legislative action but that is not beyond reasonable expectation."[1]

One is tempted to remark that the legislative reforms achieved in England and Ireland since the 1960s largely explain why the judiciary have felt able to

---

[1] [1967] 1 A.C. 361 at 406.

discard the "fundamental breach as a rule of law" method of counteracting harsh exemption clauses.[2]

## Standard Form Contracts

It is commonplace to find that the parties to a contract have reduced the terms of the bargain into written form, notwithstanding the fact that in most instances an oral bargain is enforceable without the need for its terms to be reduced into writing or evidenced by a memorandum. It is also by no means unusual to find that the offer itself is communicated by way of a standard form document which may have been drawn up by the offeror. It is also possible for the terms of the offer – which in turn will provide the parties with their contract unless the exceptions to the parol evidence rule come into play as in *Clayton Love v. B + I Transport*[3] – to have been drawn up by the offeree and remitted to members of the public, traders and other commercial organisations. This indeed is normal practice in the insurance world where the company presents applicants with their own documentation by way of the proposal form which the applicant for insurance fills in, and, upon it being submitted to the company, an offer is made to the company on its own preferred terms. Similarly, tenders for the sale of goods or the provision of services are submitted on forms provided by the offeree.

The practice of formulating offers on standard form documents (often in tandem with a stipulation that the offer and any subsequent contract shall be determined only by reference to the standard form document and that no other statement, written or oral is to be operative) can be justified on economic grounds. Both sides benefit from the use of standard, printed conditions of contract. The cost of negotiating the contract is reduced; if the same forms and terms of contract are widely used throughout an industry or trade, the number of special conditions being kept to a minimum, then this helps each side to clarify their respective intentions and reduces the chance of mistakes or misunderstandings during the negotiation.[4]

The dangers however of allowing the standard form to invariably prevail are considerable. Standard forms are valuable simply because negotiations are truncated by virtue of their use; the possibility that persons may be able to negotiate favourable terms for themselves are substantially reduced if the contract is concluded on the terms proposed. While it is theoretically possible for the person who seeks to negotiate a particular contract to go elsewhere this option, in practice, is not always open. The terms used may be universal within a trade or industry; the bargaining position of the parties may, on the facts, be so disproportionate that the weaker party has no choice but to submit; more invidious still, the party presenting the terms may enjoy a monopoly, either by

---

[2] See in particular the Sale of Goods and Supply of Services Act 1980.
[3] (1970) 104 I.L.T.R. 157.
[4] *Llewellyn* (1931) 40 Yale L.J. 704.

virtue of being the sole provider or market leader in an industry, or by way of statute. In these instances where "freedom of contract" cannot be said to exist in any real sense the contract is a contract of adhesion.[5] The terms are presented on a take it or leave it basis; the terms are drafted by one party who seeks to impose them on others in circumstances where negotiations to modify or alter them will not take place. The party is faced with a choice – contract on the terms proposed or not at all.

It is a mistake however to see all standard form contracts as being inherently unfair; it does not follow that because a contract is proposed and concluded on standard form that the bargain is at all suspect. In *Schroeder v. Macaulay*,[6] Lord Diplock distinguished between two kinds of standard form document. The first consists of contracts which set out the terms on which mercantile transactions have traditionally been performed. Examples of such transactions include bills of lading, charterparties, policies of insurance and contracts of sale in specialist commodity markets. Because these contracts have evolved over the centuries and have stood the test of time these contracts are not generally to be treated with suspicion; indeed, the terms of these contracts are to be presumed to be fair and reasonable. In contrast, the second type of standard form contract is not generally the result of negotiation but is the result of business activities being concentrated into a few hands. Contract terms are imposed by the party with stronger bargaining power. Lord Diplock gave as an example of this second type of contract the ticket cases by which railway companies in the last century obtained effective immunity from actions brought against them by members of the public.

In Ireland this analysis has been echoed in the Supreme Court. In *McCord v. E.S.B.*[7] both Henchy J. and O'Higgins C.J., commenting on the General Conditions of Contract drawn up by the E.S.B. under their statutory obligations to provide an electricity supply, mentioned that customers must contract on the terms proposed, terms which are not only not open for negotiation but are subject to unilateral variation. Henchy J. said the real question in this case was whether the Board had the power to disconnect the supply of electricity to premises when the meter has been wrongfully interfered with (in this case without the knowledge of the occupier) and the occupier has refused to give a statement in writing setting out what he knows of the wrongdoing and giving an undertaking to pay by instalments for the electricity consumed but unrecorded. Henchy J. continued:

> "Before proceeding to answer this question, it is important to point out that the contract made between the plaintiff and the Board (incorporating the General Conditions relating to Supply) is what is nowadays called a contract of adhesion: it is a standardised mass contract which must be

---

5   Kessler (1943) 43 Col.L.Rev. 629.
6   [1974] 1 W.L.R. 1308.
7   [1980] I.L.R.M. 153.

entered into, on a take it or leave it basis, by the occupier of every premises in which electricity is to be used. The would-be consumer has no standing to ask that a single iota of the draft contract presented to him be changed before he signs it. He must lump it or leave it. But, because for reasons that are too obvious to enumerate, be cannot do without electricity, he is invariably forced by necessity into signing the contract, regardless of the fact that he may consider some of its terms arbitrary, or oppressive, or demonstrably unfair. He is compelled, from a position of weakness and necessity *vis-à-vis* a monopolist supplier of a vital commodity, to enter into what falls into the classification of a contract and which, as such, according to the theory of the common law which was evolved in the *laissez-faire* atmosphere of the nineteenth century, is to be treated by the courts as if it had emerged by choice from the forces of the market place, at the behest of parties who were at arm's length and had freedom of choice. The real facts show that such an approach is largely based on legal fictions. When a monopoly supplier of a vital public utility – which is what the Board is – force on all its consumers a common form of contract, reserving to itself sweeping powers, including the power to vary the document unilaterally as it may think fit, such an instrument has less affinity with a freely negotiated interpersonal contract than with a set of byelaws or with any other form of autonomic legislation. As such, its terms may have to be construed not simply as contractual elements but as components of a piece of delegated legislation, the validity of which will depend on whether it has kept within the express or implied confines of the statutory delegation and, even if it has, whether the delegation granted or assumed is now consistent with the provisions of the Constitution of 1937."[8]

If we confine our attention to the Statutory Conditions of Supply drafted and relied upon by the E.S.B. it is of interest to note that there has been one subsequent decision in which it was held that if the sweeping powers given to the E.S.B. are not exercised with due care and consideration for the consumer then there will be liability for breach of contract. In *Farrelly v. E.S.B.*[9] the plaintiff's electricity supply was disconnected even though he had recently paid his electricity bill. The Board's employees had acted unreasonably, ignoring the plaintiff's request to wait until the receipt could be produced. Ellis J. allowed the plaintiff's appeal from the Circuit Court and awarded a total of £600 damages. In truth the providers of public utilities can and at times do utilise their powers of cut-off in a relatively sensible way but for political reasons the powers of water authorities to discontinue supply have been constrained by legislation.[10]

There are a variety of techniques that can be utilised by the judges, who, alarmed at the possibility that superior bargaining power may be abused, are

---

[8] [1980] I.L.R.M. 153 at 161.
[9] *The Irish Times*, March 10, 1983.
[10] Local Government (Delimitation of Water Supply Disconnection Powers) Act 1995.

showing an increasing willingness to protect the weak from exploitation by the strong. One method is demonstrated by the House of Lords in *Liverpool City Council v. Irwin*.[11] The Council drafted in standard form the conditions that tenants would be bound by if they became Council tenants. The express obligations imposed on the tenant were clearly set out but the document, hardly surprisingly, was silent on the obligations the Council was to undertake in respect of their tenants. Lord Wilberforce noted that it was necessary to imply terms into the contract in order to make what appeared to be a one-sided contract truly bilateral.

In *McCord v. E.S.B.*,[12] Henchy J. indicated that in cases where the contract was presented on a take it or leave it basis, the courts will be vigilant in scrutnising the powers given under the terms of the contract to the party imposing those terms on the other. It must be said, however, that this approach is not universally endorsed. McCarthy J. in *Tradax (Ireland) Ltd. v. Irish Grain Board Ltd.*[13] doubted whether the law of contract recognised a general principle that all contract terms should be read against the party who drafted them for in McCarthy J.'s view the only case where this can occur is when the *contra proferentem* rule is applied to exemption clauses. In this writer's view this broader view of the *contra proferentem* rule should apply where the standard form contract falls within Lord Diplock's second category of standard form contract, but such a situation does not currently represent the law.

Other methods of curbing reliance on standard conditions have surfaced within the context of exception clauses. If there is a conflict between a printed term and an oral statement, or typed or hand-written statement, then the printed form will generally not be applied.[14] The most revolutionary technique has been the direct attack mounted through the unconscionable bargain doctrine. If the contract has not been freely negotiated and the result achieved is seen as unfair then the transaction should, either in whole or in part, be denied effect. Lord Reid in *Schroeder v. Macaulay*[15] said "[i]f contractual restrictions appear to be unnecessary or to be reasonably capable of enforcement in an oppressive manner, then they must be justified before they can be enforced." Lord Denning M.R., on several occasions, asserted that such a common law power was available to the courts[16] and some other judges have approved this approach as desirable although these judges have stated that in the absence of a legislation the unfairness or otherwise of a contract is irrelevant: see for example, Kerr J. in *Gallaher v. B.R.S.*[17] and O'Hanlon J. in *British Leyland Exports Ltd. v. Brittain Group Sales Ltd.*[18]

---

[11] [1977] A.C. 239.
[12] [1980] I.L.R.M. 153.
[13] [1984] I.R. 1.
[14] *Evans v. Merzario* [1976] 1 W.L.R. 1078.
[15] [1974] 1 W.L.R. 1308.
[16] *Gillespie v. Roy Bowles* [1973] Q.B. 400; *Levison v. Patent Steam Carpet Cleaning Co.* [1978] Q.B. 69.
[17] [1974] 2 Lloyd's Rep. 440.
[18] [1981] I.R. 335.

Nevertheless, section 52(1) of the Sale of Goods and Supply of Services Act 1980 empowers the Minister for Industry, Commerce and Tourism to, by order, require a person acting in the course of business who uses standard form contracts (within the scope of the Act) to serve notice on the public such information as the order may specify as to the user of this form and whether or not he is willing to contract on any other terms. No orders have been made under section 52(1).

## Consumer Protection through the Criminal Law

Parliament may direct that it is in the interests of all consumers that traders are prevented from selling goods that fail to reach a satisfactory standard. This of course will be particularly so if the goods consist of foodstuffs that are unfit for human consumption and to this end the Public Health (Ireland) Act 1878, section 132 empowers the inspectorate to inspect foodstuffs that are unfit for human consumption and section 133 makes it an offence to expose for sale such foodstuffs. The Sale of Food and Drugs Acts 1875–1936 provide, *inter alia* that it is an offence to mix into foodstuffs any ingredient or material which thus renders the article injurious to health with the intent that the article will be sold. While the offence is not one of strict liability the defence outlined in section 25 of the 1875 Act will be difficult to establish: see *Duffy v. Sutton*.[19] Other legislative provisions exist in order to prevent or control the extent to which chemical substances and drugs may be used in an attempt to ensure that such substances do not find their way into foodstuffs, for example, by way of chemical or antibiotic residue in meats, cereals and dairy products.[20] The controversy over bovine spongiform encephalopathy or "mad cow" disease, and the possibility that this could enter the human food chain, led to stringent measures[21] that have kept the incidence of the disease in Ireland low in comparison with the United Kingdom.

Many pieces of public health legislation now have their origins in Brussels in the form of directives which are then implemented via delegated legislation under section 3 of the European Communities Act 1972. Although there are many examples of this process, two statutory instruments, dealing with issues of the scientific debate, provide good examples of how European Community directives may inhibit freedom of contract for the greater public good, the penalty for non-observance being criminal rather than civil in nature. For example, under the European Communities (Egg Products) Regulations 1991,[22] a person is not to produce as a foodstuff, or for use in the manufacture of a foodstuff, any egg products unless that person complies with Directive

---

[19] [1955] I.R. 248.

[20] *e.g.* S.I. No. 236 of 1986; S.I. No. 221 of 1997.

[21] *e.g.* S.I. No. 61 of 1989; S.I. No. 79 and 80 of 1997.

[22] S.I. No. 293 of 1991, implementing Council Directive 89/437/EEC of June 20, 1989 on hygiene and health problems affecting the production and the placing on the market of egg products [1989] O.J. L212/87.

89/437/EEC. Storage and transportation of egg products are also to be carried out under compliance with the Directive. The production, use in manufacture and packaging of egg products are to be carried out in establishments approved by the Minister for Industry and Commerce. Powers of entry, inspection, search and seizure are given to authorised officers, and in some instances Commissioners of Customs and Excise, and a wide range of criminal offences, to be prosecuted by the Minister, are set out. A second example of this kind of legislation is provided by the European Communities (Materials and Articles intended to come into Contact with Foodstuffs) Regulations 1991.[23] Concern over the possibility that some packaging may be carcinogenic or otherwise harmful, led to a number of directives dealing with packaging and wrappings which came into contact with human foodstuffs being regulated. The statutory instrument sets out a general prohibition on the manufacture, sale, importation or use of certain substances when used in the course of a business, for food storage or preparation. The use of vinyl chloride monomer, regenerated cellulose film, ceramics and plastics is regulated, and the Minister for Industry and Commerce has powers of entry, inspection, search and seizure and is competent to prosecute offenders.

Leaving the area of public health legislation to one side, it must also be realised that the consumer needs to be protected from producers, wholesalers and retailers who, while supplying foodstuffs and other goods which are not dangerous, would be supplying goods that fall below a standard the consumer can reasonably expect. The creation of government agencies to regulate the quality of goods and in particular foodstuffs must be seen as an attempt to improve the product the consumer can reasonably expect to buy. This can be done by laying down minimum standards that the producer or seller must meet in respect to the product. The Food Safety Authority of Ireland, established by way of the Food Safety Authority of Ireland Act 1998, is charged with the principal function of ensuring that Irish produced or distributed food meets the hightest standards of food safety and in particular that such food meets legislative standards. Powers of prosecution are contained in the legislation.[24] An alternative route is by requiring growers and wholesalers to provide a method by which the consumer can identify the producer – under pain of a fine for failure to comply with the legislation – so as to give purchasers a greater opportunity of recovering in the civil courts by way of contract or tort. The obligation on potato growers and packers to register and identify themselves on packages sold by them is an example of this kind of provision, enacted under the Registration of Potato Growers and Packers Act 1984.[25] The most significant example of the use of the criminal law as a method of consumer protection is to be found in the provisions of the Consumer Information Act 1978 which builds upon the provisions of the Merchandise Marks Act 1887.

---

[23]  S.I. No. 307 of 1991; S.I. No. 226 of 1996.
[24]  See in particular sections 11 and 57.
[25]  See (1984) *Irish Current Law Statutes Annotated* (Round Hall Sweet & Maxwell) 84/24–01.

The Act amends the 1887 Act by substituting a wide definition of "trade description" and "fair trade description" so as to broaden the offence of applying a false trade description in section 2(1)(*d*) of the 1887 Act. The definition of trade description includes descriptions or statements, direct or indirect, as to weight and size of the goods, country of origin or processing, method of manufacture, identity of manufacturer, the material from which the goods have been made, fitness for purpose: see section 2(1). The 1978 Act also creates two new offences; section 6(1) provides that if a person in the course of or for the purposes of a trade, business or profession makes a false statement or a statement which is made recklessly, as to, *inter alia*, the nature, effect, fitness for purpose of any services so provided, he shall be guilty of an offence. Section 7 also creates a new offence in relation to false or misleading indications as to the price of goods, services and accommodation. The statutory defences are restricted – see sections 3(2) and 22 of the 1978 Act – and a court has the power to order that any fine imposed may be paid to the person to whom injury or loss has been occasioned: see section 17(3) and *Director of Consumer Affairs v. Sunshine Holidays.*[26] The Director of Consumer Affairs and his Department are charged with enforcement of the legislation. It has not proved necessary to prosecute in order to resolve all complaints satisfactorily. In 1984 proceedings were taken in relation to 12 out of 541 complaints. By 1989 the figures had reached 39 prosecutions from over 700 complaints. The powers and responsibilities of the Director and his officers are set out in the legislation. These are extended from time to time – see for example, sections 55–57 of the Sale of Goods and Supply of Services Act 1980. The investigative procedure under the 1978 Act was considered in *Director of Consumer Affairs v. Joe Walsh Tours Ltd.*[27]

Under the terms of the Consumer Information Act 1978 the Minister for Industry and Commerce has the power to provide, by statutory instrument, distinct standards that must be satisfied by traders. One of the most important examples is found in the Consumer Information (Advertisements) (Disclosure of Business Interests) Order 1984.[28] This Order requires that all advertisements made in the course of a trade, business or profession must make it clear to the public that the advertiser is engaged in business. The Order was made largely to counteract "small ad" motor dealers who, by publishing individual small advertisements in the press, may lead persons to believe that the sale is a private sale which does not therefore attract the protection to the buyer afforded by the Sale of Goods Acts. The advertising media is obliged by the Order to check the advertisement and make it clear that the advertiser is a dealer (*e.g.* by adding words if necessary) and prosecutions are possible against traders and advertising agencies, newspapers and others who fail to comply with the Order. The other statutory order that is directed at unscrupulous trading is the Consumer Information (Consumer Credit) Order 1987.[29] Under this Order legally binding

---

[26] [1984] I.L.R.M. 551.
[27] [1985] I.L.R.M. 273.
[28] S.I. No. 168 of 1984.
[29] S.I. No. 319 of 1987.

definitions of consumer credit agreements are set out, and any advertisement that comes within the ambit of the Order must, if it makes reference to the cost of credit, additionally indicate the true cost of credit by means of an annual percentage rate of charge (APR). The display on premises of a credit offer must also include a statement of APR. Where the credit offer is linked to the purchase of goods or services, the APR, cash price, total credit price, and the rate and number of instalments must also be indicated. The 1987 Consumer Credit Order has been supplanted by the new Consumer Credit regime, introduced by the Consumer Credit Act 1995, mentioned in outline in Chapter 4.

## Statutory Protection and Civil Remedies

The Sale of Goods and Supply of Services Act 1980 is the most significant piece of consumer protection legislation since the founding of the State. The Act, in part, builds upon the Sale of Goods Act 1893 and the Hire Purchase Acts 1946–1960 and it also extends some degree of protection into areas of commercial activity which have been ignored altogether by the legislature; this is particularly so when the contract involved a contract for the provision of a service rather than sale or hire purchase of goods. Part VI of the Act provides some degree of protection from commercial activities that are seen as unfair, for example, unsolicited goods (section 47). The Hire Purchase Acts however have recently been replaced by the provisions of Part VI of the Consumer Credit Act 1995. It is also to be noted that in relation to credit agreements, section 42 of the 1995 Act not only does not prejudice the operation of the 1980 Act *vis-à-vis* suppliers, section 42 also gives the buyer recourse rights against the creditor in certain circumstances.

## Sale of Goods

The Sale of Goods Act 1893 was never intended to apply as a comprehensive measure under which traders and suppliers were closely controlled, by statute, from dealing with consumers in such a way as to exploit their superior bargaining power. In fact the concept of the consumer was alien to the 1893 Act for the Act was a codifying statute which put into statutory form the law as it had evolved by way of mercantile practice. As these rules had evolved in the marketplace amongst traders it is difficult not to see the relevance of Lord Diplock's bifurcation of standard form contracts[30] being directly relevant here too; in such a case (*i.e.* where both parties are traders) there is little or no reason to hold that the statutory provisions are in any sense prima facie likely to lead to unfair results. Nevertheless the 1893 Act did amend the law in several respects; section 12, considered below, was not representative of the

---

[30] In *Schroeder v. Macaulay* [1974] 1 W.L.R. 1308.

common law position, should the seller of goods not have title to them. Perhaps the most significant provisions in the 1893 Act are set out in sections 12–15, as amended by the 1980 Act. These provisions are now only to be avoided by contrary express agreement, *i.e.* by an exemption clause, if it can be shown that the buyer does not deal as a consumer and it can be shown that the provision is fair and reasonable.[31]

## Section 12

Section 12(1) of the 1893 Act sets out two obligations:

(a) an implied condition in a contract of sale that the seller has the right to sell the goods and, in relation to an agreement to sell, that the seller will have the right to sell the goods, at the time property is to pass; and

(b) an implied warranty that the goods are, and will remain free until the time when property is to pass from any encumbrances not disclosed to the buyer and that the buyer shall enjoy quiet possession except in relation to encumbrances disclosed at the time of sale.

Section 12(1) is broken when the seller has no right to dispose of the property, not simply because the goods were stolen by the seller but also if the seller purchased goods, in good faith, believing that thereby he acquired a good title to them: see *Rowland v. Divall*[32] and *O'Reilly v. Fineman*.[33] Section 12(1) is also broken if the buyer acquires a good title to the goods but a third party could have, at the time of the sale, obtained an injunction to restrain the sale because the labels attached to the goods infringed a trademark of that third party: see *Niblett v. Confectioner's Materials Co.*,[34] or infringed a patent held by another: see *Microbeads A.C. v. Vinehurst Road Markings*.[35] Because section 12(1) is a condition there is a right to reject the goods and claim the purchase price back without the buyer being obliged to make an allowance for any benefits received. Consequential loss may also be recoverable: see *Stock v. Urey*.[36] Section 12(2) enables the parties to limit the obligation in section 12(1) should the seller be unsure of his right to sell the goods. If the terms of section 12(2) are complied with and the buyer's quiet possession is disturbed at sometime in the future, the remedy sounds in damages only.

---

[31] s.55(4) of the 1893 Act, as inserted by s.22 of the 1980 Act.
[32] [1923] 2 K.B. 500.
[33] [1942] Ir.Jur.Rep. 36.
[34] [1921] 3 K.B. 387.
[35] [1975] 1 W.L.R. 218.
[36] [1957] N.I. 71.

# Section 13

Section 13 enacts an implied condition that where goods are sold by description they will correspond with the description. While at first sight this implied condition simply appears to restate the obvious – that goods expressly described in the contract must meet the description – there are several advantages for the buyer in relying on section 13 rather than the general law. Firstly, the term is labelled a condition. Rescission is available under the Statute. It is not necessary to show it is a condition expressly so agreed or under *Bentsen & Son v. Taylor*.[37] Secondly, description under section 13(3) extends to "a reference to goods on a label or other descriptive matter accompanying the goods." The packaging of the goods may form part of the description: *Re Moore & Co. v. Landauer & Co.*[38] It is also established by both English (see *Wren v. Holt*[39]) and Irish (*O'Connor v. Donnelly*[40]) cases that the goods may be sold by description even if they are before the buyer, as long as the buyer relies on the description.[41] In the Irish case of *O'Connor v. Donnelly* the plaintiff suffered injury when consuming a tin of salmon. While there was no reliance on the seller's skill and judgment so as to bring the case within section 14 both the Circuit Court and High Court affirmed the view that there can be a sale of goods by description even if the goods are shown to the buyer. Judge Davitt in the Circuit Court said that, in order to recover, the buyer must rely upon the description in establishing the essential characteristic of the goods and not simply a quality to be attributed to the goods.

A further advantage of relying on section 13 follows from the fact that if the buyer does not deal in the course of business it is now impossible to exclude liability under section 13 for failure to provide goods that correspond with their description. In some of the cases the courts indicated that an appropriately worded exclusion clause may have enabled the seller to exclude liability in such a case: see Scrutton L.J.'s remarks in *Andrews v. Singer*.[42] If, however, the buyer does not deal as consumer an exemption clause may operate as long as it is fair and reasonable.

# Section 14

Section 14 of the 1893 Act, as amended, is in many respects the cornerstone of Irish Consumer Protection Law where the quality of goods provided under a contract fall below the expected standard.

---

[37] [1893] 2 Q.B. 271.
[38] [1921] 2 K.B. 519.
[39] [1903] 1 K.B. 610.
[40] [1944] Ir.Jur.Rep. 1.
[41] *Harlingdon and Leinster Enterprises v. Christopher Hull Fine Art Ltd.* [1990] 1 All E.R. 737; *Bolands Ltd. v. Trouw Ireland Ltd.* unreported, High Court, May 1, 1978; *O'Regan and Co. v. Micro-Bio Ltd.*, unreported, High Court, February 26, 1980.
[42] [1934] 1 K.B. 17.

*Section 14(2)*

Section 14(2), as amended by the 1980 Act, provides that where a seller sells goods in the course of business there is an implied condition as to merchantability, as defined in section 14(3), except in regard:

(a) to defects specifically drawn to the buyers attention before contract; or,

(b) if an examination is made prior to contracting, to defects the examination ought to have revealed.

The definition of merchantable has troubled the courts for decades for it was not defined in the 1893 Act. The amended section 14(3) now provides a definition:

> "goods are of merchantable quality if they are as fit for the purpose or purposes for which goods of that kind are commonly bought and are as durable as it is reasonable to expect having regard to any description applied to them, the price (if relevant) and all the other relevant circumstances."

This flexible definition of merchantable quality has yet to be considered in Ireland in any reported case. There are several decisions from the United Kingdom which are of some assistance in fleshing out this concept. In many instances the problem arises in contracts for the sale of a motor vehicle. Even where a vehicle is new there are decisions which indicate that some defects are not such as to make the vehicle unmerchantable. In *Leaves v. Wadham Stringer*[43] the vehicle supplied had a leaking boot, a defective bonnet light, a loose door, some rust and a defective fanbelt. The vehicle was nevertheless held merchantable. In contrast, in *Rogers v. Parish (Scarborough) Ltd.*,[44] a new Range Rover was supplied with a misfiring engine, excessive noise from the gearbox and transfer box, and substantial defects on the bodywork. The Court of Appeal held that a motor vehicle capable of being satisfactorily driven could nevertheless constitute a breach of the merchantable quality implied condition. Given the fact that the vehicle was a prestige model, a Range Rover, the description created expectations that would not necessarily arise in a less up-market marque; the price paid was also relevant and because the price paid here was greater than an average family saloon, the buyer had a right to expect a vehicle which surpassed that which was actually supplied to him. In general, however, motor vehicles which are defective will not be merchantable if the performance of the car is prejudiced, the defect cannot be easily remedied or repair will be expensive or take some time to perform: *Bernstein v. Pamson Motors (Golders Green) Ltd.*[45] applying the leading case of *Bartlett v. Sidney Marcus*.[46]

---

43 [1980] R.T.R. 308.
44 [1987] 2 All E.R. 232.
45 [1987] 2 All E.R. 220.
46 [1965] 2 All E.R. 753.

Where the vehicle is second hand the traditional view of protection available to the consumer has been far from generous. In *Bartlett v. Sidney Marcus*, Denning M.R. indicated that a vehicle is merchantable if it is in usable condition even if not perfect. The standard has risen in relation to "exclusive" or prestige models, following *Shine v. General Guarantee Corporation*[47] and in a recent Northern Ireland case the Denning M.R. test was denied a literal application. Carswell J., in *Lutton v. Saville Tractors Ltd.*[48] held in favour of the purchaser of a three-year-old Ford Escort XR3 who found the vehicle unsatisfactory and although the defects were minor, performance was clearly affected. Given the age, the price paid, the model involved, and the low mileage, the buyer could expect a better vehicle than that provided, particularly when given an express warranty in relation to the vehicle. Carswell J. indicated that if the vehicle was an older model, with higher mileage, sold at a lower price and did not create expectations of high performance, defects of the kind detected would not have rendered it unmerchantable. On the test of merchantable quality Carswell J. indicated that the Denning M.R. test in *Bartlett v. Sidney Marcus*

> "is not universally valid in sales of second hand cars, nor would Lord Denning have intended it to be. At the end of the day a decision whether a car is of merchantable quality is a matter of fact and degree, and it is essential to take account of the factors specified in the statutory definition."[49]

The merchantable quality test can still produce some surprising results, as the case of *Harlingdon Ltd. v. Hull Fine Art Ltd.*[50] shows. A painting, wrongly thought to be by a particular German expressionist was sold for £6,000. When it was discovered to be a forgery the purchaser sought rescission as it was of a much lower value. The Court of Appeal, by a majority, held the painting still to be merchantable, mainly because the work could still be appreciated in an aesthetic sense even though its value was between £50 and £100.

*Section 14(4)*

While at common law a sale of goods creates an implied warranty as to fitness (*Shiels v. Cannon*[51]), section 14(4) of the 1980 Act gives added protection to the buyer. This provision, the successor to section 14(1) of the 1893 Act, implies a condition into every contract for the sale of goods that where the buyer, expressly or by implication, makes known to the seller any particular purpose for which the goods are bought, the goods supplied should be reasonably fit for that purpose. While the seller must sell goods in the course of a business, this

---

[47] [1988] 1 All E.R 911.
[48] [1986] N.I. 327.
[49] *Ibid.* at 336.
[50] [1990] 1 All E.R. 737.
[51] (1865) 16 I.C.L.R. 588.

alone will not entitle the buyer to succeed for the section goes on to provide that the condition does not apply if the circumstances show the buyer did not rely on it, or it would have been unreasonable for the buyer to have relied on the seller's skill and judgment. The fitness for purpose condition in section 14(4) obviously overlaps with the merchantability condition in section 14(2). A copper detonator included in a bag of coal renders the coal supplied both unmerchantable and unfit for its purpose: *Egan v. McSweeney*.[52] Foodstuffs which, unknown to the seller are unsound at the time of sale are also both unmerchantable and unfit for their purpose. In the leading Irish case of *Wallis v. Russell*[53] the plaintiff's grand daughter asked the defendant fishmonger for "two nice fresh crabs for tea." The defendant replied that he had no live crabs but that boiled ones were available; he selected two for the plaintiff's grand-daughter who took them home. Both the plaintiff and her agent – the grand-daughter – suffered food poisoning as a result of eating the crabs. The defendant indicated that he had inspected the crabs himself and would normally be able to detect (by their weight) if anything was wrong with them. Both the Court of Kings Bench and the Court of Appeal found for the plaintiff. Section 14(1) of the 1893 Act was not to be confined to manufactured goods; the intimation that the crabs were to be eaten was sufficient information disclosed to the defendant to signify the particular purpose for which they were required and it was no defence to say the defect was latent and could not be discoverable by inspection.

One problem that arises in relation to this aspect of section 14(4) follows on from *Wallis v. Russell* – when does the buyer satisfy the requirement that a particular purpose be disclosed? In *Brady v. Cluxton*[54] a woman purchased a fur coat with no intimation of the purpose for which it was required. The fur caused a skin disorder. The action for damages was dismissed because the plaintiff had not made known the particular purpose for which the coat was required; contrast the later English case of *Griffiths v. Peter Conway Ltd.*[55] This approach has been relaxed when the goods have only one purpose: underpants are to be worn next to the skin, hot water bottles are to be used to pour water into, buns, beer and coal are to be "consumed". In the case of *Stokes & McKiernan v. Lixnaw Co-op Creamery Ltd.*[56] the plaintiffs purchased alcohol to be used in testing milk. The defendants knew they were supplying a co-operative and that milk would be tested with it. The alcohol was of poor quality and gave misleading results. The purpose was held to have been made known by implication: see also *Sproule v. Triumph Cycle.*[57]

Where the goods have a multiple purpose and are required to achieve a certain objective, or are intended for a particular use, then actual disclosure may be needed. If denim fabric is to be used to make denim jeans and the seller, unaware

---

[52] (1955) 90 I.L.T.R. 40.
[53] [1902] 2 I.R. 585.
[54] (1927) 61 I.L.T.R. 89.
[55] [1939] 1 All E.R. 685.
[56] (1937) 71 I.L.T.R. 70.
[57] [1927] N.I. 83.

of this, provides cloth that is suitable for making dresses but not sturdy enough to make jeans then an action for breach of the merchantability and fitness for purpose obligations will fail: see *Brown (B.S.) & Son Ltd. v. Craiks Ltd.*[58]

The seller may escape liability if it can be shown that the buyer did not rely on the skill and judgment of the seller. In *Slater and Slater (a firm) v. Finning Ltd.*[59] the defendant supplied a camshaft to be used on a fishing vessel, knowing that the camshaft would be used on that particular boat. The boat in question was liable to an unusual tendency to produce "excessive torsional resonance" so that the camshaft became badly worn. The defendants, not having been made aware of this factor, were in no position to exercise skill and judgment in dealing with that condition. Lord Steyn drew attention to the fact that consumer law had moved some way from the position of *caveat emptor* but observed that if the plaintiff recovered here, *caveat venditor* would be allowed to run riot. If however reliance is asserted it is established that reliance may be partial; if the buyer asks an animal foodstuffs manufacturer to produce food to the buyer's formula then if the food turns out to be unfit because one of the ingredients was of poor quality, thus rendering the food toxic, there will still be liability, the seller being relied upon to the extent that the buyer relied upon the seller to select ingredients of sound quality: see *Ashington Piggeries Ltd. v. Christopher Hill Ltd.*[60] If in the *Lixnaw Co-op* case the Co-operative had tested the alcohol before purchasing, no liability under the fitness for purpose or merchantability conditions would arise. The most graphic example however is produced by *Draper v. Rubenstein.*[61] A butcher who had 17 years' experience of buying cattle in Dublin Cattle Market was held to have relied upon his own skill and judgment and accordingly could not invoke section 14 when cattle turned out to be unfit for human consumption. The fitness for purpose condition is also broken if misleading instructions on the package make otherwise suitable merchandise less effective than would have been the case if used correctly: see *Wormell v. R.H.M. Agricultural (East).*[62]

## Section 15

This section, which was not amended in any way by the 1980 Act, enacts three implied conditions. First, if the goods supplied have been sold by sample there is an implied condition that the bulk will correspond with the sample. Secondly, the buyer must be given a reasonable opportunity to inspect the sample. Thirdly, if the goods supplied match the sample in every way but the sample and the bulk are defective and thus unmerchantable, there is to be liability in respect of this defect if it would not be apparent on reasonable

---

[58] [1970] 1 W.L.R. 752.

[59] [1996] 3 All E.R. 398.

[60] [1972] A.C. 441.

[61] (1925) 59 I.L.T.R. 119; *Southern Chemicals Ltd. v. South of Ireland Asphalt*, unreported, High Court, July 7, 1978.

[62] [1987] 3 All E.R. 75. On correct use instructions see *Kearney v. Paul and Vincent Ltd.*, unreported, High Court, July 30, 1985.

examination of the sample. It is extremely difficult, even prior to the enactment of the new section 55 in 1980, to avoid liability under section 15; either the law of mistake[63] or a rule of construction (laid down in *Champanhac & Co. Ltd. v. Waller & Co. Ltd.*[64]) may be invoked by the courts so as to short circuit any exemption clause.

## Hire-Purchase

If the transaction is a hire purchase-transaction rather than a contract of sale or an agreement to sell then the hirer cannot rely on the 1893 Act; witness the decision in the Irish case of *B.P. v. Smyth*.[65] In 1946 the Oireachtas, through the Hire- Purchase Act 1946, gave consumers who found it necessary to obtain goods on hire-purchase a degree of protection from faulty and defective merchandise. While shadowing the 1893 Act, the Hire-Purchase Act 1946 in some respects went further than the Sale of Goods Act 1893.

### (1) Implied terms

Section 9 of the 1946 Act implied into contracts of hire-purchase the same implied terms as were set out in sections 12–15 of the Sale of Goods Act 1893. In one respect protection afforded by section 9 was greater in relation to the fitness for purpose condition because this term could only be excluded if the hirer's attention had been specifically drawn to the existence of the express term in the contract which excluded the implied statutory condition. Section 2(4) of the 1980 Act repealed section 9 of the Hire-Purchase Act 1946, but the implied terms were substantially re-enacted in sections 26–29 in the clarified and modified language applied to sale of goods by the 1980 Act.[66] The legislation that currently governs the hirer's rights in a hire-purchase contract is now set out in the Consumer Credit Act 1995; the 1946 and 1980 Hire-Purchase legislation has been repealed and substantially re-enacted in Part VI of the 1995 Act. Section 74 of the 1995 Act sets out implied terms as to title and these cannot be displaced by contrary agreement: section 79(2). Implied conditions as to goods let by description, merchantability and fitness for purpose, and the letting of goods by sample, are found in sections 75, 76 and 77. The exclusion of these implied conditions may be made by agreement only if the excluding provision is fair and reasonable: section 79(3).[67] Section 82 of the 1995 Act reproduces the section 13 implied condition *vis-à-vis* the sale of motor vehicles and makes it equally applicable to hire-purchase letting of vehicles. While it is therefore clear that a person who takes goods on hire-purchase terms can rely

---

[63] *Megaw v. Molloy* (1878) 2 L.R.(Ir.) 530.
[64] [1948] 2 All E.R. 724.
[65] (1931) 65 I.L.T.R. 182.
[66] *Butterley v. UDT* [1963] I.R. 56.
[67] See *Sovereign Finance Ltd. v. Silver Crest Furniture* [1997] C.C.L.R. 76.

on much the same set of rights in respect of those goods as an outright buyer of goods can, it will still be important to establish whether the contract is a contract of sale or one of hire-purchase in order to know which implied terms are to be pleaded; this will be particularly important if goods are bailed out to the hirer, through a dealer, the hirer's contract of hire-purchase being with a finance company rather than the dealer: see *Dunphy v. Blackhall Motors,*[68] the effect of which is reversed by section 32 of the 1980 Act and re-enacted in section 80 of the 1995 Act.

*(2)  Other statutory terms*

The hirer of goods obtains further protection under the Consumer Credit Act 1995; a copy of the terms of the agreement must be delivered or sent to the hirer within ten days of the agreement, otherwise the contract may be unenforceable. If the hirer has paid one third of the total hire-purchase price the goods are protected goods and under section 64 cannot be repossessed without the appropriate court order although this does not prevent the hirer from voluntarily giving the property back: see *McDonald v. Bowmaker (Ireland).*[69] The consumer may be further protected by the courts from unreasonable default clauses.[70]

# Hiring or Leasing

The rise of the leasing industry as a method of supplying moveable property to industry and commerce under an operating lease or a finance lease, has been a significant commercial development in recent years. However, because most operating leases do not give the lessee a right of purchase (a right of purchase driving the base is inconsistent with a lease in any event) the lessee did not enjoy any statutory rights should the moveables malfunction. Section 38 of the 1980 Act gave a lessee similar rights to those afforded to the hirer of goods under a hire-purchase contract: *O'Callaghan v. Hamilton Leasing.*[71] Even if the lessee loses rights to repudiate the leased property there may still be a remedy in damages: *U.C.B. Leasing Ltd. v. Holtom.*[72]

Section 38 has been repealed by the 1995 Act and Part VII of the Consumer Credit Act 1995 provides the hirer of goods in a consumer hire agreement with rights that are based upon sections 75–83 of that Act. That is, such persons enjoy rights which parallel those of a hire-purchase letting.

---

[68]  (1953) 87 I.L.T.R. 128.
[69]  [1949] I.R. 317.
[70]  Particularly acceleration clauses: see Chap. 18.
[71]  [1984] I.L.R.M. 146.
[72]  [1987] R.T.R. 362.

## Supply of Services

The most innovative aspect of the Sale of Goods and Supply of Services Act 1980 is found in Part IV. There are implied terms – the Act does not say whether they are conditions or warranties in the technical sense – set out in section 39 which are to apply to contracts where the supplier is acting in the course of a business:

> "(a) that the supplier has the necessary skill to render the service;
> (b) that he will supply the service with due skill, care and diligence;
> (c) that where materials are used, they will be sound and reasonably fit for the purpose for which they are required; and
> (d) that, where goods are supplied under the contract, they will be of merchantable quality within the meaning of section 14(3) of the Act of 1893."

Section 39 has proved to be extremely useful in the context of holiday litigation where the tour operator will often fail to make clear express promises about the quality of the holiday and incidental matters. In *O'Flynn v. Balkan Tours Ltd.*[73] the scope of the duty of care incumbent upon a tour operator was held to cover information about local ski runs within the ski resort. *McKenna v. Best Travel Ltd.*[74] indicates that the section 39 duty extends to information about the safety of a particular area or resort. So, when the plaintiff was injured during a demonstration on the West Bank, the failure to advise the plaintiff, a tourist to the Holy Land, of local conditions and suitable precautions was held to break that duty.

The application of section 39 in *Irish Telephone Rentals Ltd. v. Irish Civil Service Building Society Ltd.*[75] illustrates how useful the section may be in cases where the contract extends over a period of time. The plaintiff contracted to install and maintain a telephone system in the premises of the defendant. While the system seemed to function adequately in 1982, the time of installation, by 1985 it was causing severe difficulties because it could not cope with the increased volume of calls that resulted from the defendant's greater volume of business, a volume of business that the telephone system was supposed to handle adequately. Costello J. found that, under section 39, the contract contained an implied term that goods would be of merchantable quality. These goods installed as part of a leased telecommunications service consisted of a switchboard, console and telephone sets; they were held not to be fit for the purpose of providing a reasonably efficient telephone system. On the facts of this case it would be likely that a common law duty would also arise and, in a leasing contract, the implied conditions available under a consumer hire contract would also be available to the lessee.

---

[73] Unreported, High Court, December 1, 1995, affirmed by the Supreme Court, April 7, 1997.
[74] Unreported, High Court, December 17, 1996.
[75] [1991] I.L.R.M. 880.

However, the concept of a service contract was given a narrow interpretation by Costello J. in *Carroll v. An Post National Lottery Co.*[76] Section 39 was held not to apply when the plaintiff purchased a lottery ticket which was negligently processed by the staff at a post office for the learned judge held that "the contract is to sell a ticket which confers rights and obligations on the parties to the contract". This appears a somewhat surprising conclusion. A contract of insurance can also be so described but no-one doubts that an insurance intermediary operates in the financial services sector. Similarly, sections 39 and 40 have been held not to be applicable on issues concerning the degree of notice required to incorporate an arbitration clause into a contract.[77]

## Contracting out under the Sale of Goods and Supply of Services Act 1980

If the parties to the contract attempt to contract out of the implied terms inserted by the Sale of Goods and Supply of Services Act 1980 they will find that their right to do so is controlled by legislation. In the context of the Sale of Goods Acts 1893–1980, section 55(4) of the 1893 Act, as amended, renders ineffective any attempt to contract out of the implied conditions as to sales by description, merchantability, fitness for purpose, and the implied conditions as to sales by sample if the buyer deals as consumer. The Act also provides that an exemption clause shall in any other case not be enforceable unless it can be shown that the term is fair and reasonable. The "fair and reasonable" test also applies to attempts to contract out of section 13 (the implied term relating to motor vehicle sales), section 31 (the implied conditions in sections 27–29 which relate to non-consumer hire-purchase transactions), section 40 (implied terms relating to the supply of services) and section 46 (contractual attempts to limit or exclude liability for misrepresentation). Before the "fair and reasonable" test can operate, the person invoking the statutory rights conferred in relation to the sale or hire-purchase letting of goods by description, the sale or hire purchase letting of goods alleged to be unmerchantable or unfit for their purpose, or the sale or hire-purchase letting of goods sold by sample, must show that they dealt as consumer.

Section 3 provides:

> "1. In the Act of 1893 and this Act, a party to a contract is said to deal as consumer in relation to another party if –
> > (a) he neither makes the contract in the course of a business nor holds himself out as doing so; and
> > (b) the other party does make the contract in the course of a business; and

---

[76] [1996] 1 I.R. 443.

[77] *Carroll v. Budget Travel*, unreported, High Court, December 7, 1995.

(c) the goods or services supplied under or in pursuance of the contract are of a type ordinarily supplied for private use or consumption.

2. On –
   (a) a sale by competitive tender; or
   (b) a sale by auction –
      (i) of goods of a type, or
      (ii) by or on behalf of a person of a class defined by the Minister by order,

the buyer is not in any circumstances to be regarded as dealing as consumer.

3. Subject to this, it is for those claiming that a party does not deal as consumer to show that he does not."

Section 3 has been considered on two occasions. In *O'Callaghan v. Hamilton Leasing (Ireland) Ltd.*[78] the lessee of a drinks vending machine to be used in his take-away foods shop alleged the machine was defective within section 14 of the 1893 Act or, alternatively, section 38 of the 1980 Act. McWilliam J., allowing the lessor's appeal from a decision in the Circuit Court, held that the leasing agreement had effectively excluded liability for these defects. The plaintiff had not dealt as consumer – the goods were provided for the plaintiff's business use and section 3 did not require that the ultimate user of a product was always to be classified as a consumer. This approach was later followed in *Cunningham v. Woodchester Investments Ltd.*[79] when the acquisition of an automatic telephone system to be installed in an agricultural college was held to be a non-consumer sale, even though the college was run on a non-profit making basis.

While these two decisions of McWilliam J. are no doubt correct this approach is at odds with the decisions of the Appellate Courts in England, which in two cases in particular[80] have held that a degree of regularity in dealing is needed before the buyer will lose the status of a consumer. The net result in these English cases is to give a business purchaser the status of a consumer, even though the purchase is an incidental element in the purchaser's business activities (*e.g.* purchase of storage equipment). While the decision in *R. & B. Customs Brokers Co. Ltd. v. U.D.T. Ltd.* must be regarded as borderline, it is difficult not to agree with Pearce[81] that regarding business purchasers as consumers is a regrettable judicial development and a reversal of Parliamentary intention, which has taken place in isolation from a clear review of the policy issues invoked.

---

[78] [1984] I.L.R.M. 146.
[79] Unreported, High Court, November 16, 1984.
[80] *R. & B. Customs Brokers Co. Ltd. v. UDT and Another* [1988] 1 All E.R. 847: *Davies v. Sumner* [1984] 1 W.L.R. 1301.
[81] [1989] 3 L.M.C.L.Q. 371.

## "Fair and reasonable"

The Schedule to the 1980 Act provides that a term is fair and reasonable if that term, in all the circumstances, was a term which was "or ought reasonably to have been known to or in contemplation of the parties when the contract was made." While this test looks to all the facts and requires the court to consider the reasonable expectations of the parties, given the industry or area of commercial activity concerned, the Schedule of the Act sets out factors that particular regard may be given to:

(a) the relative bargaining position and the possibility of an alternative method of meeting the customer's requirements; or

(b) whether there was an inducement to enter this contract; could another supplier have provided the goods or service without the exception clause?; or

(c) whether the customer had actual or constructive knowledge of the existence of the term or its extent, having particular regard to custom of trade or a course of dealing; or

(d) if the term imposed an obligation on the customer, to be met by him, was compliance practicable?; or

(e) whether the goods were manufactured, processed or adapted to the customer's special order.

Factor (a) is clearly designed to see if the customer had any real chance of negotiating a different contract. Even if the supplier holds a monopoly but the customer had a choice of contract options – whether to buy insurance, for example – this may still indicate the term was fair and reasonable: see *Slattery v. C.I.É.*[82] In *Woodman v. Photo Trading Processing*[83] a film processing service which excluded liability for loss and limited its liability to replacement of the reel of film, undertook to process the plaintiff's wedding photographs. Most of the photographs where lost. In considering whether the exclusion was fair and reasonable Judge Clarke held that within the industry a code of practice recognised a two-tier level of service. The unavailability of a second level of service, under which the processor would be liable to exercise greater care (and be entitled to charge accordingly) meant that the processor could not show that the clause satisfied the statutory test of reasonableness. The issue seems to be whether the consumer could have obtained a similar service on different terms either from the same supplier or another supplier. The fact that all suppliers shelter behind similar terms does not seem to have come before the courts other than in an oblique manner: *Usher v. Intasun*[84] and *Singer Co. (U.K.) Ltd. v. Tees*

---

[82] (1972) 106 I.L.T.R. 71.
[83] (1981) 131 N.L.J. 933.
[84] [1987] C.L.Y. 418.

*and Hartlepool Port Authority*.[85] Factor (b) is similarly designed to consider whether the customer made a choice between one supplier as against another; if there was a collateral inducement – a "free gift" for taking one type of vehicle from dealer A when dealer B had the same vehicle but did not make this collateral inducement available – then the customer may be taken to have freely consented to that term. Factor (c) crosses the boundary from this notion of the substantive fairness of the transaction into the procedural fairness of using this particular term. Many of the comments made in relation to incorporation of exemption clauses are relevant here. If, however, the proferens has not on previous occasions relied upon the clause but has tried to negotiate a compromise of any claim – no doubt in order to retain the goodwill of his customers – this will indicate that the term was not fair and reasonable: see *Western Meats Ltd. v. National Ice & Cold Storage Co.*[86] and *George Mitchell (Chesterhall) Ltd. v. Finney Lock Seeds Ltd.*[87] Factor (d) deals with limitation of liability clauses that require the customer to notify the seller or supplier within a set period at the risk of losing his cause of action: see clause 16 in *Clayton Love v. B + I Transport*[88] for an example. Whether compliance was practicable is a question of fact. In *Stag Line Ltd. v. Tyne Ship Repair Group Ltd.*[89] Staughton J. had to consider whether a limiting provision in respect of a ship repair contract could pass the reasonableness test. If the contract in question required the return of the vessel to the Tyneside ship repair yard in cases of defective work, such an impracticable obligation was said, *obiter*, not to be fair and reasonable given that the vessel could break down anywhere in the world. Factor (e) seems to be ambivalent. Presumably, if the customer has laid down specific requirements this will point away from the clause being unfair or unreasonable. However, in *Edmund Murray Ltd. v. B P International Foundations*[90] an order placed by the plaintiffs for the supply of an oil rig, to specification, was given to the defendants because the defendants had specialist knowledge. In these circumstances the defendants' conditions, which excluded liability for the provision of a rig that was unsuitable *simpliciter*, were not fair and reasonable.

The leading English case of *George Mitchell (Chesterhall) v. Finney Lock Seeds Ltd.* indicates that other factors pertinent to the "fair and reasonable" test include whether the supplier could have insured against a claim without this materially affecting the price at which the goods or service could be provided. However, the cases suggest the issue is whether at the time of the formation of the contract, insurance was available to either or both parties and the terms upon which cover was available – the premiums paid and the exclusions applicable, for example. In *Singer v. Tees and Hartlepool Port Authority*[91]

---

[85] [1988] 2 Lloyd's Rep. 164.
[86] [1982] I.L.R.M. 101.
[87] [1983] 2 A.C. 803.
[88] (1970) 104 I.L.T.R. 157.
[89] [1984] 2 Lloyd's Rep. 211.
[90] (1992) 33 Con.L.R.1.
[91] [1988] 2 Lloyd's Rep. 164.

Steyn J. held that it was irrelevant whether the parties were actually insured, and in *The Flamar Pride*[92] Potter J. held that, unless the evidence indicates that prior to the conclusion of the contract the existence or extent of cover was discussed, the law will not regard the insurance position of the parties as material in commercial or consumer contracts.

The most important English decision on the reasonableness test is *Smith v. Eric S. Bush (a firm).*[93] The respondent applied to a building society for a mortgage in order to purchase a house. The building society engaged a firm of surveyors to carry out a statutory written report and valuation. The respondent paid a fee for the survey and obtained a copy of the report. The report was negligently compiled and failed to detect severe defects in the property. The purchaser relied upon the report and did not obtain a further report. The House of Lords indicated that a duty of care was owed in these circumstances to the intending purchaser by the surveyor. The surveyor was not allowed to rely upon a clause which purported to exclude liability for negligence. In cases where domestic property is purchased by an owner–occupier, it was unreasonable to allow a professional person to transfer risk to the owner–occupier given that the loss was caused by negligence and the loss could more reasonably be borne by the professional and his insurer. In contrast, a professional management contractor who limits liability for the provision of services may satisfy the fair and reasonable test if the contract is negotiated and not in standard form, the parties are seen as being at arm's length and there were others who could have been approached to contract on dissimilar terms. Both parties were able to obtain insurance against the risk so this factor was neutral in nature: see also *Chester Grosvenor Hotel v. Alfred McAlpine Management.*[94] However, the availability of insurance to either side, and the terms available to each will generally be a crucial factor, even though it is not mentioned in the Schedule: *The Salvage Association v. CAP Financial Services*[95] and *St. Albans City and District Council v. International Computers Ltd.*[96]

The only Irish case in which the substantive merits of an exemption clause have been examined is the decision of Carroll J. in *McCarthy and Others v. Joe Walsh Tours Ltd.*[97] The contract in question was a package holiday agreement containing a standard arbitration clause which obliged the consumer to submit any dispute to compulsory arbitration before an Irish Travel Agents Association arbitrator. The I.T.A.A. scheme was both compulsory and a limitation of rights, because the maximum recoverable in any claim was £5,000. Carroll J. upheld the decision of Judge Murphy in the Circuit Court, deciding that the clause was a term which limited the implied term under section 39 and, accordingly, in a

---

[92] [1990] 1 Lloyd's Rep. 429.
[93] [1989] 2 All E.R. 514.
[94] (1992) 56 B.L.R. 115; *W. Photoprint v. F.T.E.* (1993) 12 Tr.L.R. 146; *Monarch Airlines v. London Luton Airport* [1997] C.L.C. 698.
[95] [1995] F.S.R. 654. The Court of Appeal decision is unreported.
[96] [1996] 4 All E.R. 481.
[97] [1991] I.L.R.M. 813.

consumer contract, could only be enforced if specifically drawn to the attention of the consumer and if fair and reasonable. Carroll J. held that the clause could not be relied upon in this case because it was not specifically drawn to the attention of the consumer in question. However, it is arguable that the compulsory arbitration clause, if involving a limitation on liability, must be regarded as a clause limiting the rights of the consumer and that the fair and reasonable test cannot be satisfied in such circumstances. In an interesting comment on this case[98] White argues that compulsory arbitration clauses may in general fall foul of the statutory test (presumably in consumer contracts at any rate) if it gives a proferens the right to unilaterally select an arbitrator on the basis of a risk of partiality.

There are two contrasting English cases which suggest that the Unfair Contract Terms Act 1977 does not generally operate against indemnity clauses which transfer risk as opposed to clauses which limit or exclude it.[99] Nor does the 1977 Act apply to agreements which, unfairly as it turns out, settle or compromise litigation: *Tudor Grange Holdings v. Citibank N.A.*[100] These decisions would also be applicable in Ireland under the Sale of Goods and Supply of Services Act 1980.

The Sale of Goods and and Supply of Services Act 1980 also provides additional protection for the buyer in respect of a manufacturer's or supplier's guarantee. Section 16 requires, *inter alia,* that the guarantee discloses information in relation to the person supplying the guarantee, the duration of the guarantee, plus the claim procedure involved, and discloses the carriage charges the buyer must meet; non-compliance with section 16 is an offence: see section 16(6). The seller may also be liable in respect of the manufacturer's or supplier's guarantee (section 17) and section 18 provides that rights given under the guarantee do not exclude or limit the buyer's rights under statute or common law. Section 18 declares that attempts to displace these rights, or impose additional obligations on the buyer, or reserve for the guarantor or his agent the right to be sole arbiter on whether goods are defective "shall be void." Section 19 provides a right of action against the manufacturer or other supplier "as if that manufacturer or supplier had sold the goods to the buyer and had committed a breach or warranty." An extended definition of "buyer" and "manufacturer" is given under section 19.

Part VI of the 1980 Act also contains a series of additional measures designed to deal with directory entries that are made for trade or business purposes; trade directories have to be compiled according to criteria set out in section 48 and is a criminal offence for the compiler to demand payment without satisfying the provisions of section 48. Other criminal offences are created by section 49 – failure to meet prescribed terms in relation to the format to be employed in drafting invoices – or contracts or guarantees (section 51). Section 53 also

---

[98] (1991) 9 I.L.T. 92.

[99] *Phillips Products Ltd. v. Hyland* [1987] 2 All E.R. 620; *Thompson v. Lohan (Plant Hire) Ltd.* [1987] 2 All E.R. 631.

[100] [1991] 4 All E.R. 1.

empowers the Minister for Industry, Commerce & Tourism to prescribe the size or type to be used in printed contracts and guarantees; non-compliance renders the person who contravenes section 53 guilty of an offence. These provisions have not yet been employed for the Minister has yet to make any orders prescribing the size and style of the documentation in question.

## Motor Vehicles

Section 13 of the Sale of Goods and Supply of Services Act 1980 (not to be confused with section 13 of the 1893 Act as amended by the Act of 1980) sets out an implied condition which is of singular importance in contracts for the sale of motor vehicles. Section 13(2) states that, without prejudice to any other condition of warranty, there is an implied condition that at the time of delivery the vehicle is free from any defect which would render it a danger to the public, including persons travelling in the vehicle. The implied condition does not apply if the buyer is a dealer in motor vehicles, and subsection (3) provides that, if the vehicle is not intended for use in the state in which it is delivered, and a document to that effect is signed by both parties, and the agreement is fair and reasonable, the implied condition is inapplicable. The Act also provides a presumption of unfitness in certain circumstances and the implied condition cannot be excluded by contrary agreement. Another novel feature is that the condition is available for the benefit of persons travelling in the vehicle if they are injured as a result of the defect. In the first case under section 13, a decision of the High Court in *Glorney v. O'Brien*,[101] a mini was sold in poor condition for £250. The vehicle crashed three weeks later when the suspension collapsed. The Court brushed aside a claim that given the low price, the vehicle was not intended for use but for spare parts:

> "no matter how old or cheap a motor vehicle may be it must not be sold to an ordinary member of the public not in the motor trade in a condition which would render it a danger to the public including the occupants of the vehicle if driven on the road."

Damages totalling £18,650 were awarded to the driver and passenger in respect of the injuries suffered. The implied condition could presumably be used by a buyer to set aside a contract, even if the seller is not a dealer, so it provides a very useful additional remedy to motor vehicle buyers. The implied condition is also applicable to cases of hire-purchase and bailments, such as holiday car hire, fleet leasing or operating leasing of motor vehicles.

---

[101] Unreported, High Court, November 14, 1988.

## Miscellaneous Statutory Measures

In the Republic, the Oireachtas has intervened in order to regulate the extent to which a limiting clause may be relied upon in many everyday transactions.

In cases of bailment, specific rules apply under the Hotel Proprietors Act 1963. If a hotel proprietor displays a notice informing persons who book sleeping accommodation that liability for loss of the guest's property is to be regulated by the Act, the proprietor will, under section 7 of the Act, only be liable to compensate up to a maximum sum of £100. If the loss of property is the result of an act of God, act of war or is due to the actions of the guest or a person accompanying him, the proprietor is exempt from liability. The £100 ceiling does not operate if a notice is not conspicuously displayed at the reception desk, or if the loss results from the wrongful act, default or omission of the proprietor or his employee. If goods are left for safekeeping with the proprietor and they are destroyed, damaged or lost, the proprietor cannot rely on the £100 ceiling. Nor will the £100 limit apply if the guest's motor car is lost, damaged or stolen when the vehicle is brought onto hotel property. While the Act in some cases limits the proprietor's liability and is thus of benefit to him, a balance is struck by section 9 which provides that a term excluding or varying liability is void.

In contracts for the transport of goods and passengers, the Transport Act 1958 permits C.I.É. a wide discretion as to the terms upon which it wishes to contract. Section 8(3) provides that C.I.É. "may attach to any service provided by it such terms and conditions as the Board thinks fit." The Railway and Canal Traffic Act 1854 attempted to limit the content of contracts of carriage to conditions which were judged by the court to be "just and reasonable": see *Fox v. M. & S. Ry.*[102] The Act, as amended by the Transport Act 1958, prevents a court from ruling on whether the terms imposed are "just and reasonable" for sections 8(4) and (5) of the 1958 Act provide that all contracts for the carriage of merchandise which are deemed to comply with Statutory Rule and Order 13 of 1930 "shall be deemed to be carriage of that commodity under terms and conditions which are just and reasonable." This statutory presumption does not operate if a passenger is injured but it remains open to C.I.É. to limit liability for such injuries too.

Section 40(6) of the 1980 Act prevents section 39 of the Act (which imposes implied undertakings as to the quality of a service) from applying until such time and on such terms as the Minister for Transport sees proper.[103]

There is a general willingness on the part of successive governments to provide protection for public sector employers against liability for the non-provision of services or against loss occasioned by failure to provide an efficient service, even if the failure is the result of negligence. The Postal and Telecommunications Act 1983 provides in sections 64(3)(*a*) and 88(3)(*a*) that

---

[102] [1926] I.R. 106.
[103] Contrast s.3 of the U.K. Unfair Contract Terms Act 1977.

the obligations under section 39 of the Sale of Goods and Supply of Services Act 1980 – the implied terms in relation to the supply of a service – are not to apply at all in respect of claims arising from loss occasioned by the non-provision, or interruption in, or defective provision of international postal or telecommunications services. In all other cases section 39 of the 1980 Act is only to apply on such terms as the Minister for Communications shall, by order, determine: sections 64(3)(*b*) and 88(3)(*b*). The vexed question of the protection afforded by the Standard Conditions used by the E.S.B. is also pertinent here. In January 1986 the Government announced the introduction of legislation to remove the Board's virtual immunity from suit. This announcement was necessary because of the Products Liability Directive (which is discussed below at page 191) which covers the provision of electricity in Article 2. The Liability for Defective Products Act 1991, which came into force on December 16, 1991, defines a product so as to include "electricity where damage is caused as a result of failure in the process of generation of electricity" and this liability in tort for a producer of electricity can now be established under section 2 of the 1991 Act.

## Community Law

As part of the rationale for the existence of the European Communities, that is, the establishment of a single market within the area of the Community (Article 2 of the Treaty of Rome) and within the context of Article 3(a), which specifies that the activities of the Community includes "approximation of the laws of the Member States to the extent required for the proper functioning of the Common Market," the Commission has drawn up proposals for a series of measures by way of consumer protection and information. Many of these proposals have now been implemented.

### (1) The Misleading Advertising Directive

This Directive,[104] adopted in September 1984, was implemented into Irish law on June 23, 1988 by Ministerial Order. The Directive, as implemented, provides very useful additional powers to those given by the Consumer Information Act 1978 to the Director of Consumer Affairs. The preamble to the Directive, after noting that the laws in force against misleading advertising differ widely and that the dangers that result include the distortion of competition within the Common Market, continues by declaring that consumer advertising affects the consumer's economic welfare and may cause the consumer to make prejudicial decisions when acquiring goods, property, or using services. The Directive, in Article 2.1 defines advertising as "the making of a representation in any form in connection with a trade, business, craft or profession in order to promote the

---

[104] Council Directive 84/450/EEC of September 10, 1984 relating to the approximation of the laws, regulations and administrative provisions of the Member States concerning misleading advertising [1984] O.J. L250/17.

supply of goods or services" including immovable property. Article 2.2 defines misleading advertising as "any advertising which in any way, including its presentation, deceives or is likely to deceive." Article 4 requires Member States to ensure that adequate and effective means exist for the control of misleading advertising in the interests of consumers as well as competitors and the general public. The method of enforcement is to be resolved within each Member State. Article 4 allows the means of control to include legal provisions which enable persons having a legitimate interest in prohibiting misleading advertising to (a) take legal action against such advertising and/or (b) bring such advertising before an administrative authority to decide on complaints or initial proceedings. The Statutory Instrument which brings the Directive into force, the European Communities (Misleading Advertising) Regulations, 1988,[105] gives the Director of Consumer Affairs the power to request any person engaging in misleading advertising, or proposing so to do, to discontinue or refrain from such advertising. Any person, including the Director, may seek an injunction in which the court may prohibit misleading advertising: the applicant is not required to prove actual loss or damage, nor recklessness or negligence on the part of the advertiser. The question whether the advertisement is misleading or not is to be resolved by reference to Article 3 of the Directive which requires the court to have regard to the characteristics of the goods and services such as availability, nature, execution, composition, method and date of manufacture or provision, fitness for purpose, quality, origin, price, rights and attributes of the advertiser, including any copyright or patent rights the advertiser may have.

The Misleading Advertising Directive has recently been amended so as to broaden the scope of regulation to include comparative advertising.[106] While comparative advertising, that is, the comparison of goods or services marketed, distributed or supplied by an enterprise by reference to the name, mark, reputation or image of a competitor, is the subject of industry self regulation by way of the Advertising Standards Authority for Ireland, and while the Trade Marks Act 1996, section 14(6) makes derogatory use of a competitor's mark a trade mark infringement, this Directive is intended to control comparative advertising throughout the European Union, for in some countries such as Germany such advertising is unlawful. The Directive permits comparative advertising if the practice meets a list of requirements, which can be paraphrased as requiring that the advertisement must not be misleading, is based on objectively verifiable factors, compares like with like, does not cause confusion in the market or denigrate the trade marks and other indicia of a competitor, or unfairly appropriate the mark or indicia of a competitor or his reputation. The Directive sets out a requirement that national laws afford appropriate remedies and legal procedures for rightholders. The Directive must be transposed into national law by April 23, 2000.

---

[105] S.I. No. 134 of 1988.
[106] Directive 97/55/EC of European Parliament and of the Council of October 6, 1997 amending Directive 84/450/EEC concerning misleading advertising so as to include comparative advertising [1997] O.J. L290/18.

## (2) The Directive on Contracts Negotiated Away From Business Premises

This Directive, first proposed in 1977 and later amended in 1978, applies to contracts between a consumer and trader when negotiations have been initiated away from business premises – "doorstep contracts." The definition of business premises includes stalls at fairs and markets. Article 4 provides that the contract document must be signed by the consumer in his own hand and a copy given to him or forwarded immediately thereafter. The contract must contain specified information and the consumer is to have a seven-day cancellation period. The European Communities (Cancellation of Contracts Negotiated Away from Business Premises) Regulations, 1989 – implementing Directive 85/577/EEC –[107] came into effect on November 1, 1989. The Regulations set out a model cancellation form that must be used by a trader who is caught by the Regulation. Non-compliance means that the contract is void. It is possible that some unscrupulous traders may seek to avoid the Regulation by inserting into the contract a declaration that the visit to the home of the consumer, as the case may be, was done at the express request of the consumer, but the courts will be vigilant in seeking out such fictions.

The provisions of section 50 of the Sale of Goods and Supply of Services Act 1980 overlap to some extent with the Directive and the implementing Statutory Instrument. The Minister is empowered to specify circumstances in which certain "doorstep contracts" may be subject to a "cooling off period," during which time the acceptance may be withdrawn.

## (3) The Distance Selling Directive

This Directive[108] attempts to regulate the sale of products to consumers when the contract is concluded at a distance, that is, through direct marketing, telesales and Internet type sales. The willing consumer of a good or service is to be given information about the name, address and type of product provided by the supplier and details concerning price, delivery charges or other fees, before the contract is concluded. Confirmation in writing is required and an ability to revoke the contract within seven days of supply of the goods is provided. Delivery of the goods, unless otherwise stated in the contract, must take place within 30 days of the conclusion of the contract. The Directive also addresses issues of inertia selling (see section 47 of the Sale of Goods and Supply of Services Act 1980) and also regulates the use of automated dialling and fax machines and, generally speaking, prohibits "cold calling" of consumers. Transposition must take place before June 4, 2000.

## (4) The Product Liability Directive

The most significant measure of consumer protection is the Product Liability Directive,[109] adopted by the Council on July 25, 1985. While the Directive

---

[107]  S.I. No. 224 of 1989: Directive 85/577/EEC [1985] O.J. L372/31.
[108]  Directive 97/7/EC [1997] O.J. L144/19.
[109]  Council Directive 85/374/EEC [1985] O.J. L210/29: see (1991) I.C.L.S.A. 91/28–02.

does not affect any of the rights which are available through the laws in force relating to contractual and non-contractual liability (Article 13), it is clear that the Directive is an important landmark in breaking down the distinction between consumer protection through contract (liability is stricter but extends only to the purchaser) and consumer protection in tort (liability of the defendant in negligence must be shown). In order to explain why Community legislation is necessary the Directive, in the preamble, refers to divergences in national law distorting competition, affecting the free movement of goods within the Community and entailing different degrees of protection for the consumer against damage caused to health and property from defective products. While the preamble identifies "liability without fault on the art of the producer" as the sole means of adequately solving the problem of products liability *vis à vis* technological methods of production, the Directive also acknowledges that liability should not be unlimited and that harmonisation will not be immediately obtained. The Directive in several respects is predicated on the assumption that implementation of the Directive is really a first step.

Article 1 declares that the producer shall be liable for damage caused by a defect in his product. "Product" is defined in Article 2 as all moveables with the exception of "primary agricultural products"[110] and game. "Primary agricultural products" means the products of the soil, stock-farming and fisheries, excluding products that have undergone initial processing. Thus tinned salmon would be covered by the Directive, as would probably a boiled crab, but whether fresh crabs or possibly even pasteurised milk would be covered may be open to some doubt. Article 2 also includes electricity as a product. "Producer" is defined in Article 3 as:

(a) the manufacturer of a finished product; or

(b) the producer of any raw material; or

(c) the manufacturer of a component part; or

(d) any person who by putting his name, trade mark or other distinguishing feature on the product thereby identifies himself as its producer.

Importers of goods into the community are also responsible as producers: see Article 3.2. A product is said to be defective when it does not provide the safety a person is entitled to expect having regard to the presentation, expected uses and time it was put into circulation: see Article 6.

Liability under the Directive is not however strict. Article 7 provides the producer with six defences:

(a) he did not put the goods into circulation; or

---

[110] However, a Draft Directive produced by the European Commission COM (97) 478, dated October 1, 1997, intends to bring these products within the 1985 Directive.

(b) it is probable that at the time of putting the product into circulation it did not have the defect; or

(c) the product was not manufactured by him for sale or distribution for an economic purpose nor in the course of business; or

(d) the defect was due to compliance with mandatory public authority regulations; or

(e) that, given the state of technical knowledge, it was not possible at the time of distribution to discover the defect; or

(f) if the product is a manufactured component the defect is the result of a design defect in the product into which the component has been fitted.

Liability is limited to the period of three years following the day the plaintiff became aware, actually or constructively of the damage, defect and identity of the producer. Liability is also to extend only insofar as the damage occurs within 10 years of the product going into circulation by the producer unless the injured party has within that time issued proceedings. There may also be financial limits placed on the awards made under the national laws passed in order to implement the Directive: see Article 16.

Powers of derogation are given in relation to the scope of the definition of "product". Member States may include primary agricultural products and game and the "state of knowledge" defence in Article 7(e) may be omitted. Member States were obliged to bring the Directive into force not later than three years after notification. The Liability for Defective Products Act 1991 came into effect over three years late, on December 16, 1991. Section 2(1) sets out the basic liability of producers and section 2(2) defines a producer accordingly. The Act does not define "product" so as to include primary agricultural products which have not undergone initial processing because all Member States save for Luxembourg have excluded such products and to include primary agricultural products would disadvantage Irish farmers. Section 6(e) of the Act retains the "state of the art" defence despite Article 15(1)(b) of the Directive. Damages below £350 are not recoverable and where damages exceed £350 the excess of that figure only is recoverable.[111] Exclusion clauses or notice are rendered inoperative by section 10, and section 11 provides that the Act does not affect any other rights at law which the injured person may have.

*(5) The Proposed Directive on Consumer Guarantees*

This proposed Directive[112] is to be read with the Product Liability Directive for it sets out two guarantee rights. The first, a mandatory requirement, gives all consumers who shop anywhere in the E.U. a range of remedies for defective goods, including replacement rights, within two years of the sale. There is a

---

[111]  s.3.
[112]  October 16, 1996. Significant progress on this Directive was made in April 1998.

second optional provision which must afford greater rights to the consumer than the minimum mandatory provisions. A common position for this Directive is expected to be agreed before the end of 1998.

### (6) The Timeshare Directive

This Directive[113] was transposed into Irish law by S.I. No. 204 of 1997 and those Regulations came into operation on May 14, 1997. The Directive generally sets out contents requirements for timeshare contracts such as the name, address, domicile of the parties, state of construction and common parts details to be disclosed, as well as providing for language of the transaction requirements to be in the hands of the buyer. A ten-day cooling off requirement is inserted, which can be extended to three months, or three months plus ten days, if certain requirements are not met.

### (7) The Unfair Contract Terms Directive

This is undoubtedly the most important piece of consumer protection legislation to emanate from the European Community. While the Directive[114] at times appears to be quite familiar to U.K. and Irish contract lawyers, the philosophy behind the Directive is closer to French and German law insofar as the concepts of *bonne foi* and *Treu und Glauben* are essential parts of each contract regime and the Directive puts the concept of good faith at the centre of attention. The Directive is seen as an Internal Market measure,[115] giving consumers the assurance that they may conclude contracts anywhere within the Community and not find that their rights are prejudiced by virtue of each Member State providing varying degrees of consumer rights and remedies. The Directive has been transposed into Irish law by virtue of the European Communities (Unfair Terms in Consumer Contracts) Regulations 1995[116] and the Regulations are applicable to all contracts concluded after December 31, 1994, as long as the contract is between a consumer and the seller of goods or supplier of services and the sale or supply is for purposes related to the seller or supplier's business. These provisions broadly shadow section 3(1) of the Sale of Goods and Supply of Services Act 1980. Contracts relating to employment, succession rights, family law and company or partnership formation are not included within the scope of the Regulations. Mandatory or statutory provisions that must be included in a contract or International Treaty are not covered, and where some provisions "shrink" the core of a contract in the sense that they define the main subject matter of the contract (*e.g.* a red VW polo) or address the adequacy of the price (as distinct from permitting a price variation), those clauses are also not open for review under the 1995 Regulations. However these core exclusions must be set out in plain intelligible language for them to be immune from

---

[113] Directive 94/47/EC [1994] O.J. L280/83.
[114] Council Directive 93/13/EEC [1993] O.J. L095/29.
[115] Article 100A – see opening recital to the Directive.
[116] S.I. No. 27 of 1995.

scrutiny and the U.K. Office of Fair Trading has commented that for core exclusions to work and thus avoid scrutiny under the Directive, core terms have to be brought to the attention to the consumer.[117]

The Regulations do not apply if the term in question has been individually negotiated and a term is always to be regarded as not having been individually negotiated where it has been drafted in advance and the consumer has thus not been able to influence its substance. Even if a specific term, or an aspect of that term, has been individually negotiated the Regulations may apply to the rest of the contract if it is assessed to be a pre-formulated standard contract. The onus of proof rests upon the seller or supplier to show the term was individually negotiated.[118]

The key to defining an unfair contract term is found in article 3(2) of the 1995 Regulations which provides:

> "For the purpose of these Regulations a contractual term shall be regarded as unfair if, contrary to the requirement of good faith, it causes a significant imbalance in the parties' rights and obligations under the contract to the detriment of the consumer, taking into account the nature of the goods or services for which the contract was concluded and all circumstances attending the conclusion of the contract and all other terms of the contract or of another contract on which it is dependent."

The good faith requirement, when put into this context, appears to point to the circumstances surrounding the formation of the contract. It may be, for example, that a contract is one-sided in terms of the fairness of the exchange, but if the consumer is openly and fairly treated by the seller or supplier then it may be that the contract term in question will not be unfair; it remains possible however for a court to conclude that even if the consumer has entered into a contract without there being any hint of duplicity or oppression by the other party, the consumer's position is so out of balance with the other party, and so detrimental, that the clause is unfair. Whether good faith is present or absent is a matter for the courts and the Regulations, in Schedule 2, set out four non-exhaustive guidelines for the courts, which are as follows:

> "In making an assessment of good faith, particular regard shall be had to
>
> – the strength of the bargaining positions of the parties,
> – whether the consumer had an inducement to agree to the term,
> – whether the goods or services were sold or supplied to the special order of the consumer, and
> – the extent to which the seller or supplier has dealt fairly and equitably with the consumer whose legitimate interests he has to take into account."

---

[117]   O.F.T. *Unfair Contract Terms Bulletin* No. 1, p. 8.
[118]   S.I. No. 27 of 1995, Article 3.

This statement broadly corresponds with the Schedule to the 1980 legislation; the fourth factor in particular is something of an unconscionability catch-all provision which could make factors like degree of notice, availability of insurance, the risk to the consumer and the consumer's ability to avoid the harm, extremely relevant.

Once we move away from the good faith requirement, the Regulations give the issue a more specific focus by listing some 17 examples of terms in consumer contracts that may be unfair. This list, found in Schedule 3 to the Regulations, is a grey-list and the Regulations require the specific clause to be set against the good faith requirement. The U.K. Office of Fair Trading (O.F.T.) has categorised the most common unfair terms encountered by the O.F.T. in the following way:

> Entire agreement clauses – These exclude from the contract anything said or promised by a salesman or agent of the company.
>
> Hidden clauses – Consumers are not bound by terms they could not get to know before signing a contract, but it is regrettably common for consumers not to have sight, or any notice, of the full terms and conditions until after they have signed a contract.
>
> Penalty clauses – A number of consumer contracts have one-sided clauses which penalise consumers, for example by permitting a company to retain deposits with no counterbalancing penalties on the company if it does not comply with its obligations.
>
> Exclusion clauses – These exclude liability for every possible eventuality, and are very common.
>
> Variation clauses – Typically these give the supplier the right to put up prices with no realistic right for the consumer to withdraw without penalty."[119]

Some of the "grey-list" provisions are extremely beneficial to Irish consumers. Disclaimers in relation to physical injury or death caused while using a mode of transport or an amusement ride, for example, will now be rendered ineffective in most instances. The U.K. experience indicates that one-sided contracts for car hire, mobile phones, home installations like double-glazing and paving, satellite t.v. packages, and for some financial services, can be significantly re-addressed as long as the monitoring of such standard contracts is done effectively by the enforcement agency. In Ireland this role is filled by the Office of the Director of Consumer Affairs.

Note also that the Regulations also require clear and intelligible drafting of contract terms in standardised contract documents.

---

[119] O.F.T. *Unfair Contract Terms Bulletin* No. 1, p. 9.

## (8)  *The Package Holidays Directive*

This Directive,[120] transposed into Irish law by the Package Holidays and Travel Trade Act 1995 adds to the existing law relating to misrepresentation and disclaimers in holiday contracts by setting out minimum standards for brochure content, pre-contractual disclosure provision of information as well as obligations to be met before the package commences, a number of essential terms, a booking transfer right and restrictions on the right to vary prices.

---

[120]  Council Directive 90/314/EEC of June 13, 1990 on package travel, holidays and package tours [1990] O.J. L158/59.

# 9 Importance and Relative Effect of Contractual Terms

## Introduction

Not all contractual terms are of the same weight and importance. At one time the common law position was different. All covenants were independent in the sense that if one party failed to perform or satisfy a covenant or condition, the contractual obligations of the other party subsisted; that other party could not use the failure of the condition as an excuse for his own non-performance. He was obliged to perform and sue the other for all loss occasioned by any breach of contract. If both parties broke the agreement and one party sued, the defendant could not plead that the plaintiff's own breach of contract excused the defendant. The defendant's remedy was a cross-action for damages. So, a promise by A to pay £1,000 for a piece of land owned by B was described in the language of the day as an independent covenant. Should B fail to convey land he could not excuse non-performance by asserting that A had broken his own covenant to pay £1,000 at a date prior to the agreed date for completion; B's remedy was an action for the £1,000. Lord Mansfield identified this as a source of some injustice; should A be unable to pay £1,000 this would oblige B to convey without giving him any realistic hope of obtaining the consideration promised by A. In *Kingston v. Preston*[1] Lord Mansfield laid down that covenants could be broken down into tree types:

(1) conditions could be dependent; here B alleges a failure by A to show that a named event has occurred and that the event was a condition precedent, preventing B's obligation from accruing at all;

(2) covenants designed to be performed simultaneously with those of the other contracting party were described as concurrent conditions; this concurrent covenant was dependent in the sense that if the plaintiff alleged failure to perform by the defendant the plaintiff could not recover damages unless the plaintiff pleaded performance of his obligation or at least a willingness to perform;

(3) covenants could be independent. These covenants were actionable without reference to the obligations of the plaintiff.

While section 28 of the Sale of Goods Act 1893 provides a statutory instance of a concurrent obligation – payment of price and delivery and concurrent

---

[1]  (1773) 2 Doug. 689.

obligations[2] – the issues raised are complicated indeed, and generally fall to be decided from first principles of common law rather than as the result of parliamentary guidance. Professor Corbin[3] provided the clearest explanation of this difficult area of law. Corbin explained that covenants have to be distinguished from promises. The old terminology of dependent/independent/concurrent covenant operated when one person tried to rely on the failure of another person to show that some stipulated event had not occurred and that the failure of this condition permitted that person from withholding the performance promised. In *Kingston v. Preston* itself it was held that the failure of the plaintiff to provide security in respect of a business owned by the defendant entitled the defendant to refuse to transfer the business to the plaintiff; the defendant did not wish to part with his business and stock-in-trade and become an unsecured creditor. The covenant was such that the defendant's obligation to transfer was dependent upon the plaintiff's obligation to provide adequate security.

The principle upon which the courts distinguished between dependent and independent covenants was the subject of the leading case of *Davidson v. Gwynne*.[4] Lord Ellenborough observed:

> "unless the non-performance alleged in the breach of the contract goes to the whole root and consideration of it, the covenant broken is not to be considered as a condition precedent, but as a distinct covenant for the breach of which the party injured may be compensated in damages."[5]

This approach was adopted in several nineteenth century English and Irish cases. It was clearly held in *Cripps v. Smith*[6] that a breach of warranty, or independent covenant, is to be the subject of a cross-action by the injured party and is not to be the basis for rescission of the contract. In *Garrick v. Bradshaw*[7] the dichotomy between independent and dependent covenants was extensively considered and *Boone v. Eyre*[8] was cited with obvious approval. In *Fearnley v. London Guarantee Insurance Co.*[9] May C.J. presented the issue in graphic terms:

> "where, as in the present case, a defendant sued for the non-performance of promises contained in an instrument relies on the breach by the plaintiff of some term in the same instrument to be performed by him, as an answer to the action. . . . the point to be ascertained is, did the default of the plaintiff affect the essence of the contract between the parties?"[10]

---

2  *MacAuley and Cullen v. Horgan* [1925] 2 I.R. 1.
3  (1919) 28 Yale L.J. 739.
4  (1810) 12 East 381.
5  *Ibid.* at 389.
6  (1841) 3 Ir.L.Rep. 277.
7  (1846) 10 Ir.L.Rep. 129.
8  (1779) 1 Hy.Bl. 273; *Clements v. Russell* (1854) 7 Ir.Jur. 102.
9  (1881) 6 L.R. (Ir.) 219, 232, 394. The House of Lords disagreed (1882) 5 App.Cas. 911.
10  (1881) 6 L.R. (Ir.) 219 at 242.

In *Fearnley v. London Guarantee Insurance Co.* the issue was whether the plaintiff could enforce an insurance policy, a fidelity policy whereby the plaintiff sought an indemnity from his insurers because of fraudulent embezzlement by the plaintiff's employee. The defendant pleaded, *inter alia*, that a condition precedent to liability on the policy was that the plaintiff should diligently prosecute the employee in question. The Court of Exchequer and two members of the Court of Appeal held that on its true construction, the obligation was not a condition precedent to recovery on the policy because the obligation upon the insurer to indemnify the employer operated independently. While both Ball L.C. and Morris C.J. felt that the covenant was dependent, the members of the Court of Appeal stressed that the issue was one of construction of the contract.

A contrasting contemporary decision can be found in *In Re Application of Butler*.[11] Under a valid contract for motor insurance Butler was required to give notice as soon as practicable of any motor accident in which he was involved. The policy declared that his covenant, *inter alia*, was a condition precedent. Butler failed to notify the company of an accident in which he was involved and the Supreme Court held that he was not entitled to recover on the foot of the insurance policy for notification was a condition precedent to the insurer's obligation to pay out on the policy. The failure to notify was not of itself a breach of contract by Butler but it justified the company's refusal to pay. While the insurer may waive the condition precedent there is no obligation to show non-compliance has been prejudicial: see Gannon J. in *Galecrann Teoranta v. Payne*.[12] If the condition is independent the courts hold that, even if one of the conditions has not been met, this will not justify a refusal to satisfy the other condition. Corbin cites *Constable v. Cloberie*[13] as the leading case. Here the plaintiff promised to sail with the next favouring wind. The defendant in turn promised to pay if the ship reached Cadiz and returned. While sailing with the next wind was both a condition and a contractual promise it was not a dependent condition nor a contractual promise which, if broken, justified the defendant in witholding the promised sum.

One feature of dependent covenants, when they are external to the contract, is that the person bound by, or prejudiced by non-observance of the covenant, does not, as such, commit a breach of contract. (See *In Re Application of Butler*[14] for a clear illustration of this point.) However, English and Irish judicial practice is to identify a dependent or independent covenant as part of the contractual nexus, that is, an obligation which is to be performed by one of the parties. In deciding whether an agreement is subject to the occurence of an event, the non-performance of that event postponing the very existence of a contract, the practice within an industry or profession may be pertinent. The

---

[11] [1970] I.R. 45: *Board of Ordnance v. Lewis* (1854) 7 Ir.Jur. 17.
[12] [1985] I.L.R.M. 105.
[13] (1662) Palmer 397.
[14] [1970] I.R. 45.

"subject to contract" cases in real property transactions are perhaps the best examples of such a process, for until the contract is signed or exchanged the majority of property sales do not have any legal force at all. The contract only comes into existence upon the contingent event. One of the most interesting features of "subject to contract" agreements is that it is entirely within the control of the parties to decide whether or not to proceed and execute the agreement: a capricious or unmeritorious decision not to sign the contract or to exchange contracts is not a basis for relief for the aggrieved party.

If in particular the condition fixed is something over which the parties can have no control – *e.g.* a statement that A will pay B £20,000 for an acre of farmland if the local authority grants B's application to re-zone the land for industrial use – it may be that A's statement will be held to be a condition and that until this event occurs there is no contract. In *Pym v. Campbell*[15] an action brought upon an alleged agreement to pay for an interest in an invention failed when the defendant was able to show that the existence of the contract was conditional upon one Abernathie, an engineer, approving the invention. Abernathie failed to give his approval so no contract existed which could form the basis of the plaintiff's claim. In *Macklin & McDonald v. Greacen & Co.*[16] the defendant agreed to sell land to the plaintiffs providing the Northern Bank, who occupied the site, gave permission. This permission was not forthcoming. The plaintiffs' action for breach of contract failed; Griffin J. in the Supreme Court pointed out that because the defendant had not expressly or impliedly promised that the bank would give permission there could not be liability in contract. Even if the event in question is within the power of one party to secure, a condition precedent may still be held to exist: *Myton Ltd. v. Schwab-Morris.*[17] In this case Goulding J. held that an agreement which required the purchase of land to pay a deposit involved a condition precedent and that until the payment was made no contract existed. The result in this case was, on the facts, a fair one for the defendant purchaser had registered a caution against the vendor's property and this result meant the caution could be removed. However, the reasoning of Goulding J. is open to criticism: the purchasers duty to pay a deposit is part of the purchaser's contractual obligations, rather than an external condition upon which the contract's very existence will turn. If the event stipulated is within the power of one of the parties, it does not follow that there is an obligation to bring the stipulated event into being. Only if there is an express or implied obligation, or a duty, which requires one party to do, or abstain from doing, anything which may affect the happening of the stated event will the courts intervene.

In *Thompson v. ASDA-MFI Group Plc*[18] the plaintiff was a member of a pension scheme which gave him the option of increasing his shares. However, under the rules of the pension scheme, the option expired if the pensioner's

---

15  (1856) 6 El & Bl. 370.
16  [1983] I.R. 61.
17  [1974] 1 W.L.R. 331.
18  [1988] 2 All E.R. 722.

employer ceased to be a member of the Group. The defendants sold their shareholding in W. Ltd.; the plaintiff's employer and the plaintiff therefore ceased to have any rights of purchase. Scott J. indicated that the plaintiff company were not bound by contract not to dispose of its shareholding in W. Ltd. *Thompson v. ASDA-MFI Group Plc* is an illustration of a condition subsequent. Here the contract and contractual rights of the parties subsist until some stipulated, or contingent, event occurs. In this instance, the plaintiff had a right to purchase shares until his employer ceased to be a part of the ASDA-MFI Group. When this occurred the contractual right was terminated.

Conditions subsequent will be anticipated in situations where the buyer of goods takes delivery but wishes to have the goods inspected or examined to see if they comply with a description or statement about merchantability or fitness for purpose.[19] In contracts for the sale of land for potential development, the purchaser may stipulate that if the application for planning permission is unsuccessful, the purchaser is to have the option of returning the property and obtaining the return of his purchase money.[20] Conditions subsequent are much less common than conditions precedent. Conditions precedent are more complex in effect. If a condition precedent is not met, this may prevent the contract itself from coming into existence, as in *Macklin & McDonald v. Greacen & Co.*, or it may simply control the remedies available to the parties. In *Gregg & Co. v. Fraser & Sons*[21] a contract provided that before an award of damages for breach of contract could be awarded by a civil jury there had to be a valid and enforceable award from an arbitrator or umpire. It was held that this clause was, implicitly, a condition precedent and that until it was satisfied a jury award could not be made.

It is common to find that the condition is held to also involve a promissory element. There may be an express promise that the condition will be fulfilled or it may be implied that efforts will be made to ensure that the condition precedent is satisfied as in *Rooney v. Byrne.*[22] In this case, the purchaser of real property, under a contract subject to him obtaining satisfactory finance, was held to be under a duty to make efforts to find and accept satisfactory finance and not entitled to exercise a discretion to accept or refuse finance. Whether the condition precedent, to use Corbin's analysis, contains a promissory element is a question of construction. It may be that an express or implied statement to this effect can be detected. If the parties, or their agents, clearly considered the condition created an obligation then the condition is sometimes said to be a "fundamental term:" see *Damon Cia v. Hapag Lloyd S.A.*[23]

The Irish case of *Tradax (Ireland) Ltd. v. Irish Grain Board Ltd.*[24] illustrates that it will not be easy to find such an implied term if the condition itself is not

---

[19] *Head v. Tattersall* (1871) L.R. 7 Exch. 7.
[20] *Dorene Ltd. v. Suedes (Ireland) Ltd.* [1981] I.R. 312.
[21] [1906] 2 I.R. 545, 570.
[22] [1933] I.R. 609.
[23] [1985] 1 All E.R. 475.
[24] [1984] I.R. 1.

stated in the contract. The majority of the Supreme Court, McCarthy J. dissenting, could not find an implied obligation upon the buyers of grain to open a letter of credit in favour of the seller. In distinguishing the facts of the case from the English cases (see, for example *Ian Stach Ltd. v. Baker Bosley Ltd.*[25]) the majority of the Supreme Court rejected the view that his implied fundamental term could exist because it was inconsistent with the express terms of the contract.

So, where we use the term condition in the sense of contractual promise we can see that the courts face a difficult task of construction or interpretation; the principles of construction the courts have developed are of the utmost importance in resolving disputes over interpretation. In relation to express terms in the contract section 11(2) of the 1893 Act, as amended by the 1980 Act, provides:

> "whether a stipulation in a contract of sale is a condition, the breach of which may give rise to a right to treat the contract as repudiated, or a warranty, the breach of which may give rise to a claim for damages but not to a right to reject the goods and treat the contract as repudiated, depends in each case on the construction of the contract. A stipulation may be a condition, though called a warranty in the contract."

The issue of whether an express term is a condition is not a matter a of law but one of interpretation. The test for deciding whether a term is a condition or not, in cases where parties have not expressly so provided, is to be found in the words of Bowen L.J. in *Bentsen & Son v. Taylor*[26]:

> "[t]here is no way of deciding that question except by looking at the contract in the light of the surrounding circumstances, and then making up one's mind whether the intention of the parties, as gathered from the instrument itself, will best be carried out by treating the promise as a warranty sounding only in damages, or as a condition precedent by the failure to perform which the other party is relieved of his liability."[27]

Therefore, the test for a condition requires the courts to look at the contract document and surrounding circumstances – at the time of contracting and not subsequent events – and try to fix the intention of the parties. A term may be held a condition even if the remedy of rescission is not affixed to the obligation.[28] In the recent decision of the House of Lords in *Total Gas Marketing v. Arco British Ltd.*[29] the designation of an obligation to be "conditional" upon the defendants entering a separate agreement was held to make that event a condition precedent even in the absence of a stipulation entitling the plaintiffs,

---

[25]   [1958] 2 Q.B. 130.
[26]   [1893] 2 Q.B. 274.
[27]   *Ibid.* at 281.
[28]   *Bunge Corporation v. Tradax S.A.* [1981] 1 W.L.R. 711.
[29]   *The Times*, June 26, 1998.

in the event of the default of the defendants, to regard their obligations as terminated or discharged for non-occurance of the condition precedent.

If, however, the obligation was an implied obligation under the Sale of Goods Act 1893 the situation becomes more complicated. If the goods sold were not the seller's to sell (section 12), did not meet the contract description (section 13), were unmerchantable or unfit for their purpose (section 14), or having been sold by sample did not accord with the sample (section 15), then the buyer had a right to reject the goods because these implied statutory obligations were statutory conditions for, as we have seen, the effect of this dichotomy was to provide a right of rescission if the obligation was a condition, but a right to damages only if the obligation was a warranty. This was graphically illustrated by *Re Moore & Co. v. Landauer*.[30] The contract was for the sale of 3,100 cases of Australian canned fruit packed 30 tins to a case. Some cases were delivered with less than 30 tins to a case, some with more. The total number of tins delivered met the contract requirement. No loss resulted for failure to meet the contract description yet the buyer was held entitled to rescind simply because section 13 (requiring goods to answer their description) was broken by defective packing of goods.

This rigid and inflexible result could be avoided by an exemption clause, but in the absence of such a clause the courts could not overturn the statute because (so it was thought prior to 1975) *all* contract terms, express or implied, in sale of goods cases were either conditions or warranties. After 1893, there was no room for an old approach in which the courts could sometimes ask, is the breach likely to go to the root of the contract? Is the innocent party to the contract likely to be substantially deprived of the fruits of the contract? *A fortiori*, the actual effects of breach where also not relevant.

The problem that bedevils this classification is this: who is to decide which category the obligation falls into? If the parties have taken the trouble to "label" each obligation then the courts will respect this, but, in the real world, persons are not so fastidious. As a result, obligations and their importance, came to be an area for the exercise of judicial discretion. So, in *Ritchie v. Atkinson*[31] a vessel left the Port of St. Petersburgh with a short cargo. Loading was broken off because of the danger of hostilities breaking out between Britain and Russia. On its arrival in Britain the merchant refused to pay the shipowners their freight, claiming that the obligation to deliver a full cargo was a condition precedent to the merchant's obligation. To uphold such a plea would have permitted the merchant to obtain free transportation of his goods. The Court of Kings Bench held the breach of contract had minor consequences for the merchant. The obligation to deliver a full cargo was independent and the merchant was obliged to pay freight on a *pro rata* basis; any loss suffered by the defendant as a result of the short cargo was to be actionable in damages. While some of the nineteenth century decisions such as *Graves v. Legg*[32]

---

[30] [1921] 2 K.B. 519.
[31] (1808) 10 East 295.
[32] (1854) 9 Exch. 709.

indicate that the nature of the term may change depending upon the consequences of breach, the issue of interpretation of the contract as a whole, and a search for the presumed intention of the parties ultimately became the basis upon which the contract term was classified. Palles C.B., in *Fearnley v. London Guarantee Insurance Co.*,[33] indicated that the classification given by the parties is not necessarily dispositive, for if the label given is inconsistent with the entire contract it will not be given effect. This is not to say, however, that the courts are free to ignore or override the clear intention of the parties, but rather the courts will infer that the entire agreement should be compatible with the classification adopted, for if doubts arise, the courts are likely to give effect to the most natural interpretation to be placed on the contract as a whole.

In the Irish case of *Knox v. Mayne*[34] the Court of Exchequer upheld a plea of condition precedent. The sellers of a cargo of maize sued the defendant purchasers for non-acceptance. The purchaser was to have "privilege of having shipment to direct port" to be nominated by him. The sellers shipped the final cargo without requesting a port of discharge, whereupon the defendants took delivery but refused to pay for the final cargo. The plaintiffs argued that it was for the defendants to show loss resulted from the breach. It was held that the right of selection had to be given to the defendants. The failure was failure of a condition precedent, not a collateral or independent covenant. Two further examples serve to illustrate the difficulties encountered here. It is established that if a farmer acquiring land under an agistment or conacre agreement fails to pay the contract price this constitutes breach of a dependent covenant; the landowner may treat this failure as terminating his own obligation to permit user of the land: see *Carson v. Jeffers*.[35] On the other hand, *Carson v. Jeffers* must be contrasted with *Athol v. Midland Gt. W. Ry. Co.*[36] The lessor covenanted to permit the plaintiff lessees use of a conduit for draining excess water from the land leased to them. The defendant lessor diverted the conduit. An action by the plaintiffs was met with the plea that they had not paid rent and that payment was a condition precedent to the defendant's obligation to permit user of the conduit. The plea failed; each obligation was held to be independent.

## The Sale of Goods Act 1893

It is necessary to mention the effects of the Sale of Goods Act 1893 on the common law rules outlined above. Although this Act should not have influenced the courts in non-sale of goods cases, it had a "spill over" effect which is only now being expunged from the common law.

---

[33] (1881) 6 L.R. (Ir.) 219, 232, 394; (1880) 5 App.Cas. 911.
[34] (1873) I.R. 7 C.L. 557.
[35] [1961] I.R. 44.
[36] (1867) I.R. 3 C.L. 333.

## Conditions and Warranties

The 1893 Act was not designed to be a radical measure of reform; it was primarily designed to codify the rules that had evolved at common law. But the difficulties surrounding the question of discharge of contractual obligations were met by invoking a new theoretical framework which, while it relied heavily on the dependent/independent convenant dichotomy, led to the temporary obliteration of the old common law rules, even in non-sale of goods transactions.

The 1893 Act divided obligations into conditions and warranties. Unfortunately, the draftsman did not define such obligations but, contented himself with setting out the consequences of breach of each obligation. A condition is a term, breach of which entitles the innocent party to elect to rescind the contract and sue for damages or affirm the contract and sue for damages.[37] Under section 11(1)(c), the right to rescind was lost once delivery of goods had taken place and the contract executed. (The revised section 11 in the 1980 Act abandons this restriction on the right to rescind.) If the term is a warranty the innocent party has a remedy in damages only. A warranty is defined in section 62(1) as something "collateral to the main purpose of such contract." This technical use of the word "warranty", which connoted at common law a contractual representation, has been a source of some confusion and students should bear in mind that "warranty" may mean different things according to context.

## The *Hong Kong Firs* Case

The first indication that the condition/warranty dichotomy was not all embracing was given by the English Court of Appeal in the *Hong Kong Firs* case.[38] A contract for the charter of a cargo ship for a period of two years was broken because the vessel was unseaworthy. Repairs were necessary and the vessel was out of service for 20 weeks. The charterers sought to rescind the contract claiming the obligation to provide a seaworthy vessel was a condition. (The charterers wanted to repudiate because a lowering of freight charges would permit the charterers to acquire another vessel at a lower cost). The Court of Appeal rejected this view of the bargain. The Court looked to the pre-1893 case law and held that a seaworthiness obligation was not a condition in the sense that failure to supply a seaworthy vessel discharged the charterer's obligation to take the vessel and pay freight or the cost of hire. Upjohn L.J. observed that to hold a seaworthiness obligation was a condition would lead to absurdities:

> "If a nail is missing from one of the timbers of a wooden vessel or if proper medical supplies or two anchors are not on board at the time of sailing, the owners are in breach of the seaworthiness stipulation. It is contrary to common sense to suppose that in such circumstances the

---

[37] *White Sewing Machine Co. v. Fitzgerald* (1894) 29 I.L.T.R. 37.
[38] *Hong Kong Fir Shipping Co. Ltd. v. Kawasaki Kisen Kaisha Ltd.* [1962] 2 Q.B. 26.

parties contemplated that the charterer should at once be entitled to treat the contract as at an end for such trifling breaches."[39]

So, in non-sale of goods cases the condition/warranty dichotomy was challenged; unless there was conclusive evidence that the parties intended breach of such a term to lead to a right to rescission or damages only, the courts will now ask:

> "Does the breach of the stipulation go so much to the root of the contract that it makes further commercial performance of the contract impossible, or in other words is the whole contract frustrated: If yes, the innocent party may treat the contract as at an end. If nay his claim sounds in damages only."[40]

The problem with this approach is that it is very litigation oriented. It has been attacked as inconsistent with the 1893 Act and undesirable because it leads to uncertainty and unpredictability of result. The *Hong Kong Firs* case was thought to be applicable only in contracts where the 1893 Act could not apply. Since the decision in *Cehave N.V. v. Bremer Handelgesellschaft*,[41] it is established that even in sale of goods cases the courts should not give the extreme remedy of rescission unless the parties have clearly so agreed or unless a precedent binds a court so to hold. In *Cehave N.V.* the Court of Appeal set out a series of questions that should be asked:

(1) Does the contract *expressly* confer a right of termination for such a breach? If so the courts must respect this and allow rescission even if loss resulting is minimal or non-existent.

(2) If no to question 1, does the contract impliedly give a right to rescission or only a right to damages? Again an affirmative answer will be conclusive, as *Schuler A.G. v. Wickman Tools*[42] shows. However, it may be that the unreasonableness of the result or absence of loss will point towards the next question coming into play.

(3) Does a statute or *stare decisis* point towards the obligation being a condition or warranty? The *implied* obligations under the 1893 Act (as amended by the 1980 Act) remain conditions or warranties so *Re Moore & Co. v. Landauer*[43] would still be decided in the same way; similarly, case law determines that a statement that a ship will be ready to load is a condition: see *Behn v. Burness*[44]; so too is an expected date of arrival stipulation: see *The Mihalis Angelos*[45]; see also the decision in *Toepfer (Hamburg) v. Verheijdens Veervoeder*

---

[39] *Hong Kong Fir Shipping Co. Ltd. v. Kawasaki Kisen Kaisha Ltd.* [1962] 2 Q.B. 26 at 70.
[40] *Ibid.* at 70.
[41] [1976] Q.B. 44.
[42] [1921] 2 K.B. 519.
[43] [1973] 2 All E.R. 39.
[44] (1863) 3 B & S 751.
[45] [1971] 1 Q.B. 164; *The Baleaes* [1993] 1 Lloyd's Rep. 215.

*Commissiehandel (Rotterdam)*,[46] in which the Court of Appeal held an obligation to make prompt payment to be a condition, illustrating that if the court feels that commercial practice requires the obligation to be a condition the contract term will be so construed. See also *Gill & Duffus S.A. v. Berger & Co.*[47] in which the House of Lords held that failure by the buyer under a C.I.F. contract to pay the price when presented with documents constitutes a fundamental breach of contract entitling the seller to rescind and sue for damages. In *Barber v. NWS Bank plc*[48] the Court of Appeal held that an express term in a contract of hire-purchase which declared, wrongly, that the defendants were the owners of a car which was the subject of a conditional sale agreement was a condition. The term was fundamental to the contract and could be broken in one way only. The plaintiff could thus rescind the contract for breach of condition when the true state of affairs were discovered.

If we have another look at the facts of *Knox v. Mayne*[49] it is likely that a modern Irish court, influenced by these English authorities, would not be so ready to hold the destination clause to be a condition and would now perhaps test the case by asking the fourth question posed in *Cehave N.V.*:

(4) Has the breach gone to the root of the contract so as to deprive the injured party of that which he contracted for? Unless this central or core obligation can no longer be obtained – several English judges and commentators call this *the fundamental term* – damages will be deemed to be the most appropriate remedy. This trend is only part of a broader movement towards conferring wide discretionary powers on the courts in the area of remedies.

The facts of *Laird Brothers v. Dublin Steampacket*,[50] the leading Irish authority on this question, are instructive. The plaintiffs agreed to build a ship to be delivered by August 1, 1897. Payment was to be made by instalments. The contract provided that the sixth and final instalment of £5,000 was not to be paid unless the vessel was completed on the agreed date. The vessel was not completed until September 1897. The defendants had not suffered loss but they argued that under the terms of the contract completion on the due date was a condition precedent to the payment of the last instalment. Andrews J. regarded the matter as one of construction and posed the following question:

> "are the words of the clause, . . . so precise, express and strong, when taken in connection with the entire contract, that the intention prima facie so unreasonable, is the only one compatible with the terms employed?"[51]

It would appear that the court was reluctant to give the contract term its plain and ordinary meaning – which would have favoured the defendants –

---

[46] *The Times*, April 26, 1978.
[47] [1985] 1 Lloyds Rep. 621.
[48] *The Times*, November 27, 1995.
[49] (1873) I.R. 7 C.L. 557.
[50] (1900) 34 I.L.T.R. 97.
[51] *Ibid.* at 100.

because, as Andrews J. said "[i]t is impossible to hold that this delay went to the root of the matter so as to render the performance of the rest of the contract by the plaintiffs a thing different in substance from what the defendants stipulated for." Yet, as we have seen, such a question can only be asked *after* the court has ascertained what the parties have agreed upon; a clear statement of intention must be given effect even if the result is unreasonable. It appears to this writer that Andrews J. went some way towards modifying the terms of this agreement by ruling that an unreasonable contract provision can only be given effect if an unreasonable result is the only possible interpretation that can be placed on the term.

In *Bunge Corporation v. Tradax S.A.*[52] the House of Lords upheld the decision of the Court of Appeal in which it had been held that an express obligation requiring the shippers of goods to give 15 days' notice of their date for the cargo to be available was a condition, breach of which entitled the owner to rescind the charterparty. While the contract did not expressly cede the remedy of rescission, this type of obligation – a time obligation – was held to be normally so important in commercial transactions that, for the sake of certainty, predictability and uniformity of approach, it will be interpreted as having been intended as a condition in the sense of an express promise which, if broken, gives the injured party the right to rescind the contract without reference to the actual effects of the breach.

The movement towards holding that time obligations in mercantile contracts will generally be held to be conditions has been further emphasised by the House of Lords, in *Cie Commercial Sucres et Denrées v. Czamikow Ltd., The Naxos.*[53] The contract was concluded on standard terms used exclusively between sugar dealers and incorporated rules of the Refined Sugar Association of London. Under the contract, the buyer was entitled to call upon the seller to load, the seller to be given not less than 14 days of notice that the buyer's vessels were expected to be ready to load. Due notice was given, but the seller failed to deliver the sugar. The buyer then rescinded the contract for breach, brought a replacement cargo and sued for consequential loss. The House of Lords had to consider whether the rules relating to boarding were contractual obligations which were binding on the seller once due notice was given by the buyer, and whether the obligation was in the nature of a condition. While both the Commercial Court and the Court of Appeal held in favour of the seller, the House of Lords reinstated the view of the arbitrators that the obligation in question was contractual and in the nature of a condition. In giving the leading judgment Lord Ackner followed *Bunge* and, classifying the contract as mercantile and the obligation as a time obligation, went on to consider the findings of the arbitrators. In the view of the arbitrators, the obligation was of the "utmost importance", because prompt performance of delivery obligations would be vital to both parties, and a prompt right to cancel for default would

---

[52]   [1981] 1 W.L.R. 71.
[53]   [1990] 3 All E.R. 641.

be essential to allow the buyer to mitigate loss by securing delivery from another source. The case is a compelling one because the rules in question, and the contract generally, were far from specific on the issue of remedies. Lord Brandon, dissenting, pointed out that similar time obligations were clearly warranties. The majority of the House of Lords however was clearly influenced by the arbitrators who had ruled that demurrage would not be an adequate remedy in such circumstances. The contract was therefore not symmetrical and, despite Lord Brandon's view that the result of the majority judgment was to create illogical consequences, the value of certainty and predictability of result was seen as of paramount importance.

If we put to one side complicated transactions such as those in *Bunge* and *The Naxos*, and, bearing in mind Ormond L.J.'s statement in *Cehave* that the courts should be slow to hold an express term in a condition, we can see that the *Hong Kong Firs* test means that the judges, appraised of all the facts and the results of the actual breach, are to have the power to determine which remedy is the most appropriate one in this particular dispute. While some flexibility of approach is sometimes demonstrated by the judges (*Regent O.H.G. Aisenstadt und Barig v. Francesco of Jermyn St.*[54]) this will not always prove possible. There have been relatively few cases in which the fourth element or question in the *Hong Kong Firs* test has been *applied*, because the courts have tended to find that the obligation, expressly or by implication, has been intended to be a condition. However, the House of Lords in *The Gregos*[55] held that an obligation to redeliver a vessel at the end of a time charter was an innominate term; a short delay would not justify giving the obligation the status of a condition. Similarly, in one of the only two reported Irish cases in which *Hong Kong Firs* has been applied, Costello J. was able to hold that the obligation in question was to be tested by reference to the consequences of the breach in the case at bar. In *Irish Telephone Rentals Ltd. v. Irish Civil Service Building Society Ltd.*[56] the plaintiffs purported to rescind a contract for the supply of a telephone system on the ground that it malfunctioned. Costello J. found that the goods supplied were not in compliance with the implied term found in section 39 of the Sale of Goods and Supply of Services Act 1980, and, specifically, that the goods were not of merchantable quality. It is important to note that section 39 obligations are implied terms – the Act does not assign them the status of condition or warranty in the context of supply of services even though merchantable quality is an implied condition in sale of goods, leasing and hire-purchase contracts. Costello J. cited the following extract from the judgment of Diplock L.J. in *Hong Kong Firs*:

> "The contract may itself expressly define some of these events, as in the cancellation clause in a charter party; but, human prescience being limited, it seldom does so exhaustively and often fails to do so at all. In

---

[54] [1981] 3 All E.R. 327.
[55] [1995] 1 Lloyd's Rep. 1.
[56] [1991] I.L.R.M. 880; see also *Taylor v. Smyth* [1990] I.L.R.M. 377.

some classes of contracts such as sale of goods, marine insurance, contracts of affreightment, evidenced by bills of lading and those between parties to bills of exchange, parliament has defined by statute some of the events not provided for expressly in individual contracts of that class; but where an event occurs the occurrence of which neither the parties nor parliament have expressly stated will discharge one of the parties from further performance of his undertakings, it is for the court to determined whether the event has this effect or not.

The test whether an event has this effect or not has been stated in a number of metaphors all of which I think amount to the same thing: does the occurrence of the event deprive the party who has further undertakings still to perform of substantially the whole benefit which it was the intention of the parties as expressed in the contract that he should obtain as the consideration for performing those undertakings?"[57]

Declaring that in his view this test was to be applied to the case before him, Costello J. held that the delays afforded in communications by virtue of the defective system were of a serious nature and justified giving the plaintiff the right to rescind.

This interesting application of *Hong Kong Firs*, however, is not free from difficulty. Costello J. also held that the defendants were in breach of an express term that the goods supplied would be provided and maintained in good working order. If express terms of this kind are in any event normally held to be conditions, even if the consequences of the section 39 breach had not been serious, the separate breach of an express condition should, arguably, have given the plaintiff a right to rescind anyway. The answer to this, of course, is that "good condition" express promises are normally characterised as innominate terms, after the decision in *The Hansa Nord*[58] and Costello J.'s decision should be seen in this context.

---

[57] [1962] 2 Q.B. 26 at 65–66.
[58] [1976] Q.B. 44; *The Aktiou* [1987] 1 Lloyd's Rep. 283.

# Part 3

# Invalidity

# 10  Mistake

## Introduction

There are insuperable difficulties for any writer faced with the task of producing a neat and intelligible exposition of the law of mistake in contract.[1] The current law is beset with jurisdictional problems that can only be resolved by future decisions or legislation. Effective analysis of the law is hampered by the fact that judges do not use terms consistently: this is particularly true of the expressions "common," "mutual" and "unilateral." Cheshire and Fifoot[2] use this threefold classification as the basis of their analysis, whilst conceding that the courts do not use these terms precisely. Several judges have used the terms "common" and "mutual" as synonyms: Dixon J. in *Nolan v. Nolan*[3] even used the terms "mutual" and "unilateral" interchangeably, regarding any distinction as "largely one of phraseology". In the case of *O'Neill v. Ryan and Others*[4] Costello J. stressed that a preliminary problem of terminology can be an impediment to clear analysis, "for whilst the courts and text-book writers have used such descriptive terms as 'common,' or 'mutual' or 'unilateral' to categorise the mistake which has affected the parties contract, unfortunately these adjectives have not been used consistently with the same meaning." Costello J. is clearly correct in pointing out the lack of uniformity, but the terms common, mutual and unilateral can provide the student with a proximate, if at times unreliable, conceptual structure. I do not, however, intend to use the Cheshire and Fifoot classification which, even in an ideal world, would be unsatisfactory.

Instead, it is proposed that we look to what the courts do rather than what they say they do. We will first of all examine the case law in order to discover when a mistake will be operative, either at common law or in equity. As a second step we will consider the rules that have emerged in relation to the remedies of damages, rescission, rectification and specific performance. Students must bear in mind the fact that if a mistake is operative it does not follow that the party pleading mistake will be entitled to any or all of these remedies. An operative mistake may give rise to the remedy of rescission without allowing the court to change or rectify the contract. Further, even if a mistake is held not to prevent a contract coming into existence the court may decline to award specific performance on the ground that the party labouring under the mistake should not be obliged to perform the contract – he may instead be held liable in damages.

---

[1]  See, *e.g.* Stoljar, *Mistake and Misrepresentation* (1968); Kerr, *Fraud and Mistake* (1954).
[2]  Cheshire, Fifoot and Furmston, *Law of Contract* (13th ed., 1996), pp. 235–236.
[3]  (1954) 92 I.L.T.R. 94.
[4]  [1991] I.L.R.M. 672.

## Operative Mistake

### (1) Mistake of law

One, or indeed both, of the contracting parties may mistakenly believe that a statute or an agreement has certain consequences; this may in turn produce an agreement based upon on misunderstanding of law. Once the true legal position is established an attempt may be made to avoid the contract by pleading its invalidity because of mistake. The legal maxim *ignorantia juris neminen excusat* may come into effect here. It would be inconvenient to allow persons to avoid contractual obligations because of a misunderstanding of the law, particularly in cases where the correct legal position could have been discovered quite easily. Thus it is often said that a mistake of law cannot be operative, either at common law or equity. In *O'Loghlen v. O'Callaghan*[5] the plaintiff leased property to the defendant under an arrangement which permitted the defendant to deduct the rates and pay them to the local authority. *Both* plaintiff and defendant calculated the rate by reference to a section of the relevant Act which was later found to be inapplicable. As a result a lower rate than that calculated had been payable and the plaintiff sued for £100, being the difference between the rent actually paid and the rent payable had the rates been calculated correctly. It was held that at common law the defendant was not obliged to pay the difference; the mistake as a mistake of law was not operative.

The modern law of restitution however tends to skate over this distinction between mistakes of law and mistakes of fact. One specific example of this has surfaced in the Irish courts. If a local authority charges an excessive rate because of a misinterpretation of the rating legislation, or if the local authority charges an amount of money for a service or for the transfer of an interest in land which is in excess of the amount that should have been charged because of a misinterpretation of the enabling legislation, can the overpayment be reclaimed or used by way of set off? While at first sight the older cases[6] suggest that this is not possible, the decision of the Privy Council in *Kiriri Cotton Co. v. Dewani*[7] has been followed. In *Dolan v. Nelligan*[8] Kenny J. approved the speech of Lord Denning in *Kiriri Cotton* when his Lordship said: "If there is something more in addition to a mistake of law, if there is something in the defendant's conduct which shows that, of the two of them, he is the one primarily responsible for the mistake then it may be recovered back, they are not *in pari delicto*." In *Rogers v. Louth County Council*[9] the Supreme Court also approved *Kiriri Cotton Co.* In the High Court decision in *Lord Mayor of Dublin v. The Provost of Trinity College Dublin*,[10] Hamilton J. held that monies paid by the College in rates could be set off against monies due; the monies paid were in excess of

---

[5] (1874) I.R. 8 C.L. 116; *Gee v. News Group Newspapers, The Times*, June 8, 1990.
[6] For a review of the old law, see Kerr, *Fraud and Mistake* (1954), pp. 133–137.
[7] [1960] A.C. 192.
[8] [1967] I.R. 247.
[9] [1981] I.L.R.M. 143.
[10] [1986] I.L.R.M. 283.

the lawful rate. Hamilton J., after citing the above decisions said: "where money is paid, whether under a mistake of fact or law, justice requires that such money should be recoverable if the law so permits." While the Supreme Court later allowed an appeal there is nothing in the decision of the Supreme Court to suggest disapproval of Hamilton J.'s decision on this particular point. In *Avon C.C. v. Howlett*,[11] the Court of Appeal was required to consider whether overpayments of salary could be recovered from an employee. The employee argued that the error arose due to a misinterpretation of his contract of employment and his entitlement to sick pay and was therefore a mistake of law. Slade L.J. in his leading judgment noted that since *Cooper v. Phibbs* had been decided the courts had not been enthusiastic about upholding this distinction. The mistake was accordingly characterised as one of fact not law. The overpayment was held irrecoverable on the grounds of estoppel and not because it was made under a mistake of law. This entire area has been recently considered by the English Law Commission.[12]

A mistake made by a legal adviser when executing a document will still be operative and may be avoided by the client: *Monaghan C.C. v. Vaughan*.[13] English cases suggest that a solicitor who misinterprets the effect of a statute makes a mistake of law which will not be operative.

### (2) Mistake of law in equity

In equity a distinction has been drawn between a mistake as to the general law, that is, the ordinary law of the country as found in public statutes for example, and private law, the law as found in agreements, wills and Private Acts of Parliament. In *Cooper v. Phibbs*[14] the plaintiff and defendant contracted to permit the plaintiff to lease a salmon fishery in Sligo. Both parties assumed that the defendant's father had earlier owned the Sligo fishery which had descended to them by will. In fact, a Private Act of Parliament made the plaintiff tenant for life. He sought to avoid the contract because in point of law he was already the owner. Lord Westbury, in giving judgment in the House of Lords declared:

> "private right of ownership is a matter of fact; it may be the result also of a matter of law; but if parties contract under a mutual mistake and misapprehension as to their relative and respective rights, the result is that the agreement is liable to be set aside as having proceeded upon a common mistake."[15]

In *Leonard v. Leonard*,[16] Manners L.C. indicated that equity would not hold the plaintiff bound by an agreement to settle a dispute as to private ownership

---

[11] [1983] 1 W.L.R. 605.
[12] Law Com. No. 120, *Restitution of Payments made under a Mistake of Law* (1991).
[13] [1948] I.R. 306.
[14] (1865) 17 Ir. Ch.R. 73; (1867) L.R. 2 H.L. 149.
[15] (1867) L.R. 2 H.L. 149 at 170; see Matthews, (1988) 105 L.Q.R. 599.
[16] (1812) 2 Ball & B. 171.

of land where the other party knew facts, unknown to the plaintiff, which influenced the plaintiff's decision to compromise an action. This decision however is based on fraud rather than a common or cross-purposes mistake.

### (3) Common mistake of fact

Not all mistakes of fact will justify rescinding a contract concluded under such a misapprehension, whether it be shared by both parties or not. The common law took a very restrictive view of such cases and the conventional wisdom holds that only if the mistake relates to the existence of the subject-matter of the contract, or to the existence of a person or a relationship essential to the whole transaction will it be fundamental enough to operate at common law. If parties contract to buy and sell corn which, unknown to both parties has perished, the transaction will be void[17]; if people who are not married enter into a separation agreement in the belief that they are married, the separation agreement will be void.[18] A life insurance policy or annuity, taken out in the mistaken belief that the person in question is still alive, will be void: see *Strickland v. Turner*.[19] In *Pritchard v. Merchants and Tradesmans Mutual Life Assurance*[20] a life assurance policy had lapsed due to non-payment of the premium. The beneficiary sought to revive the policy by paying the premium, and while payment was made, both parties discovered that the assured, at the date of renewal, was in fact dead. An action to enforce the policy failed because the policy was void; the premium, however, was recoverable by action. Costello J. in *O'Neill v. Ryan and Others*[21] approved the decision in *Scott v. Coulson*[22] which is of a similar effect. However, it must not be assumed that the parties will always be able to invoke a plea of common mistake for it may be that the agreement will, expressly or impliedly, transfer or allocate risk to one of the parties. The position is different if one party warrants the existence of the person or goods as in *McRae v. Commonwealth Disposals Commission*[23] or is prepared to assume the risk that circumstances are otherwise: *March v. Pigot*.[24] This involved a colourful set of facts. Two young men resolved to contract that whoever was able to prove that his father lived longer than that of the other would pay a sum to the other – a contract to "run" the life of one father against that of the other. Unknown to the parties, one father had already died. The contract was not void for the parties were taken to have accepted that the risk of either parent already being dead was not to invalidate the contract.[25]

However, despite the narrow common law basis for holding contracts to be void *ab initio*, there are some judicial pronouncements that contemplate a

---

[17] *Couturier v. Hastie* (1856) 6 H.L.C. 673.
[18] *Galloway v. Galloway* (1914) 30 T.L.R. 531.
[19] (1852) 7 Exch. 208.
[20] (1858) 3 C.B.N.S. 622.
[21] [1991] I.L.R.M. 672.
[22] [1903] 2 Ch. 249.
[23] (1951) 84 C.L.R. 377.
[24] (1771) 5 Burr. 2802.
[25] This wagering contract predated the Gaming Act 1845.

broader role for the common law. In *Kennedy v. Panama New Zealand and Australian Royal Mail Co.*,[26] a case concerned with innocent misrepresentation, Blackburn J., borrowing from civil law systems the doctrine of *error in substantibus*, distinguished between (operative) mistakes of substance in the subject matter, and (inoperative) mistakes as to attributes, or quality. In using language that was also to be found in English jurisprudence on the vexed question of rescission for breach of obligation, Blackburn J. drew the common law and civil law position together when he wrote,

> "the principle of our law is the same as that of the civil law; and the difficulty in every case is to determine whether the mistake or misapprehension is as to the substance of the whole consideration, going, as it were, to the foot of the matter, or only to some point, even though a material point, an error as to which does not affect the substance of the whole consideration."[27]

These lines of authority are not altogether incompatible but the cases are likely to reveal different approaches to a plea of common mistake, as a matter of legal philosophy. Some judges view pleas of mistake with hostility because a valid plea leads to the contract being void, and it is not always evident that justice is served by transferring the entire loss from one person to another, particularly when an express clause could have been utilised to achieve the same result.

In the leading English case of *Bell v. Lever Brothers.*[28] Bell and another former employee of the defendants had negotiated "golden handshake" payments in the belief that Lever Brothers could not terminate the contract of employment in any other way, a belief also held by Lever Brothers. In fact, Bell was guilty of misconduct which would have justified summary dismissal. Lever Brothers claimed that this mistake was operative and that they could recoup the £50,000 paid. The House of Lords ruled that the mistake was not fundamental enough to justify rescission. Professor Waddams has argued in his *Law of Contracts*[29] that on the facts the conclusion may be correct; a large part of the payment was reward for services rendered rather than being attributable to "buying out" the contract of employment. Nevertheless dicta in the Lords, particularly the speech of Lord Atkin, suggests that a shared mistake as to the quality of goods will never be operative; if two parties contract to transfer a painting which they believe to be an old master and it turns out to be a modern copy, the mistake will not be operative unless there is an express warranty or a misrepresentation. There is oblique Irish authority supporting this view of the position at common law. In *Megaw v. Molloy*[30] a mistake was held operative

---

[26] (1867) L.R. 2 Q.B. 580.
[27] *Ibid.* at 589.
[28] [1932] A.C. 161.
[29] (2nd ed., Canada Law Book, Toronto, 1984), pp. 285–289.
[30] (1878) 2 L.R. (Ir.) 530.

but in so concluding Ball C. said that this "is not the case of a seller and purchaser intending to sell and buy the same horse with a misapprehension as to his soundness", thereby implying that such a mistake would not be fundamental enough to induce the common law courts to declare the transaction void.

There are cases, however, which suggest that a fundamental mistake may, generally, render a contract void *ab initio* even though this approach is difficult to square with Lord Atkin's speech in *Bell v. Lever Brothers*. The Privy Council in *Sheikh Brothers v. Ochsner*[31] held that a contract, under which the lessee of agricultural land promised to deliver a minimum of 50 tons of sisal per month, was void for common mistake. Both parties wrongly thought the land in question was capable of producing that minimum figure. While attempts to limit the impact of *Sheikh Brothers* have in the main been successful – Cheshire and Fifoot simply footnote this case as turning entirely on a statutory provision,[32] an argument this writer cannot agree with – a recent Circuit Court decision has endorsed this wider view of common mistake. In *Western Potato Co-operative Ltd. v. Durnan*[33] Judge Clarke held that a contract for the sale of seed potatoes was void because both parties erroneously believed the seed potatoes were sound. Judge Clarke approved the following statement in Anson's *Law of Contract*:

> "Where the parties contract under a false and fundamental assumption, going to the root of the contract, and which both of them must be taken to have in mind at the time they entered into it as the basis of their agreement, the contract may be void."[34]

A recent application of *Bell v. Lever Brothers* illustrates that the test, although difficult to satisfy, is not without vitality. In *Grains & Fourrages SA v. Huyton*[35] the sellers and buyers of goods had these goods tested but being unhappy that the tests were perhaps not accurately carried out the parties agreed to read the test certificates in a particular way. Unfortunately both were in error about the same matter, the tonnage of the goods, and when this came to light the buyer sought to reopen the matter. Mance J. held that the common mistake was a fundamental one and that *Bell v. Lever Brothers* was satisfied, citing Lord Atkin,[36] who observed whilst giving judgment in *Bell v. Lever Brothers* that he agreed with counsel's submission that

> "whenever it is to be inferred from the terms of the contract or its surrounding circumstances that the consensus has been reached on the basis of a particular contractual assumption and that assumption is not true, the contract is avoided."

---

[31] [1957] A.C. 136.
[32] (13th ed., 1996), p. 243.
[33] [1985] I.L.R.M. 5: see Clark, (1984) 19 Ir. Jur. 101.
[34] Citing the 25th ed., p. 296.
[35] [1997] 1 Lloyd's Rep. 628.
[36] [1932] A.C. 161 at 225.

If the parties have provided for the event by way of an express term and particularly an exemption clause, it would be inappropriate to apply a common mistake analysis. Similarly, where a foreseeable event materialises and the contract fails to provide for this, the fact that the party pleading common mistake has failed to anticipate the event may be a factor which militates against a plea of common mistake. Fault has been identified as a valid consideration when a plea of common mistake has been raised according to the High Court of Australia in *Pakullus & Another v. Cameron*.[37] As Costello J. in *O'Neill v. Ryan and Others*[38] said, however, "the circumstances in which a shared common mistake will nullify a contract are extremely limited . . . a shared common mistake will not result in a void contract" save in exceptional circumstances.

### *(4) Common mistake of fact in equity*

The equitable rule in relation to shared or common mistake seems to have been wider and more flexible. The leading case of *Cooper v. Phibbs*,[39] decided before the fusion of the common law and equity, is often said to be authority for the view that a common mistake can be relieved against on such terms as the court sees fit. In *Cooper v. Phibbs* the House of Lords set aside the lease, declared the appellant the owner while ordering that the respondents were entitled to a lien on the property in respect of money paid improving it. The only difficulty that *Cooper v. Phibbs* presents rests on the fact that the mistake in that case would probably have been operative, even at common law, by analogy with *Couturier v. Hastie*.[40] This weakens the case if it is the primary support for the modern doctrine of equitable mistake. *Cooper v. Phibbs*, however, does not stand alone as support for a broader equitable jurisdiction. The decision of the Court of Appeal in *Huddersfield Banking Co. Ltd. v. Henry Lister & Co.*[41] is a very substantial basis upon which to predicate a broader equitable approach. A mortgagee agreed that certain pieces of industrial machinery were not affected by a mortgage which included rights over fixtures and upon this basis the mortgagee and a receiver agreed to a sale of these items as chattels. It later transpired that the equipment should properly have been regarded as fixtures and the mortgagee sought a declaration that the mortgagee's consent was liable to be set aside for common mistake. Lindley L.J. regarded equity as being able to proceed in this case in much the same way as the courts of common law, citing, *inter alia, Strickland v. Turner* and *Cooper v. Phibbs*. Kay L.J. said that the equitable jurisdiction to set aside agreements can operate

> "not merely for fraud, but in case [consent] was based upon a mistake of material fact which was common to all the parties to it."

---

37  (1982) 43 A.L.R. 243.
38  [1991] I.L.R.M. 672.
39  (1867) L.R. 2 H.L. 149.
40  (1856) 6 H.L.C. 673.
41  [1895] 2 Ch. 273; *Cue Club Ltd. v. Navaro Ltd., Irish Times Law Report*, February 17, 1997.

This case can be regarded as really within the narrow line of cases anticipated as void at common law but it seems symptomatic of a more liberal equitable jurisdiction to *set aside* transactions rather than declare contracts void *ab initio*, and supporters of the common law approach, such as Lord Atkin, have asserted that *Huddersfield Banking* does not evidence a broader equitable doctrine, at least in an historical sense. Nevertheless a series of English Court of Appeal decisions establish that while the common law doctrine of mistake may not operate, equity can set aside a transaction on such terms as the court sees fit. In *Solle v. Butcher*[42] a lease entered into when both parties believed the property not subject to rent restriction legislation was declared voidable and the contract was set aside on terms, the decree giving the tenant the option of leaving the flat or staying on at a rent that, in the view of the Court of Appeal, accurately reflected the value of the property. In *Grist v. Bailey*[43] a contract to sell a house under the mistaken belief that a tenant was protected under the Rent Acts was also declared voidable, the purchaser being entitled to repudiate or take at a fair market value of £2,250 rather than the agreed price of £850. These cases have prompted Lord Denning M.R. to summarise the law as follows: "common mistake even on a most fundamental matter does not make a contract void at law but voidable in equity." Although the modern English case law has not been ruled on by the Supreme Court the Irish ancestry of the leading case of *Cooper v. Phibbs* suggests that the Irish courts would decline to follow the narrower doctrine of mistake, as espoused in *Bell v. Lever Brothers*, preferring instead the *Solle v. Butcher* line of authority.

In *O'Neill v. Ryan and Others*[44] Costello J. provided a most useful summary of the English law on common mistake and, citing Denning L.J. in *Solle v. Butcher*, apparently approved the proposition that:

> "a contract is also liable in equity to be set aside if the parties were under a common misapprehension either as to facts or as to their relative and respective rights, provided that the misapprehension was funda-mental and that the party seeking to set it aside was not himself at fault."[45]

In *Associated Japanese Bank (International) Ltd. v. Credit du Nord SA and Another*[46] Steyn J. attempted to reconcile the equitable and common law approaches to what the learned judge described as "common or mutual mistake". The defendant bank had guaranteed certain sale and leaseback transactions in which the plaintiffs purchased and leased back four machines, the seller/lessee being a Mr. Bennett. In fact Bennett had defrauded the plaintiffs for the machines did not exist, and the issue was whether the guarantee of Bennett's obligations under the lease were enforceable by the plaintiff against the defen-

---

[42] [1950] 1 K.B. 671.
[43] [1967] Ch. 532. See however Hoffmann L.J. in *William Sindell plc v. Cambridgeshire County Council* [1994] 3 All E.R. 932 at 952.
[44] [1991] I.L.R.M. 672.
[45] [1950] 1 K.B. 671 at 693.
[46] [1988] 3 All E.R. 902.

dant. The plea of common mistake gave Steyn J. the opportunity to examine the current state of English law and the learned judge held that the leading case of *Bell v. Lever Brothers* was essentially concerned with common law mistake and that the equitable jurisdiction, set out in *Solle v. Butcher*, "is not circumscribed by common law definitions". Steyn J., however, did not view *Solle v. Butcher* as effecting the soundness of *Bell v. Lever Brothers* when the issue is common mistake at common law. Steyn J. regarded the existing state of English law to be capable of coherent enunciation and application. Steyn J. argued that the first step to be taken is to look to see if the contract has made provision for the contingency; only if the contract is silent is there room for a plea of mistake. As a later step, a plea of common mistake at law must be considered and if the case can be accommodated within the narrow test, as found in Lord Atkin's speech in *Bell v. Lever Brothers*, then the contract is void *ab initio*. If this is not possible the court may go on to consider whether the contract may be set aside in equity. On the facts before him Steyn J. held that the contract was void *ab initio*: the non-existence of the machines, the subject matter of the main contract was of fundamental importance to the collateral guarantee, and the closeness to *res extincta* cases was also noted by the learned judge.

This is not, however, likely to be a precursor to widespread judicial acceptance of common mistake pleas. Steyn J. stressed that "the first imperative must be that the law ought to uphold rather than destroy apparent bargains", and even judges who have favoured the *Solle v. Butcher* line of authority have been slow to intervene, as the case of *Amalgamated Investments v. John Walker*[47] illustrates. In this case two parties were mistaken as to the likelihood of a building being declared a "listed building", which had the effect of reducing its value as a commercial property. The need for certainty and security of commercial transactions will be viewed as more important than the interests of one distressed litigant. In such cases the buyer should include a term that if at a later date the building is listed the buyer can rescind the contract. To similar effect is the decision of the Court of Appeal in *William Sindell plc v. Cambridgeshire County Council*.[48] The defendants sold land to the plaintiffs who intended to build on it. While the defendants had disclosed what they knew about the site, the plaintiffs discovered that a drain was incorporated into the site via an easement. When property values halved the plaintiffs sought to rescind, *inter alia*, on the ground of common mistake. The Court of Appeal held that the purchasers took the risk, in accordance with the terms of the contract and settled principles of law. Evans L.J. pointed out that while the equitable rules were more likely to trigger rescission the fact that the contract dealt with this issue, allied to the relatively minor financial consequences for the builder, meant that the contract subsisted.

---

[47] [1976] 3 All E.R. 509.
[48] [1994] 3 All E.R. 932.

## (5) Mistake as to the terms of the agreement

In these cases, which are often described as instances of mutual mistake, the parties are negotiating about different things. A wants to buy wheat; B wants to sell barley. At first sight there can be no contract. Indeed, Ball L.C. said in *Megaw v. Molloy*[49] that a "dealing where the parties are not intending the same subject matter, evidently cannot be an agreement." This is not correct. The essential factor to be noted is whether the party pleading mistake has a reasonable expectation that the contract would include the terms contended for. In *Stapleton v. Prudential Assurance*[50] the plaintiff entered a life insurance contract believing that by paying two shillings a month for 11 years she would be paid £25 at the end of the period. In fact the contract provided that such a sum would be payable on her death; at the end of 11 years the policy was convertible into a free paid policy after 25 years. The plaintiff, when she learnt of the mistake sought to get back the premiums paid. Sullivan P. held that while Stapleton laboured under a bona fide mistake this would not justify rescinding the contract: see *Jameson v. National Benefit Trust Ltd.*[51] which also illustrates that self-induced mistakes as to the terms of a bargain will not ground relief for the mistaken party. The courts are concerned to discover what the parties said and did during negotiations. If the intention of one party, objectively ascertained, indicates assent to a particular term, that term will be included in the bargain. The courts will not permit the reasonable expectations of one party to be defeated if they exist because of the conduct of the other party. This is often described as the rule in *Smith v. Hughes*[52]:

> "if whatever a man's real intention may be, he so conducts himself that a reasonable man would believe he was assenting to the terms proposed by the other and that other party upon that belief enters into a contract with him, the man thus conducting himself would be equally bound as if he has intended to agree to the other parties terms."[53]

If the agreement is clear in its terms then the defendant cannot avoid the agreement by pleading, or indeed convincing the court, that the defendant felt that the agreement would produce a quite different result. In *Mespil Ltd. v. Capaldi*[54] an action for possession of rented premises was commenced by the plaintiff lessor for breaches of covenant. Prior to these proceedings commencing the defendants had settled existing litigation in respect of the premises under an agreement which referred to a "full and final settlement of all matters". The defendants pleaded that they had intended to settle all matters outstanding, including all current disputes which were not the subject of proceedings.

---

[49] (1878) 2 L.R. (Ir.) 530.
[50] (1928) 62 I.L.T.R. 56.
[51] (1902) 2 N.I.J.R. 19.
[52] (1871) L.R. 2 Q.B. 597.
[53] *Ibid.* at 607, *per* Blackburn J.; *Jennings v. Carroll* (1849) 2 Ir. Jur. 275.
[54] [1986] I.L.R.M. 373; Maher (1987) 9 D.U.L.J. 113.

O'Hanlon J. held that the contract was not capable of having this extended application, and, citing *Smith v. Hughes*, the learned trial judge held that because both sides were not under the same misapprehension as to the effect of the agreement "there was an element of mutual mistake involved in the trans-action", which could not however operate so as to defeat the plaintiff's legitimate expectations. On appeal however the Supreme Court held that the agreement was void for mutual mistake. While the Supreme Court upheld the distinction between a mistake as to the impact or effect of the bargain – which is not effective – and a mistake as to the true nature of the agreement – which may be effective – the Supreme Court characterised this mistake as falling into the second category. Henchy J. expressed the principles at issue here as follows:

> "When a person enters into an agreement, giving the other person the impression that he understands the nature and effect of the agreement, the general rule is that he will not be allowed to say later that he should not be bound by the agreement because he did not at the time understand its import or effect. That is undoubtedly correct law. Business relations would be thrown into undesirable uncertainty, if a party to an agreement who at the time gave no indication that he did not understand what he was doing, could later renounce the agreement on subjective considerations. If he freely and competently entered into the agreement he will not normally escape being bound by it, by saying that he misunderstood its effect. The position is essentially different when, as in the case here, there was a mutual or bilateral mistake as to the true nature of the agreement. Different and more fundamental principles of the law of contract come to be applied in such circumstances. It is of the essence of an enforceable simple contract that there be a consensus *ad idem*, expressed in an offer and an acceptance. Such a consensus cannot be said to exist unless there is a correspondence between the offer and the acceptance. If the offer made is accepted by the other person in a fundamentally different sense from that in which it was tendered by the offeror, and the circumstances are objectively such as to justify such an acceptance, there cannot be said to be the meeting of the minds which is essential for an enforceable contract. In such circumstances the alleged contract is a nullity."[55]

The Supreme Court indicated that not only were the persons who had negotiated the settlement at cross purposes, the written agreement itself was capable of being interpreted as a settlement of all disputes, but all surrounding circumstances justified the plaintiffs in their view that the settlement was limited: Henchy J. regarded the case as one in which there was "latent ambi-guity and mutual misunderstanding".

The objective test can of course work the other way; if the agreement, objectively judged, cedes to the plaintiff a benefit which was unintended by the defendant, the defendant will not be able to claim that the contract should be

---

[55] [1986] I.L.R.M. 373 at 376–377.

enforced on the terms actually intended by the defendant. Two modern Irish cases provide clear illustrations of this particular aspect of this rule. In *Clayton Love v. B & I Transport*[56] the appellants intended to contract with the respondents for the transport of frozen scampi. The appellants intended the scampi would be loaded at sub-atmospheric temperatures. The respondents intended loading would take place at atmospheric temperature. Applying *Smith v. Hughes*, the Supreme Court held that because of the way the respondents had conducted themselves during negotiations they were bound to load the cargo on the terms anticipated by the appellants. They were therefore liable for the deterioration of the goods. In the important case of *Lucy v. Laurel Construction*[57] Mr. Lucy agreed to purchase a house to be built by Laurel Construction. The site plan indicated the plot would be 170 feet long. The plan was in error; the builders only intended to sell a plot 120 feet long. At no time was Mr. Lucy ever told this and all he knew of the builders' intention was disclosed on the faulty site plan. When the builders discovered the mistake they sought to have the plan altered to reflect their intention. Mr. Lucy was held entitled to retain the bargain as initially struck. The site plan was the only objective manifestation of the other party's intentions; Mr. Lucy had done nothing irregular or dishonest and Kenny J. declined to rectify the contract.

There are cases in which the courts have held that no contract exists because of mistake. In *Megaw v. Molloy*[58] the plaintiff employed a broker to sell maize for him. The maize he intended to sell had been imported on board the "Emma Peasant". The plaintiff had imported another cargo of maize on the "Jessie Parker", which was of a superior quality than that on board the "Emma Peasant". On the morning of the sale a sample purporting to be from the "Emma Peasant" was displayed but this sample was accidentally taken from the "Jessie Parker". The defendant purchased the cargo after inspecting the sample but later refused to take delivery when he discovered the true quality of the cargo. The plaintiff sued for non-acceptance. The defendant did not plead that the quality of the goods sold did not meet the sample for there was an express disclaimer of a warranty as to quality; he instead successfully argued that there was no contract at all. The vendor intended to sell the cargo on the "Emma Peasant"; the purchaser intended to buy the bulk out of which the sample had been taken, that is, the corn on the "Jessie Parker". Ball L.C. said there was "a misapprehension as to the very substance of the thing in contract, not as to any quality or incident or merit or demerit of it – *error in corpore*." This distinction between a mistake as to quality as against identity is often difficult to draw, as *Gill v. McDowell*[59] shows, and it has been criticised as unsatisfactory in practice. Another way of looking at *Megaw v. Molloy* would be to consider who was responsible for the error? It would be monstruous to allow the party responsible for creating the mistake, whether by a deliberate falsehood or pure

---

[56] (1970) 104 I.L.T.R. 157; *Diamond v. Council for Catholic Maintained Schools* [1994] N.I.J.R. 77.

[57] Unreported, High Court, December 18, 1970.

[58] (1878) 2 L.R. (Ir.) 530.

[59] [1903] 2 I.R. 463.

negligence, to compel the purchaser to take delivery of the wrong cargo and any express clause would hardly pass the "just and reasonable" test in the sale of Goods and Supply of Services Act 1980. Contrast *Megaw v. Molloy* with *Scott v. Littledale*.[60] Here the defendants had sold tea "ex Star of the East". The sample provided was of a lower quality than the cargo and the defendants sought to plead mistake. The defence failed and they were held liable for non-delivery. In this situation the defendants had been careless and to allow a plea of mistake would not only deprive the plaintiffs of their bargain – albeit a bargain more advantageous than they thought – but also allow the defendants to ride free from the consequences of their own carelessness. Yet this approach is not always relied upon. If the remedy sought is specific performance the courts may refuse to grant the remedy against even the person responsible for the error if this would, on balance, work an injustice: see *Browne v. Marquis of Sligo*.[61]

An interesting illustration of this discretionary aspect of mutual mistake is afforded by the *Minister for Education v. North Star Ltd*.[62] The plaintiff sought specific performance of an agreement to sell a strip of land which was to provide vehicular access to a proposed development. The defendant agreed to the sale, but regarded it as essential that two other access points be provided. The plaintiff abandoned any attempt to develop these two other access points due to the hostility of local residents. Even though Lynch J. regarded this as a case of mutual mistake, and seemed of the view that the mistake itself was not known to the plaintiff, the change of intention was relevant to the remedy sought. "It is a fundamental principle of equity that he who seeks equity must do equity and the plaintiff is disqualified from the equitable remedy of specific performance by the plaintiff's abandonment of an intention to seek vehicular access via [the two other access points.]"

*(6) Mistake in executing a deed or contract*

Three situations must be kept apart.

(i) Where one party at the time of the agreement assents to a term but notices that the other party has misstated the term when executing the contract document or memorandum of agreement. Here the error may favour the party who notices the slip of the pen. In *Nolan v. Graves & Hamilton*[63] the plaintiff agreed to buy a row of houses sold by auction. Evidence showed that the plaintiff had agreed to pay £5,550; the auctioneer erroneously wrote the price to be £4,550. The plaintiff was not entitled to take at the lower price. The contract was rectified to reflect the bargain actually struck. Similarly, a separation agreement that gave income tax advantages to the wife when it was intended that these would accrue to the husband was rectified upon proof that the wife was aware that the agreement did not carry into effect the intent of both parties; *Nolan v. Nolan*.[64]

---

[60] (1858) 3 E. & B. 815.
[61] (1859) 10 I.R. Ch. R. 1.
[62] Unreported, High Court, January 12, 1987.
[63] [1946] I.R. 377.
[64] (1954) 92 I.L.T.R. 94: contrast *J.D. v. B.D.* [1985] I.L.R.M. 688.

(ii) Where the contract is executed and one party later comes into court claiming that, as worded, the document does not accurately reflect the bargain struck. Here the party seeking relief will not always claim sharp practice on the part of the other. In *Peter Cremer GmbH v. Cooperative Molasses Traders Ltd.*[65] the applicants sought a declaration, *inter alia*, that a contract contained an agreement to arbitrate. While the contract document itself was silent on this point Costello J. commented that "once the terms actually agreed to have been established I do not think that an error in the preparation of a formal contract effects the legal consequences." A form of rectification occurred via the exceptions to the parol evidence rule: the contract document was held to be only part of the contract and was to be read with telex correspondence which referred to arbitration.

It will not always prove possible to avoid altering the contract document itself. The nineteenth century Irish case of *Fallon v. Robins*[66] provides a good illustration of this problem. Fallon agreed to take a lease from Robins. The lease, drafted by Fallon's solicitor, was to run for 31 years and it was intended that Fallon would have a right to terminate the lease after three years. The lease was ambiguously worded and Robins purported to take advantage of the termination clause. Smith M.R. held that unless the lease failed to accurately set out the intention of both parties it could not be *rectified*; as we shall see however an Irish court can order rescission on the authority of *Mortimer v. Shortall*[67] in such cases. Nevertheless, in *Fallon v. Robins*, Smith M.R. interpreted the ambiguous clause to permit Fallon a right of termination only. *Lucy v. Laurel Construction*[68] illustrates this point too; unless the conduct and words of one party indicate assent on the terms now sought, a mistake which is not communicated to the other party will not be operative and the document will not be rectified.

The decision of the Supreme Court in *Irish Life Assurance Co. Ltd. v. Dublin Land Securities Ltd.*[69] will be of great assistance in delimiting the scope of rectification in mutual mistake cases. The plaintiff company wished to sell its portfolio of ground rents which totalled some 11,055 properties. The plaintiff company also owned lands at Palmerstown, Co. Dublin, which had been the subject of compulsory purchase orders and the plaintiff did not wish these properties to be included so as to later obtain compensation for compulsory purchase. In preparing the portfolio for sale the legal department of the plaintiff company failed to delete the Palmerstown lands from the portfolio. The defendant company acquired the portfolio but were not told that lands at Palmerstown were to be excluded; although an agent acting for the defendant was informed of the intention to exclude certain lands, this knowledge was not, in these circumstances, such as to give notice to the purchaser. When the error in the contract came to light, the plaintiff company sought rectification of the contract. Rectification was refused. The approach approved by the Supreme Court is that the court will not

---

[65] [1985] I.L.R.M. 564.
[66] (1865) 16 Ir. Ch. Rep. 422.
[67] (1842) Connor & Lawson 417.
[68] Unreported, High Court, December 18, 1970.
[69] [1989] I.R. 253.

reform a contract made in writing in the absence of convincing proof that the contract, as the result of a mistake, has failed to give effect to the common intention of the parties previously manifested in outward accord.[70]

In contrast, however, stands the decision of Vice-Chancellor Chatterton in *Young v. Halahan*.[71] The plaintiff assigned, by way of a lease, part of his land to a railway company. This was done by execution of two separate deeds in February and March 1871 respectively. The plaintiff subsequently sold part of the estate, including the land assigned to the railway company, by auction. The contract of sale failed to exclude all the land so assigned, and the defendant was only given express notification of the first lease executed in February. The purchaser brought proceedings at law for breach of covenant on the ground that part of the property sold to him had been already leased to the railway company. In equity, however, the defendant sought rectification of the contract so as to exclude the lands leased to the railway company. While this was a case in which the error was solely attributable to the defendants, equitable relief was granted. The crucial factor was the user and occupation of the lands in question by the railway company and the defendant's knowledge of this user and occupation. The real contract between the parties was held to be for the sale of an agreed parcel of lands, minus those lands occupied by the railway company, and the conveyance was rectified accordingly. In *Irish Life Assurance Co. Ltd. v. Dublin Land Securities Ltd.*[72] the purchaser had, in no sense, walked the lands, nor had he any substantial information about the Palmerstown lands.

(iii) Where the party pleading mistake shows that, despite the apparent assent of both parties to the written terms of the agreement, the document does not carry into effect what may be described as "the contract formula". Authority for this proposition stems from the unusual case of *Collen Brothers v. Dublin County Council*.[73] The Council agreed to grant a construction contract to the plaintiffs' the price to be calculated on the defendants' bills of quantities minus a list or bill of reductions designed to lower costs. By a clerical oversight the contract price was £357 less than it should have been. The plaintiffs sought rectification. Ross J. was prepared to permit rectification, dismissing the claim of the Council that the plaintiffs were to bear the cost of the mistake; the intention of the parties, when analysed, was that the tender for the original amount of the priced section, less the amount of the priced bill of reductions, should be accepted. The sum of £167,000 was erroneously taken to be that figure and erroneously embodied in the contract. "In what way does this differ from an error in adding the figures? In no way." If, however, the parties complete the contract in the mistaken belief that they have actually agreed a price for the work, then the case goes beyond the realm of a miscalculation. In *Fanning v. Wicklow County Council*[74] the plaintiffs claimed the balance due

---

[70] [1989] I.R. 253 at 263, *per* Griffin J.
[71] (1875) I.R. 9 Eq. 70.
[72] [1989] I.R. 253.
[73] [1908] 1 I.R. 503.
[74] Unreported, High Court, April 30, 1984; *Lachhani v. Destination Canada (U.K.) Ltd.* (1997) 13 Const. L.J. 279.

under an agreement to build houses for the defendant. The offer and acceptance did not correspond, and in this case O'Hanlon J. was constrained to hold that no contract had been concluded. The plaintiffs were however able to recover on a *quantum meruit* basis.

### (7) Mistake as to title and the nature of an interest in real property

*Cooper v. Phibbs*[75] establishes that equity will set aside on terms any leasing contract where both parties mistakenly believe that title to the land is vested in someone other than the prospective lessor. In *Gardiner v. Tate*[76] a contract was held unenforceable at common law against a defendant who had been misled by the plaintiff's agent into believing that an interest purchased at an auction was a legal estate in land when in fact it was an equitable leasehold interest.

### (8) Mistake as to identity

The Irish courts have not considered this problem to any great extent. For the sake of completeness the following propositions, based largely on English case law, can be advanced.

If one party contracts face to face with another, believing that other person to be someone else, the contract is voidable. In *Lewis v. Averay*[77] a rogue obtained possession of a motor car by falsely representing that he was the television actor, Richard Greene, of the "Robin Hood" series. He showed a false pass from Pinewood Studios and apparently bore a strong resemblance to the actor. Convinced that he was dealing with the actor the owner took a cheque signed "R. A. Green". The cheque bounced. The car turned up with the defendant who had purchased it from the rogue. The Court of Appeal held that the initial owner could not successfully recover the vehicle on the ground of mistake. The contract between himself and the rogue conferred a voidable title upon the rogue which had been transferred to the defendant. This conclusion reached is a proposition of law. Denning M.R., citing *Corbin*, was prepared to follow American practice where "the courts hold that if A appeared in person before B impersonating C an innocent purchaser from A gets the property in the goods against C." The fraudulently induced mistake does not operate to make the transaction a nullity; a similar rule has been advanced and applied in the Irish cases of *Re French's Estate*[78] and in *Re Ambrose's Estate*.[79]

The rule is otherwise if the contract is concluded by post. The decision of the House of Lords in *Cundy v. Lindsay*[80] was to hold the transaction void, thus preventing the purchaser from the rogue from obtaining a good title. Lord Cairns, in giving judgment, seemed persuaded by the view that if "minds do not meet", no "consensus" or contract can result, but this is not strictly true –

---

[75] (1867) L.R. 2 H.L. 149.
[76] (1876) I.R. 10 C.L. 460.
[77] [1972] 1 Q.B. 198.
[78] (1887) I.R. 2 Eq. 234.
[79] [1913] I.R. 506; [1914] I.R. 123.
[80] (1878) 3 App. Cas. 459.

see *Lucy v. Laurel Construction* discussed above. Denning L.J. (as he then was) said in *Solle v. Butcher*[81] that the "void" contract in *Cundy v. Lindsay* would now be held to be voidable on terms. This seems on balance a preferable solution given that the court could adjust the rights of the parties under the terms of the decree. Legislation on this point is necessary. If it were possible for the original owner to recover damages in tort in such a case, section 34 of the Republic's Civil Liability Act 1961 would permit damages payable by the purchaser from the rogue to be reduced "by such amount as the court thinks just and equitable having regard to the degrees of fault of the plaintiff and defendant." Devlin L.J. in *Ingram v. Little*[82] suggested a similar reform be initiated in England and *Cundy v. Lindsay* has been held not to be authority for the proposition that fraudulent transmission of documents between two innocent parties does not prevent a contract from being formed: *Citibank NA v. Brown Shipley & Co. Ltd.*[83] The limitation of *Cundy v. Lindsay* is to be very much welcomed.

The mistaken identity cases have been declared to be inapplicable to situations where the contract is concluded in writing and the entire agreement is reduced into writing. In *Hector v. Lyons*,[84] the contract was concluded in the name of an infant. The infant's father brought an action seeking specific performance, but was met with the objection that the person named in the contract was not the litigant. Infants cannot obtain the remedy of specific performance, so the infants father pleading the mistake *inter presentes* cases sought a declaration that he was the contracting party. The submission was rejected on the ground that written documents should be regarded as conclusive and the indentity of the vendor and purchaser is to be established by the names in the written contract.

Not all mistaken identity cases are instances where one party knows of the other's mistaken belief. For this reason the mistaken identity cases are not always instances of "unilateral mistake", to use Cheshire and Fifoot's classification. In *Smallman v. O'Moore & Newman*[85] the two defendants carried on a partnership until 1954 when they converted the firm into a limited company. The plaintiff had dealt with the defendants as a partnership and although the defendants circularised their suppliers informing them of their change in legal status, the plaintiffs failed to note the new position, even though the second defendant signed cheques in favour of the plaintiffs in the company name. The plaintiff sued the defendants personally for the price of goods supplied, claiming that they were individually liable as if they remained partners in an unincorporated firm. The defendants successfully pleaded that the only contracts struck were between the company and the plaintiff even though the plaintiff thought he was contracting with someone else. Davitt J. held that the plaintiff could not rely on his own mistake in order to render the defendants personally liable. This decision should be contrasted with *Boulton v. Jones*.[86]

---

[81] [1950] 1 K.B. 671.
[82] [1961] 1 Q.B. 31.
[83] [1991] 2 All E.R. 690.
[84] *The Times*, December 19, 1988.
[85] [1959] I.R. 220.
[86] (1857) 2 H. & N. 564.

# Remedies available for an Operative Mistake

A mistake operative at common law leads to the contract being declared void *ab initio: Cundy v. Lindsay*. Technically the party arguing mistake may seek a decree in the court in cases where the other party is pressing for performance, or title to goods or chattels transferred is in question. Equitable remedies in mistake cases prior to the Irish Union of Judicature Act 1877 were (and are) a good deal more sophisticated. Despite the fact that we no longer have separate courts of common law and equity, students should bear in mind that the remedies available have evolved from these distinct streams of law. At the risk of repetition we shall now turn to consider those remedies.

## *(1) Rescission – both at law and in equity*

At law, a mistake which is common to both parties and which relates to a fundamental matter of fact, such as the continued existence of goods (see section 6 of the Sale of Goods Act 1893), or a person in insurance cases, will prevent a contract coming into being. The contract price paid will be returnable. Where parties are contracting at cross purposes, that is where both persons contract to buy and sell different things, the contract may be invalid if the party pleading mistake reasonably but erroneously believes that a certain state of affairs exists: see *Megaw v. Molloy*[87] and *Leonard v. Leonard*.[88] If rescission is to be available, however, the mistake should refer to an essential or fundamental term in the contract and must not be an error in relation to the effect the contract will have. A mistake as to terms may ground relief but a mistake as to the results will most certainly not. In *Reen v. Bank of Ireland Finance Ltd. & Lucey's Garage (Mallow) Ltd.*[89] an action for breach of contract was settled on terms which the plaintiff's solicitor erroneously believed would include all legal costs involved. This was incorrect, and, further, the solicitor for the defendant was aware that further expenses would accrue for the plaintiff. The plaintiff claimed the contract was liable to be set aside for mistake. McMahon J. dismissed the action remarking that the offer and acceptance corresponded and that there was no mistake as to the terms of the agreement:

> "This is a case of a man entering into an agreement which he intended to make but which he would not have made but for a misunderstanding as to a matter extraneous the agreement, namely his client's position *vis à vis* other parties in the litigation."[90]

Had there been a unilateral mistake as to terms, *e.g.* the defendant's solicitor knew that the plaintiff was contracting in the belief that the defendant's solicitor had warranted or promised that the settlement would have the effect the plain-

---

[87] (1878) 2 L.R. (Ir.) 530.
[88] (1812) 2 Ball & B. 171.
[89] [1983] I.L.R.M. 507.
[90] *Ibid.* at 509–510.

tiff believed, then at common law the contract would be rescinded: *Smith v. Hughes*. One of the most important English decisions on this point is *Hartog v. Colin and Shields*.[91] The plaintiff received an offer from the defendant offering to sell to the plaintiff Argentine hareskins at 10$^{1}$/₄d a pound. In the trade, hareskins were sold by the piece, and, given that there are approximately three pieces to a pound, the offer was a most favourable one for the plaintiff. The plaintiff accepted but then sued for non-delivery. The defendant resisted the action by claiming that the offer was so obviously incorrect that the plaintiff must have realised that there was an error and sought to take advantage of it. The action for non-delivery failed. Singleton J. held that the offer was such that the plaintiff could not have reasonably supposed that it set out the offeror's real intention; the contract was invalid. However, if the mistake in the offer, objectively ascertained, would not have been apparent to a reasonable offeree, and if the offeree reasonably interprets the agreement in another way the contract will not necessarily be liable to rescission: *O'Neill v. Ryan and Others*.[92]

Rescission in equity is a much more fluid doctrine. The Sligo fishery case of *Cooper v. Phibbs* illustrates, that mistakes that are operative at common law, can be treated differently in equity. Brady L.C. in the Court of Appeal in Ireland said that as a precondition to equitable relief "there must be something unconscientious on either one side or the other in order that the aid of this court should be called for." The modern English cases suggest that unconscientious dealing is not a precondition for relief, but rather, that ethical factors may help set the terms upon which rescission will be ordered.[93]

A decree of rescission may be given in cases where one party has sought rectification of the contract, the court refusing this relief. In *Mortimer v. Shortall*[94] Sugden L.C. (later Lord St. Leonards) said "a mistake on one side may be a ground for rescinding a contract but it is not a ground for taking from a man part of a property demised to him." So in *Gun v. McCarthy*[95] Gun offered to let property to McCarthy for £33.10s. The offer was accepted but, as Flanagan J. later found, the figure was inserted by mistake. Gun intended the rent to be £55.10s. McCarthy knew the figure was so low that an error had been made. McCarthy did not know the intended figure. Flanagan J. refused to grant rectification and increase the rent. This would have obliged McCarthy to be bound by a contract which he had not assented to; instead Flanagan J. ordered rescission. In *Webster v. Cecil*,[96] a similar English case, the court instead rectified the bargain, giving the purchaser the option of taking the property under the terms of the amended contract or rescinding the contract. This may not always be possible if there is no real contract struck; witness the decision of the House of Lords in *Cummins v. Boylan*,[97] dismissing an appeal from the Court

---

[91] [1939] 3 All E.R. 566.
[92] [1991] I.L.R.M. 672.
[93] *Solle v. Butcher* [1950] 1 K.B. 671.
[94] (1842) Connor & Lawson 417.
[95] (1884) 13 L.R. (Ir.) 304.
[96] (1861) 30 Beav. 62.
[97] (1901) 35 I.L.T.R. 170.

of Appeal in Ireland. In *Ferguson v. Merchant Banking Ltd.*[98] a case with facts very similar to *Irish Life Assurance Co. Ltd. v. Dublin Land Securities Ltd.,* discussed above, the error came to light before completion and the purchaser sought specific performance, leaving the defendant to counterclaim for rectification or, in the alternative, recission. While the *Irish Life* case disposed of the rectification element in the counterclaim, Murphy J. considered the issue of rescission, a remedy not sought by the vendor in *Irish Life.* Murphy J. indicated that rescission would not be granted where the mistake is by one party and it is not shared or in any way contributed to by the other party, that other party being unaware that the agreement is not in its terms consensual.

The remedy of rescission can be lost for a variety of reasons. If the parties cannot be returned to their pre-contractual position, the now superceded common law rule was that rescission would not be ordered. Equity would permit the rights of the parties to be adjusted by the decree. In *Cooper v. Phibbs*[99] the House of Lords ruled that the defendants, who mistakenly believed they owned the fishery, possessed a lien against the land for improvements made; the plaintiff was ordered to pay rent for property he had enjoyed.

Rescission may be refused if there is a delay in seeking equitable relief: the facts of *Stapleton v. Prudential Assurance*[100] illustrate this point graphically. Rescission will also be refused if the mistake renders the contract voidable, but before the contract is repudiated a bona fide purchaser acquires an interest in the goods. The Irish case of *Anderson v. Ryan,*[101] discussed in the next chapter, is authority for this proposition.

## (2) Rectification

Before the Judicature Acts a court of common law, faced with a bargain that was not accurately recorded in a written instrument, was obliged to refer the case to a court of equity to enable rectification. Since 1877 the process is simpler. In *Borrowes v. Delaney*[102] the Court of Exchequer, on discovering that a contract document contained a mistake, simply treated the contract as if it had been rectified. Dowse B. indicated that this remedy is available even though no express request for rectification had been made by either party. Once the true facts become known the courts will respond accordingly.

The burden of proof resting on the party seeking rectification will be a heavy one. Although parol evidence is admissible Sugden L.C. in *Mortimer v. Shortall*[103] suggested that parol evidence alone will not show conclusively that the written document is inaccurate:

"There is no objection in law to rectify an instrument by parol evidence, when you have anything written to go by; but where you depend upon

---

[98] [1993] I.L.R.M. 136.
[99] (1867) L.R. 2 H.L. 149.
[100] (1928) 62 I.L.T.R. 56.
[101] [1967] I.R. 34.
[102] (1889) 24 L.R. (Ir.) 503.
[103] (1842) Connor & Lawson 417.

the recollection of witnesses, and the defendant denies the case set up by the plaintiff, to be the true one, there appears to be no remedy."

This onus demands rather too much of the plaintiff. The modern case of *Nolan v. Graves & Hamilton*[104] suggests that if oral evidence shows conclusively that the instrument is defective, rectification will be ordered.

The jurisdiction of a court to order rectification was succinctly stated by Kenny J. in *Lucy v. Laurel Construction*[105] to exist:

(a) where there is a shared or common mistake made by the two parties in the drafting of a written instrument which is to give effect to a prior oral agreement;

(b) when one party sees a mistake in a written agreement and, aware that the other party has not seen it, he signs knowing it contains a mistake.

A good example of case (b) is provided by the facts of *Nolan v. Graves & Hamilton*, which are related above.[106] This case also decides that if the instrument as it stood was sufficient to satisfy the Statute of Frauds, the rectified instrument will also be deemed within the Statute. The actual decision in *Nolan v. Graves & Hamilton* has been doubted by Professor Dowrick.[107] Instead of ordering specific performance of the rectified agreement, Mrs. Nolan, who had tried to take advantage of the auctioneer's slip of the pen, was given the option of either taking the property under the terms of the amended instrument or rescinding. Professor Dowrick pointed out that under section 27(7) of the Union of Judicature Act 1877, specific performance of a rectified agreement can be ordered. Mrs. Nolan should have been ordered to take the property; after all she had agreed to purchase on the terms of the rectified agreement, unlike the tenant in *Gun v. McCarthy*, above. On the other hand, if the court cannot establish a common intention, as in *R. McD. v. V. McD.*[108] where the parties to a settlement of a matrimonial dispute simply overlooked the question of whether liability to pay costs formed part of the agreement, rectification will not be possible.

The remedy of rectification is not dispensed liberally to litigants. In *McAlpine v. Swift*,[109] Manners L.C. pointed out that equity will not rectify for mistake unless the court is sure that rectification will not work an injury. For this reason, the courts will not rectify a contract document if it appears that the parties have failed to reach a prior agreement on the terms to be inserted into the rectified instrument. As the contrasting cases of *Webster v. Cecil* and *Gun v. McCarthy* show, compulsory rectification in such a case compels one party to labour under a bargain he did not assent to and the judiciary view this as unacceptable. It is clear that this solution is often reached when the courts

---

[104] [1946] I.R. 377.
[105] Unreported, High Court, December 18, 1970.
[106] [1946] I.R. 377.
[107] Irish Supplement to Cheshire and Fifoot's *Law of Contract* (1954).
[108] [1993] I.L.R.M. 717
[109] (1810) 1 Ball & B. 285.

strike down exemption clauses, unconscionable bargains and insert implied terms into contracts. It may be that legislation which would permit the courts to vary or cancel contracts concluded by way of a mistake would provide a sensible solution to many mistake cases. The New Zealand Contractual Mistakes Act, s.7 contains just such a provision as part of its discretionary remedy system.[110] One English judge has hinted that in cases of unconscionable conduct a court may be prepared to adopt a much more flexible approach to remedies. In *Commission for New Towns v. Cooper*[111] Stuart Smith L.J. said, *obiter*

> "I would hold that where A intends B to be mistaken as to the construction of the agreement, so conducts himself that he diverts B's attention from discovering the mistake by making false and misleading statements, and B in fact makes the very mistake that A intends, then notwithstanding that A does not actually know, but merely suspects that B is mistaken, and it cannot be shown that the mistake was induced by any misrepresentation, rectification may be granted. A's conduct is unconscionable and he cannot insist on performance in accordance to the strict letter of the contract; that is sufficient for rescission. But it may also not be unjust or inequitable to insist that the contract be performed according to B's understanding, where that was the meaning that A intended B should put upon it."[112]

The prospect that judges will take a more creative, case by case approach to remedies and contractual mistake is a tantalising one.

The recent Northern Ireland case of *Rooney & McParland v. Carlin*[113] illustrates how limited the present remedy of rectification is. Carlin commenced nuisance proceedings against the plaintiffs who operated a quarry in County Armagh. The action was compromised by counsel for both parties. Counsel for the plaintiffs purchased land from Carlin believing that the land purchased was all the property Carlin owned in the vicinity. This belief was also shared by Carlin's counsel. The folio number and the map annexed to the agreement correctly identified and set out the property sold. In fact Carlin owned another field worth some £800 which was not included in the sale. The plaintiffs sought rectification so as to include this field, arguing that they were not obliged to pay further sums of money for this additional property. Kelly J. at trial permitted rectification. This decision was reversed by the Court of Appeal. Lord Lowry in his speech said that there was no mistake as to terms; neither counsel knew of the existence of the field and to talk of a mistaken common intention here was to confuse motive, object and belief with intention. Rectification was refused. Were the courts able to (a) reduce the price payable

---

[110] See the cases of *Conlon v. Ozolins* [1984] 1 N.Z.L.R. 489 and *Engineering Plastics Ltd. v. Mercer* [1985] 2 N.Z.L.R. 72.
[111] [1995] 2 All E.R. 929.
[112] *Ibid.* at 946.
[113] [1981] N.I. 138.

to reflect the lower value of the property purchased or (b) to order rectification upon condition a higher price is paid, a fairer result would ensue in such a case.

One important practical point that has fallen for extensive judicial consideration in recent years is this: is rectification available only in respect of a concluded legally enforceable contract, which predates execution of the written document in repsect of which rectification is sought? Alternatively, can rectification of a document be obtained, even though the document itself marks the formulation of an enforceable and binding contract? Until recently, Irish law tended to favour the first view. The leading case on this point was the decision in *Lucey v. Laurel Construction Co.*[114] Kenny J., following *Rose v. Pim*[115] and other English cases, held that a concluded oral contract must exist. The English Court of Appeal in *Joscelyne v. Nissen*[116] have relaxed this requirement. It is sufficient for the party seeking rectification to show "a continuing common intention" to contract on particular terms, falling short of a concluded contract, and that the parties have outwardly expressed this. The Northern Ireland Court of Appeal, in *Rooney & McParland v. Carlin*[117] has discussed and approved *Joscelyne v. Nissen*. The Supreme Court, in *Irish Life Assurance Co. Ltd. v. Dublin Land Securities Ltd.*[118] also approved *Joscelyne v. Nissen*, and overruled *Lucey v. Laurel Construction Co.* on this specific point. Both Keane J. and the Supreme Court approved the speech of Lord Lowry in *Rooney & McParland v. Carlin* where his Lordship said that the following principles are applicable:

"1. There must be a concluded agreement antecedent to the instrument which is sought to be rectified; but
2. The antecedent agreement need not be binding in law (for example, it need not be under seal if made by a public authority or in writing and signed by the party if relating to a sale of land) nor need it be in writing: such incidents merely help to discharge the heavy burden of proof; and
3. A complete antecedent concluded contract is not required, so long as there was prior accord on a term of a proposed agreement, outwardly expressed and communicated between the parties, as in *Joscelyne v. Nissen*."[119]

However the onus resting upon the party seeking rectification is a heavy one, for that person must adduce convincing proof, manifested in some outward expression of accord, which shows that the common continuing intention of both parties was in favour of the term omitted from the written document. In the *Irish*

---

[114] Unreported, High Court, December 18, 1970.
[115] [1953] 2 Q.B. 451.
[116] [1970] 2 Q.B. 86.
[117] [1981] N.I. 138.
[118] [1989] I.R. 253.
[119] [1981] N.I. 138, at 146. Those are in fact the statements of principle by Russell L.J. in *Joscellyne v. Nissen*.

*Life* case itself, the evidence admitted that the seller wished to exclude certain land, but the vagueness of the statements made by the seller could in no sense attribute the necessary continuing common intention upon both parties.

## (3) Damages

If one party contracts under a mistaken belief as to the terms of the bargain a remedy in damages is not available unless the court can also find that a warranty or fraudulent or negligent misrepresentation was made. For this reason, the plaintiff, in the case of *Harlingdon Ltd. v. Hull Fine Art Ltd.*[120] was constrained to plead misrepresentation and breach of implied condition when a painting which was thought to be an original by the German expressionist Munter turned out to be a forgery. A right to damages may also arise under the Sale of Goods and Supply of Services Act 1980 in limited cases. In exceptional cases a court may be prepared to hold that the seller of goods who fails to disabuse a buyer of some mistaken belief may render the seller liable in damages for fraud. In *Gill v. McDowell*[121] the seller of a hermaphrodite member of the oxen family – "when looked at from the back [it] appeared to be a heifer, but when looked at from certain other directions appeared to be a bullock" – was held liable in damages to the purchaser of the beast. The seller had taken the oxen to a market and sold it without informing the buyer of its unusual characteristics. This is something of a "rogue" decision because the Court of Appeal denied that a misrepresentation had been made; fraudulent intent seems to have provided the basis of the decision. The precedent value of *Gill v. McDowell* is not high. It is possible for the parties to stipulate that any mistake in the contract is to be actionable in damages only and in *Phelps v. White*[122] such a clause was upheld.

Submissions for statutory reform of the law of mistake have included suggestions that the courts be given a discretionary power to award damages in lieu of rescission or rectification. Again, the New Zealand Contractual Mistakes Act permits a court to grant relief by way of restitution or compensation.

It should be noted that both the Misrepresentation Act (Northern Ireland) 1967 and the Sale of Goods and Supply of Services Act 1980, reforming aspects of the law of misrepresentation in the Republic, permit the courts to grant damages in lieu of rescission. To extend this discretionary power into cases of mistake would seem a natural progression, one which would improve the remedial powers of a court faced with operative mistake.

## (4) Specific performance

The fact that the defendant has made a mistake cannot, of itself, give him a defence to an action for specific performance. If there has been a misrepresentation or an ambiguity in the contract the court may decline to award specific

---

[120] [1990] 1 All E.R. 737.
[121] [1903] 2 I.R. 463.
[122] (1881) 5 L.R. (Ir.) 318; 7 L.R. (Ir.) 160.

performance: see *Tamplin v. James*.[123] If the plaintiff has not acted equitably, specific performance may be refused as part of the overall discretionary nature of the remedy.[124]

## *Non Est Factum* – "it is not my deed"

This plea was initially confined to cases where a blind or illiterate person signed the contract after its effect had been misrepresented to him. The plea expanded so as to become available to all persons who signed an instrument which turned out to be a different document to that which they had assumed or had been told they were signing. The plea is useful to the signor because if it is successful the contract is void and not merely voidable. Third parties cannot acquire title to goods where *non est factum* is successfully pleaded by the initial owner. Cherry C.J. in *Bank of Ireland v. McManamy*[125] explained that:

> "The principle of the cases is not, however, that fraud vitiates consent, but rather that there is an entire absence of consent. That the mind of the party who signs under a fundamental error does not go with the act of signing, and that there is consequently no contract at all in fact."[126]

*Bank of Ireland v. McManamy* establishes that fraud need not be shown although this will exist in most cases: see also *Siebel & Seum v. Kent*.[127]

The facts of *McManamy* are worth recounting. The respondents, all 23 of them, were members of a co-operative creamery in County Roscommon. They were approached by the creamery manager who, so the defendants said, wanted them to sign forms to order manure and other creamery requirements. The documents were in fact bank guarantee forms. The jury found the defendants were not negligent. An action for a new trial was refused on the ground that it was not necessary for the jury to find fraud; the jury had declined to answer this question.

Although the rationale for the plea is somewhat metaphysical – the mind of the signor did not accompany his hand – there are practical considerations here. As a matter of policy the plea is to be kept within narrow bounds. A party signing must show that the error was "fundamental" in nature. Signing a bank guarantee when one thinks the document is an application for a load of manure is a fundamental misconception; a guarantee of a debt for £100,000 when one thinks the sum was only £100 is also a fundamental error. *Saunders v. Anglia Building Society*,[128] the leading English case, holds that to assign a house to X for £3,000 when the document is thought to be an assignment of the same house to Y

---

[123] (1880) 15 Ch.D. 215.
[124] *Minister For Education v. North Star Ltd.*, unreported, High Court, January 12, 1987.
[125] [1916] 2 I.R. 161.
[126] *Ibid.* at 173.
[127] Unreported, High Court, June 1, 1976.
[128] [1971] A.C. 1004.

by way of gift is not a fundamental enough error to ground *non est factum*. If the signor successively shows a fundamental error he must also show he has not been careless at the date of signing the contract. To sign a document without reading it is carelessness which will prevent the signor from relying on *non est factum*. In *U.D.T. v. Western*,[129] the English Court of Appeal held that someone who signs a loan proposal form in blank, leaving another person to fill in the details, acts carelessly. There is one important exception to this rule. In the case of *Petelin v. Cullen*[130] the High Court of Australia ruled that if A misrepresents a document's effect to B and B signs without reading it, then the document will not be valid if A tries to rely on it. Should A transfer his interest to C, an innocent third party, carelessness or negligence will be material here. *Saunders v. Anglia Building Society*[131] illustrates this point well. The Building Society, an innocent third party, was not to bear the loss resulting from Mrs. Gallie's negligence in signing a document unread. In *Bank of Ireland v. McCabe and McCabe*[132] the defendants were held not to be able to utilise a *non est factum* defence in relation to a deed of guarantee when they claimed the guarantee was not applicable to a given transaction. Citing *Saunders v. Anglia Building Society*, Flood J. said there was no evidence that the defendants had taken reasonable steps to have the document explained to them so as to acquire knowledge of its effect.

However, in *Lloyds Bank Plc v. Waterhouse*[133] the Court of Appeal placed a somewhat interesting interpretation upon the lack of negligence element that the signor must satisfy. The defendant signed a bank guarantee in favour of the plaintiff in order to enable his son to buy a farm. The defendant believed the form was only applicable to the loan made in respect of the form when in fact it was a guarantee of all monies advanced to the defendant's son. The defendant was illiterate, but able to sign his name to the form. He did not advise the plaintiff of his disability. The Court of Appeal held *non est factum* could be pleaded. The defendant was under no duty to advise the bank of his disability and he was able to show that he had asked a series of questions in order to try and discover the implications of the guarantee, but the bank had been negligent in responding to these inquiries and this misled the defendant. This is a somewhat liberal application of *non est factum* which is attributable to the negligence of the plaintiff bank outweighing the lack of candour by the defendant, who was apparently "too shy" to inform the plaintiff of his disability.

---

129 [1976] Q.B. 813.
130 (1975) 132 C.L.R. 355.
131 [1971] A.C. 1004.
132 Unreported, High Court, March 23, 1993.
133 [1991] Fam. Law. 23.

# 11 Misrepresentation

## Introduction

A misrepresentation is made when one contracting party has uttered a statement of fact which is untrue. We have discussed in Chapter 5 the extent to which the Irish courts are prepared to go in holding a precontractual statement to be a part of the contract. In such cases the injured party can sue for breach of a contractual term. The remedy available will depend on whether the promise takes effect as a warranty, condition or intermediate term.[1] The misrepresentation may also produce a remedy in tort. Should a court refuse to hold the statement to be a contractual term, the injured party may still be able to recover damages or repudiate the contract if the misrepresentation can be deemed fraudulent, negligent or innocent. As we shall see, the remedy available depends largely on which category the statement falls into. As in the law of mistake equitable principles and remedies differ from those developed by the common law courts. Limited measures of statutory reform have recently come into operation in both parts of Ireland. As a result it is possible for a misleading statement to take effect in one of three ways; it can produce a remedy in contract; alternatively, the statement can produce a remedy in tort; thirdly, it could produce a remedy under Part V of the Sale of Goods and Supply of Services Act 1980. In most instances the plaintiff will plead breach of contract, tortious misrepresentation, or breach of statute as alternative causes of action. It is also worth recalling that where false or reckless statements are made in the course of a trade, business or profession a remedy may be available under sections 6(1) and 17(3) of the Consumer Information Act 1978. It is also of course possible for the representor to commit criminal offences by making false statements in relation to a contract: witness the conviction in *Arthur Guinness Son & Co. v. Killeen*[2] in respect of false trade descriptions under the Merchandise Marks Act 1887. Notwithstanding this bewildering array of remedies there is still ample scope for further legislative activity by the Oireachtas.

In this Chapter we will confine our attention to the contractual, tortious and statutory remedies available to someone who has entered a contract as a result of a misrepresentation.[3]

---

[1] See Chap. 9.
[2] (1898) 32 I.L.T.R. 107.
[3] Other remedies may be available through the law relating to fiduciaries and in restitution. On the question of liability for express terms, see Chaps. 5 and 9.

## The Statement

For a statement to take effect as a misrepresentation, several criteria have to be met. The statement must not be a statement of law. We have discussed this problem in the context of the law of mistake and it is suggested that the exception drawn in *Cooper v. Phibbs*[4] is operative in misrepresentation cases also, that is, misrepresentations as to private rights under contract may still ground relief to the representee. This distinction was discussed and upheld by Keane J. in *Doolan v. Murray, Murray and Others*[5] where the learned judge indicated that a misrepresentation relating to a right or easement could be actionable on the ground that "a misrepresentation as to private rights may still afford a cause of action".

A statement of opinion will, in certain cases, be outside the law of misrepresentation. If the person uttering the statement knows it is false or had the opportunity to check its accuracy he will be bound, particularly if the representee was unable to investigate the facts for himself. If I say, "in my opinion, the car is sound" and I know the vehicle is only fit for the scrapheap, I have misstated my true opinion; this constitutes a misrepresentation of fact. In *Esso Petroleum v. Mardon*,[6] the appellants were held to have made a misrepresentation when they told a prospective tenant that, in their opinion, a filling station would sell 200,000 gallons per annum at the end of a two-year period. The English Court of Appeal said Esso were liable for a misrepresentation nonetheless. The appellants were said to have misrepresented that they had exercised care and skill in calculating this figure. It should be noted that Esso were in the best position to estimate "throughput".

The distinctions between statements of future intention, statements of opinion and actionable misrepresentations are extremely difficult to draw in situations where the contractual subject-matter is itself speculative or aspirational. Many of the leading cases involve statements about the development potential of land, or a business venture, or a corporate body to be operated in the future. In general, the element of futurity can be exploited by the alleged misrepresentor as long as it can be shown that the intention or the opinion was held at the time of the statement being made. Two contrasting Commonwealth cases illustrate this problematical area very well. In *Buxton v. The Birches Time Share Resort Ltd.*,[7] the defendant read very attractive promotional material which painted an attractive picture of a timeshare development which the plaintiff wished to undertake. The development, by way of chalet units, began and the defendant booked two weeks in that chalet unit. However, the contract document provided made it clear that the entire development of later units and certain facilities depended on successful completion of the staged development. The early phase was not a complete success. Some timeshare weeks remained

---

[4] (1867) L.R. 2 H.L. 149.
[5] Unreported, High Court,December 21, 1993.
[6] [1976] Q.B. 801.
[7] [1991] 2 N.Z.L.R. 641.

unsold, and the defendant refused to proceed. Summary judgment was given against him and on appeal the judgment was upheld. Hardie Boys J. observed that "a statement of intention will be a misrepresentation if the intention did not in fact exist when the statement was made but what appears to be a statement concerning the future may in reality be or it may imply a representation as to a present fact." The brochures clearly painted a brighter picture than the reality, but the learned judge did not find any basis for an implied misrepresentation of fact. At the legally significant date – entry into the contract – the full speculative nature of the venture was known: success "depended entirely on the success of the marketing of the project, a matter to a large degree beyond the control of the promoters. The risk involved was obvious, and those who purchased must have been prepared to run it. Mr. Buxton having chosen to do so cannot now repudiate his contract when the risk appears to have materialised."

In the Ontario case of *447927 Ontario Inc. v. Pizza Pizza Ltd.*[8] the plaintiffs, franchisees of a pizza restaurant, unsuccessfully sought damages in respect of a franchise agreement which the plaintiffs claimed had been concluded on the basis of misrepresentation and breach of warranty. The defendants, through their franchise sales manager, had stated the earnings level to be anticipated from a retail outlet, but the plaintiff could not show any error of the kind disclosed in respect of the calculations and on this point *Esso Petroleum Co. v. Mardon* was distinguishable. In any event, the agreement executed contained an integration clause, that is, a clause that excluded pre-contractual statements and negotiations and made the written contract the entire contract. This express clause was operative and in particular negated the existence of any warranties by the defendant franchisor. In the Ontario High Court, Arderson J. specifically drew attention to this factual difference between the case at bar and *Esso Petroleum Co. v. Mardon*. However, where the statement is made verbally and is clearly a statement of fact which induced the contract, the British Columbia Court of Appeal, in *Zippy Print Enterprises Ltd. v. Pawliuk*[9] held that an integration clause will be denied effect.

While this line of case law is supportable, there is the possibility of abuse by allowing advertising material to set out very laudatory claims which raise expectations that are then deflated, or negatived, by contract terms. No doubt the courts will strive to prevent fraud or negligently-made assertions and will require fairness during contract negotiations, but there remain some instances where *caveat emptor* will prevail. It is significant, for example, that in the *Harlingdon Ltd. v. Hull Fine Art Ltd.*[10] case, the decision involving the forged Munter painting, the plaintiff did not pursue a claim of actionable misrepresentation, presumably on the ground that the statement about origin was a statement of opinion only.

If neither party is in a position to verify the statement, an opinion that turns out to be wrong will not always be actionable. In *Smith v. Lynn*[11] the plaintiff

---

8  (1987) 44 D.L.R. (4th) 366, affirmed (1990) 64 D.L.R. (4th) 160.
9  [1995] 6 W.W.R. 99.
10  [1990] 1 All E.R. 737.
11  (1954) 85 I.L.T.R. 57.

and defendant were both interested in buying the same house. The plaintiff outbid the defendant at auction. Both parties had read an advertisement stating that the property was "in excellent structural and decorative repair". Six weeks after the plaintiff bought the property he put it back on the market. The plaintiff used the same advertisement and when asked by the defendant why the property was being resold, the plaintiff replied that the sale was due to personal reasons. The defendant purchased; after the sale it was discovered that the house was infested with woodworm! The defendant refused to proceed with the purchase pleading that the plaintiff has misrepresented that the house was sound. The defence failed. The advertisement was held to be a statement of opinion, an advertising "puff" not intended to have legal consequences. Both parties had inspected the premises and, in the view of the court, the defendant could not avoid the bargain. The case of *Hummingbird Motors v. Hobbs*[12] is to similar effect. Here a statement by the defendant about the mileage of a motor vehicle sold to the plaintiff company was held not to be a warranty. However, statements of opinion that lack an objective quality, which are made by a person who has the facts upon which the opinion is based, cannot be made with impunity. In *Doheny v. Bank of Ireland*[13] the defendant was held liable on a "glowing" reference it gave in respect of a bank customer whom the bank represented to be "respectable and trustworthy". The defendants had bounced several cheques written by the customer and knew that she had a record of dishonesty. The plaintiff, a landlord who had let property to the customer, was held able to recover damages for rent arrears and damage to property. Similarly, letting agents for units in a shopping centre who expressed the view that all units would be let by Christmas were held to have crossed the thin line between an aspirational "puff" and a statement of fact: *Donnellan & Donnellan v. Dungoyne Ltd.*[14]

In *Smith v. Lynn* the court also formed the view that the defendant had not relied on the statements made. He purchased on the strength of his own examination of the building. A statement will not constitute a misrepresentation if it is not read or heard by the other party or if it is not relied upon. In *Grafton Court Ltd. v. Wadson Sales Ltd.*[15] the defendants took a lease in a shopping complex. They pleaded that the plaintiff developer had represented that the other tenants would be high quality commercial concerns. The defendants pleaded that the other tenants did not meet this standard. Finlay P. held that if this statement had been made the defendant had not relied on it. When the lease was signed the other units were occupied. The true facts were known to the defendant when the contract was entered into. In some cases the misrepresentor may purport to rectify the earlier misrepresentation; the onus upon the misrepresentor is to show that at the time of contracting, rectification of the misrepresentation was plainly brought to the attention of the representee. It is

---

[12] [1986] R.T.R. 276.
[13] *Irish Times*, December 12, 1997.
[14] Unreported, High Court, August 15, 1994.
[15] Unreported, High Court, February 17, 1975.

not enough to plead that the misrepresentation could have been discovered if a search had been undertaken, or that the misrepresentee was invited to verify the statement but declined to do so.[16]

In *Sargent v. Irish Multiwheel*[17] it was held that the representee does not have to inform the representor that he has seen the misleading statement; it is enough to show the fact of reliance. Sargent was therefore able to sue on an advertisement which represented that a van which he later purchased was English-assembled. A statement will also be actionable even if it is only one reason why the representee entered the contract. In *Edgington v. Fitzmaurice*[18] the plaintiff purchased debentures partly due to a misrepresentation in the brochure and partly because of a self-induced mistaken belief that the debentures were such as to provide preferential creditor status in the event of the company failing. It was held sufficient to maintain an action on the misrepresentation to show that the misrepresentation was one of the reasons why the subsequent contract was entered into. However, the courts stop short of a test of total subjectivity. According to *Smith v. Chadwick*[19] the misrepresentation must have been of a kind that would have induced a reasonable person to enter into the contract but this has been doubted in England,[20] the view being taken that the issue of whether a reasonable person would have been induced was relevant to issues of proof – did the representee act in reliance?

A very curious result occurred in *Cody v. Connolly*.[21] The plaintiff inspected a mare and was told that it would do all kinds of work. The plaintiff, however, before buying, had the mare inspected by a vet, despite the defendants saying "what do you want to do that for? Didn't I tell you she was all right." The sale was concluded. The mare was badly winded. The vet did not discover this during the examination. The plaintiff sued for misrepresentation. O'Byrne J. held that the inspection could not affect the plaintiff's rights against the defendant because it was not part of the contract that the animal be inspected. This seems beside the point. If the plaintiff purchased only after the inspection he would be placing his faith on the vet, not the seller's representation. The defendant should not have been liable in my view. The proper action would have been to sue the vet for his negligent inspection.

It is not unusual for the contract to attempt to place an obligation on the representee to verify all statements made to him. In *Pearson v. Dublin Corporation*[22] the plaintiff was about to tender to the corporation for a construction contract. He was told by the defendant's agent that a wall had been built on the construction site and that the foundations of the wall were nine feet

---

[16]  *Redgrave v. Hurd* (1881) 20 Ch.D. 1; *Buxton v. The Birches Time Share Resort Ltd.* [1991] 2 N.Z.L.R. 641.

[17]  (1955) 21–2 Ir.Jur.Rep. 42.

[18]  (1885) 29 Ch.D. 459.

[19]  (1884) 9 App.Cas. 187.

[20]  Scott J. in *Musprime Properties Ltd. v. Adhill Properties Ltd.* (1990) 36 E.G. 114.

[21]  [1940] Ir.Jur.Rep. 49.

[22]  [1907] A.C. 351.

deep. This statement was untrue and it adversely affected the price contained in the tender, which the defendants accepted. The contract provided that the plaintiff had to verify all representations for himself and not rely on their accuracy. Palles C.B. held that this provision was effective and he refused to leave an issue to the jury, dismissing the action. The House of Lords granted a new trial. The statement was made by the agent fraudulently; several members of the House of Lords said that, in general, a person cannot avoid the effect of his or her agent's fraudulent statements by inserting a clause in the contract that the other party shall not rely on them. Any other rule would encourage fraudulent practices. The decision in *Pearson v. Dublin Corporation* was discussed in *Dublin Port and Docks Board v. Brittania Dredging Co. Ltd.*[23] The defendants contracted to perform dredging work for the plaintiffs. The material to be dredged was stated in the contract to be of a particular quality but the survey upon which this representation was based was itself inaccurate. The material was much coarser and the cost of extraction was higher, thereby affecting the profitability of the contract. However, the contract provided that the defendants were deemed to have inspected the site and the plaintiffs were not liable for any misrepresentation. The Supreme Court characterised this misrepresentation as innocent, not fraudulent. The survey was provided honestly and in good faith. The clause could therefore be operative. More recently, Slade J. observed[24] that the rule "*caveat emptor* has no application to a case where a purchaser has been induced to enter the contract of purchase by fraud", but the general usefulness of exclusion clauses is outlined by *447927 Ontario Inc. v. Pizza Pizza Ltd.*[25] where it was stated, *obiter*, that an exclusion clause could be relied upon to exclude liability for misrepresentations that did not find their way into the contract document. However, some protection against exclusion clauses in sale of goods, hire-purchase, bailment and contracts for services is found in Irish statute law. Section 46 of the Sale of Goods and Supply of Services Act 1980 limits the effectiveness of such disclaimer clauses to cases where a clause is "fair and reasonable in the circumstances of the case" (see above, Chapter 8).

A representee who becomes aware of the untruth of a statement before he enters into the contract has no remedy; he has not relied upon the statement because he has notice of its falsity. Notice means actual and not constructive notice. In *Phelps v. White*[26] the plaintiff was told that timber on land he intended to lease would be part of the property transferred. This was untrue. The plaintiff was furnished with documentation which would have revealed the misrepresentation. The Court of Appeal in Ireland refused to hold the plaintiff had notice of the misrepresentation. In *Gahan v. Boland & Boland*[27] the defendants falsely but innocently represented that their property would not be affected by any new roads to be built in the area and, in reliance, the representee purchased

---

[23] [1968] I.R. 136.
[24] *Gordon v. Selico* [1986] 1 E.G.L.R. 71.
[25] (1987) 44 D.L.R. (4th) 366.
[26] (1881) 7 L.R.(Ir.) 160.
[27] Unreported, Supreme Court, January 20, 1984.

the property. After completion the plaintiff sought to rescind the contract of sale on the grounds of a contractual misrepresentation. The defendants argued that as the plaintiff was a solicitor and intending purchaser he was obliged to pursue inquiries which would have led to him being informed of the true position. The Supreme Court granted rescission, holding that only actual and not constructive notice will debar a purchaser from repudiating a contract on the ground of misrepresentation.

In the Northern Ireland case of *Lutton v. Saville Tractors Ltd.*[28] an interesting point of law arose out of a contract for the sale of a second-hand motor vehicle. The plaintiff purchased the car, partly on the basis that the vehicle had not been involved in an accident, and the salesman innocently misrepresented that the vehicle had not been so involved. The plaintiff rescinded the contract because it proved defective. Shortly after proceedings commenced, the untruth of the assurance about involvement in an accident was discovered. Carswell J. nevertheless held that the innocent misrepresentation could be relied upon:

> "it is a well established principle of the law of contract that a person who refuses to perform a contract on one ground, may, if that is inadequate, subsequently rely upon another ground which justifies his refusal to perform provided it in fact existed at the time of the refusal: *Benjamin's Sale of Goods*, 2nd Edition, paragraph 1725."[29]

In this case the learned judge also held that where an employee makes a representation in the course of employment this will be actionable against the employer. On the question of whether an agent's knowledge of fraud can bind a principal, see the old Irish case of *Sankey v. Alexander*,[30] and the recent English case of *Stroves and Another v. Harrington and Others*[31] in which Browne-Wilkinson V.C. considered the circumstances in which knowledge acquired by a purchaser's solicitor can be imputed to the purchaser, thereby effecting an estoppel. A novel application of estoppel by misrepresentation occurred in *Lease Management Services Ltd. v. Purnell Secretarial Services.*[32] Here a finance company used contract documents which deceived customers into thinking they were dealing with a company associated with an international trading group when there was no such link. The use of this misleading trade practice gave rise to an estoppel by representation so that it was bound by statements made by employees of the supplier of the goods.

---

[28] [1986] N.I. 327.
[29] *Ibid.* at 334.
[30] (1874) 9 Ir.Rep.Eq. 259.
[31] [1988] 1 All E.R. 769.
[32] [1994] C.C.L.R. 127.

## The Causes of Action

### *(1) Fraudulent misrepresentation*

A fraudulent misrepresentation is actionable in the tort of deceit. In the leading English case of *Derry v. Peek*,[33] Lord Herschell said "without proof of fraud no action of deceit is maintainable." In that case the House of Lords held that fraud is proved when it is shown that a false representation has been made knowingly, or without belief in its truth, or recklessly, without caring whether it is true or false.

In *Fenton v. Schofield*[34] the vendor of land represented that over the last four years a river running over the land had yielded 300–350 salmon a year and that he had spent £15,000 renovating the property. Both statements were untrue as the vendor well knew. A purchaser paid £17,000 for the land. The value of the property was calculated by assuming each statement to be true. When the purchaser learnt of their untruth he sued in deceit, recovering damages based on the difference between what the land was worth and what it was represented to be worth. In *Carbin v. Somerville*[35] the vendor of a house in Clontarf misrepresented that the house was dry. The Supreme Court held the plaintiff, who purchased the house on the strength of this assurance, entitled to rescind the contract.

The facts of *Pearson v. Dublin Corporation*[36] show that fraud can exist even when the representor does not necessarily know that his statement is false. When the agent told the plaintiff that the foundations of a wall stood on the site the agent did not know if this was true or false: the statement was nevertheless fraudulent.

An action in deceit may lie even if the representor has no intention to cause loss to the representee. In *Delany v. Keogh*[37] Keogh, an auctioneer, was employed by Bradley, a solicitor, to sell Bradley's interest in leasehold property. The conditions of sale stated that while the rent was £25 per annum the landlord had accepted £18. Before the sale Keogh was told by the landlord that the full rent of £25 would be charged to the purchaser of the lease. Bradley advised Keogh that in his view the landlord would be estopped from charging the full rent. Keogh was advised not to change the conditions of sale. The plaintiff purchased the lease. The Kings Bench Division refused to find Keogh liable in deceit because it could not be shown that Keogh intended to mislead. The Court of Appeal reversed this decision. Holmes L.J. found that the misrepresentation stemmed from a failure to make known that he had reason to believe that the landlord would charge the higher rent. While Keogh believed what Bradley had told him this would not absolve him. Keogh should have mentioned, after reading out the conditions, that while he had been informed

---

[33] (1889) 14 App.Cas. 337.
[34] (1966) 100 I.L.T.R. 69.
[35] [1933] I.R. 227.
[36] [1907] A.C. 351.
[37] [1905] 2 I.R. 267.

by the landlord that a higher rent would be charged it was Keogh's solicitor's opinion that the landlord was legally estopped.

Holmes L.J. also distinguished the leading case of *Derry v. Peek*:

> "The directors of a Tramway Co. that had authority to use steam power with the consent of the Board of Trade, believing that this consent would be given as a matter of course issued a prospectus in which it was stated that they had the right to use steam power without reference to any condition. It was held that this was not actionable, inasmuch as the statement was made in the honest belief that it was true. This is, I think old law; but if the directors had known, before they issued the prospectus that the Board of Trade had refused to consent or had announced its intention to refuse, the case would have been like this, and the directors would have no defence; nor in such a case would their position have been improved if their solicitor had assured them that there would be no difficulty in obtaining from Parliament an amending Act removing the condition."[38]

### (2) Negligent misstatement

In *Derry v. Peek* the House of Lords ruled that there is no liability in deceit for a false statement made carelessly and without reasonable grounds for believing it to be true. In the absence of a contract, negligently made statements could be the subject of an award of damages only if a fiduciary relationship existed between the parties, such as solicitor and client. In 1963 the House of Lords declared that liability in the tort of negligence could arise from a negligent misstatement. In *Hedley Byrne v. Heller*[39] a bank negligently represented a company to be on a sound financial footing. This caused the appellant to invest in the company which later collapsed. The Law Lords stated *obiter* that where a "special relationship" exists, a duty of care will arise between the parties. *Esso Petroleum v. Mardon*[40] establishes that liability will arise under this cause of action where the misstatement results in a contract between the parties.

The *Hedley Byrne* principle has been considered by the courts in Ireland. In *Bank of Ireland v. Smith*,[41] Kenny J. cited *Hedley Byrne* although the learned judge found the misrepresentation in that case would ground liability in contract. In *Stafford v. Keane Mahony Smith*,[42] Doyle J. discussed the *Hedley Byrne* principle, as extended in *Esso Petroleum v. Mardon*. Doyle J. noted that *Hedley Byrne* had been approved by Davitt P. in *Securities Trust Ltd. v. Hugh Moore & Alexander Ltd.*[43] Doyle J. declared that:

---

[38] [1905] 2 I.R. 267 at 290.
[39] [1964] A.C. 465.
[40] [1976] Q.B. 801.
[41] [1966] I.R. 646.
[42] [1980] I.L.R.M. 53; *Hazylake Fashions v. Bank of Ireland* [1989] I.R. 601.
[43] [1964] I.R. 417. See generally McMahon & Binchy, *Irish Law of Torts* (2nd ed., 1990).

"In order to establish the liability for negligent or non-fraudulent misrepresentation giving rise to action there must first of all be a person conveying the information or the representation relied upon; secondly, that there must be a person to whom that information is intended to be conveyed or to whom it might reasonably be expected that the information would be conveyed; thirdly, that the person must act upon such information or representation to his detriment so as to show that he is entitled to damages."[44]

The action in *Stafford v. Keane Mahony Smith* was brought against an estate agent who had represented that certain property would be a good investment. The plaintiff purchased the house but later had to resell it at a loss. The action failed because Doyle J. found that any representations made were not made to the plaintiff but to his brother.[45] In *Doolan v. Murray, Murray and Others*[46] the plaintiff entered into building work on property she had purchased from the first two defendants because she believed that a right of way was a pedestrian right of way only. The third defendant had assisted in bringing the plaintiff's belief into being but the right of way was more extensive than the third defendant had stated. The work had to be removed. Keane J. held that the plaintiff could not succeed against the first two defendants in either contract or tort, but that liability against the third defendant in negligent misstatement could be made out. This case is an interesting one because in most actions of this kind the defendant is a professional person or someone who holds themselves out as possessing special knowledge or skill: recent English and Irish case law has explored the issue of whether a solicitor, for example, will be in a special relationship with someone other than his immediate client and the courts hold that, exceptionally, this may be so.[47] Similarly, liability in tort has been visited upon auctioneers who, acting for a vendor, make careless statements to inexperienced or naive prospective purchasers about the development potential of the property: *McAnarney v. Hanrahan*[48] and *McCullagh v. P B Gunne (Monaghan) plc.*[49] The third defendant in *Doolan v. Murray, Murray and Others* was not a professional person but a lay person who had created the right of way and had been a previous owner of the property.

## (3) Innocent misrepresentation

Prior to the *Hedley Byrne* decision it followed that all misrepresentations that were not fraudulent were classified as innocent misrepresentations. The fact that a misrepresentation was negligently made could not (in the absence of a

---

[44] [1980] I.L.R.M. 53 at 64.
[45] Contrast *Irish Permanent Building Society v. O'Sullivan and Collins* [1990] I.L.R.M. 598.
[46] Unreported, High Court, December 21, 1993.
[47] *White v. Jones* [1995] 2 A.C. 207; *Doran v. Delaney* [1998] 2 I.L.R.M. 1; *Woodward v. Wolferstans (a firm), The Times,* April 8, 1997.
[48] [1994] 1 I.L.R.M. 210.
[49] Unreported, High Court, January 17, 1997.

fiduciary relationship[50]) avail the injured party. While *Hedley Byrne* has qualified this proposition it is still true to say that an innocent, non-fraudulent misrepresentation secures limited redress to the representee. It is at this point that jurisdictional factors become important. At common law the victim of an innocent misrepresentation could only repudiate the agreement if there was a total failure of consideration, that is, if the thing contracted for was not supplied at all or it was a totally different item from that envisaged at the time of agreement. The courts of equity permitted rescission upon proof that the misrepresentation was material in that it induced the contract. It was unnecessary to show a failure of consideration. This essential difference was overlooked in *Carbin v. Somerville*[51] when Fitzgibbon J. in the Supreme Court held the vendor entitled to repudiate only if the statement was fraudulent or a total failure of consideration resulted. This proposition overlooks the equitable jurisdiction in which rescission would be ordered if an innocent misrepresentation were made. If the representation made is contractual in nature then the fact that the contract is executed is a barrier to rescission unless the barrier is removed by section 44 of the Sale of Goods and Supply of Services Act 1980. Fitzgibbon J. may well have been alluding to this difficulty in *Carbin v. Somerville*, a point we shall refer back to below.

Equity ordered the drastic remedy of rescission because historically an award of damages in lieu of rescission was not part of an equitable court's array of remedies. Because the common law courts took a restrictive view of the cases in which an innocent misrepresentation would be operative, many victims of an innocent misrepresentation were denied a remedy in damages unless the statement could be elevated into a contractual term or a collateral warranty. In *Connor v. Potts*[52] the plaintiff agreed to purchase two farms, innocently misrepresented to be 443 acres in all. The price was calculated at £12.10s. an acre. The farms fell 67 acres short of the figure represented. The plaintiff was held entitled to specific performance of the contract; the price payable by the plaintiff was reduced by calculating £12.10s. 67. Similarly in *Keating v. Bank of Ireland*[53] an abatement of price was held to be allowable when the purchaser agreed to buy property following a misrepresentation. It was further held that the vendor could not insist upon the closing of the sale prior to the abatement being calculated under an arbitration clause which formed the basis of the agreement. In *O'Brien v. Kearney*[54] the misrepresentee was able to counterclaim for specific performance at the abated price, using the misrepresentation as the successful basis for resisting the misrepresentor's action for specific performance, the misrepresentor seeking to have the issue of abatement being resolved subsequently.

---

[50] *Nocton v. Lord Ashburton* [1914] A.C. 932.
[51] [1933] I.R. 227. To make this observation accurate one has to add that the contract had been executed.
[52] [1897] I.R. 534.
[53] [1983] I.L.R.M. 295. Often this remedy will be prescribed in lieu of rescission by the contract.
[54] Unreported, High Court, March 3, 1995.

## (4) Statutory right to damages

While pre-contractual statements are increasingly likely to be characterised as contractual terms (see Kenny J. in *Bank of Ireland v. Smith*[55]) the Oireachtas has recently created a right to damages in cases of innocent misrepresentation. Section 45(1) of the Sale of Goods and Supply of Services Act 1980 provides:

> "Where a person has entered into a contract after a misrepresentation has been made to him by another party thereto and as a result thereof he has suffered loss, then, if the person making the representation would be liable to damages in respect thereof had the misrepresentation been made fraudulently, that person shall be so liable notwithstanding that the misrepresentation was not made fraudulently, unless he proves that he had reasonable ground to believe and did believe up to the time the contract was made that the facts represented were true."

This section is based upon section 2(1) of the English and Northern Ireland Misrepresentation Acts. It was seen as desirable to supplement the restrictive range of remedies available following an innocent misrepresentation which induces a contract because rescission is neither appropriate nor indeed possible in the majority of cases. Section 2(1) enables the representee to claim damages, as in *Gosling v. Anderson*[56] when the Court of Appeal held the purchaser of a flat entitled to damages when it was shown that planning permission to enable garages to be built had not in fact been obtained. The proviso to section 45(1) enables the misrepresentee to avoid liability if the court can be persuaded that the representee believed, and had a reasonable ground for believing, the truth of the statement. This defence is somewhat wide and in this writer's view it would be preferable to hold the mispresentor liable in damages simply upon proof that the statement was false. The New Zealand Contractual Remedies Act 1979, for example, provides an interesting contrast to the U.K. and Irish model for section 6 of that Act provides a right to damages if the statement is false and was relied upon.

The proviso has been interpreted narrowly on the one occasion when it has been considered in detail by an English Court. In *Howard Marine & Dredging Co. Ltd. v. A Ogden & Sons (Excavations) Ltd.*[57] the plaintiffs were the owners of barges hired out to the defendant to enable them to dump excavated spoil at sea. The capacity of the barges was stated at 1,600 tonnes by the plaintiff's marine manager, a figure based on recollection of the figure in Lloyds Register. The Lloyds Register was incorrect and the true capacity was 1,055 tonnes, a figure that was discernable by looking at the shipping documents, which the marine manager had seen. In an action for non-payment, the defendants counterclaimed under section 2(1) of the 1967 Act. A majority of the Court of

---

[55] [1966] I.R. 646.
[56] (1972) 223 E.G. 1473.
[57] [1978] 2 All E.R. 1134; Brownsword (1978) 41 M.L.R. 735.

Appeal held the proviso inapplicable on the ground that the plaintiffs could not show that it was reasonable for their marine manager to rely on recollection rather than to consult the shipping documents in question. The case is also of interest because the Court of Appeal did not hold that a duty of care in tort is a *sine qua non* of liability – indeed, Denning M.R., dissenting, was of the view that the marine manager owed no duty of care and had not been careless. This point was clearly made by Moriarty J. in *O'Donnell v. Truck and Machinery Sales*[58] where he pointed out that the English legislation was to govern disputes where no duty of care existed. Furthermore, Moriarty J. followed the earlier English case of *Gran Gelato Ltd. v. Richcliff (Group) Ltd.*[59] in holding that even if there is fault on the part of the misrepresentee liability will result, the fault of the misrepresentee may lead to damages being reduced under section 45(1) by way of a finding of contributory negligence under the Civil Liability Act 1961.

The remedy under section 45(1) was enacted in order to supplement the shortcomings of the range of remedies then otherwise available. It does not as such create a new statutory cause of action for persons who would otherwise have to satisfy other criteria. In *Resolute Maritime Inc. v. Nippon Kaiji Kyokai*,[60] Mustill J. held that the representee could not use section 2(1) of the 1967 Act to make an agent liable in damages under section 2(1) for any misrepresentation made by the agent within the scope of his authority. Mustill J. reasoned that the law of tort, through deceit and *Hedley Byrne*, conferred upon the misrepresentee a cause of action and that the law would develop along irrational lines if the misrepresentee could always side-step the "special relationship" requirement in *Hedley Byrne* by simply invoking the Statute. This approach has wider ramifications. The view previously held about the scope of section 2(1) of the English Act and its relationship with the rule in *Bain v. Fothergill*[61] has come under attack. According to *Watts v. Spence*[62] all the victims of a misrepresentation made in relation to the vendor of a real property's capacity to make a good title had to do, in order to avoid the above rule (which limited damages to expenses incurred) was to invoke section 2(1). In *Sharneyford Supplies Ltd. v. Edge*,[63] Mervyn Davies J. refused to follow *Watts v. Spence* on this point because the Statute did not remove the requirement that, before *Bain v. Fothergill* could be avoided, the vendor must be shown to have been in default. This aspect of section 2(1) of the English Act is not germane to the Irish situation because section 43 confines section 45(1) to contracts for the sale of goods, hire-purchase and the supply of a service.

The usefulness of the statutory right to damages has been re-enforced by the decision of the Court of Appeal in *Production Technology Consultants v. Bartlett*.[64] The defendant made an innocent misrepresentation in relation to

---

[58] [1997] 1 I.L.R.M. 466.
[59] [1992] Ch. 560.
[60] [1983] 1 W.L.R. 857.
[61] (1874) L.R. 7 H.L. 158.
[62] [1976] Ch. 165.
[63] [1987] 1 All E.R. 588, reversing [1985] 1 All E.R. 976.
[64] [1988] 1 E.G.L.R. 182.

land, the sale of which was made on the basis of the misrepresentation. The falsity of the representation became known to the plaintiff just prior to completion but the plaintiff still closed the purchase. The defendant submitted that in closing the sale the plaintiff lost any right to damages by affirmation of the contract – the plaintiff must rescind and seek damages. The Court of Appeal rejected this submission. Affirmation of a contract may lead to loss of the right to rescind, but, following *Arnison v. Smith*,[65] does not result in loss of a right to damages. However, section 2(1) of the English 1967 Act has been held to be inapplicable to contracts *uberrimae fidei* unless there is a misrepresentation in the sense of an express statement rather than simple non-disclosure. The authority in question is the decision of the Court of Appeal in *Banque Financiere de la Cite S.A. v. Westgate Insurance Co. Ltd.*,[66] although the decision of the Court of Appeal was affirmed on other grounds by the House of Lords,[67] their Lordships declining to deal with this point, amongst others.

There remains one very important matter. What measure of compensation is available under section 45(1)? The section itself points to a tortious measure – "shall be so liable" seems to refer back to the measure in deceit. In *F & H Entertainments v. Leisure Enterprises*[68] the tort measure was favoured. In *Davis & Co. v. Afa Minerva*[69] it was held that all consequential loss arising from the malfunctioning of a burglar alarm could be recoverable and it was not necessary to distinguish between the statutory cause of action and contractual warranties: see also Denning M.R. in *Jarvis v. Swans Tours*.[70] Nevertheless, it is generally agreed that if the measure of compensation cannot include damages for loss of bargain, in appropriate cases, the statutory right to damages is not flexible enough. In contrast, section 6 of the New Zealand Contractual Mistakes Act 1979 directs the contract measure will always be the measure of compensation! There is, as yet, no conclusive answer to this question in Ireland. In England while *Watts v. Spence*[71] indicates that damages for loss of bargain may be available, this case has not been followed in *Sharneyford Supplies Ltd. v. Edge*. Yet in that case Mervyn Davies J. expressly kept this point open: "I do not decide whether or not such damages for innocent misrepresentation embrace any element for loss of bargain." However, the matter seems to have been settled, for the moment, by a two-judge Court of Appeal, in *Royscott Trust Ltd. v. Rogerson and Another*.[72] Here the Court of Appeal held that the tortious, rather than the contractual, measure should be awarded under the statutory cause of action. The Court of Appeal went on to hold that the relevant tortious measure is that for deceit rather than negligence. This means that the plaintiff is able to recover any loss which flowed from the defendant's

---

[65] (1889) 41 Ch.D. 348 at 371, *per* Cotton L.J.
[66] [1989] 2 All E.R. 952.
[67] [1990] 2 All E.R. 947.
[68] (1976) 120 S.J. 331.
[69] (1974) 2 Lloyd's Rep. 27.
[70] [1973] 2 Q.B. 233.
[71] [1976] Ch. 165.
[72] [1991] 3 All E.R. 294; *Naughton v. O'Callaghan* [1990] 3 All E.R. 191.

fraud, even if it could not be foreseen.[73] So, in the case in question, a finance company were held entitled to recover all losses incurred when financing a car purchase agreement with a car dealer, even if the losses were unforeseeable.

# Remedies

## *The equitable right of indemnity*

Although an action for damages is not permitted for an innocent misrepresentation some limited pecuniary remedy is permitted to a representee where the terms of the contract have required the representee to make this expenditure. The courts have been careful to limit the right of indemnity for it is often difficult to distinguish expenditure required by the contract from expenditure envisaged by the contract. In the New Zealand case of *Power v. Atkins*[74] the plaintiff agreed to purchase a hotel after an innocent misrepresentation had been made to him. The plaintiff repudiated the contract when he discovered the true facts. The plaintiff sued for the return of the deposit paid and expenses such as board and lodging, advertising, train fares, preliminary expenses, an accountant's fee for investigating the account, a valuer's fee, the cost of investigating legal title. Salmon J. permitted recovery of the deposit as well as legal fees incurred in researching title. The accountants fee was irrecoverable but a fee paid to a valuer of stock in trade was allowable on proof that the contract required this valuation be made. All other expenses were rejected as being appropriate to a claim in damages. The difficulty and uncertainty surrounding this doctrine is illustrated by the fact that another New Zealand judge in the case of *Duncan v. Rothery*,[75] also decided in 1912, held legal fees to be irrecoverable in the equitable action for an indemnity. The leading English case is *Whittington v. Seale Hayne*.[76] The defendants leased farm premises to the plaintiff, representing that the premises were in sanitary condition. The lease required the plaintiff to carry out any repairs required by the local council. The water supply was polluted, causing an outbreak of disease which wiped out the commercial value of the plaintiff's poultry and made the farm manager and his family ill. The local authority required the drains to be repaired and the house made fit for human habitation. The plaintiffs sought to recover the value of stock, consequential loss in the form of lost sales and loss of the breeding potential of the stock, and medical and removal expenses. Because the only payment rendered necessary by the lease was the repairs done to the premises, the amounts recoverable were limited to such repairs, the other items being, in reality, a claim for damages.

---

[73] *Smith New Court Securities v. Scrimgeour Vickers (Asset Management) Ltd.* [1996] 4 All E.R. 769. Their Lordships were less than enthusiastic about the *Royscot* decision above.

[74] [1921] N.Z.L.R. 763.

[75] [1921] N.Z.L.R. 1074.

[76] (1990) 82 L.T. 49.

The 1980 Act, section 43, does not permit an action for damages when real property forms the subject matter of a contract.

*Rescission – when will the right to rescind be lost?*

(i) **When the contract is executed.** In *Legge v. Croker*[77] the defendant innocently misrepresented that a leasehold interest he was about to sell to the plaintiff was not subject to any public right of way. The transfer was executed. Manners L.C. held that an executed lease could not be set aside, even under the wider equitable jurisdiction to rescind, unless there is a fraudulent misrepresentation. This statement was taken up by later courts and forged into a doctrine commonly known as the doctrine in *Seddon v. North Eastern Salt*[78]; this rule provides that where a contract has been executed, it will only be set aside in equity where there has been equitable fraud. The rule was not confined to cases where land formed the subject-matter of the contract. In *Lecky v. Walter*[79] the plaintiff purchased bonds, issued by a Dutch company. The plaintiff had been told that the bonds were secured and that in the event of a liquidation his claim would take priority as a security. The bonds were not so secured and were in fact virtually worthless. The plaintiff's action for rescission failed. It was held that an executed contract can only be repudiated if the representation is fraudulent or if the plaintiff has suffered a total failure of consideration. In *Lecky v. Walter* the plaintiff could not make out a case under either of these exceptions.

The rule has been attacked: see in particular the English Court of Appeal's decision in *Leaf v. International Galleries*.[80] Section 1(*b*) of the English Misrepresentation Act 1967, giving effect to the Law Reform Committee's recommendation for reform, provides that no matter what the subject-matter of the contract may be, the fact that a contract has been executed should not impede rescission. Section 44(*b*) of the Sale of Goods and Supply of Services Act 1980 is based on the desire to sweep away the rule but, again, section 43 of the Act prevents this. Most of the cases that arise under *Seddon* are cases involving land and such contracts are outside the 1980 Act. Even the decision in *Lecky v. Walter* would not be different – shares are choses in action and cannot be goods – see *Lee & Co. (Dublin) Ltd. v. Egan (Wholesale) Ltd.*[81] – so further reforms are necessary here too.

(ii) **Affirmation.** Should the misrepresentee obtain full knowledge of the facts and the existence of a misrepresentation, and if the misrepresentee is aware of his right to rescind,[82] then any declaration of intent to proceed, or any

---

[77] (1811) 1 Ball & B. 506.
[78] [1905] 1 Ch. 326.
[79] [1914] I.R. 378.
[80] [1950] 2 K.B. 86.
[81] Unreported, High Court, December 18, 1979. This point may well have been overlooked in *Donnellan Donnellan v. Dungoyne Ltd.*, unreported, High Court, August 15, 1994.
[82] *Peyman v. Lanjani* [1984] 3 All E.R. 703.

action which is evidence of such an intention, will be held to be an affirmation of the contract. The misrepresentee thus loses any right to rescind the contract. However, in *Lutton v. Saville Tractors Ltd.*[83] Carswell J. held that the right to rescind is only lost if the misrepresentation is known to the misrepresentee, so, the fact that the plaintiff was unaware of the existence of a misrepresentation at the time he retained the defective motor vehicle (the alleged acts of affirmation) could not constitute an affirmation: loss of the right of rescission, due to affirmation of the contract by the misrepresentee, does not prevent the misrepresentee from obtaining a remedy in damages: *Production Technology Consultants v. Bartlett.*[84]

**(iii) Delay in seeking relief or "laches".** Because rescission will generally be sought in equity the equitable doctrine that litigants should seek equitable relief promptly may operate here. The doctrine of laches, as well as the Statute of Limitations Act 1957 may prevent equitable relief. The courts have shown a willingness to hold that the victim of a fraudulent misrepresentation need not be as prompt as someone who has contracted on the strength of an innocent misrepresentation. In *O'Kelly v Glenny*[85] the plaintiff, in ignorance of the full value of her interest in her deceased father's estate, sold the interest to her solicitor who fraudulently misrepresented her position. Ten years later an action setting the transfer aside was brought. Laches was held not to prevent rescission: see also *Murphy v. O'Shea.*[86] If the defrauded party, on learning of the fraud, fails to rescind within a reasonable time however acquiescence will be imputed; delay of 27 and 54 years would clearly be fatal to a claim of rescission: see *Hovenden v. Lord Annesley.*[87]

The victim of an innocent misrepresentation is not treated so indulgently. In *Leaf v. International Galleries*[88] an innocent misrepresentation that a picture, "Salisbury Cathedral", was painted by *the* John Constable was made at the time of sale. Five years later the purchaser learnt this was untrue. He claimed rescission on the ground of innocent misrepresentation. The Court of Appeal held the action must fail. By analogy with other sale of goods cases the right to rescind is lost if it is not sought within a reasonable time after the sale. Five years was not a reasonable time. Jenkins L.J. noted that the proper remedy was breach of warranty and not rescission; it may be that the plaintiff sued for rescission to avoid a finding that the statement as to the identity of the painter was not a contractual term: see also *Mihaljevic v. Eiffel Tower Motors.*[89]

In *Dillon Leech v. Maxwell Motors Ltd.*[90] the plaintiff purchased a car on the basis of an oral representation that the vehicle was reliable and suitable for

---

83 [1986] N.I. 327.
84 [1988] 1 E.G.L.R. 182.
85 (1846) 9 Ir.Eq.R. 25.
86 (1845) 8 Ir.Eq.R. 329.
87 (1806) 2 Sch. & Lef. 637.
88 [1950] 2 K.B. 86.
89 [1973] V.R. 545.
90 [1984] I.L.R.M. 624.

long journeys; these statements were untrue. There were several incidents in which the vehicle demonstrated its unreliability, yet the plaintiff retained the vehicle. While this delay no doubt prejudiced his equitable right to rescind, Murphy J. was able to hold that the defendants had subsequently accepted the purchaser's offer to effect a return of the vehicle. The courts have also been obliged to consider in sale of goods cases whether a right to rescind can be lost through acceptance of the goods. *Lutton v. Saville Tractors Ltd.*[91] seems to indicate a broader view of this issue for Carswell J. held that section 35(1) of the Sale of Goods Act 1979 did not operate against the buyer when the buyer co-operates with the seller in seeking to have the goods repaired.

It should also be noted that in Ireland a second ground in *Leaf v. International Galleries* for refusing rescission would have been the rule in *Seddon's* case; the Republic's 1980 statute would now remove such an objection if *Leaf v. International Galleries* were an Irish case occuring after 1980: section 44(*b*).

**(iv)   Third party rights.**   Although one early Irish case holds a fraudulent conveyance by A to B to be void and not merely voidable (see *O'Connor v. Bernard*[92]) it is now established that fraud renders a contract voidable and not void unless the party seeking to invalidate the transfer of property can show that the misrepresentation had the further effect of rendering the contract void at common law, as in *Cundy v. Lindsay*[93] as limited by the decision in *Citibank NA v. Brown, Shipley & Co. Ltd.*[94]

Rescission will not be available if a third party acquires an interest in the property and can show he is a bona fide purchaser for valuable consideration. The leading Irish case is *Anderson v. Ryan*.[95] Davis owned a mini. He answered a newspaper advertisement offering a Sprite motor car for sale. The parties agreed to swap vehicles, no money changing hands. The Sprite was a stolen vehicle. Davis was dispossessed of the Sprite but the gardai eventually returned the Mini to Davis. The Mini had been the subject of two subsequent deals. The defendant purchased the vehicle from a person representing himself to be Davis. This person was, in all probability, the person who had misrepresented that he owned the Sprite. The defendant in turn sold the Mini to the plaintiff Anderson who was dispossessed by the gardai. Anderson sued Ryan claiming that under sections 12(1) and 21(1) of the Sale of Goods Act 1893, Ryan lacked title to the goods at the time of the transfer of the property to him, Anderson. The Circuit Court judge found for Anderson. The decision was reversed on appeal to the High Court. Henchy J. found the essential issue to be whether Ryan had a good title to the car when he sold it to Anderson. Davis, the original owner had parted with the vehicle as a result of a fraudulent misrepresentation but this rendered the contract voidable. Because the contract between Davis

---

[91]   [1986] N.I. 327.
[92]   (1838) 2 Jones 654.
[93]   (1878) 3 App.Cas. 459.
[94]   [1991] 2 All E.R. 690.
[95]   [1967] I.R. 34.

and the rogue had not been avoided before the sale between Anderson and Ryan had been concluded, Ryan had, under the terms of section 23(1) of the 1893 Act, a valid, if voidable, title. This title was transferred to Anderson. As Henchy J. observed, the seizure of the Mini by the gardai was a wrongful act and redress should be sought from that direction.

If property is transferred to a person who subsequently cannot be traced, rescission can be effected by informing the police of the fraud in the hope that property can be recovered; this will prevent further transactions involving the property from passing a good title to the transferee, even if he is an innocent third party; *Car and Universal Finance Co. v. Caldwell.*[96]

(v) **Rescission – total or partial?** Where a person has been induced into giving a guarantee for past and future debts on the basis of an apparently fraudulent misrepresentation that the guarantee relates to future debts only, the High Court of Australia held in *Vadasz v. Pioneer Concrete (SA) Pty. Ltd.*[97] that rescission in equity would not extend to the guarantee entirely. Rescission in part was ordered because the guarantor had the benefit of performance by the misrepresentor and the effect of the High Court's order was to leave the guarantor in the position represented.

(vi) **Power to award damages in lieu of rescission.** The Sale of Goods and Supply of Services Act 1980, section 45(2), permits a court to declare a contract subsisting and award damages in lieu of rescission if the court is "of opinion that it would be equitable to do so". This statutory restriction on the right to rescind seems sensible given the restrictions developed by the courts on the right to rescind: see *Cehave N.V. v. Bremer Handelsgesellschaft GmbH.*[98] It should be noted that until recently it was thought that the court may award damages in lieu of rescission only if the remedy of rescission was still available to the representee. If rescission has been lost because of lapse of time, affirmation or waiver, it is not possible to award damages under section 45(2). This is unfortunate; the discretion should not be so limited, particularly in cases where the doctrine of laches applies. In *Lutton v. Saville Tractors Ltd.*[99] Carswell J., *obiter*, considered whether the case could have been an appropriate instance in which damages should have been awarded in lieu of rescission. Carswell J. did not however give any guidance on the factors that will lead a court to award damages in lieu of rescission. Nor did the learned judge provide any indication of the appropriate measure of damages under section 2(2), for it is by no means certain that the deceit measure found in section 2(1) is also recoverable under section 2(2). However, guidance on both these points has been provided in two recent English cases. In *Thomas Witter Ltd. v. TBP*

---

[96] [1965] 1 Q.B. 525.
[97] (1995) 184 C.L.R. 102; contrast *TSB Bank v. Camfield* [1995] 1 All E.R. 951.
[98] [1975] 3 All E.R. 739.
[99] [1986] N.I. 327.

*Industries Ltd.*[100] Jacob J. held that the right of a judge to grant damages under section 2(2) would survive the loss of any right to grant rescission. In *William Sindall plc v. Cambridgeshire County Council*[101] two members of the Court of Appeal indicated that the measure of damages under section 2(2) is rooted in the notion of indemnity for a breach of warranty and that to award all consequential loss, the section 2(1) measure, would be inappropriate in such situations. Both of these decisions provide welcome illumination on these points of law.

**(vii) Specific performance.** Should the plaintiff be responsible for making a misrepresentation the defendant may avoid an action for specific performance by pleading the plaintiff's misrepresentation. This is discussed by Delany.[102] The representee may be permitted to obtain an injunction preventing the representor from continuing an action. Such an injunction was awarded to a misrepresentee in *Costello v. Martin*.[103]

## Section 46 – the Exemption Clause

Section 46 attempts to control the extent to which persons may make false statements and then attempt to avoid or limit liability by way of an exemption clause. While *Pearson v. Dublin Corporation*[104] is authority for the proposition that a fraudulent misrepresentation cannot be negatived by an express disclaimer from liability for false statements, there were no special rules governing the use of exemption clauses where one party was responsible for a misrepresentation. Section 46 provides:

> "If any agreement (whether made before or after the commencement of this Act) contains a provision which would exclude or restrict (a) any liability to which a party to a contract may be subject by reason of any misrepresentation made by him before the contract was made, or (b) any remedy available to another party to the contract by reason of such a misrepresentation, that provision shall not be enforceable unless it is shown that it is fair and reasonable."

The "fair and reasonable" test has been considered above,[105] and the factors set out are of general application.

Of special interest under section 46 are the English decisions which consider the English counterpart to section 46. In *Walker v. Boyle*[106] the vendor of land

---

[100] [1996] 2 All E.R. 573.
[101] [1994] 3 All E.R. 932.
[102] [1951] Ir.Jur. 51.
[103] (1867) 1 Ir.Rep.Eq. 50.
[104] [1907] A.C. 351.
[105] See Chap. 8.
[106] [1982] 1 W.L.R. 495.

misrepresented that there were no disputes in relation to the boundaries of the land to be sold. This was an incorrect statement. The contract provided that "no error, mis-statement or omission in any preliminary answer concerning the property . . . shall annul the sale." This exclusion clause, despite the fact that it was a term in the English Law Society Standard Conditions of Sale for many years, was denied effect. In *Southwestern General Property Co. v. Marton*[107] the misrepresentation appeared in an auctioneer's particulars of sale and gave readers of the particulars the impression that planning permission would be available in relation to a site if a suitable development were proposed. The catalogue attempted to exclude liability for any misrepresentation contained therein. The exclusion clause was denied effect. Here the sale was concluded by auction and the purchaser had bid for the property at short notice. There was no possibility of the purchaser making the normal inquiries before he was bound. A similar conclusion was reached in *Production Technology Consultants v. Bartlett.*[108] In Ireland, section 46 cannot operate within the context of contracts for the sale of land and it remains possible for the agreement itself to control the misrepresentee's range of remedies following certain innocent misrepresentations. See the provisions of Condition No. 21 of the 1978 edition of the General Conditions of Sale of the Incorporated Law Society of Ireland, discussed in *Keating v. Bank of Ireland.*[109]

## The Duty to Disclose and Silence as a Misrepresentation – *Uberrima Fides*

In the early part of this chapter we talked of a misrepresentation in terms of being a false "statement". Can silence constitute a statement? It is generally held that silence or failure to disclose a material fact may constitute a misrepresentation only in exceptional cases. If I have made a statement which, while true at the time it was uttered, is subsequently rendered false by subsequent events, my failure to advise of the change will constitute a misrepresentation.[110] On the other hand, if I agree to sell goods there is no obligation on me, the seller, to advise the buyer of material facts which may influence his decision to purchase. The case of *Gill v. McDowell*[111] conditions this second proposition somewhat. The purchaser of the hermaphrodite animal thought he was buying a cow or a bull. The seller failed to disclose the true facts. Because the animal was sold in a market where cow or bulls were sold, the seller was held to be under a duty of disclosure. The decision may have been different had the buyer purchased the animal while visiting the seller's property. The fact that the Irish courts have developed a duty of disclosure in the context of contracts to sell

---

[107] (1982) 263 E.G. 1090.
[108] [1988] 1 E.G.L.R. 182.
[109] [1983] I.L.R.M. 295.
[110] *Davies v. London and Provincial Marine Ins. Co.* (1878) 8 Ch.D. 469.
[111] [1903] 2 I.R. 463.

animals, a not unreasonable development in a primarily agricultural society, is further illustrated in *Kennedy v. Hennessy*.[112] Gibson J. there declared that to sell a yearling heifer in calf without disclosing this fact – such an animal being less valuable because of the dangers of such an early pregnancy – may be actionable if the seller has knowledge of this. The parties may themselves create a contractual duty to make full disclosure of all material facts and if this subsequently turns out not to have been done the contract may be avoided: *Munster Base Metals Ltd. v. Bula Ltd.*[113] In *Geryani v. O'Callaghan*[114] the purchaser of property rescinded a contract of purchase upon discovery that certain defects had not been disclosed. While Costello J. held that the general law did not make such disclosure obligatory, the conditions of contract, specifically the Law Society General Conditions of Sale, made disclosure necessary under the terms of the contract.

The obligation to disclose has been considered in the context of sale of leasehold property which is subject to restrictive covenants. In *Power v. Barrett*[115] the plaintiff, lessee of premises in Abbey St., Dublin, wanted to sell his lease, which was to his knowledge subject to a covenent that the lessee would not carry on any dangerous, noxious or offensive trade. He sold his interest to a chandler, who wanted to store oil on the premises. This would breach the restrictive covenant. The defendant pulled out of the contract when he learnt of the covenant. Chatterton V.C. refused to order specific performance against the chandler: "if a purchaser states the object which he has in purchasing and the seller is silent as to a covenant in a lease prohibiting or interfering with that object, his silence would be equivalent to a representation that there was no such prohibitory covenant." This rule applies to sales of leasehold interests only. The duty of disclosure applies even to clauses the "representor" is unaware of: *Flight v. Barton*.[116] Equity has required the vendor of property to disclose any unusual defects in title, a proposition laid down in 1885 and reaffirmed in *Rignall Developments Ltd. v. Hill*.[117] A more celebrated example of a duty of disclosure in a property context is found in the New York case of *Stambovsky v. Ackley*.[118] The plaintiff sought the return of a deposit paid by him to the defendant in order to purchase a large Victorian house. The plaintiff withdrew from the contract when he discovered that the house was haunted by three ghostly figures attired in colonial dress. On appeal, it was held that there was a duty of disclosure and that silence constituted misrepresentation on the part of the defendant.

A general duty to disclose does apply to fiduciary relationships. A failure to disclose material facts was held fatal in *Dunbar v. Tredennick*[119] where the

---

[112] (1906) 40 I.L.T.R. 84.
[113] Unreported, High Court, July 27, 1983.
[114] Unreported, High Court, January 25, 1995.
[115] (1887) 19 L.R.(Ir.) 450.
[116] (1832) 3 My. & K. 282.
[117] [1988] Ch. 190.
[118] 572 N.Y.S. (2d) 672 (1991).
[119] (1813) 2 Ball & B. 304.

transfer was between agents and trustees on the one hand, and principal and beneficiary on the other. Members of a family are also under an obligation to disclose all material facts: *Leonard v. Leonard*,[120] and the obligation is imposed in a diverse range of transactions, such as agreements to vary the terms of a will, or settle or transfer property. In some instances the duty to make full and frank disclosure will operate within a family context because statute requires. The leading English cases involve agreements struck during matrimonial proceedings. Should an agreement be made, one spouse failing to disclose to the other party, and the court, some material circumstance, such as an intention to remarry, then the settlement may be liable to amendment: *Livesy v. Jenkins*.[121] In certain types of commercial contract, exceptional circumstances may need to be disclosed. For example, in suretyship contracts, the creditor may be under a duty to disclose to a guarantor facts of which the creditor is aware which make the risk to which the guarantor is to be exposed an unusual one, or a risk materially different to that which the surety would normally expect. So, in *Levett v. Barclays Bank plc*[122] the plaintiff was not told that the arrangements between the debtor and the bank made the plaintiff's treasury stock, the property being put up by the plaintiff, virtually worthless. The contract was set aside.

The most common instances of actionable non-disclosure concern insurance contracts. It is often said that when the prospective insured makes an application for insurance he is in the best position to know the circumstances surrounding the application. This is certainly true in cases of life assurance and health insurance. The applicant is in the best position to know his age, health, and plans for the future. A failure to answer truthfully *and* disclose all material facts may each invalidate the insurance policy. If the contract is one of marine insurance the Marine Insurance Act 1906 still has effect in Ireland. This Act, largely a codification of mercantile practice, states the general duty, in section 18(1), as follows:

> "Subject to the provisions of this section, the assured must disclose to the insurer, before the contract is concluded, every material circumstance which is known to the assured, and the assured is deemed to know every circumstance which, in the ordinary course of a business, ought to be known by him. If the assured fails to make such disclosure, the insurer may avoid the contract. Every circumstance is material which would influence the judgment of a prudent insurer in fixing the premium, as determining whether he will take the risk."

There are provisions within the Marine Insurance Act 1906 that have recently been held to apply to both marine and non-marine insurance policies. The decision of a very strong Court of Appeal in *PCW Syndicates v. PCW*

---

[120] (1812) 2 Ball & B. 171.
[121] [1985] A.C. 424; *Border v. Border* [1986] 2 All E.R. 918.
[122] [1995] 2 All E.R. 615.

*Reinsurers*[123] deals extensively with the relationship between the pre-1906 common law and provisions of the Act, particularly section 18. On the issue of materiality, it is material, for example, that the vessel to be insured has grounded[124] or that the cargo is to be carried on deck, a circumstance which is unusual and renders the cargo vulnerable.[125] In the case of *Seaman v. Fonereau*[126] the insured was held bound to disclose rumours that the vessel was leaking, and missing the next day, even though no actual proof was known to the insured. The duty of disclosure is mutual, and applies both to insurer and insured, but it is not *ipso facto* a basis for the award of damages.[127] Fortunately for the assured there are limits on the duty, for the basis of the duty to disclose is an assumption that the assured is in the best position to know material circumstances. The assured does not have to disclose matters of common knowledge for, as section 18(3)(b) puts it, "the insurer is presumed to know matters of common notoriety or knowledge, and matters which an insurer in the ordinary course of his business, as such, ought to know . . . ". For this reason O'Hanlon J. in *Brady v. Irish National Insurance Co. Ltd.*[128] held that a boat-owner's failure to inform his insurers of his intentions to lay up the boat over the winter and effect maintenance and repairs and using the galley during this time, did not entitle the company to avoid the policy. It was a matter of "common notoriety" that this occurred within the boat-owning fraternity. The decision was affirmed by the Supreme Court on this point. The decision of the Supreme Court[129] is noteworthy for the fact that both Finlay C.J. and McCarthy J. were critical of the use by the insurer of a marine insurance contract in the context of a pleasure craft in use on the Shannon and other inland waterways. This observation however has to be seen in the light of recent case law in which the courts have drawn attention to the fact that the 1906 Act, in many respects, does not create a regime that only operates in marine insurances cases: some of these provisions are declaratory of the common law only. One new English case, decided within the spirit of the line of Irish cases that begin with *Aro Road*, discussed below, is particularly welcome. In *Economides v. Commercial Insurance*[130] the Court of Appeal held that the duty of disclosure involves only a duty to be honest. In satisfying the test of subjectivity which is found in section 20(5) of the 1906 Act the representor does not have to go further and impliedly represent that there are objectively reasonable grounds in existence which justify that belief. Further it is only actual knowledge that is relevant to the duty of disclosure. Constructive knowledge is not imposed on the representor.

---

[123] [1996] 1 W.L.R. 1136.
[124] *Russell v. Thornton* (1860) 6 H. & N. 140.
[125] *Alluvials Mining Machinery Co. v. Stowe* (1922) 10 Lloyds L.R. 96.
[126] (1743) 2 Stra. 1183; *Lynch v. Hamilton* (1810) 3 Taunt. 37.
[127] *Westgate Insurance Co. Ltd. v. Banque Financiere de la Cité SA* [1990] 2 All E.R. 947.
[128] [1986] I.L.R.M. 669.
[129] [1986] I.R. 698.
[130] [1997] 3 W.L.R. 1066; Clarke [1998] C.L.J. 24.

In many insurance contracts, however, the insurer may seek to place an even heavier duty onto the shoulders of the insured. The insured, when completing the proposal form, may be asked questions, often about matters of fact which the insured may not be in a position to answer authoritatively or accurately, and will then be obliged to warrant that the answer is factually correct. The accuracy of all replies is said to be "the basis of the contract" and gives the insurer a possible ground for repudiation of the policy should the answer subsequently turn out to be inaccurate. However, the courts seek to narrow these basis of contract clauses wherever possible, either by denying the clause the character of a promissory warranty, as in *Fearnley v. London Guarantee Insurance Co.*,[131] or by reading any ambiguous warranties *contra proferentem.* In *Brady v. Irish National Insurance Co. Ltd.*[132] the majority of the Supreme Court held that use of a gas cooker in a galley while the vessel was laid up was within the concept of customary overhaul of the vessel and thus did not represent breach of an express warranty that the vessel would not be available for use during the laid up period. The basis of contract clause can operate very harshly if the promise made relates to some matter about which the promisor has no special knowledge. In life assurance policies a warranty that the insured is in good health may be obtained. Should the insured not be in good health and the condition or illness manifests itself later, the insurer could repudiate the policy if the facts indicate that the latent condition or illness must have existed, unknown to all, on the date the warranty was given. Again, the Supreme Court has been protective of the insured when an insurer asserts the existence of an absolute warranty.

In *Keating v. New Ireland Assurance Company plc*[133] the defendant sought to avoid a life insurance policy on the ground, *inter alia*, that the policy contained an absolute warranty by the insured that he was in good health, when, unknown to the insured he was suffering from angina (the insured believed he was suffering from a gastric disorder of no importance). In this case the alleged warranty was to be found in the policy and a declaration in the proposal form that the answers given "are true and complete". The Supreme Court held that the words used did not create the warranty claimed. McCarthy J., with whom Finlay C.J. and Hederman J. concurred, rejected the interpretation placed upon this contract of insurance by the insurers. In interpreting the words found in the contract itself, "the policy is conditional upon full and true disclosure," McCarthy J. stated that the principles which govern the interpretation of a contract of insurance include the proposition that "if insurers desire to found the contract upon any particular warranty, it must be expressed in clear terms without any ambiguity," and, further, that "if there is any ambiguity, it must be read against the persons who prepared it."[134] Disclosure required disclosure of facts known to the insured and, in this case, the insured was unaware of his

---

[131] (1880) 5 App.Cas. 911.
[132] [1986] I.R. 698.
[133] [1990] I.L.R.M. 110.
[134] *Ibid.* at 119.

medical condition so the warranty was not breached. The case represents a considerable improvement in terms of consumer protection, for the Supreme Court now, essentially, requires the basis of contract warranty to be absolutely explicit before it will be enforced. McCarthy J. posed the following rhetorical question:

> "If the proposal form were to contain a statement by the proposer that the statements and answers written in the proposal together with the written statements and answers made to the company's medical examiner shall form the basis of the proposed contract "even if they are untrue and incomplete for reasons of which I am totally unaware," would there be any takers for such a policy?"[135]

However, if a basis of contract clause is made out, the answers given must be accurate. It is not necessary for the misstatement to be material in the sense that it would be an important factor which would influence the terms upon which risk would be assessed or the premium fixed. A graphic illustration is afforded by *Keenan v. Shield Insurance Company Ltd.*[136] The policy was a household building and contents policy. The proposal form asked whether there had been any previous claim, to which he answered in the negative. In fact a claim for £53 in respect of fire damage to a pump had been made in the previous year. While this was a trivial and non-material misstatement, the plaintiff had warranted that the particular answers were true and complete in every respect, and as Blayney J. observed, even if the answer given was a trivial inaccuracy "that would be no obstacle to the defendant repudiating the policy in view of the inaccuracy of the answers in the proposal form having been warranted by the plaintiff." Another very hard case, which illustrates the unfairness of the rule, is *Farrell v. S.E. Lancs. Insurance Co. Ltd.*[137] Farrell purchased a bus. An insurance broker filled in the proposal form on Farrell's behalf, misstating that Farrell had paid £800 for the vehicle when in fact only £140 was paid. The "basis of contract" clause invalidated the application. While this kind of clause can operate in life policies, as in *Life Association of Scotland v. McBlair*,[138] the effects are to some extent ameliorated by sections 61–64 of the Insurance Act 1936.

It is often difficult to disentangle cases where the insured has falsely and fraudulently answered a question or has falsely and fraudulently failed to correct an impression created by an earlier, untruthful answer. Care should be taken to consider whether the facts of the case involve uttering a falsehood rather than a clear case of non-disclosure. An example of the former is provided by *Abbot v. Howard*.[139] An applicant for life insurance was asked if he had been treated for certain diseases. He replied "No." The answer was

---

135 [1990] I.L.R.M. 110 at 119–120.
136 [1987] I.R. 113. An appeal to the Supreme Court failed: [1988] I.R. 89.
137 [1933] I.R. 36.
138 (1875) 9 Ir.Rep.Eq. 176.
139 (1832) Hayes 381.

false. The contract of insurance was held void because of the misrepresentation. If the insurer discovers that a fraudulent misrepresentation has been made and that the applicant has received payment the Supreme Court's decision in *Carey v. W.H. Ryan Ltd.*[140] suggests that the insurer can seek a declaration that the contract is avoided and may trace the monies paid out on the foot of the policy.

Where however the case involves simple non-disclosure of a material fact, fraud is not always material to the inquiry at all. The test is not intention to defraud but whether the misrepresentation related to a material fact. The duty to disclose all facts that a reasonable insurer would think material to the risk requires a lot of the insured; he is required to know what the insurer thinks material.

Nevertheless, Kenny J. in the Supreme Court, in *Chariot Inns Ltd. v. Assicurazioni Generali S.P.A. & Coyle Hamilton, Hamilton Phillips*[141] stated the test thus:

> "It is not what the person seeking insurance regards as material, nor is it what the insurance company regards as material. It is a matter or circumstance which would reasonably influence the judgment of a prudent insurer in deciding whether he would take the risk and, if so, in determining the premium which he would demand. The standard by which materiality is to be determined is objective, not subjective. The matter has, in the last resort, to be determined by the court: the parties to the litigation may call experts in insurance matters as witnesses to give evidence of what they would have regarded as material but the question of materiality is not to be determined by the parties."[142]

The *Chariot Inns* case represents the approach taken by Irish and English courts for decades, but in *Pan Atlantic Insurance Co. v. Pine Top Insurance Co.*[143] the majority of the House of Lords, in a marine insurance case, reformulated the test so as to require that the information not disclosed be material in the sense that the prudent insurer would like to know this fact, even if it did not ultimately influence the decision to take the risk. This broadening of materiality is immediately countered by another requirement, that the insurer should be required to show that the non-disclosure induced the insurer into entering the contract. This decision has not been considered by an Irish court, and two Law Lords dissented strongly, and it may be that *Pan Atlantic* would not be followed here.

In *Chariot Inns* the Supreme Court held that a prudent insurer, in relation to an application for insurance on a building, would expect the applicant to disclose that a fire had occurred in a building owned by an associated company

---

[140] [1982] I.R. 179.
[141] [1981] I.L.R.M. 173.
[142] *Ibid.* at 174.
[143] [1994] 3 All E.R. 581.

less than two years prior to the application. Similarly, an application for household insurance may be avoided if the applicant fails to disclose that he has criminal convictions: *Schoolman v. Hall*.[144] Sometimes however the applicant may feel a sense of grievance for it has been held that there may be no obvious correlation between the fact not disclosed and the risk to be covered. An obvious example of this is found in *Lambert v. Co-operative Insurance Society Ltd*.[145] The policy was an All Risks policy which provided cover in respect of jewellery owned by the plaintiff and her husband. When completing the proposal form the plaintiff failed to disclose that her husband, some years earlier, had been convicted of a dishonesty offence, and, later, her husband was convicted again of dishonesty offences but this was not disclosed at renewal of the policy. When a claim was made in respect of lost or stolen items the defendant refused to meet the claim. Because the test of materiality is that which the prudent insurer, not the reasonable insured, thinks material, the defendants were held to be entitled to refuse to meet the claim. McKenna J. found the law to be unsatisfactory, and seemed to be of the view that a reasonable insured would, like Mrs. Lambert, think her husband's convictions to be irrelevant, and it must be conceded that the courts have, traditionally, been most accommodating to insurers in non-marine insurance cases. Refusal by another company to take a fire insurance application when the applicant sought car insurance has been held material in *Lockyer & Woolf Ltd. v. Western Australian Insurance Co*.[146] In *London Assurance v. Mansel*[147] failure to disclose that other companies had turned down an application for life cover was held material to an application for life assurance. In *Mansel* it was also held that it did not matter that the applicant did not think the refusal was material because he felt the applications were turned down on grounds other than the state of his, the applicant's, health. The position of the insured is made all the more difficult by virtue of the fact that the Supreme Court, in *Carna Foods Ltd. v. Eagle Star Insurance Co*.[148] has recently reaffirmed that there is no implied obligation on the insured to explain why an application for a new policy, or a renewal, has been turned down.

Many cases on materiality are straightforward. In life policies, it is relevant for the insurer to know the medical history of the assured as in *Kelleher v. Irish Life Assurance Co. Ltd.*,[149] when a life policy was avoided on the ground that the insured failed to disclose that he had previously suffered from cancer and had suffered radiation damage as a result of treatment. Similarly, in *Curran v. Norwich Union Life Insurance Society*[150] an incorrect declaration made by an applicant that he was in good health, when shortly before the application being made the applicant suffered a minor epileptic attack, probably as a result of a

---

[144] [1951] 1 Lloyd's Rep. 139.
[145] [1975] 2 Lloyd's Rep. 485.
[146] [1936] 1 K.B. 408.
[147] (1879) 11 Ch.D. 363.
[148] [1997] 2 I.L.R.M. 499.
[149] Unreported, High Court, December 16, 1988.
[150] Unreported, High Court, October 30, 1987.

head injury the year before, rendered the policy unenforceable at the option of the insurer. However, the issue of materiality is a matter for the judge to rule on. There can be evidence, adduced by the insurer in the form of testimony given by other underwriters, but essentially the materiality of the fact withheld is to be decided by the judge. In *Aro Road and Land Vehicles Ltd. v. The Insurance Corporation of Ireland Ltd.*,[151] the facts of which are set out below, the Supreme Court overruled the judge at first instance, who had indicated that, while she did not feel that the fact withheld was material, expert testimony to the contrary was to be adopted. McCarthy J. observed that to defer to expert testimony is incorrect, for it is the judge who is "the sole and final arbiter" on materiality.

In cases where a life assurance contract is taken out, the insured misstating his age, the common law renders the contract void. The courts could not form an opinion as to the terms upon which the policy would have been effected if there had not been a misrepresentation and permit limited recovery: *Irish National Assurance Co. v. O'Callaghan*.[152] The Oireachtas stepped in to pass the Insurance Act 1936, s.64 of which permits such a calculation in contracts of industrial assurance, defined as life assurance contracts: see on the 1936 Act *McCarthy v. New Ireland Assurance Co.*[153] If however the policy is a policy for health cover which involves the insurer making payments in order to replace lost earnings while the insured is out of work, the policy may require the insured to give a full disclosure of his medical condition. In *Harnedy v. Century Insurance*[154] the court had to consider whether this kind of obligation is material or not. Harnedy failed to disclose that he was suffering from a heavy cold; this cold in fact was a symptom of a more serious condition that eventually led to him claiming on a disability insurance policy. Evidence from brokers suggested that the practice would have been to suspend the policy. McWilliam J. held the insurer had not established materiality.

The insurance companies are given other advantages by the courts over the insured, over and above the use of "basis of contract" clauses. In *Farrell*,[155] the broker was seen as agent of the insured, not the insurer, thereby fixing the insured with the loss occasioned by the broker's mistake. Knowledge of surrounding circumstances will bind the insurance company's agents only in relation to facts made known while the agent is employed by the insurance company: *Taylor v. Yorkshire Insurance*.[156] If the broker acts as agent for the applicant and he fills in the application form incorrectly or fails to disclose a material fact the policy will not bind the insurance company. The applicant will be able to recover in an action against the broker: *Chariot Inns Ltd. v. Coyle Hamilton, Hamilton Phillips*.[157] Should the insured's broker fail to inform the insurer when, after effecting the insurance, the broker learns of facts which

---

[151] [1986] I.R. 403.
[152] (1934) 68 I.L.T.R. 248.
[153] (1941) 75 I.L.T.R. 225.
[154] Unreported, High Court, February 22, 1983.
[155] [1933] I.R. 36.
[156] [1913] 2 I.R. 1.
[157] [1981] I.L.R.M. 173.

may render the insurance contract invalid for material non-disclosure, the broker may be liable to his client. In *Latham v. Hibernian Insurance Company Ltd. and Peter J. Sheridan and Company Ltd.*[158] the second defendant obtained building insurance on behalf of the plaintiff, his client, from the first defendant. Shortly afterwards the second defendant discovered that the plaintiff had been guilty of dishonesty offences which rendered the insurance, in respect of a retail grocery and tobacconist shop, potentially invalid. In failing to inform the insurer the second defendant was in breach of the contractual duty owed to the plaintiff. The plaintiff lost the opportunity to consider whether to continue to trade, without insurance in all likelihood, or close the business altogether, thereby avoiding the loss of the premises as a result of fire. In general, constructive knowledge of the falsity of a representation made to an insurance company will not bind them. In *Griffin v. Royal Liver Friendly Society*[159] the applicant for a burial insurance policy falsely stated he was in good health. The insured was examined by a doctor who failed to notice the true medical condition of the applicant. The company were held not to have constructive knowledge so as to estop them from declaring the policy void. The fact that an employee or agent of the insured obtains knowledge of the true facts from someone other than the insured or the insured's agent may be enough to sustain the insurance contract as long as that information is received in the course of that person's duty and employment: *Woolcott v. Excess Insurance.*[160] If information is obtained by the employee or agent purely in the course of socialising with friends, Blayney J. has held, in *Latham v. Hibernian Insurance Company Ltd. and Peter J. Sheridan and Company Ltd.,*[161] that this knowledge will not generally suffice to impute knowledge to the insurer, although it is submitted, this must be a very general rule to be viewed in the light of each individual case.

On the other hand, an applicant is not obliged to do the insurance company's job for it. If the insured informs the company of all the circumstances surrounding an application and the company fails to pursue the matter and inquire further, the policy may still be valid: *Kreglinger and Fernau Ltd. v. Irish National Insurance Co. Ltd.*[162] It should be noted that in this case no false statement was made; in contrast, the plaintiff in *Griffin v. Royal Liver Friendly Society* was guilty of a fraudulent misrepresentation. The court was obviously reluctant to permit an estoppel to work in such a case.

## Modification of the standard of disclosure in Ireland

The standard fixed by the courts over the last 150 years, is onerous; the insured must disclose every material circumstance within the knowledge of the assured, and the proper question is, whether any particular circumstance was

---

[158] Unreported, High Court, March 22, 1991; for restitution of premiums paid to the company, see *Byrne v. Rudd* [1920] 2 I.R. 12.
[159] (1842) 8 Ir.Jur.Rep. 29.
[160] [1979] 1 Lloyd's Rep. 231.
[161] Unreported, High Court, March 22, 1991.
[162] [1956] I.R. 116.

in fact material? and not whether the party believed it to be so.[163] From time to time suggestions for reform have centred around a revised definition of material, such as, a fact which would be considered material to a reasonable insured: Law Reform Committee *5th Report*, 1957 (U.K.). While no movement has been made on the legislative front either in Ireland or the United Kingdom, the Supreme Court, in two recent cases, has substantially modified the standard of disclosure. In *Aro Road and Land Vehicles Ltd. v. Insurance Corporation of Ireland Ltd.*[164] the policy in question, property insurance in respect of goods being transported by road from Dublin to Maize, Co. Antrim, was negotiated over the phone between the insured and an agent of the insurer. No proposal form was completed – no details were requested other than identity of the goods and destination. After the goods had been destroyed by armed gunmen who burnt the vehicle, the insurer sought to avoid the policy because it had not been revealed that the managing director of the plaintiff company had been convicted of receiving stolen goods some nineteen years before. In holding the policy valid the Supreme Court reaffirmed that the general duty of disclosure is based upon the standard of that which a reasonable and prudent insurer would consider material in deciding to take the risk and on what terms. Henchy J., however, said that the rule has exceptions. In particular, "over-the-counter" insurance, effected by way of intermediaries such as airlines, shipping companies and travel agents, are insurance contracts where full disclosure is not a practical or reasonable possibility and in these instances the company is willing to provide insurance without requiring full disclosure. Henchy J. found that, looking at the circumstances in which this policy was concluded, the insurer's agent was "indifferent" about matters such as the personal circumstances of the managing director of the insured company. McCarthy J., with whom Walsh J. and Hederman J. agreed, was even more forthright in qualifying the standard of disclosure in cases of "one-off" or over-the-counter insurance concluded with a minimum of formality. McCarthy J. indicated that where there is no proposal form, and relevant questions are not asked to spur the memory, materiality may be tested by a standard other than that of the prudent insurer

> "if the judgment of an insurer is such as to require disclosure of what he thinks is relevant but which reasonable insured, if he thought of it all, would not think relevant, then, in the absence of a question directed towards the disclosure of such a fact, the insurer, albeit prudent, cannot properly be held to be acting reasonably. A contract of insurance is a contract of the utmost good faith on both sides."

McCarthy J. returned to this theme of the mutality of the good faith obligation later in the judgment when he observed that the managing director's criminal conviction many years before had been forgotten by him. It was no longer a

---

[163] Kenny J. in *Chariot Inns* [1981] I.L.R.M. 173.
[164] [1986] I.R. 403.

factor influencing his behaviour. The learned judge observed that the test remains one of "utmost good faith":

> "how does one depart from such a standard if reasonably and genuinely one does not consider some fact material; how much the less does one depart from such a standard when the failure to disclose is entirely due to a failure of recollection?"[165]

It is important to note that both Henchy J. and McCarthy J. considered these observations to be applicable to cases of honest failure to recollect: the concession would not be available in cases of fraudulent concealment of material facts. The Supreme Court returned to this area in *Keating v. New Ireland Assurance Company plc.*[166] Because the insured was unaware of the nature of his medical condition he was held not to be in breach of the duty of disclosure. McCarthy J. again emphasised that the duty of disclosure was based on good faith and the superior knowledge of the insured: —

> "one cannot disclose what one does not know, albeit that this puts a premium on ignorance. It may well be that wilful ignorance would raise significant other issues; such is not the case here. If the proposer for life insurance has answered all the questions asked to the best of his ability and truthfully, his next-of-kin are not to be damnified because of his ignorance or obtuseness which may be sometimes due to a mental block on matters affecting one's health."[167]

The approach outlined above and the restrictions placed on the basis of contract clause in *Keating's case* are very much to be welcomed. Insurers should be required to be specific and efficient when insurance contracts are under negotiation: basic fairness so requires. Most recently, the Supreme Court, in *Kelleher v. Irish Life Assurance*[168] held that the defendants had abridged the duty to make full disclosure from the way in which they had formulated the proposal form and presented the package to a large group of potential customers via a special promotional deal. However, these decisions are not unprecedented. Two Irish judges from the last century adopted forthright positions on this issue and it is to be welcomed that the Supreme Court have rediscovered this kind of radicalism. In *Rose v. Star Insurance Company*[169] Richards B. said:

> "it is most unjust to allow a company to disturb insurances after having taken the money of the party. The parties ensuring [*sic*] are frequently country gentlemen, ladies, and other persons knowing nothing about the

---

165 [1986] I.R. 403 at 413–414.
166 [1990] I.L.R.M. 110.
167 *Ibid.* at 116.
168 [1993] I.L.R.M. 643.
169 (1850) 2 Ir.Jur. 206.

law. The papers are generally filled in in the office of the company, and signed merely as a matter of form."

Earlier still, Smith B., dissenting in *Abbott v. Howard*[170] wrote:

"Here, *ex hypothesi*, are two innocent parties; the Company and the Insured. Of these, which is in default? Which has been, in some degree negligent and remiss? Those who have not made an enquiry which they could have made; and which might have produced information, that we will assume to have been material? Or he, who innocently, (keep this in mind,) having answered the questions asked, happens to stop there, without any fraudulent motive for so doing? Where, if any, is the negligence or default? I should say, on the part of the innocent Company. – And on whom is the loss and penalty to attach? On the found to be not less innocent Insured. – Is this conformable to the rules usually applied to the case of two innocent persons, one of whom must suffer?"[171]

However, the duty of utmost good faith extends to all facets of the insurance contract. In *Fagan v. General Accident*[172] the duty was held to extend even to the making of a claim and where the insured inflated the claim by 100 per cent Murphy J. held this to constitute a breach of duty entitling the insurer to repudiate the contract.

*Contra Proferentem*

Two Irish cases provide clear guidance on the position to be adopted in the interpretation and construction of insurance contracts. In *Rohan Construction Ltd. and Rohan Group plc v. Insurance Corporation of Ireland Ltd.*[173] Keane J. observed:

"It is clear that policies of insurance, such as those under consideration in the present case, are to be construed like other written instruments. In the present case, the primary task of the court is to ascertain their meaning by adopting the ordinary rules of construction. It is also clear that, if there is any ambiguity in the language used, it is to be construed more strongly against the party who prepared it, *i.e.* in most cases against the insurer. It is also clear that the words used must not be construed with extreme literalism, but with reasonable latitude, keeping always in view the principal object of the contract of insurance. (See *MacGillvray and Parkington on Insurance Law* (7th ed.), pp. 433 *et seq.*)"[174]

---

[170] (1832) Hayes 381.
[171] *Ibid.* at 410–411.
[172] Unreported, High Court, February 19, 1993.
[173] [1986] I.L.R.M. 419.
[174] *Ibid.* at 423. The Supreme Court allowed an appeal in part but this principle was not doubted: [1988] I.L.R.M. 373.

In *Brady v. Irish National Insurance Company Ltd.*[175] Finlay C.J. also reaffirmed the proposition that where an express warranty is vague it is to be construed against the party relying upon it.

In *In Re Sweeney & Kennedy's Arbitration*[176] the High Court used the *contra proferentem* rule to facilitate the insured's claim on a motor vehicle insurance policy. The proposal form asked "are any of your drivers under 21 years of age or with less than 12 months of driving experience." The applicant answered "No." While this was true at the date of application the insured later hired a driver below 21 years of age who had less than 12 months' experience. Kingsmill Moore J. refused to hold that the "basis of contract" clause could operate here; in cases of ambiguity the question in a motor insurance proposal form should be drafted precisely. It was possible for the insured to ask whether the applicant intended to use young inexperienced drivers and, in the absence of specific questions, the insurer should bear the loss. The *contra proferentem* rule may not always be used. In *Young v. Sun Alliance*[177] the English Court of Appeal refused to read an exclusion from cover *contra proferentem*, preferring instead to adopt a "plain and ordinary meaning" approach.

---

[175] [1986] I.R. 698.

[176] [1950] I.R. 85.

[177] [1976] 3 All E.R. 561; *Contrast Gaelcrann Teo v. Payne* [1985] I.L.R.M. 190 with *Capemel v. Lister* [1989] I.R. 319.

# 12 Duress

## Introduction

Despite the recent spate of decisions which establish the concept of economic duress, this plea has traditionally been kept within narrow limits by the common law judges. It is invoked by a party to a contract who claims that he was forced into entering the contract or modifying a term contained in a contract. This is, of course, consistent with the restrictive circumstances in which duress will succeed as a defence to a criminal charge.[1] The Privy Council, in the case of *Barton v. Armstrong*,[2] an appeal from the High Court of Australia, has ruled that duress may render a contract void. In that case threats to the safety of a man or his family were sufficient to vitiate consent to the contract. While it may seem that duress can only operate at common law where the danger apprehended is assault or injury to the person, it is suggested that the courts of equity have taken a more liberal position on the plea of duress, although the cases are isolated instances of duress.

In *Lessee of Blackwood v. Gregg*[3] an old man of 92 was abducted by relatives. He later executed a deed in favour of one of the captors. The deed was not read over to the old man. The trial judge was held by the Court of Exchequer to have correctly left it for the jury to decide whether the personal restraint imposed on the old man constituted duress. In *Rourke v. Mealy*,[4] Palles C.B. indicated that a person threatened with the prosecution of a near relative unless he or she undertakes to pay a debt owed by the relative, may, in certain instances, be able to plead duress in equity. There are also English cases which support the operation of a duress plea in this context. In *McClatchie v. Haslam*[5] the plaintiff's husband, employed as the secretary of a building society, misappropriated funds. Fearing a prosecution of her husband, she executed a mortgage of her own property to provide security; although she was not sure that a prosecution would commence, the mortgage was set aside. Kekewich J. expressed the view that

> "this lady, though in one sense she executed this deed freely and voluntarily, did not execute it so freely and voluntarily as to defeat her right now to say that she did it under duress, and in order to free her

---

[1] *D.P.P. v. Lynch* [1975] A.C. 653, overruled in *R. v. Howe* [1987] A.C. 417; *R. v. Gotts* [1992] 1 All E.R. 832.

[2] [1976] A.C. 104; the view now is that the contract is voidable not void: see *Byle v. Byle* (1990) 65 D.L.R. (4th) 641 and *Cockerill v. Westpac Banking Corp.* (1996) 142 A.C.R. 227.

[3] (1831) Hayes 277; *Armstrong v. Gage* (1877) 25 Grant Ch.Cas. 1.

[4] (1879) 13 I.L.T.R. 52; *Williams v. Bayley* (1866) L.R. 1 H.L. 200.

[5] (1891) 17 Cox C.C. 402.

husband from the criminal prosecution which she believed under the circumstances to be imminent."[6]

Other cases where equity has refused to enforce bargains concluded under duress include instances where the legal process itself is abused. Attempts to detain persons in order to extract payments through bogus legal claims, as in *Scott v. Scott*,[7] have not been tolerated in equity, and in *Nicholls v. Nicholls*[8] Lord Hardwicke stated that

> "though a man is arrested by due process of law, if a wrong use is made of it against the person under such arrest, by obliging him to execute a conveyance which was never under consideration before, this Court will construe it as duress, and relieve against a conveyance executed under such circumstances."[9]

Perhaps the broadest and most frequently established plea of duress operates in the context of marriage contracts. In *Griffith v. Griffith*[10] a young man was threatened with imprisonment and dishonour unless he married a young girl he was alleged to have made pregnant while on a camping holiday on Howth Head. His father and the local priest joined with the girl's mother in pressing him into a contract of marriage. When it became known that the plaintiff was not the father of the child he successfully claimed that his contract of marriage was void for duress. The court indicated that if he were the father a petition for a decree of nullity would not have been successful. The Irish civil courts in recent years have adopted a more expansive view of the situations in which a marriage will be declared void *ab initio* for duress and *Griffith v. Griffith* has been disapproved by O'Hanlon J. in *M.K. (McC) v. McC*.[11] A marriage took place between the petitioner (who was pregnant by the respondent) under extreme pressure from both parents. O'Hanlon J. taking a broader view of the civil law jurisdiction in relation to duress, held "the will, not merely of one partner but of both husband and wife, was overborne by the compulsion of their respective parents and that they were driven unwillingly into a union which neither of them desired." An extensive review of the many recent Irish marriage cases would be out of place in a book devoted to general principles of contract and readers should examine specialist works on Family Law, and the Supreme Court decision in *D.B. v. N.O'R.*[12]

---

[6] (1891) 17 Cox C.C. 402 at 406; *Northern Bank Ltd. v. McCarron* [1995] N.I. 258.
[7] (1846) 9 Ir.Eq.R. 451.
[8] (1737) 1 Atk. 409.
[9] *Ibid.*
[10] [1944] I.R. 35.
[11] [1982] I.L.R.M. 277.
[12] [1991] 1 I.R. 289. See also *U.F. v. J.C.* [1991] I.R. 330; *B.C. v. L. O'F.* unreported, High Court, November 24, 1994.

The most important Irish decision on duress is *Smelter Corporation of Ireland v. O'Driscoll.*[13] The plaintiff company sought specific performance on an option agreement which gave them a right to purchase O'Driscoll's land in County Cork. The option had been given reluctantly. The agent of the plaintiff company believed that if O'Driscoll did not sell to them directly, the County Council intended to make a compulsory purchase order. When the agent communicated this to O'Driscoll he felt he had no alternative but to give the option. In fact, the County Council did not intend to purchase the land. O'Higgins C.J. in the Supreme Court said "in these circumstances it appears to me that there was a fundamental unfairness in the transaction." The unfairness stems from O'Driscoll's belief that he was going to lose his land, one way or another. He could not be said to have consented to the agreement. Specific performance was refused. The case is perhaps to be regarded as an illustration of the reluctance of equity to grant specific performance of a contract which is struck in circumstances of substantial unfairness, or where the enforcement of the contract would be oppressive to the defendant, or where consent cannot be said to have been given: *P.M.P.S. Ltd. v. Moore.*[14] As such, it must be conceded that these isolated instances of equitable jurisdiction do not constitute a coherent, unified system of jurisprudence. However, the law of restitution, and in particular the action for money had and received, has been a fruitful source of legal principle that can transcend the narrow, factual, constraints on the development of the law of duress. One such example is found in cases where money payments are made as a result of coercion.

In *Great Southern and Western Railway Co. v. Robertson*[15] a railway company was under statutory obligation to transport soldiers and their equipment at a rate of two pence per ton per mile. They charged the plaintiff, a carrier who had agreed to act as agent for the military, a higher rate. The plaintiff paid the excess, some £601, under protest. He was held entitled to recover the excess as money had and received to his use. In these cases the party exercising duress often does so because of some misinterpretation of the legal position. This will not justify the exercise of coercion and, further, restitution will be ordered even though it is generally true to state that a mistake of law will not be operative. The oppressive conduct of the payee will justify an award of restitution even if the mistake of law was shared by both parties. In *O'Loghlen v. O'Callaghan*[16] and *Jackson v. Stopford*[17] this rule against holding money paid under a mistake of law to be recoverable was affirmed.[18]

There seems to be a trend towards widening the circumstances in which recovery of money paid under a mistake of law will be ordered. In *Rogers v.*

---

[13] [1977] I.R. 305.
[14] [1988] I.L.R.M. 526; see also *O'Reilly v. Minister for Industry and Commerce and others* [1994] E.L.R. 48.
[15] (1878) 2 L.R.(Ir.) 548; *Scott v. Midland Gt. W. Ry. Co.* (1853) 6 Ir.Jur. 73.
[16] (1874) I.R. 8 C.L. 116.
[17] [1923] 2 I.R. 1.
[18] See Law Com. No. 120 (1991).

*Louth County Council*[19] money was paid to the defendants in order to redeem an annuity. This figure was calculated in good faith according to guidelines distributed by the Department of Local Government. After payment was made the Supreme Court ruled this basis of assessment inaccurate. The plaintiff sought to recover £953.53 as an overpayment. On a case stated to the Supreme Court by the Circuit Court it was held that the sum was recoverable. Despite the fact that both parties knew the (albeit erroneous) calculation was the result of advice from an independent source the Supreme Court declared the parties not to be *in pari delicto*. This, it is submitted, is beside the point. The case relied upon in *Rogers* is an authority on illegality, not mistake of law, *viz. Kiriri Cotton Co. v. Dewani.*[20] The factors that will justify a court refusing to follow the rule against non-recovery were stated in *O'Loghlen v. O'Callaghan*[21] to be "mala fides . . . fraud or imposition" *per* Whiteside C.J. It is hardly accurate to describe a demand for payment made by a local authority in the mistaken belief that this payment is due as a case of "imposition" but, nevertheless the Supreme Court in *Rogers v. Louth County Council*[22] broadened the notion so as to include such payments. Indeed in that case Griffin J. said overpayment could be recoverable in an action for money had and received where it was paid involuntarily, "that is, as the result of some extortion, coercion and compulsion". The facts of *Rogers and Dublin Corporation v. Trinity College Dublin*[23] suggest that the implicit sanction – fear of proceedings such as an execution against property – may satisfy the "compulsion" element, even though the payment itself may not have been made under protest.

Apart from isolated instances where coercion was able to ground relief by way of restitution, or could be a contributory factor in showing that the bargain was unconscionable, very few jurisdictions acknowledged a distinct doctrine of duress in contracts. The courts in the United States and, to a lesser extent, those in Australia and Canada, have often acknowledged that contracts negotiated or re-negotiated under a practical compulsion may not be enforceable if the party coerced seeks to have the transaction declared void.[24] It is only within the last 25 years that the English courts have, somewhat hesitantly, acknowledged that coercion of the will may provide a distinct basis for holding a contract invalid. The first instance decision of Kerr J. in *The Siboen & Sibotre*[25] has provided the basis for this development. A contract for the charter of a ship was re-negotiated on the strength of fraudulent misrepresentations about the perilous economic position of the charterer. Although the case was decided on the basis of fraud, Kerr J. emphatically rejected the view that English law restricted its doctrine of duress to threats of the imposition of violence, and

---

[19] [1981] I.L.R.M. 143; *Woolwich Equitable v. I.R.C.* (No. 2) [1993] A.C. 70.
[20] [1960] A.C. 192.
[21] (1874) I.R. 8 C.L. 116.
[22] [1981] I.L.R.M. 143.
[23] [1985] I.L.R.M. 283.
[24] Sutton (1974) 20 McGill L.J. 254; Beatson (1974) 33 C.L.J. 97.
[25] [1976] 1 Lloyd's Rep. 293.

duress of goods. In *North Ocean Shipping v. Hyundai Construction*,[26] Mocatta J. also approved the view that coercion may be operative if the coercion means that the will of the person promising is overborne. Mocatta J. was willing to hold that a promise to pay an additional sum of money in order to secure the completion of a ship which was being built by the defendant company could be procured by duress; to threaten to break the contract unless the payment is made or promised would possibly create serious financial difficulties for the party threatened and may involve the breach of some further contract entered into by that party on the strength of the delivery dates set out in that contract, dates that will not be met if the contract is broken. The Privy Council approved of these developments in *Pao On v. Lau Yiu Long*[27] although in all three of these cases no complete case for relief had been made out, indicating perhaps that it will be difficult to set out a case for relief via duress. In a later case however, the House of Lords, by a majority of three to two, upheld the view that a payment obtained by a trade union by threatening industrial action, specifically the "blacking" of a cargo on board a ship, constituted duress. In *Universe Tankships of Monrovia v. International Transport Workers Federation*[28] the union threatened to "black" the appellant's vessel unless it was paid a sum of money which the union would disburse amongst seamen employed on "flag of convenience" ships. Lord Diplock, giving the leading judgment for the majority, declared of duress:

> "the rationale is that his apparent consent was induced by pressure exercised on him by that other party which the law does not regard as legitimate, with the consequence that the consent is treated in law as revocable unless approbated either expressly or by implication after the illegitimate pressure has ceased to operate on his mind. It is a rationale similar to that which underlies the avoidability of contracts entered into and the recovery of money enacted under colour of office, or under undue influence or in consequence of threats of physical duress."[29]

Lord Scarman, dissenting, took a more structured view; while the *threat* may indeed be coercive it can be "legitimated" by looking at the broader question: is the *demand* made an acceptable one? Can pressure within this context be upheld as a justifiable use of bargaining power? Lord Scarman indicated that four factors were relevant as evidential matters[30]:

(1) Did the person protest?

(2) Was there an alternative course open to him?

(3) Was he independently advised?

(4) After entering the contract did he take steps to avoid it?

---

[26] [1979] Q.B. 705.

[27] [1980] A.C. 614.

[28] [1982] 2 All E.R. 67.

[29] *Ibid.* at 75–76.

[30] *Ibid.* at 88. This analysis was adopted by Tipping J. in *Shivas v. Bank of New Zealand* [1990] 2 N.Z.L.R. 327; see also *Gordon v. Roebuck* (1989) 64 D.L.R. (4th) 568.

The traditional hostility of English judges to trade union objectives and the use of industrial action in support of collective bargaining is no doubt a narrower issue than that raised by the facts of *Universe Tankships* – the workers to benefit were not even members of the Union – but there is a danger that the "overborne will" theory may intrude into industrial relations law generally. The House of Lords, in *The Evia Luck (No. 2)*[31] has reaffirmed the application of the "overborne will" theory, holding that the threat to black a vessel may be illegitimate, even if the threat is not tortious or even unlawful under the law of the place where the blacking is to be implemented, in this case the law of Sweden. Hostility to the "overborne will" theory has surfaced in some jurisdictions, particularly in Australia where many of the leading cases that are shaping the restitutionary character of this cause of action have formed a distinctive jurisprudence. A New South Wales court, in *Crescendo Management Property v. Westpac Banking Co.*[32] and a Victoria court have presented a test of illegitimate pressure in contra-distinction to "overborne will". In the Victoria case of *Deemcope Property v. Cantown Property*[33] the court stressed the need to locate conduct other than ordinary commercial pressures and leverages; in the absence of unlawful threats of unconscionable conduct the transaction will be sustained.

The English courts have shown a ready facility for applying duress to other kinds of industrial action, when taken by workers in a concerted manner and at a time when the employer in question has little option but to agree to the demands made by the workforce. In *B & S Contracts v. Victor Green Publications*[34] the plaintiffs agreed to pay an additional sum to the defendants, who had been engaged to erect an exhibition stand. The sum would be used to pay the defendants' workers who were demanding increased payments for the work. The defendants indicated that if the sum was not paid they would cancel the contract under a cancellation clause. The Court of Appeal held the cancellation clause could not have been available in these circumstances and that the payments obtained had been paid under duress. The clearest English decision in which a plea of economic duress has been sustained in favour of a contracting party who has been coerced into re-negotiating a contract is *Atlas Express Ltd. v. Kafco (Importers and Distributors) Ltd.*[35] In June 1986 the defendant company engaged the plaintiff company to deliver cartons on behalf of the defendant to branches of Woolworths. The estimated contract price payable to the plaintiff proved uneconomic, due to a miscalculation by the plaintiff's depot manager, and the plaintiff in November 1986 obtained the defendant's consent to a new higher rate. The defendant agreed to the new rate because they were dependant upon the contract with Woolworths, were unlikely to find another carrier, and feared that if the plaintiff company refused to deliver the cartons the defendant would be sued by Woolworths. In holding that the

---

[31] [1991] 4 All E.R. 871.
[32] [1988] N.S.W.L.R. 40.
[33] [1995] 2 V.R. 44.
[34] [1984] 1 I.C.R. 419.
[35] [1989] 1 All E.R. 641; *The Alev* [1989] 1 Lloyd's Rep. 138.

defendant's consent to the November 1986 agreement had been given unwillingly and under compulsion, Tucker J. further held that the defendant's apparent consent to the agreement was induced by pressure which was illegitimate. Tucker J. also held that the defendant's November 1986 agreement was unenforceable for lack of consideration. Most English cases indicate that it will be difficult to establish duress and the "coercion of the will so as to vitiate consent" theory has been described by Atiyah as "unsatisfactory" because it deflects attention away from the central issue, "the permissible limits of coercion in our society".[36] If the pressure is the result of outside pressure by third parties such as a bank then coercion will not be present according to Deputy Judge Millet in *Alec Lobb (Garages) Ltd. v. Total Oil.*[37]

Several judges have been concerned to distinguish economic duress from commercial pressure which is not sufficient to vitiate consent.[38] An excellent case which distinguishes between these two situations is *Walmsley v. Christchurch City Council.*[39] Here the plaintiff had been engaged to produce a souvenir programme for a Golden Jubilee Airshow organised by the defendant. Due to production difficulties, the programme was substandard and rejected by the defendant, who then pressed the plaintiff to provide and pay for a reprinting, the plaintiff to be entitled to any profits over and above a guaranteed minimum amount. Weeks after the Airshow, the plaintiff sought to claim that consent to the new arrangement was coerced. Hardie Boys J. rejected this plea. Even though the defendant had obtained the consent of the plaintiff by a threatened breach of contract, in refusing to accept the programme, the proof-reading errors were such that the defendant was in law entitled to reject the programme. Further, the fact that the plaintiff had time to consult his business partner and legal advisers pointed away from duress. Delay in rescinding the contract was also relevant here.

If the payment is made or promised "under protest" this will not be essential and the presence or absence of protest is not conclusive: *per* Lord Scarman in *Pao On.* If the person making the promise has an alternative course of action – the possibility of quick and effective legal action to remove the threat of pressure for example – this may signify consent and the absence of duress.[40] Perhaps the most controversial issue is motive. Mocatta J. in *North Ocean Shipping* held it immaterial whether the person making the demand and uttering the threat was aware that the person addressed had no effective alternative because the person making the demand had full knowledge of the difficulties the threatened action would produce. It is submitted that if we are concerned with notions of legitimacy and the motive of the person threatening, rather than simply the will of the party threatened, then this factor should be of great

---

[36] (1983) 99 L.Q.R. 356.
[37] [1985] 1 W.L.R. 173.
[38] *Magnacrete Ltd. v. Douglas Hill* (1988) 48 S.A.S.R. 565; *Alec Lobb (Garages) Ltd. v. Total Oil* [1985] 1 W.L.R. 173.
[39] [1990] 1 N.Z.L.R. 199.
[40] *per* Griffiths L.J. in *B&S Contracts v. Victor Green Publications*, [1984] 1 C.R. 419.

importance. It was clearly material in *D & C Builders v. Rees*[41] that the builders were known to be in a difficult financial position when they "agreed" to accept a reduced settlement of their claim: see also *Osorio v. Cardona*.[42] It is however clear that if the person threatened does not immediately seek relief once the pressure is removed, then he is likely to be held to have consented to the demand: *North Ocean Shipping v. Hyundai Construction*[43] and *Walmsley v. Christchurch City Council*.[44]

The most recent discussion in the English courts, *CTN Cash and Carry v. Gallaher Ltd*[45] concerned a threat to refuse the buyers to utilise credit facilities that the sellers had extended to the buyers, as a privilege, unless the buyers paid a disputed sum of money. Although it later transpired that the buyers were not liable in law to pay this money, the Court of Appeal held that the payment made was not improperly obtained. The sellers were bona fide of the view that the sums were due and the threat to discontinue the credit facility, while coercive, was not unlawful. However, the Court of Appeal, in a refreshing discussion of the boundaries of duress, conceded that in certain circumstances a threat to do something that was coercive could be improper even though not in its own terms being unlawful.

One English judge has indicated that in his view the likelihood of an employer–employee agreement being voidable for economic duress must be remote indeed: see Popplewell J. in *Hennessy v. Craigmyle*,[46] in which it was held that the court had no jurisdiction to hear an unfair dismissal claim because the claim had earlier been settled by agreement. In the Ontario case of *Stott v. Merit Investment Corporation*,[47] the Ontario Court of Appeal provided a compelling illustration of just how difficult it will be to make out a claim of economic duress in this context. The plaintiff, a financial securities salesman employed by the defendant, was obliged to meet shortfalls on his customer accounts and after pressure was brought to bear by his supervisor, he signed a document acknowledging his indebtedness, fearing that otherwise he could not find employment in the industry. He was at this time financially embarrassed and in no position to terminate his employment. The majority of the Ontario Court of Appeal found that even if his consent was coerced, the plaintiff had remained in employment and thus approbated the agreement. In his dissenting judgment, Blair J.A. drew a quite different inference from the plaintiff's apparent inactivity: "it is unrealistic to suggest that at all times [Stott] had the option of resigning, exposing himself and his family to the hazards of unemployment, bankruptcy and litigation which he could not afford."

---

[41] [1966] 2 Q.B. 617; see a prescient comment by Winder (1966) 82 L.Q.R. 165 and an earlier comment at (1940) 3 M.L.R. 97 by the same writer.
[42] (1985) 59 B.C.L.R. 29.
[43] [1979] Q.B. 705.
[44] [1990] 1 N.Z.L.R. 199; contrast *Byle v. Byle* (1990) 65 D.L.R. (4th) 641.
[45] [1994] 4 All E.R. 714; Smith (1997) 56 C.L.J. 343.
[46] [1985] I.R.L.R. 446; *McConville v. ESB* [1995] E.L.R. 46.
[47] (1988) 48 D.L.R. (4th) 288.

# Part 4

# Equitable Intervention

# 13   Equitable Intervention

## Introduction

The doctrine of undue influence enables a court to set aside contracts, transfers of property *inter vivos* and dispositions by will whenever it appears that one party has not freely consented to the transaction. The doctrine is designed to discourage victimisation and sharp practice, particularly on the part of persons who are in positions of trust and confidence and who may abuse the power they acquire over other persons.

### *(1)   The presumption of undue influence*

Persons who acquire a considerable amount of influence over others often do so because of the very nature of the relationship that exists between them. A patient may place trust and confidence in his physician: *Aherne v. Hogan.*[1] A trustee who employs an agent to carry out his obligations places that agent in a fiduciary relationship *vis à vis* the beneficial owner of the property: see *Murphy v. O'Shea*[2] and *King v. Anderson.*[3] A solicitor will normally hold some degree of influence and dominion over a client: *Lawless v. Mansfield.*[4] In these cases it goes without saying that the solicitor, trustee, or physician should not misrepresent or trick the other party into conveying property to them. Equity also requires all transactions between these persons to be justified by the party in whom trust and confidence is placed. In certain cases the courts go so far as to say that there is an absolute incapacity to contract. In *Atkins v. Delmege*[5] a purchase of property was set aside when the purchaser turned out to be the legal representative of the estate, the sale being ordered by a court. The solicitor, in such circumstances was declared to be incapable of purchasing. The general rule is that once the purchaser falls into a category of person in whom trust and confidence is reposed he is obliged to show that the sale was fair and freely assented to. In *Molony v. Kernan*[6] it was held that before an agent could take a lease from his principal the agent must show that full information was given to the principal and that the contract was entered into in good faith.

Undue influence will also be presumed where property is transferred to a religious association by a devotee. In *White v. Meade*[7] the plaintiff, then aged

---

[1]   Dru. *temp.* Sug. 310: Clark, *Inequality of Bargaining Power* (1987); Sheridan, *Fraud in Equity* (1956).
[2]   (1845) 8 I Eq.R. 329.
[3]   (1874) 8 Ir.Eq.R. 625; *Tate v. Williamson* (1886) L.R. 2 Ch. 55.
[4]   (1841) 1 Dr. & War. 557.
[5]   (1847) 12 Ir. Eq. R. 1.
[6]   (1832) 2 Dr. & War 31; *Patten v. Hamilton* [1911] 1 I.R. 46.
[7]   (1840) 2 Ir.Eq.R. 420.

18, entered a religious establishment as a lodger. It was envisaged that if the plaintiff decided at a later date to take holy orders she could do so after being allowed to consult with friends. The defendants prevailed on her to take holy orders while actively preventing her from seeking guidance from her brother. The Order also managed to get the plaintiff to transfer £1100 and a large amount of realty to the Order. The transfer was set aside. It is not necessary to show that the religious order practiced coercion. It is enough to show that the religious devotee was unable to freely consent to the transaction because he or she was incapable of exercising independent judgment. *Allcard v. Skinner*[8] shows that even if a court does not impute improper motive or unconscionable behaviour to the party taking under the contract or transfer, the transaction will be set aside unless it can be shown to be fair and freely consented to. The facts of *Allcard v. Skinner* were as follows: the plaintiff, a woman in her mid-thirties, was introduced by the spiritual adviser to the defendant, a lady superior of a Protestant enclosed sisterhood. There was a similar link between the charitable body and the spiritual adviser. After some years, the plaintiff entered the sisterhood and in furtherance of vows gave property to it which was used for charitable purposes. Under the rules of the sisterhood, obedience to the defendant was a central tenet. After eight years, she left the sisterhood. Some six years later, she sought the return of that portion of her donated property that was unspent on the date of her departure from the sisterhood. While no pressure had been placed upon the plaintiff other than the ordinary rules and vows of poverty and obedience, and no improper use had been made of the monies, undue influence was presumed. Lindley L.J. explained the basis of the doctrine in the following terms:

> "What is the principle? Is it that it is right and expedient to save persons from the consequences of their own folly? – or is it that it is right and expedient to save them from being victimised by other people? In my opinion the doctrine of undue influence is founded upon the second of these two principles. Courts of Equity have never set aside gifts on the ground of folly, imprudence or want of foresight on the part of the donor."[9]

A presumption in appropriate cases is seen as a useful foil to victimisation. Nevertheless, delay in seeking relief, and acts of affirmation carried out during the six-year interval, together prevented the plaintiff from succeeding in *Allcard v. Skinner*. There are however some instances in which gifts to religious bodies have been held to be freely and voluntarily given. In *Kirwan v. Cullen*[10] a gift to the Catholic Church was upheld. The executor of the donor's estate alleged that one of the trustees of the property conveyed had been the religious confessor of the donor; the transaction was upheld when it was shown that the trustee in question had ceased to be the donor's confessor

---

[8] (1887) 36 Ch.D. 145.
[9] *Ibid.* at 182–183.
[10] (1854) 2 Ir. Ch.Rep. 322.

two years before the gift was made. It remains of course possible for the court to hold that, while the religious mentor did not have a confidential relationship with the donor in a formal sense, undue influence was in fact exercised. In *Murphy v. O'Neill*[11] the jury found that undue influence was exercised by a priest over a member of the Church although the priest had not been the confessor of the victim and the victim was resident in the next parish.

Other relationships the courts view with suspicion include parent and child, guardian and ward. In *Wallace v. Wallace*[12] and *Croker v. Croker*[13] transfers of property by a son in favour of his father were set aside because the father was unable to show that the transfers were freely made. In *McMackin v. Hibernian Bank*[14] a guarantee signed by a young girl living with her mother was set aside because of the undue influence of the mother. This presumption also applies to instances of guardian and ward. *Mulhallen v. Marum*[15] is a very colourful illustration of the presumption in this context. The plaintiff, a young man of 18 years, went to live with his married sister and her husband. The plaintiff was supplied with horses, clothing, money and other essentials by his sister's husband. He was then effectively placed in the custody of his sister's husband and upon his reaching full age was persuaded to transfer lands, including valuable mining rights, to him. These transactions were set aside on the basis that the transfers had been made to a person standing in the position of guardian, receiver of rents of the plaintiff's land, agent and tenant of the plaintiff, all of which separately could be viewed as a basis for imputing undue influence in a proper case.

The most compelling modern cases in which transactions have been re-opened as a result of undue influence have involved music artists who, while unknown and unsuccessful, and under the influence of advisers who have a fiduciary relationship with the artist, have entered into recording contracts, music publishing contracts, and have executed copyright assignments. In *O'Sullivan and Another v. Management Agency & Music Ltd. and Others*[16] the artist Gilbert O'Sullivan was able to successfully set aside publishing and recording contracts which were entered into by the artist following advice of his manager, the contracts in question being unduly restrictive and concluded with recording and publishing companies with whom the manager was closely linked. In *John and Others v. James and Others*[17] Elton John and Bernie Taupin were also able to successfully plead the existence of a fiduciary relationship between themselves and music publishers, so when the agreements were not exploited by the publishers in a manner which was conscientious and fair to the artists, there could be an account ordered of profits made by the fiduciary.

---

[11] [1936] N.I. 16.
[12] (1842) 2 Dr. & War. 452: persons *in loco parentis; O'Connor v. Foley* [1905] 1 I.R. 1.
[13] (1870) 4 I.L.T.R. 181.
[14] [1905] 1 I.R. 296.
[15] (1843) 3 Dr. & War. 317.
[16] [1984] 3 W.L.R. 448.
[17] [1991] F.S.R. 397; See Tatt [1987] 9 E.I.P.R. 132; Woolcombe [1987] 9 E.I.P.R. 187. On account of profits see *Warman International Ltd. v. Dwyer* (1995) 182 C.L.R. 544.

There are other instances where the courts may eventually hold that the burden of showing the propriety of the transaction rests upon the party seeking to uphold it. The value of the presumption is that it results in the transaction being set aside if the onus is not discharged. This is a reversal of the burden of proof in most civil actions where it normally rests on the person impugning the transaction. This evidentiary matter was considered by the Northern Ireland Court of Appeal in *R. (Proctor) v. Hutton, Re Founds Estate.*[18] An action was brought by executors of Mrs. Founds estate to set aside legacies on the ground of undue influence having been exerted by a niece of the deceased. Jones L.J. said:

> "The presumption of undue influence may arise in two sorts of cases. The evidence may show *a particular relationship* for example that of solicitor and client, trustee and *cestui que trust,* doctor and patient or religious adviser and pupil. Those cases or some of them, depending on the facts, *may of themselves* raise the presumption. Such examples, as regards undue influence, have much in common with the doctrine of *res ipsa loquitur* in relation to negligence. But then there is the other sort of case, the precise range of which is indeterminate, in which *the whole evidence,* when meticulously considered, may disclose *facts* from which *it should be inferred* that a relationship is disclosed which justifies a finding that there is a presumption of undue influence. In other words the presumption enables a party to achieve justice by bridging a gap in the evidence where there is a gap because the evidence is impossible to come by."[19]

Lord Lowry, L.C.J. agreed:

> "The relationships which raise the presumption are left unlimited by definition, wide open for identification on the facts and in all the circumstances of each particular case as it arises . . . it is a common but not a necessary feature of the relationship that the person on whose part undue influence is alleged assumed a responsibility for advising the donor even managing his property. There are certain relationships which are recognised as giving rise to the presumption, but there are also those which, upon a consideration of the particular facts, may raise the same presumption."[20]

This second instance of a presumption operating in favour of the party seeking to invalidate the transaction can be illustrated by peripheral family relationships which may give one person the opportunity to gain dominance over the other. Brother and brother: *Armstrong v. Armstrong*[21]; brother and

---

[18] [1978] N.I. 139.
[19] Unreported, Court of Appeal, April 30, 1979 affirming Lowry L.C.J. in [1978] N.I. 139; emphasis added.
[20] *Ibid.*
[21] (1873) I.R. 8 Eq. 1.

sister and uncle and nephew: *Gregg v. Kidd*[22]; brother-in-law and sister-in-law: *Evans v. Elwood*.[23] These are all cases where the presumption may come into effect after evidence has been given to show that a relationship of trust and confidence developed between these persons. In the case of *McGonigle v. Black*[24] this second instance of a presumption arising on the facts was held to operate by Barr J. An elderly farmer, living alone following the death of relatives, contracted to sell his property to a near-neighbour and the transaction was set aside, Barr J. citing with approval the speech of Lord Lowry L.C.J. in *R. (Proctor) v. Hutton, Re Founds Estate*. After looking at all the facts, Barr J. concluded that this was "a grossly improvident transaction which was brought about by undue influence persistently exercised by the defendant over Mr. McGonigle who, because of a combination of bereavement, inability to cope, loneliness, alcoholism and ill-health, was vulnerable to manipulation and was so manipulated by the defendant to the vendor's obvious disadvantage."

Particular difficulties arise in relation to pleas of undue influence when a husband and wife relationship is under scrutiny. It has been held in several cases that no presumption of undue influence arises out of the simple fact of the relationship created by way of marriage (*e.g. Bank of Montreal v. Stuart*[25] cited by Murnaghan J. in *Northern Banking Co. v. Carpenter*).[26] If however the person seeking relief can show that one spouse was under the dominion of the other then the party holding power over the other will be required to show that the transaction was the result of the exercise of free will and independent judgment. The same proposition applies in relation to the banker-customer relationship. In *Lloyds Bank v. Bundy*[27] the Court of Appeal held that, while in most cases a bank will only be involved in a creditor–debtor relationship with its customers, there may be situations in which there may be obligations placed upon the bank to ensure that customers have a full and complete explanation of a transaction when they enter into a financial transaction with the bank. The scope of this duty of fiduciary care remains as yet undefined. While Peter Pain J. in *Horry v. Tate & Lyle Ltd.*[28] held that an insurance company settling an accident compensation claim with an employee of the insured was obliged to disclose all relevant information, and perhaps ensure the employee obtained independent advice, or run the risk of the settlement being overturned, it has been held in *O'Hara v. Allied Irish Banks*[29] that *Lloyds Bank v. Bundy* does not create a right to damages if a bank fails to ensure that a guarantor receives a full and comprehensive explanation of the nature of, and circumstances affecting, a guarantee. It is however safe to say that if a bank does not provide

---

[22] [1956] I.R. 183.
[23] (1874) 8 I.L.T.R. 118.
[24] Unreported, High Court, November 14, 1988.
[25] [1911] A.C. 120.
[26] [1931] I.R. 268; *F. v. F.* unreported, High Court, October 24, 1985.
[27] [1975] Q.B. 326.
[28] [1982] 2 Lloyd's Rep. 416.
[29] *The Times*, February 7, 1984.

a full and detailed explanation of a guarantee given by one of its customers in favour of another customer the instrument may not be enforceable. In *Midland Bank plc. v. Cornish*[30] a wife executed a mortgage in favour of a bank, in order to provide security for her husband's business debts, without having been given a clear explanation of the impact of the mortgage. The Court of Appeal held that the bank, having chosen to provide advice to a customer, was under an obligation to provide a full explanation, and, upon proof that an unfair advantage had been taken, a presumption of undue influence arose.[31] While the Court of Appeal found that no unfair advantage could be shown and, following *National Westminster Bank v. Morgan,*[32] no presumption could thus arise, the bank were liable in damages under *Hedley Byrne.* Until very recently, English Courts took a very restrictive view of the obligation a financial institution has resting upon it to ensure that a full explanation of the nature *and* advisibility of a transaction is given to persons with whom the institution deals. There are much stronger Canadian and Australian lines of authority which require financial institutions to ensure that guarantors, particularly elderly persons or other persons who are keen to help the customer of that institution (typically a son of the guarantors) are given an adequate explanation of the instrument: see *Morrison v. Coast Finance*[33] and the High Court of Australia's decision in *Commercial Bank of Australia v. Amadio.*[34] In *Amadio* two members of the High Court of Australia in particular were anxious to explain that when a bank knows that the proposed guarantor is potentially at a disadvantage – here, elderly parents without a good command of English, guaranteeing business debts of their son, the dominent member of the family, in circumstances where the bank feared that the business activities were not likely to succeed – the institution extracting the guarantee is vulnerable. Mason J. indicated that the bank will be guilty of unconscionable conduct, if it does not disclose to would be guarantors such facts as to enable them to form a judgment for themselves and advising them to seek independent advice. Dean J. observed that at least the bank, in this case, was bound to inquire whether the transaction had been adequately explained. This line of reasoning has been consolidated by *National Australia Bank v. Noble.*[35] The respective parents of a married couple, of Italian extraction with limited powers of understanding English, gave security for a building company run by their son. They gave a guarantee and mortgaged land without being told that the bank had formed the view that the building company was in a poor financial condition. The documents however were explained fully by the bank manager. Applying *Amadio*, the Federal Court of Australia held the mortgage invalid for the unconscionable behaviour of the bank in not explaining the full facts of the background to the securities provided to the bank.

---

[30] [1985] 3 All. E.R. 513.
[31] On related pleas of *non est factum* and negligent misstatement, see *Lloyd's Bank plc v. Waterhouse* [1991] Fam.Law 23.
[32] [1985] A.C. 686.
[33] (1965) 55 D.L.R. (2d.) 710.
[34] (1983) 151 C.L.R. 447.
[35] (1991) 100 A.L.R. 227.

One English case takes a similar line. In *Avon Finance Co. v. Bridger*[36] the parents of a young man signed a legal charge over their property in order to guarantee loans made by a licenced moneylender to their son. They had not received an explanation of the instruments signed from either the lender or their son. Lord Denning held the case fell within the inequality of bargaining power principle he had earlier enunciated in *Bundy* itself. The son's failure in particular to explain the instrument was a risk that could most appropriately be taken by the lender – a kind of *de facto* agency arose here. While a later Court of Appeal, in *Coldunell Ltd. v. Gallon*[37] attempted to confine *Avon Finance* to its own facts, the Court of Appeal, in *Midland Bank plc v. Shephard*[38] has endorsed the view that when a creditor, pressing for a security for a debt, gives the task of explaining an instrument to a person who is in a position to obtain consent to that instrument by fraud or misrepresentation, and there is fraud or mispresentation, the instrument will not be enforced in favour of the creditor. However, both *Midland Bank v. Shephard* and *Bank of Baroda v. Shah*[39] indicate that creditors and their solicitors are only required to advise a surety that it would be desirable to seek independent advice. It is only when the creditor leaves the surety in the hands of a person who, to the knowledge of the creditor, may exercise some influence over the surety, that the security may be in danger through this agency principle. The Commonwealth cases go further by making the security vulnerable when it is an oppressive or unconscionable transaction even if the creditor advises the surety to seek independent advice. The operation of the agency concept is graphically illustrated by *Barclay's Bank plc v. Kennedy and Another*.[40] The Court of Appeal held that where a husband charges the matrimonial home after the creditor permits the husband to obtain his wife's consent, the husband in law will be held to act as agent for the creditor. The creditor must not be in any better position than the husband, so if the husband exercises undue influence or induces signature by misrepresentation, the creditor will suffer the consequences.

In 1993 the House of Lords took a new tack, deciding that concepts of agency, or the possible evolution of a "special equity" for spouses providing security for a business debt out of the family home, did not afford a coherent basis for regulating suretyship transactions. In *Barclay's Bank v. O'Brien*[41] the House of Lords reformulated the evidentiary requirements of undue influence and, allied with the concept of notice, sought to balance the interests of the financial services industry with the need for transactions to be procedurally irreproachable. In *O'Brien* Lord Browne-Wilkinson indicated that the

---

[36] (1979) 123 S.J. 705.
[37] [1986] 1 All E.R. 429.
[38] [1988] 3 All E.R. 17.
[39] [1988] 3 All E.R. 24.
[40] *The Financial Times*, November 15, 1988.
[41] [1993] 4 All E.R. 417; *Smith v. Bank of Scotland, The Times*, June 23, 1997.

following classification of undue influence, laid down by the Court of Appeal in *Bank of Credit and Commerce International v. Aboody*[42] was to be adopted:

> Class 1: actual undue influence. Here the claimant must affirmatively show the undue influence alleged.

> Class 2: presumed undue influence. This class breaks into two parts. Firstly, Class 2A under which the relationship itself raises the presumption (e.g. solicitor and client). Secondly, Class 2B under which the presumption arises when the facts prove, *de facto*, repose of trust and confidence by the complainant in the wrongdoer and the transaction is manifestly disadvantageous to the complainant.

Building upon this classification (which is mirrored in Irish case law) their Lordships reaffirmed the view that a husband and wife, or a cohabiting couple, do not come within Class 2A. However, if one spouse can show that financial decisions were left by that party for the other to address, then a Class 2B presumption may be made out, and the transaction may be rendered voidable as between those persons. However, if the issue is whether a transaction between the dominated spouse and a third party – classically a bank and a married woman – is liable to be invalidated, the analysis becomes more complex. Should the bank be aware of undue influence as of fact then the transaction will not be enforceable; but, in the absence of such knowledge, is the bank to be denied the right to enforce any security interest it has *vis-à-vis* the dominated spouse? The decision of the House of Lords, in *Canadian Imperial Bank of Commerce Mortgages plc v. Pitt*[43] makes it clear that if the transaction is an everyday transaction, of some benefit to the spouse, and that it has no unusual provisions or surrounding circumstances (a remortgage ostensibly to obtain funds to buy a holiday home for example) the bank can enforce its interest even if the wife is the victim of actual, *i.e.* Class 1 undue influence, for in such a case it is the husband who is the wrongdoer. However, if the parties are known to be closely linked by marital, sexual or other strong emotional ties and the transaction involves the use of property as security for existing or future indebtedness, such circumstances will fix the bank with constructive notice that undue influence exists: in such a case

> "unless the creditor who is on inquiry takes reasonable steps to satisfy himself that the wife's agreement to stand surety has been properly obtained, the creditor will have constructive notice of the wife's rights" [*i.e.* to have the transaction set aside for misrepresentation or undue influence][44]

Thus, the bank should have clear procedures to ensure that the transaction is clearly understood by the "wife". A private meeting in the bank, with the "husband" being excluded will satisfy this reasonable steps test. Merely sending

---

[42] [1990] 1 Q.B. 923.
[43] [1993] 4 All E.R. 433.
[44] *Ibid.* [Author's addition]

documents to the home of the parties without ensuring that they are explained will not suffice (the facts of *O'Brien* itself). Current practice appears to be to make sure that documents are sent to a reputable firm of solicitors, the lender obtaining from the solicitor a certificate that the transaction has been adequately explained to all the parties to the transaction. Even if there are irregularities in the way in which the clients are advised, as in *Massey v. Midland Bank plc*,[45] where the firm was selected by the dominant spouse and he was present at the time the transaction was explained, the bank will avoid constructive notice of the dominated spouse's equity for it can rely on the professional competence of the client's solicitor and any certificate provided: *Banco Exterior v. Mann*.[46] As Hoffman L.J. put it in *Bank of Baroda v. Rayarel*,[47] the "bank's legal department is not obliged to commit the professional discourtesy of communicating directly with the solicitor's client and tendering such advice itself. Nor is it obliged to inform the solicitor of his professional duties."

While most cases involve suretyship, some cases involve new loans which are not on their face to the advantage of the spouse, the duty of inquiry still arising according to *Allied Irish Bank plc v. Byrne*[48] and *Halifax Mortgage Services v. Stepsky*.[49] Nor is the relationship necessary to trigger the duty one of marriage or cohabitation: emotional links created by virtue of being the parents of a child sufficed in *Massey* while in the most radical of these cases, *Credit Lyonnais v. Burch*,[50] a complex relationship between an older man and a female employee was able to come within the *O'Brien* mechanism.

It is evident that the *O'Brien* case means that difficulties that may arise when family property is used as a finance tool have been addressed by the adoption of new practices that make it likely that the transaction will stand, in the absence of some omission by the lending institution. Some commentators favour the view that *O'Brien* does not recognise the special position of the family home and that it does not go far enough as a protective mechanism. Fehlberg[51] in particular criticises the *post O'Brien* decisions, saying that there is an overemphasis on suretyship being for the "common good" and that the cases tend to underestimate the degree of pressure under which a "dependant spouse" within the *O'Brien* schema may actually be. More protective laws like Canadian "homestead" legislation, or consumer credit type "cooling off" and explanatory document legislation would also be useful. Fehlberg's arguments are brought home by a careful reading of *Northern Bank Ltd. v. McCarron*.[52]

---

45 [1995] 1 All E.R. 929.
46 [1995] 1 All E.R. 936.
47 [1995] 2 F.L.R. 376, approved in *Barclays Bank v. Thomson* [1997] 4 All E.R. 816. The banks legal department is required to ensure a reply is given by the nominated solicitor: *Cooke v. National Westminster Bank, The Times*, July 27, 1998.
48 [1995] 2 F.L.R. 325.
49 [1996] 2 All E.R. 277.
50 [1997] 1 All E.R. 144; *Hooley and O'Sullivan* [1997] L.M.C.L.Q. 17; contrast *Banco Exterior v. Thomas* [1997] 1 All E.R. 46.
51 (1994) 57 M.L.R. 467; (1996) 59 M.L.R. 675.
52 [1995] N.I. 258. Carswell L.J. applies the law with all the probity one would expect from such a good judge, but the result in the case still seems shocking to this reader.

Returning to the issue of non-coercive transactions we should note that it is easier to make an allegation of undue influence than to sustain it as a defence.

The leading English case of *National Westminster Bank v. Morgan*[53] is most frequently cited for Lord Scarman's observations on the doctrine of inequality of bargaining power and his Lordship's questioning of the need for such a general principle in English law. What is often overlooked is the application of principles of undue influence to the facts of the case. Mrs. Morgan was in no sense "victimised": the financial arrangement made by the bank in that case offered her the best prospect available of salvaging the family home and was struck on the kind of terms a borrower, in the perilous condition of the Morgans, could expect from a respectable lender. The contrast between *Morgan* and *Amadio* lies in the unconscionable behaviour of the bank in the latter case and the absence of any such unconscionable behaviour in *Morgan*. The decision of the Court of Appeal in *Woodstood Finance Ltd. v. Petrou*[54] confirms the view that in the absence of undue influence between husband and wife, proved by way of dominion or victimisation by one over the other, a normal loan transaction made by a bank, as part of a general banker-customer relationship, will be upheld.

There is little direct Irish authority on whether this duty to explain, or ensure that an explanation is given, exists. The decision of the majority of the Supreme Court in *Northern Banking Co. v. Carpenter*[55] at first sight seems applicable but in that case (in which a husband lodged title deeds of his wife's property as security for loans made to him) the bank simply failed to show that the wife knew of or signed any instrument relating to her property. In *Bank of Nova Scotia v. Hogan*[56] the Supreme Court cited with approval the reasoning in *O'Brien* but on the facts there was no evidence of undue influence or misrepresentation, actual or presumed. The Supreme Court also referred to the Australian approach with approval so a definitive view is yet to emerge in Ireland. The concern of the Irish courts to see that transactions are concluded on equal terms (see *Grealish v. Murphy*[57] and *Macken v. Munster & Leinster Bank*,[58]) suggests that the broader equitable approach favoured in Canada and Australia will prevail in Ireland.

## (2) Undue influence as of fact

If the presumption does not arise automatically and if the court does not feel that the facts shown raise an inference that the transaction was not freely consented to, it is necessary to convince the court that the transaction should not stand. The courts will not presume that undue influence exists if, at first sight, one person is in no position to hold dominion over another. In a sense the

---

[53] [1985] A.C. 686.
[54] [1986] F.L.R. 158.
[55] [1931] I.R. 268.
[56] [1997] 1 I.L.R.M. 407.
[57] [1946] I.R. 35.
[58] [1959] I.R. 313.

courts presume that the parties deal on an equal footing. In the case of *Mathew v. Bobbins*[59] the English Court of Appeal ruled that the relationship of employer/employee does not give rise to the presumption that the employer stands in a dominant position *vis à vis* the employee. The Court of Appeal reasoned that twentieth century employment protection legislation has readjusted an inbalance that clearly existed in the last century. Mr Bobbins was held not to have been prevailed upon by his employer when he "agreed" to sign a document which changed his status from a tenant into a licensee of accommodation provided by his employer. It is open to doubt whether employment legislation, either in Ireland or in Great Britain, has reached the level of sophistication or effectiveness contemplated in this case.

Similarly, the Privy Council in *Glover v. Glover*[60] held that debtor/creditor and mortgagor/mortgagee relationships do not give rise to a presumption. Lord Porter said that in cases where no presumption ordinarily arises:

> "certain matters are always regarded as relevant and sometimes conclusive, amongst which the following are worthy of special mention:
>
> (1) that the transaction in question was a voluntary gift;
> (2) that the transaction, if amounting to a contract was for a manifestly inadequate consideration;
> (3) the existence of a marked disparity in age and position between the parties to the transaction."[61]

Because the House of Lords have recently emphasised that "victimisation" is the essence of undue influence it will be difficult to grant relief if, as in *National Westminster Bank plc. v. Morgan*[62] itself, there is proof that the transaction was understood by the person allegedly influenced (even if no full explanation was given) and the transaction itself in its substantive terms is not unfair.

In *O'Flanagan v. Ray-Ger Ltd.*[63] an agreement between two sole shareholders of a company, transferring property to the defendant, was set aside for undue influence. There was a marked disparity in terms of business acumen, the defendant being dominant and the more astute. Negotiations took place away from business premises in circumstances where the very considerable persuasive powers of the defendant partner could freely operate. The agreement was improvident, virtually a gift transaction because of the poor health of the transferor who, to the knowledge of both parties, was terminally ill. In these circumstances Costello J. held that the plaintiff, executor of the estate of the transferor, had proved undue influence as a fact. Indeed, in this writer's view, the facts are so compelling that it would have been possible to hold that the

---

59 *The Times*, June 21 1980; contrast the Canadian decision in *Blackmore v. Cablenet Ltd.* [1995] 3 W.W.R. 305.
60 [1951] 1 D.L.R. 657.
61 *Ibid.* at 664–665.
62 [1985] A.C. 686.
63 Unreported, High Court, April 28, 1983.

whole evidence would raise the presumption of undue influence in the second sense in which Jones L.J. talked of the presumption arising in *R. (Proctor) v. Hutton, Re Founds Estate*, as well as coming within Class 2B in *Barclay's Bank v. O'Brien*.[64]

## (3) Discharging the onus of proof

Once the presumption operates, the party seeking to uphold the transaction must show that consent was freely given and that the party with whom he contracted did so with his eyes open. The cases suggest that this can be done by advising that independent advice be sought from a respectable source. In *McMackin v. Hibernian Bank*[65] a bank was denied enforcement of a bank guarantee because the guarantor, their client's daughter, should have obtained legal advice; the case where the guarantor is also a client of the bank is considerably *a fortiori: Lloyds Bank v. Bundy*.[66] The case of *Smyth v. Smyth*[67] holds that it is enough if the party seeking to enforce the bargain shows that it was contemplated that independent legal advice would be given before the contract was completed. This may be a dangerous precedent to rely on. The best advice would be to advise the other person to seek and obtain independent legal advice. If the advisor turns out to be a trusted friend or respected member of the community this may suffice.

In fact, sales in which no advice was sought or given have been upheld. What the doctrine boils down to is the protection of persons who are not able to freely consent to a transaction. If, after hearing the evidence, the court feels that the bargain should stand, no *a priori* test will stand in the way. This is shown vividly by *Smyth v. Smyth*. In *McCrystal v. O'Kane*[68] there was evidence of a sale at a substantial, but not gross, undervalue, and in the absence of other vitiating factors Murray J. held that there was not a sufficient basis for finding undue influence as of fact, particularly when the defendant vendor was advised twice to obtain independent advice by the solicitor acting for both vendor and purchaser.

In *McCormack v. Bennett*[69] Finlay P. upheld a transfer of farm property made by an elderly couple to a daughter, who in return, agreed to look after them for the rest of their lives. The disposition was challenged on the ground that no independent advice was given. The action was dismissed:

> "The presence of full and satisfactory independent advice is not the only way of proving that a voluntary deed even though it may be on the face of it improvident resulted from the free exercise of the donor's will . . .
> I think it is a reasonable inference from the evidence which I have heard

---

[64] [1978] N.I. 139 Court of Appeal judgment of April 30, 1979.
[65] [1905] 1 I.R. 296.
[66] [1975] Q.B. 326.
[67] Unreported, High Court, November 22, 1978: *Noonan v. O'Connell*, unreported, High Court, April 10, 1987.
[68] [1986] N.I. 123.
[69] Unreported, High Court, July 2, 1973; *Provincial Bank v. McKeever* [1941] I.R. 471.

that he was a sufficiently astute man to know that no form of bargain or commercial transaction was likely to secure for himself what they really needed and that was personal care and attention granted largely through affection and kindness by a member of their family."

As a general rule it is more difficult for administrators of an estate to convince a court that the deceased was unable to freely consent, particularly if the deceased later seems to have approved the consequences of her action: see *Kirwan v. Cullen*.[70] This reluctance to "second guess" the deceased, particularly when he or she seems mentally competent, is evident in *McCormack v. Bennett* also. However, if the facts are equivocal the disposition may be overturned. In *Carroll & Carroll v. Carroll*[71] the elderly transferor of a family pub appeared to the court to have been misled by his son, the transferee, and his assurances to his daughters that they would "have a home" were compatible with lack of knowledge that he had actually executed a transfer of property as well as an act of concealment by the transferor. In these circumstances the presumption of undue influence was not rebutted.

## (4) Delay in seeking relief

A party who later approves and seeks to take advantage of a bargain will be bound by it, even if it was suspicious at the time it was entered into: *De Montmorency v. Devereux*,[72] affirmed by the House of Lords.

In cases where the presumption operates but there is no evidence of fraud or overbearing conduct, relief must be sought promptly. In *Allcard v. Skinner*[73] relief was refused because of a delay of six years in seeking relief. Where fraud or overbearing conduct exists as of fact a delay of 12 years was held not to be fatal in *O'Kelly v. Glenny*.[74] Time begins to run from the date of emancipation from the dominion of the other party.

In many of these cases, the agreement has been carried into effect, often over a period of many years. Where land has been exploited, for example, the court may order an account of profits and may allow the person who has benefited from the undue influence some degree of remuneration, or an allowance for improvements made: see *Mulhallen v. Marum*.[75] In the more recent English cases[76] in which recording and publishing contracts were overturned, several years after these contracts had been in operation, an inquiry into profits made was ordered and the court allowed the deduction of reasonable out of pocket expenses incurred in exploiting these works, as well as an allowance for skill and labour exercised on behalf of the artist, including a profit element. Considerable

---

[70] (1854) 2 Ir.Ch.R. 322.
[71] Unreported, High Court, March 5, 1998.
[72] (1840) 2 Dr. & Wal. 410.
[73] (1887) 36 Ch.D. 145.
[74] (1846) 9 Ir.Eq.R. 25.
[75] (1843) 3 Dr. & War. 317.
[76] *e.g. O'Sullivan and Another v. Management Agency and Music Ltd. and Others* [1984] 3 W.L.R. 448; *John and Others v. James and Others* [1991] F.S.R. 397.

flexibility in the granting of equitable reliefs is available, the concept of fair compensation in equity being available as well as an inquiry into an account of profits.[77]

## Unconscionable Bargains

The Irish courts of equity have intervened in unconscionable bargains by setting aside the transaction or amending the terms in order to produce what the court sees as a fairer transaction. Historically the courts, both here and in England, have protected persons who mortgaged or sold an interest in family property by obliging the mortgagee or purchaser to show the bargain to be a fair one.[78] This jurisdiction extended into cases where an aged or illiterate person for example, sold property, of which they were in possession, for an inadequate consideration.[79] The equitable doctrine relating to expectant heirs and reversioners, as these persons came to be known, has in part, produced a wider equitable jurisdiction.

In the case of *Slator v. Nolan*,[80] Sullivan M.R. after reviewing the early cases declared:

> "I take the law of the Court to be that if two persons – no matter whether a confidential relation exists between them or not – stand in such a relation to each other that one can take an undue advantage of the other, whether by reason of distress or recklessness or wildness or want of care and where the facts show that one party has taken undue advantage of the other, by reason of the circumstances I have mentioned – a transaction resting upon such unconscionable dealing will not be allowed to stand."[81]

In *Slator v. Nolan* itself, a young man, in want of money because of his youthful excesses, was able to set aside a sale of his inheritance.

These cases proceed on a finding that the parties were not equal at the time the contract was struck, largely as a result of the individual circumstances into which one of the parties has fallen. In *Rae v. Joyce*[82] a pregnant woman who mortgaged a reversionary interest in real property at an undervalue was held entitled to set the transaction aside. The mortgagee, a Dublin moneylender, was clearly the more commercially astute; the delicate medical condition of the

---

[77] Contrast *Cheese v. Thomas* [1994] 1 All E.R. 35 with *Mahoney v. Purnell* [1996] 3 All E.R. 61.

[78] The doctrine is traced in Chap. 1 of Clark, *Inequality of Bargaining Power* (Carswell, Ontario, 1987). The leading Irish cases are *Scott v. Dunbar* (1828) 1 Moll. 457; *Woodroffe v. Allen* (1832) Hayes & Jo. 73; *Cook v. Burtchaell* (1842) 2 Drur. & War. 165; *Ormsby v. Lord Limerick* (1849) 2 Ir.Jur. 301.

[79] e.g. *Garvey v. McMinn* (1846) 9 Ir.Eq.Rep. 526.

[80] (1876) I.R. 11 Eq. 367.

[81] *Ibid.* at 409.

[82] (1892) 29 L.R. (Ir.) 500.

mortgagor and her needy circumstances, allied to a rate of interest fixed at 60 per cent, convinced the Irish Court of Appeal that the bargain should be set aside, a rate of interest of five per cent being substituted instead. The mortgagee was unable to show that the bargain was not a hard one.

Although sharp practice, misrepresentation and collusion often appear in these cases, the basis of relief is not fraud in any real sense of a fraudulent misrepresentation. If a bargain is harsh in its terms and if one party is clearly in a stronger bargaining position, equity will intervene. The hardness of the bargain was stressed to be the foundation of intervention in *Benyon v. Cook*[83] but it is not clear whether this is of general application and whether it is compatible with Selborne L.C.'s speech in *Aylesford v. Morris*[84] when the Lord Chancellor stressed that equitable intervention "depended on an unconscientious use of the power arising out of these circumstances and conditions." A further retrenchment has occurred in the Privy Council. In *Hart v. O'Connor*,[85] it was emphasised that a contract will not be overturned simply because the bargain is on its terms unfair if there is no evidence of unconscionable dealing. To put it another way, a bargain that is one-sided cannot be interfered with if the conscience of the party benefiting most is not affected. It is tolerably clear that the Irish courts have favoured a more protective and paternalistic position than that countenanced in *Hart v. O'Connor*.

The Irish courts are extremely protective of elderly persons who sell or dispose of farmland outside the family unit. In *Buckley v. Irwin*,[86] McVeigh J. in the Northern Ireland Chancery Division refused to grant a decree of specific performance in favour of the plaintiff who had purchased the defendant's farm at undervalue. The parties were not equally competent in business matters; the plaintiff was described as "sharp-eyed and experienced", the defendant characterised as "a person who would require protection and guidance in carrying out business affairs". In *Grealish v. Murphy*[87] a transfer of land made by an elderly, intransigent and illiterate farmer, again at undervalue in favour of a younger man, was set aside by Gavan Duffy J. on the ground that the parties were not on an equal footing.

At this point we should consider whether the basis of invalidity is always a finding that the weaker party has been "overreached". Many cases turn upon the fact that one party, while he or she cannot be said to be insane, is unable, for reasons of idiocy, senility, illness or lack of business acumen, to understand the implications of the contract. *Grealish v. Murphy* is such a case. Here the transaction was drafted and explained to the old man by his lawyer. While Gavan Duffy J. held that the lawyer had not done everything he could have done to bring home to his client the implications of the transaction, it is difficult to see how this would be possible if the old man was incapable of grasping the consequences of the contract. In these situations invalidity results from the fact

---

[83] (1875) L.R. 10 Ch.App. 389.
[84] (1873) L.R. 8 Ch.App. 484.
[85] [1985] 2 All. E.R. 880.
[86] [1960] N.I. 98; *Stronge v. Johnston* [1997] N.I.J.B. 56.
[87] [1946] I.R. 35.

that the bargain is so improvident that no reasonable person would enter into it. The best modern authorities are provided by *Lyndon v. Coyne*[88] and *J.H. v. W.J.H.*[89] In *Lyndon v. Coyne* the aged owner of land transferred the property to his nephew in return for a promise by the nephew to permit the old man and his wife to remain on the property for their lives, and for periodic payments of cash. Given the health and age of the old man the instrument was a foolish and improvident one. There was no revocation clause included in the instrument; payments were likely to end at an early date – the old man died three months later – and the instrument as a whole was curiously drafted, suggesting to the court that it was not understood by the old man. O'Byrne J. set the deed aside. More pertinent still is the decision in *Rooney v. Conway*.[90] An elderly man sold his farm outside the family at undervalue to a young man who had befriended and helped him in his old age. The sale was set aside even though there was no evidence of improper or unconscionable behaviour. It was expressly stated that in cases where the sale is at gross undervalue and between persons not on equal footing, and the transaction is thus improvident, it is not necessary to show improper behaviour or equitable fraud by the stronger party before the relief can be granted.

Similar decisions can be found in English law but the equitable jurisdiction seems to be more frequently utilised in Ireland. The traditional equitable jurisdiction to grant relief against unconscionable bargains in England is summarised in *Fry v. Lane*[91] as depending upon three factors; the poverty and ignorance of the plaintiff, the consideration being at undervalue, and the lack of independent advice. In *Cresswell v. Potter*[92] a matrimonial home was held by both husband and wife. When the marriage broke down, the wife was persuaded to execute a conveyance of her interest in the property to her husband, in return for an indemnity against liability under the mortgage and for nothing else. The wife claimed that she believed the document was necessary in order to realise her interest in the matrimonial property, by enabling it to be sold. There was no fraud, no misrepresentation, and no undue influence. Megarry J. held that all three *Fry v. Lane* factors existed. The wife was a member of the "lower income groups" and thus poor and ignorant. The sale was at an undervalue and, finally, made without independent advice. More recently, in *Watkin v. Watson Smith*,[93] an old man of 80, with diminished powers of judgment, concluded a quick sale of property at £2,950, the estimated value of the property being £29,500 or ten times more than the price. By adopting the more flexible approach to *Fry v. Lane* as countenanced by *Cresswell v. Potter*, the sale was set aside. In place of poverty and ignorance, the first limb of the *Fry v. Lane* test, the court substituted the old age and diminished judgment of the seller.

---

[88] (1946) 12 Ir.Jur.Rep. 64.
[89] Unreported, High Court, December 20, 1979; see also *Carroll and Carroll v. Carroll*, unreported, High Court, March 5, 1998.
[90] Unreported, March 8, 1986, a decision of the Northern Ireland Chancery Division.
[91] (1888) 40 Ch.D. 312.
[92] [1978] 1 W.L.R. 255.
[93] *The Times*, July 3, 1986.

Unconscionable bargains are sometimes concluded by commercial organisations with persons of little or no business experience. The Canadian courts, for example, have utilised this jurisdiction to set aside settlements of insurance claims when the bargain is unfair. A recent illustration of this is afforded by *Doan v. Insurance Corporation of British Columbia.*[94] A loss adjuster settled a claim on behalf of an insurance company and the plaintiff, a road accident victim, for $60,000. The injury was a serious one and the plaintiff and his family were unsophisticated and relied entirely on the advice of the loss adjuster. The injury worsened and an application was brought to set aside the settlement. Paris J. cited the leading case of *Harry v. Kreutziger*[95] where McIntyre J. held that:

> "Where a claim is made that a bargain is unconscionable, it must be shown that there was inequality in the position of the parties due to the ignorance, need or distress of the weaker party which would leave him in the power of the stronger, coupled with proof of substantial unfairness in the bargain."[96]

Paris J., following this test, held the settlement to be unconscionable and set it aside, assessing damages at a total figure of $312,000.

It will be difficult to obtain relief from an allegedly unfair bargain if the transaction is struck between commercial organisations. If improper pressure is imposed then economic duress may be relevant but, in general terms, the courts take the view that a predominantly market economy does not require that unsound business decisions should be amended by allowing one party to invoke the unconscionable bargain jurisdiction unless there existed a duty of fiduciary care (*Lloyds Bank v. Bundy*).[97] Nevertheless, Costello J. in *O'Flanagan v. Ray-Ger Ltd.*[98] indicated that even business transactions are not sacrosanct, when, in the context of an agreement between the two sole shareholders in a company, he considered *Grealish v. Murphy* to be potentially applicable although, on the facts, undue influence was established. In *McCoy v. Greene & Cole,*[99] Costello J. reiterated the view that unconscionable bargains may exist within the context of commercial transactions (albeit within the context of a family business) but that the onus of showing that the contract is unfair rests upon the person seeking relief.

*Upholding the unconscionable bargain*

*Rae v. Joyce*[100] suggests that in cases of the sale of a reversionary interest the purchaser must show that the bargain is, in point of fact, fair, just and reason-

---

[94] (1987) 18 B.C.L.R. (2d.) 286.
[95] (1978) 95 D.L.R. (3d.) 231.
[96] *Ibid.* at 237, applying, *inter alia, Waters v. Donnelly* (1884) 9 O.R. 391.
[97] [1975] Q.B. 326.
[98] Unreported, High Court, April 28, 1983.
[99] Unreported, High Court, January 19, 1984.
[100] (1892) 29 L.R. (Ir.) 500.

able. *Kelly v. Morrisroe*[101] decides that where an eccentric and elderly owner of property sells to a younger person the onus of showing that the bargain was fair rests on the purchaser. As in cases of undue influence the purchaser will discharge this onus by convincing the court that the vendor contracted with his eyes open and was given the market value of the property. The prudent purchaser will advise the vendor to seek independent advice before contracting. In cases where the presumption of unconscionable bargain is raised, and no independent advice has been sought, or the party seeking to support the bargain has not advised the weaker party to obtain independent advice, the bargain can be upheld if the contract can be shown to be fair and reasonable, both as regards the circumstances in which it was struck, and the relative mutuality or fairness of the exchange.

In *Smyth v. Smyth*[102] the trustee of real property purchased part of the land from the beneficial owner, a young man who suffered from a drink problem. The young man had first raised the question of a sale. The sale took an "inordinate" length of time to complete, so there was no question of the bargain being concluded without giving the vendor time for reflection. Costello J. refused to find the bargain invalid. He rejected evidence that the consideration paid was inadequate and despite the fact that no independent solicitor was consulted – one solicitor acting for both parties – the transaction was, in the learned judge's view, neither unconscionable nor improvident.

It is clear that the judges will take radically different positions on the implications to be drawn from the evidence – witness the old but seminal case of *O'Rorke v. Bolingbroke*,[103] an appeal to the House of Lords from the Court of Chancery in Ireland, and the English Court of Appeal decision in *Re Brocklehurst (deceased)*.[104] Many academic commentators are critical of the unconscionability doctrine because of the uncertainty surrounding its application to individual cases, yet it is sometimes difficult to see how else the courts could deal with the cases in which unconscionability is pleaded.

---

[101]  (1919) 53 I.L.T.R. 145.
[102]  Unreported, High Court, November 23, 1978.
[103]  (1877) 2 App. Cas. 814.
[104]  [1978] 1 Ch. 14.

# Part 5

# Public Policy

# 14 Illegal Contracts

## Introduction

A contract may be rendered invalid because the transaction runs into conflict with some important value or principle which must be upheld, at the cost of rendering a bargain void or unenforceable.[1] These cases are often divided into two categories: the first category is reserved for cases which are illegal in the purest sense; these transactions infringe a statutory or common law rule to the extent that the whole contract is rendered invalid. Cases falling into the second category, often described as void contracts, do not produce the cataclysmic effects that attend illegal contracts. It is possible for the courts to remove or "sever" the unpalatable or void term while enforcing the rest of the transaction. This distinction seems well established, particularly in English law.[2]

Many writers regard the distinction with distrust but, in general, the cases fall into line with the classification. A further consequence of the distinction concerns collateral transactions which may also be invalid if the main contract is illegal. Megarry J. observed in *Spector v. Ageda*[3] "[a] transaction may simply be void, or it may be unenforceable, and in either case other connected transactions may nevertheless be perfectly valid and enforceable. But illegality is another matter; for it may be contagious."[4]

## Illegal Contracts at Common Law

### (1) Contracts to commit a crime or tort

Contracts which are *contra bonos mores* are absolutely illegal. So, contracts to publish libellous material, knowing the material has this character,[5] to commit a physical assault on a third party[6] or a criminal conspiracy to defraud investors,[7] are clearly illegal. Sometimes the guiding principle is expressed somewhat differently; a person is not to benefit from his or her wrong, even if the level of moral guilt is minimal. So, persons who have been convicted of manslaughter

---

[1] See, generally, Winfield, (1928) 42 Harvard L.R. 76; Grodecki, (1955) 71 L.Q.R. 254; Furmston, (1966) 16 U.T.L.J. 267.

[2] *Bennett v. Bennett* [1952] 1 K.B. 249; *Lee v. Showmans Guild* [1952] Q.B. 329; *Goodinson v. Goodinson* [1952] 2 Q.B. 118.

[3] [1973] 1 Ch. 30.

[4] *Ibid.* at 42.

[5] *Apthorp v. Neville & Co.* (1907) 23 T.L.R. 575.

[6] *Allen v. Rescous* (1676) 2 Lev. 174.

[7] *Scott v. Brown Doering* [1892] 2 Q.B. 724.

have generally not been permitted to recover under the will of the deceased and even social welfare widows' pensions have been denied when widowhood was the consequence of the unlawful killing by a wife of her husband.[8] The principle was extended to cover the personal representatives of the deceased in *Beresford v. Royal Insurance Co.*[9] Here the insured took his own life. A life assurance policy was in existence, but the policy did not contain a clause which prevented payment if the insured took his own life and therefore the policy should have been payable to the estate of the deceased for the benefit of relatives and creditors. While the House of Lords held the policy valid for certain purposes, the payment of the assured sum to the estate was not sanctioned. Suicide, as a criminal act, would have been committed for the benefit of the wrongdoer's estate and it was not considered desirable that such wrongful acts be permitted or encouraged, even indirectly. Furmston[10] has argued that contracts of insurance which indemnify the insured for his unlawful acts should, in certain instances, be enforceable. Nevertheless, the English case of *Gray v. Barr*[11] takes the rule of public policy even further. The defendant was convicted of manslaughter but was acquitted of murder. The widow of the deceased sued the defendant in negligence for causing the death of her husband. The Court of Appeal refused to allow the defendant to rely on an insurance policy covering "home accidents". This seems to be both undesirable and improper. If the defendant had already been acquitted of the intentional offence of murder the Court of Appeal acted irregularly when it imputed intentional improper conduct to him. However, the rationale for such an extreme position is found in the dictum that "a man is not to be allowed to have recourse to a court of justice to claim a benefit from his crime, whether under a contract or a gift."[12] In cases where no crime has been established, the party pleading illegality will have to discharge the onus of proof. So, in *Gray v. Hibernian Insurance Co.*[13] a publican was acquitted of arson, despite two alleged accomplices giving testimony that the publican had commissioned them to set fire to a public house in order to extract insurance. In the Circuit Court during malicious injuries proceedings the accomplices again gave evidence but meanwhile the publican had died. The Circuit Court judge indicated that the accomplices were probably telling the truth; on this basis an insurance settlement with the widow of the publican was repudiated. In the High Court Barron J. held that the onus rested on the defendant to prove the illegal bargain and that the burden of proof was, on these facts, a heavier standard of proof than the balance of probabilities, given the fact of the initial acquittal and the non-availability of the deceased to rebut the "accomplice" evidence in the later proceedings. The settlement was held to be enforceable.

---

[8] *Re Giles* [1972] Ch. 544; *R. v. N.I.C. ex p. O'Connor* [1980] Crim L.R. 579.
[9] [1937] 2 K.B. 197.
[10] (1966) 16 U. of Toronto L.J. 267.
[11] [1971] 2 Q.B. 554; Fleming (1971) 34 M.L.R. 176. It is clear that this application of public policy prejudices innocent third parties and is undesirable for this reason.
[12] *per* Lord Atkin in *Beresford v. Royal Insurance Co.* above, n.9.
[13] Unreported, High Court, May 27, 1993.

Nor will the courts award a contractual remedy to a plaintiff when enforcement of a contract would, directly or indirectly, lead the defendant into doing something prohibited by the law then being in force. So, in *Namlooze Venootschap De Faam v. Dorset Manufacturing Co.*[14] the plaintiff company sought to recover in an action for goods sold and delivered. While the contract was itself unexceptional, the Emergency Powers (Finance) (No. 7) Ord. 1941 prohibited the transfer of foreign exchange beyond the State without the permission of the Minister for Finance. The contract provided for payment abroad in Dutch guilders but permission was not sought by the defendants for the transfer. Dixon J. felt unable to award the contract price for to do so would be to compel the defendants to do an act prohibited by law and would be contrary to public policy. This reasoning was subsequently approved by the Supreme Court in *Fibretex (Societe Personnes Responsobilite Limite) v. Beleir Ltd.*[15]

However, in *Westpac Banking Corporation v. Dempsey*[16] Morris J. noted that exchange control legislation did not make acts done in contravention of these statutes a nullity. All the legislation did was make payment in circumstances where exchange controls were not satisfied temporarily prohibited. So, upon evidence that exchange control legislation after the decision in *Namlooze* and *Fibretex* had been effectively dismantled, the learned judge permitted enforcement of a foreign judgment obtained in England because Irish enforcement proceedings had started shortly after the removal of all E.C. controls.

## (2) Contracts prejudicial to the administration of justice

It should be noted that a person who protects or shelters a felon is at common law guilty of a criminal offence. Contracts which serve to subvert the cause of justice, while not of themselves criminal, are illegal and cannot give rise to enforceable contractual obligations. In *Brady v. Flood*[17] the defendant was paid a sum of money to get criminal charges of conspiracy dropped. Brady C.B. refused to hear litigation arising from this transaction because it was clearly illegal.

As a matter of public policy it is of the utmost importance that criminal proceedings, once commenced, should be completed without interference from persons who may have some personal interest in the case. Although the courts view agreements to compromise civil suits favourably, agreements relating to a criminal offence are viewed differently. The public interest requires persons accused of criminal offences to be prosecuted, particularly if the offence committed is serious. In the leading English case of *Keir v. Leeman*[18] an agreement to compromise criminal proceedings arising from a riot was held to be illegal; Lord Denman indicated however that if the criminal proceedings commenced can also be the subject of a civil action it will be possible to execute a valid compromise. In cases of assault, which has the dual characteristic of being

---

[14] [1949] I.R. 203.
[15] (1958) 89 I.L.T.R. 141.
[16] Unreported, High Court, November 19, 1992.
[17] (1841) 6 Circuit Cases 309.
[18] (1846) 9 Q.B. 371; *Edgcomb v. Rodd* (1804) 5 East. 294.

a tort and a crime, a compromise of proceedings will be enforceable. The decision in *Nolan v. Shiels*[19] illustrates that this exception will be viewed restrictively. The plaintiff, victim of an indecent assault, was given a cheque for £50 in return for her promise not to prosecute the defendant's friend who had committed the offence. Judge Pigot refused to allow an action on the cheque; he noted that if the offence committed had been the less serious offence of common assault *Keir v. Leeman* would have allowed an action to succeed on the dishonoured cheque. An extremely vivid illustration of this principle is found in *Parsons v. Kirk*.[20] Here a payment of money was agreed in return for an undertaking by a petitioner to withdraw his petition. The petition had questioned the election of a member of Parliament, alleging that there had been bribery of voters. The consideration was held to be void. Clearly the investigation of such an important issue was in the public interest and could not be made the subject of a private bargain.

If no prosecution has commenced and the promissory note is given in exchange for a promise not to take the matter further, the case of *Rourke v. Mealy*[21] suggests that an action may succeed. The plaintiff held a negotiable instrument which he suspected had been forged by a relative of the defendant. He informed the defendant of his suspicions, whereupon the defendant made himself personally liable on the instrument in consideration for the plaintiff's promise not to charge the relative with forgery. The plaintiff was held entitled to sue the defendant on the instrument. This was not an agreement to stifle a prosecution for no proceedings were in progress; nor did the public interest require the truth of an allegation of forgery to be ascertained. Similarly, in the 1885 case of *Re Boyd*,[22] a grocer, who had been both customer and agent of Leatham and Howard, owed them considerable sums of money. They received notice of Boyd's impecuniosity and approached him with a view to settling accounts. Boyd, in the face of pressure, transferred goods and gave an equitable mortgage over property to Leatham and Howard; there was a suspicion on their part that Boyd had embezzled monies belonging to them. The three members of the Court of Appeal allowed an appeal against a finding that this agreement was illegal. There was no agreement to stifle a prosecution; as Sullivan L.C. said: "a threat of prosecution will not invalidate a security thereupon given, if there was no agreement to abandon the prosecution ultimately".[23]

A person who fraudulently abuses judicial proceedings to obtain the benefits of bankrupt status should be brought to justice; an agreement between a creditor and the defrauding debtor, in which proceedings to set aside a discharge as fraudulently obtained are compromised for a promise to pay the debt, is illegal: *Daly v. Daly*.[24] An alternative way of rationalising these decisions is to hold

---

[19] (1926) 60 I.L.T.R. 143.
[20] (1853) 6 Ir.Jur.(N.S.) 168.
[21] (1879) 4 L.R.(Ir.) 166.
[22] (1885) 15 L.R.(Ir.) 521; *Brook v. Hook* (1871) L.R. 6 Ex. 89.
[23] *Ibid.* at 542, citing *Ward v. Lloyd* (1843) 7 Sc. N.R. 499.
[24] (1870) I.R. 5 C.L. 108.

that there is a failure of consideration for an unlawful consideration is not recognised in the eyes of the law.

A rather surprising result was reached in *Bagot v. Arnott*.[25] The plaintiff had lent large sums of money to S, who, in return for a further advance, gave bills of sale to the plaintiff as security, instructing the plaintiff to sell the property covered by the bills to realise the security. Bagot knew that S had committed forgery and would use the advance to flee abroad and avoid prosecution. The goods were seized by other creditors. The plaintiff successfully sued in tort to recover the goods. The Court of Common Pleas held that, notwithstanding Bagot's knowledge that S intended to use part of the funds to evade prosecution, *the purpose* behind the advance was to obtain security for earlier bona fide debts, not to enable S to leave the country. The case is best regarded as an authority on the enforceability of monies lent in order to discharge illegal contracts, considered below.

The common law judges have also viewed contracts which encourage speculative litigation as undesirable. Where the effect of a transaction, such as an assignment of causes of action, is to make litigation uncertain or unworkable, public policy requires these transactions to be void: *Investors Compensation Scheme Ltd v. West Bromwich B.S.*[26] Both the common law and several ancient statutes have sought to suppress arrangements that constitute trafficking in litigation by way of maintenance and champerty. If a third party lends assistance to a litigant in circumstances which are viewed as improper he is guilty of the crime of maintenance. Lord Denning M.R. defined maintenance as

> "Improperly stirring up litigation and strife by giving aid to one party to bring or defend a claim without just cause of excuse."[27]

In *Uppington v. Bullen*[28] Bullen, a solicitor, took a conveyance of lands from Fleming, a client, the conveyance being for £400. However, by a separate agreement it was provided that the £400 would be made up of £100 cash, the balance being the costs of an action being run by Bullen on behalf of Fleming, as plaintiff. The conveyance was set aside, Sugden L.C. observing that this was unlawful maintenance.

Where, however, a person other than the litigant stands to gain from the litigation – by agreeing to pay legal fees in return for an agreed portion of the damages awarded, if any, the contract is described as champertous. Strictly speaking, lawyers who agree to fund litigation on a contingency fee basis are guilty of champerty. In *Littledale v. Thompson*,[29] Whaley was a party to a dispute concerning the right to a clerical living or advowson. Thompson agreed that if Whaley continued to press his claim to the advowson, Thompson would pay

---

[25] (1867) I.R. 2 C.L. 1.
[26] *The Times*, November 11, 1996.
[27] *Re Trepca Mines Ltd.* (N.Z.) [1963] Ch. 199 at 219.
[28] (1842) 2 Dr. & War. 184.
[29] (1878) 4 L.R.(Ir.) 43.

legal fees if Whaley would in turn convey the advowson to him, if successful. Littledale, Whaley's executor, sued Thompson when he failed to pay the fees. The action was dismissed as being part of a champertous contract. An agreement to assist a litigant to recover property, via litigation, is tainted it seems.

In *McElroy v. Flynn*[30] the plaintiff sought a declaration that a contract between himself and the defendants was valid. The plaintiff, a specialist in tracing next-of-kin, contacted the defendants after seeing an advertisement which requested information on the whereabouts of the relatives of a deceased person, the advertisement being placed by the British Treasury Solicitor in an attempt to dispose of the estate: the defendants were cousins of the deceased. The agreement provided that 25 per cent of the shares in the estate would be paid to the plaintiff in consideration of the plaintiff informing the defendants of their entitlement. Blayney J. held the agreement void as being champertous:

> "the real agreement here was that the plaintiff should do more than merely inform the defendants of the name of the deceased. I consider that the plaintiff agreed in addition to assist actively in the recovery of the defendant's shares in the estate and that the agreement accordingly is void."

This distinction between contracting to provide information, which is lawful, and contracting to assist in prosecuting the claim and procuring evidence, which is unlawful, was affirmed by the Supreme Court in *Fraser v. Buckle*.[31] O'Flaherty J. in particular indicated that Irish law had not changed on this point for over a century, and that heir locator contracts, as a particularly speculative enterprise that is clearly open to abuse and fabricated claims, are viewed with hostility in England and in many U.S.A. jurisdictions and are not to be encouraged. However, despite several recent English cases in which legal aid "collateral" contracts have been held unenforceable[32] it is evident that some changes in judicial attitude to these common law policies are taking place to avoid apparently sensible arrangements being invalidated because legal proceedings are in danger of being scandalised.

If however the proceedings cannot be said to be proceedings in a court of law, or are proceedings which are not in the nature of litigation, an agreement in relation to such proceedings may be enforceable. In *Pickering v. Sogex Services (U.K.) Ltd.*[33] a contingency fee payable to surveyors who had achieved a considerable reduction in local authority rate charges was held recoverable because negotiations before a local valuation court were not part of a process of litigation; nor was a district valuation court a court of law. If however,

---

[30] [1991] I.L.R.M. 294. The fraud of the plaintiff in concealing material facts should be seen as an essential element in the ratio of this case.

[31] [1996] 2 I.L.R.M. 34; Capper (1997) 60 M.L.R. 286.

[32] *Joyce v. Kammac* (1988) Ltd., *The Times*, October 16, 1995; *Mohamed v. Alaga & Co.*, unreported, April 2, 1998; *Norglen Ltd. v. Reeds Rains Prudential Ltd.*, *The Times*, December 1, 1997; *Thai Trading Co. (a firm) v. Taylor*, *The Times*, March 6, 1998.

[33] (1982) 263 E.G. 770; *Porter v. Kirtlan* [1917] 2 I.R. 138.

legislation has been passed to relax the prohibition against maintenance and champerty, as is the case in relation to permitting trustees in bankruptcy and liquidators to conclude certain types of agreement enabling litigation to be pursued for the benefit of creditors, some unusual arrangements that are not embraced by the statutory exemption may still fall foul of these common law proscriptions. In *Grovewood Holding plc v. James Capel and Co.*[34] Lightman J. held that while insolvency law allowed the sale of bare causes of action, the sale of interests in the fruits of litigation were still unlawful. In England there is a strong line of authority which has cast doubt on the future of these concepts in a closely regulated modern society.[35] The House of Lords, in *Norglen Ltd. v. Reeds Rains Prudential Ltd.*[36] has held that an assignment of a cause of action by a company to an individual is not to be rendered invalid by virtue of the underlying intention, namely to support the litigation by obtaining legal aid, the view being taken that abuses of legal aid were to be counter-manded by the relevant regulatory agencies, not the common law concept of public policy. Furthermore, in *Thai Trading Co. (a firm) v. Taylor*[37] the Court of Appeal upheld an arrangement to finance litigation on a contingency fee basis as long as the successful solicitor was only seeking normal fee levels and disbursements rather than, say, 50 per cent of damages obtained.

At least in a formal sense, Irish law looks seriously antiquated on these issues.

### (3) Agreements which serve to defraud the Revenue

Attempts are sometimes made to reduce the tax liability of the vendor of real property by misstating the purchase price. In *Starling Securities v. Woods*[38] the plaintiff purchased real property under an oral contract which would have been enforceable had it not become apparent to McWilliam J. that the consideration had been misstated in order to defraud the Revenue Commissioners. Collusive arrangements between employers and employees in which the employee is given "expenses" in order to reduce his liability to P.A.Y.E. or P.R.S.I. contributions are also illegal. Indeed, an employee party to such an agreement has been held unable to recover arrears of wages and unable to bring an action for redundancy payments or unfair dismissal: see the English cases of *Napier v. N.B.A.*[39] and *Tomlinson v. Dick Evans "U" Drive.*[40]

In the first edition of this book the author expressed the hope that the *Tomlinson case* would not be followed in Ireland. The Employment Appeals Tribunal has however adopted the reasoning in *Tomlinson* in *Lewis v. Squash Ireland Ltd.*[41] Lewis was employed as managing director of the respondent

---

[34] [1994] 4 All E.R. 417.
[35] *Giles v. Thompson* [1994] 1 A.C. 142.
[36] *The Times,* December 1, 1997.
[37] *The Times,* March 6, 1998, overruling *Aratra Potato Co. Ltd. v. Taylor* [1995] 4 All. E.R. 695.
[38] Unreported, High Court, May 24, 1977.
[39] [1951] 2 All E.R. 264.
[40] [1978] I.C.R. 638.
[41] [1983] I.L.R.M. 363.

company. Apart from his £14,000 annual salary Lewis was paid annually £2,000, as "expenses". Following his dismissal Lewis sued for compensation for an alleged unfair dismissal under the Unfair Dismissals Act 1977. The Tribunal expressed concern about the £2,000 element in the salary paid to the plaintiff and formed the view that the payment was in fact remuneration, though described as expenses, in order to minimise the P.A.Y.E. obligations of the employee. Applying the earlier English cases, the E.A.T. found that Lewis knew that his salary was being misdescribed and that P.A.Y.E. returns made by the employer would not refer to the £2,000 as remuneration. The scheme was therefore illegal and while severance of the illegal portion of the salary was mathematically possible, the fact that the parties knowingly incorporated this term into the contract made it impossible to sever this illegal term and enforce the rest of the contract. Even though the employee may be seeking to enforce a statutory cause of action and not a common law cause of action i.e. unfair dismissal and not wrongful dismissal – the E.A.T. refused to limit the illegality doctrine, holding that culpability *vis à vis* the contracting parties would no doubt be taken into account by the Revenue Commissioners when they decided whether both parties were to be prosecuted for tax evasion. This writer still feels the *Tomlinson* position is unacceptable; the method of payment in these cases is, generally, the sole responsibility of the employer. The employer can also benefit from the wrongful act – often more so than the employee – for P.R.S.I. contributions, levied as a proportion of the employee's salary are often reduced for the employer as well as the employee, to say nothing of the fact that payments "under the table" may be made to discourage other workers from making claims for increases in salary. The basic fear of comparability claims was alleged to be at the heart of the *Lewis* strategem itself. In the more recent case of *Hayden v. Sean Quinn Properties Ltd.*[42] the employee was given a tax free "expenses" top up, to bring his income up to the level obtained in his previous employment and even though the court seemed to have decided that the employer was the prime mover, the *Napier* case was followed and the defendant was denied a remedy for wrongful dismissal because "the plaintiff allowed himself to agree to something which would benefit the defendant at the expense of the Revenue": *per* Barron J. Finally, the position of the court is fundamentally unfair for the penalty smacks of double jeopardy. A worker who has worked for many years in one job could find statutory redundancy or unfair dismissal rights prejudiced by the fact that the worker recently worked weekends on a "tax-free" basis by being paid out of petty cash.

### (4) Agreements which serve to corrupt public officials

In *Lord Mayor of Dublin v. Hayes*[43] the defendant was appointed Marshall of the City of Dublin, a position which also gave him the post of Registrar of Pawnbrokers. This entitled the defendant to collect fees which he agreed to

---

[42] Unreported, High Court, December 6, 1993.
[43] (1876) 10 I.R.C.L. 226.

transfer to the City Treasurer. It was clear that the appointment was made in exchange for the defendant's promise. The promise was held unenforceable because such a contract would tend to encourage corrupt practices amongst public officials.

The desire to encourage public officials to discharge their duties conscientiously and without hope for a separate reward has been seen as a principle of public policy and morality that transcends national borders. For this reason, an English court has held that a contract governed by English law, but which would have the effect of corrupting public officials of a foreign state, is not enforceable in England in appropriate circumstances.[44]

### (5) *Contracts tending to encourage immorality*

Even if the conduct contemplated by the contract is not itself illegal, as would be the case in an arrangement to procure the seduction of a girl below the age of consent, a contract that promotes some illicit sexual behaviour is illegal. Illicit sexual behaviour simply means sexual intercourse which takes place outside the confines of marriage. The older common law cases draw an important distinction; a contract that contemplates an obligation to provide future sexual intercourse is illegal while a contract that is made in consideration for sexual favours already conferred is not illegal; it may be invalid for want of consideration. This can be overcome if the promise is in a deed under seal. In *Reade v. Adams*[45] a deed was executed providing an annuity to any children of an illicit union should the woman marry another man. The annuity was held enforceable; the deed did not require the woman to continue illicit sexual intercourse in order to retain the annuity: contrast the badly reported case of *Quidihy v. Kelly*.[46]

The English courts, faced with the trend towards stable relationships being formed outside marriage, have decided to respond by permitting one partner to acquire rights in the other partner's property through the doctrines of estoppel, contractual licence, and constructive trust: see in particular *Tanner v. Tanner*[47] and *Pascoe v. Turner*.[48] The words of Sable J. in *Andrews v. Parker*,[49] a Queensland decision, are instructive:

> "Are the actions of people to-day to be judged in the light of the standards of the last century? As counsel for the plaintiff said, cases discussing what was then by community standards sexual immorality appear to have been decided in the days when for the sake of decency the legs of tables wore drapes ... I do not accept that immoral today

---

44 *Lemenda Trading Co. Ltd. v. African Middle East Petroleum Co. Ltd.* [1988] 1 All E.R. 513.
45 (1855) 2 Ir.Jur.(N.S.) 197.
46 (1788) Vern & Scriv. 515.
47 [1975] 1 W.L.R. 1346.
48 [1979] 2 All E.R. 945.
49 [1973] Qd. R. 93.

means precisely what it did in the days of *Pearce v. Brooks*. I am, I believe entitled to look at the word under modern social standards."[50]

This dictum was cited with approval in the New South Wales case of *Seidler v. Schallhofer*.[51] An agreement made between a cohabiting couple, who were contemplating a trial run for a future marriage, involved the joint purchase of a house as joint tenants, the female party borrowing money from the male party to enable her to pay her part of the consideration. The agreement provided that if at the end of a fixed period the parties decided that it was best that they not marry then the male party would buy out the female party's interest. The agreement was upheld. Given that community standards of morality had changed (both statute law and law reform agencies in Australia were referred to so as to provide evidence that quasi-marital relationships are common in Australia) an agreement of this kind was not to be denied legal effect on grounds of public policy.

A prostitute would nevertheless have extreme difficulty in recovering a fee if she performed her part of a bargain to provide sexual favours on credit terms. On the other hand, in the recent Australian case of *Barac v. Farnell*,[52] the plaintiff broke her arm while employed as a receptionist in a brothel. It was held that there was no public policy interest in existence which prevented her from recovering compensation for her injuries. Incidental transactions may also be invalid. In *Pearce v. Brooks*[53] a contract for the hire of a carriage to a prostitute who, to the knowledge of the owner intended to use it in furtherance of her "immoral vocation", was breached when the carriage was returned in a damaged condition. The owner's action failed; his knowledge of the immoral purpose behind the contract meant he "participated" in the illegality. However, in *Armhouse Lee Ltd. v. Chappell*[54] the defendants had provided a telephone sex line service to the public, placing advertisements for their services with the plaintiffs. The defendants refused to pay, calling in aid a defence that to allow recovery would be to encourage sexual immorality over the telephone line at a price. The defence was rejected, the Court of Appeal stating that no general moral code condemned these sex line services. Contracts should be upheld and it was not for judges to impose their standards of morality onto the public in the area of a civil law dispute.

A contract designed to promote unlawful gambling is just as illegal as one aimed at furthering illicit sexual activity. In *Devine v. Scott and Johnston*[55] the plaintiff let premises in Belfast to Johnston who intended to carry on an unlawful bookmaking business. The plaintiff's agent was fixed with knowledge which bound the principal. An action to recover arrears of rent was dismissed.

---

[50] [1973] Qd. R. 93 at 104.
[51] [1982] 2 N.S.W.L.R. 80. Single sex cohabitation agreements are generally unenforceable, but one Californian case goes the other way: *Whorton v. Dillingham* 248 Calif.Rep. 405 (1988).
[52] (1994) 125 A.L.R. 241.
[53] (1866) 1 Ex. 213.
[54] *The Times*, August 7, 1996.
[55] (1931) 66 I.L.T.R. 107.

In contrast, the E.A.T. in *Donohue v. Simonetti*[56] found the applicant to have been dismissed without the requisite notice from her employment as a cashier in an amusement arcade. The Tribunal rejected as a defence the defendant's claim that their gaming activities were probably unlawful because, at that time, litigation concerning illegal gaming machines was pending before the Supreme Court.

Even so, it is submitted that the contract of employment would not be rendered unlawful by the fact that the employer ran his business in such a way as to commit a criminal offence for the 1956 Statute, considered below, does not prohibit contracts of employment but certain activities that may themselves be committed by the employer through the employee. A contract to hire a room for illegal gambling directly raises an illegal mutual purpose; a licensed gaming machine proprietor who employs persons who, following the employer's instructions may break the criminal law, does not necessarily, even indirectly, taint the contract of employment. If however both employer and employee are aware that the employer's business is itself illegal – the employee knows that the employer's business activity or objective is itself contrary to the criminal law – then the employee cannot enforce any rights under that contract. The employee cannot for example recover social security pensions for his illegal employment was not insurable, even if deductions have in fact been made and remitted to the Revenue (*McHugh v. Ministry of Labour for Northern Ireland*)[57] unless there is statutory guidance on this point.

### (6) Contracts to trade with enemies of the State

A contract between nationals and enemy aliens is contrary to public policy. In *Ross v. Shaw*[58] a contract to purchase yarn to be supplied from a mill in Belgium could not be lawfully performed once the mill was occupied by German troops during World War I. The plaintiff's action for non-delivery failed.

### (7) Contracts that breach foreign law

The courts refuse to enforce a contract that is illegal according to the law of the place where it is to be performed. In *Stanhope v. Hospitals Trust Ltd.*[59] the plaintiff in Natal posted Irish sweepstake tickets to the Dublin office where the draw was to take place. The tickets were not included in the draw. Sweepstakes were illegal in Natal; the contract was illegal according to the law of the place where the contract was formed; it was not illegal under Irish law and could be enforceable in Ireland. A joint enterprise to violate foreign and domestic

---

[56] U.D. 639/1981.
[57] [1940] N.I. 174.
[58] [1917] 2 I.R. 367. Related transactions include contracts which involve performance in another country of acts contrary to law in that country or public policy in that country: *Regazzoni v. K C Sethia (1944) Ltd.* [1958] A.C. 301; *Lemenda Trading Co. Ltd. v. African Middle East Petroleum Co. Ltd.* [1988] 1 All E.R. 513; see generally Binchy, *Irish Conflict of Laws* (1988).
[59] (1936) Ir.Jur.Rep. 25.

customs laws will be illegal and unenforceable by both parties: *Whitecross Potatoes v. Coyle.*[60]

## Statutory Illegality

Rules of public policy, whether designed to further social or economic objectives, are articulated by the legislature in the Acts of the Oireachtas or Statutory Instruments. Contractual arrangements that fall foul of these policy objectives may be invalidated by legislation, either expressly or impliedly. The distinction drawn by the courts between a void and an illegal contract is not always relied upon by the legislature.

Legislation expressly proscribes contracts in many situations. In the Republic, the now repealed Moneylenders Acts 1900–1933 made contracts entered into by unlicensed moneylenders unenforceable; charging of compound interest was also unlawful. The Family Home Protection Act 1976, s.3(1), provides "[W]here a spouse, without the prior consent in writing of the other spouse, purports to convey any interest in the family home to any person except the other spouse, then, [subject to legislative exceptions] the purported conveyance shall be void." The Consumer Credit Act 1995 requires hire-purchase contracts to be evidenced in writing; otherwise the transaction is unenforceable; *Henry Forde & Son Finance Ltd. v. John Forde & General Accident Fire & Life Assurance Co.*[61] In employment contracts the Holidays (Employees) Act 1973 makes contracts to give up rights to holiday pay void; so too are contracts to give up rights to minimum periods of notice under the Minimum Notice and Terms of Employment Act 1973, s.5(3), as applied by the Employment Appeals Tribunal in *Foley v. Labtech Ltd.*[62] In this case the employee was entitled to compensation under section 4 following failure by the employer to give the statutory minimum notice, notwithstanding a term in the contract entitling either side to terminate the contract without notice after the first four months of employment. An employer cannot contract with employees to bargain away redundancy payments and compensation for unfair dismissal; attempts to avoid equal pay legislation are also rendered void by legislation – see section 5(1) of the Anti-Discrimination (Pay) Act 1974 and the decision of the Supreme Court in *P.M.P.A. Insurance Co. v. Keenan.*[63]

Licensing legislation of various kinds is a fruitful source of examples of statutory invalidity. Section 36(1) of the Road Transport Act 1933 provided that "it shall not be lawful for any person to enter into an agreement for the carriage for reward of merchandise by any other person unless such other person is a licensee under a merchandise licence." In *O'Shaughnessy v. Lyons*[64]

---

[60] [1978] I.L.R.M. 31.
[61] Unreported, High Court, June 13, 1986.
[62] M 259/1978.
[63] [1983] I.R. 330.
[64] [1957] Ir.Jur.Rep. 90.

the plaintiff agreed to train as well as transport the defendant's greyhounds to and from race meetings. Justice O'Briain refused to permit an action to recover the agreed fee for this work because such a contract was in breach of section 36(1). Similarly, section 11 of the Money Lenders Act 1933 provided protection for lenders which, if not observed, led to the loan being unenforceable as against principal debtor and surety: *Handelman v. Davies*.[65] In contrast however the legislature may expressly provide that, notwithstanding the illegality, the entire contract is not to be rendered unenforceable. This is necessary where the legislation creates rights for individuals who would otherwise have to run the gauntlet of showing that a statute has not worked an implied prohibition. Two examples should suffice. The Consumer Information Act 1978 in section 25 provides: "A contract for the supply of any goods or the provision of any services shall not be void or unenforceable by reason only of a contravention of any provision of the [Merchandise Marks Acts 1887–1970] or this Act." Section 50 of the Social Welfare (Consolidation) Act 1981 enables the Minister for Social Welfare to direct that the employment is to be insurable for the purposes of entitling a worker injured as the result of an accident arising out of, and in the course of, his employment to occupational injuries benefits "notwithstanding that, by reason of a contravention of or non compliance with [a statute] passed for the protection of employed persons or of any class of employed person the contract . . . was void or the employed person was not lawfully employed." This section, in a piece of legislation designed to supplant the old Workmans Compensation Acts, stands in contrast to cases where unlawful employment originally prevented the worker from recovering workmen's compensation should the worker be injured: see *Pountry v. Turton*,[66] applied in *McHugh v. Ministry of Labour for Northern Ireland*.[67]

An Act may go further than rendering an agreement unlawful. In *Gray v. Cathcart*[68] the defendant had taken a lease of an insanitary house in Belfast. The Belfast Corporation Acts made it an offence to occupy insanitary premises. The landlord's action to recover arrears of rent failed; Johnston J. said:

> "Everyone commits a misdemeanour who does any act forbidden by a statute: accordingly when these parties entered into an agreement to occupy a house which had been condemned it was a contract to do that which the statute says you could not do. It was a contract to do an illegal thing, and though the parties might go through the form yet such a contract is not binding and cannot be sued upon."[69]

It does not follow however that simply because conduct is by statute made a criminal offence any contract in which one party acts in breach of such a

---

[65]  (1937) 71 I.L.T.R. 268.
[66]  (1917) B.W.C.L. 601.
[67]  [1940] N.I. 174; *Barac v. Farnell* (1994) 125 A.L.R. 241.
[68]  (1899) 33 I.L.T.R. 35.
[69]  *Ibid.*

statute will automatically render the contract illegal. Johnston J. was in error if the above reasoning is advanced as the *modus operandi* to be invariably followed by the courts. If the statute expressly makes such contracts void the courts have no option but to follow this provision. If however, the legislature has not spelt out the consequences of entering into a contract it is not to be assumed that a contract will be invalid. The courts must ask; does this statute impliedly prohibit a contract of this nature? The court should inquire into the purpose behind the statute; licensing arrangements are often designed simply to raise revenue for the Government or to regulate an industry. Changing social and religious values may lead to a statutory prohibition being changed or repealed; see the 1695 statute forbidding Sunday trading repealed by the Statute Law Revision (Pre–Union Irish Statutes) Act 1962 and *Brady v. Grogan*.[70]

In *Smith v. Mawhood*[71] statute prohibited the sale of tobacco by unlicensed dealers. The plaintiff was an unlicensed dealer and in an action brought against the defendant for tobacco sold and delivered the defendant pleaded that the contract was illegal. Parke B. said "the question is, does the Legislature mean to prohibit the act or not?" The Court of Exchequer held that this was not the legislative intention but the prohibition was merely a revenue–raising measure. In *O'Brien v. Dillon*[72] the exceptional nature of *Smith v. Mawhood* was recognised and the general rule was stated to be, in the words of Lord Ellenborough in *Langton v. Hughes*[73] that, "what is done in contravention of the provisions of an Act of Parliament cannot be made the subject matter of an action."[74]

In fact, even this approach is now recognised as being too broad. If the Act is clear and declares the contract to be illegal, then there is little room for doubt that illegality in the strict sense will be intended: see Megarry J. in *Spector v. Ageda*.[75] But the trend in recent years has been marked by a reluctance to readily infer a legislative intention to prohibit contracts.

The leading English decision on statutory illegality is *St. John Shipping Corporation v. Joseph Rank*.[76] The plaintiffs sued for freight owed by the defendants who had contracted for the plaintiffs to transport their cargo. The master of the vessel overloaded the vessel contrary to statute, calculating that even after paying the maximum fine a profit would still be made by carrying excess cargo. Devlin J. held for the plaintiffs. This contract was lawful at the time it was entered into. The breach of statute, which occurred during performance, did not run foul of any express or implied provision invalidating contracts. The matter is one of construction of the statute; Devlin J. said that the test is not is there an illegal act during performance of the contract but rather, does the illegal performance thereby turn the contract into one which is

---

[70] (1842) Armstrong 278.
[71] (1845) 14 M. & W. 452.
[72] (1858) 9 Ir. C.L.R. 318. For specific statutory control of corruption amongst office-holders, see *Fitzgerald v. Arthure* (1839) 1 Ir.Eq.R. 184.
[73] (1813) 1 M. & S. 593.
[74] *Ibid.* at 596.
[75] [1973] 1 Ch. 30.
[76] [1957] 1 Q.B. 267; *SCF Finance v. Masri (No. 2)* [1987] 2 W.L.R. 58.

prohibited by statute? The test here is determined by reference to the statute in question. If the statute expressly or implicitly prohibits the contract being sued upon here then the intention of the parties is not material to the issue. As Devlin J. pointed out, a contract to actually overload the ship with bunkering may have been illegal but a contract to carry a cargo in circumstances in which the vessel was thus overloaded would not be unlawful. In the latter case of *Archbolds (Freightage) Ltd. v. Spanglett Ltd.*[77] an action brought by the owner of goods for their value when lost while in the possession of the defendant haulier was met with a plea that the contract of carriage was illegal because here the haulier was not suitably licensed under the Road Traffic Acts. The defendants tried to rely on the argument that the contract was illegal under statute but, noting the distinction in *St. John Shipping*, the Court of Appeal rejected the defence. While the Road Traffic Acts may prohibit the use of an unlicensed vehicle on the highway and may indeed prohibit all contracts for the use of unlicensed vehicles it did not follow that statute impliedly prohibits contracts for the carriage of goods by unlicensed vehicles, for this kind of transaction is seen as collateral in character. As Pearce L.J. pointed out, if this defence was to succeed it would affront common sense. A taxidriver operating without a licence could dump a passenger in the middle of nowhere at dead of night and in an action brought by the passenger for breach of contract could plead in defence the "status" of unlicensed carrier. The public policy interest that would be served by such a situation was stated by Pearce L.J. to be non-existent, and such a solution would "injure the innocent, benefit the guilty and put a premium on deceit". This observation was cited with approval by Morris J. in *Westpac Building Corporation v. Dempsey.*[78]

In *Hortensius Ltd. and Durack v. Bishops and Others*[79] the trustees of the Trustee Savings Bank, Dublin, used depositors funds in order to purchase investment opportunities from the plaintiffs, the use of such funds not being a business use recognised by the Trustee Acts 1863–1979. The plaintiffs built upon this fact to argue that a contract and certain mortgages and charges entered into were void and unlawful, as being illegal contracts. Costello J. held that there was no question of statutory illegality on the facts of this case. The prohibition found in section 15 of the Trustee Act 1863 did not make illegal contracts for the purchase of loans, it prohibited the trustees from entering into such contracts. Costello J. held that there was an important distinction between a statutory provision which made it illegal for a trustee to enter into certain types of contract and a statutory provision which made certain kinds of contract illegal. The prohibition in section 15 was in the former category and the intention of Parliament was to make trustees liable in the law relating to breach of trust and not make any such contracts entered into by a trustee in breach of statutory duty. As Costello J.'s approach illustrates, the issue is essentially one of construction of the statute in the light of surrounding

---

[77] [1961] 1 Q.B. 374; *Cotronic (U.K.) v. Denzione* [1991] B.C.C. 200.
[78] Unreported, High Court, November 19, 1992.
[79] [1989] I.L.R.M. 294.

circumstances; the courts lean against finding that the Act, on its construction, has this effect because it means treating persons who intend to break the law in the same way as persons who do so unwittingly. The possibility that a lawbreaker will not only be fined but lose the fruits of a contract also contributes towards a restrictive approach to the implied prohibition problem; such a conclusion punishes a person twice over.

The Supreme Court's decision in *Gavin Lowe Ltd. v. Field*[80] is instructive. The plaintiffs sued on a dishonoured cheque which had been given to them by the defendants who had purchased a cow from the plaintiff. The beast was bought after it had been put on the market in such a way as to be "exposed for sale"; Public Health legislation made it an offence to "expose for sale" a diseased animal; the cow had later to be destroyed because it was tubercular. The statute did not in terms make it an offence to sell diseased livestock; it was therefore possible to buy cattle that were diseased as long as the transaction did not involve an act of "exposure for sale". The plaintiff argued that he was entitled to recover on the dishonoured cheque; he argued that the purpose behind the legislation was not to make contracts for the sale of diseased live-stock illegal but to protect the public health by making it an offence to expose for sale diseased meat. The majority of the Supreme Court accepted this argument and permitted recovery on the cheque. Sullivan C.J. held that because the Acts did not make it an offence to sell, the defence of illegality would only succeed if the unlawful act of exposure and the sale amounted "to a unity of design". In the Chief Justice's view this was not so. Murnaghan and Geoghegan JJ. concurred. A more satisfactory view is advanced by the dissenting members of the Supreme Court. Meredith J. held it to be "an absurdity" to reach such a conclusion; the prohibition of an act preparatory to sale was designed to preclude the sale itself from being legal. "Prohibition of the bud is then prohibition of the blossom."[81] O'Byrne J. agreed: "It seems difficult to justify such a construction as would recognise the validity of a contract arising out of exposure for sale, though the exposure itself is made a criminal offence."[82]

The "unity of design" approach favoured by the majority is not of any great value for it seems to this writer to be far too vague. A more recent approach to problems of statutory illegality, in contrast, however, is blessedly simple for it requires the legislature to spell out the implications of a statute for any contracts that may arise in the course of some illegal activity. In *Yango Pastoral Co. Property v. First Chicago (Australia) Ltd.*[83] a mortgage granted in favour of the mortgagee bank by the mortgagor was alleged to be void because the bank, as an unlicensed body, was committing criminal offences for which a daily maximum fine could be imposed upon conviction. The mortgagor claimed the mortgagee could not enforce the security. The High Court of Australia rejected this, even though the activity prohibited was clearly

---

[80] [1942] I.R. 86.
[81] *Ibid.* at 100.
[82] *Ibid.* at 107.
[83] (1978) 139 C.L.R. 411; *Fitzgerald v. FJ Leonhardt Property* (1997) 7 A.L.J.R. 653.

central and not collateral to the bank's primary trading activity – lending money on security. Mason and Aickin JJ. opined that there is much to be said for the view that once a statutory penalty has been provided for an offence the role of the common law in determining the legal consequences of the commission of the offence is thereby diminished. This approach was recently endorsed by Leggatt J. in *Stewart v. Oriental Fire and Marine Insurance Co.*[84] but this decision has been overruled in *Phoenix General Insurance Company of Greece S.A. v. Administratia Asigurarilor de Stat,*[85] a decision that must now be regarded as providing the definitive statement on how pleas of statutory illegality must be approached. The Insurance Companies Act 1974, intended as a piece of protective legislation, required the insurance business to be carried on only by authorised insurers. Phoenix, prior to January 1978, were authorised insurers. However, in that year, new regulations were introduced which reclassified the various kinds of insurance. These regulations were very complex and Phoenix continued to underwrite in the same way. Phoenix entered into reinsurance contracts with the defendants and when claims were submitted by Phoenix, the defendants refused to pay. The defendants claimed that the contracts of reinsurance were illegal because Phoenix had not obtained the necessary authorisation. The Court of Appeal, however, held that under transitional arrangements Phoenix were, in fact, authorised, reversing Hobhouse J. on this point. The Court of Appeal went on to consider what the position would have been had the insurer not been authorised. The Court of Appeal noted that public policy would be best served by holding that the illegality would not render the contract void because the purpose behind the legislation was very much one of protecting the unwitting consumer who would not be in a position to know if the insurer was authorised or not, but in the context of this statute there was no room for public policy. The unilateral prohibition of unauthorised insurers did not simply prohibit the business of effecting contracts of insurance for which the insurer had no authority, it extended to "carrying out contracts of insurance". As Kerr L.J. noted,

> "this extension of prohibition has the unfortunate effect that contracts made without authorisation are prohibited by necessary implication and therefore void. Since the statute prohibits the insurer from carrying out the contract (of which the most obvious example is paying claims) how can the insured require the insurer to do an act which is expressly forbidden by statute."[86]

This case illustrates how poor drafting can unwittingly subvert the very objective behind a statute itself. Fortunately, this case is, as the Court of Appeal observed, a decision based very much on its own facts, and most statutes, when not expressly providing for the consequences of illegality on contracts, do

---

[84] [1984] 3 W.L.R. 741.
[85] [1987] 2 All E.R. 152.
[86] *Ibid.* at 176.

leave room for a more purposive interpretation, as in *Archbolds (Freightage) Ltd. v. Spanglett Ltd.*[87] In *Marrinan v. O'Haran*[88] Pringle J. followed the *Spanglett* case. The issue before the Court in *Marrinan v. O'Haran* was whether the plaintiff would be prevented from obtaining a commission payable for services rendered in introducing to the defendant a property owner who gave the defendant sole agency rights to sell property which the owner was anxious to sell. The defendant was not a licensed house agent, and was thus acting contrary to section 7 of the Auctioneers and House Agents Act 1947 which provides that it is a criminal offence to carry on, hold out or represent oneself as a house agent, or act as a house agent without a licence. Pringle J. indicated that he would not have prevented the plaintiff from recovering "as there was no evidence that he knew that the defendant had no auctioneer's licence and the contract itself was not expressly forbidden by statute." Even if the party pleading illegality can point to some default by the defendants or their agents or employees, the protection afforded by statute and the underlying policy will be closely scrutinised and, in the absence of a clear express prohibition *of the contract* under statute, the underlying policy will be given effect.[89]

## Gaming and Wagering Contracts

The Gaming and Lotteries Acts 1956–1986 are the most important Acts regulating the way in which gambling is carried on within the Republic. While an analysis of this legislation is outside the scope of this book, section 36 of the 1956 Act governs the consequences of the contractual relationship created by gaming and wagering.

### (1) Wagering

The legislation does not define a wager but case law has produced the following definition, taken from Cheshire, Fifoot and Furmston's *Law of Contract:*

> "Staking something of value upon the result of some future uncertain event such as a horse race, or upon the ascertainment of the truth concerning some past or present event, such as the population of London, with regard to which the wagering parties express opposite views."[90]

It is of the essence of a wager that one party is to win and the other to lose upon the determination of the event. For this reason a bet placed with "the Tote", that is, the Racing Board established by the Totaliser Act 1929, is not a

---

[87] [1961] 1 Q.B. 374.
[88] Unreported, High Court, June 17, 1971.
[89] *Hughes v Asset Managers plc* [1995] 3 All E.R. 669.
[90] 13th ed., p. 334.

wager. This was decided by Pringle J. in *Duff v. Racing Board*.[91] Because the Racing Board are legally bound to pay all the money received to successful ticketholders it follows that the Board can neither win nor lose.

English case law establishes that multipartite arrangements are not wagers: *Ellesmere v. Wallace*.[92] The Alberta case of *Breitmeier v. Batke*[93] on the other hand suggests that an arrangement between three persons may be a wager. Fridman, author of the leading Canadian text, suggests that the Canadian authority is to be preferred for "the true test surely is whether one person can win and others lose." Irish cases should follow this test in my view. Nevertheless a tripartite wager may often be a lottery.

Trading ventures which induce subscribers to join a venture may fall foul of the Pyramid Selling Act 1980 and a number of recent highly publicised cases in England, such as *One Life Ltd. v. Roy*,[94] the *Titan* case[95] and *Re Vanilla Accumulation Ltd.*[96] indicate that many dubious product marketing ventures are illegal. Indeed, the Director of Consumer Affairs has warned Irish consumers to avoid a particular International Pyramid Scheme called Golden Circle.[97] Even apparently innocent promotional ventures may fall foul of the law against unlawful lotteries. In *Flynn v. Denieffe and Independent Newspapers*[98] the Supreme Court struck down a game of no skill as being a lottery, notwithstanding that all participants did not have to purchase a newspaper and thus they did not provide a payment when playing the "Scoop" game.

Many transactions resemble a wager; a contract of insurance is "a bet on the outcome of a future uncertain event". It is not a wager if the assured has an insurable interest in the subject matter; to insure a ship's cargo against destruction during a voyage is a valid contract of insurance if the assured has an interest in the cargo. It is a wager if not.[99]

Stockbroking arrangements often fall into the category of wagers. "Contracts for differences" involve an agreement between two persons who agree that they will ascertain the difference in price of certain shares on one day and their price at a later date. If the parties do not intend that the shares will be purchased the "contract for differences" will be void. Similarly in *Byers v. Beattie*[100] the plaintiffs agreed to purchase and sell shares which were owned by the defendant. The agreement provided that if the price for which the shares were later sold

---

[91] Unreported, High Court, November 19, 1971 applying *Tote Investors Ltd. v. Smoker* [1968] 1 Q.B. 509.

[92] [1929] 2 Ch. 1.

[93] (1966) 56 W.W.R. 678.

[94] *The Times,* July 12, 1996.

[95] *Re Senator Hanseatische Verwattungsgesellschaft* [1997] 1 W.L.R. 515.

[96] *The Times,* February 24, 1998.

[97] *The Irish Times,* March 21, 1998.

[98] *Irish Times Law Report,* February 23, 1993, following *Imperial Tobacco Ltd. v. A.G.* [1981] A.C. 718.

[99] See *Church and General Insurance Co. v. Connolly and McLoughlin,* unreported, High Court, May 7, 1981; *Fuji Finance v Aetna Life Insurance* [1996] 4 All E.R. 608 illustrates how new insurance products must be carefully structured to avoid this trap.

[100] (1867) I.R. 1 C.L. 209.

was greater than that paid by the defendants, the defendants would pay the difference plus any charges and commission to the plaintiffs. The plaintiffs sued for sums due under this agreement. The arrangement was held a wager.

### (2) Gaming

At common law gaming was legal if the element of chance was negligible and the outcome of the game turned upon the skill of the players. The present legislation defines "gaming" as "playing a game (whether of skill or chance or partly of skill and partly of chance) for stakes hazarded by the players."[101] Section 4 of the 1956 Act makes gaming unlawful if:

(a) the chances of all of the players, including the banker, are not equal; or
(b) if a portion of the stakes are retained by the banker otherwise than as winnings; or
(c) gaming is conducted by way of slot machines.

Later sections make gaming at a circus, travelling show, carnival, public house, amusement hall and funfair lawful gaming in specific instances.

### (3) Lotteries

Section 21(1) of the Gaming and Lotteries Act 1956 provides "[n]o person shall promote or assist in promoting a lottery." Private lotteries, lotteries at dances and concerts, carnivals and other events, as well as lotteries under permit or licence are lawful. Lotteries on football games are outside the terms of the 1956 Act; see section 32 of the Betting Act 1931. The Irish Hospitals Sweepstakes before its dissolution,[102] was a lawful agreement under The Public Hospitals Act 1933 and was enforceable in the Republic's courts *(Stanhope v. Hospitals Trust Ltd. (No. 2)*[103] as is the National Lottery: see National Lottery Act 1986, section 32.

## Consequences of a Gaming or Wagering Contract.

Section 36 of the Gaming and Lotteries Act 1956 provides:

"(1) Every contract by way of gaming or wagering is void.
(2) No action shall lie for the recovery of any money or thing which is alleged to be won or have been paid upon a wager or which has been deposited to abide the event on which a wager is made.
(3) A promise express, or implied, to pay any person any money paid by him under or in respect of a contract to which this section applies or

---

[101] 1956 Act, s.2. On netting contracts see the Netting of Financial Contracts Act 1995 discussed by Foy in (1996) 3 C.L.P. 72 and Chap. 5 of Foy, *The Capital Market, Irish and International Laws and Regualtions* (1998). The Act is fully annotated by Hoy in *Irish Current Law Statutes Annotated.*
[102] By the Public Hospitals (Amendment) Act 1990.
[103] (1936) Ir.Jur.Rep. 25.

to pay any money by way of commission, fee, reward or otherwise in respect of the contract or of any services connected with the contract is void and no action shall lie for the recovery of any such money."

Subsection 4 allows the winner of a lawful game to sue for the prize provided it is not a stake.

The section is based in part upon section 18 of the Gaming Act 1845, which is repealed in Ireland, in the Schedule to the 1956 Act. The following points must be made about the meaning of the 1956 Act, as gathered from litigation on section 18 of the Gaming Act 1845.

By declaring every contract by way of gaming or wagering void the Oireachtas has reaffirmed that, while the transaction is not illegal, no rights can accrue to either party. Thus in *Pujolas v. Heaps*[104] a bookmaker, licensed under betting shops legislation, refused to pay out to a punter who had won his bet. The punter was unable to recover his winnings in an action. If the loser pays by cheque and then cancels it, no action will lie on the dishonoured cheque. The legislation confers a privilege upon the loser; if he choses to waive this privilege by paying the winner, the loser has no right to recover the money paid; see also the badly reported case of *Phelan v. Stewards of the Kilmacthomas Races*.[105]

The opening limb of section 36(2) produces an interesting problem of construction. One view of this subsection holds that it adds nothing to section 36(1); as a result, a subsequent contract to pay the sum due on a wager may be enforceable if given for good consideration. In *O'Donnell v. O'Connell*[106] the defendant owed debts to the plaintiff, a bookmaker. The plaintiff said he would list the defendant as a defaulter, which would have damaged his creditworthiness at the track. The plaintiff compromised his admittedly hopeless action on the debt and refrained from listing the defendant in return for a promissory note. The plaintiff successfully sued on the promissory note. The trial judge, Molony C.J. following the now overruled[107] English Court of Appeal decision in *Hyams v. Stuart King*[108] held that the 1845 Act did not invalidate an action brought on a promise given for some act of forbearance. The better view of the legislation is that subsequent transactions are rendered unenforceable by what is now section 36(2). The House of Lords so ruled in *Hill v. William Hill (Park Lane) Ltd.*[109] It is to be hoped that the flagrant evasion of the policy underlying the Act leads to a future Supreme Court overruling *O'Donnell v. O'Connell*. In any event, *O'Donnell v. O'Connell* is certainly inconsistent with two earlier Irish cases: *O'Donnell v. O'Sullivan*,[110] and *Walker v. Brown*.[111]

---

[104]  (1938) 72 I.L.T.R. 96.
[105]  (1896) I.C.T. 36.
[106]  (1923) 57 I.L.T.R. 92.
[107]  In *Hill v. William Hill (Park Lane) Ltd.* [1949] A.C. 530.
[108]  [1908] 2 K.B. 696.
[109]  [1949] A.C. 530.
[110]  (1913) 47 I.L.T.R. 253.
[111]  (1897) 31 I.L.T.R. 138.

The second part of section 36(2) has also received a narrow interpretation. At first sight it should mean that where money has been deposited with a stakeholder no action will succeed. In *Graham v. Thompson*[112] money was deposited with a stakeholder. The plaintiff repudiated the agreement before the money was paid but after the result of the event was known. It was not clear whether the plaintiff was the winner or loser. It was held that whenever the loser of an illegal wager repudiates at any time before the wager is paid he can recover his part of the stake in an action for money had and received. The second part of section 36(2) prevents any person, whether he be winner or loser, from recovering the other person's part of the stake: *McElwain v. Mercer.*[113] This interpretation of the words of section 18 of the 1845 Act has carried over into the 1956 Act as the case of *Crean v. Deane*[114] shows.

Section 36(3) deals with the case of a contractual arrangement in which a principal engages an agent to place bets on his behalf. If the agent advances his own money to cover the stake and he is promised, expressly or impliedly, recompense, he cannot recover in an action against the principal. Nor is the principal liable to pay a commission, fee or reward to the agent. Section 36(3) substantially recites section 1 of the Gaming Act 1892, which prevents the ordinary rule that an agent is liable to be indemnified for all lawful acts from extending into wagering transactions.

On the other hand, the principal may have the right to recover if the agent places the bet but refuses to pay over the winnings: *Griffith v. Young.*[115] If the agent fails to place the bet and the wager would have been successful the principal has no remedy for breach of contract: *Cohen v. Kittell.*[116]

If money is paid to a stakeholder the stakeholder becomes an agent for both parties; as we have seen the stake is recoverable if the agent's authority to pay is revoked before payment is made. The agent will be liable if he then pays the stake to the other party. No action will lie for the recovery of sums actually paid to the winner, in breach of the stakeholder's authority. In *Toner v. Livingston,*[117] A made a bet with B regarding the weight of a bullock owned by A. A deposited £20 with a stakeholder to abide the result. The bullock was never weighed but the stakeholder paid the £20 to B. A sued B for money had and received; the action failed, being caught by the words of what is now section 36(3) of the 1956 Act.

## Money lent for gaming and wagering

In *Anthony v. Shea,*[118] Anthony lent Shea £43 knowing Shea was to use it for gaming. Even though it was not proved that the money was so used Anthony was unable to recover from Shea's estate. The gaming transaction in question

---

[112]   (1867) I.R. 2 C.L. 64.
[113]   (1859) 9 I.C.L.R. 13.
[114]   [1959] I.R. 347.
[115]   (1810) 12 East 513.
[116]   (1889) 22 Q.B. 680.
[117]   (1896) 30 I.L.T.R. 80.
[118]   (1951) 86 I.L.T.R. 29.

may have been lawful gaming but this point was not made; the English textbooks state that money lent for lawful gaming is recoverable.[119]

*Cheques and other securities.*

The party who takes a negotiable instrument which has been given for a gambling debt can sue upon it if he can show he is a "holder in due course".[120]

# The Consequences of Common Law and Statutory Illegality

The common law rules which circumscribe the remedies available to persons who have entered a contract which is illegal at common law also apply where the contract is illegal under statute. Legislators do not frequently resolve the problems which arise here by stipulating that such and such an illegal contract is to give rise to the following consequences. This often leads to unfortunate results as we shall see. Three situations must be distinguished:

*(1) Where the contract is unlawful on its face*

A contract which creates an illegal consideration is unlawful on its face. When the plaintiff in *Littledale v. Thompson*[121] promised to convey a right to an advowson in return for the defendant's promise to pay the costs of the plaintiff's litigation the contract was champertous on its face. All parties to such an agreement are prevented from suing to enforce any promise under that contract. If a contract is illegal on its face the contract is said to be illegal at its inception. In *Gray v. Cathcart*[122] the landlord was held unable to recover arrears of rent because the insanitary premises could not be lawfully let. Similarly, under section 44 of the Land Act 1936, a sub-lease of certain lands could only be lawful if the consent of the Land Commission was obtained. No such consent was sought or given. The landlord was held unable to recover arrears of rent because the lease was illegal; the landlord sought to avoid the illegality by invoking estoppel, but the High Court held that estoppel cannot be used to avoid an illegal contract.[123] The leading case is *Murphy & Co. Ltd. v. Crean*.[124] The plaintiffs agreed to lease premises to Crean who was to carry on the business of publican, taking all the stout needed for this purpose from the plaintiffs. The licence necessary was transferred, with the consent of the local justices, to the defendant. The contract however also contained a provision which later obliged the defendant to transfer the licence to any person in

---

[119] See Cheshire, Fifoot and Furmston's *Law of Contract* (13th ed.), pp. 349–351, especially *CHT Ltd. v. Ward* [1965] 2 Q.B. 63. The Gaming Act 1892 was repealed by the 1956 Act thus clearing the way for an application in Ireland of the dictum in *CHT Ltd. v. Ward* [1965] 2 Q.B. 63.

[120] Bills of Exchange Act 1882, s.29(1).

[121] (1878) 4 L.R.(Ir.) 43.

[122] (1899) 33 I.L.T.R. 35.

[123] *Dempsey v. O'Reilly* (1958) Ir.Jur.Rep. 75; *O'Kane v. Byins* [1897] 2 I.R. 591.

[124] [1915] 1 I.R. 111.

another public house nominated by the plaintiffs. Irish licencing legislation does not permit transferability of a liquor licence to a person not in occupation of the premises. This rule is designed to prevent someone whom the licensing justices have deemed a fit person from transferring the licence to someone who may not be of good character. This illegal covenant rendered the whole agreement unenforceable. The plaintiffs were held unable to prevent the defendant from selling stout manufactured by another company. The Supreme Court, in *Macklin & McDonald v. Greacen & Co.,*[125] reaffirmed this general approach by refusing to grant specific performance in relation to a contract for the sale of a liquor licence, the sale to be independent from the sale of premises. The leading English case of *Re Mahmoud and Hispani*[126] shows that in this situation the rule can operate harshly. The plaintiff agreed to sell linseed oil to the defendant who falsely represented that he, the defendant, had a licence to purchase the oil. Such a licence was necessary under statute. The defendant refused to take delivery and was sued for non-acceptance. The action failed. The innocent party was held unable to sue on a contract unlawful at its inception. *Re Mahmoud* was followed in the Queensland case of *Olsen v. Mikkelsen.*[127] The plaintiff purchased seeds from the defendant who supplied them without giving an invoice, an offence under statute. The seeds failed to germinate. The contract was held illegal at formation so the plaintiff could not sue for breach of warranty. *Anderson v. Daniel*[128] also points to how far-reaching statutory illegality can be. The plaintiff sued for the price of fertilisers sold and delivered to the defendant. The defendant pleaded non-compliance with legislation which made it necessary to deliver to the buyer a notice indicating the composition of the fertilisers. The Court of Appeal held that the legislation in question was not revenue legislation, and had as its objective the protection of the public. There was no legislative basis for upholding the vendor's submission that analysis was on these facts extremely burdensome and thus, an apparently unmeritorious purchaser was able to retain the goods without having to pay for them.

There are comparatively few Irish cases in which a statute has been held to declare that a particular transaction is not to be actionable. In *Irvine v. Teague*[129] loans made to the defendant and secured by way of mortgage were held to infringe the provisions of section 24 of the Charitable Loan Societies Act 1843 which declared that "it shall not be lawful" to lend more than £10 to one borrower at one time. This infringement prevented the Treasurer of the Society from enforcing the mortgage.

In the English case of *Ashmore v. Dawson*[130] the plaintiffs owned a piece of heavy engineering equipment which had to be transported by lorry. The defendant hauliers agreed to transport the machinery, a perfectly valid agreement. The defendants, to cut costs, intended to use a particular lorry which

---

125 [1983] I.R. 61.
126 [1921] 2 K.B. 716.
127 [1937] Qd. R. 275.
128 [1924] 1 K.B. 138.
129 (1898) 32 I.L.T.R. 109.
130 [1973] 1 W.L.R. 828.

did not meet the capacity requirements set out in legislation. The plaintiff's transport manager was present when the machinery was loaded onto the vehicle; he was held to know that the statutory restrictions were being broken. In the view of the majority of Lords Justices in the Court of Appeal the knowledge and acquiescence of the transport manager meant that he "participated" in the illegal performance. Phillimore L.J. went further; he found that the contract was deliberately given to the defendants knowing that it would be performed in this manner, rendering the agreement unlawful at its inception. The decision in *Devine v. Scott and Johnston*[131] provides another Irish example of this type of illegal contract.

### (2) Where the contract is lawful on its face but one person only intends to perform unlawfully

Again, *Ashmore v. Dawson*, above, is in point. Had the transport manager not been present or if it had been shown that he did not know of the restrictions on transporting goods by lorry the plaintiffs would have been able to sue on the contract for the rule is that the party intending illegal performance is unable to avoid the rule, *ex turpi causa non oritor actio*, but the innocent party, that is a party who does not know or participate in the illegality, has the full range of remedies available for him because, from his perspective, the contract was lawful. The burden of proving a joint illegal intent lies upon the party pleading the illegality.

The decision of Finlay P. in *Whitecross Potatoes v. Coyle*[132] emphasises the importance of distinguishing contracts which one party only intends to perform illegally. Coyle, a farmer in Meath agreed to sell potatoes to the plaintiffs, a company in England who intended to use the potatoes in their chain of fish and chip shops. Each party suspected that the U.K. and Irish governments were about to impose restrictions on the export and import of potatoes. The agreement provided that if this occurred a higher price would be payable. This clause was consistent with two modes of performance; the plaintiffs explained that Coyle was going to purchase potatoes in Northern Ireland and deliver these to them, thereby getting around the problem of import restrictions. This would be perfectly lawful. The defendant however explained that he intended no such thing; he intended to smuggle the potatoes into Northern Ireland, the higher price covering transport costs. Finlay P. held that Coyle alone intended to perform the contract in an illegal manner. The plaintiffs were therefore entitled to recover for non-delivery of the potatoes.

These distinctions are not always drawn. In *Martin v. Galbraith*[133] the Supreme Court had to consider whether an employee could recover for overtime worked in breach of legislation limiting hours worked in excess of 48 hours a week. The majority of the Supreme Court held such an action must

---

[131] (1931) 66 I.L.T.R. 107.
[132] [1978] I.L.R.M. 31.
[133] [1942] I.R. 37.

fail; statute made it an offence for the employer to require this work to be done, although the employee did not commit an offence. Murnaghan J. stated: "parties to a contract which produces illegality under a statute passed for the benefit of the public cannot sue upon the contract unless the legislature has clearly given a right to sue."[134] This analysis is too simplistic for if the contract is illegal in relation to overtime an employee could not sue to recover unpaid wages earned during the 48-hour period of lawful employment! The correct questions to ask would be, have the parties agreed at formation that unlawful overtime would be worked? If not, has the employer exacted unlawful performance from the employee who knew of the breach of statute? Are the parties equally at fault?

## Judicial Attitudes to Illegality

The general attitude of the courts when faced with an illegal transaction was succinctly stated by Lindley L.J. in *Scott v. Brown Doering*,[135] an English case followed in several Irish decisions:

> "*Ex turpi causa non oritur actio* . . . No court ought to enforce an illegal contract or allow itself to be made the instrument of enforcing obligations alleged to arise out of a contract or transaction which is illegal if the illegality is duly brought to the notice of the court and if the person invoking the aid of the court is himself implicated in the illegality."[136]

It is clear that damages will not be awarded for breach of an illegal contract; indeed, in *McDonnell v. Grand Canal Co.*[137] an injunction preventing a company from carrying into effect an intention to enter an illegal contract was issued. It is less clear why the courts go further by preventing restitutionary relief in cases where property has been transferred as part of the illegal transaction; Lindley L.J. said in *Scott v. Brown Doering* that any legal rights a party has apart from the illegal contract may be recognized. The case of *Brady v. Flood*[138] suggests that ownership alone may not be enough to permit restitution. Brady sued Flood for the recovery of banknotes which Flood had been given in return for a promise to get criminal charges against Brady's sons dropped. This agreement was illegal as interfering with the administration of justice. Brady C.B. said: "I will not try this case. You are parties to an illegal contract and whoever has got the money I will allow him to keep it."[139]

The judges shelter behind another Latin maxim: *In pari delicto potior est conditio possidentis*, which means that where both parties are equally in fault

---

[134] *Ibid.* at 54.
[135] [1892] 2 Q.B. 724.
[136] *Ibid.* at 726.
[137] (1853) 3 Ir.Jur.(N.S.) 197.
[138] (1841) 6 Circuit Cases 309.
[139] (1841) 6 Circuit Cases 309 at 311. See also *Taylor v. Chester* (1869) L.R. 4 Q.B. 309.

the condition of the possessor is best. Nevertheless, there are signs that if the contract is illegal and the illegality is neither socially nor morally reprehensible – as in a case where the contract is illegal because one party fails to get a licence or complete a document – restitution and/or damages may be ordered. See the controversial case of *Bowmaker v. Barnet's Instruments*.[140] Here Smith sold three machine tools under a contract to the plaintiffs, who then let them to the defendants on hire-purchase. The initial sale to the plaintiffs was illegal. The defendants wrongly sold machine tools one and three to third parties and failed to pay hire charges due under the contract in respect of machine tool two. The plaintiffs sued for conversion; the defendants resisted the action on the ground that the initial illegal contract also attached to the hiring contracts. The Court of Appeal noted that neither the plaintiff nor the defendant were aware of the technical illegality but there was an illegality. Nevertheless, the action in conversion succeeded. The wrongful sale of tools one and three had the effect in law of terminating the defendant's right to possession and, because it was conceded that ownership passed to the plaintiff from Smith notwithstanding the initial illegality, the plaintiffs could, fortunately, rely on their rights of ownership and were not constrained to plead the illegal contract. Du Parq L.J. indicated that there was no public policy objection to allowing the owner of goods to recover in conversion, even if there were unlawful dealings in the goods at some time in the past. *Bowmakers Ltd. v. Barnets Instruments* is a difficult case because the agreement in respect of machine tool two was not concluded with a clause giving an automatic right of repossession to the owner for non-payment of hire charges, and non-payment of rental is not a basis for liability in conversion *simpliciter*. Hamson[141] has argued that *Bowmakers Ltd. v. Barnet Instruments* would, on this point, now permit recovery of possession under an illegal lease for non-payment of rent, as long as a clause to that effect were contained in the lease. *Bowmakers Ltd.* has its defenders both in respect of the practicality and justice of the result and legal principle.[142]

The *in pari delicto* rule has unfortunate consequences. First of all, the party responsible for the illegality may use it to his advantage in circumstances which are quite unfair. In *Daly v. Daly*[143] the defendant, a discharged insolvent debtor, had obtained his discharge through fraud. The plaintiff, one of his creditors, learned of the fraud and upon confronting the defendant obtained a promise that the defendant would pay the initial debt in full, even though the discharge extended to this sum. The plaintiff dropped proceedings to set the discharge aside for fraud. The action on the new promise failed.

The application of the rules on illegality may conflict with other policy considerations, particularly when a statute is the source of the initial prohibition. In *Martin v. Galbraith*[144] the statute prohibiting excessive overtime was

---

140  [1945] K.B. 65.
141  (1949) 10 C.L.J. 249.
142  *e.g.* Coote (1972) 35 M.L.R. 38.
143  (1870) I.R. 5 C.L. 108.
144  [1942] I.R. 37.

designed to ensure, *inter alia*, the payment of wages at fair rates to employees. As O'Byrne J., dissenting, pointed out, the interpretation placed on the legislation defeated the intention of the Oireachtas. A similar United States decision has been criticised by Furmston.[145] The judges are often aware that the effect of holding the contract to be illegal is to prejudice the very class of persons that public policy has identified as worthy of protection. In *Phoenix General Insurance Co. of Greece SA v. Administratia Asigurarilor de Stat*[146] Kerr L.J. stressed that each case must turn upon distinct factual and policy considerations.

> "one merely has to contrast moneylending contracts with a contract of insurance to see why it is good public policy to refuse to enforce the former but bad policy in the case of the latter. In both cases the legi- lation is designed to protect the customer, but the protection he requires is wholly different. In cases of moneylending the contract leaves virtually every subsequent obligation to be performed by the borrower, whereas in contracts of insurance the position is precisely the opposite."[147]

Kerr L.J. went on to contrast food legislation which is also intended to protect consumers: if food is purchased on the foot of an illegal contract and the food causes illness, the policy of the law would also be subverted if there could be no liability in contract due to illegality. However, as in *Phoenix* itself, the statute, in cases of express prohibition leave no room for flexibility. In cases of implied prohibition under statute, or instances of common law illegality, many judges are alive to this issue. One legislative improvement that could be considered by the Oireachtas would be to vest in the judiciary a general residual discretion to depart from the *ex turpi causa* rule, where an application produces unfortunate consequences, as it did in the *Phoenix* case.

## Exceptions to Ex Turpi Causa and In Pari Delicto

### (1) Where the parties are not equally at fault

The first "exception" is not really an exception at all. In the Northern Ireland case of *Sumner v. Sumner*[148] Megaw J. accepted that if one party to the illegal contract entered into the bargain because of fraud, duress or undue influence on the part of the other he may have a remedy. The courts will generally permit recovery of money paid. So too, participation in the illegal contract will not be a bar to relief if the participator can show that he was a member *of the class* which the statute was designed to protect: see the old English case of *Browning v. Morris*.[149] In *Martin v. Galbraith*,[150] Meredith J. dissenting, was in favour of holding the

---

[145] (1966) 16 U.T.L.J. 267 at 288, criticising *Coules v. Pharris* (1933) 250 N.W. 404.
[146] [1987] 2 All E.R. 152; *Byrne v. Rudd* [1920] 2 I.R. 20.
[147] *Ibid.* at 175.
[148] (1935) 69 I.L.T.R. 101.
[149] *Browning v. Morris* (1778) 2 Comp. 790; *Kiriri Cotton Co. v. Dewani* [1960] A.C. 192.
[150] [1942] I.R. 37.

employee entitled to recover because the employee was not *in pari delicto*; he did not commit an offence. It can also be argued that an employee who refused to work in an illegal manner may fear dismissal so he is not *in pari delicto: cf. Mathew v. Bobbins.*[151] In one case the English Court of Appeal permitted a person innocently breaking exchange control regulations to recover in an action for deceit, if a successful plea of illegality would permit the rogue to retain the benefits of his fraudulent conduct: *Shelley v. Paddock.*[152] Contrast cases where the plaintiff was aware of the illegality, *e.g. Thackwell v. Barclays Bank plc.*[153]

Two important English cases indicate that there is a considerable movement afoot in respect of judicial attitudes to the *in pari delicto* rule. The fact that one party only is to benefit from the disgraceful act may be a powerful indicator in future cases that the parties are not *in pari delicto,* even if the non-benefiting contracting party is aware of, or even assists in, furthering the illegal purpose. In *Saunders v. Edwards*[154] the plaintiffs agreed to purchase a flat from the defendant, acting upon a fraudulent misrepresentation which induced the contract. In order to minimise their stamp duty on the purchase of the property, the plaintiffs obtained the defendant's participation in a conveyance which valued the contents at £5,000, thereby reducing the liability of the plaintiffs for stamp duty. The contents were worth between £500 and £1,000, at most, and the misdescription was an attempt to defraud the revenue. The plaintiff's action was brought in the tort of deceit, the plaintiffs realising that enforcement of the contract itself would not be available but, on the merits, the plaintiffs were held entitled to damages for the tort of deceit. The moral culpability of the plaintiffs was outweighed by the fraud perpetrated by the defendant; the misrepresentation was an unanswerable tort and unconnected to the contract. Even if there had been no subsequent arrangement to mislead the revenue, the loss to the plaintiff would still have been occasioned by the defendant's fraud.

In *Euro Diam Ltd. v. Bathurst*[155] the Court of Appeal went even further by holding that an insurance contract was enforceable in favour of the plaintiff, even though the plaintiff had assisted in enabling a customer to defraud the German revenue authorities. Euro-Diam Ltd. had sold diamonds to a German company on the foot of invoices that misstated the price and led to a lower rate of German import tax being levied. Euro-Diam Ltd. effected a related contract of insurance but did not rely on the lower figure and had declared the full value of the goods to the insurers. The diamonds were stolen and the contract of insurance sought to be relied upon. While the issue of the invoice was reprehensible, the related contract of sale was not being sued upon; the false invoice did not assist Euro-Diam Ltd., and involved no deception of the insurers. There was no public policy consideration which required the contract of insurance in this particular case to be caught by the *ex turpi causa* defence.

---

[151] *The Times,* June 20, 1980.
[152] [1980] 2 W.L.R. 647.
[153] [1986] 1 All E.R. 676.
[154] [1987] 2 All E.R. 651.
[155] [1988] 2 All E.R. 23.

A further illustration of the exceptional circumstances which may cause the courts to relax the *in pari delicto* rule is afforded by the facts of *Howard v. Shirlstar Container Transport Ltd.*[156] where a pilot who took an aircraft from Nigeria, in breach of air traffic control regulations, was held entitled to recover his previously agreed fee for doing so, because the acts were committed in order to escape from an apparently life-threatening situation to the pilot and his wireless operator. The Court of Appeal held that the conscience of the Court would not be affronted by allowing recovery in such exceptional circumstances.

## (2) Repentance

If the transaction is illegal at formation but has yet to be performed, repudiation of the illegal transaction may permit the repudiating party to recover property transferred. A person who parts with property in an attempt to defraud creditors may recover those assets if he repents before any creditors are affected. In *Tribe v. Tribe*[157] a father transferred assets as a pre-emptive move to put those assets out of the reach of creditors. The transfer, to his son, was part of a bogus sale. When the anticipated litigation with the creditors did not materialise the father asked for the assets back but the son refused to comply, arguing that for the father to succeed he would have to reveal the illegal purpose. The Court of Appeal held that because no creditors had been defrauded the father could "repent" and be reimbursed, notwithstanding the illegality. There are no Irish cases on this point.[158]

## (3) Independent cause of action

Case law exists which suggests that property in goods passes when parties to a contract for the sale of goods (the contract being illegal) transfer physical possession to the purchaser: *Singh v. Ali,*[159] a decision of the Privy Council. Indeed, property may pass under an illegal contract even if a third party holds the goods according to *Belvoir Finance Co. v. Stapleton,*[160] an English Court of Appeal decision. In *Hortensius Ltd. & Durack v. Bishops* and *Others,*[161] the decisions in *Singh v. Ali* and *Belvoir Finance v. Stapleton* were cited with approval by Costello J. Thus, if the loan purchase transactions in *Hortensius Ltd.* had been illegal contracts which could not have been enforced by the trustees in question, "once the consideration provided in them has been paid, and the property referred to in them transferred to the trustees, they are not void contracts." Execution of the illegal agreement gave good title to choses in action and properties transferred to them by the agreements, thereby allowing the trustees rights of enforcement albeit by a somewhat circuitous route. An

---

[156] [1990] 3 All E.R. 366.
[157] [1995] 4 All E.R. 236; Creighton (1997) 60 M.L.R. 102.
[158] The leading English case is *Kearley v. Thompson* (1890) 24 Q.B.D. 742; Merkin (1981) 97 L.Q.R. 420.
[159] [1960] A.C. 167.
[160] [1971] 1 Q.B. 210.
[161] [1989] I.L.R.M. 294.

action in detinue, a tort independent of contract, will be possible if the transferor later interferes with goods. The Privy Council have decided that the registered owner of land who lets property under an illegal landlord and tenant agreement can rely upon his title to recover possession. The tenant would not be able to plead the illegal contract as a defence to an action in trespass based on the plaintiff's ownership: *Amar Singh v. Kulyubya.*[162] Contrast *Brady v. Flood*[163] if banknotes are transferred.

## Separate Transactions

In order to permit a limited remedy the courts may view a transaction as divisible into separate contracts, thereby isolating or limiting the effects of the illegality. In *McIlvenna v. Ferris and Green*[164] the defendants ordered construction of a building. Under Emergency Powers Legislation such work could only be lawfully carried out under licence. No licence was obtained. The plaintiff's action for work performed under the written contract failed; the court permitted the plaintiff to recover for additional work ordered just after the regulation had been rescinded on the basis that this was the subject of a separate contract. Another Irish decision in point is *Sheehy v. Sheehy.*[165]

It is common in building contracts for the parties to expressly covenant that all necessary planning permission has been obtained by the owner of the site. In *Strongman (1945) Ltd. v. Sincock*[166] a similar agreement was held to give rise to a remedy in damages when it transpired that the necessary permission had not been obtained. The action here was brought upon a collateral contract, separate and distinct from the illegal construction contract. In *Namlooze Venootschap De Faam v. Dorset Manufacturing Company,*[167] Dixon J. held that the free transfer of foreign exchange was prohibited under statute. While an award of damages could not be made, for this would result in the statute being ignored, it remained possible for the plaintiff to establish a right to damages by showing a failure by the defendant to use due diligence in obtaining the consent of the Minister for Finance to a transfer of foreign exchange out of the jurisdiction.

### Contracts of Loan

Loans made in order to enable the borrower to make or perform an illegal contract, or to pay a debt contracted under an illegal contract, are also illegal if the lender is aware of the purpose for which the loan is sought.[168] If a loan is sought

---

162 [1964] A.C. 142.
163 (1841) 6 Circuit Cases 309.
164 [1955] I.R. 318.
165 [1901] 1 I.R. 239.
166 [1955] 2 Q.B. 525.
167 [1949] I.R. 203.
168 *Cannan v. Bryce* (1819) 3 B. & Ald. 179; *Fisher v. Bridges* (1854) 3 E. & B. 642.

in order to discharge a loan which itself was illegal, then that second transaction will also be tainted and unenforceable if the earlier illegality was known to the second lender: *Spector v. Ageda*.[169] However, the fact that the lender knows that the loan may be used to evade lawful creditors which is not itself unlawful, does not bring the case within this principle, at least when the loan is made in order to obtain security for an earlier bona fide debt: *Bagot v. Arnott*.[170]

### Contracts of guarantee

If the main contract between A and B is illegal in circumstances which make it impossible for A to sue B, can a contract of guarantee be enforceable by A, the creditor, against C, the guarantor? The question was answered in the negative in *Devine v. Scott and Johnston*.[171] Devine, landlord under an illegal letting to Johnston, was held unable to recover rent from either Johnston or Scott, the guarantor of Johnston's indebtedness.

## Severance

In *Devine v. Scott and Johnston* only a part of the demised premises were used for the illegal purpose. The plaintiff suggested that the court could permit recovery of a portion of the rent, calculated by reference to the proportion of the property used in a lawful manner. The court rejected the view that such a power exists at common law. Furthermore, if a covenant contained in the contract is illegal this is said to taint the entire contract. The case of *Murphy & Co. Ltd. v. Crean*[172] illustrates this. The plaintiffs were not attempting to enforce the illegal covenant requiring Crean to transfer the licence but this illegal clause precluded enforcement of other covenants which, taken alone, were unobjectionable. The weight of authority, both in England and Ireland, is against extending the doctrine of severance beyond cases which are in restraint of trade.

There is support for the other view however. In *Carolan v. Brabazon*[173] the plaintiff sought specific performance of a lease which contained a covenant requiring the tenant to pay poor law rates. This covenant was illegal by Act of Parliament. Sugden L.C. said *obiter* that it may have been possible to grant specific performance of the lease minus the term as to payment of the poor law rate. In *Furnivall v. O'Neill*,[174] O'Neill, an arranging debtor, entered into a secret arrangement in 1879 with Furnivall, a creditor, under which Furnivall was promised payment in full. This agreement was illegal. In 1880 this promise was repeated and a contract executed reciting the obligation. This contract also recorded other debts due to O'Neill which were legitimate. O'Neill sought to

---

[169] [1973] 1 Ch. 30.
[170] (1867) I.R. 2 C.L. 1.
[171] (1931) 66 I.L.T.R. 107: *Rooney v. Armstrong* (1847) 10 Ir.L.Rep. 291.
[172] [1915] 1 I.R. 111.
[173] (1846) 9 Ir.Eq.R. 224.
[174] [1902] 2 I.R. 422.

recover on the 1880 instrument. Andrews J. held that the promise to pay the illegal sums formed the main and operative consideration for the 1880 deed, and was thus fatal to the action. Had the illegal promise been incidental or peripheral then, like *Carolan v. Brabazon*, severance may have been possible.

One English case decides that severance may be possible in cases of statutory illegality: *Ailion v. Spiekermann*.[175] Templeman J. in that case refused to follow the practice of other judges by "washing" his hands of the illegal contract because he said that such a solution was particularly unsatisfactory where one party is an unwilling victim. This case is to be welcomed; if severance is a legitimate device to do some measure of justice in restraint of trade cases this is no reason why it should not be available in other contracts where public policy is infringed. Indeed, *Ailion v. Spiekermann* and the Court of Appeal's decision in *Shelley v. Paddock*[176] are indicative of a new and refreshing trend towards illegality cases; the English courts now seem reluctant to readily brand each party equally at fault, thereby making a restitutionary remedy available to the less culpable party. Indeed, the Privy Council in *Carney v. Herbert*[177] established that severance is possible where the illegal promise forms a collateral or incidental part of the transaction and no compelling social, economic or moral imperative would be subverted by enforcement of the rest of the transaction. Thus severance will be available in regard to illegal contracts where the source of the illegality is a technical or regulatory provision, as in *Carney v. Herbert* itself (but cf. section 60 of the Irish Companies Act 1963) but severance is less likely where the illegal provision is contrary to public policy or private morality. So, while the spirit of *Carney v. Herbert* is to be welcomed it would not lead an Irish court into adopting a different approach to *Lewis v. Squash Ireland Ltd.*.[178] The employee would still not be able to recover for wrongful dismissal or a redundancy payment, or compensation for unfair dismissal. Nor is it likely that the facts of *McHugh v. Ministry of Labour for Northern Ireland*[179] would go the other way after *Carney v. Herbert*.

## Flexible Remedies – Possible Reforms

Some English judges have argued the need for the evolution of a public conscience test to give the courts a more discretionary power to react to any illegal purpose that the court takes note of: *Thackwell v. Barclays Bank*.[180] Lords Goff and Keith, dissenting in *Tinsley v. Milligan*,[181] championed this approach but the majority of the House of Lords in that case regarded such reforms as a matter for statutory reform. While some statutory reforms have given the

---

[175] [1976] Ch. 158.
[176] [1980] 2 W.L.R. 647.
[177] [1985] A.C. 301.
[178] [1983] I.L.R.M. 363.
[179] [1940] N.I. 174.
[180] [1986] 1 All E.R. 676.
[181] [1993] 3 All E.R. 65.

courts a very broad power to adjust remedies where appropriate – witness the New Zealand Illegal Contracts Act 1970, section 7 of which gives the courts the power to grant relief "by way of restitution, compensation, variation of the contract, validation of the contract in whole or in part for any particular purpose, or otherwise howsoever as the court in its discretion thinks just" – it is not likely that, in the absence of statutory reform, such a public conscience test would evolve through case law in Ireland. However, not all judges are as timorous as the majority in *Tinsley v. Milligan*. In *Nelson v. Nelson*,[182] *Tinsley v. Milligan* was not followed by the High Court of Australia, that Court adopting a novel approach involving the surrender by the wrongdoer of the value illegally obtained in order to give practical effect to the purpose behind the statute and the "clean hands" doctrine.

## Pleading Illegality

If the illegality appears on the face of the contract document it is not necessary that illegality be pleaded as a defence. The courts will not enforce the agreement: *Murphy & Co. Ltd. v. Crean*.[183] If the agreement is not illegal on its face the party seeking to resist the action should plead illegality if he wishes to avoid liability on this basis: *Whitecross Potatoes v. Coyle*.[184] A person may be reluctant to do this, for obvious reasons; a confession of illegality often invites a prosecution later. If, however illegality is not pleaded but during the course of the trial it becomes clear to the trial judge that an illegal contract is disclosed he is not obliged to disregard the illegality. In *Starling Securities v. Woods*,[185] McWilliam J. refused to enforce a contract formed with an illegal object in mind, even though illegality was not expressly pleaded as a defence: see also *Lewis v. Squash (Ireland) Ltd*.[186]

---

182 [1996] 184 C.L.R. 538.
183 [1915] 1 I.R. 111.
184 [1978] I.L.R.M. 31.
185 Unreported, High Court, May 24, 1977.
186 [1983] I.L.R.M. 363.

# 15  Void Contracts

## Contracts Void at Common Law

As we saw in the previous chapter, there are instances where the judiciary may refuse to enforce a contract on the ground that the contract, or an individual clause or objective, is contrary to public policy. Where the contract is held to be illegal at common law, the entire contract is incapable of grounding a cause of action, even if the obligation which is being relied upon by the plaintiff is itself unobjectionable. Further, while the courts are increasingly discriminating in respect of the principle of severance if the source of the illegality is a statute, or if the party resisting severance has been guilty of fraud, there is still a substantial difference between cases in which contracts are illegal at common law and contracts which are held to be void because they infringe public policy. In a leading English case the distinction was stated thus:

> "There are two kinds of illegality of differing effect. The first is where the illegality is criminal, or *contra bonos mores*, and in these cases, which I will not attempt to enumerate or further classify, such a provision, if an ingredient in a contract, will invalidate the whole, although there may be many other provisions in it. There is a second kind of illegality which has no such taint; the other terms in the contract stand if the illegal portion can be severed, the illegal portion being a provision which the court, on grounds of public policy, will not enforce."[1]

It is generally accepted that there are three kinds of contract which fall into the second category referred to in the above quotation.

## (1) Agreements to oust the jurisdiction of the courts

Persons who seek to become members of a professional or trade association may find that part of the agreement dictates that in the event of a dispute the decision of the association shall be final. Such a provision is invalid; attempts to uphold agreements and at the same time deny recourse to the ordinary courts are also invalid; the public interest requires that disputes be amenable to the jurisdiction of the courts: *Lee v. Showman's Guild of Great Britain*.[2] The basic distinction that must be observed is between clauses that attempt to reserve

---

[1] Somervell L.J. in *Goodinson v. Goodinson* [1954] 2 Q.B. 118 at 120–121 citing *Bennett v. Bennett* [1952] 1 All E.R. 413.
[2] [1952] 2 Q.B. 329.

issues of law for the sole decision of a private tribunal or arbitrator, and clauses which give the private tribunal or arbitrator sole competence on issues of fact. The right of the parties to seek review of an arbitration on the basis of an error of law must be upheld, and any clause to the contrary will be void.

In contrast, there is a venerable line of authority which holds that the parties can make provision for a tribunal to seek to establish the salient facts and, to this end, a clause making the arbitration a condition precedent will be upheld as long as the clause does not seek to close off the ordinary courts altogether. The leading case is *Scott v. Avery*,[3] a decision of the House of Lords in 1856, and, while *Scott v. Avery* has been followed in Ireland on numerous occasions,[4] the Irish courts have sometimes been reluctant to extend this decision. In *Mansfield v. Doolin*[5] a clause provided that if a dispute broke out over a building contract the award of an architect was to be a condition precedent to any proceedings. The arbitrator's award was held not to constitute a condition precedent but the clause was classified as being simply an agreement to refer a dispute to arbitration which did not take away the right to sue in the ordinary courts immediately. The distinction is generally agreed to be a somewhat elusive one. When the question of the impact of the decision in *Scott v. Avery* came directly before the Irish Court of Kings Bench, and then the Court of Appeal, in *Gregg & Co. v. Fraser & Sons*,[6] it was said by both Lord Chief Barron Palles and Fitzgibbon L.J. to lay down nothing new. Fitzgibbon L.J. said *Scott v. Avery* laid down that "[i]t is lawful for parties to contract that no action shall be brought upon until arbitrators have decided, and that effect must be given to a contract which amounts to that." Indeed, the Arbitration Act 1980, section 5, enables a court to restrain proceedings brought in the courts when it is established that an arbitration clause has not been observed,[7] thereby strengthening a similar provision in section 12 of the Arbitration Act 1954. Furthermore, under the Arbitration Act 1954, section 35(1), the High Court is given a supervisory jurisdiction; in particular, the arbitrator "may, and shall if so directed by the court", state questions of law or the terms of an award for decision by the court as a special case. This section re-affirms the inability of parties to absolutely prohibit recourse to the courts at least on questions of law. Indeed, in *Winterthur Swiss Insurance Co. v. I.C.I.*,[8] O'Hanlon J. indicated that in certain instances the court may exercise its discretion to refuse to stay proceedings before a court on the ground that arbitration may not prove the best method of resolving a dispute between the parties. The power of the parties to a contract to make arbitration a condition precedent to an action in the ordinary courts may be restricted in many instances, as a result of the

---

[3] (1856) 5 H.L. Cas. 811.
[4] *Mansfield v. Doolin* (1868) 4 I.R.C.L. 17; *Gregg & Co. v. Fraser & Sons* [1906] 2 I.R. 545.
[5] (1868) 4 I.R.C.L. 17.
[6] [1906] 2 I.R. 545.
[7] See *Mitchell v. Budget Travel* [1990] I.L.R.M. 739; *Parkarran Ltd. v. M. & P. Construction Ltd.* [1996] 1 I.R. 83; *Doyle v. Irish National Insurance Co. plc*, unreported, High Court, Kelly J., January 30, 1998.
[8] [1990] I.L.R.M. 159.

decision of Carroll J. in *McCarthy v. Joe Walsh Tours Ltd.*[9] The arbitration clause in question was found in a holiday contract, concluded on the industry standard form contract, and sought to make arbitration a binding element of the contract. Carroll J. held that because the clause and the arbitration scheme provided only limited relief, the clause was a limitation clause which could not be relied upon because it had not been specifically drawn to the attention of the consumer and did not meet the requirements of section 40 of the Sale of Goods and Supply of Services Act 1980. It remains open to a court to hold that such a clause is also not "fair and reasonable", even if incorporated into the contract. A recent Australian case holds that contractual provisions that fetter a person's recourse to the courts are equally as bad as express prohibitions: *Novamaze Property Ltd. v. Cut Price Deli Property.*[10]

Several of the leading English cases concern the issue of whether a spouse may give up a statutory right to maintenance payments. The tendency has been to hold that such clauses are invalid because such a clause would force the separated spouse onto social security and thus oblige the taxpayer to provide support.[11] In Ireland the scope of such clauses has been discussed by Walsh J. in *H.D. v. P.D.*[12] In considering whether a contractual separation agreement under section 8 of the Family Law (Maintenance of Spouses and Children) Act 1976 is final, Walsh J. stated "it is not possible to contract out of the Act by an agreement made after the Act came into force or by an agreement entered into before the legislation was enacted." This judgment was followed by Barr J. in *J.H. v. R.H.*,[13] allowing a wife to make an application for revision of maintenance under the 1976 Act, notwithstanding a full and final settlement clause in the separation agreement. Barr J. held that this power operates even in regard to matters arising under the Judicial Separation and Family Law Reform Act 1989. The test in operating such a revision power is whether the husband has failed to provide maintenance which is proper in all the circumstances.

## (2) Contracts which subvert the sanctity of marriage

(a) It is said to be a matter of public interest that persons enter into contracts of marriage and affiliated transactions for reasons which are likely to produce satisfactory marriages. Marriage brokerage contracts, in which a fee is paid to a marriage bureau in return for an undertaking to find a wife or husband, are void: see the English case of *Hermann v. Charlesworth.*[14] In the old Irish case of *Williamson v. Gihan*,[15] Williamson, an impecunious young man, obtained the help of his friend Gihan in spiriting away a young heiress to Scotland

---

[9] [1991] I.L.R.M. 813.
[10] [1995] A.T.P.R. 37.
[11] *Hyman v. Hyman* [1929] A.C. 60; *Bennett v. Bennett* [1952] 1 All E.R. 413.
[12] Unreported, Supreme Court, May 8, 1978.
[13] *Irish Times Law Report*, October 30, 1995;
[14] [1905] 2 K.B. 123.
[15] (1805) 2 Sch. & Lef. 357.

where Williamson married the young lady. He promised Gihan £500, payable from his wife's property for services rendered. Williamson was held not entitled to fetter his wife's estate in these circumstances. It seems that the court frowned upon contracts of marriage that resulted from elopement – despite the fact that the then Lord Chancellor Lord Eldon had procured his wife in this manner – fearing that even collateral transactions between the groom and others would lead to fortune-hunting.

(b) Unilateral contracts in which one person promises not to marry any person other than the promisee are void: *Lowe v. Peers*.[16] However, this line of authority is not to be taken too far. The Supreme Court of Canada in *Caron v. Caron*[17] upheld a separation agreement which made financial provision for the female spouse until she either remarried or cohabited as man and wife with any person for a period of more than 90 days. Wilson J., who gave the leading judgment, observed that although the clause may have had the effect of discouraging remarriage, it was not to be seen as analogous to a promise not to marry or a promised payment if the promisor marries a particular person.

(c) Contracts for future separation. Prior to the removal of the constitutional prohibition in Article 41. 3.2° against divorce in the Republic of Ireland, the petition for a decree *a mensa et thoro*, or judicial separation, was (and is) an important but frequently expensive way in which the parties to a marriage may get the courts to make financial and property adjustments when a marriage has broken down. The parties may instead wish to make their own arrangements. Nevertheless a contract which provides that one party is to pay a certain sum to support the other in the event of future separation will be void as weakening the marriage bond: *Marquess of Westmeath v. Marquess of Salisbury*.[18] A more recent illustration is provided by the English case of *H. v. H.*[19] The litigation arose out of an agreement between two couples who, as part of a spouse-swapping arrangement, divorced their respective spouses and then married the eligible spouse of the other couple. Prior to the remarriage it was agreed that each man would support and provide a home for the new partner. Ewbank J. refused to enforce an agreement of this kind for it involved the breaking up of two marriages.

Some change in the law in this area is imminent in the United Kingdom. The Lord Chancellor's Department and the Cabinet have approved the introduction of legally binding pre-marriage contracts under which the parties contract on asset distribution should the marriage later break down. While this reform is supported on the ground that much acrimonious litigation is avoided, doubts about the fairness and relevance of such solutions exist,[20] especially if the marriage subsists for many years.

---

[16] (1768) 4 Burr. 2225.
[17] (1987) 38 D.L.R. (4th) 735.
[18] (1830) 5 Bli.(N.S.) 339; *H. v. W.* (1857) 3 K. & J. 382.
[19] (1983) 127 S.J. 578.
[20] See "Cabinet backs move to make pre-nuptial contracts legal" *The Times*, May 18, 1998.

If however the parties are not living together but they decide to resume cohabitation, agreeing that if the reconciliation thereby effected should later break down then the wife will be paid a certain sum, this will be enforceable. In *McMahon v. McMahon*,[21] Holmes L.J. said of such an agreement, "far from endangering the unity of the family, it restored it." But for this clause the initial separation would have continued. These agreements preclude further action for financial support, even if the defendant who relies upon the agreement is guilty of adultery: see *Ross v. Ross*[22] in which Andrews J. distinguished actions for a decree *a mensa et thoro* from cases where adultery precludes reliance on a provision restraining divorce actions.

Separation agreements which unwittingly tend to encourage immoral practices are not *per se* void: see *Lewis v. Lewis*.[23]

(d) Prior to the passing of the Fifteenth Amendment to the Constitution, contracts to obtain a divorce outside the jurisdiction may also have been in conflict with Irish public policy because of the constitutional ban on divorce. A recent illustration of public policy being utilised to enforce the marriage contract, albeit in a rather mechanical fashion, is afforded by *Dalton v. Dalton*.[24] An application to have a separation agreement made a rule of court under section 8 of the Family Law (Maintenance of Spouses and Children) Act 1976 ran into difficulty because the contract contained a clause whereby the parties agreed to obtain a divorce *a vinculo* outside the jurisdiction. Because both spouses were domiciled in Ireland, the divorce would not be recognised in Irish law. The application failed because to grant the application would be contrary to public policy. The court did not immediately consider the option of granting the application after deleting the offending clause, something it clearly had jurisdiction to do, but in a later application by the parties, the clause was deleted and the agreement accepted under section 8 in this amended form.[25]

Cohabitation agreements, whether in contemplation of marriage or not, are contrary to public policy and void. In *Ennis v. Butterly*[26] the parties were married, but not to each other. The plaintiff alleged a contract whereby she would move into a house bought by them, give up her employment and take on the role of home-maker. She also alleged an agreement to marry upon the granting of a divorce to each of them. Dealing with the contract to marry argument first, Kelly J. held that such a contract was statute-barred by section 1 of the Family Law Act 1981, which abolished this cause of action. Further, at common law, such contracts, by married persons, are void: *Wilson v. Carnley*.[27] Irish law, Kelly J. held, did not recognise cohabitation contracts where the provision of "wifely services"[28] is the consideration. Kelly J. followed the

---

[21] [1913] 1 I.R. 428.
[22] [1908] 2 I.R. 339.
[23] [1940] I.R. 42; contrast *Jackson v. Cridland* (1859) 10 I.C.L.R. 376.
[24] Unreported, High Court, September 9, 1981.
[25] See reporter's note to the above judgment.
[26] [1997] 1 I.L.R.M 28.
[27] [1908] 1 K.B. 729.
[28] Above, n.26 at 39.

English case of *Windeler v. Whitehall*[29] in which Millett J. had declared cohabitation or "palimony" contracts contrary to public policy in England. Kelly J. observed:

> "Given the special place of marriage and the family under the Irish Constitution, it appears to me that the public policy of this State ordains that non-marital cohabitation does not and cannot have the same constitutional status as marriage. Moreover, the State has pledged to guard with special care the institution of marriage. But does this mean that agreements, the consideration for which is cohabitation, are incapable of being enforced? In my view it does since otherwise the pledge on the part of the State, of which this Court is one organ, to guard with special care the institution of marriage would be much diluted. To permit an express cohabitation contract (such as is pleaded here) to be enforced would give it a similar status in law as a marriage contract. It did not have such a status prior to the coming into effect of the Constitution, rather such contracts were regarded as illegal and unenforceable as a matter of public policy. Far from enhancing the position at law of such contracts the Constitution requires marriage to be guarded with special care. In my view, this reinforces the existing common law doctrines concerning the non-enforceability of cohabitation contracts. I am therefore of [the] opinion that, as a matter of public policy, such agreements cannot be enforced."

With respect, views of this kind make it essential that legislative changes to contract and property law are made soon. The regualtion of private morals should not be undertaken by the courts in this negative way. Patterns of behaviour and social order that may well have had some resonance in the mind of a victorian chancery judge seem quite at odds with the everyday experiences of persons on the verge of the third millenium.

## (3) Contracts in restraint of trade

This venerable common law doctrine has been succinctly stated by Diplock L.J. in the English Court of Appeal in the following terms:

> "A contract in restraint of trade is one in which a party (the covenantor) agrees with any other party (the covenantee) to restrict his liberty in the future to carry on trade with other persons not parties to the contract in such manner as he chooses."[30]

---

[29] [1990] 2 F.L.R 505.

[30] *Petrofina (Great Britain) Ltd. v. Martin* [1966] Ch. 146 at 180; cited with approval by Lords Hodson and Morris in *Esso Petroleum Co. Ltd. v. Harpers Garage* (Stourport) Ltd. [1986] A.C. 269.

The Irish judiciary have followed this approach, most notably in the case of *John Orr Ltd. and Vescom B.V. v. John Orr*[31] where Costello J. summarised the restraint of trade doctrine in these terms:

> "All restraints of trade in the absence of special justifying circumstances are contrary to public policy and are therefore void. A restraint may be justified if it is reasonable in the interests of the contracting parties and in the interests of the public. The onus of showing that a restraint is reasonable as between the parties rests on the person alleging that it is so. Greater freedom of contract is allowable in a covenant entered into between the seller and the buyer of a business than in the case of one entered into between an employer and an employee. A covenant against competition entered into by the seller of a business which is reasonably necessary to protect the business sold is valid and enforceable. A covenant by an employee not to compete may also be valid and enforceable if it is reasonably necessary to protect some proprietary interest of the covenantee such as may exist in a trade connection or trade secrets. The courts may in some circumstances enforce a covenant in restraint of trade even though taken as a whole the covenant exceeds what is reasonable, by the severance of the void parts from the valid parts."[32]

One problematical issue about the scope of the restraint of trade doctrine remains unresolved, notwithstanding the deliberations of the Supreme Court in *Kerry Co-operative Creameries Ltd. and Another v. An Bord Bainne Co-operative Ltd. and Another.*[33] Does the doctrine only operate if an express covenant of a restrictive nature is before the court, or can the doctrine be applicable in relation to a contractual provision that has the effect of restraining freedom to trade? The argument arose in the context of a proposed rule change which required the members of a co-operative society to trade with the society or run the risk that non-trading members would find that shareholdings would be diluted by being excluded from bonus share distributions, by termination from membership of the society and by loss of voting rights. McCarthy J. favoured the view that the restraint of trade doctrine could be applicable to such a situation, and he rejected the view that the doctrine is only applicable to express covenants or conditions in a contract. O'Flaherty J. took the opposite view and held that there had to be a covenant in restraint of trade, or something akin to a covenant. Finlay C.J. declined to state his views on this point. Whatever the final outcome of this point it is sufficient, for present purposes, to state that the modern doctrine of restraint of trade is designed to strike at commercial and professional practices which unduly restrict the covenantor's freedom to carry on a business or profession; not all restrictive covenants operate in such a way as to incur the wrath of the judges.

---

[31] [1987] I.L.R.M. 702.
[32] *Ibid.* at 704.
[33] [1991] I.L.R.M. 581.

**Historical antecedents.** Restrictive commercial practices were not unknown in late medieval times. Commercial arrangements between traders designed to artificially inflate prices – known as badgering, forestalling, regrating and engrossing – were made criminal offences under statute. The Elizabethan desire to control food prices made the prohibition of such transactions necessary. When commercial attitudes changed these offences were repealed in 1844 under 7 & 8 Vict. c. 24, which extended into Ireland. The establishment of Guilds, Craft Associations and Corporations also led to restrictive practices designed to regulate and protect members of those associations. An Act of 1846, 9 & 10 Vict. c. 76, also attempted to bring these older medieval practices into step with the needs of *laissez faire* capitalism by abolishing the privileges held by trading organisations in Ireland; the Act provides that it shall be lawful for any person to carry on any lawful trade or profession and take apprentices. Fines and penalties could not be extracted by the Guilds.[34]

These isolated pieces of legislation serve the same policy objectives as the common law restraint of trade doctrine. The courts however had to struggle with the problem, often unaided by statute. In the landmark case of *Mitchel v. Reynolds*[35] it was laid down that a general restraint was bad; partial restraints were valid. Thus a covenant not to carry on trade throughout England was invalid; a provision limiting the prohibition to a town or district was valid if good and adequate consideration was provided.

This general/partial distinction began to wear a little thin when commercial and industrial innovations meant that the consequences of carrying on trade in a remote part of England, or indeed the world, could have severe implications for persons some distance away. The *Mitchel v. Reynolds* doctrine was revised in a series of decisions handed down between 1893 and 1916, the most important of which is *Nordenfelt v. Maxim Nordenfelt*.[36] In this case Nordenfelt, the vendor of a business, in which guns and other munitions were manufactured, agreed that, upon the sale of the business to a company formed to purchase the munitions business, he would not, for a period of 25 years, carry on business, or be engaged, directly or indirectly, with any other manufacturer of guns, mountings, or munitions. This agreement entered into in 1886 was revised two years later when the purchasing company merged with another company to form Maxim Nordenfelt. During this time, the original vendor had been engaged as managing director at a handsome salary; the evidence indicated that Nordenfelt had freely consented to the changes wrought by the 1888 re-arrangement. Despite the world-wide nature of the covenant, it could be justified.[37] Lord

---

34  See generally, Holdsworth, *History of English Law*, Vol. 8., pp. 56–62.
35  (1711) 1 P.Wms. 181.
36  [1894] A.C. 535.
37  Lord MacNaghten observed of the original Nordenfelt business;
"His customers were comparatively few in number, but his trade was world-wide in extent. He had upon his books almost every monarch and almost every state of any note in the habitable globe": [1894] A.C. 535 at 559. For a world-wide restrain in the pharmaceutical industry see the Northern Ireland case of *Norbrook Laboratories Ltd. v. Smyth*, unreported, N.I. High Court, September 30, 1986.

MacNaghten restated the law of restraint of trade so as to abandon the general/partial distinction, preferring instead to hold that all interference with liberty of action in trading, and all restraints of trade in themselves are contrary to public policy and void. To this general rule exceptions may arise if a restriction can be held to be reasonable "in reference to the interests of the parties concerned and reasonable in reference to the interests of the public."

**The modern doctrine.** In the leading case of *Esso Petroleum Co. Ltd. v. Harpers Garage (Stourport) Ltd.*[38] – hereafter *Esso* – the House of Lords gave a comprehensive analysis of the existing rules of restraint of trade. Lord Reid in his speech stressed that the following questions are to be asked:

(1) Does the restraint go further than to afford adequate protection to the party in whose favour it was granted? if so, the covenant is prima facie void;

(2) Can it be justified as being in the interests of the party thus restrained?

(3) Is the covenant contrary to the public interest?[39]

The onus of showing the restraint to be in the interests of the party thus restrained, or, to put it another way, that the covenant is reasonable as between the parties, is upon the person seeking to uphold the transaction. If the agreement is alleged to be unenforceable because it is contrary to the public interest, notwithstanding its reasonableness *inter partes*, the burden of proof is upon the party alleging the invalidity of the covenant.[40]

It should be stressed that while public policy is at the heart of this doctrine two separate policy considerations are at issue here; first of all, the courts view it as being a cardinal rule of public policy that a person be held to a contract freely entered into: *Murphy v. O'Donovan.*[41] On the other hand a man is not to be permitted unduly to fetter his freedom to contract and earn a living for himself and his family: *Langan v. Cork Operative Bakers T.U.*[42] The desire of the courts to uphold both of these often conflicting objectives means, as Lord Morris said in *Esso*, that "a certain adjustment is necessary". Lord Pearce, in the same case, stressed the essentially pragmatic nature of the doctrine.

> "The rule relating to restraint of trade is bound to be a compromise, as are all the rules imposed for freedom's sake. The law fetters traders by a particular inability to limit their freedom of trade so that it may protect the general freedom of trade and the good of the community."[43]

---

[38] [1968] A.C. 269.
[39] See [1968] A.C. 269 at 300.
[40] See [1968] A.C. 269 at 319, *per* Lord Hodson.
[41] [1939] I.R. 457.
[42] (1938) Ir.Jur.Rep. 65.
[43] [1968] A.C. 269 at 324.

**Restraints outside the doctrine of restraint of trade.** Not all contracts that restrain or prevent a contracting party from entering into agreements must be tested by reference to the restraint of trade doctrine.

Exclusive dealing arrangements between commercial traders are valid if they are commonplace and incidental to everyday trading activities; a contract by a restaurant owner to take all the Beaujolais he may require from one retailer does not fall within the doctrine.[44] The practice, in former times common in the Cork area, of trading in a public house as a tenant, agreeing to take all the stout and beer from the landlord company may no doubt be restrictive of the freedom of the tenant to obtain supplies from other companies but is not an arrangement that must be justified as reasonable as between the parties and the public interest. In *Murphy & Co. v. O'Donovan*[45] the defendant took an assignment of a lease, the lease containing a covenant that the premises would be operated as a public house that would only take supplies of stout and porter from the plaintiff lessors. The defendant sought to avoid the covenant by arguing that as it was a restraint on competition, the covenant was void. The covenant, entered into by a person of full age and competent understanding, was enforceable and was not, in the view of Johnston J., to be equated with the *Nordenfelt* case. Indeed, the marketplace, by evolving its own rules relating to fair trading, requires that freedom of contract be upheld when no anti-competitive practice is evident.

Restrictive covenants in which the purchaser of an interest in land agrees that he will not use the land for a particular commercial or industrial purpose are also *per se* enforceable.[46] There are similar lines of authority in respect of restrictions found in leasehold property transactions, the general view being that the lessee of property who takes property under a lease which contains a restrictive covenant, does not come within the restraint of trade doctrine because the freedom to carry on the trade is only acquired under the lease, and it is not contrary to public policy for such transactions to be left unscrutinised, save in exceptional circumstances.[47] Although it is difficult to distinguish these cases from other transactions which fall under the restraint of trade doctrine Lord Wilberforce in *Esso* explained these exceptions as due to the fact that they have "passed into the accepted and normal currency of commercial or contractual or conveyancing relations".

Covenants in employment contracts that restrict or deter an employee from working for a rival concern when he leaves employment are within the doctrine; covenants that restrict an employee while in employment are not. In *McArdle v. Wilson*[48] the contract of workmen employed in a factory in Tyrone obliged them to give two weeks' notice if they wished to terminate employment. The contract provided that if more than five employees gave notice then the notice

---

[44] *Servais Bouchard v. Princes Hall Restaurant* (1904) 20 T.L.R. 574.
[45] [1939] I.R. 457; *Murphy Co. v. Crean* [1915] 2 I.R. 115.
[46] Wylie, *Irish Land Law*, (3rd ed., 1997), Chap. 19.
[47] e.g. *Clegg v. Hands* (1890) 44 Ch.D. 503; *Ravenseft Properties v. Director General of Fair Trading* [1978] Q.B. 52.
[48] (1876) 10 I.L.T.R. 87.

of other employees would not be accepted. The provision was clearly designed to reduce the effectiveness of strike action; failure to observe the covenant was to result in the docking of one week's wages. An action to recover wages retained failed; the Court of Exchequer found the covenant valid; Palles C.B. went further and held the doctrine of restraint of trade inapplicable. So, too, a provision obliging an employee to repay training expenses incurred should he terminate his contract of employment has been held outside the doctrine of restraint of trade because no restriction operated once the employee had left work: *Schiesser International (Ireland) Ltd. v. Gallagher.*[49]

The House of Lords decision in *Schroeder Music Publishing Co. Ltd. v. Macauley*[50] did not involve a contract of employment, but one for exclusive services, the agreement unduly restricting the freedom of one party during the currency of the agreement. *Schroeder Music Publishing Co. Ltd. v. Macauley* has commenced a line of case law in which little known composers and musicians have been able to have publishing agreements, copyright assignments and management contracts declared to be invalid as unreasonable restraints of trade. These cases include *Silverton Records Ltd. v. Mountfield*[51] in which the Stone Roses were able to overturn recording agreements because the terms were one-sided and capable of operating for many years due to extension option clauses. A publishing agreement that could also operate indefinitely was also set aside, the publisher's rights to alter and adapt the works being substantively unfair. This line of cases may, by analogy, lead to a decision in which restrictions operating during a contract of employment may be held within the restraint of trade doctrine.[52]

The most recent illustration of the restraint of trade doctrine being held to be applicable in exclusive services contracts can be found in *Watson v. Prager.*[53] Here the boxer Michael Watson sought to avoid an exclusive services contract between himself and his manager, the manager/promoter Mickey Duff. The plaintiff pleaded that the agreement which tied him to the defendant was potentially very prejudicial because the defendant was seen to be subject to several conflicts of interest, as he also promoted boxing events. Scott J. held that because *Nagle v. Feilden*[54] decided that the current rules of a sporting association could be scrutinised by reference to the restraint of trade doctrine, the analogous manager/boxer contract was also to be tested.

**Contracts traditionally within the doctrine.** The courts have consistently reaffirmed the view that the categories of restraint of trade are not closed. So, if the court takes the view that a plaintiff has a legitimate proprietary interest

---

49  (1971) 106 I.L.T.R. 22.
50  [1974] 1 W.L.R. 1308.
51  [1993] E.M.L.R. 152; see also *Zang Tumb Tuum v. Johnson* [1993] E.M.L.R. 61 and contrast *Panayiotou v. Sony* [1994] E.M.L.R. 229.
52  Heydon 85 L.Q.R. 229 at 235.
53  [1991] 3 All E.R. 487.
54  [1966] 1 All E.R. 689; *Macken v. O'Reilly* [1979] I.L.R.M. 79.

then a covenant will be upheld even if the plaintiff falls outside the category of a traditional "restraint" plaintiff. So, in one recent English case[55] a restraint covenant could be subjected to the scrutiny of the doctrine, the contract relating to a joint venture even though no employment relationship or business transfer was involved.

*(i) Employment contracts.* The freedom of an employee to carry on an activity which adversely affects a former employer may be circumscribed by agreement. In fact the common law furnishes some degree of protection to an employer, and in several Irish cases the conduct of the employee breached a common law rather than a contractual duty. The common law, through the implied obligation to serve an employer faithfully, makes it a breach of contract for an employee to prepare a list of customers while intending to use this list after the contract of employment has ended. An employee who solicits orders from his employer's customers, intending to meet the orders personally rather than *qua* employee, also breaches this implied term. The facts of *Arclex Optical Corporation v. McMurray*[56] and *Stanford Supply Co. Ltd. v. O'Toole*,[57] (in which employees solicited orders to be met by their own concerns while still employed by the plaintiff companies), are in point.

It is sometimes said that the common law implied term is not the most accurate explanation for judicial protection being made available here. Sometimes the courts consider that on the facts there exists a confidential relationship between the parties and that this relationship creates an obligation for one person not to abuse trust or confidence, to the prejudice of the other. While these cases may involve employment contracts – which in part helps explain why the implied contract is sometimes advanced as the basis of the jurisdiction – the duty not to abuse confidential information can operate as between business partners too. The leading Irish case must be considered to be *House of Spring Gardens Ltd. v. Point Blank Ltd.*[58] In that case a licensee of bullet-proof vests breached an agreement by manufacturing a similar product, thereby infringing the plaintiff's copyright and breaking the licensing agreement. Costello J., in a judgment approved by the Supreme Court who dismissed the licensee's appeal, stated that the court must consider whether a confidential relationship exists and whether the information imparted can properly be required as confidential information. In considering these facts it is relevant to consider the degree of skill, time and labour involved in compiling the information. If the owner has expended skill, time and labour in compiling this information, use of this information may be treated as confined for a specific purpose, and for that purpose only, if the court holds a confidential relationship exists. Even if the information could be gleaned from other sources there may still be a breach of duty if the information has been compiled by the plaintiff,

---

[55] *Dawnay Day & Co. v. D'Alphen, The Times*, June 24, 1997.
[56] [1958] Ir.Jur.Rep. 65.
[57] Unreported, High Court, December 11, 1972.
[58] [1985] F.S.R. 327.

although in this context the decision of McWilliam J. in *Nu Glue Additives and Bika (Ireland) Ltd. v. Burgess Galvin & Co.*[59] suggests the remedy may be limited to damages rather than injunctive relief.

In these cases the employer may seek an interlocutory injunction restraining the employee until the merits of the action can be heard. The injunction is the primary remedy here although an account for profits made, or payment of damages, can also be ordered.

An employer may also wish to extract an express covenant from his employees. The many advantages for the employer may include greater predictability – the employee *knows* that he cannot solicit – and certainty of remedy. More importantly, the employee may not be able to carry on his trade or profession for a period after leaving employment. It is essential that the employer show he has a legitimate commercial interest capable of protection; he must also show that the covenant goes no further than is necessary in order to protect that interest. In a modern commercial context it is often quite difficult for the employer to establish that the express covenant has been broken. In *Meadox Medicals Inc. v. V.P.I. Ltd.*[60] the defendant company had been formed by two former employees of the plaintiffs in order to manufacture and market medical equipment. The employees were researchers who marketed products which rivalled those manufactured by the plaintiff company. McWilliam J. found that while the defendant's product was an improved product it had been made by using trade secrets, know-how and other information, in breach of their contractual undertaking not to use this kind of knowledge within one year after leaving employment.

If the employee has acquired trade or professional secrets which would prejudice the employer's business if, upon termination of employment, these secrets could be used by the employee, either for his own or another's benefit, the employer can prevent the employee from entering future employment in that field or industry. The secret need not be expensive or complex. In *Forster & Sons v. Suggett*[61] the works engineer for the plaintiff company who manufactured glass bottles knew the correct proportion of gas and air to be introduced into the furnaces during the manufacturing process. He was successfully prevented from working in the glass-making industry for a period of five years after leaving employment; the restraint covered the whole of the United Kingdom. An employer cannot by contract prevent an employee from using the skill he ordinarily employs in his trade, even if the employer has contributed towards developing this talent; so in *Arthur Murray Dance Studios of Cleveland Inc. v. Witter*[62] the plaintiffs could not prevent the defendant from working for a rival studio simply because they taught the defendant to become a proficient dance instructor. No "secret" information or skill was conferred upon the defendant. Problems arise where the information acquired is not a trade secret.

---

[59] [1983] I.L.R.M. 372.
[60] Unreported, High Court, April 22, 1982.
[61] (1918) 35 T.L.R. 87.
[62] (1952) 105 N.E. 2d. 685.

Unless the information is used in such a way as to breach the implied duty of fidelity owed by an employee to the employer (as in *A.F. Associates v. Ralston*[63] when employees, on resignation, took confidential customer files with a view to using them to start a rival business by soliciting customers of the employer) confidential information may be used by former employees for their own purposes even if such use directly harms the business of their former employer. In *Faccenda Chicken Ltd. v. Fowler*[64] the defendants, former employees of the plaintiff company, started to directly compete in the business of selling fresh chickens from refrigerated vans. The defendants knew the pricing policy of the plaintiff and the routes, delivery days and names and addresses of the plaintiff's customers as a result of their former employment and, using this knowledge, began to undercut the plaintiff company. Because this case did not involve the deliberate copying of lists or other documents and because no employment relationship existed at the time of use the plaintiff could not invoke the implied contractual term to serve the employer faithfully. Further, the fact that no express term had been included in the contract was held not to be material for the Court of Appeal held that even where confidential information that is not a trade secret (*i.e.* knowledge of a process, method of manufacture or the like) may prove commercially harmful to the employer if used by a former employee, former employees may not be prevented from using it for their own advantage even by an express covenant. The Court of Appeal left open the question whether such information can be protected from use if the former employee seeks to sell it to a third party for gain rather than use it himself in order to earn a living.

The most common interest an employer can advance as worthy of protection has been described as his "customer connection". Businessmen, partnerships and corporations view customers and clients as part of their assets and, as such, the former employee who solicits orders may imperil the stability of the venture. If the employee has a close working relationship with members of the public the chances of the customers "following" the employee are substantial. It is legitimate to try and prevent this. Instances where the "customer connection" may be shown to exist include travelling salesmen (*Arclex Optical Corporation v. McMurray*[65]); warehouse manager (*Waterworth v. Eaton*[66]); laundry manageress (*Franklin Steam Laundry Co. v. Anderson*[67]); solicitor (*Mulligan v. Corr*[68]); hairdresser (*Oates v. Romano*)[69]; milk roundsman (*Home Counties Dairies v. Skilton*[70]).

If the employee does not have close contact with the public a restraint will not be allowed to operate. The position of a laundry manageress who has close contact with the public can be contrasted with a menial employee who works

---

[63] [1973] N.I. 229.
[64] [1985] I.C.R. 589: *Baker v. Gibbons* [1972] All E.R. 759.
[65] [1958] Ir. Jur. Rep. 65.
[66] (1905) 40 I.L.T.R. 27.
[67] (1903) 3 N.I.J.R. 85.
[68] [1925] I.R. 169.
[69] (1950) 84 I.L.T.R. 161.
[70] [1970] 1 All E.R. 1227.

in the laundry pressing clothes. Even if there is some degree of contact with the public it does not follow that the employee will have sufficient "pull" to entice away former customers; a law firm would not expect to find its business falling away if a receptionist left to work for a rival firm. In *Dosser v. Monaghan*[71] the defendants were musicians who had formerly played in a band owned by the plaintiff. They had agreed not to enter into similar employment within 50 miles of Great Yarmouth, Redcar, Southport, New Brighton and Belfast, towns in which the band played regularly. Best L.J. refused to grant an interlocutory injunction preventing the defendants from breaching the covenant; given the fact that the defendants were obscure members of the band the covenant was not reasonable. "It would be different if the musicians were famous."

*(ii) Covenants on the sale of a business.* Again, certain obligations are implied upon the sale of a business. The rule which dictates that a man must not derogate from his grant prevents the vendor of a business from directly soliciting his former customers: *Trego v. Hunt*,[72] *per* Lord MacNaghten. If the vendor wishes to open up a shop next door to his former business, trading in exactly the same product, he can do so. As a result, the purchaser of a business will include a term in the contract limiting the freedom of the vendor to compete. Again, a covenant must be shown to be reasonable as between the interests of the parties and in the public interest. In *Nordenfelt*, the House of Lords upheld a worldwide covenant preventing the vendor of a munitions firm from trading for a period of 25 years. On the other hand, if the covenant is designed to go further and prevent the vendor from competing with the purchaser it may be rejected. In *British Reinforced Concrete v. Schieff*[73] the plaintiffs, manufacturers of road reinforcements used throughout the U.K., purchased a business which made steel road reinforcements. The owner of the business sold covenanted not to act as servant of any person concerned in the business of manufacturer or sale of road reinforcements in any part of the U.K. The covenant was held too wide; the defendant dealt only in a particular kind of reinforcement; he manufactured the product and was not responsible for retail activities. Younger L.J. observed that it is only the business *sold* which is the legitimate subject of protection. In Ireland *Trego v. Hunt* was extended in *Gargan v. Ruttle*[74] to prevent a former partner soliciting customers of the old "firm".

In general, the position of a professional person or trader who has been a partner in a professional or business organisation is seen as being governed by the sale of a business interest line of authority, as distinct from being an employee covenant. So, in cases where a solicitor, a doctor, an accountant, a designer, or other professional person, becomes a partner, then the partnership deed may validly seek to prevent the partner from competing, or taking the firm's clients when leaving the partnership. While in some cases there may be

---

[71] [1932] N.I. 209.
[72] [1896] A.C. 7; *Gargan v. Ruttle* [1931] I.R. 152.
[73] [1921] 2 Ch. 563; *Allied Dunbar (Frank Weisinger) Ltd. v. Frank Weisinger, The Times,* November 17, 1987.
[74] *Oswald, Hickson Collier & Co. (a firm) v. Carter-Ruck* [1984] 2 All E.R. 15.

some nice issues of fact, such as who were the firm's customers,[75] the general view is that these agreements are to be more readily enforceable than employment covenants.[76] There may however be other considerations which make the covenant unenforceable, as in *Kerr v. Morris*[77] where the Court of Appeal had to consider whether a medical partnership which limited the power of a retiring partner to practice infringed legislation regulating the National Health Service, but as long as the activity of the professional concerned is seen as a partnership activity, the covenant will not be as closely scrutinised as an employee restraint. However, in the case of a salaried partner who does not participate fully as a partner, *i.e.* does not share fully in the profits, or losses, of the partnership, the courts may regard the partner as being, in reality, an employee and thus may deprive the covenant of the benefit of the arm's length presumption that attaches to goodwill covenants. So, in *Briggs v. Oates*[78] the defendant was held, as a salaried partner, to be an employee.

Another problematical contemporary development in this context is the advent of profit sharing, or share transfers in a company to employees as part of their remuneration. Does this sharing element put the employee in the same kind of position as the vendor of a business for the purpose of enforcement of a restraint clause? There is an English case which indicates that this will be so in appropriate circumstances.[79]

*(iii) Exclusive dealing arrangements.* Members of an industry may decide to amalgamate in order to support and protect their common interests. In the agricultural community it is common for producers to form co-operative ventures, the rules of which may have to satisfy the restraint of trade doctrine. The leading case is *McEllistrem v. Ballymacelligott Co-operative Agricultural and Dairy Society*,[80] a decision of the House of Lords on Appeal from the Court of Appeal in Ireland. The appellant was a member of a co-op in Kerry, the co-op being formed to develop and improve dairy farming in the district. Members of the society were bound by its rules which provided that while the society was bound to take and market all the milk produced by its members, the members were precluded from selling milk to any other local creamery. Members could not resign from the creamery unless the Co-operative's committee consented. The Court of Appeal in Ireland felt bound by two earlier decisions and upheld the rules; these cases, *Athlacca Co-operative Creamery v. Lynch*[81] and *Coolmoyne & Fethard Co-operative Creamery v. Bulfin*[82] were overruled. The House of Lords reasoned that while the respondents were

---

75   *Whitehill v. Bradford* [1952] Ch. 236: *Deacons (a firm) v. Bridge* [1984] 2 All E.R. 19; *John Mitchell Design plc v. Cook* [1987] I.C.R. 445; *Clarke v. Newland* [1991] 1 All E.R. 397.
76   [1986] 3 All E.R. 217.
77   [1987] Ch.D. 90.
78   [1991] 1 All E.R. 407.
79   *Systems Reliability Holdings plc v. Smith* [1990] I.R.L.R. 377.
80   [1919] A.C. 548.
81   (1915) 49 I.L.T.R. 233.
82   [1917] 2 I.R. 107.

entitled to protect their venture by ensuring stability, both of supply and in the
lists of their customers, the restraint went further than was necessary to ensure
this; it was no answer to say that the restraint operated locally and that the
appellant could carry on farming in another part of Ireland:

> "in a sparsely inhabited agricultural neighbourhood, with scanty means
> of communication, a prohibition of trade in every township within a
> radius of ten miles, might have precisely the same effect upon the
> business of a small trader, as if the preclusion extended to the remotest
> corners of Donegal; . . . "[83]

In *Kerry Co-operative Creameries and Another v. An Bord Bainne Co-
operative Ltd. and Another*[84] the plaintiffs, members of the first defendant, a
co-operative society established for the purpose of assisting Irish dairy farmers,
*inter alia*, by arranging for the export sale of dairy produce, proposed to
change its rules so as to dilute the shareholding and related rights of members
who declined to trade with Bord Bainne, but marketed export sales products
themselves. The proposed rule change obtained the necessary two-thirds
majority at a special general meeting, but the plaintiffs objected and sought to
have the rule change declared an unlawful restraint of trade. Costello J.,
holding the doctrine applicable, found the changes to be reasonable. The new
rules required members to make a commercial decision as to the benefits of
trading with Bord Bainne or otherwise. Further, the duty to trade with Bord
Bainne was of a limited nature – indeed it replaced a broader duty to provide
all produce to the Board – and, given Bord Bainne's legitimate interest in securing continuity of supply, the rule changes did not fall within *McEllistrem*. The
Supreme Court also upheld the restraint as reasonable, although O'Flaherty J.,
as mentioned above, was not persuaded that the doctrine applied in the absence
of a restraint covenant.[85] McCarthy J., utilising Article 45 of the Constitution
in interpreting the common law, concluded,

> "I am satisfied that the restraint as I have outlined it is also a reasonable
> one; indeed, I have difficulty in understanding any argument that it is
> unreasonable that a co-operative dairy society may not use any legiti-
> mate means available to it, to secure that those of its members who trade
> through it will benefit and greatly benefit by such trading as compared
> with those of its members who decide to go it alone, in whole or in part.
> As to the second consideration of public good, it is clear as a legitimate
> opinion to be held by the majority of the members that the national

---

[83] [1919] A.C. 548 at 562, *per* Lord Birkenhead L.C.
[84] [1991] I.L.R.M. 851.
[85] O'Flaherty J. distinguished *Stenhouse Australia Ltd. v. Phillips* [1974] A.C. 391; *Wyatt v.
Kreglinger* [1933] 1 K.B. 793 and *Bull v. Pitney Bowes* [1966] 3 All E.R. 384. See also the
case of *Sadler v. Imperial Life Assurance* [1988] I.R.L.R. 388.

interests are best served by the promotion and expansion of Bord Bainne."[86]

*(iv) Solus Agreements.* The most frequently litigated exclusive dealing arrangement in recent years involves contracts between petroleum wholesalers and retailers, the arrangement obliging retailers to take all the petrol and motor oils they may require from one particular wholesaler. These contracts, known as "solus" agreements are common, both in the Republic and Northern Ireland. There are important formal differences between the law on each side of the border.

A solus agreement typically involves a promise given by a wholesaler who undertakes to keep retailers supplied with petrol if the retailer in turn agrees to take all the petrol he will require from the wholesaler alone. The retailer may also promise to keep his filling station open at all reasonable hours and to take a minimum gallonage. The retailer may in return be given a rebate on petrol supplied, as well as interest-free loans and help in purchasing petrol pumps. There are substantial advantages to the wholesaler under such agreements. Distribution costs are kept down and the wholesaler can better predict customer demand in the future. The retailer, apart from the financial advantages, is also guaranteed some degree of security of supply.

In the Republic the solus agreement was investigated by the Fair Trade Commission, predecessor of the Restrictive Practices Commission,[87] who reported in 1961,[88] that, while the solus system was generally of benefit to the public, the profitability of the retail trade led to an undesirable proliferation of outlets that could not then be controlled under existing planning legislation. A statutory instrument was passed in order to discourage the expansion of the solus system. The maximum period an agreement could run was for five years; nor could retailers obtain price advantages under a solus agreement for the instrument made it unlawful for wholesalers to, directly or indirectly, discriminate as between retailers although rebates are paid to retailers who sign solus agreements.[89]

The Statutory Instrument of 1961 produced a change in policy on the part of petrol distributors in the Republic. Wholesalers decided not to invest in retailers, who could obtain substantial advantages and ride free of the tie after a relatively short time. This led to wholesale distributors purchasing their own retail outlets. Statutory Instrument No. 294 of 1961 was modified in 1972 so that a solus agreement could run for a maximum period of 10 years.[90] A ban on the acquisition of retail outlets by wholesalers, known as company-owned outlets, was also imposed. The Commission in its 1979–80 report[91] recom-

---

[86] [1991] I.L.R.M. 851 at 871.
[87] Now replaced by the Competition Authority under the Competition Act 1991.
[88] Pr. 6000.
[89] S.I. No. 294 of 1961.
[90] Following a second Inquiry into the motor spirit distribution trade: (I Prl. 1931) (1971) S.I. No. 150 of 1972.
[91] 1944. The Fair Trade Commission Inquiry, which was published in 1990, is the most recent investigation of the motor spirit distribution industry (Pl. 7951).

mended no change be made in the maximum period of 10 years and that restrictions on the acquisition of outlets by companies remain, with some modifications. While the author cannot give here a detailed outline of the effects of the legislation it should be noted that in Statutory Instrument No. 70 of 1981 the Minister continued the 10-year maximum period for the duration of solus agreements but altered the terms and conditions a solus agreement may contain. While the wholesaler was not entitled to discriminate between solus and non-solus retailers, wholesalers could provide training facilities for solus retailer staff, advance loans to rebuild, repair or extend stations and any similar service or facility, without being obliged to provide these facilities to non-solus retailers. Statutory Instrument No. 70 of 1981 also entitled the wholesaler to charge a lower price to solus retailers as long as the differential was "reasonable and justifiable" in the circumstances. Limitations on the acquisition of company-owned retail outlets remained in force.

In the most recent report, the Fair Trade Commission considered that while the 10-year maximum period was long and had anti-competitive aspects, there was a net benefit to the public in the form of wholesaler investment in independent outlets which would otherwise not be made. However, given the fact that the European Commission[92] in 1983 had passed legislation in the form of a Regulation which gave petrol outlets a similar exemption under Article 85(3), there was no real point in continuing to regulate solus agreements under domestic law. To date, this report has not been implemented directly *in toto*, but the repeal of the Restrictive Practices Acts by the Competition Act 1991 means that the Statutory Instruments governing solus agreements are no longer in force. The Council Regulation of 1984, the Competition Act 1991 and the common law, together, now govern such agreements. These statutory provisions do not mean that the common law rules, as enunciated in *Esso* by the House of Lords, are superfluous in the Republic. If other factors make a tie oppressive it may still be held an unreasonable restraint of trade, notwithstanding that it is to last for under 10 years. Factors that are important here are the duration of the tie, mutuality of obligation and the position of the wholesaler in the industry. There are signs that a court may permit a new wholesaler, attempting to establish himself in the market, to extract slightly better terms for himself. The desire to stimulate new competition explains this factor. While it is possible for the courts to look forward and anticipate future events like inflation and O.P.E.C. price increases – see *Amoco Australia Property. v. Rocca Brothers,*[93] – a solus agreement that is fair and reasonable at the time of agreement cannot be unenforceable if subsequent events produce this result: *Shell U.K. v. Lostock Garage.*[94]

The leading Irish case is the decision of Kenny J. in *Continental Oil Company of Ireland Ltd. v. Moynihan.*[95] Moynihan, a retailer, entered into a solus agreement in 1970 agreeing to take petrol at the plaintiff's scheduled prices.

---

[92] Regulation 1984/83, reproduced at p. 169 of Pl. 7951.
[93] [1975] A.C. 561.
[94] [1977] 1 All E.R. 481.
[95] (1977) 111 I.L.T.R. 5.

The agreement was to run for five years; Moynihan was obliged to buy all his petrol from the plaintiffs and to give 48 hours' notice of his requirements. He was to take the largest possible consignments, not less than 800 gallons. The station was to be kept neat and clean and the number of pumps was not to be reduced. Moynihan benefited from the agreement by purchasing pumps on interest-free hire-purchase terms. Moynihan refused to take any further supplies from the plaintiffs when they operated a differential pricing scheme that threatened Moynihan's already slender profit margins. Kenny J. upheld the plaintiff's claim for an injunction to restrain the defendant from taking supplies from elsewhere. Viewed at the date of agreement Kenny J. held the agreement reasonable as between the parties and refused to find that enforcement of this agreement was against the public interest. While this may be correct, a later decision of the Court of Appeal in England puts a new light on *Moynihan's* case; if the differential pricing scheme operates harshly it is possible to deny an injunction on the grounds that the wholesaler has not acted fairly and should thus be denied an equitable remedy.[96]

While it is material to the question of reasonableness to decide if there is a prohibition on the retailer selling or leasing the premises to a third party without the wholesaler's consent (see *Irish Shell Ltd. v. Burrell*[97]) the duration the tie has to run is perhaps the most important factor in determining reasonableness; in *Esso* the House of Lords held a 21-year tie unreasonable but a four-year five-month tie valid; the Ontario Court of Appeal however upheld a 10-year tie, with an option to renew for a further 10 years, on the particular circumstances of the case before it: *Stephens v. Gulf Oil Canada Ltd.*[98]

Many of the cases involving solus agreements have been cases in which the company taking the benefit of the "tie" has sought interlocutory relief, *e.g. B.P. Ireland Ltd. v. Shreelawn Oil Co. Ltd.*[99] and *Irish Shell Ltd. v. Dan Ryan Ltd.*[100] and it is clear that the English cases are influential, notwithstanding the legislative gloss in Ireland that results from the Competition Act 1991. Indeed, in the only recent Irish case in which the limits of the restraint of trade doctrine has been thoroughly examined Costello J. gave his view of the correct solution to a question that has troubled academic lawyers and judges since *Esso Petroluem Co. Ltd. v. Harpers Garage (Stourport) Ltd.*[101] was decided. According to a majority of the Law Lords in *Esso Petroleum* the doctrine of restraint of trade does not apply to cases where, at the time of contracting, the trader does not enjoy the freedom to carry on the trade in question. If therefore a lease is executed under which X *acquires* from the company a lease of a station as well as the freedom to carry on the trade of petroleum retailer, and the lease also contains a solus tie, it is arguable that the doctrine does not apply for only by

---

[96] *Shell U.K. v. Lostock Garage* [1977] 1 All E.R. 481.
[97] Unreported, High Court, June 17, 1981.
[98] (1976) 65 D.L.R. (3d.) 193.
[99] [1983] I.L.R.M. 372.
[100] Unreported, High Court, April 25, 1985.
[101] [1968] A.C. 269.

signing the lease does the trader *acquire* the freedom to carry on the trade; at that time, that is, just prior to signing, he has no freedom to trade. While this dogmatic proposition has been affirmed as a prima facie rule in *Cleveland Petroleum Co. v. Dartstone Ltd.*[102] by the Court of Appeal, the Privy Council, in *Amoco Australia Property v. Rocca Brothers*[103] (mindful that this proposition could provide a neat method of evading the restraint of trade doctrine altogether) held that the reasonableness of the covenant had to be established even in such a case. In *Irish Shell Ltd. v. Elm Motors,*[104] *Costello* J., after considering these three decisions, distinguished *Esso* from *Amoco* on the ground that in the former case the garage proprietor never owned the land leased to him while in *Amoco* the proprietor had earlier owned the land. Holding that the case before him fell outside the restraint of trade doctrine (even though the site was partly owned by the lessee proprietor before the lease containing the tie was granted to the lessee proprietor), Costello J. said:

> "As a general principle the common law doctrine of restraint of trade does not apply to restraints on the use of a particular piece of land when imposed by a conveyance or lease of the land in question. This exemption would not, however, apply if the restriction is contained in a demise when the lessor has obtained the land as part of a transaction which enables the restriction to be imposed. If such a transaction takes place the restraint must pass the test of reasonableness laid down in the doctrine."[105]

It does not seem to have been argued that the tie in *Irish Shell Ltd. v. Elm Motors Ltd.* requiring the lessee to purchase motor fuels from the lessor for the duration of the lease – 42 years – was unenforceable by virtue of the statutory provisions already discussed that is, Statutory Instrument No. 70 of 1981.

## Resale Price Maintenance and Restrictive Commercial Practices

Agreements between producers or retailers which keep the price of goods or services at a certain level are not invalid at common law unless the person challenging the agreement is able to show the price level maintained is unreasonable or is designed to produce a monopoly. In *Cade v. Daly*[106] an agreement between members of The South of Ireland Mineral Water Manufacturers and Bottlers Trade Protection Association that no member would sell beer and minerals below a scheduled price was upheld; the agreement operated within one district of Cork and was to run for a short period.

This position reflects a reluctance to protect consumers against artificial pricing arrangements. In the Republic, prices of many essential goods have in

---

[102] [1969] 1 W.L.R. 116.
[103] [1975] A.C. 561.
[104] [1984] I.R. 200.
[105] *Ibid.* at 213.
[106] *Cade v. Daly* [1910] 1 I.R. 308.

the past been controlled by legislation; see, *e.g.* the Prices Act 1958 and statutory instruments limiting the price payable for milk. The Restrictive Trade Practices Acts 1953–1987 made it the task of the Commission established by the Acts to establish fair trading rules in relation to the supply and distribution of goods and services.[107] The legislation was upgraded in 1972 by the passing of the Restrictive Practices Act 1972 and later, in 1978, the Mergers, Takeovers and Monopolies (Control) Act 1978 added a further level of control.

The Restrictive Practices Acts were used to counteract certain anti-competitive practices, most notably through the use of a statutory order prohibiting below-cost selling as a means of combatting the trend towards the increasing control of the grocery trade by a small number of multiple supermarket outlets.[108] Despite a revision and extension of existing competition and consumer protection laws through the Restrictive Practices (Amendment) Act 1987, a decision to completely restructure the law of competition was made by the Fianna Fail/Progressive Democrat Coalition Government, and this has resulted in the Competition Act 1991, a fairly short piece of legislation which promises to have profound consequences for Irish competition law.

The basic model for the 1991 Act has been provided by sections 85 and 86 of the Treaty of Rome. Article 85 applies to anti-competitive agreements and practices which may affect trade between Member States within the European Community, and in a number of recent Irish cases, the Irish courts have been required to consider whether Article 85 has been infringed. Similarly, Article 86, which provides a means of counteracting practices which affect trade between Member States and constitute abuse of a dominant position, has been considered by Irish courts, most notably in *Kerry Co-operative Creameries Ltd. and Another v. An Bord Bainne and Another.*[109] In cases where the agreement or practice does not have an Article 85 or 86 dimension because it does not involve trade between Member States, Irish competition law, prior to the implementation of the Competition Act 1991, was heavily dependent upon public agencies for investigation and enforcement. The 1991 Act however takes a different tack by giving the relevant agency, the Competition Authority, certain powers of scrutiny, investigation, licensing of agreements and certification of agreements and practices, but the Act envisages that recourse to the courts in respect of anti-competitive practices and agreements, and any abuse of a dominent position, will generally be the prerogative of aggrieved persons. Section 6 of the Act confers a cause of action for relief against any undertaking which is a party to the offending agreement upon any aggrieved person – generally a competitor, trader or consumer, but the expression is not defined.[110]

---

[107] Report on Travel Companies and Tour Operators (1984) Pl. 2601.

[108] Restrictive Practices (Groceries) Order, 1987 (S.I. 1987 No. 142); Restrictive Practices (Confirmation of Order) Act 1987.

[109] [1991] I.L.R.M. 851.

[110] See Cregan, Annotation to Competition Act 1991 in *Irish Current Law Statutes Annotated* (Sweet & Maxwell). The enforcement mechanisms have been enhanced through the Competition (Amendment) Act 1996. See Lucey, Annotation in *Irish Current Law Statutes Annotated*.

The most important section in respect of competition rules is section 4. Section 4(1) provides that

> "all agreements, decisions or concerted practices between undertakings or associations of undertakings which have as their object or effect the prevention, restriction or distortion of competition in trade in any goods or services in the State or in any part of the State are prohibited and void."

Section 4(1) goes on to specify particular examples of prohibited and void agreements, decisions or concerted practices. These are agreements, decisions or concerted practices which

(a)  directly or indirectly fix purchase or selling prices or any other trading conditions;

(b)  limit or control production, markets, technical development or investment;

(c)  share markets or sources of supply;

(d)  apply dissimilar conditions to equivalent transactions with other trading parties, thereby placing them at a competitive disadvantage;

(e)  make the conclusion of contracts subject to acceptance by the other parties of additional obligations which by their nature or according to commercial usage have no connection with the subject of such contracts.

Section 4(1) catches price-fixing, production-fixing, market-sharing, exclusive purchasing and distribution agreements, franchising agreements, intellectual property licensing agreements, and agreements which contain restrictive covenants, amongst others. The Competition Authority can license and thereby exempt anti-competitive agreements if the agreements meet certain criteria found in section 4(2); the agreement must contribute to improving the production or distribution of goods or services, or promote technical or economic progress, it must allow consumers a fair share of the benefits, it must not impose terms which are not indispensible for the attainment of the objectives of the agreement, and it must not afford the undertaking with the possibility of eliminating competition. The Competition Authority may also, under section 4(4), give a certificate that an agreement, decision or concerted practice does not infringe section 4(1).

Once a section 4(2) licence or a section 4(4) certificate is given, the right of action under section 6 is not available. The potential scope of section 4 is clearly enormous.[111] The volume of work involved in vetting, licensing and certification has led to amendments in the 1996 Act whereby *certificates* could also cover categories of agreement: prior to the 1996 Act only category *licences* could be issued. The workload of the Authority is voluminous.[112]

---

[111]  Brown (ed.), *Competition Law and Regulation in Ireland* (Competition Press, Dublin 1991).

[112]  See generally, Maher (1993) 28–30 Ir.Jur. 21.

While section 4 of the 1991 Act is based on Article 85 of the Treaty of Rome, section 5 of the 1991 Act is a rough approximation of the Article 86 abuse of a dominant position provision found in the Treaty of Rome. Examples of abuse can be found in section 5 and these include the imposition of unfair purchase or selling prices, imposition of unfair trading conditions, limitations on production, markets or technical developments, but the precise identification of abuse will be a matter for the Minister and the Authority, under section 14, or the courts, following a section 6 action brought by an aggrieved person. One of the first instances of ministerial action was the reference of the proposed purchase of the *Sunday Tribune* by Independent Newspapers; Independent Newspapers, in the event of the acquisition proceeding, would control three of Ireland's five Sunday newspapers. The Competition Authority recommended that the acquisition should be permitted. A ministerial order prohibiting the transaction was subsequently made.[113] In its first decision on whether certain agreements are designed to prevent, restrict or distort competition, the Authority ruled that a non-competition clause in a partnership sale agreement, which bound the seller not to engage in a similar business for three years within a 20-mile radius, would have no effect on competition in the circumstances of the case.[114]

The interface between restraint of trade and the Competition Acts remains somewhat ill-defined. There is some evidence that the courts are sticking to certain basic tenets of restraint of trade[115] while the Competition Authority is evolving an approach which is closer to E.U. competition law and more directly influenced by economic theory. For example, in *Sibra Building Company v. Palmerstown Centre Development Ltd.,* Keane J. reaffirmed the view that covenants to fetter a future freedom are outside the scrutiny of the doctrine; the Competition Authority takes no such view. Also, in *Apex Fire Protection Ltd. v. Murtagh*[116] the Competition Authority, while upholding a confidentiality covenant in an employment contract, struck down non-competition clauses imposed upon a former employee who intended to enter the market. The Authority also took a very strict view of duration restraints, opting for an "absolute necessity" rather than a reasonableness test. The basis upon which injunctive relief may be available for breach of the Competition Acts has been tentatively explored[117] by the Supreme Court, and the possibility of an award of damages for breach of the provisions of the Competition Acts is a very real option for the Irish courts (see *Blemings v. David Patton Ltd.*[118] and *Carna Foods Ltd. v. Eagle Star Insurance*),[119] even if the plaintiff in such an action is party to a contract that would otherwise be enforceable.

---

113 Report, March 1992, Pl. 8795.
114 Decision of April 9, 1992, Nallen/O'Toole Agreement.
115 Unreported, High Court, November 24, 1992.
116 [1993] E.L.R. 201; see generally the Competition Authority, *Employee Agreements and the Competition Act, Iris Oifigiúil,* September 18, 1992.
117 *Premier Dairies v. Doyle* [1996] 1 I.L.R.M. 363.
118 Unreported, High Court, January 15, 1997.
119 [1997] 2 I.L.R.M. 499.

*Trade union rules affecting union members*[120]

It is established that because the relationship between a trade union and its members is based on contract, the rules of a union which control or restrict the freedom of union members to earn a living are subject to the restraint of trade doctrine: see *Doyle v. Trustees of the Irish Glaziers and Decorative Glass Workers T.U.*[121] In the leading case of *Langan v. Cook Operative Bakers Trade Union*[122] a trade union gave financial assistance to members who wished to emigrate and find work abroad. The rules provided that a member who returned to the district was bound not to work as a baker in that locality. The plaintiff was held able to repudiate the agreement upon making restitution of the sums advanced, the agreement being an unreasonable restraint of trade. While these decisions would appear to be incompatible with the spirit of section 3 of the Trade Union Act 1871, for that section effectively excluded all union agreements from the restraint of trade doctrine, it is easy to endorse the justice of the result in *Langan's* case.

## Recent expansion of the restraint of trade doctrine

While employment and sale of a business contracts are the classical instances in which the restraint of trade doctrine will operate the categories of restraint of trade are never closed; English case law has held the rules of the Football Association,[123] Pharmaceutical Society of Great Britain[124] and the Test and County Cricket Board,[125] to be subject to review under the doctrine. These cases involve persons who complain about rules to which they did not consent. Indeed, the rules of the Irish Football League, which laid down maximum signing-on fees and wages for part-time professional footballers, were held an unreasonable restraint of trade in *Johnston v. Cliftonville Football & Athletic Club Ltd.*[126] Even though these rules, agreed between the football club and the Irish league were, in a formal sense, consented to by the plaintiff when he registered as a league player with the club. In *Watson v. Prager*[127] the rules of the British Boxing Board of Control, which regulated contracts between managers and boxers, were not only held to be subject to the restraint of trade doctrine, *pace, Schroeder Music Publishing Co. Ltd. v. Macaulay,*[128] but the contract between the boxer and the manager could also be regulated during the currency of the agreement.

In the field of equestrian sports, the rules of the Jockey Club were scrutinised by reference to the restraint of trade doctrine in *Nagle v. Fielden*[129] and

---

[120] Wedderburn, *The Worker and the Law* (3rd ed.), pp. 788–817.
[121] (1926) 60 I.L.T.R. 78.
[122] [1938] Ir.Jr.Rep. 65.
[123] *Eastham v. Newcastle United Football Club* [1964] Ch. 413.
[124] *Pharmaceutical Society of Great Britain v. Dickson* [1970] A.C. 403.
[125] *Greig v. Insole* [1978] 1 W.L.R. 302.
[126] [1984] N.I. 9.
[127] [1991] 3 All E.R. 486.
[128] [1974] 1 W.L.R. 1308.
[129] [1966] 2 Q.B. 633.

a decision to refuse a trainer's licence to the plaintiff on the ground of her sex were held an unlawful restraint of trade. *Nagle v. Fielden* is a fairly conventional application of the rules of restraint of trade but the decision of the Supreme Court in *Eddie Macken v. O'Reilly*[130] breaks new ground in several respects. The plaintiff, a world famous show jumper, complained that the rules of the Equestrian Federation of Ireland, which obliged Irish competitors to ride only Irish bred horses, constituted an unreasonable restraint of trade. The rules were protective measures designed to promote the Irish horse breeding industry. Hamilton J. held that the rules, because they denied Macken the opportunity to compete on the best available horses, Irish or otherwise, constituted an unreasonable restraint of trade. In the Supreme Court, O'Higgins C.J. and Kenny J., the only judges who found it necessary to discuss the restraint of trade doctrine, ruled that even if the rules did prejudice the plaintiff, they were still to be enforced because the wider public interest required that Macken's individual interests be overridden. O'Higgins C.J. ruled:

> "The trial judge disregarded entirely the undisputed evidence as to the effect a change of policy would have on the horse breeding industry and on equestrian sport in Ireland. This ought to have been considered as a balance to the harm or inconvenience caused to the plaintiff."[131]

With respect, the rules on restraint of trade as they stand do not require such a "balancing process"; if the rule is unreasonable *inter partes* it is unnecessary to consider the public interest; indeed most cases are decided entirely on reasonableness *inter partes*. The view that individual interests which are unreasonably prejudiced must be sacrificed if they conflict with wider public interests is a novel doctrine. The general approach to the common law doctrine of restraint of trade is largely individualistic; if the agreement is not shown to be reasonable *inter partes* then the restraint falls at the first hurdle and there is no room for a balancing process of this kind. However, there are signs of a modified Irish doctrine emerging, as a result of the *Eddie Macken* case and the observations of McCarthy J. in *Bord Bainne*[132] where, it will be recalled, the learned judge observed that Article 45 of the Constitution could influence the interpretation of the restraint of trade doctrine. While McCarthy J. held that the rules of Bord Bainne were reasonable *inter partes* and that the public interest would best be served by the development of Bord Bainne, McCarthy J. may well have been prepared to uphold the rules, even if unreasonable *inter partes* because of the greater public interest that the Bord Bainne rules supported.

## Construction of covenants in restraint of trade

It is often said that employment restraints, because they are "negotiated" between persons who are in unequal bargaining positions, are viewed restrictively; it is

---

[130] [1979] I.L.R.M. 79.
[131] *Ibid.* at 91.
[132] [1991] I.L.R.M. 581.

clear that an employer and employee restraint is treated with greater suspicion than a restraint imposed on the sale of a business. In *John Orr Ltd. and Vescom B.V. v. John Orr*[133] Costello J. observed that "greater freedom of contract is allowable in a covenant entered into between the seller and the buyer of a business than in the case of one entered into between an employer and employee."

The courts recognise that goodwill covenants may be a reasonable means of permitting the purchaser to enjoy the benefits of the business acquired, while in employment cases all the employer purchases is the services of the employee and, further, the deeper pocket of the employer is more likely to be able to fund litigation than that of the employee. While in some instances the employee may possess considerable clout – Lord Denning observed that "a managing director can look after himself"[134] – there are reasons which indicate that the restrictive interpretation of employment covenants is perhaps a sound policy. Employers sometimes rely on provisions which exceed protection of their legitimate interests and the courts should not help an employer who has not drafted the covenant with precision. Two Irish cases support this view; the first is *Oates v. Romano*.[135] The second, *Coleborne v. Kearns*,[136] concerned an employee who worked in a shop which involved him in close contact with the community. The employer extracted a covenant that prevented him from working in a similar shop within 15 miles of the employer's shop for seven years should he "leave" employment. The court refused to interpret "leave" as also covering dismissal by the employer.

If however the employer can show he has a legitimate interest to be protected the courts often permit the employer to enforce the covenant, even if it, literally construed, would cover less meritorious cases. The employee will often place an extended, quite fantastic and literal interpretation on a covenant hoping that this will lead the court to strike the covenant as invalid. In *Home Counties Dairies v. Skilton*[137] an employer was able to enforce a covenant against a milk roundsman who worked as a roundsman for a rival concern, even though literally construed the covenant against working as a dairy produce salesman would prevent him from selling cheese in a grocer's shop. The Court of Appeal ruled that the covenant must be construed by reference to the commercial background in which the contracting parties operated. A useful exercise is to compare *Oates v. Romano*[138] with *Marion White v. Francis*.[139] In the first case the covenant was interpreted literally and held to be too wide because it would have precluded the defendant, a hairdresser, from working as a receptionist or having even a financial interest in the plaintiff's business. In *Marion White v. Francis* on the other hand, the clause indicated that the employee could not be

---

[133] [1987] I.L.R.M. 702 at 704.
[134] *Littlewoods Organisation v. Harris* [1978] 1 All E.R. 1026 is illustrative of the difference between key employees and other workers.
[135] (1950) 84 I.L.T.R. 161.
[136] (1911) 46 I.L.T.R. 305.
[137] [1970] 1 All E.R. 1227.
[138] (1950) 84 I.L.T.R. 161.
[139] [1972] 1 W.L.R. 1423.

engaged as agent servant or assistant or in any other capacity whatsoever in the business of ladies hairdresser. The Court of Appeal rejected the contention that the clause could prevent the employee from working as a bookeeper in a backroom, or be a shareholder or director in a hairdressing company. The covenant was held to be directed at active participation which was directly connected to the hairdressing business and had to be read in such a context.

The same principle is applicable to restraints in general, regardless of the kind of relationship involved. In *Clarke v. Newland*[140] two general practitioners engaged in a partnership executed a deed which obliged a retiring partner "not to practise within the practice area" within three years. The defendant argued that the covenant was too wide because it prevented him from practising in a hospital or as a consultant. This interpretation was rejected in favour of an interpretation limiting the covenant to practising as a general practitioner, because the objective behind the clause was the protection of one partner against rivalry in trade and, further, the clause had to be construed by reference to the context and factual matrix at the time when the agreement was made.

## Severance of void provisions – basic principles

Even if the courts place a very liberal interpretation on covenants in restraint of trade the court may well decide to limit the scope of a restraint by strict application of the doctrine of severance.[141] The doctrine of severance is not intended to give the courts a free hand to redesign or reshape a covenant that fails to meet a test of proportionality. As Younger L.J. said in a leading case, the doctrine is "permissible in a case where the covenant is not really a single covenant but is in effect a combination of several distinct covenants. In that case and where the severance can be carried out without the addition or alteration of a word, it is permissible but in that case only."[142] This principle is strictly adhered to in employment cases, but seems to be relaxed somewhat in sale of business cases. In *John Orr Ltd. and Vescom B.V. v. John Orr*[143] Costello J. had to consider the enforceability of a restraint clause which bound the defendant who had sold his interest in the first plaintiff company to the second plainiff company. The share transfer agreement obliged the defendant to enter into a service agreement, and for one year after leaving employment, not to compete with the business of the second defendant, on a world-wide basis, and not to solicit customers of either the first or second plaintiff. Costello J. found this covenant to be too wide and, holding that it was legitimate to protect the purchaser from solicitation of the first plaintiff's customers by the defendant, the learned judge severed that part of the solicitation clause that

---

140 [1991] 1 All E.R. 397; *Norbrook Laboratories Ltd. v. Smyth*, September 30, 1986.
141 See generally Heydon, *The Restraint of Trade Doctrine*, pp. 122–136.
142 *Attwood v. Lamont* [1920] 3 K.B. 571 at 593; *N.I.S. Fertilizers Ltd. v. Neville*, unreported, N.I. High Court., February 10, 1986; *Marshall v. NW Financial Management*, *The Times*, June 24, 1997.
143 [1987] I.L.R.M. 702.

operated *vis-à-vis* the acquiring company, Vescom B.V. However, the finding of the court in relation to the competition clause is inconclusive because counsel for the plaintiffs submitted that the restraints were reasonable and did not suggest that the court had a power to redraft covenants which were too wide. Costello J. held the restraints, as world-wide restraints covering business activities of the second defendant, were excessive and in these circumstances were unenforceable.

If the restraint is too wide in relation to the *geographical* area to be covered the court may limit the scope of the covenant by cutting down the area, insofar as this can be done by eliminating towns, districts or even countries through a "blue pencil" test. In *Mulligan v. Corr*[144] the defendant, a solicitor's apprentice, agreed that when he left the plaintiff's employment he would not practice (a) within 30 miles of Ballina and Charlestown; and (b) within 20 miles of Ballaghadreen. The Supreme Court considered reducing the geographical area by severing (b), leaving covenant (a) enforceable. It was held that even if severance were performed the area covered by covenant (a) was still excessive.

The issue of geographical scope is a very difficult issue that can only be decided on a case by case basis. In an important English case a restraint preventing the branch manager and a consultant employed by an employment agency was held excessive even though it operated within 1,000 metres of their previous place of employment. The area covered was, in effect, most of the City of London and, as such, an impermissible restraint.[145] Even a relatively small geographical area may be excessive, depending on circumstances. Twenty miles was too wide where the customers constituted a static group that was unlikely to move away from the former district in any large numbers: *N.I.S. Fertilizers Ltd. v. Neville.*[146]

In *Skerry, Wynne & Skerry's College Ireland Ltd. v. Moles*[147] a teacher who agreed not to teach within seven miles of Belfast, Dublin and Cork when he left employment with the plaintiffs as a shorthand typing instructor was held bound. The court severed the geographical restraint by deleting Dublin and Cork. It was also argued that the covenant was too wide in terms of duration. The "evil" the plaintiffs were entitled to protect themselves against was the possibility that when the teacher left he would take his students with him. The defendant argued that the restraint, to apply for three years, was indefensible because the courses offered by the plaintiffs ran for 12 to 18 months, Barton J. dismissed this argument. It is suggested that the case is wrongly decided on this point. If the employer can show he has a legitimate interest to protect but the covenant is excessively long, a court cannot substitute a reasonable period for the unreasonable period. If however, the plaintiff seeks an injunction the

---

[144] [1925] I.R. 169; *Sadler v. Imperial Life Assurance* [1988] I.R.L.R. 388; *Ronbar Enterprises Ltd. v. Green* [1954] 1 W.L.R. 815.
[145] *Office Angels Ltd. v. Rainer Thomas, The Times*, April 11, 1991; *Spence v. Marchington* [1988] I.R.L.R. 392.
[146] Unreported, High Court, February 10, 1986 (N.I.).
[147] (1907) 42 I.L.T.R. 46.

same result may follow from the way in which the courts implement this discretionary remedy. In *Cussen v. O'Connor*,[148] the plaintiffs employed the defendant as a commercial traveller, obliging him not to work for any rival business for either (a) 10 years after commencement of employment in 1889; or (b) two years after termination of employment. The defendant left employment in 1892; the covenant therefore had seven years to run, an unduly long time. Andrews J. instead of striking down the restraint, ruled that the court had a discretion to determine how long the injunction was to run; in the view of the learned judge a reasonable period would be two years. So, although the court could not reduce the plaintiff's substantive rights to reasonable proportions it could limit the scope of the primary remedy available.

There is a suggestion in the judgment of McWilliam J. in *E.C.I. European Chemical Industries Ltd. v. Bell*[149] that the courts may now be prepared to "tailor" a restraint which is clearly too wide in terms of area and duration, once the employer can show he has a legitimate interest worthy of protection. In that case the plaintiffs had inserted an excessively wide covenant, adding that if the covenant was held invalid "the said covenant shall be given effect to in its reduced form as may be decided by any court of competent jurisdiction." After noting the conflict between the English cases of *Commercial Plastics v. Vincent*[150] and *Littlewoods v. Harris* McWilliam J. expressed *obiter* a preference for the later decision. While one can sympathise with McWilliam J. who was clearly concerned that the employee should not use trade secrets to the positive detriment of the former employer, in principle the courts should not allow the employer "two bites at the cherry", *i.e.* draft a wide restraint which will no doubt discourage employees from engaging in quite acceptable and lawful activities after leaving employment, and then invite the courts to redraft the contract when one employee challenges through the courts the validity of the covenant: see *Davies v. Davies*.[151]

The American courts take a more adventurous view of the doctrine of severance and openly admit that they have the jurisdiction to shape and restrict area, duration and activity restraints to reasonable proportions.

There is one final point which should be mentioned. Most employment restraints are governed by reasonableness *inter partes*, as are covenants for the sale of a business. The question of reasonableness in the public interest does not generally arise. In the English case of *Hensman v. Traill*[152] a covenant preventing a doctor from competing was struck down as being unreasonable in regard to the public interest and *inter partes*: had the covenant been reasonable *inter partes* it would still have been defeated, it being contrary to the public

---

[148] (1893) 32 L.R.(Ir.) 330.
[149] [1981] I.L.R.M. 345: contrast *John Orr Ltd. and Vescom B.V. v. John Orr* [1987] I.L.R.M. 702.
[150] *Commercial Plastics v. Vincent* [1965] 1 Q.B. 623; *Littlewoods v. Harris* [1978] 1 All E.R. 1026, criticised by Phillips, (1978) 13 Ir.Jur. 254.
[151] (1887) 36 Ch.D. 359.
[152] *The Times*, October 22, 1980; *Kerr v. Morris* [1987] Ch.D. 90.

interest to prevent a doctor practising in such circumstances. In *Johnston v. Cliftonville Football & Athletic Club Ltd.*[153] an attempt to justify maximum wage payments as being in the public interest was made by the Irish League: if wages could be freely negotiated there was, the League argued, a danger that the two biggest and wealthiest clubs would attract the best players through lucrative contracts and this would lead smaller clubs to overreach themselves financially in an attempt to retain their best players. Murray J. held that this consequence was not established by the defendants, on the evidence.

## Repudiatory breach and enforceability

The enforceability of a restraint clause may also be in doubt in cases where the party seeking enforcement has been guilty of a repudiatory breach of contract. So, where an employee has a fixed-term contract and the company employing him is compulsorily wound up, thereby effecting a wrongful dismissal, the employer is not entitled to the benefit of the restraint by virtue of the repudiation of the contract of employment.[154] This principle was more applied in *Briggs v. Oates*.[155] The defendant was employed by a firm of solicitors for a fixed period. The partnership came to an end and the employment of the defendant accordingly terminated. A restraint preventing the defendant from practising for five years within five miles of the partnership office was held unenforceable. The breach must however be repudiatory.[156] *Briggs v. Oates* was used as the foundation for an argument that where the restraint purported to operate when a repudiatory breach took place on the part of the employer, the entire clause was unenforceable even if the event that brought the clause into play was innocuous (*e.g.* the resignation of the employee).[157] In *Rock Refrigeration Ltd. v. Jones*[158] the Court of Appeal has rejected this argument.

---

[153] [1984] N.I. 9.
[154] *Measures Bros. Ltd. v. Measures* [1910] 2 Ch. 248.
[155] [1991] 1 All E.R. 407.
[156] *Spence v. Marchington* [1988] I.R.L.R. 392.
[157] *D. v. M.* [1996] I.R.L.R. 192.
[158] [1997] 1 All E.R. 1.

# Part 6

# Capacity to Contract

# 16 Contractual Capacity

## Introduction

Most systems of law seek to protect persons falling into particular categories of "disability" by rendering them unable to contract freely. When this occurs, the individual bargain is thereby invalid although it may be that some limited remedy may still be available; see for example section 2 of the Sale of Goods Act 1893, which provides that the supplier of goods that are non-necessaries may recover a reasonable price from an infant or mentally disordered person to whom the goods have been provided. In certain instances, statute may close off contractual remedies even under an executed contract, but general tortious remedies, or the law of restitution, or equitable principles, may still provide a prospect of some limited recovery from the person lacking full contractual capacity.

## Infants or Minors

At common law a person attained the age of majority at 21 years of age: this age was selected because it was felt to be the age at which it became possible to expect a youth to be able to wear and carry a full set of armour.[1] Following upon the Law Reform Commission, *Report on The Age of Majority, the Age for Marriage and some Connected Subjects*,[2] the Oireachtas enacted the Age of Majority Act 1985. The Act follows a strong international trend towards reducing the age of majority.[3] Section 2(1) provides:

> "Where a person has not attained the age of twenty-one years prior to the commencement of this Act, he shall attain full age –
> (a) on such commencement if he has attained the age of eighteen years or is or has been married, or
> (b) after such commencement when he attains the age of eighteen years, or in case he marries before attaining that age, upon his marriage."

The Act came into force on March 1, 1985. Therefore section 2 provides that any person who was aged 18 years or was a married person on that date, or had

---

[1] Harland, *The Law of Minors in Relation to Contracts and Property* (Butterworths, Sydney 1974), s.106.
[2] (1977) L.R.C. 2. In the U.K. see the Report of the Committee on the Age of Majority (Cmnd. 3342) (1969), and Law Commission Report No. 134.
[3] See generally, Hartwig (1996) 15 I.C.L.Q. 780; Hartland, *The Law of Minors in Relation to Contracts and Property* (1974) in Chap. 2 examines the general position in common law jurisdictions. The law in Canada is based on the common law and various provincial statutes: see Percy (1975) 53 Can. Bar. Rev. 1.

been married before that date, attained full age on March 1, 1985. Where a person married after that date, or attained full age after March 1, 1985, then such a person will attain full age on marriage or eighteenth birthday, as the case may be.[4]

While the decision to reduce the age of majority to 18 has attracted wide agreement, as the Law Reform Commission's Report pointed out, and is compatible with developments elsewhere, the decision to confer full age upon a person by virtue of marriage was described by one commentator as arguably a policy of debatable merit.[5] As this commentator points out, the policy of encouraging banks and other institutions to deal with young persons may be a laudable one but there are still difficulties of definition and it is arguable that the Act may expose immature and inexperienced young persons to legal liabilities at a time when they require more protection rather than less. The 1985 Act does not, however, alter any of the rules relating to an infant's liability in contract and it is to this (as the law stands) quite unsatisfactory area of the law of contract that we now turn.

Professor Treitel points out that the law relating to infants' contractual liability attempts to strike a balance between two conflicting objectives; first of all, the courts seek to protect an infant from the consequences of his own inexperience in commercial matters. On the other hand, the judges seek to protect commercial men who unwittingly contract with infants, particularly if the infant has misrepresented that he is of age.[6] However, the position under the Infants Relief Act 1874, and the general case law surrounding infants' contracts, is generally agreed to favour the infant unduly. While in Ireland the 1874 Act continues to present an obstacle to a rational reappraisal of the law, in the United Kingdom, the Minors Contracts Act 1987 has adjusted many of the worst features of the law, in particular providing sweeping and largely discretionary relief against a minor who has had property transferred to him on the foot of a contract.[7] We will consider the 1987 Act below.

The general rule at common law is that an infant's contract is voidable; voidable in this context bears two meanings. First of all, certain contracts are valid unless repudiated by the infant. Other contracts are voidable in the sense that unless the infant affirms the transaction within a reasonable time after coming of age the transaction does not bind him. Certain contracts are valid at common law; these are contracts for necessaries and beneficial contracts of service.

## Necessaries

The following statement, found in *Coke upon Littleton*, a seventeenth century English text, is perhaps one of the most enduring propositions in the common law:

---

[4] In the U.K. the age of majority fell from 21 to 18 as from January 1, 1970: Family Law Reform Act 1969, s.1.

[5] Commentary to the Age of Majority Act 1985, in *Irish Current Law Statutes Annotated*, at 85/2–11 (Binchy).

[6] Treitel, *The Law of Contract* (9th ed., 1995), p. 150.

[7] s.3(1).

"An infant may bind himself to pay for his necessary eat, drink, apparel, necessary physic, and such other necessaries, and likewise for his good teaching or instruction, whereby he may profit himself afterwards, but if he bind himself in an obligation or other writing, with a penalty for the payment of any other, that obligation shall not bind him."

Necessaries are defined in the Sale of Goods Act 1893, section 2, as "goods suitable to the condition in life of such infant or minor . . . and to his actual requirements at the time of the sale and delivery." Many of the old cases were decided before juries, who favoured the interests of the trader, by giving an extended meaning to necessaries. It is now the role of the judge to say first of all whether an item is capable of being classified as a necessary. Certain items are incapable of being necessaries. In *Skrine v. Gordon*[8] the defendant, who represented himself to be a member of the Surrey Staghunt, agreed to buy a hunter from the plaintiff for £600. The price was never paid. Lawson J. ruled that the issue of whether this was a necessary or not should never have been left to a jury: "luxuries or amusement are quite different from necessaries." So, in the leading English case of *Ryder v. Wombwell*[9] jewelled cuff-links were held incapable of being classified as necessaries. One Australian case holds that a bicycle may be a necessary if used to convey the infant to and from his place of work 11 miles away: *Scarborough v. Sturzaker*.[10] Early Canadian case law suggests that a motor car cannot be a necessary even if used for business purposes: *Nobles v. Bellefleur*.[11] However, in *First Charter Financial Bank v. Musclow*[12] Craig J. found that in more recent times the access to a motor vehicle must generally be regarded as a necessary and this view must be correct, certainly if the vehicle is to be used for essential activities such as travel, whether work-related or for general domestic purposes. Whether a flashy sports model or a racing car would be caught by the argument that these are items of luxury or amusement must, however, remain an open question. Vehicles which are to be used for entreprenurial business activities must, however, be regarded as incapable of being necessaries, for the common law does not regard trading contracts to be enforceable, even if apparently for the benefit of the infant.[13] It is clear that a heavy lorry cannot be a necessary: *Mercantile Union v. Ball*,[14] not least because of the traditional reluctance of the common law to allow an infant to enter trade, thereby running the risk of financial ruin. The necessaries test will vary depending upon the circumstances of the infant. While a motor boat may not be a necessary for most infants – see *Prokopetz v. Richardsons Marina*[15] – it is conceivable that a young person supplied with such a boat in a

---

[8] (1875) I.R. 9 C.L. 479.
[9] (1868) L.R. 4 Ex. 32.
[10] (1905) 1 Tas.L.R. 117.
[11] (1963) 37 D.L.R. (2d.) 519.
[12] (1974) 49 D.L.R. (3d.) 138.
[13] *Cowern v. Nield* [1912] 2 K.B. 419.
[14] [1937] 2 K.B. 498.
[15] (1979) 93 D.L.R. (3d.) 442: Clark (1980) 26 McGill L.J. 110.

remote lakeland region may come within the rubric of an infant supplied with necessaries. The Law Reform Commission Report[16] contains an example which readers may find enlightening. A computer supplied to a 17-year-old who uses the machine in pursuit of his studies in computer science at the university may be a necessary (after all, books supplied to students are, according to *Soon v. Wilson*[17]) but the same computer, supplied to a 17-year-old who uses the machine to play computer games, will not be a necessary. Similarly, a set of encyclopedias sold to an infant television researcher or journalist may be a necessary but, in general, would not be if supplied to an infant with a mere thirst for knowledge. Guns supplied to an infant game-keeper may, according to the case of *Dickson v. Buller*,[18] be necessary goods.

If the goods can be classified as necessaries the supplier must go further and show that the infant was not adequately supplied with such goods; this will be a difficult burden to discharge. In *Nash v. Inman*[19] 11 fancy waistcoats supplied to an Oxford undergraduate were held not to be necessaries, the father of the infant being able to show to the court that his son was adequately supplied with clothing.

> "If a man satisfies the needs of the infant or lunatic by supplying to him necessaries, the law will imply an obligation to repay him for the services so rendered, and will enforce that obligation against the estate of the infant or lunatic. The consequence is that the basis of the action is hardly contract. Its real foundation is an obligation which the law imposes on the infant to make a fair payment in respect of needs satisfied. In other words, the obligation arises *re* and not *consensu* . . . the sum he recovered was based on a *quantum meruit* . . . this is very ancient law, and is confirmed by the provisos of section 2 of the Sale of Goods Act 1893 – an Act which was intended to codify the existing law . . . the plaintiff has to shew, first, that the goods were suitable to the condition in life of the infant; and, secondly, that they were suitable to his actual requirements at the time – or, in other words, that the infant had not at the time an adequate supply from other sources."[20]

The words of section 2 of the 1893 Act indicate that an infant can only be liable for necessary goods if they have been supplied; even then, the section provides the infant is only liable to pay a "reasonable price" for such goods. A contract to purchase goods which will be used to carry on a trade are not necessaries as the English case of *Whittingham v. Hill*[21] and the Nova Scotia case of *Jenkins v. Way*[22] show. Contracts for necessary services are also valid.

---

[16] (1985) L.R.C. 15.
[17] (1962) 33 D.L.R. (2d.) 428.
[18] (1859) 9 I.C.L.R. (Appendix).
[19] [1908] 2 K.B. 1.
[20] Fletcher-Moulton L.J. at [1908] 1 K.B. 1 at 8, and see the same judge in *Re J.* [1909] 1 Ch. 574 at 577. Contrast Buckley L.J. in *Nash v. Inman* [1908] 1 K.B. 1 at 12.
[21] (1619) Cro.Jac. 494.
[22] (1881) 14 N.S.R. 394.

An infant widow will be liable on a contract to obtain funeral services for her deceased husband: *Chapple v. Cooper*.[23] A contract to enable an infant to gain instruction and earn his living as a professional billiards player will be enforceable, even if partly executory in nature: *Roberts v. Gray*.[24] Legal advice which results in substantial benefits to an infant may also be a necessary service: *Helps v. Clayton*.[25]

If the service or goods provided are made available to the infant upon terms that are not universally favourable the contract may not be enforceable, even though the goods or service, viewed in isolation, are undoubtedly a necessary. In *Fawcett v. Smethurst*[26] a contract for the hire of a motor vehicle was held in the circumstances to be one for necessaries but because the hire was concluded on terms which included an express term placing the responsibility for loss or damage to the vehicle on the infant hirer in all circumstances, this was held to make this particular contract unenforceable because the contract, viewed as a whole, was not advantageous to the infant.

## Beneficial Contracts of Service

This category of enforceable contract has evolved relatively recently. It seems to have originated in the nineteenth century when the courts began to view contracts of apprenticeship and related transactions as enforceable at common law: contrast *Horn v. Chandler*[27] with *De Francesco v. Barnum*.[28] Many cases that are treated as beneficial contracts of service are difficult to disentangle from the category of necessary services. A contract of service will bind the infant if, viewed as a whole, the contract is seen as beneficial to the infant. The fact that one or more terms may be to the disadvantage of the infant will not be conclusive. In *Shears v. Mendeloff*[29] an infant boxer appointed the plaintiff to be his manager. The agreement provided that the manager would get 25 per cent. of the infant's earnings. The manager had not expressly covenanted to obtain fights for the plaintiff and the infant had to pay his own expenses. Avory J. in the English High Court held this contract of service not to be beneficial to the infant; it may be different if the infant receives instruction as a boxer: see the Australian case of *McLaughlin v. D'Arcy*.[30] The provision of education and instruction will not be dispositive, even if no alternative source of instruction was available on improved terms. In *Toronto Marlboro Hockey Club v. Tonelli*[31] a young hockey

---

23  (1844) 13 M. & W. 252.
24  [1913] 1 K.B. 520; see Mathews (1982) 33 N.I.L.Q. 148.
25  (1864) 17 C.B.(N.S.) 553.
26  [1914] 84 L.J.K.B. 473.
27  (1670) 1 Mod. 271.
28  (1890) 45 Ch.D. 430. The first edition of *Simpson on Infants*, published in 1875, does not contain an analysis of any such separate category.
29  [1914] 30 T.L.R. 342.
30  (1918) S.R.N.S.W. 585.
31  (1979) 96 D.L.R. (3d.) 135.

player signed a standard form contract which tied him to a junior hockey club. This method of recruitment to the lucrative world of North American ice hockey was the only established method of advancement and the terms offered were the only terms available, for all junior clubs used the same terms. There were penalty provisions and compensation clauses which obliged Tonelli to pay over a percentage of his earnings to the plaintiffs when his contract expired, should he be signed by a senior professional team. The Ontario Court of Appeal, by a majority of two to one, held Tonelli was not bound by this contract.

If the contract in question is incidental to the means whereby an infant earns his living it may be enforceable. In *Doyle v. White City Stadium*,[32] Jack Doyle, then an infant, obtained a licence to box from the British Boxing Board of Control. The terms of the licence provided that should the licensee be disqualified in a contest his purse would be forfeited. Doyle, never the most scientific of pugilists, was disqualified for a low blow during a title fight. He challenged the rules, alleging that they could not bind him. The English Court of Appeal upheld the rules. It was generally in Doyle's interest that the rules prohibit or discourage illegal blows, even if on this occasion the rules operated against him.[33]

The most significant examination of this category of potentially enforceable contract is the decision of the Court of Appeal in *Chaplin v. Leslie Frewin (Publishers) Ltd.*[34] The plaintiff, a son of Charlie Chaplin, had fallen out with his father and, while marrying during his infancy, was dependent solely upon national assistance payments for the support of himself and his wife. He entered into an agreement with the defendants whereby the defendants would publish a ghost-written autobiography of the plaintiff in which the plaintiff would make revelations about his famous father and his family life. The plaintiff was paid a substantial advance and he co-operated with the writers. After the book was written it proved to be a most unflattering work about the Chaplin family, and the plaintiff, prior to publication, sought to have the publishing contract, including an assignment of copyright, declared unenforceable as being a contract of service which was not to his benefit because it was potentially libellous. The Court of Appeal held that the contract was to be viewed as akin to a beneficial contract of service and that the general test of substantial benefit could be satisfied. The royalties payable and the advance already made, in the view of the majority of the Court of Appeal,[35] outweighed the negative aspects of the agreement, namely the potential for litigation it created and the adverse publicity that would attach: as one judge observed, "the mud may cling but the

---

[32] [1935] 1 K.B 110.

[33] Hanworth M.R. said the rule "is applicable on both sides and cannot be looked at merely from the particular point of view of one person such as the plaintiff in this case."

[34] [1966] Ch. 71.

[35] Denning M.R. at 88 dissented:

"I cannot think that a contract is for the benefit of a young man if it is to be a means of purveying scandalous information. Certainly not if it brings shame and disgrace on others; invades the privacy of family life; and exposes him to claims of libel . . . it would be better for him to take his mother's advice: 'Get a job and go to work.'"

profits will be secured."[36] The contract enabled the plaintiff to make a start in the world of journalism and it mattered not that the work was scurrilous and lacked literary merit.

In *Keays v. The Great Southern Railway*[37] the plaintiff, a child of 12, held a season ticket, issued at a reduced rate, which exempted the defendants from liability for injuries caused by their negligence. The season ticket was purchased to enable the plaintiff to travel to and from school. The plaintiff was injured while travelling on the defendants' line, the injuries being the result of negligence. Hanna J., after construing the contract as a whole, ruled that the terms of the contract were so harsh as to entitle the infant to repudiate it:

> "The contract in this case is very unfair to the infant because it deprives her of practically every common law right that she has against the railway company in respect of the negligence of themselves or their servants. For that reason, I think it is not for her benefit."

Even a contract entered into by an infant which does not as such enable the infant to obtain schooling, instruction or a living may fall into this category. In *Harnedy v. The National Greyhound Racing Association*[38] an exemption clause which purported to prevent an infant greyhound owner from suing in respect of injuries to the dog was held not to be beneficial and could be repudiated.

## Voidable Contracts

The common law courts recognised that contracts in which an infant was capable of being subjected to a series of recurring obligations were voidable in the sense that the infant was bound unless he repudiated the contract within a reasonable time.[39] These contracts fall into five distinct categories.

(i) There is Irish support for the proposition that an insurance contract which involves a periodic obligation to pay premiums is a voidable contract: see *Stapleton v. Prudential Assurance*.[40] If the premium has been paid and the risk has begun to run, the infant cannot repudiate the contract and obtain the return of premiums paid.[41] If the contract is void, for infringing the Life Assurance Act 1774, for example, premiums will be repayable.[42]

(ii) An infant is also liable on contracts to take shares or to meet "calls" made upon shareholders. This obligation was explained by Parke B. in the leading English case of *North Western Railway Co. v. McMichael*[43] as turning

---

[36] *per* Danckwerts L.J. at 95.
[37] [1941] I.R. 534: contrast *Clements v. London and North Western Railway* [1894] 2 Q.B. 482.
[38] [1944] I.R. 160.
[39] *Carter v. Silber* [1892] 2 Ch. 278, affirmed [1893] A.C. 360.
[40] (1928) 62 I.L.T.R. 56.
[41] *Ibid.*; see also *Ritchie v. Salvation Army Assurance* [1930] I.A.C.Rep. 20.
[42] *Gardner v. Hearts of Oak Assurance* [1928] I.A.C.Rep. 20.
[43] (1850) 5 Ex. 114.

upon the fact that the infant acquires an interest in something of a permanent nature rather than a mere chattel. The exception may implicitly rest on the need to facilitate the development of joint stock companies in general and railways in particular. *McMichael's* case was followed in *Midland Railway v. Quinn.*[44] If the infant is to avoid liability he must show and plead that he repudiated the contract within his infancy or a reasonable time thereafter: *Dublin and Wicklow Railway Co. v. Black.*[45] An action to recover money paid by the infant on the foot of such an obligation will fail unless the infant can show a total failure of consideration: *Steinberg v. Scala (Leeds) Ltd.*[46] followed in *Stapleton's* case.

(iii) An infant who agrees to enter a partnership will be bound by that contract unless he repudiates openly within a reasonable time; *Griffiths v. Delaney,*[47] however, establishes that the supplier of goods delivered to the partnership cannot recover the price from an infant partner. Should an infant partner sue other partners for specific performance the action will fail for want of mutuality – the courts do not award specific performance against an infant. The infant will be able to sue should he affirm the partnership agreement upon coming of age: *Shannon v. Bradstreet.*[48]

(iv) Family settlements and those made by an infant in contemplation of marriage may be avoided within a reasonable time after coming of age. Indeed, in *Paget v. Paget*[49] the plaintiff agreed with his father upon the terms of a resettlement of family property. At the time of the transaction the plaintiff, unknown to himself, was only 20 years of age. Ten years later he learnt that he was an infant at the date of execution of the settlement and repudiated immediately. He was held to have done so in time. Any delay after learning the true facts would have been fatal to the right to repudiate: *Allen v. Allen.*[50] Contrast the position where an infant spouse signs a consent form permitting the other spouse to sell the family home; under section 10(1) of the Family Law Act 1981, the consent is not voidable on the grounds of infancy alone.

(v) A lease taken by an infant is voidable. If the infant repudiates within a reasonable time after coming of age he will not be liable to pay rent due in the future. The case of *Blake v. Concannon*[51] is authority for the view that if the infant has used and enjoyed the property before repudiation he will be liable to pay for the use and enjoyment of the demised property; the desire to prevent unjust enrichment of the infant is evident in *Mahon v. Farrell*[52] which supports the view that an infant assignee is liable in similar circumstances. However, the view advanced in *Blake v. Concannon* has not been accepted in other jurisdictions and, in particular, Jessel M.R. declined to accept it in one English

---

[44] (1851) 1 I.C.L.R. 383.
[45] (1852) 8 Exch. 181.
[46] [1923] 2 Ch. 452.
[47] (1938) 4 Ir.Jur.Rep. 1.
[48] (1803) 1 Sch. & Lef. 64: *Milliken v. Milliken* (1845) 8 Ir.Eq.R. 16.
[49] (1882) 11 L.R.(Ir.) 26.
[50] (1842) 2 Dr. & War. 307.
[51] (1870) I.R. 4 C.L. 323.
[52] (1847) 10 I.L.R. 527.

case.[53] The view that is advanced in the leading English case of *North Western Railway Co. v. McMichael*[54] is contradictory. Parke B. indicated that the rule applicable in cases where an infant waives or repudiates the permanent interest is that the interest is at an end, as is any liability due upon it, even though avoidance of the contract may not have taken place before liability accrued. In the present writer's view, the Irish rule is preferable, at least when use and enjoyment of property has occurred. Cheshire, Fifoot and Furmston's *Law of Contract*,[55] however, favours the view of Parke B. There are decisions the other way. In *Kelly v. Coote*[56] a lease which devolved to an infant by operation of law was held to make an infant liable to pay rent even though the infant tenant had not moved into possession.

There are other kinds of contract which have been described as voidable contracts. In these contracts the transaction is not binding until it is affirmed. Most of the cases involve transactions which were not within the category of necessary goods and services and, for all practical purposes, this category of voidable contract did not survive the Infants Relief Act 1874.

# Infants Relief Act 1874

This statute, still in force in Northern Ireland and the Irish Republic, is a controversial piece of legislation; Treitel calls it: "a somewhat mysterious statute. No convincing reason has ever been advanced to explain exactly why it was passed."[57] One may add that few convincing observations have been advanced to conclusively show what it achieves.

## *Section 1*

> "All contracts, whether by specialty or by simple contract, henceforth entered into by infants for the repayment of money lent or to be lent, or for goods supplied or to be supplied (other than contracts for necessaries), and all accounts stated with infants shall be absolutely void. . . ."

[Section 1 goes on to except contracts valid under statute and contracts valid at common law or in equity.]

Several points must be made about section 1.

(i) Contracts in which money is lent to an infant and in which goods are supplied to an infant are rendered "absolutely void" by this section; cases in which the infant supplies goods or lends money are outside the section. It has been argued by Treitel[58] that the exception in favour of contracts for necessaries

---

53  *Re Jones* (1881) 18 Ch.D. 109 at 118.
54  (1850) 5 Ex. 114.
55  (13th ed.,1996), p. 449.
56  (1856) 5 I.R.C.L. 469: *Slator v. Brady* (1863) 14 I.C.L.R. 61.
57  (1957) 73 L.Q.R. 194.
58  73 L.Q.R. 194 at 198–199.

includes money-lending contracts in which the infant borrows money in order to purchase necessaries. In *Bateman v. Kingston*[59] the plaintiff sued upon a promissory note given by the defendant; the money lent upon the note was used to purchase necessaries. Lawson J. refused to allow an action on the notes *which bore interest*. It was suggested by Lawson J. that if notes were given to a trader in return for necessaries an action on the note may lie in such a case. The view that section 1 validates a loan to purchase necessaries seems inconsistent with *Bateman v. Kingston* and Treitel has since withdrawn this argument.

(ii) It is doubtful whether an infant can sue upon such a contract. Although the common law rule was otherwise the wording of section 1 on this point – "absolutely void" – seems to be irrefragable. English textbook writers, however, tend to favour the view that an infant can sue on the "absolutely void" contract.

(iii) The orthodox view is that an infant cannot recover back property transferred under an "absolutely void" contract. In order to recover the infant must show that there has been a total failure of consideration. In *Pearce v. Brain*[60] the infant plaintiff exchanged a motorcycle for a motor car. The car broke down four days later. The plaintiff sought to recover his motorcycle. The action failed; the plaintiff had used the car and was thus unable to show a total failure of consideration.

(iv) The English case of *Stocks v. Wilson*[61] is authority for the proposition that property will pass under an "absolutely void" contract. The Supreme Court of British Columbia, on the other hand, has ruled that property will not pass under an "absolutely void" contract to an infant buyer unless the infant has paid the purchase price: see *Prokopetz v. Richardson's Marina*.[62] The English view, because it protects innocent purchasers from an infant, is to be preferred.

(v) A guarantee of a loan made to an infant, which is "absolutely void", is itself unable to create a liability for an adult guarantor, according to the English case of *Coutts & Co. v. Brown-Lecky*.[63] This decision has not escaped criticism and in the British Columbia case of *First Charter Financial Bank v. Musclow*[64] Craig J. thought the decision to be wrong. The 1874 Act was designed to protect infants and it is difficult to see why an adult should be able to avoid a guarantee simply because the principal debtor can plead the 1874 Act as a defence. In fact the injustice of the decision in *Coutts & Co. v. Browne-Lecky* has been recognised by the United Kingdom Parliament. Section 2 of the Minors Contracts Act 1987 now provides that where a guarantee is given in respect of another's obligation under a contract, and the obligation is unenforceable by virtue of the minority of the contracting party, "the guarantee shall not for that reason alone be unenforceable against the guarantor."

---

[59] (1880) 6 L.R.(Ir.) 328.
[60] [1929] 2 K.B. 310; *Valentini v. Canali* (1889) 24 Q.B.D. 166.
[61] [1913] 2 K.B. 235.
[62] 1979 93 D.L.R. (3d.) 442; Clark, (1980) 26 McGill L.J. 110.
[63] [1947] K.B. 104.
[64] (1974) 49 D.L.R. (3d.) 138.

(vi) In cases where an infant trader acquires goods, those goods are not classifiable as necessaries. It appears from the Irish case of *Re Raineys*[65] that the infant cannot be adjudicated a bankrupt in respect of non-necessary goods caught by section 1 of the 1874 Act, even if the infant has suppressed the fact of infancy in order to induce others to contract with him.

*Section 2*

This obscure section provides:

> "No action shall be brought whereby to charge any person upon any promise made after full age to pay any debt contracted during infancy, or upon any ratification made after full age of any promise or contract made during infancy, whether there shall or shall not be any new consideration for such promise or ratification after full age."

Most of the reported cases deal with persons who contract to marry whilst an infant, and who make a new contract, not merely a ratification of the old, upon coming of age.[66] Section 2 has been considered in the Irish case of *Belfast Banking Co. v. Doherty*.[67] Doherty was sued upon a bill of exchange drawn by Wilson in consideration for a loan made to Doherty while Doherty was an infant. Doherty accepted the bill of exchange when he attained his majority. Wilson indorsed the bill of exchange to the plaintiffs who took without knowledge of the circumstances surrounding acceptance by Doherty. The Queen's Bench Division held that while section 2 would have prevented Wilson from recovering upon a promise to pay for a debt contracted during infancy it was not to be extended so as to prejudice a bona fide holder for value. The decision in *Belfast Banking Co. v. Doherty* is not, however, of any great significance following the enactment of section 5 of the Betting and Loans (Infants) Act 1892. This section declares that a fresh promise given after the coming of age to pay a loan contracted during infancy, that loan being void at law, and any negotiable instrument given in respect of such a loan, is to be void as against all persons. So, while the *Belfast Banking* case would still be effective in relation to an adult acceptor of a bill of exchange in respect of necessaries supplied to the acceptor while still an infant, the case would be decided differently today.

# Miscellaneous

*(i) An infant's liability in tort.*   It was held in *O'Brien v. McNamee*[68] that an infant over the age of seven may be liable in tort so long as the tort in question (a) does not require malice to be shown; (b) does not arise out of a breach of

---

[65] (1878) 3 L.R.(Ir.) 459.
[66] *Coxhead v. Mullis* (1878) 3 C.P.D. 439; *Northcote v. Doughty* (1879) 4 C.P.D. 385; *Ditcham v. Worrall* (1880) 5 C.P.D. 410.
[67] (1879) 4 L.R.(Ir.) 124.
[68] [1953] I.R. 86.

contract. As we have seen, many incidents can produce liability in tort as well as contract.[69]

The test developed to distinguish viable tort actions against an infant from those that are too closely linked to contract has been summarised by Pollock; the minor

> "cannot be sued for a wrong, when the cause of action is in substance *ex contractu*, or is so directly connected with the contract that the action would be an indirect way of enforcing the contract [but if the act is] independent of the contract in the sense of not being an act of the kind contemplated by it, then the infant is liable."[70]

The test is artificial in the extreme. The cases of *Jennings v. Rundall*[71] and *Burnard v. Haggis*,[72] discussed in the leading English texts, illustrate this point. One obvious way in which an infant might be held liable in tort, where he has fraudulently misrepresented his age or creditworthiness for example, would be to sue in deceit. It was held in the Irish case of *Bird v. Wilson*[73] that an infant does not "misrepresent" that she is of age simply by signing a contract.

Even if an infant positively asserts that he is of age, thereby inducing an adult to contract with him, the decision in *R. Leslie v. Sheill*[74] suggests that, because the statement is directly linked to the contract, no liability in deceit can arise. Irish case law, such as it is, suggests that the same rule will apply. In *Bateman v. Kingston*[75] the plaintiff pleaded that he had taken promissory notes from an infant, the infant fraudulently misrepresenting that he was of age. Lawson J., following the English case of *Bartlett v. Wells*,[76] held that the infant could not be liable in deceit. The only Irish authority the other way is a dictum of Crompton J. in *McNamara v. Browne*[77] where it was observed that an infant who gave a bond after holding himself out as of age may be liable on the bond.

If the infant retains property transferred the court will order restitution: *R. Leslie v. Sheill*, above. However, if the infant does not retain the property but has, for example, sold the property and merely has in his possession the proceeds of sale, then restitution is not possible on the ground that restitution stops where repayment begins.[78] Nor can the infant be ordered to make restitution in respect of the value of goods consumed. In the United Kingdom

---

[69] See Chap. 11.

[70] *Contracts* (12th ed.), p. 63.

[71] (1799) 8 Term Rep. 335. On the liability of adults for minors' torts see Law Reform Commission Report No. 17 (1986).

[72] (1863) 14 C.B.N.S. 45; *Ballet v. Mingay* [1943] K.B. 281.

[73] (1851) 4 Ir.Jur.Rep. 58.

[74] [1914] 3 K.B. 607.

[75] (1880) 6 L.R.(Ir.) 328.

[76] (1862) 1 B. & S. 836.

[77] (1843) 5 I.L.R. 460.

[78] *Ibid. per* Lord Sumner. The case of *Stocks v. Wilson* [1913] 2 K.B. 235 indicates that proceeds of sale may be disgorged from the infant but this decision is out of step with established authority.

section 3(1) of the Minors Contracts Act 1987 confers a broad discretion upon the courts, in cases where a contract is unenforceable by virtue of the minority of one party, when just and equitable to do so, to require the minor to transfer to the other party property acquired under the contract, or any property representing it. This power stops short of ordering the infant to pay compensation out of funds that have not been obtained by selling property transferred to the infant under the contract, for example, but it marks a significant expansion of proprietary relief in order to counteract unjust enrichment.

*(ii) An infant's liability in quasi-contract.* An action brought for the recovery of money paid or property transferred to an infant will be successful if the infant retains possession of the banknotes or chattel, even if property in the goods has passed to the infant. In cases like this there can be no question of the infant being forced to perform a contract; all the adult seeks is a limited restitutionary remedy. The cause of action, however, is, in *substance*, contractual.

In *Stocks v. Wilson*,[79] Lush J. suggested that if the infant has obtained property by way of fraud then equity will require the infant to account for the proceeds should he part with the goods. This observation was rejected by the Court of Appeal in *R. Leslie v. Sheill*[80] a year later. *R. Leslie v. Sheill* has been followed in other jurisdictions but the matter has still to be ruled upon by an Irish court. It is suggested that a fraudulent infant should be liable to account in such situations. There is an Australian case in point. In *Campbell v. Ridgely*[81] an infant fraudulently misrepresented that he was of age, thereby inducing the plaintiff to do work for him and also supply building materials. The plaintiff sued claiming (a) the value of the materials, £382, or in the alternative; (b) return of so much of the materials still in the infant's possession; and (c) an inquiry into the value of the goods not in possession. The defendant challenged ground three as an impermissible basis of relief. Although the later case of *R. Leslie v. Sheill* would suggest the defendant's challenge should have succeeded the Supreme Court of Victoria rejected the view that an account for the value of property fraudulently obtained and disposed of cannot be ordered against an infant.

It is hoped that this wider view of equitable restitution prevails in Ireland.[82]

*(iii) Estoppel.* Fraud by an infant will not operate an estoppel: *Levene v. Brougham.*[83]

---

[79] [1913] 2 K.B. 235.
[80] [1914] 3 K.B. 607.
[81] (1887) 13 V.L.R. 701.
[82] *Peters v. Tuck* [1915] 11 Tas.S.R. 30 suggests that an infant can be ordered to pay the value of banknotes bailed with him.
[83] (1909) 25 T.L.R. 265.

## Infants – Suggestions for Reform

The law relating to an infant's liability in contract and tort is generally recognised as being fraught with anachronistic and extremely irrational distinctions, distinctions which at times seem to ignore the underlying policy objective of preventing young persons from being exposed to liabilities that may unduly prejudice them – witness *Coutts & Co. v. Brown-Lecky*, above. Indeed, it is certainly arguable that the law is so complex that reforms may necessitate the complete repeal of all statutes which attempt to grant immunities from suit to infants. Protection from improvident, unconscionable or unfair transactions is available from the courts on equitable grounds, and, so this argument runs, with a modern expansion of the unconscionable bargain jurisdiction it may be that specific rules on infants' contracts are unnecessary and that the power of a court to protect young persons from unconscionable or oppressive bargains may produce more satisfactory solutions. In the Ontario case of *Toronto Marlboro Hockey Club v. Tonelli*[84] the majority of the Ontario Court of Appeal, using *Schroeder v. Macauley*,[85] decided an infant's contract dispute on unconscionability grounds. In fact readers should note that two old Irish cases, *Aylward v. Kearney*[86] and *Dawson v. Massey*,[87] suggest that equity will protect young (not necessarily infant) persons from oppressive bargains. While this argument in favour of total repeal may at first sight seem an attractive one, it has not found favour with any of the law reform agencies, nor has it provided the basis for legislation. The Irish Law Reform Commission, *Report on Minors' Contracts*[88] considered this course of action undesirable, primarily because it was likely to lead to considerable uncertainty in the law until the courts developed a coherent set of principles in relation to such contracts. After an expansive review of solutions enacted or proposed in several jurisdictions the Law Reform Commission recommended that legislation should seek to implement a policy "of qualified enforceability, which seeks to impose contractual responsibility on minors to the extent that it would be fair to do so, but no further". The Law Reform Commission proposed that legislation should introduce a general principle of restitution whereby a contract made by a minor with an adult party would be enforceable by the minor against the adult, but unenforceable by the adult against the minor. The parties would be entitled to apply to the court for compensation based on restitutionary rather than contractual principles. Restitution is to be interpreted widely, and, while the main objective is to reform the existing law which generally precludes an adult from recovering property or receiving compensation, it is also the intention of the Law Reform Commission to enable infants to obtain restitutionary relief in circumstances in which the law currently denies the infant a remedy – see

---

[84] (1979) 96 D.L.R. (3d.) 135.
[85] [1974] 1 W.L.R 1308.
[86] (1814) 2 Ball & B. 463.
[87] (1809) 1 Ball & B. 219.
[88] (1985) L.R.C. 15.

*Stapleton v. Prudential Assurance.*[89] The legislation should, in the Commission's view, include a power to grant to any party such relief by way of compensation or restitution as is proper, and upon doing so, to discharge the parties from further obligations specified by the contract if the court considers it proper to do so. The Report specifies that in making such orders the court should have regard to:

(a) the subject-matter and nature of the contract;

(b) the nature and value of property involved in the transaction;

(c) age, mental capacity and experience of the minor, when contracting, and at the time of the hearing;

(d) experience and knowledge of the minor relative to the contract;

(e) relative economic circumstances of the parties, at the time of contract and hearing;

(f) circumstances surrounding the transaction and the reasonableness or fairness of the bargain;

(g) value of actual benefits obtained under the contract;

(h) the amount of any benefit retained at the date of the hearing;

(i) the expenses or losses sustained or likely to be sustained;

(j) all other relevant circumstances.

The Commission, in the Report, went on to recommend the abolition of the concept of necessaries because it was felt that the concept is a difficult one that is not easily or readily understood or justifiable. The restitutionary principle, in the view of the Law Reform Commission, is able to accommodate transactions involving necessaries, but the Report recommended that specific reference be made in the legislation to whether the goods or services were suitable to the condition in life and actual needs of the minor, so that the courts can take account of such factors when determining an appropriate compensatory or restitutionary award.

The Report also set out a series of specific recommendations. The Law Reform Commission recommended that no action upon any debt contracted during infancy should be possible – even if a new promise "to pay" the debt is made when of full age – and the same rule should apply *vis-à-vis* loans made to infants even for necessaries. Ratification of undertakings made during infancy, however, should be possible if the infant comes of age. A validation procedure should be available which would enable a court to approve contracts entered into by minors upon an application by any party to the contract – but not the parents of the minor – if the court thinks it correct to do so. Factors the court should have particular regard to are:

---

[89]  (1928) 62 I.L.T.R. 56.

(a)  the age of the minor;

(b)  the nature, subject-matter and terms of the contract;

(c)  the reasonable likelihood of performance by each party;

(d)  the requirements of the minor;

(e)  the financial resources of the minor;

(f)  the wishes of the guardians of the minor.

This validation procedure would probably be used by young entertainers – rock musicians, sports-stars and the like – and must be seen in context; the Law Reform Commission recommended that employment contracts should bind infants if for their benefit. It would be anomalous if this closely related kind of transaction could not bind the infant in any circumstance. The Report also suggested legislation to clarify the existing law in relation to certain matters. Property should pass when the infant seller of goods or property transfers such property to the adult, even if the adult is aware of the infancy of the seller (subject to the restitutionary principle *vis-à-vis* the infant seller and the immediate purchaser). The restitutionary principle should apply to cases of misrepresentation as to full age but the existing law in relation to tort liability should remain. The Law Reform Commission also favoured the view that an adult guarantor should not be able to avoid liability simply upon proof that the infant principal debtor was a minor.

While one may quibble with one or two of the recommendations, total abolition of the concept of the contract for necessaries for example, the Report of the Law Reform Commission represents an admirable and balanced attempt to remedy some of the worst inequities that arise in the entire law of contracts and the general thrust of the Report – the restitutionary principle – is a coherent basis for reforming legislation.

## Convicts

The Forfeiture Act 1870, section 8, makes a convict incapable of making any contract, express or implied. The statute was discussed in *O'Connor v. Coleman*,[90] a case in which a solicitor attempted to recover legal fees from a convicted person.

---

[90]  (1947) 81 I.L.T.R. 42. See generally, Hogan, Byrne, McDermott, *Prisoners' Rights – A Study in Irish Law* (1981), pp. 97–98.

# Mental Incompetents

The modern authorities in England favour the view that a contract entered into by someone who is insane is voidable. Such a person has contractual capacity and he may be bound by a contract unless he was known to be insane by the other party, who, accordingly, took advantage of the other's infirmity. This rule, requiring knowledge of insanity, can be traced to the old common law cases. There is, however, authority for the view that a contract entered into by a person who, unknown to the other, was insane at that time, will be invalid in equity. The insane person must show that at the time he was so insane as to be incapable of understanding the contract. The Australian case of *Gibbons v. Wright*[91] and the British Columbia case of *Moore v. Confederation Life Association*[92] are in point.

The first approach, adopted by the English common law courts in the latter part of the nineteenth century, is at first sight irrational; how can a person consent to a bargain when it is established by the evidence that the transaction was not understood by that mentally ill person? The answer lies not so much in the rejection of the consensus theory, but in the need for commercial certainty. Bargains fully performed would be liable to be subsequently overturned in circumstances where persons dealing with the mentally disturbed could not be expected to know of that other's illness and inability to consent. In fact the view that an executed contract cannot be overturned on the ground that one party was so insane as to be incapable of understanding what was being done was later, in *Imperial Loan Co. v. Stone*,[93] extended to all transactions, executed or executory, although the inconvenience that would result if the contract was declared void (in this writer's view) does not justify the extension effected by *Imperial Loan Co. v. Stone*.[94]

It is, however, clear that *Imperial Loan Co. v. Stone* simply sets out the modern common law approach to pleas of mental incompetency and that the cases of *Gibbons v. Wright* and *Moore v. Confederation Life Association* are representative of a more venerable common law and equitable doctrine. Those cases establish that it does not follow that the *Imperial Loan Co.* case – even though it was decided by the Court of Appeal after the Union of Judicature Acts – delimits the situations in which a transaction involving a mentally unsound person will be overturned. The decision of the Privy Council in *Hart v. O'Connor*[95] recognises that all transactions struck with a person who, by virtue of mental illness, is unable to understand and thus consent to the transaction, will have to be tested by reference to unconscionability, in addition to *Imperial Loan Co.* Therefore there now exist alternative grounds for relief.

---

[91] (1953) 91 C.L.R. 423.
[92] (1918) 25 B.C.R. 465.
[93] [1892] 1 Q.B. 559.
[94] For a more considered view of the law, see the present writer's work, *Inequality of Bargaining Power* (Carswell, Ontario, 1987), pp. 111–142.
[95] [1985] 3 W.L.R. 214.

However, the Privy Council have adopted criteria that indicate that before the bargain can be overturned it must be unfair in two senses. There must be procedural unfairness – sharp practice, victimisation, pressure and the like – as well as substantive unfairness or "contractual imbalance" as Lord Brightman described it. Their Lordships all agreed with Lord Brightman that "equity will not relieve a party from a contract on the ground that there is contractual imbalance not amounting to unconscionable dealing." So, when old Mr. O'Connor, being of unsound mind, sold trust property at undervalue, on unusual terms, without fully independent advice, the sale was not to be subsequently overturned because the buyer was unaware of Mr. O'Connor's condition and the buyer had not acted in any way unfairly. The Privy Council overruled *Archer v. Cutter*[96] and the decision of the New Zealand Court of Appeal, below, in *O'Connor v. Hart*[97] on the ground that the wider view – that a contract to buy property from a mental incompetent can be overturned because the price is a substantial undervalue – is not truly representative of equitable practice.

In Ireland there is authority for the wider view that did not prevail in *O'Connor v. Hart*. In *Hassard v. Smith*[98] an action to set aside a lease on the ground that the lessor was of unsound mind failed. While it was clear that the lessee believed the lessor to be of sound mind, Chatterton V.-C. declared that for a contract with a person in the condition of the plaintiff to be upheld in equity the defendant lessee must show it was "fair and bona fide"; more importantly, Chatterton V.-C. accepted that the disparity between price paid and market value may itself provide proof that the transaction was not honest, that the buyer may know that the price is so unrealistic that the purchase is not a fair exchange and that the seller has been victimised.

This wider protective approach – it is akin to protection from improvident bargains – represents a reasonable compromise between promoting commercial certainty and general contractual principles, and it is to be hoped that the "fair and bona fide" test is not subjected to the same interpretation in Ireland as it was in *Hart v. O'Connor*. The Irish courts have gone further than the English courts in holding that persons of diminished or retarded intellectual capacity are to be protected from entering into improvident bargains even if there is no proof of unfair dealing by the other: *Grealish v. Murphy*[99] and *Rooney v. Conway*.[100]

Should there be a supply of necessary goods or services then the fact of supply will make the mentally infirm person liable to pay on a *quantum meruit* basis. Indeed, section 2 of the Sale of Goods Act 1893, in the context of goods supplied, makes this obligation an obligation to pay a "reasonable price" but, in relation to services, the same basic obligation arises in law: *Nash v. Inman*.[101]

---

[96] [1980] 1 N.Z.L.R. 386.
[97] [1983] 1 N.Z.L.R. 280: Hudson [1984] Conv. 32.
[98] (1872) I.R. 6 Eq. 429.
[99] [1946] I.R. 35.
[100] Unreported, N.I. High Court, March 8, 1982.
[101] [1908] 1 K.B. 1.

# Drunkards

Contracts struck with persons who are so drunk as to be incapable of understanding the bargain are voidable. It is also said that the other, sober party must be shown to have known of this condition. It is likely that this will be far easier to prove than in cases of insanity. However, in cases where the contract is negotiated in writing, or possibly at an auction,[102] there is the prospect of more difficult issues presenting themselves; should the contract not be promptly repudiated when sobriety returns, the contract will be binding.[103] If the degree of intoxication falls short of the required standard the contract will also be viewed as potentially unconscionable according to the case of *White v. McCooey*.[104] A drunkard, like an infant and an insane person, is bound to pay a reasonable price for necessaries supplied: Sale of Goods Act 1893, section 2.[105]

# Married Women

The Married Women's Status Act 1957 swept away in the Republic the rules and concepts that conferred upon married women limited contractual and property rights. Section 2(1) declares that the capacity of a woman to contract is unchanged upon marriage. The Act does give a married woman additional advantages.[106]

# Corporations

An incorporated body of persons, unlike unincorporated associations such as a club, is a competent contracting party, the law recognising the corporation as a juristic entity distinct from the natural persons who constitute the corporation. Corporations may be established in a variety of ways.[107]

(i) At common law a corporation could be formed by royal charter; Trinity College Dublin and the Queen's University were established by Royal Charters issued by Elizabeth I and Queen Victoria respectively; see the discussions in *Gray & Cathcart v. Provost of Trinity College*[108] and *MacCormack v. The Queen's University*.[109]

(ii) Corporations may also be established under statute; obvious examples of such corporations are "semi-state" bodies such as the Electricity Supply Board.[110]

---

[102] *Hawkins v. Bone* (1865) 4 F. & F. 311.
[103] *Nagle v. Baylor* (1842) 3 Dr. & War. 60; *Bawll Grain Co. v. Ross* (1917) 37 D.L.R. 620.
[104] Unreported, High Court, June 24, 1976; *Black v. McGonigle*, unreported, High Court, November 14, 1988; *McCrystal v. O'Kane* [1986] N.I. 123.
[105] *Re Byrne* [1941] I.R. 378.
[106] ss.7 and 8.
[107] See generally, Usher, *Company Law in Ireland* (1986).
[108] [1910] 1 I.R. 370.
[109] (1867) I.R. 1 Eq. 160.
[110] See generally Golding (1978) 13 Ir.Jur. 302.

(iii) Thirdly (and more commonly), a company may be formed by compliance with the provisions of the Companies Acts 1963–90. In this manner the majority of commercial trading companies are established. The company must have articles of association (governing items of internal administration) and a memorandum of association (which states the objects of the company, its scope of operation and the extent of the company's powers).

The extent to which the officers and directors may bind the company by entering into contracts with third persons will, in the first instance, depend on whether the transaction falls within (*intra vires*) the objects of the company.

### (1) The doctrine of ultra vires

A statutory corporation (*i.e.* (ii) & (iii) above) can exercise only those powers expressly or impliedly conferred by the statute itself. The doctrine of *ultra vires* declares an act done which is not authorised by the incorporating statute or the objects clause in the memorandum of association to be void at law.

Thus a company that is empowered to manufacture, sell or hire railway carriages, plant and equipment is not able to validly consent to purchase the right to construct a railway: *Ashbury Railway Carriage Co. v. Riche.*[111] On the other hand the memorandum at issue in *Martin v. Irish Industrial Benefit Society*[112] was held wide enough to permit advances to non-members of a building society.

Attempts to avoid the *ultra vires* doctrine pass on drafting the objects of the company so widely as to empower the directors to carry on any business which in their opinion might be carried on advantageously in connection with the main business (whatever that may be): *Bell Houses Ltd. v. City Wall Properties Ltd.*[113] Alternatively an extremely detailed memorandum may be drawn so as to include every conceivable activity.

### (2) Statutory modification

The only real result of the *ultra vires* doctrine in the modern context is to prevent a third party, honestly dealing with a company, from being able to sue on a contract. The harshness of this led the Oireachtas to enact section 8(1) of the Companies Act 1963:

> "Any act or thing done by a company which if the company had been empowered to do the same would have been lawfully and effectively done, shall, notwithstanding that the company had no power to do such act or thing, be effective in favour of any person relying on such act or thing who is not shown to have been actually aware at the time when he so relied thereon, that such act or thing was not within the powers of the company . . . "

---

[111] (1875) L.R. 7 H.L. 653.
[112] (1960) Ir.Jur.Rep. 42.
[113] [1966] 2 Q.B. 656, 694.

In *Northern Bank Finance Corporation Ltd. v. Quinn & Achates Investment Co.*[114] the plaintiffs sought to enforce a guarantee signed by an officer of the second defendant. The memorandum stressed that the second defendant's main objects were to acquire and hold securities, investments and other property; the incidental objects were to "sell, exchange, mortgage assign . . . generally deal in" such securities. Keane J. held that the transaction, namely signature of a guarantee, was *ultra vires*. In considering whether section 8(1) applied, Keane J. held that the officer of the plaintiffs had inspected the memorandum and had formed the erroneous belief that the transaction was *ultra vires*; in Keane J.'s view:

> "Where a party is shown to have been actually aware of the contents of the memorandum but failed to appreciate that the company were not empowered thereby to enter into the transaction in issue, s.8(1) has no application."[115]

In the first edition of this book this writer submitted that Article 6 of the European Communities (Companies) Regulations 1973[116] was overlooked in *Quinn & Achates* but, in *Company Law in the Republic of Ireland*, Keane J. (writing extrajudicially of course) states that this Article was not relied on in that case "presumably because the company was not a limited company".[117]

### (3) Other remedies

The question whether a company may sue upon an *ultra vires* transaction which the company has executed, conferring a valuable benefit upon a third party, was considered in *Crone v. Dublin C.C.*[118] Water rates were fixed *ultra vires*; the defendants argued that the fact that they had supplied water to the plaintiff entitled them to recover on an implied contract. A majority of the Supreme Court held that no implied contract existed and the action failed.

It may be possible to plead an estoppel *in pais*; this was considered by Keane J. in the *Quinn & Achates* case.[119]

---

[114] [1979] I.L.R.M. 221.
[115] *Ibid.* at 230.
[116] S.I. 1973 No. 163.
[117] Page 103. The U.K. *ultra vires* rule is now found in s.35 of the Companies Act 1985.
[118] (1958) 95 I.L.T.R. 79.
[119] [1979] I.L.R.M. 221.

# Part 7

# Third Party Rights

# 17 Privity of Contract

## Introduction

The doctrine of privity of contract prevents a contract from being enforceable in favour of, or against, someone who is not a party to that contract. While this is, in general, the basic rule, the English Law Commission, in Consultation Paper No. 121,[1] emphasise that there are three aspects to the doctrine:

(i) a person cannot enforce rights under a contract to which he is not a party;

(ii) a person who is not a party to a contract cannot have contractual liabilities imposed on him;

(iii) contractual remedies are designed to compensate parties to a contract, not third parties.

The doctrine resembles the rule (already considered in Chapter 2) requiring consideration to move from a promisee before a promise can be enforced by that person. Furmston[2] has convincingly argued that these two propositions are in fact two different ways of saying the same thing. A "stranger to the consideration" (*i.e.* a person who has not rendered himself liable upon the contract) does not provide consideration for any promise addressed to him. By the same token, the fact that a gratuitous promise is addressed to a person does not make that person a promisee; the test used to identify persons who are privy to a bilateral contract is whether that person is bound to do anything under the contract. Nevertheless, the weight of authority is in favour of regarding the law as having two distinct rules:

> "My Lords, in the law of England certain principles are fundamental. One is that only a person who is a party to a contract can sue on it. . . . A second principle is that if a person with whom a contract not under seal has been made is to be able to enforce it, consideration must have been given by him to the promisor or to some other person at the promisor's request."[3]

Indeed, in the case of *Coulls v. Bagot's Trustee*[4] the High Court of Australia confirmed the view that there are two distinct rules, indicating that a promise made to two promisees makes the promisees each contracting parties, and that a promise thus made is enforceable by both separately, even if only one promisee

---

[1] *Privity of Contract: Contracts for the Benefit of Third Parties* (1991); The Final Report is *Contracts for the Benefit of Third Parties* (1996).
[2] (1960) 23 M.L.R. 373.
[3] Viscount Haldane L.C. in *Dunlop Pneumatic Tyre Co. Ltd. v. Selfridge & Co.* [1915] A.C. 847.
[4] (1967) 40 A.L.J.R. 1.

furnishes consideration. Although the decision has been criticised,[5] it does represent an example of a judicial desire to ensure that the expectations of parties to a contract are not frustrated by technical rules that do not serve the interests of justice.

## Origins

The cases of *McCoubray v. Thompson*[6] and *Barry v. Barry*,[7] discussed in Chapter 2, indicate that the doctrine is designed to prevent persons who are simply the objects of a gratuitous promise from suing others in contract. The doctrine is not popular and many writers have argued that it is in fact a common law doctrine of fairly recent origin. The leading English case is the decision of the Court of Queen's Bench in *Tweddle v. Atkinson*.[8] An action was brought by a son-in-law to recover a sum of money from the estate of his deceased father-in-law. The sum had been promised in return for a similar promise given by the plaintiff's own father upon the plaintiff's marriage. The action failed. *Tweddle v. Atkinson* stands in marked contrast to a series of earlier English cases, particularly *Dutton v. Poole*[9] where similar family arrangements were held to be enforceable by third parties. These older cases are to be regarded as having been overruled by *Tweddle v. Atkinson* and the later case of *Dunlop v. Selfridge*,[10] a House of Lords decision in which the plaintiff company, who had sold their tyres to a wholesaler under the terms of a contract which provided that the tyres would not be resold at a price below the recommended retail price, was held not to be entitled to enforce the term against the defendant retailer for reason of lack of consideration and the privity rule.

The most important Irish common law decision is probably *Murphy v. Bower*.[11] The plaintiffs, railway contractors, undertook construction work for a railway company. The company employed Bower as an engineer to supervise the work. The construction contract stipulated that Bower would issue certificates as work was completed, thereupon entitling the plaintiffs to payment. Bower refused to certify the work. The Court of Common Pleas dismissed the plaintiffs' action against Bower. It should be noted that the plaintiffs had not engaged the engineer; nor was Bower's employer, the railway company, a plaintiff in the action. Monahan C.J. observed: "it has been decided that where the foundation of the right of action is rested upon contract, no one can maintain an action who is not a party to the contract."[12]

---

[5] Coote [1978] C.L.J. 301.
[6] (1868) 2 I.R.C.L. 226.
[7] (1891) 28 L.R.(Ir.) 45.
[8] (1861) 1 B. & S. 393.
[9] (1678) 2 Lev. 210; *Carnegie v. Waugh* (1823) 1 L.J.(O.S.) K.B. 89.
[10] [1915] A.C. 847.
[11] (1868) I.R. 2 C.L. 506. See also *Waugh v. Denham* (1865) 16 I.C.L.R. 405; *Corner v. Irwin* (1876) 10 I.R.C.L. 354.
[12] *Ibid.* at 512.

## Equity's Response to Actions Brought by Third Parties

The courts of equity adopted a characteristically flexible position. In the early case of *Shannon v. Bradstreet*[13] a tenant for life with a power to lease entered into an agreement to execute a lease in favour of Shannon. Shannon entered into possession but no lease was formally executed (which prevented the possibility of the lease binding successors as a covenant running with the land). On the death of the tenant for life the remainderman sought ejectment claiming the lease did not bind him. Lord Redesdale gave judgment for Shannon, holding that in equity a remainderman is bound by a leasing agreement made by a predecessor in title.

This isolated example of equity recognising that a third party may be bound by a contract pales into insignificance when contrasted with the line of authority commencing with the English case of *Tomlinson v. Gill*,[14] a decision of Hardwicke L.C. Gill promised a widow that if she would appoint him administrator of her deceased husband's estate he would personally meet any debts the estate could not discharge. An action brought by a creditor on this promise succeeded: "the plaintiff . . . could not maintain an action at law, for the promise was made to the widow; but he is proper here, for the promise was for the benefit of the creditors and the widow is a trustee for them."[15]

While traditionally the equitable concept of the trust does provide a right of action to a beneficiary who may sue the trustee should he not discharge his duties it has been said that, in this context, the trust is not apparent. In *Tomlinson v. Gill* there was no express intention to create a trust; nor was a trust fund established. Corbin, in his exhaustive review of these early cases,[16] observed of this case that "there was merely a contract between two persons in which one promised to pay a debt owed to a third party; the promisee – the widow – was called a trustee of the promise merely to allow the action in equity to succeed against the promisor."[17]

The trust concept has been discussed in several Irish cases. In *Drimmie v. Davies*[18] a father and son agreed to establish a dental practice. The partnership deed obliged the son to pay annuities to his mother and his siblings in the event of the father predeceasing him. The executor of the deceased partner's estate and the beneficiaries sued to enforce the promise. The executor's action succeeded; Chatterton V.-C. in a judgment upheld by the Court of Appeal ruled that the defence of privity between promisor and beneficiaries did not prevail in equity and, following the Judicature Act, the equitable rule prevailed, namely, "the party to whose use or for whose benefit the contract had been entered into has a remedy in equity against the person with whom it was expressed to be

---

[13] (1803) 1 Sch. & Lef. 64.
[14] (1756) Amb. 330: *Les Affréteurs Reunis SA v. Leopold Walford Ltd.* [1919] A.C. 801.
[15] (1756) Amb. 330 at p. 335.
[16] (1930) 46 L.Q.R. 12.
[17] *Ibid.* p. 21.
[18] (1899) 1 I.R. 176.

made." Note also Holmes L.J.'s judgment in the Court of Appeal. The fact that the trustee himself – the executor – was prepared to sue makes this statement *obiter dictum*: see *Beswick v. Beswick*.[19] If the executor/promisee is unwilling to bring proceedings such a dictum may be invaluable.

In *Kenney v. Employer's Liability Insurance Corporation*[20] a bank, mortgagees of Kenney's estate, appointed B as a receiver to hold and pay over to them rents and profits. B took out insurance with the defendant to cover acts of default. B defaulted and Kenney, who had paid out to cover B's default, sued on the insurance policy. The majority of the Court of Appeal held Kenney entitled to sue on the contract. Holmes L.J. for the majority said the case fell within the trust principle established in *Drimmie v. Davies*. Walker L.J., dissenting, said that B did not intend to confer a beneficial right on the mortgagor, nor did B intend to make himself a trustee for the mortgagor. In general, however, the courts, by the early years of this century, had carved out a most subversive doctrine. The intention to benefit a third party, once demonstrated, led the courts to readily infer a trust to benefit that third party. The House of Lords, in *Les Affréteurs Reunis SA v. Leopold Walford Ltd.*,[21] gave such a development its approval, holding that a broker who had negotiated a charter-party could enforce a promise contained therein whereby the owners of the vessel promised to pay the broker a commission, even though the broker was not privy to the contract.

There is one nineteenth century Irish case that goes the other way. In *Clitheroe v. Simpson*,[22] John Simpson, father of both the defendant and Alice Clitheroe, late wife of the plaintiff, agreed by deed with the defendant that in consideration of the defendant agreeing to pay Alice Clitheroe £100, John Simpson would convey land to the defendant. The sum was not paid; the plaintiff, executor of his wife's estate, sued but the action failed. Morris C.J. observed that even if a trust had been pleaded, which it was not, he did not think any circumstances existed which would bring the case within that exception to the privy rule. Lawson and Harrison JJ. concurred. This case (decided by judges from a predominantly common law background) was described by Corbin as one in which the judges looked for a trust fund, "and finding none denied the plaintiff a remedy. The possibility of regarding the promisee as a trustee of the contract right did not occur to the Court."

While the primacy of the *Drimmie v. Davies* line of authority has not been directly challenged in the Irish courts the practice of utilising the concept of the trust as a means of avoiding the privity doctrine has fallen into disfavour. Lord Wright described it as "a cumbrous fiction" when used in this context.[23] The Privy Council in *Vandepitte v. Preferred Accident Insurance Corporation of New York*[24]

---

[19]  [1968] A.C. 58.
[20]  [1901] 1 I.R. 301; *Walsh v. Walsh* [1900] 1 N.I.J.R. 53.
[21]  [1919] A.C. 801.
[22]  (1879) 4 L.R.(Ir.) 59.
[23]  (1939) 55 L.Q.R. 189 at 208.
[24]  [1933] A.C. 70; *Green v. Russell* [1959] 2 Q.B. 226.

refused to allow a third party to sue on an insurance contract because it could not be shown that the insured intended to benefit the third party. In fact the position taken in *Vandepitte* closely resembles that of Walker L.J. dissenting in *Kenney*, above. In the case of *O'Leary v. Irish National Insurance Co. Ltd.*[25] the court left open the question whether an intention to create a trust must be shown before a third party can recover but Barrington J., in *Cadbury Ireland Ltd. v. Kerry Co-op Creameries Ltd.*,[26] held that such an intention must be present. In that case a promise contained in a document agreed between the defendant company and the State, made when the defendant company sought to acquire a semi-state company in the Kerry district, was not actionable by the plaintiff company even though the interests of the plaintiff company were intended to be protected by the State when agreeing to sell the semi-state company to the defendants. If at the time of the promise the beneficiary does not exist, it may sometimes be more difficult to persuade the court to uphold the trust concept than would otherwise be the case. In *Inspector of Taxes Association v. Minister for the Public Service, Ireland & the Attorney-General*,[27] Murphy J. refused to hold that the plaintiff Association could avail of a conciliation and arbitration scheme. Following the *Kerry Co-op* case the judge found it impossible to infer "that the various Staff Associations who were parties to the original C. & A. agreement purported to contract by implication as trustees on behalf of other associations which might be formed hereafter". There are nevertheless individual employment cases where relatives of an employee have been held entitled to recover benefits payable under the rules of their deceased relative's trade union.[28]

The trust concept is out of favour, both in England and Ireland, because it strikes many judges as intellectually dishonest. More importantly perhaps, the use of this "cumbrous fiction" can unduly interfere with perfectly sensible arrangements by preventing the parties from being able to rescind or vary them by agreement. This occurs because the "beneficiary", as the possessor of an equitable interest, must often consent to a variation: *Re Schebsman*.[29] Nevertheless it is suggested that the case of *McKay v. Jones*[30] (the facts of which are given in Chapter 3) should be considered as wrongly decided. The possibility that the boy's parents were trustees of the contract promise does not seem to have been argued.

## Agency

If an agent is appointed and given the authority to contract on behalf of a principal then any transaction within the scope of such authority will bind the

---

25 [1958] Ir.Jur.Rep. 1.
26 [1982] I.L.R.M. 77.
27 Unreported, High Court, March 24, 1983, affirmed by the Supreme Court [1986] I.L.R.M. 296.
28 Contrast *Kelly v. Larkin* [1910] 2 I.R. 550 with *Rooney v. T.O.S.I.* (1913) 47 I.L.T.R. 303.
29 [1944] Ch. 83.
30 (1959) 93 I.L.T.R. 177.

principal. Before the agency exception can operate there must normally exist an intention to create the relationship of principal and agent: *Sheppard v. Murphy*.[31] The doctrine of the undisclosed principal, however, allows enforcement of a promise by a principal if the contract has been made by an agent within the agent's authority, even if the agent has, to all intents and purposes, contracted in his own name and for his own benefit. Commercial convenience is the most obvious explanation for such a rule. In most agency cases, however, the link between the agent and principal will be apparent.

In *Pattison v. Institute for Industrial Research and Standards*[32] a trade union negotiating on behalf of its members obtained a promise from the defendant to pay an additional allowance to the plaintiff, an employee of the defendant. McWilliam J. held that the plaintiff could enforce this promise. The decision can only be explained as resting on a finding that the union negotiated as agent for its members.

The agency exception has produced a controversial series of decisions in recent years. In *The Eurymedon*[33] machinery was to be transported by ship from England to New Zealand. The consignors in England contracted with a carrier, the contract providing that liability of the carriers, their employees, agents and independent contractors would be limited. The carriers employed the defendant stevedores to unload the machinery, which was damaged due to the stevedores' negligence. The majority of the Privy Council held the stevedores entitled to rely on a limitation clause even though it was contained in a contract between consignor and carrier. The Privy Council, following the earlier case of *Scruttons Ltd. v. Midland Silicones*,[34] held if the following four conditions can be satisfied the third party will take the benefit of such a clause:

(1) the contract must make it clear that the stevedore is intended to be protected;

(2) the contract clearly provides that the carrier has the status of agent for the purpose of obtaining the benefit of the contract for a principal;

(3) the carrier has the authority to contract on the stevedore's behalf;

(4) there are no difficulties in relation to consideration.

The minority in *The Eurymedon* were unable to find that the contract also contained an offer addressed to the stevedore; the dissenting members of the Board expressed misgivings about using a legal fiction to avoid the privity doctrine (in much the same way as their predecessors had in *Vandepitte* when faced with the trust argument). Nevertheless *The Eurymedon* has been followed in *The New York Star*,[35] also a Privy Council decision. *The Eurymedon* has, as a

---

[31] (1867) 1 Ir.R.Eq. 490.
[32] Unreported, High Court, May 31, 1979; *Keighley, Maxsted & Co. v. Durant* [1900] A.C. 240.
[33] [1975] A.C. 154.
[34] [1962] A.C. 446.
[35] [1980] 3 All E.R. 257; see, however, *International Technical Operators Ltd. v. Miida Electronics Inc.* (1986) 28 D.L.R. (4th) 641.

general exception, also found favour in areas of law that go beyond the carriage of goods. The principle has been applied recently in relation to the negotiation of an insurance contract: *National Oilwell (UK) Ltd. v. Davy Offshore Ltd.*[36] However the most striking illustration of the principle is the use made of it by O'Sullivan J. in the controversial litigation in *Hearn and Matchroom Boxing Ltd. v. Collins.*[37] One of the issues facing the court was whether an agreement made between the second plaintiff and Stephen Collins could be the subject of enforcement by the first plaintiff, a defence of privity being raised by the defendant. After mentioning the four elements set down by the majority in *The Eurymedon*, O'Sullivan J. found that all four factors were satisfied. As a management contract the parties were aware that only a human person could manage a boxer and Matchroom Boxing, in the judge's view, was contracting as agent for Barry Hearn. The company clearly acted within the scope of its authority and the "consideration which moved from Barry Hearn as an individual was his undertaking to extend the management agreement and also of course to be bound by its terms and provide appropriate services to Stephen Collins thereunder". While *The Eurymedon* is normally seen as a decision on bailment and the law relating to exclusion clauses in contract and tort, O'Sullivan J.'s decision gives it a broader application. However, we should return to the law of bailment for a moment. We have seen earlier in this book specific illustrations of how the law of bailment produces a *sui generis* example of a contracting party, the bailor, being held to impliedly consent to the terms of a later contract entered into with sub-bailees by the original bailee.[38]

In *Fox v. Higgins*,[39] Gibson J. also encountered difficulties when confronted with a contractual arrangement intended to bind persons outside the original bargain. The plaintiff was employed by the Rev. Busby, school manager, as a teacher in a national school. The Rev. Busby resigned; the defendant Higgins replaced him as school manager. Before the defendant was confirmed as manager Fox fell ill and was away from work for several months. Fox, on his return to work, was told that his contract of employment ended when the Rev. Busby resigned. Gibson J. found that Higgins was bound by the National Board rules to enter into a contract with all teachers employed at the commencement of his own service as school manager; this was described as "a kind of triangular pact" by which in certain circumstances the new manager is bound "in the same way and to the same effect as if he had signed the contract".

These tripartite contracts are exceptional: *Halpin v. Rothwell & U.D.T.*[40] It is a matter of construction whether an arrangement binds all parties equally or whether the relationship between contracting parties subsists in a series of

---

[36] [1993] 2 Lloyd's Rep. 582.
[37] Unreported, High Court, February 3, 1998.
[38] *Morris v. C. W. Martin & Sons Ltd.* [1966] 1 Q.B. 716; *Singer (U.K.) v. Tees and Hartlepool Port Authority* [1988] 2 Lloyd's Rep. 215; *Spectra International plc v. Hayesoak* [1998] 1 Lloyd's Rep. 153.
[39] (1912) 46 I.L.T.R. 22.
[40] [1984] I.L.R.M. 613.

separate transactions; the speech of O'Higgins C.J. in *Henley Forklift (Ireland) Ltd. v. Lansing Bagnall & Co. Ltd. et al.*[41] is instructive.

## Covenants Running with the Land

Conveyancing practice and a wealth of case law establishes that covenants that "touch and concern" real property may be enforced against, and indeed be enforced by, persons who are not parties to the original transaction. Considerations of space do not permit an extensive review of this exception to the privity doctrine. The law is discussed with great clarity in Wylie, *Irish Land Law.*[42] An illustration of the *Tulk v. Moxhay*[43] principle is afforded by the decision of Murphy J. in *Whelan and Whelan v. Cork Corporation.*[44]

### The De Mattos principle

*De Mattos v. Gibson*[45] lays down a broad principle of equity which indicates that a person with notice of a right or interest, who acquires property, whether movable or immovable, will not be able to ignore that right of a third party if the third party has given valuable consideration for the interest. The precise scope of the principle is in doubt but the existence of this principle is not. However, in *Law Debenture Corporation v. Ural Casplan Ltd.*[46] Hoffmann J. held that *De Mattos* only applies to give a negative injunction to restrain the person with notice from acting in a way that is inconsistent with the rights of the third party.

There are no Irish cases dealing with the applicability of such covenants to contracts for the sale of chattels.

### Limitation clauses – A canadian exception

A majority of the Supreme Court of Canada, in *London Drugs Ltd. v. Kuehne & Nagel International Ltd.*[47] has identified a separate exception to the privity doctrine based upon the intention of the parties, fairness, business and insurance practices. Where a limitation clause was intended to benefit a third party – an employee of a contracting party for example – the courts will allow the benefit of the clause to defeat or restrict liability in tort or contract. While this exception may operate in *The Eurymedon* context, the Supreme Court of Canada preferred a method that did not involve the artificiality of *The Eurymedon* reasoning.

---

[41] Unreported, Supreme Court, December 3, 1979; *Herlihy v. Sullivan* (1896) 30 I.L.T. 536.
[42] (3rd ed., 1996) Chap. 19.
[43] (1848) 2 Ph. 774.
[44] [1991] I.L.R.M. 19.
[45] (1859) 4 De G. & J. 276; *Lord Strathcona S.S. v. Dominion Coal Co. Ltd.* [1926] A.C. 108; *Swiss Bank Corp v. Lloyds Bank* [1979] Ch. 548.
[46] [1993] 2 All E.R. 355, citing *Barker v. Stickney* [1919] 1 K.B. 121.
[47] [1992] 97 D.L.R. (4th) 261; Waddams (1993) 109 L.Q.R. 349.

## Statutory Exceptions to the Privity Doctrine

In England the Law Revision Committee recommended in a 1937 Report[48] that legislation be enacted conferring sweeping rights of action upon third-party beneficiaries. This Report has been ignored by the United Kingdom Parliament but two recommendations have been adopted by the Oireachtas.

The first recommendation builds upon section 11 of the Married Women's Property Act 1882. By adopting the trust concept, discussed above, Parliament in 1882 gave widows and children of a deceased man the right to sue upon a policy of life insurance. Section 7 of the Married Women's Status Act 1957 extends this right of action to endowment policies also. This right of action applies to policies whether the policy is "expressed to be for the benefit of" or "by its express terms purporting to confer a benefit upon the wife, husband or child of the insured."[49]

More importantly, perhaps, section 8 of the 1957 Act creates a cause of action in all contracts other than those covered by section 7 if the contract is expressed to be for the benefit of a wife, husband or child of one of the contracting parties, or if the contract purports to confer a benefit upon such a third party. As a result the contract will be enforceable by the third party in his or her own name.

The facts of *Jackson v. Horizon Holidays*[50] illustrate the usefulness of section 8. Jackson booked a holiday in Ceylon for himself and his family. The accommodation provided was unsatisfactory so on his return to England Mr. Jackson sued to recover damages for the disappointing holiday. He recovered damages to compensate not only himself but all members of the family. *Jackson* makes good sense but the Court of Appeal's reasoning has been attacked as incorrect in law[51] and disapproved by the House of Lords in *Woodar Investment v. Wimpey Construction.*[52] However, in *Linden Gardens Trust Ltd. v. Lenesta Sludge Disposals Ltd.*[53] the House of Lords indicated that there are exceptional situations in which a plaintiff may recover damages for breach of contract even though the recoverable loss may be that of a third party. Lord Griffiths in particular canvassed a very broad right of recovery on behalf of third parties and his judgment sets out a very sound and common-sense approach to the issue of third-party rights. However, the status of the *Jackson* case in English law remains uncertain. In Ireland the 1957 Act provides a clear solution. Under section 8 the wife and children of a contracting party would, on similar facts, be able to sue in contract in their own name. Section 8 does permit the contract to be rescinded by the contracting parties at any time before

---

[48] Cmd. 5449.
[49] See Dowrick, (1958) 21 M.L.R. 98.
[50] [1975] 1 W.L.R. 1468.
[51] P. Wylie, (1975) 26 N.I.L.Q. 326.
[52] [1980] 1 All E.R. 571, cited with approval by Finlay C.J. in *Burke and Others v. Lord Mayor of Dublin* [1990] 1 I.R. 18.
[53] [1993] 3 All E.R. 417; *Darlington B.C. v. Wittshier Northern Ltd.* [1995] 3 All E.R. 895.

the beneficiary adopts it; the third party is also bound by any defences the defendant may have against the other contracting party.

If a tenancy agreement between a male tenant and a landlord envisages that the tenant's wife is to live on the premises it may be that the wife will fall within the scope of section 8, depending of course on the terms of the letting agreement. If the wife of the tenant is injured because the premises turn out to be defective she should in such a case be able to sue the landlord under section 8. This point does not seem to have been argued in either *Chambers v. Cork Corporation*[54] or *Coughlan v. Mayor of Limerick*.[55] However, in *Burke and Others v. Lord Mayor of Dublin*[56] the first plaintiff, a minor, sought damages to compensate for aggravation of his asthma condition, his condition being the result of living in unfit housing conditions, the tenants being his parents. The plaintiff's counsel argued that because local authority differential rents were calculated by reference to the number of children resident therein, it was possible to argue that the contract was expressed to be for the benefit of, or, by its express terms, purported to benefit, the infant plaintiff. The argument was rejected by the Supreme Court. The need for an express reference is a considerable barrier to the operation of section 8, but the words of section 8 seem to permit no other result in a case such as *Burke and Others v. Lord Mayor of Dublin*. However, the alternative argument, based upon *Jackson v. Horizon Holidays*, suggests that family holiday contracts, contracts for restaurant services, taxi services, and the like, will be capable of giving a right of action to persons envisaged as being recipients of the service, even if the consideration and the contract involve one of the recipients only. McCarthy J., while holding *Jackson v. Horizon Holidays* to be inapplicable, approved the idea that these situations call for special treatment, citing Lord Wilberforce in *Woodar Investment v. Wimpey Construction*.

Section 76(1) of the Road Traffic Act 1961 gives a person claiming against an insured motorist certain remedies against the insurer. If judgment is obtained against the insured, section 76(1)(*b*) and (*c*) provides that an application to execute judgment against the owner or user may be brought: *Herlihy v. Curley*.[57] Should the claimant not recover judgment against that person then section 76(1)(*d*) provides that the claimant may apply to institute proceedings against the insurer or guarantor, in lieu of the owner or user of the vehicle, if:

(1) the owner or user is outside the State, or cannot be found or is immune from process; or

(2) for any other reason it is just and equitable that the application be granted.

Case law indicates a considerable overlap between these two provisions, e.g. *Norton v. General Accident*.[58]

---

[54] (1959) 93 I.L.T.R. 45.
[55] (1977) 111 I.L.T.R. 114.
[56] [1990] 1 I.R. 18.
[57] [1950] I.R. 15.
[58] (1941) 74 I.L.T.R. 123; *Hayes v. Legal Insurance Co. Ltd.* [1941] Ir.Jur.Rep. 40.

In *Hayes v. Legal Insurance Co. Ltd.*[59] and in *O'Leary v. The Irish National Insurance Co.*,[60] Budd J. expressly left open the question of whether this provision confers a right of action on third parties against insurance companies in the same way that English statute law did. This argument has the advantage of sidestepping the trust doctrine which, as we have seen, was disapproved of by the Privy Council in *Vandepitte v. Preferred Accident Insurance.*[61] The privity of contract doctrine has also proved to be very problematical in another commercial context. Where goods, typically a motor vehicle, have been "sold" on hire-purchase terms, the hirer, often unaware of the complex legal nature of the transaction into which he has entered, attempts to obtain a contractual remedy from the wrong source. Because the hirer's contractual arrangements are generally with a finance company rather than the dealer there have been cases in which the dealer has escaped liability in respect of defective goods by pleading the privity doctrine: *Dunphy v. Blackhall Motors.*[62] The Hire-Purchase Acts 1946 to 1980, recently supplanted by the 1995 Act closed this gap in the law. Section 80 of the 1995 Act provides that, in respect of agreements where the antecedent negotiations were conducted by another person, that person, along with the owner of the goods shall be deemed to be a party to the agreement. That person and the owner are jointly and severally liable to the hirer for any misrepresentation made in the course of the antecedent negotiations.

The Sale of Goods and Supply of Services Act 1980, by section 13(2), enacts an implied "condition" in sales by a dealer of a motor vehicle to the effect that the vehicle is, at the time of delivery, free from any defect which would render it a danger to the public including persons travelling in the vehicle. The provision goes further by providing in subsection 7 that a person using the vehicle with the consent of the buyer, who suffers loss as a result of breach of subsection 2 "may maintain an action for damages against the seller in respect of the breach as if he were the buyer".[63] Section 34 extends the section 13 implied "condition" to contracts involving the hire-purchase of motor vehicles. Section 14 of the Act also makes a finance house liable for breach of contract and a dealer's misrepresentations if goods are sold by a dealer to a consumer, the dealer being paid the purchase price by a finance house, the purchaser repaying the finance house.

## Further Reforms?

Apart from piecemeal legislative reforms the doctrine of privity remains intact. The judges are anxious to limit possible injustices: see *Beswick v. Beswick*[64] as

---

[59] (1941) Ir.Jur.Rep. 40.
[60] [1958] Ir.Jur.Rep. 1.
[61] [1933] A.C. 70.
[62] (1953) 87 I.L.T.R. 128.
[63] See *Glorney v. O'Brien*, unreported, High Court, November 14, 1988.
[64] [1968] A.C. 58.

applied in *Snelling v. John G. Snelling Ltd.*[65] There are signs that further judicial reforms may be forthcoming; witness Lord Scarman's speech in *Woodar Investment v. Wimpey Construction* where, after noting Parliament's failure to implement the 1937 Report, the learned judge said: "[I] hope the House [of Lords] will reconsider *Tweddle v. Atkinson* and the other cases which stand guard over this unjust rule."[66]

The English Law Commission has more recently considered[67] the topic of third-party rights and has made a number of significant recommendations about the kind of reform programme that would prove to enhance the English law of contract *vis-à-vis* third-party rights. The approach canvassed by the Law Commission builds upon existing law and is divorced from the related issue of reform of consideration. A series of legislative measures are proposed. The essence of the Law Commission's provisional proposals is said to be to allow actions by third parties when to do so gives effect to the intentions of the contracting parties. The third party must be able to show that the contracting parties intended that the third party receive the benefit of the promised performance and also that they intended to create a legal obligation enforceable by the third party; the circumstances surrounding the transaction are to be relevant when deducing the intention of the parties. However, the rights created against a contracting party are to be governed by the contract and may be subject to conditions precedent. Rights are to extend to both the promised performance due and any remedies for default, as well as the ability to rely on limitations on the liability of third parties. The Law Commission also considered the issue of ascertainability and recommended that rights be created for a third party not ascertained or in existence (contrast section 8 of the Married Women's Status Act 1957 and the position of Burke in *Burke and Others v. Lord Mayor of Dublin*). A number of ancillary issues were addressed by the Consultation Paper such as defences and overlapping remedies. In the Law Commission's Report, *Privity of Contract: Contracts for the Benefit of Third Parties*,[68] the Law Commission produced a nine-section draft statute that will remove this "pestilential nuisance".[69] In relation to contracts, a third party beneficiary ("C") will be able to sue the promisor ("A") directly, without having to join the promisee ("B"). C will be entitled to obtain reliance loss and, alternatively, C's expectation interest where appropriate. Under the proposal C is not a party to the contract but C enjoys the rights of a contracting party. However, for C to maintain an action C must satisfy one of two tests. The first limb is that C should be expressly stated by A and B to have a right of action against A, or where the issue is C's right to rely on an exemption clause, that C is to be afforded resort to the clause. The second limb operates where there is

---

[65] [1973] 1 Q.B. 87; Rules of the Superior Courts, Order 16.
[66] [1980] 1 All E.R. 571 at 590. Also Steyn, LJ. in *Darlington B.C. v. Wiltshier Northern* [1995] 3 All E.R. 895 at 904–905.
[67] Consultation Paper No. 121 (1991).
[68] No. 242 (1996).
[69] Adams and Brownsword (1993) 56 M.L.R. 722.

no express agreement on the point between A and B. However, if the contract between A and B purports to confer a benefit on the third party and, on its construction the court holds that the parties intended to give C, the third party, a direct right of action against A, or have resort to an exemption clause, where applicable then C may rely on the contract. For the beneficiary to come within either limb he or she need not be named but they must be a member of a class or answer a particular description; nor need the beneficiary be in existence at the time of contracting. While A and B may control the issue of C's entitlement, *e.g.* by excluding the right, the power of A and B to vary C's rights, or cancel the contract will be constrained if C has acted in reliance or C has communicated agreement to the rights ceded to C. Some critics of these proposals have drawn attention to some omissions and difficulties[70] but the reform is welcome.[71]

---

[70] See generally Tettenborn (1996) J.B.L. 602; Andrews (1997) C.L.J. 25; Hemsworth (1998) C.L.J. 55.
[71] Reynolds (1997) 113 L.Q.R. 53.

# Part 8

# Discharge

# 18   Discharge of Contractual Obligations

## Introduction

Contracts may be discharged in a variety of ways. The most obvious method will be through performance but disputes about what was required by the contract and whether the relevant standard was attained will be foreseeable. The contract may also be discharged as a result of breach of contract by one party, but in many cases the contract survives notwithstanding the breach. The contract may also be terminated by operation of law through the frustration doctrine. The contract may also be terminated by agreement or, exceptionally, by waiver or estoppel of a legal right.

## Discharge of a Contract through Performance

*Entire contracts*

Before a contract may be discharged by performance it must be established that performance complies exactly with the terms of the contract. Only the most insignificant deviations imaginable will be excused under the maxim *de minimis non curat lex*.

Two picturesque examples of the general position were given by Jessel M.R. in *Re Hall & Baker*[1]:

> "If a man engages to carry a box of cigars from London to Birmingham, it is an entire contract, and he cannot throw the cigars out of the carriage half-way there, and ask for half the money; or if a shoemaker agrees to make a pair of shoes, he cannot offer you one shoe and ask you to pay half the price."[2]

*Re Moore & Co. v. Landauer & Co.*[3] illustrates how demanding this obligation may turn out to be. In this case the seller delivered tinned fruit to the buyer. The contract description indicated that the tins were to be packed 30 tins to each case. While the correct number of tins in total were delivered, some cases contained only 24 tins. The seller was held not to be entitled to payment, for the breach of the obligation to deliver in cases of 30 tins was a basis for repudiation of the contract by the buyer, *inter alia*, on the ground of breach of section 13 of the Sale of Goods Act 1893. Normally, however, the issue of

---

[1]   (1878) 9 Ch. D. 538.
[2]   *Ibid.* at 545.
[3]   [1921] 2 K.B. 519.

413

whether a contract is entire or not will arise when the party who has provided less than full performance is subject to a series of obligations, often over a period of time. In the Irish case of *Nash & Co. v. Hartland*[4] it was pointed out that whether a contract is entire or not is a matter of construction. If the contract, expressly or impliedly, sets out that precise and exact performance by one party must be rendered before any obligation accrues to the other, the contract is entire.

The leading English case is *Cutter v. Powell.*[5] Cutter was engaged as a second mate to serve on a voyage from Jamaica to Liverpool. He was given a promissory note for 30 guineas, payable 10 days after the vessel arrived in Liverpool, should he serve faithfully in that post. Cutter died *en route*. His widow sued, claiming entitlement to a proportionate part of the sum on a *quantum meruit* basis. The action failed. The normal rate of pay for a second mate on such a voyage was £8. The higher rate was explained as being "a kind of insurance": per Kenyon M.R. The bargain here was an exceptional one. If Cutter served and arrived in Liverpool he would be paid nearly four times the normal rate; if not, he would recover nothing.

In the case of *Brown v. Wood*[6] the Irish Court of Exchequer distinguished *Cutter v. Powell* from the case at bar. The plaintiff agreed to take yarn from the defendant and manufacture cloth from it. Under the terms of the agreement, the plaintiff gave monies as security for the defendant's yarn and undertook to deliver the cloth as it was completed, whereupon the plaintiff would be paid manufacturing expenses and a profit element. While several consignments of cloth were delivered, the plaintiff failed to convert all the yarn, and he disposed of it. While the plaintiff had not completed all the work set by the contract, it was held that the plaintiff was entitled to payment for that part of the work actually completed and delivered, as well as the monies advanced as security for the defendant's yarn. The defence was one of entire contract. As a matter of construction and justice, the contract was held not to be entire. The plaintiff was held entitled to recover for completed goods delivered, and to be entitled to the return of the monies paid by him as security for the yarn; the defendant was held entitled to retain monies given as security for the yarn not processed and to an action for non-delivery of the work not completed.

The entire contract, as Beck has pointed out,[7] has been confused with a lump sum contract. The courts all too readily presume that if it is agreed that a lump-sum will be payable after performance the parties had made an entire contract. This, Beck argues, is a *non sequitur*; it is possible that the parties also intend that periodic payments or payment for partial completion can be claimed while work is in progress. This view is illustrated by the judgment of Whiteside C.J. in *Collen v. Marum*,[8] a case in which a builder agreed to

---

[4]  (1840) 2 Ir.L.R. 190.
[5]  (1795) 6 Term Reports 320; *Vigers v. Cook* [1919] 2 K.B. 475.
[6]  (1864) 6 Ir.Jur. 221; *Taylor v. Laird* (1856) 1 H. & N. 266.
[7]  (1975) 38 M.L.R. 413.
[8]  (1871) 5 Ir.C.L.R. 315.

construct a house for a fixed sum. Whiteside C.J. said in such a case the contract is entire and indivisible and that "the employer is not bound to pay for half or quarter of a house for the court and jury can have no right to apportion that which the parties themselves have treated as entire."[9]

The courts hold that a lump-sum building contract and an entire contract are synonymous; despite Beck's comments[10] it is understandable that this should be so, otherwise a builder would be encouraged to abandon work in progress should a more lucrative contract come along, safe in the knowledge that he can recover for the work completed. Before the courts will permit this it must be shown that the employer has acquiesced to the deviation from precise performance: *per* Whiteside C.J.[11] The case of *Coughlan v. Moloney*[12] takes the test a little further by requiring the builder to show an implied agreement to pay for the work done. The plaintiff there agreed to build a house for the defendant for £200, to be completed by Christmas 1902. No provision for periodic payments were made. The work was left incomplete and in October 1903 the defendants wrote asking for an account to be submitted so that "the matter should be finally wound up". No reply came; the builder sued for the value of work completed, the defendants having engaged another builder to finish the work. The action for work completed failed; if the employer has a half-completed structure on his land he has no choice whether to accept or reject the work. It would be absurd to require the employer to leave the structure in that condition; so, if he used materials left on the site he impliedly promises to pay for their value; he does not impliedly pay for work completed. In *Coughlan v. Moloney* the letter of October 1903 was held not to be a new contract for the builder did not provide consideration for this new promise.

The English case of *Sumpter v. Hodges*[13] provides a clear statement of the relevant legal principles. Here a builder undertook to build two houses and a stable on the defendant's land for a lump sum. The builder indicated that he was unable to complete the work due to a cash shortage. The trial judge found that the plaintiff had abandoned the work and was not entitled to recover on a *quantum meruit*. A. L. Smith L.J. indicated that the trial judge was correct: "the law is that, where there is a contract to do work for a lump sum, until the work is completed the price of it cannot be recovered."[14] If the work completed is adopted by the person who initially commissioned it, in circumstances where there is an option to adopt or reject the work, it may be possible to infer a new contract in appropriate circumstances. However, if the Commissioner has no option but to accept the work, then no inferred new contract is possible. Both Chitty and Collins L.JJ. agreed. Chitty L.J. noted that the mere fact that a person remains in possession of land does not give rise to an inference that

---

[9] (1871) 5 I.C.L.R. 315 at 319.
[10] (1975) 38 M.L.R. 413.
[11] (1871) 5 Ir.C.L.R. 315 at 320.
[12] (1905) 39 I.L.T.R. 153.
[13] [1898] 1 Q.B. 673.
[14] *Ibid.* at 674.

half-completed works on the land will be paid for. The Commissioner is not obliged to keep unfinished buildings on his land for such a construction would be a nuisance on the land.

The position taken in *Coughan v. Moloney* and *Sumpter v. Hedges* is a harsh one; after all, the employer gets a substantial benefit which he does not have to pay for. To mitigate the effects of the general rule the courts have developed a doctrine called "substantial performance". If the work has been carried out in its essential respects the party rendering substantial performance will be entitled to the contract price, subject to the employer being able to set-off all sums necessary to engage another person to complete the work. Two factors are important here:

(1) the nature of the defects;

(2) the cost of remedying the defects as against the contract price.

In *Hoenig v. Isaacs*[15] a builder agreed to redecorate the defendant's flat for £750; work was not completed and the cost of remedying the defects was £55. The English Court of Appeal held that because the defects were insignificant – a bookcase had to be completed – the builder was entitled to total payments of £695.

In *Hoenig v. Isaacs* Denning L.J. expressed the law in the following way:

> "the first question is whether, on the true construction of the contract, entire performance was a condition precedent to payment. It was a lump sum contract, but that does not mean that entire performance was a condition precedent to payment. When a contract provides for a specific sum to be paid on completion of specified work, the courts lean against a construction of the contract which would deprive the contractor of any payment at all simply because there are some defects or omissions. The promise to complete the work is, therefore, construed as a term of the contract, but not as a condition. It is not every breach of that term which absolves the employer from his promise to pay the price, but only a breach which goes to the root of the contract, such as an abandonment of the work when it is only half done. Unless the breach does go to the root of the matter, the employer cannot resist payment of the price. He must pay it and bring a cross-claim for the defects and omissions and is usually calculated by the cost of making them good."[16]

In contrast it has been held that where a central heating system was installed improperly, payment being agreed at £560, the system emitting fumes and working inefficiently, these defects, which would cost £124 to put right meant that the deviation fell short of substantial performance: *Bolton v. Mahadeva*.[17]

---

[15] [1952] 2 All E.R. 176.
[16] *Ibid.* at 180.
[17] [1972] 2 All E.R. 1322.

There is authority for the view that substantial performance will not apply if the builder refuses to complete or abandons work he acknowledges to be due; only if the parties genuinely dispute whether the work completed meets the contract standard can the compromise of substantial performance operate. In *Kincora Builders v. Cronin*,[18] the only Irish case in which substantial performance has been considered, Pringle J. held that where a builder refused to insulate an attic this would constitute an abandonment, denying him a remedy under substantial performance.

The English law Commission in a Working Paper[19] pointed out that the result of the present law is to create a strong possibility of an employer being unjustly enriched if a builder, through lack of funds, is unable to complete work. Sweeping restitutionary changes were proposed if it could be shown that one party to a lump-sum contract has conferred substantial advantages on the other. The Law Commission in its final report[20] agreed that where a builder conferred a benefit on the other party, payment should be made unless the contract excludes this. The dissent of one member of the Commission to such a proposal draws attention to the danger of allowing compensation where the builder refuses to complete for no good reason. The dissenting member had this to say of the proposal that a party in breach of an entire contract should be entitled to some payment if a net benefit has been conferred on the other contracting party, unless the contract expressly provides to the contrary.

> "Experience has shown that it is all too common for such builders not to complete one job of work before moving on to the next. The effect of the report is to remove from the householder almost the only effective sanction he has against the builder not completing the job."[21]

If money is paid in advance under an entire contract and some benefit has been conferred upon the party making advance payment, restitution of the total price paid is not possible, for there will not have been a total failure of consideration. Damages will be awarded, calculated by reference to the cost of having the work completed by a third party.[22]

## (1) Statutory modifications

The position reached in *Coughlan v. Moloney*, a building contract, is echoed by section 30(1) of the Sale of Goods Act 1893 which provides that while the buyer of goods who takes delivery of a quantity of goods which are less than he consented to take may reject them, he is obliged to pay for them at the contract rate should he accept the goods: see section 31 and *Norwell & Co. v. Black*.[23]

---

[18] Unreported, High Court, March 5, 1973.
[19] Working Paper No. 65 (1975).
[20] Law Comm. No. 121 (1983).
[21] Brian Davenport Q.C., at p. 36.
[22] *Whincup v. Hughes* (1871) L.R. 6 C.P. 78.
[23] (1930) 65 I.L.T.R. 104.

If certain services have already been rendered by A to B, A then terminating the contract without having been paid on a *quantum meruit* basis, there can be no question of B electing to accept or reject partial performance. The Apportionment Act 1870 does give some limited redress. Under the combined effect of sections 2 and 5 "rents, annuities, dividends and other periodical payments", including "salaries and pensions" shall be considered as accruing from day to day. A lump-sum payment for one period of employment is not a periodical payment so *Cutter v. Powell* would be outside this Act; see also *Creagh v. Sheedy*,[24] which seems to be decided *per incuriam*.

If the claimant *terminates* employment his termination does not prevent him from relying on the Act. In *Treacy v. Corcoran*,[25] Treacy was employed as a clerk, the remuneration being payable half yearly. In April 1872 he resigned. Corcoran took over the job and at the end of the half year Corcoran was paid £115, the sum payable for the whole of the period. Treacy was held entitled to a proportion of that sum, based on the 34-day period he was in employment. If the claimant is in *breach* of contract, English cases suggest the Act will not apply.[26]

## (2) Divisible contracts

If a contract is held to be made up of a series of separate obligations, the contract providing that payment is to be due during the process of performance, the contract is divisible. In the building industry contracts are generally drafted so as to entitle the builder to payment as certain stages are completed; to ensure performance the contract normally provides that a proportion of the total price – 15 to 20 per cent – will be retained until some time after the work has been completed.

If work is to be done on part of a building or some other structure a presumption may arise in favour of the contract being divisible rather than entire. A trade custom in favour of a shipwright being entitled to call for repair work to be payable in instalments explains the leading case of *Roberts v. Havelock*.[27]

In the case of *Verolme Cork Dockyard Ltd. v. Shannon Atlantic Fisheries Ltd.*[28] the plaintiffs claimed for £28,000, alleged to be due for repair work performed on the defendants' fishing boat. The defendants pleaded that the work was not completed and that the contract was entire. Finlay P. on the evidence held that the contract contained a term requiring a substantial payment on account to be made when a reasonably high proportion of the work had been carried out.

## (3) Fault of one party preventing performance

While an entire contract must be performed precisely there will be a remedy available in *quantum meruit* should one party fail to perform his obligations

---

[24] [1955–6] Ir.Jur.Rep. 86.
[25] (1874) I.R. 8 C.L. 40.
[26] e.g. *Clapham v. Draper* (1885) Cab. & El. 484.
[27] (1832) 3 B. & Ad. 404.
[28] Unreported, High Court, July 31, 1978.

because of some act or default on the part of the other. In the case of *Arterial Drainage Co. Ltd. v. Rathangan River Drainage Board*[29] contractors agreed to drain land for the defendant Board, the contract being entire. The contract provided that if the contractors failed to carry out work with due diligence the employer could terminate the contract. The defendant purported to exercise this right. It appears that the work was not performed as quickly as envisaged because the defendant had failed to make land and plans available to the contractors. The Court of Common Pleas, distinguishing *Cutter v. Powell*, held that the defendants default prevented the plaintiffs from performing their obligations. The plaintiffs were therefore entitled to treat the contract as rescinded and sue for the value of work completed.

### (4) Tender of performance

When one party unsuccessfully attempts to render performance this is known as a tender. The effects of a tender differ according to the nature of the outstanding obligation.

If the obligation is to pay a sum of money, the creditor refusing to accept the sum, this does not discharge the debtor's obligation to pay. Should the debtor pay the sum into court the creditor may recover the sum by way of action but interest will not be payable; the debtor will recover his costs.[30]

Even if the obligation is an obligation to pay money and the contract does not make provision for the form in which payment is made, one party may accept a cheque, or credit card payment as the method of payment. Should the payment be dishonoured there may be either an action for the recovery of the original debt or an action on the dishonoured payment. Whether such actions are available is a matter of interpretation. In *P.M.P.S. Ltd. v. Moore*[31] the question arose as to whether acceptance of a bill of exchange operated as a conditonal or absolute acceptance. While the general presumption is that the acceptance is conditional only, thereby making a tender of the bill incapable of discharging the underlying debt in the case of dishonour, Murphy J. indicated that an exception will arise where the bill tendered is drawn by the creditor himself and endorsed back to the creditor.

The debtor must meet any contractual terms set as to the place, time and manner of payment. The Northern Ireland case of *Morrow v. Carty*[32] establishes that attempted payment of a deposit required in cash by offering a cheque will not be sufficient. In the Republic of Ireland the Decimal Currency Act 1969 defines legal tender within the State as follows; silver coins are legal tender up to the sum of £10 (section 8(1)); a tender of bronze coins and silver coins up to a value of 10p. is legal tender for any sum up to £5 (section 8(2)); bronze coins

---

[29] (1880) 6 L.R. (Ir.) 513; *Planché v. Colburn* (1831) 8 Bing. 14.
[30] *Griffiths v. Board of Ystradyfodwg* (1890) 24 Q.B.D. 307: Rules of the Superior Courts 1986, Order 22.
[31] [1988] I.L.R.M. 526; Gill (1987) 6 I.L.T. 81.
[32] [1957] N.I. 174.

are legal tender up to a sum of 20p. Banknotes are legal tender up to any amount. United Kingdom banknotes and coins are not legal tender in the Republic because they are not issued under the Coinage Acts 1926–1950, or the 1969 Act. However, these legislative provisions are apparently doomed by the prospect of monetary union. The Economic and Monetary Union Act 1998 has outlined the repeal of these provisions by June 30, 2002 (sections 9 and 10), and from the beginning of January 1999 the currency of the State is declared to be the euro, the Irish pound being a subdivision thereof (section 6).

If the tender consists of an attempt to perform actions other than payment of money, the delivery of goods for example, non-acceptance may discharge the obligations of the promisor. Thus if goods are due and they are tendered during a reasonable hour, a refusal to accept may amount to a repudiation entitling the seller to treat the contract as discharged: Sale of Goods Act 1893, ss.29(4), 31(2), 37. The essential issue is whether the tender gives the buyer the opportunity to adequately inspect the goods.

### (5) Time of performance

While at common law any time fixed for the performance of a contract was held to be "of the essence of the contract", failure to perform entitling the other party to terminate and sue for damages,[33] the equitable rule, which now prevails makes it clear that normally time for performance is not of the essence; see the Judicature Act 1877, s.28(7), and *Mayne v. Merriman*.[34] In Ireland, time will be of the essence if the contract provides; this is frequently done in conveyancing. In *Crean v. Drinan*[35] the plaintiff purchaser stipulated a completion date in connection with the purchase of property. It had also been stipulated that an assignment of an interest held by third parties would be obtained by the closing date. While it was held that the failure to close on the completion date did not itself discharge the agreement, the failure to obtain the deed of assignment by that date did discharge the contract. Applying the leading case of *Aberfoyle Plantations v. Cheng*,[36] Barrington J. held that where a conditional contract of sale fixes the date by which the condition must be met the date so fixed must be strictly adhered to. The contract accordingly was discharged when the defendant failed to obtain the assignment stipulated by the plaintiff. The plaintiff was entited to the return of his deposit. However, each agreement will turn on its own facts. In *Sepia Ltd. and Opal Ltd. v. M. & P. Hanlon Ltd. and Another*[37] the defendants agreed to sell two parcels of land, Block A and Block B, to the plaintiffs. Block A was the subject of a contract which expressly fixed the closing date and expressly made time of the essence.

---

[33] *Bowes v. Shand* (1877) 2 App.Cas. 455. This rule was particularly strong in cases of delivery of goods: *Clements v. Russell* (1854) 7 Ir.Jur. 102.

[34] Unreported, High Court, February 3, 1980.

[35] [1983] I.L.R.M. 82.

[36] [1960] A.C. 115. In some commercial property sales time may be of the essence as a matter of implication: *O'Brien v. Seaview Enterprises*, Unreported, High Court, May 31, 1976.

[37] Unreported, High Court, January 23, 1979.

The agreement was subject to the plaintiffs obtaining planning permission. Should the permission not be obtained by the closing date, the defendant vendor would have been able to treat the contract as at an end and the purchaser's deposit would have been forfeited. In this case the planning permission difficulty was not such as to excuse non-performance of the obligation to close the Block A contract.

The English courts have recently restated the view that where a contract expressly makes time of the essence equitable principles cannot be used to overlook non-compliance with the literal terms of the bargain. In *Union Eagle Ltd. v. Golden Achievement Ltd.*[38] a contract for the conveyance of a flat in Hong Kong provided for completion on or before 5 p.m. on a given day. Non-compliance would give the vendor a cancellation right and the right to forfeit the deposit. The purchaser was 10 minutes late. Proceedings by the purchaser to obtain specific performance ultimately failed in the Privy Council, equity not intervening to absolve the purchaser from the effects of the "time of the essence" clause and the cancellation provision; there was nothing in the nature of a penalty involved here and the Privy Council refused to evolve an unconscionability remedy on the ground that such relief would cause uncertainty and fly in the face of the contract itself.

If the contract does not originally make time of the essence, one party may subsequently serve a notice that as from a stated date time shall be of the essence. In *Nolan v. Driscoll*[39] the plaintiff, in December 1975, agreed to purchase the defendant's house; due to problems relating to registration of title the sale was still incomplete two years later; on March 2, 1977 the defendant, being of the view that a sufficient title had been shown, served notice that he now wished to make time of the essence, and that completion should take place at the end of the month. McWilliam J. upheld the defendant's view that he was entitled to terminate when the plaintiff failed to meet the closing date and refused to order specific performance against him. However, if there is a date fixed for closing, it may be that the parties will subsequently extend or in some way alter the closing date. In *Sepia Ltd. and Opal Ltd. v. M. & P. Hanlon Ltd. and Another*,[40] while the contract in respect of Block A contained an express term making time of the essence, the later contract for Block B, which was silent on this point, superseded the original closing date in the Block A contract, and provided that the closing date for both contracts was to be one of two fixed dates, at the option of the purchasers. When both dates passed, the defendant vendors wrote a letter making time of the essence and giving three months' notice of the closing date fixed. Costello J. stated the applicable principles as follows:

---

[38] [1997] A.C. 517, applying *Steedman v. Drinkle* [1916] 1 A.C. 275. See Stevens (1998) 61 M.L.R. 255.
[39] Unreported, High Court, April 25, 1978.
[40] Unreported, High Court, January 23, 1979.

"If a stipulation as to time is not of the essence of a contract, then when one party has been guilty of undue delay the other may give notice requiring the contract to be performed within a reasonable time specified in the notice. In considering the reasonableness of the time so limited the court will consider not merely what remains to be done at the date of the notice but all the circumstances of the case, including the previous delay of the purchaser and the attitude of the vendor to it. If the notice is a reasonable one the vendor may at its expiration treat the contract as at an end if the purchaser refuses to complete."[41]

In this case the purchasers had been dilatory in order to progress their application for planning permission to the stage of grant of the permission prior to closing. The notice period was reasonable, given that the delays in respect of the planning permission were also in part due to the plaintiff's tardiness and the fact that the defendants had no hand or part in this process and the very consistent attitude of the defendants. They had been sympathetic to the plaintiffs but had pressed for closing on the dates fixed. More recently, the English courts have been presented with the opportunity to further refine these principles. For example, when the closing date arrives, the purchaser may, if it is apparent that there will be a delay, be immediately presented with a notice making time of the essence. The vendor is not obliged to wait for a reasonable period before serving the notice. However, the time set must be a reasonable one.[42] In accordance with the rules on tender, the duty to complete by tendering the purchase price is strict and cannot be excused by, for example, a dispute over the monies due under the contract.[43] A further basis upon which the contract may be terminated, even in the absence of an express notice, either at the time of contracting or following a delay, is where the purchaser or vendor has been guilty of a frustrating delay. The vendor or purchaser, if innocent of fault, is entitled to treat the contract as discharged by operation of the doctrine of frustration.

In landlord and tenant cases the House of Lords has indicated that the attitude to all time obligations, whether the property is commercial or otherwise, will be governed by the general rule that, in the absence of an express term, time is not of the essence. The decision in *United Scientific Holdings Ltd. v. Burnley Borough Council*[44] is to be seen as the leading case on time covenants generally.

In commercial contracts the courts are reluctant to hold time of the essence unless the contract so requires: see section 10(1) of the Sale of Goods Act 1893. Due to the nature of the commodity sold time will be of the essence in contracts for the sale of a business as a going concern. Non-observance of time obligations in a commercial contract may permit the innocent party to regard the other party as being in breach, thereby entitling the innocent party to treat

---

[41] Citing *Stickney v. Keeble* [1915] A.C. 386; *Ajit v. Sammy* [1967] 1 A.C. 259.

[42] *Behzadi v. Shaftesbury Hotels Ltd.* [1991] 2 All E.R. 477, disapproving *Smith v. Hamilton* [1950] 2 All E.R. 928. The decision in *British and Commonwealth Holdings v. Quadrex Holdings Ltd.* [1989] 3 All E.R. 492 is something of a transitional decision after the *Behzadi* case.

[43] *Carne v. Debono* [1988] 3 All E.R. 485.

[44] [1977] 2 All E.R. 62, followed in *Hynes v. Independent Newspapers* [1980] I.R. 204.

the contract as at an end, if the obligation is a condition or the obligation, as an intermediate stipulation, has been broken in a way that goes to the root of the contract.[45]

## Discharge through Agreement

Post-contractual representations which purport to have the effect of abrogating or modifying contractual terms present acute difficulties, due in the main to a failure on the part of judges to use and define terms like "rescission", "variation" and "waiver" with any degree of precision; the term "waiver", for example bears at least six meanings.[46] Additional difficulties are presented by jurisdictional factors; modern equitable lines of authority provide solutions which differ from those developed by the courts of common law.

### (1) Rescission through accord and satisfaction

For a contract to be terminated by mutual agreement (accord), consideration (satisfaction) must be present. No difficulty arises where the transaction is executory on both sides; mutual promises not to sue for non-performance generate consideration from both parties. Even if the agreement is partly executed on both sides the same rule applies. In general, the form in which the contract is discharged is not relevant. A deed may be rescinded by a simple contract and need not be contained in a deed. However, if there is a written instrument which records the terms of the executory or partly executed contract in order to make the agreement enforceable as a matter of statute law, as in section 2 of the Statute of Frauds (Ireland) 1695, then it may be necessary to record the terms of any agreement which is intended to vary or supplement any prior agreement in the same way as the initial agreement. If these oral terms are not recorded in a memorandum in writing, to use the example of the Statute of Frauds, then the agreement continues and the oral variation will not be enforceable.[47] In contrast, if the oral agreement is intended to extinguish or abrogate an executory or partly executed contract for the sale of land, this can be done by an oral agreement. If the intention is to abrogate the written contract, which does comply with statutory formalities, and replace it with an entirely oral agreement which is incompatible with the earlier agreement, then both the earlier and later agreements are unenforceable for different reasons. In relation to the first, it is rescinded verbally but the second is unenforceable for failure to comply with the statute in question.[48] If the intention is simply to supplement

---

[45] *Hong Kong Fir Shipping Co. v. Kawasaki Kishen Keisha* [1962] 2 Q.B. 26.

[46] Dugdale and Yates (1976) 39 M.L.R. 680.

[47] *McQuaid v. Lynam* [1965] I.R. 564; *Morris v. Baton & Co.* [1918] A.C. 1; *Scott v. Midland Great Western Railway* (1853) 6 Ir.Jur. 73; *Ruck v. Brownrigg* (1849) 2 Ir.Jur. 142.

[48] *Morris v. Baron & Co.* [1918] A.C. 1; *Jackson v. Hayes* [1939] Ir.Jur.Rep. 59; *Travers Construction Ltd. v. Lismore Homes Ltd.*, unreported, High Court, March 9, 1990.

or vary orally a written agreement, then the written agreement will remain enforceable.[49] These strict rules may be relaxed by way of the notice of waiver.[50]

If one party has completely performed his part of the contract a promise given by that person will not rescind the contract. So, if A has delivered wheat to B and B has yet to pay for the goods, a promise by A not to sue B is ineffective unless recorded in a deed under seal or B gives some nominal consideration for A's promise.[51]

It suffices for the purpose of the discharge of the initial cause of action, if the satisfaction agreed upon – for example, a cash debt of £500 is to be satisfied by the debtor transferring to the creditor a motor vehicle owned by the debtor in full satisfaction of the cash debt – is promised without the actual performance having been executed.[52] This is subject, of course, to qualification. The creditor may make the discharge conditional upon actual receipt of the satisfaction promised by the debtor.

Section 62 of the Bills of Exchange Act 1882, in force in both parts of Ireland, provides that no satisfaction is necessary for the renunciation of a debt owed to the holder of a bill of exchange or promissory note. So a straightforward way of avoiding the general rule would be for the creditor to take a bill or note in satisfaction of the debt and then renounce the debt.[53]

### (2) Variation

Consideration must also be present if a contractual term is deleted or altered, leaving the rest of the contract untouched: *Fenner v. Blake*.[54]

The variation, to be effective, may have to overcome certain evidentiary hurdles. Section 2 of the Statute of Frauds (Ir.) 1695 and section 4 of the Sale of Goods Act 1893 come into play here. A variation may have to be recorded in writing. The leading Irish case is *McQuaid v. Lynam*[55]; Kenny J. said:

> "It is essential to distinguish between the case in which the parties to an agreement intend that agreement to find expression in a written contract and that in which the parties make an oral contract which is intended to be binding. If in the later case of memorandum or note in writing is required by the Statute of Frauds, that memorandum or note does not become the contract."

After reading section 2, Kenny J. continued:

---

[49] *UDT Corporation (Jamaica) Ltd. v. Shoucair* [1969] 1 A.C. 340.
[50] See the discussion in *Wright v. Griffith* (1851) 3 Ir.Jur. 138, in which *Goss v. Nugent* (1833) 5 B. & Ad. 58 is examined in the context of waiver.
[51] *Drogheda Corp. v. Fairtlough* (1858) 8 Ir.C.L.R. 98: *Foakes v. Beer* (1884) 9 App. Cas. 605.
[52] *Cartwright v. Cooke* (1832) 3 B. & Ad. 701; *British Russian Gazette Ltd. v. Associated Newspapers Ltd.* [1933] 2 K.B. 616.
[53] See Trietel, *The Law of Contract* (9th ed., 1995), p. 96.
[54] [1900] 1 Q.B. 427.
[55] [1965] I.R. 564.

"[W]here the parties intend their agreement to find expression in a written document, a subsequent oral variation of the contract is not effective unless it is evidenced by a memorandum or note in writing . . . But in the other type of case, where the oral agreement is intended to be the contract, evidence may be given of an agreed variation even if there is a memorandum or note of the contract but not of the variation."[56]

However, if no formal requirement to reduce the contract into writing exists then an oral variation of the contract can be proved in the usual way: *Saphena Computing Ltd. v. Allied Collection Agencies.*[57]

### (3) Waiver

If a contractual term is subject to a variation then as a matter of contract the terms of the agreement are altered. If however there is a request for some degree of forbearance, such request being agreed to, no change occurs *vis-à-vis* the contractual obligation. In this context it is common to describe the conduct of the party granting the concession as waiver of a contractual right.

Again the Statute of Frauds becomes material to the discussion. Waiver of a contractual right does not have to be evidenced in writing unlike a variation, because in strict theory the right continues to exist while it may be unenforceable – a jurisprudential oddity.

The case of *McKillop v. McMullen*[58] illustrates the effect of a waiver on a contractual obligation. The defendant agreed to sell land to the plaintiff subject to the defendant acquiring a right of way over a road to be built upon the land; planning permission was to be a condition precedent to the sale. When the closing date agreed upon arrived the defendant vendor failed to rescind; in fact he later requested performance. Shortly after this he, without notice, rescinded the contract. Planning permission was granted shortly after. Murray J. held that when the defendant allowed the date for completion to pass, insisting that the parties complete at some later date, that this was a waiver of his right to terminate for failure to obtain planning permission at the date of completion; the waiver was not unqualified however. The right to terminate could be exercised upon giving reasonable notice of a new date; failure to give such notice meant that the waiver remained effective.

Waiver may also affect the range of remedies available to the party forbearing to enforce his rights. In *Car & General Insurance Corp. v. Munden*[59] the plaintiffs, insurers of the defendant's motor vehicle, required in clause 2 of the contract that no admission, offer, promise, payment or indemnity would be given by the insured without the consent of the plaintiffs who were also to have a right to sue in respect of an accident involving the insured. The insured's

---

[56] [1965] I.R. 564 at 573.
[57] [1995] F.S.R. 616.
[58] [1979] N.I. 85.
[59] [1938] I.R. 584.

vehicle collided with a bus injuring the insured and damaging the vehicle. The insured signed a release note issued by the bus company who paid compensation for his personal injuries. The plaintiffs believed that this broke clause 2; the right of subrogation was thereby extinguished. The plaintiffs therefore claimed to be entitled to recover £130 paid in respect of damage to the vehicle. It was held that while clause 2 may have been broken, payment of the £130 constituted a waiver of the right to refuse to indemnify the defendant. The waiver only prevented the plaintiffs from terminating the agreement and obtaining resitution; they were entitled to recovery damages, which, because of difficulties of proof, were nominal in this case.

This result seems a curious one. It is difficult to see how waiver may be possible in cases of this nature where that person is unaware that the right to terminate has come into play: when the insurance company paid out they were unaware of Munden's non-observance of clause 2. In contrast the Court of Appeal in *Peyman v. Lanjani*[60] held that before a contracting party can be held to have affirmed an agreement and waived a right to rescind it, knowledge of the right to elect whether to affirm the contract or rescind must be shown. If there is simply knowledge of the facts without knowledge that on these facts rescission is possible then waiver cannot be said to take place if that party simply refrains from a particular course of action. The decision of Carswell J. in *Lutton v. Saville Tractors Ltd.*[61] is to similar effect. The purchaser of a motor car obtained a warranty that the vehicle had not been involved in a motor accident. After taking delivery of the vehicle, it proved unsatisfactory and the purchaser took the vehicle back on several occasions to have it repaired. Eventually, he returned the vehicle on the basis of unsatisfactory performance. After rescission, the purchaser discovered that the vehicle had been involved in an accident. The purchaser could not have affirmed the contract in respect of this misrepresentation because he had no knowledge of the true state of affairs at the time of the alleged affirmation.

It is not an act of waiver to intimate that one may be prepared in certain circumstances to waive some contract right: *per* Barrington J. in *S.A. Fonderies Lion M.V. v. International Factors (Ireland) Ltd.*[62]

On the waiver of constitutional rights and in particular constitutional fundamental freedoms in employment contracts see *Murphy v. Stewart*[63] and the discussion in Kerr and Whyte, *Irish Trade Union Law.*[64]

## (4) Estoppel

It may be that the equitable doctrine of promissory estoppel will, in time, present a universal doctrine which will eliminate the distinctions between variation and

---

[60] [1985] 2 W.L.R. 154.
[61] [1986] N.I. 327.
[62] [1985] I.L.R.M. 66.
[63] [1975] I.R. 97.
[64] (1985), pp. 31–33.

waiver; Denning L.J. in *Charles Rickards Ltd. v. Oppenheim*[65] described forbearance, waiver and variation as "a kind of estoppel". This thematic approach was reiterated by Lord Denning M.R. in *Crabb v. Arun District Council,*[66] a dictum later approved by Finlay P. in *Smith v. Ireland.*[67]

### (5) Reform

Dugdale and Yates[68] have suggested that post-contractual statements should be analysed in two ways: firstly, consensual agreements altering terms of the contract shall be effective without consideration; secondly, conduct which the representor knows should induce a change in position should, if the statement is unambiguous, affect the remedies available to the representor. This scheme seems eminently sensible and would eliminate most of the sterile distinctions that plague this area.

# Discharge Following a Breach of Contract

It is generally accepted that a breach of contract does not of itself terminate a contract. Such a result would be unsatisfactory because a person could, by his own act, put an end to his contractual obligations. The innocent party has an option when a breach of contract occurs; he may elect to treat the breach as discharging his contractual duties as well as the primary obligations of the other party to perform. He may also decide to waive the right to repudiate, choosing instead to treat the contract as remaining in existence. In this second situation the innocent party may recover damages for any loss occasioned by the breach. However, upon a failure to accept the breach as one which terminates the contract, the innocent party is obliged to provide the agreed price should the party in breach perform obligations due under the contract, after making provision for any damages occasioned by the breach of contract.[69]

Of course the right to terminate does not arise in every case. If the term broken is a warranty, the remedy of termination is not available.[70]

Although academics and judges are at variance on the correct terminology to apply, the right to terminate will arise in three situations:

---

[65] [1950] 1 K.B. 616.
[66] [1976] Ch. 179.
[67] [1983] I.L.R.M. 300; the extension of the public law concept of legitimate expectation into contractual matters such as the employment contract will accelerate this process in Ireland: *e.g. Duggan v. Ireland* [1989] I.L.R.M. 710.
[68] (1976) 39 M.L.R. 680.
[69] *Sim v. Rotherham M.D.C.* [1987] Ch. 216.
[70] *Cripps v. Smith* (1841) 3 Ir. L.Rep. 277; *Garrick v. Bradshaw* (1846) 10 Ir.L.Rep. 129; see the discussion of *Poussard v. Spiers and Pond* (1876) 1 Q.B.D. 410 and *Bettini v. Gye* (1876) 1 Q.B.D. 183 in *Fearnley v. London Guarantee* (1880) 5 App.Cas. 911 and in the lower court (1881) 6 L.R.Ir. 219.

(1) where the breach amounts to a repudiatory breach of contract;

(2) where the breach is a fundamental breach; that is, it goes to the root of the contact so as to deprive the innocent party of the commercial benefits envisaged;

(3) where the term broken is such as to amount to breach of a condition.

## *(1) Repudiatory breach*

A repudiatory breach involves a decision by one party that he will not perform his contractual obligations. In *Mersey Steel and Iron Co. v. Naylor Benzon*[71] the purchaser of goods refused to pay for goods delivered by a company that was the subject of winding-up proceedings, the purchaser being wrongly advised that effective payment was only possible with leave of a court. The evidence disclosed that the plaintiffs were in fact anxious to discharge the debt. The House of Lords refused to find a repudiatory breach. In contrast, the House of Lords held, in *Athlone Rural District Council v. A. G. Campbell & Son (No. 2)*[72] that the appellants were guilty of repudiatory breach. Contractors agreed to excavate a well under the terms of a contract which made the issue of an engineer's certificate a condition precedent to payment for their work. After the work was completed in part, the contractors (following an unsuccessful action for damages) wrote indicating their willingness to complete their work. The local authority replied that they would not require the work to be done. This letter of reply was held to be a repudiatory breach of contract. The contractors were held entitled to recover damages for breach of contract or mount a claim in *quantum meruit.*

The decision in *Decro-Wall International SA v. Practitioners in Marketing Ltd.*[73] provides an instructive statement on the relevant principles. Here the defendants were appointed sole distributors of the plaintiffs' goods within the United Kingdom. The defendants, as the plaintiffs knew, were short of working capital and relied upon payment from customers to meet the plaintiffs' invoices. Payment was consistently late, but it was never in doubt that payment would at some time be made. Instead of charging the defendants with the consequential loss incurred, namely bank interest charges on monies borrowed, the plaintiffs terminated the distributorship. The defendants alleged wrongful repudiation; the plaintiffs alleged that the late payment by the defendants was repudiatory. The Court of Appeal reiterated that the test was whether the breach goes to the root of the contract. This, as a matter of degree, obliges the court to consider all the facts of the case. Here the loss was minor; some £20 on each unpaid bill. The delay in payment was, on average, an eight-day delay. The contract did not make time of the essence in respect of payment, and the plaintiffs did not give notice that if late payment continued the contract would

---

[71] (1884) 9 App.Cas. 434.
[72] (1912) 47 I.L.T.R. 142.
[73] [1971] 2 All E.R. 216.

be terminated. The recent decision of the Court of Appeal in *Nottingham Building Society v. Eurodynamics Systems plc*[74] is to similar effect. Here the defendants provided computer software to the plaintiff but a dispute about the contract developed. The plaintiff refused to pay invoices and the defendants purported to accept this repudiation. The Court of Appeal held that in no sense could the plaintiff be taken to have repudiated the contract through a refusal to pay disputed invoices.

A more controversial decision is presented by the case of *Woodar Investment v. Wimpey Construction.*[75] A contract for the sale of land to Wimpey by Woodar was subject to a condition that should the property *later* become subject to compulsory purchase proceedings the purchaser would have the right to terminate; land prices fell dramatically and Wimpey, who were anxious to re-negotiate the price, purported to rescind because part of the land was later compulsorily purchased, even though these particular proceedings were in progress when the contract of sale was concluded. Woodar's agent indicated that his company would not accept the rescission, indicating that: "We will retire to our battle stations and it goes without saying I am sure that you will abide by the result as I will." All members of the House of Lords held the rescission to be wrongful but by a majority (three to two) it was held that there was no repudiatory breach; while the fall in land prices provided a motive for termination, the conduct of Wimpey did not of itself manifest an intent to breach the contract – termination was purportedly effected under the agreement itself. As Lord Wilberforce said in the leading speech for the majority: "unless the invocation of that provision were totally abusive, or lacking in good faith, the fact that it has proved to be wrong in law cannot turn it into a repudiation."[76] A similar view applies in Ireland. In *Continental Oil Company v. Moynihan*[77] it was argued that a differential pricing arrangement, introduced by the plaintiffs during the currency of a solus agreement was a breach entitling the defendant retailer to treat the contract as discharged. Kenny J. dismissed this argument by holding that the conduct of the plaintiffs did not evidence an intention to repudiate the contract.[78] While this may be so, it is clear that there are other grounds upon which termination may be available. Kenny J.'s judgment seems incomplete on the question of discharge of a contract, as we shall see. In *House of Spring Gardens Ltd. v. Point Blank Ltd.*[79] the Supreme court upheld the decision of Costello J. in which the learned judge decided that a repudiatory breach of contract had occurred. The defendants attempted to redesign a bullet-proof vest in such a way as to create a product that did not

---

[74] [1995] F.S.R. 605.
[75] [1980] 1 All E.R. 571; contrast *Federal Commerce and Navigation Co. Ltd. v. Molena Alpha Inc.* [1979] A.C. 757.
[76] [1980] 1 All E.R. 571 at 574.
[77] (1977) 111 I.L.T.R. 5.
[78] Intention is judged objectively: *Nottingham Building Society v. Eurodynamics Systems plc* [1995] F.S.R. 605.
[79] [1985] F.S.R. 327; [1985] I.R. 611.

infringe the plaintiff's copyright. Had this exercise been successful the defendants would not have been in breach of contract. Counsel for the defendants argued however that the breach could not be repudiatory because the defendants had evinced an intention not to infringe the copyright; rescission should not therefore be available. This argument was rejected. Griffin J., in the Supreme Court, found that misleading correspondence written by the defendants, allied to suppression of information by the defendants, to the prejudice of the plaintiffs, indicated an intention to defraud the plaintiffs. These facts led to an irresistible inference that the defendants had no intention to perform their contractual obligation to pay royalties to the plaintiffs.

While a repudiatory breach may occur during performance of the agreement it is less obvious that such a breach may also occur before performance is due. Further, the innocent party may immediately sue and recover damages even though at the date of judgment the agreed time for performance may be months or even years away.

In the famous case of *Hochster v. De La Tour*[80] the defendant engaged the plaintiff to work as a courier. Agreement was struck on April 12; the plaintiff was to start work on June 1. On May 11 the defendant informed the plaintiff that his services would not be required. The plaintiff immediately sued. Counsel for the defendant argued that the announcement was only an offer to rescind and that until the date of performance the offer may be retracted. Further, until that date arrives there can be no breach of contract. The argument failed. The view that the plaintiff was obliged to remain inactive until June 1 and that he could not find alternative employment for that period, without sacrificing his right to sue, proved unattractive to the court. The plaintiff should be encouraged to mitigate his loss and the best way of doing this is to characterise a statement of intent not to perform as itself a breach of contract; the innocent party loses a right to expect the contract to be kept open for performance.[81] While this may be so, it is difficult to see why the plaintiff should be able to immediately sue, particularly when granting an immediate right to action makes the assessment of damages speculative.[82]

The doctrine in *Hochster v. De la Tour* is known as the doctrine of anticipatory breach. It has been accepted in Ireland. In *Leeson v. North British Oil and Candle Co.*[83] the defendants contracted to supply the plaintiff's nominees with up to 300 casks of paraffin over a winter season. In January the plaintiff was told that due to a strike it would not be possible to supply the paraffin for about two months, by which time of course demand would be negligible. The plaintiff refused to take further orders from his own customers fearing that if his own supplier could not meet orders the plaintiff would possibly leave himself open to actions for breach of contract. The plaintiff sued recovering

---

[80] (1853) 2 E. & B. 678.
[81] *Frost v. Knight* (1872) L.R. 7 Ex. 711.
[82] *Melachrino v. Nicholl and Knight* [1920] 1 K.B. 693.
[83] (1874) 8 I.R.C.L. 309.

damages for orders already submitted as well as for loss of orders that he would have accepted but for the defendants' statement that he would not be able to meet future orders. The defendants argued on appeal that the plaintiff's refusal to accept orders was precipitous; he should have placed the orders with the defendant on the chance that supply of paraffin might be obtained elsewhere. The Court of Queens Bench dismissed the appeal holding that the statement made entitled the plaintiff to immediately rescind the contract and recover all profits lost.

Until recently it was thought that, upon an anticipatory breach, a positive act of acceptance was required by the non-repudiating party. This could consist of bringing a claim for damages or some form of communication to the repudiating party. Mere inactivity was thought never to be an act of acceptance. After *Vitol SA v. Norelf Ltd.*[84] this question depends on individual circumstances. The point here is that if the breach is not accepted, the injured party may not be successful in obtaining damages if the court says communication of acceptance of the breach was not made.[85] If communication of acceptance is made, the fact that damages may be difficult to assess is not a bar to relief. Not all "anticipatory" breaches will give rise to a right to accept the contract as at an end.[86] Minor breaches will not suffice whether for damages or rescission: the "substantial failure of performance test" is used but this seems to cover fundamental breach and breaches of condition.

The law of partnership can provide some interesting illustrations of the law of repudiatory breach. While a partnership deed will no doubt contain clauses permitting withdrawal from, or termination of, the partnership, there may arise differences which make continued co-operation impossible. In *Bothe v. Amos*[87] the partners, a married couple, found that differences arose between them in their married life together and the wife left her husband. It was held that by her departure she had abandoned her marriage and the partnership. In a more recent Irish case[88] all the members of an accountancy firm fell out and effectively ignored their obligations under the partnership agreement. Barrington J. held that while the agreement was not terminated under the terms of the deed, or as a result of any of the standard causes, such as death, bankruptcy, expulsion or completion of the joint venture, the partnership can be terminated by conduct which is inconsistent with the continuance of the partnership.

### (2) Fundamental breach

In this context "fundamental breach" is used to describe a breach of contract which is sufficiently serious to entitle the injured party to repudiate the contract;

---

[84] [1996] 3 All E.R. 193.
[85] *Johnstone v. Milling* (1886) 16 Q.B.D. 460.
[86] See Treitel, *The Law of Contract* (9th ed., 1995) pp. 771–774.
[87] [1975] 2 All E.R. 321.
[88] *Larkin v. Groeger and Eaton*, unreported, High Court, April 26, 1988. Counsel used the idea that conduct may "repudiate the partnership" but Barrington J. did not adopt this expression.

this has nothing to do with the vexed question of the applicability of an exception clause after a fundamental breach: see *Clayton Love v. B. + I. Transport.*[89]

Certain breaches of contract are so cataclysmic that the innocent party may regard himself as free to terminate the contract. In *Robb v. James*[90] the plaintiffs purchased fabrics at an auction, the conditions of the sale requiring payment of the price and collection within 24 hours. They failed to comply with these terms and the defendants sold the goods to a third party. The plaintiffs failed in an action for breach of contract. Their failure to pay the price and collect was described by May C.J. as a breach of "the most essential term of the contract . . . under such circumstances, the seller may treat the contract as abandoned by the purchaser, and may detain and resell the goods."[91]

In this context, the question of the objectively ascertained intent of the party in breach is irrelevant; hence the present writer's reservations about Kenny J.'s dictum in *Continental Oil Company v. Moynihan*, discussed above. This is illustrated graphically by the judgment of Finlay P. in *Dundalk Shopping Centre Ltd. v. Roof Spray Ltd.*[92] The plaintiffs engaged the defendant company to spray a waterproof substance over the roof of a shopping centre. Due to various delays, and the defendants' negligence, the work was carried out inefficiently. Water seeped into the building. It was held that failure to make the roof watertight was a breach of a fundamental term of the contract, namely "to provide an effective waterproofing of this roof within a reasonable time". This breach entitled the plaintiffs to terminate the contract and obtain damages for consequential loss. Far from evidencing an intent to break the contract, the conduct of Roof Spray Ltd. showed they intended to perform the contract; however, their defective performance was sufficiently serious as to entitle the employer to treat the contract as discharged through breach.

The two most important factors in identifying a fundamental breach are:

(1) the seriousness of the breach and effect of breach;

(2) the likelihood of this recurring in the case of contracts with future obligations to be performed by the party in breach.

Other factors that will be significant include whether damages may be an adequate remedy, and the motive behind the desire to terminate. If termination is sought to avoid a bad bargain, the claim will be less meritorious.[93] In essence, the issue is the same, and the test to be applied is the same as that which arises when the court concludes that an express term is neither a condition, nor a warranty, *strictu sensu.*[94]

---

[89] (1970) 104 I.L.T.R. 157; see generally Chap. 7.
[90] (1881) 15 I.L.T.R. 59.
[91] *Ibid.* at 60.
[92] Unreported, High Court, March 21, 1979.
[93] *Hong Kong Fir Shipping Co. Ltd. v. Kawasaki Kishen Kaisha Ltd.* [1962] 2 Q.B. 26.
[94] *Ibid.*

An excellent application of this approach is demonstrated by Lardner J. in *Taylor v. Smith and Others*.[95] The plaintiff, owner and lessor of business premises, agreed to compromise a complex set of proceedings which he had brought in 1981 against the various defendants in respect of an earlier 1975 agreement to purchase the premises by the first defendant and resolve other points of disagreement, such as arrears of rental due to the plaintiff, the release of debts alleged to be payable by the plaintiff to other defendants and obtain the vacation of a *lis pendens* registered in respect of the property, this latter obligation resting upon the plaintiff. However, the plaintiff was unable to obtain the consents required and Lardner J. held that the delay was an unreasonable one. However, did the unreasonable delay in respect of completion of the sale by Taylor allow the defendants to regard the contract as repudiated? Lardner J. ruled that the obligation to transfer the freehold was not severable, and had to be seen in the light of the other, diverse obligations, which the vendor could observe:

> "a consideration of the nature of this contract and of its terms leads me to conclude that its various provisions were intended to be a settlement or compromise agreement which comprehended them all, that they were interdependent and were intended to constitute an entire contract."[96]

After noting that it was not contended that the vendors breach made the entire contract repudiatory, the defendants insisting that certain obligations survived the delay and were binding, the learned judge advanced the view that, where a delay in an entire contract which consists of a number of heterogeneous obligations occurs, the question of whether the innocent party can treat the contract as discharged is to be tested by reference to the *Hong Kong Firs* test. Lardner J. said the court, in this context, must consider the effect of the breach upon the contract as a whole and whether the effect of the delay deprived the innocent party of substantially the whole benefit of the contract. Lardner J. held the breach here did not entitle the defendants to treat the contract as discharged. Because no loss had been occasioned, the defendants were held not entitled to damages.

### (3) Breach of condition

Any term which the parties or statute has deemed to be sufficiently important to entitle the innocent party to repudiate the contract when that term is broken may conveniently be described as a condition (sometimes it is called a fundamental term). For example, the Sale of Goods Act 1893 classifies the obligation to give a good title, as a condition. It may be that the innocent party will lose his right to repudiate the contract for a breach of condition. Section 11(1)(c) of the 1893 Act prevented a purchaser from rescinding the contract:

---

[95] [1990] I.L.R.M. 377; *Clarke v. Kilternan Motor Co.*, unreported, High Court, December 12, 1996.
[96] [1990] I.L.R.M. 377 at 388.

(1)  if the contract was non-severable and the buyer accepted the goods or a part thereof; or

(2)  if the contract was for the sale of specific goods, property having passed to the seller.

In the Irish Republic the 1980 Act has repealed ground (2): section 11(3). In all other cases a breach of condition by the seller may be waived by the buyer or he may elect to treat the breach as a breach of warranty and not as a ground for treating the contract as repudiated: section 11(1).

### (4) Employment contracts

While a breach of contract may entitle the innocent party to rescind the contract it does not follow that the contract is discharged by the breach alone. The innocent party may affirm the contract in the hope that precise performance may later be rendered. In contracts of employment the position is somewhat different. Because specific performance of a contract of employment is traditionally unavailable, the innocent party has often no practical option but to accept the breach. An employee wrongfully dismissed must take alternative employment should it come along.[97] However, in some cases the employee may wish to keep the contract alive for certain purposes, such as establishing social welfare, redundancy or pension entitlements, and in *Thomas Marshall (Exports) Ltd. v. Guinle*[98] Megarry V.C. indicated that repudiation of the contract by an employee does not terminate the contract but, rather, gives the employee the usual choice to accept or reject repudiation. If the employee takes alternative employment, the employee will be taken to have accepted the option to rescind the contract,[99] but if the employee does not, then damages may be reduced because of failure to mitigate.[100] Not every breach of the contract of employment will entitle termination. The test advanced in the English case of *Pepper v. Webb*[101] has been accepted by Hamilton J.: "A person repudiates the contract of service if he wilfully disobeys the lawful and reasonable orders of his master."[102] Not all acts of disobedience justify termination by the other party. In the case of *Brewster v. Burke*[103] an employee's refusal to bury a dead horse was held not to be a sufficient act of misconduct as to justify summary dismissal. A tour bus courier who works for a rival concern in his own time should be disciplined but not dismissed: *Mullen v. C.I.É.*[104]

Certain breaches of contract are sufficiently serious so as to entitle the employer or employee to treat the contract as discharged. Refusal to pay wages

---

[97]  This however is a practical requirement because the employee is obliged to mitigate loss.
[98]  [1979] Ch. 227; Rose [1981] *Current Legal Problems* 235.
[99]  *Dietman v. London Borough of Brent* [1987] I.C.R. 737.
[100]  *Gunton v. Richmond Upon Thames London Borough* [1980] 3 W.L.R. 714.
[101]  [1969] 2 All E.R. 216.
[102]  *Ibid.* at 218 *per* Karminski L.J.
[103]  [1985] 4 J.I.S.L.L. 98: *Lyons v. Johnson* U.D. 579/1983.
[104]  U.D. 54/1979.

would entitle an employee to terminate the contract; the issue of strike notice may entitle the employer to regard this as a breach of contract, although Irish law differs from the English authorities on this point. In *Simmons v. Hoover Ltd.*[105] the English Employment Appeal Tribunal held that participaton in a strike was a fundamental breach of contract entitling the employer to dismiss an employee without notice. On the other hand, the Supreme Court in *Becton Dickinson Ltd. v. Lee*[106] held that issue of a strike notice, if the period of notice was sufficiently long to comply with the notice requirements necessary to terminate the contract, would not entitle the employer to treat the employee as guilty of a fundamental breach. Walsh J. in his speech expressly approved of Lord Denning M.R.'s theory, advanced in *Morgan v. Fry*,[107] in which the Master of the Rolls argued that due notice and participation in a strike suspend a contract of employment.

There is also Irish authority for the view that in certain cases a fundamental breach of an employment contract may automatically terminate the contract. In *Carvill v. Irish Industrial Bank*,[108] O'Keefe J. said:

> "There can be some breaches of contract so fundamental as to show that the contract is entirely repudiated by the party committing them, and that such an act might be relied upon in an action for wrongful dismissal, not as justifying the dismissal, but as supporting the plea that the dismissed servant had himself put an end to the contract."[109]

Indeed, one English commentator has agrued that a breach of contract automatically terminates that contract unless the innocent party chooses to waive the breach.[110] This theory must be regarded as unsound given the recent decision of the House of Lords in *Photo Production Ltd. v. Securicor Transport Ltd.*[111] Their Lordships expressly over-ruled *Harbutt's Plasticine*[112] and Lord Wilberforce observed that the "deviation" case of *Hain Steamship Co. Ltd. v. Tate & Lyle Ltd.*,[113] in which a similar rule is enunciated, must be regarded as *sui generis*. Thomson's thesis was based on the correctness and general applicability of these two cases. In Ireland the decision of Costello J. in *Industrial Yarns Ltd. v. Greene*[114] puts the matter beyond doubt. Claims for redundancy payments were challenged by an employer on the ground that there had been no dismissal or lay-off by reason of redundancy; rather, the claimants had terminated their own contracts of employment by resignation. Costello J. emphatically rejected

---

[105] [1977] I.C.R. 61.
[106] [1973] I.R. 1.
[107] [1968] Q.B. 710.
[108] [1968] I.R. 325.
[109] *Ibid.* at 345.
[110] Thomson (1975) 38 M.L.R. 346, (1978) 41 M.L.R. 137.
[111] [1980] 2 W.L.R. 283.
[112] *Harbutt's Plasticine v. Wayne Tank Corp.* [1970] 1 Q.B. 447.
[113] [1936] 41 Com.Cas. 350.
[114] [1984] I.L.R.M. 15.

this argument and in so doing re-integrated the rules relating to discharge of contracts of employment with the ordinary principles of repudiatory breach:

> "If there is no contractual power (express or implied) in the contract of employment to suspend the operation of the contract for a limited period then by ceasing to employ an employee and refusing to pay him wages the employer has been guilty of a serious breach of contract amounting to a repudiation of it. At common law that repudiation would not automatically bring the contract of employment to an end; the employee is free to accept that the repudiation has terminated the contract or not to do so (see: *Gunton v. Richmond-upon-Thames London Borough* [1980] 3 W.L.R. 714 for a recent view on the effect of an employer's repudiation of the contract of employment). If he accepts the repudiation of the contract then there has been a constructive dismissal of the employee at common law and the contract has been terminated by the employer. But if the employee responds to the employer's lay-off notice and adopts the lay-off procedures (instead of immediately accepting the employer's repudiation of the contract) and it is shown that the statutory condition for their initiation by the employer did not exist, then, it seems, the employee is entitled to treat the repudiation of the contract (which occurred when the cesser of employment began) as having terminated the contract of employment, and to base his claim for redundancy payment on that fact."[115]

### (5) Consequences of breach

In general, the innocent party must act promptly and decisively. In *An Bord Iascaigh Mhara v. Scallan*[116] the plaintiffs supplied the defendant with a fishing boat on hire-purchase terms, the agreement specifying that a particular type of winch would be fitted to the vessel. No such winch was provided but in July 1967 the defendant took possession, nevertheless. Some attempts were made to bring the winch into a satisfactory state, but these efforts came to nothing; the defendant continued to use the vessel until October 1968 when he abandoned it in Wexford harbour. While the plaintiffs were clearly in breach of section 9(2) of the Hire-Purchase Act 1946, Pringle J. held that the defendant should have repudiated the contract shortly after it became clear the winch could not be made to work satisfactorily; the defendant approbated the contract and thus could not rescind. Contrast *Dillon-Leech v. Maxwell Motors Ltd.*[117] and *Lutton v. Saville Tractors Ltd.*[118]

As we have seen, the right to rescind a contract for the sale of goods may be lost under section 11 of the 1893 Act, as amended by the Sale of Goods and Supply of Services Act 1980.

---

[115]   [1984] I.L.R.M. 15 at 20–21.
[116]   Unreported, High Court, May 8, 1973.
[117]   [1984] I.L.R.M. 624.
[118]   [1986] N.I. 327.

The consequences of a breach which entitles one party to terminate the contract and its effect upon certain contractual obligations has been clarified by the *Photo Production* case.[119] Photo Production engaged Securicor to provide a security service for their factory. Securicor engaged a worker who maliciously burnt down the premises. The contract contained an exculpatory clause absolving Securicor from the actions of their employees unless the conduct could have been foreseen and avoided by the exercise of due diligence on their part. The House of Lords reversed the decision of the Court of Appeal, rejecting the view that because the fire automatically terminated the contract, the limiting provision was unavailable to Securicor. Their Lordships explained that a limiting clause may operate so as to qualify or exclude liability for what would otherwise be a breach of contract. Lord Diplock in his speech described each party's obligation to perform as "primary legal obligations". These obligations may be the result of express agreement or through implication of law (statutory or otherwise). Upon breach, the innocent party may elect to terminate his own primary obligation to perform and in certain cases he may also terminate these obligations which the party in breach has yet to perform. This does not mean that all obligations are at an end. This is particularly true of an exemption clause. Lord Diplock argued that when primary obligations are discharged they are replaced by secondary obligations, the most obvious of which is the obligation to pay monetary compensation. Further, the decision to terminate the contract leads to the discharge of the unperformed primary obligations of the party in breach. While these primary and secondary obligations may be modified they cannot be eliminated or controlled if this would lead to the contract being deprived of all promissory content.

It should be mentioned that some contractual obligations only become effective after an alleged failure to perform a primary obligation; choice of forum clauses and arbitration clauses are examples: see Lord Diplock in *Photo Production*. In *Doyle v. Irish National Insurance Co. plc*[120] Kelly J. addressed the issue whether an insurance company, which had repudiated a policy of motor insurance for non-disclosure of a material fact, could invoke an arbitration clause in that self same contract. Kelly J. affirmed the leading case of *Heyman v. Darwins*[121] where it was said that a repudiated contract "survives for the purpose of measuring the claims out of the breach, and the arbitration clause survives for determining the mode of their settlement". Kelly J. held that these observations hold true in case of rescission for misrepresentation or non-disclosure also. It should also be mentioned that the Irish courts have not endorsed the view advanced in *Boston Deep Sea Fishing and Ice Co. v. Ansell*[122] which permits an employer who terminates a contract of employment on inadequate grounds to rely on other sufficient grounds for termination even though those grounds were unknown at the date of termination. The view that an employer

---

[119] [1980] 2 W.L.R. 283.
[120] Unreported, High Court, January 30, 1998.
[121] [1942] A.C. 356.
[122] (1888) 39 Ch.D. 339.

would thus be able to successfully defend an action for wrongful dismissal was examined in *Carvill v. Irish Industrial Bank*.[123] O'Keefe J. held that only where the wrongful act amounts to a repudiation of the contract of employment will the *Boston* principle hold good in Irish law. In *Glover v. B.L.N.*,[124] Kenny J. went further, arguing that the *Boston* principle should be expunged from Irish law. This view is to be supported; further, the English courts have rejected this rule in cases of *unfair* dismissal: *W. Devis & Sons Ltd. v. Atkins*,[125] a decision of the House of Lords. The E.A.T. in the Republic may permit an employer, who becomes aware after the dismissal of facts which support the decision to dismiss, to use these new facts, if they indicate misconduct similar to the grounds relied on at the date of dismissal.[126] It is still not clear whether a fundamental breach ends a contract, without more. The issue arose recently in *Hearn and Matchroom Boxing Ltd. v. Collins*.[127] Here the Court found that the first plaintiff had breached his contract with the defendant by seeking to persuade the World Boxing Organisation to provide one of his clients, Chris Eubank, with a particular status, the effect of which would have been to cause substantial loss of earnings to Stephen Collins in relation to a title defence. Because the plaintiffs were still contractually bound to Collins, as well as Eubank, this represented a fundamental breach of contract by the first plaintiff. Apart from this breach, the first plaintiff had conducted himself at a purse bid ceremony in such a way as to undermine the financial merits of the fight in question, a separate fundamental breach. On this basis the defendant regarded the contract as at an end; the Hearn/WBO correspondence was unknown to the defendant and in fact only came to light after trial of the action had commenced. In his judgment O'Sullivan J. seems to have given the *Boston* case some renewed life. After observing that there are different legal consequences "where there have been breaches of an agreement as distinct from fundamental breaches" and citing *Carvill* and *Glover*, the learned judge observed:

> "If a fundamental breach comes to light after dismissal it may still be relied upon by the employer to make a claim, not that this subsequently known ground was relied upon as a reason for or otherwise justified the dismissal, [*sic*] but rather that the contract at the time of the dismissal had already been repudiated."

Note that the facts of the case do not disclose an employment contract but a services contract, so the *Carvill* case is being given a broader application than before. Furthermore, this observation is clearly *obiter* because the subsequently known ground actually occurred after the fundamental breach that the defendant actually relied upon, took place.

---

[123]  [1968] I.R. 325.
[124]  [1973] I.R. 388.
[125]  [1977] A.C. 931.
[126]  *Loughran v. Rights Commissioner*, U.D. 206/1978.
[127]  Unreported, High Court, February 3, 1998.

# Judicial Review

The powers of a statutory body, when that body has been given powers to enter, vary, or terminate, contractual relationships with others are said to be subject to certain responsibilities. The courts have held that this is so in relation to the powers of the Voluntary Health Insurance Board,[128] Telecom Éireann[129] and Bus Éireann,[130] for example. Professional bodies are similarly constrained to exercise powers in accordance with constitutional requirements[131] and the public nature of these duties, whether statutory or otherwise, can be challenged by way of judicial review. Judicial review procedures have the advantage of greater speed but the courts do attempt to limit[132] judicial review to matters that are public law in nature and matters of a private nature derived solely from contract are excluded.[133] The courts also indicate that judicial review applications are not to be used to challenge or second guess properly constituted decisions of statutory bodies.[134] Public law remedies are discretionary and not available as of right.[135]

# Discharge by Operation of Law – The Doctrine of Frustration

This modern doctrine has evolved in order to deal with cases where contractual obligations can no longer be performed as a result of circumstances beyond the control of either party. The common law required a person who had agreed to perform contractual obligations to discharge those obligations; the fact that it was extremely difficult or even impossible to do so did not excuse non-performance. Thus in *Leeson v. North British Oil and Candle Ltd.*[136] the fact that the defendants could not obtain paraffin from their own supplier because of a strike did not excuse their failure to supply the plaintiff. Similarly in *Gamble v. The Accident Assurance Co.*[137] the executor of the estate of Gamble sued upon a life insurance policy which provided that if the insured met with an accident he should inform the insurers within seven days. Gamble died in a drowning accident and could not of course meet this obligation. The Court of Exchequer held that the agreement envisaged that Gamble, in his lifetime, was to arrange for a third party to notify the insurers if he met with an accident which caused his immediate demise. Pigot C.B. in his judgment expressly approved the leading English case of *Paradine v. Jane.*[138]

---

128 *Callinan v. VHI*, unreported, High Court, April 22, 1993 reversed in part by the Supreme Court, July 28, 1994..
129 *Zockoll Group Ltd. and Others v. Telecom Éireann, Irish Times Law Report*, January 19, 1998.
130 *Rafferty v. Bus Éireann*, unreported, High Court, November 21, 1996 .
131 *Geoghegan v. Institute of Chartered Accountants* [1995] 3 I.R. 86.
132 *Beirne v. Commissioner of An Garda Síochána* [1993] 1 I.L.R.M. 1.
133 *Ibid*; *Healy v. Fingal County Council*, unreported, High Court, January 17, 1997.
134 *Radio Limerick One Ltd. v. Independent Radio and Television Commission*, unreported, High Court, October 14, 1996.
135 *Bane v. Garda Representative Association* [1997] 2 I.R. 449.
136 (1874) 8 I.R.C.L. 309.
137 (1869) I.R. 4 C.L. 204.
138 (1647) Aleyn 26: Simpson (1975) 91 L.Q.R. 247.

In *Paradine v. Jane* the plaintiff had let lands to the defendant under the terms of a lease which required the lessee to pay rent on a quarterly basis. The lessee was ejected from possession by armed force, the lands then being occupied by the military during the English Civil War. In an action for arrears of rent the lessee pleaded that these circumstances excused non-payment of rent. The plea was rejected. A distinction was drawn between a general duty imposed by law upon a lessee and a duty taken on by way of contract. In this later case

> "when the party by his own contract creates a duty or charge upon himself he is bound to make it good, if he may, notwithstanding any accident by inevitable necessity because he might have provided against it by his contract."[139]

However, if the transaction is an executory one, and premises are destroyed by fire, there is early Irish authority in the form of *Re Walter John Carew*,[140] for the proposition that the purchaser is not obliged to pay the price and take a conveyance; the risk falls upon the vendor. This, however, is not a decision which represents a direct attack on *Paradine v. Jane*, but it provides an illustration of judicial awareness of the harshness of the doctrine of absolute contractual obligations, at least when viewed from the perspective of the party who is faced with the prospect of being bound by the contract. It is however not a reliable decision because it is now accepted that risk passes to the buyer upon signature, not completion, of a contract of purchase, and insurance should be organised accordingly.

The view that contractual obligations were absolute in the sense that supervening events could never provide a lawful excuse for non-performace was questioned in *Taylor v. Caldwell*.[141] The defendants agreed to let a music hall to the plaintiffs for four days. Just before the first day arrived the music hall was destroyed by fire, the accident occurring without the fault of either party. The plaintiffs sued to recover money spent in advertising the scheduled performances. Blackburn J. held that the destruction of the music hall discharged the contract, viewing the agreement as subject to an implied condition that the building remained in existence. The licensor was excused from failing to provide a music hall and the licensee was excused from payment of fees due to the licensor. In so holding, Blackburn J. used the analogy of a contract involving a person who dies after agreeing to write a book. Such a contract is thereby discharged; the executors cannot be liable upon a personal contract of this nature. The point is illustrated by *Kean v. Hart*.[142] The plaintiff and one Lyster were appointed agents. The contract provided for notice of

---

[139]  (1647) Aleyn 26 at 27.
[140]  (1851) 3 Ir.Jur. 232; contrast *Paine v. Meller* (1801) 6 Ves. 349.
[141]  (1863) 3 B. & S. 826.
[142]  (1869) I.R. 3 C.L. 388.

termination of six months. Shortly after the commencement Lyster died. The plaintiff was then given notice that the agency would end six months hence. He claimed the period of notice was insufficient. The Court of Exchequer Chamber dismissed the action, Whiteside C.J. observing that regardless of notice Lyster's death itself terminated the contract.

Because these cases do not seem very easy to reconcile, it is important to establish the rationale for judicial intervention in frustration cases. Lord Hailsham has observed that five theories of the basis for the doctrine have been advanced at various times.[143] On the theoretical basis of this doctrine, Blackburn J. in *Taylor v. Caldwell* said:

> "When from the nature of the contract it appears that the parties must from the beginning have known that it could not be fulfilled, unless when the time for the fulfilment of the contract arrived some particular specified thing continues to exist, so that when entering into the contract they must have contemplated such continued existence, as the foundation of what was to be done, then, in the absence of any express or implied warrant, that the thing shall exist, the contract is not to be considered a positive contract but subject to the implied condition that the parties shall be excused, in case, before breach, performance becomes impossible, from the perishing of the thing without the default of the contractor."[144]

This dictum was approved by O'Connor M.R. in 1912 in the case of *Cummings v. Stewart (No. 2)*[145] in which it was held that the lapse of patent rights held by the plaintiff patentee discharged the defendant, who held an exclusive licence to work the patents, from an obligation to pay royalties to the plaintiff. However, the implied term theory is no longer widely supported, as we shall see.

### (1) Frustration of the business venture

The cases of impossibility of performance (because of the physical destruction of a person, an object or structure) present difficulties when they are invoked so as to justify non-performance because subsequent events, while they do not make performance impossible, make it impossible to secure the commercial benefits envisaged at the date of agreement. In these cases of unanticipated difficulty, if it threatens to destroy the basis of the contract or make the contract as performed something fundamentally different to that envisaged at the time of agreement, then the contract may be treated as discharged.[146]

The English "coronation" cases are the best examples of this situation. When the coronation procession of Edward VII had to be cancelled due to the

---

143   *National Carriers Ltd. v. Panalpina (Northern) Ltd.* [1981] 1 All E.R. 161 at 165, citing Lord Wilberforce in *Liverpool City Council v. Irwin* [1976] 2 All E.R. 39.
144   (1863) 3 B. & S. 826.
145   [1913] 1 I.R. 95.
146   See *Jackson v. Union Marine Insurance Co. Ltd.* (1874) L.R. 10 C.P. 125 for the origins of the test in this particular context.

illness of H.R.H. many arrangements in which persons obtained the right to view the procession from hotels and rooms overlooking the route came before the English courts. In *Krell v. Henry*[147] the plaintiff let his flat to the defendant in order to enable him to view the procession. A £25 deposit was paid, the defendant owing £50 which was to be paid on the very morning the ceremony was cancelled. The plaintiff sued for the outstanding sum. The rooms were still available; the defendant could have used the rooms but of course because the procession had been cancelled the purpose implicit in the arrangement would not be attained. The Court of Appeal held the contract frustrated; Vaughan-Williams L.J. in his speech observed that the basis of the contract was the position of the rooms in relation to the coronation procession. The cancellation prevented performance and thus discharged the defendant's obligation to pay the outstanding sum of £50.

The fact that the test advanced in these cases can produce seemingly incompatible results is illustrated by the contrasting case of *Herne Bay Steam Boat Co. v. Hutton*.[148] The defendant had chartered a steamboat in order to view the Naval Review on two set days, and to sail around the fleet. The Naval Review was cancelled due to the illness of Edward VII. The fleet, however, remained at anchor. The defendant was sued for the balance due on the charter and pleaded the King's illness discharged the contract. The Court of Appeal held that this was not a defence. The Court found that the Naval Review was not the foundation of the contract. Sterling L.J. pointed out that while the Naval Review was cancelled, there remained the opportunity to view the fleet and enjoy the cruise, notwithstanding. While the boundary between these cases may be a narrow one, it is clear that the hire contract in *Herne Bay* was not tied to the presence of the monarch – it was expressed to be basically a contract to hire a boat – in the same way that the room hire agreement in *Krell v. Henry* was only entered into because of the anticipated procession. In general terms, the fact that property or goods cannot be used for the anticipated purpose is not sufficient to discharge the contract unless an express term so provides. So, the fact that goods intended to be exported by the buyer to a country that prohibits the importation of those goods will not necessarily frustrate the contract.[149]

The courts have emphasised that a contract will not be frustrated simply because increased costs or labour disputes make it impossible for one party to perform the contract without incurring serious financial losses. It would be undesirable for a businessman to agree to perform a contract for a fixed amount and permit him to seek relief through the doctrine of frustration if, during performance, unanticipated difficulties arise. In the old case of *Revell v. Hussey*,[150] Manners L.C. expressed the point thus:

---

[147]  [1903] 2 K.B. 740.
[148]  [1903] 2 K.B. 683.
[149]  *Congimex Companhia etc. v. Tradax Export SA* [1983] 1 Lloyd's Rep. 250.
[150]  (1813) 2 Ball & B. 280.

"Suppose a case that very frequently occurs of a colliery, where the company has contracted to supply iron works at a price agreed on; surely it can be no ground to rescind it that subsequent circumstances have occurred to render it very prejudicial; that the coals may have greatly increased; that the expenses working the mine may have been considerably increased."[151]

The Suez Canal cases are perhaps the best known illustrations of the principle that a contract will not be frustrated simply because of a supervening event which results in extra expense or inconvenience for a contracting party. In *Tsakiroglou & Co. v. Noblee and Thorl*,[152] the sellers of ground nuts agreed to ship the goods *c.i.f.* from Port Sudan to Hamburg. Freight charges if the journey was undertaken via the Suez Canal were £7 10s. a ton. Because of war conditions, the Canal was later closed to shipping, thereby necessitating a journey via the Cape of Good Hope at £15 a ton. The closure of the Canal, and the extra time and cost involved were held by the House of Lords not to frustrate the contract. There was no basis for an implied term that the Canal was the only permissible route; nor did the extra time involved cause any deterioration in the goods shipped, nor did the delay result in loss of any seasonal market.

In the leading English case of *Davis Contractors v. Fareham U.D.C.*[153] contractors agreed to build houses for a sum of £94,000. The work, expected to take eight months to complete, took some 22 months, mainly due to materials shortages and labour difficulties. The work cost £115,000. The contractors claimed that these events terminated the contract, entitling them to claim for the value of the work on a *quantum meruit* basis, which was greater than the contract price. The House of Lords dismissed the claim. Lord Radcliffe in his speech remarked that hardship or material loss does not of itself bring the doctrine into play. "There must be as well such a change in the significance of the obligation that the thing undertaken would, if performed, be a different thing from that contracted for."[154] Additionally, it must be pointed out that these ordinary commercial risks may be covered by contract terms; a failure to provide for these contingencies should not readily be rectified by invoking a plea of frustration. In *Amalgamated Investments v. John Walker*[155] a building which was sold as a warehouse was listed as a historic building. This event, which occurred shortly after contracts were exchanged, prevented commercial development of the building and reduced its value from £1,710,000, the contract price, to £200,000. While it may be possible to explain the Court of Appeal's refusal to hold the contract frustrated as in part due to the purchasers' failure to show that this listing could not be revised, there was a reluctance to

---

[151] (1813) 2 Ball & B. 280 at 284.
[152] [1961] 2 All E.R. 179.
[153] [1956] A.C. 696.
[154] *Ibid* at 729.
[155] [1977] 1 W.L.R. 164; *E. Johnson & Co. (Barbados) Ltd. v. NSR Ltd., The Times*, July 24, 1996.

reallocate ordinary commercial risks when the contract draftsman had failed to do so. This approach was endorsed by McWilliam J. in *McGuill v. Aer Lingus and United Airlines.*[156] The plaintiffs booked internal holiday flights within the United States with the second defendants. At the time of booking the second defendants were aware that their employees had served strike notice, but, fearing that if they disclosed this the plaintiffs would book flights with another carrier, the defendants did not tell the plaintiffs or insert an exception clause into the agreement. When the strike commenced the plaintiffs had to be carried on other flights with other airlines and as a result their holiday itinerary was cut short. The defendants pleaded frustration. While McWilliam J. refused to hold that a strike may never constitute a frustrating event it could not be pleaded on the facts of this case.

*McGuill* also illustrates the point that in some senses the frustrating event may exist, in an undiscovered state, at the time the contract is formed. An even more striking instance of this is provided by *Gamerco SA v. ICM/Fair Warning Agency.*[157] Here a rock concert in Madrid was cancelled when it was found that building materials used in construction of the stadium made this unsafe. The condition only came to light after the concert had been arranged. A more surprising conclusion was that the local concert promoters were able to plead frustration at all, for it is arguable that local agents should impliedly warrant that the venue they find for the band is satisfactory, but Garland J. declined to allocate a foreseeable risk of this kind to the concert promoter so that, when Madrid City Council cancelled the permit, the cancellation was held a frustrating event.

It is sometimes said that the event in question should have been unforeseen or unexpected. However, in *Ocean Tramp Tankers Corp. v. O Sovracht, The Eugenia*[158] Denning M.R. pointed out that, essentially, this means that the parties should not have made provision for the event in the contract. It is by no means necessary to prove that the event in question was not foreseen by the parties because frustration is a flexible enough doctrine to apply in a proper case. The decision in *Neville and Sons Ltd. v. Guardian Builders Ltd.*[159] is in point. The defendant purchased a plot of land in order to develop it. The land bordered two local authorities, and in order to obtain satisfactory access to the development, planning permissions and the goodwill of adjoining property owners had to be secured. The defendant agreed to give building work to the plaintiff. The site ran into difficulties in respect of access and the plaintiff obtained the contractual right to carry out the work. However, the parties knew at the time of the agreement that satisfactory access could only be obtained if Dublin County Council sold a strip of land to the defendant; for compensation reasons the sale did not occur. As Murphy J. said, at the time of the agreement, the site was landlocked and both parties believed the vital strip of land would be sold, so as to facilitate the developer, at some time in the near future. "The

---

[156] Unreported, High Court, October 3, 1983.
[157] [1995] E.M.L.R. 263.
[158] [1964] 1 All E.R. 161.
[159] [1995] 1 I.L.R.M. 1.

change that took place between the date of the contract and the time for its performance was the frustration of this expectation." The failure of a contemplated event may just as much frustrate a contract as a cataclysmic occurrence. The crucial fact to note is that even though the parties, objectively, could have anticipated difficulties in obtaining permission, the contract did not contain a provision dealing with the contingency. The Supreme Court however overturned Murphy J., holding that there was no frustrating event. Using principles of risk allocation the Supreme Court took the view that the plaintiff was entitled to damages. This is one of those cases that straddles the law relating to frustration, mistake and implied terms[160] and in his judgment Blayney J. echoed *Davis Contractors* by observing that the access difficulties made the contract "more onerous but that was all".

A contract cannot normally be discharged through the doctrine of frustration if a contract term covers the events which are alleged to constitute frustration. In *Mulligan v. Browne*,[161] Dr. Browne was employed as a physician by the trustees of a charity established to provide a hospital in Ballyshannon, County Donegal. His contract of employment provided that if there were insufficient funds to allow the hospital to continue in operation then the contract could be discharged by giving three months' notice. The hospital ran into severe difficulties and in 1974 the trustees purported to terminate Dr. Browne's employment. Dr. Browne argued that his employment was permanent in the sense that it could not be terminated except in specific cases which had not occurred. Gannon J. held that the severe difficulties into which the hospital had fallen discharged the plaintiff's contract. The Supreme Court overturned Gannon J. on this point; Kenny J. pointed out that in this case the contract expressly provided for the contingency: "if it is dealt with in the contract then it was within the contemplation of the parties and the doctrine [of frustration] cannot apply."

If, however, the events are literally within the scope of the provision it remains open for a court to hold that the events that have occurred are so cataclysmic that the parties could not have intended the clause to cover such a profoundly different set of circumstances. In one English case a clause in a charterparty obliging the vessel to sail "with all possible despatch, dangers of navigation excepted" was held inapplicable when the vessel ran aground, the ship being under repair for over six months. The delay was held to frustrate the commercial purpose behind the charter: *Jackson v. Union Marine Insurance Co. Ltd.*[162]

### (2) Theoretical basis of frustration

Despite the approval of the implied contract theory in the 1912 Irish case of *Cummings v. Stewart (No. 2)*[163] it is now generally recognised that there are alternative explanations for the frustration doctrine. Indeed the implied contract

---

[160] Smith (1994) 110 L.Q.R. 400.
[161] Unreported, High Court, July 9, 1976; unreported, Supreme Court, November 23, 1977.
[162] (1874) L.R. 10 C.P. 125.
[163] [1913] I.R. 95.

theory seems distinctly out of favour today and is in reality a convenient explanation, cobbled together by the judges at a time when the judges were keen to preserve the twin illusions that the judges do not make law and that the judges do not interfere in bargains struck. The only Irish case in which the theoretical basis of frustration has been extensively discussed is *Mulligan v. Browne*.[164] In his judgment Kenny J. said of the concept of frustration:

> "During the past seventy years it has been developed and refined by many decisions of the House of Lords and the Privy Council. The expression 'the contract is frustrated' so commonly used to-day is misleading: the doctrine relates, not to the contract but to the events or transactions which are the basis of the contract. It is these which make performance of the contracts impossible. This aspect of the doctrine was explained by Lord Wright in *Constantine Line v. Imperial Smelting Corporation* [1942] A.C. 154:
>
>> 'In more recent days, the phrase more commonly used is "frustration of the contract" or more shortly "frustration." "Frustration of the contract" however is an elliptical expression. The fuller and more accurate phrase is "frustration of the adventure or of the commercial or practical purpose of the contract." The change in language corresponds to a wider conception of impossibility, which has extended the rule beyond contracts which depend on the existence, at the relevant time of a specific object . . . to cases when the essential object does indeed exist, but its condition has by some casualty been so changed as to be not available for the purposes of the contract, either at the contract date or if no date is fixed, within any time consistent with the commercial or practical adventure.'

There has been considerable judicial controversy as to its foundation. At least three possible bases for it have been suggested each of which can claim eminent judicial support. The first is that it depends upon an implied term in the contract (Viscount Simon in *Constantine Line v. Imperial Smelting Corporation* [1942] A.C. 154) or upon 'the presumed common intention of the parties' (Viscount Maugham in the same case). The second rejects wholly the implied term theory and rests the doctrine on the true construction of the contract.

> 'It appears to me that frustration depends, at least in most cases, not on adding any implied term but on the true construction of the terms which are, in the contract, read in light of the nature of the contract and of the relevant surrounding circumstances when the contract was made.'

Lord Reid in *Davis Contractors v. Fareham U.D.C.* [1956] A.C. 696:

---

[164] Unreported, High Court, July 9, 1976; unreported, Supreme Court, November 23, 1977.

'So perhaps, it would be simpler to say at the outset that frustration occurs whenever the law recognises that, without default of either party, a contractual obligation has become incapable of being performed because the circumstances in which performance is called for would render it a thing radically different from that which was undertaken by the contract'

(*per* Lord Radcliffe in the same case). The third theory – associated with Lord Wright – is that where the dispute between the parties arises from an event which they never thought of, the court imposes the solution that in the circumstances is just and reasonable (Lord Wright's '*Legal Essays and Addresses*' at p. 258 and *Denny Mott and Dickson Ltd. v. Fraser and Co. Ltd.* [1944] A.C. 265 at p. 275)."

While on the facts it was not necessary for Kenny J. to select any of these three theories it is fair to say that subsequent dicta in the House of Lords tends to favour the second and third theories. In *National Carriers v. Panalpia (Northern) Ltd.*, the most recent case in which the juristic basis of frustration was considered, both Lord Hailsham L.C. and Lord Roskill favoured the view of Lord Radcliffe in *Davis Contractors*, as quoted above by Kenny J. in *Browne v. Mulligan*. Indeed, in *Neville and Sons Ltd. v. Guardian Builders Ltd.*[165] Murphy J. also cited Lord Radcliffe's dictum as proof of the extent to which the courts have moved away from the implied term theory "to an objective test based on the construction of the contract".

### (3) Frustration and illegality

Several of the cases can be explained as being decided in this way because any attempted performance would involve a breach of either the civil or the criminal law. Gannon J. used this reasoning to support his view in *Browne v. Mulligan*. If the trustees continued to operate the charity this would involve them in a breach of their duties as trustees.

In *O'Cruadhlaoich v. Minister for Finance*[166] the plaintiff had been appointed a judge by the first Dáil Éireann. The appointment was for life. These courts were later abolished by statute passed by the Government of Saorstát Éireann. O'Cruadhlaoich sued for salary due to him under the contract of employment. The action was dismissed. Following the leading case of *Reilly v. R.*[167] it was held that the abolition of the post by statute discharged the contract of employment.

In *Ross v. Shaw*[168] it can be argued that the German occupation of Belgium operated so as to make lawful performance impossible, thereby frustrating the contract. The boundary between illegality and frustration can be narrow indeed. A reluctance to award damages for a breach of contract when statute

---

[165] [1995] 1 I.L.R.M. 1.
[166] (1934) 68 I.L.T.R. 174.
[167] [1934] A.C. 176.
[168] [1917] 2 I.R. 367.

renders the transaction void was demonstrated by Dixon J. in *Namlooze Venootschap De Faam v. Dorset Manufacturing Co.*[169] A more recent illustration is provided by the dissenting judgment of Costello J. in *Dunne v. Hamilton.*[170] The Supreme Court was required to consider whether the enactment of the Family Home Protection Act 1976 prevented a conveyance, signed without his wife's consent, but not executed by the husband prior to the enactment of the Act from being specifically enforceable. The majority of the Supreme Court allowed the purchaser's appeal against Gannon J.'s decision that section 3 of the Act meant that any conveyance in consequence of a decree of specific performance would be void. While the case really turns on principles of statutory interpretation Costello J. agreed with Gannon J., holding that the 1976 Act discharged the vendor from his obligations under the contract. By the exercise of the wife's power to stop the sale, the contract was discharged by operation of law and, further, these new facts (the 1976 Act) did not expose the vendor to liability in damages.

### (4) Self-induced frustration

It is essential that the event or events are outside the control of either party. It is not essential that it be conclusively shown that the only explanation for the event does not involve carelessness or fault. In *Constantine Line v. Imperial Smelting Corporation*[171] a vessel on charter exploded and sank. Three possible causes of the accident were advanced, one of which involved a finding of negligence by the shipowners. The Court of Appeal held that it was incumbent on the shipowners to show that the accident occurred without default. The House of Lords rejected the view that such a heavy burden of proof rests on the party pleading frustration. Where the loss is unexplained, fault will not be attributed to either of the parties. The burden of proof rests upon the party alleging self-induced frustration. Their Lordships held the contract automatically discharged by the explosion.

The leading Irish authority on the doctrine of self-induced frustration is *Herman v. Owners of S.S. Vicia.*[172] The plaintiffs were engaged for a round-trip voyage from the United States to Britain and back again. Due to war conditions it was necessary for the owners of the vessel to obtain "travel warrants" in order to ensure safe access to British ports. The vessel docked in Dublin on the way to Britain. The owners of the vessel failed to obtain the necessary documentation from the British authorities. The owners pleaded that this frustrated the contracts of employment entered into with the plaintiffs. It is clear that failure to obtain the necessary documentation was due to the neglect of the defendants themselves; this is then a perfect example of "self-induced" frustration. It is possible to view *Gamble v. The Accident Assurance Co.*[173] in a similar light.

---

[169] [1949] I.R. 203.
[170] [1982] I.L.R.M. 290.
[171] [1941] 2 All E.R. 165.
[172] [1942] I.R. 304.
[173] (1869) I.R. 4 C.L. 204.

In *Byrne v. Limerick Steamship Co. Ltd.*[174] the defendants engaged the plaintiff to serve on board a ship going to England. The British authorities refused to allow Byrne a war permit. The defendants claimed that this frustrated the contract. The submission failed; the party pleading frustration in these circumstances must show that he took reasonable steps to have the decision reversed. There was no evidence that the employer had pointed out additional factors which may have caused the British authorities to reverse the decision. To this extent then, the refusal was "self-induced".

The standard of conduct insisted upon by the courts in a plea of frustration can be extremely high. In *Maritime National Fish Ltd. v. Ocean Trawlers Ltd.*[175] the defendant chartered a fishing vessel from the plaintiff but in order to utilise the vessel as a trawler, a licence to use an otter trawl had to be obtained from the Minister for Fisheries. The licence was obtained on an annual basis from 1928 to 1932, but when the defendant sought five licences for his five trawlers for the 1935 season the Minister indicated that only three licences would be issued and the defendant was asked to name the three vessels in question. The plaintiff's trawler was not one of them. In an action for hire charges, the defendant pleaded frustration. The Privy Council held that the contract was not frustrated. It was the decision of the defendant not to include the relevant vessel and their own election, not the decision of the Minister, was the basis of the failure to obtain a licence for that particular vessel. Similarly, if goods are to be shipped to a particular country where they are to be weighed, the fact that the foreign law later prohibits the landing of the goods will not necessarily frustrate the contract, if, for example, it would be possible to weigh the goods in another jurisdiction.[176]

### (5) Contracts of employment

Events which have been held to discharge a contract automatically include the sinking of a vessel upon which the employee serves: *Kearney v. Saorstát and Continental Shipping*[177]; conscription has also been held to effect the discharge of a contract of employment as has a prison sentence: *Hare v. Murphy Brothers.*[178] While the sentence must of course have the effect of making performance of the contract of employment impossible, it has been recently held that the sentence itself does not automatically bring the contract to an end. In *Chakki v. United Yeast,*[179] Chakki was sentenced to a term of imprisonment. His wife telephoned his employer to inform the employer that her husband would not be coming into work. A replacement driver was engaged. On appeal the sentence was suspended but the employer refused to re-engage Chakki. It was held that

---

174  [1946] I.R. 138.
175  [1935] A.C. 524.
176  *Congimex Companhia v. Tradax Export* [1983] 1 Lloyd's Rep. 250.
177  (1943) Ir.Jur.Rep. 8.
178  [1974] I.C.R. 603.
179  [1982] 2 All E.R. 446.

the employer had acted precipitously, especially when Chakki was about to start his annual holidays when the sentence was imposed. The employer should have waited for some days before engaging a replacement. However, *Chakki* has been said to be of doubtful authority by Kilner Brown J. in *Morris v. Southampton City Council*.[180] Here a prison sentence prevented the employee from carrying out his contract. The fault of the employee in deliberately doing something which led to an inability to carry out his contract was said to be repudiatory conduct and thus incapable of bringing the contract into the frustration concept. These contrasting decisions were confronted by the Court of Appeal in *F. C. Shepherd & Co. Ltd. v. Jerrom*.[181] An apprentice was sentenced to not less than six months borstal training when he was halfway through a four-year apprenticeship. The Court of Appeal had to consider whether the contract of the apprenticeship was repudiated and, if not, whether the case was one of self-induced frustration. The contract was held to have been frustrated because of the length of the sentence in the context of the length of the apprenticeship. The employee was held not to be able to plead self-induced frustration in order to assist him in establishing a right to compensation for unfair dismissal. Thus *Chakki*[182] remains good law.

The courts have frequently been troubled by the possibility that illness of the employee may discharge the contract of employment. In *Flynn v. Great Northern Railway Co.*[183] a van driver's contract of employment was held to have been frustrated when medical evidence was introduced to show that his medical condition was such as to make it impossible for him ever to return to his job: see also *Donovan v. Murphy & Sons*.[184] The position differs if the evidence does not conclusively show a return to work is out of the question. In *Nolan v. Brooks Thomas*,[185] a decision of the Employment Appeals Tribunal, Nolan claimed compensation for unfair dismissal and, in the alternative, redundancy or wrongful dismissal. Nolan was employed as a woodcutter/machinist from October 1969, suffering a severe injury at work in July 1973. He was only fit for work after prolonged treatment in March 1978. In August 1977 the employer purported to discharge Nolan. The work reduced his capacity for normal manual work considerably: the employment in question was potentially dangerous even to a fully fit person; the period of absence from work was considerable – almost five years. Applying the test evolved in the leading English cases of *Marshall v. Harland and Woolf*[186] and *Egg Stores v. Leibovici*,[187] the nature of the employee's incapacity viewed at the date of purported dismissal (August 1977) made it appear likely that further performance of Nolan's

---

[180]  [1982] I.C.R. 177.
[181]  [1986] 3 All E.R. 589; *Alghussean Establishment v. Eton College* [1991] 1 All E.R. 267.
[182]  [1981] 2 All E.R. 446.
[183]  (1953) 89 I.L.T.R. 46.
[184]  184/1977.
[185]  U.D. 379/1979.
[186]  [1972] 1 W.L.R. 899.
[187]  [1976] I.R.L.R. 376.

obligations in the future would be impossible or at least radically different from those undertaken by him. Similarly, in *Mulvaney v. Riversdale Concrete Products Ltd.*[188] the contract of employment of the plaintiff, a labourer, was held to have been discharged by law. He had last worked in 1974 and at the time of the employer going into liquidation, March 1981, he was still unfit for work. The E.A.T. held the contract had been frustrated "long before the respondent company went into liquidation". No redundancy payment was payable, the employer having discharged the onus to show frustration.

The most exhaustive Irish examination of the frustration concept is the decision of the E.A.T. in *Donegal County Council v. Langan.*[189] The employee, a general labourer, was employed since 1974. In 1985 he was incapacitated due to lumbar pain and was still on sick leave, submitting certificates, when, in April 1988, the Council wrote that it did not intend to re-employ him. In July 1988 he was medically certified as fit. In an action for unfair dismissal, the employer pleaded frustration. The tribunal indicated that among the matters to be taken into account in deciding if a contract is frustrated are:

"(i) the length of the previous employment.

(ii) how long it has been expected that the employment would last.

(iii) the nature of the job.

(iv) the nature, length and effect of the illness or disabling event.

(v) the need of the employer for the work to be done.

(vi) whether wages have continued to be paid.

(vii) the actions of the employer in relation to the employment.

(viii) whether consideration was given to retaining the employee on the books if not in employment.

(ix) whether the employer discussed with the employee and his trade union the employee's problems and prospects.

(x) whether adequate medical investigation was carried out (*e.g.* employers should ask their own or their employee's doctor for reports to establish the real medical facts and if there is conflicting medical evidence, to seek an independent source).

(xi) whether, in all the circumstances a reasonable employer could be expected to wait any longer."

In this case Langan was not a key worker. He had been paid only for the first 12 weeks of absence. There was no consultation with him or his union, nor was a medical examination undertaken prior to termination, and he was fit for work within three months of termination. In these circumstances, frustration had not been established by the employer.

It has been held that extraneous factors such as an increase in an employer's insurance premiums due to an employee's disability may lead to the contract

---

[188] U.D. 457/1981.
[189] U.D. 143/89. See also *Lafreniere v. Leduc* (1990) 60 D.L.R. (4th) 577 on the issue of proof.

being discharged through frustration, even if the worker is able to perform his duties satisfactorily: *Duggan v. Thomas J. O'Brien and Co. Ltd.*[190] This case should be regarded as wrongly decided on this point because it is a factor outside the test advanced in *Egg Stores*, as approved in *Nolan v. Brooks Thomas*.

In the case of *Mooney v. Rowntree Mackintosh Ltd.*[191] the E.A.T. indicated that the doctrine is inappropriate in cases where an employee is intermittently absent from work due to a series of minor ailments. Frustration may also be unsuitable in cases where a short term periodic contract cannot be performed due to a serious illness of the employee.[192]

### (6) Frustration of a lease

The concept of a leasehold interest in land has caused difficulties in relation to the doctrine of frustration. Because a lease creates an estate or interest in land it is argued that while a building situated on the land may perish in a fire or earthquake the *estate* itself endures. In Ireland the Landlord and Tenant Law Amendment Act (Ireland) 1860 (Deasy's Act) creates contractual rights to enter onto an estate in favour of a tenant; the Act does not confer an estate in land upon the tenant.[193] The Act provides a statutory solution to many frustration problems by enacting that in the absence of any express covenants to repair a tenant may surrender his tenancy if the premises are destroyed or rendered uninhabitable by fire or some other inevitable accident: section 40.

If however the premises are rendered uninhabitable by some event which is outside section 40 it is by no means clear that the theoretical differences between English and Irish leasehold interests would lead to the doctrine of frustration being held more readily applicable in Ireland. The majority of the House of Lords in the *Cricklewood* case[194] held a lease could not be frustrated, no matter how cataclysmic the event. In *National Carriers Ltd. v. Panalpina (Northern) Ltd.*[195] their Lordships have clearly overruled *Cricklewood*. Frustration of a lease will rarely occur however. In *National Carriers* the appellants were lessees of a warehouse under a 10-year lease, commencing in January 1974. Due to the danger of an adjoining building collapsing the local authority closed the main access road in May 1979, thereby preventing the appellants from using the building as a warehouse. It was estimated that the street would be reopened in January 1981. The appellants claimed the lease was frustrated. While the House of Lords by four to one held that frustration may occur the facts of this case did not disclose a change of circumstances grave enough to justify holding the lease frustrated.

---

[190] U.D. 156/1978.
[191] 473/1980.
[192] *Notcutt v. Universal Equipment Co. (London) Ltd.* [1986] 3 All E.R. 582.
[193] *Irish Land Law* (1997, 3rd ed.) Chap. 1.
[194] *Cricklewood Property and Investment Trust Ltd. v. Leighton's Investment Trust Ltd.* [1945] A.C. 221.
[195] [1981] 1 All E.R. 161, following *Highway Properties Ltd. v. Kelly Douglas & Co. Ltd.* (1971) 17 D.L.R. (3d) 710.

There is an unreported Irish case in which O'Higgins C.J. held that a lease may be frustrated. The reasoning of the Chief Justice is not entirely satisfactory in this case of *Irish Leisure Industries Ltd. v. Gaiety Theatre Enterprises Ltd.*[196] The defendant lessors agreed to let theatre premises to the plaintiffs for three years, the lease to commence six months from the date of execution of the lease. However, the existing tenant obtained a six-year extention of the lease by making an application under the Landlord and Tenant Act 1921. This prevented the plaintiffs from obtaining use of the theatre. O'Higgins C.J. held the plaintiffs lease to be frustrated. Judgment on this question was given orally; the only report of the case deals with assessment of damages. This suggests that the case is one in which the defendant lessor was in fact in breach.

It is suggested that the Oireachtas should declare the doctrine of frustration applicable to leases generally.[197]

*(7)  Effects of the doctrine of frustration*

If a contract is frustrated the common law courts decreed that all future obligations are thereby discharged. So in *Kearney v. Saorstát and Continental Shipping*,[198] Mr. Kearney's contract of employment ended with the sinking of his ship, thereby preventing his widow from obtaining compensation under the Workmen's Compensation Acts when he later died.

In *Krell v. Henry*[199] the licensee was discharged from an obligation to pay the balance of £50 because that obligation had not fallen due before cancellation of the procession. It should be noted that the licensee's cross-action to recover the sum already paid was discontinued: because that obligation had arisen before cancellation, frustration could not provide a right to restitution on the ground that the licensee would ever enjoy the benefits of the contract. Indeed, if the licensee's obligation to pay had occurred before frustration an action to recover this sum would have been successful: see *Chandler v. Webster*[200] where the Court of Appeal held that in frustration cases, the loss lies where it falls at the date of frustration. In cases where hire charges had been pre-paid prior to the cancellation of the coronation procession, actions to recover the monies were unsuccessful.[201] The injustice that this may cause is particularly striking in cases where the contract is entire. In *Appleby v. Myers*[202] the plaintiff agreed to install machinery on the defendant's premises and to maintain the machinery for two years after installation. A price of £459 was agreed. When installation was almost complete, a fire destroyed the premises and the installation. The plaintiff brought an action for £419 for work done and

---

[196]  Unreported, Supreme Court, February 12, 1975.
[197]  As in other jurisdictions, *e.g.* Ontario Landlord and Tenant Act 1980. See generally, Robertson, (1982) 60 Can. Bar. Rev. 619.
[198]  (1943) Ir.Jur.Rep. 8.
[199]  [1903] 2 K.B. 740.
[200]  [1904] 1 K.B. 493 applying the earlier case of *Blakeley v. Muller & Co.* [1903] 2 K.B. 760.
[201]  *Blakely v. Muller & Co.* [1903] 2 K.B. 760; *Civil Service Co-operative Society Ltd. v. General Steam Navigation Co.* [1903] 2 K.B. 756.
[202]  (1867) L.R. 2 C.P. 651.

materials sold and delivered, but the action failed. While the contract was discharged as a result of *Taylor v. Caldwell*, the obligation to pay the price had not fallen due at the date of the fire and no payment of any kind was available to the plaintiff.

A right that has come into existence before frustration then cannot be discharged by the event itself; frustration is only prospective in its effects. So in *Herman v. Owners of S.S. Vicia*[203] the obligation to repatriate the seaman was an "accrued right" that could not be discharged through frustration. In that case Hanna J. observed that a successful plea of frustration would only prevent the employer from being liable in damages for wrongful termination.[204] Section 40 of Deasy's Act also makes this clear; the accident which entitles the tenant to surrender the lease serves to discharge the tenant from all *future* obligations.

The common law position is far from satisfactory. The decision in *Chandler v. Webster* obliged the hapless licensee to produce the sum due even though he had no chance of obtaining even a partial benefit. The House of Lords in the *Fibrosa* case[205] overruled *Chandler v. Webster* and held that if a party to a frustrated contract can show that no tangible benefit has resulted from the contract then restitution of money paid will be ordered.[206] This result is almost as unfair as *Chandler v. Webster* for the payee may have spent a considerable amount of time and/or money in furtherance of the contract – witness *Fibrosa* itself where the respondents were ordered to repay £1,000 to the appellants, even though the respondents had incurred costs in respect of the manufacture of specialist machines which could not be delivered to Poland, a country occupied by an enemy power.

The Law Reform (Frustrated Contracts) Act 1943, which is applicable in Northern Ireland, permits some degree of apportionment in these cases; the Act has been adopted in several jurisdictions in the Commonwealth and similar legislation is in force within the United States. In Ireland the courts have not as yet been faced with choosing between *Chandler v. Webster* and *Fibrosa*; it is desirable that the Law Reform Commission and the Oireachtas provide some legislative guidelines on this question, perhaps by adding an amendment to the Civil Liability Acts 1961–64. It is notable that in the only English case in which the 1943 Act has been exhaustively considered, Robert Goff J. adopted a somewhat critical position. The learned judge pointed out that the Act does not give a general power to apportion loss between the parties. Nor is the statute designed to either put the parties in the position they would have been in if the contract had been performed or restore them to their pre-contractual position. The judge's reasoning in this case, *B.P. Exploration Co. (Libya) Ltd. v. Hunt*

---

[203] [1942] I.R. 304.
[204] *Flynn v. Great Northern Railway Co. (Ir.)* (1953) 89 I.L.T.R. 46.
[205] *Fibrosa Spolko Akcyjnia v. Fairbairn Lawson Combe Barbour Ltd.* [1943] A.C. 32.
[206] The various Commonwealth statutes are critically examined by Stewart and Carter [1992] C.L.J. 66 who find all of them seriously flawed.

*(No. 2)*,[207] was approved by the House of Lords.[208] In the only other English case in which the 1943 Act was discussed, *Garmerco SA v. ICM/Fair Warning Agency Ltd.*[209] the discretion to allow the payee to retain some monies for out-of pocket expenses was not exercised by the court even though some loss was suffered. When the Law Reform Commission and/or the Oireachtas ultimately consider the law of frustration it is hoped that the 1943 Act is not utilised in its present raw state.

In the Republic of Ireland, section 7 of the Sale of Goods Act 1893 remains in force. The common law rules on contracts of insurance, carriage of goods by sea and voyage charters (which are excluded from the U.K. Law Reform (Frustrated Contracts) Act 1943) remain applicable in the Republic. It cannot, however, be disputed that some kind of general legislative measure is overdue. The choice seems to be between a measure which is similar to the U.K. Act, or some more radical legislative initiative. Section 265 of the Second Restatement Contracts empowers the courts to "grant relief on such terms as justice requires, including protection of the parties reliance interests". Such a measure is an improvement on the U.K. Act in one significant way. The U.K. Act does not give the court the power to order one party to transfer a monetary amount to the other party, in order to compensate the transferee for wasted expenditure if, for example, the transferee was only to be paid at the end of the contract, which has been frustrated prior to completion.[210]

---

[207] [1982] 1 All E.R. 925.
[208] [1982] 1 All E.R. 986.
[209] [1995] E.M.L.R. 263.
[210] It is doubtful whether *Appleby v. Myers* (1867) L.R. 2 C.P. 651 would be decided differently under the 1943 U.K. Act: see *Parsons Brothers Ltd. v. Shea* (1965) 53 D.L.R. (2d) 86.

# Part 9

# Remedies Following Breach of Contract

# 19 Damages

## Remedies in General

While the judges are at times said to be concerned with the interpretation and enforcement of contractual obligations rather than the creation of new obligations for contracting parties,[1] in this particular context, the enforcement of contractual rights by way of a binding judicial pronouncement that one contracting party must perform a contractual obligation is not, in fact, the primary remedy available to the victim of a breach of contract to which that victim is privy. The remedy of specific performance is not freely available and even when the contract in question falls within the traditional ambit of specific performance, the best example being contracts for the sale of an interest in land, there are a variety of discretionary or residual factors that may deny the plaintiff the promised performance. Further, there are instances where the contract in question involves an obligation or range of obligations that are traditionally seen as inappropriate subjects for specific performance, such as contracts of employment and contracts for the sale of goods. The common law system of remedies is at times quite out of kilter with the expectations of ordinary citizens. For example, when consumer goods malfunction, most consumers are concerned about having the goods adequately and promptly repaired by the seller or manufacturer, but the common law and statutory rules do not give the consumer any such right. The remedy available in respect of breach of a particular obligation often depends on the condition/warranty/innominate term classification addressed elsewhere in this book.[2]

Where the contract is wholly or partly executory, the primary remedies of damages or specific performance may not be realistic propositions. The loss to the plaintiff may not be capable of calculation, particularly in a speculative venture such as a business franchise, and specific performance may not be available at all. The plaintiff may still, however, seek a remedy in the form of a declaration that the contract has been rescinded, and this may be valuable if property has been transferred or a third party interest makes the situation somewhat complicated. We have already considered rescission as a remedy in the context of mistake and misrepresentation. It remains possible, however, for a contract to deny to the injured party the right to rescind or treat the contract as terminated for breach by the other by way of an exemption clause; many contracts seek to address both the consequences of agreement and the consequences of breach, and the skills of the contract lawyer must include an awareness of how the interests of the client can best be protected. For example,

---

[1]  Jessel M.R. in *Printing and Numerical Registering Co. v. Sampson* (1875) L.R. 19 Eq. 462 at 465.
[2]  See Chap. 9.

the contract may require payment of a deposit; the contract should specify the consequences of breach or non-performance on whether, for example, that deposit is forfeit or refundable. Care must be taken to avoid the rules on penalties. Other matters that will obviously occupy the contract lawyer will be the availability, or otherwise, of damages for consequential loss, for the express terms of the contract may be a useful way of narrowing, or broadening, the common law rules on recovery, in particular the rules on remoteness of damage.

## Purpose Behind and Award of Damages

An award of damages following a breach of contract is designed to compensate the injured party and not necessarily to punish the party in breach. The motive underlying such an award should be contrasted with the measure of compensation; this was explained by Parke B. in *Robinson v. Harman*[3] as being designed to put the plaintiff "so far as money can do it . . . in the same situation . . . as if the contract had been performed." While this maxim will not always explain the precise measure of damages in every case, it should be noted that it is designed to secure for the innocent party compensation in excess of money spent in furtherance of the contract. In contrast, damages assessed in tort actions are generally designed to return the injured party to his or her position before the tort occurred: *restitutio in integrum*.[4]

A simple example may make this clear. A purchases a book for £200 from B who misrepresents that it is worth £500. The book is in fact worth £150. The measure of damages in tort will be £50. B's tort has resulted in A parting with £200; A retains a book worth £150; an award of damages of £50 is necessary to return A to the pre-tort position. In contrast an action brought in contract for breach of warranty will produce an award of £350. A has a book worth £150; A, because of B's promise, thought the book was worth £350 more than this. A is therefore entitled to be put in this position through an award of £350, the difference between the actual value of the book and the value as warranted.

This distinction is not always kept clear; witness Finlay P.'s observation in *Hickey & Co. Ltd. v. Roches Stores (Dublin) Ltd. (No. 1)*.[5] The rationale for differing rules as between contract and tort are in part explained by the fact that contractual liability is generally strict and can in several cases be adjusted by the parties, while in tort the duty of care is shaped by considerations of public policy and the presence or absence of ethical factors such as carelessness and fraud. There are, of course, cases in which the measure of damages will be the same regardless of the cause of action, as the English Court of Appeal case of *Esso Petroleum v. Mardon*[6] indicates. Nevertheless the rules on remoteness of damage, mitigation of loss and the possibility of an award of punitive damages

---

[3] (1848) 1 Ex. 850 at 855.
[4] See the excellent explanation given of these principles by Costello J. in *McAnarney & McAnarney v. Hanrahan & T.E. Potterton* [1994] 1 I.L.R.M. 210.
[5] Unreported, High Court, July 14, 1976; Clark, (1978) 26 N.I.L.Q. 128.
[6] [1976] Q.B. 801.

are not identical in contract and tort, thereby increasing the chances of differing awards being made, depending on the cause of action. This is particularly likely in litigation surrounding a misrepresentation or breach of an express term. In *Archer v. Brown*[7] this point was re-emphasised by Peter Pain J. when he stated that while damages in the tort of deceit may allow the plaintiff to recover all damages that flow directly from the fraudulent misrepresentation, the same facts, if an action is brought in contract, may produce a different measure of compensation, for damages are limited by the "reasonable contemplation" test, as set out in *Hadley v. Baxendale*.[8] The House of Lords, in *Smith New Court Securities Ltd. v. Scrimgeour Vickers (Asset Management) Ltd.*[9] has held that in cases of fraudulent misrepresentation the defendant will be liable for all loss flowing from the fraud, as long as the plaintiff has acted so as to mitigate the loss. Further, liability may be assessed by reference to the actual loss incurred not necessarily the loss valued at the date of the transaction. However, if the plaintiff can only show that the defendant was negligent then the degree of culpability of the defendant is less and the appropriate measure of recovery will be the indemnity measure. Whether the section 2(1) deceit measure in cases of statutory misrepresentation (see section 45(1) of the Sale of Goods and Supply of Services Act 1980) is the correct measure is now in some doubt: in this case the House of Lords was noticeably tepid in its support for *Royscott Trust Ltd. v. Rogerson*.[10]

## Classification of the Measure of Compensation

Fuller & Purdue, in an extremely influential article, *"Reliance Interest and Contract Damages"*[11] advanced the view that while damages in contract are compensatory three distinct types of loss are commonly involved:

### (1) The expectation loss

If P purchases goods on a rising market, the seller subsequently deciding not to deliver to P but sell elsewhere, it would be unsatisfactory simply to entitle P to claim back the purchase price for, as the terminology involved here indicates, P's expectation that the contract will be performed is seen as a legitimate area of compensation. If the price of the self same goods has risen P should be able to buy substitute goods. The measure of damages here will be the difference between the contract price and the price of the substitute goods at the later relevant date – normally the date of breach. Compensating the buyer on this basis also has the advantage of discouraging the seller from breaking the

---

[7] [1985] Q.B. 401, applying *Doyle v. Olby (Ironmongers)* [1969] 2 Q.B. 158; see also *Royscot Trust Ltd. v. Rogerson* [1991] 3 All E.R. 294.
[8] (1854) 9 Ex. 341.
[9] [1996] 4 All E.R. 769.
[10] [1991] 3 All E.R. 294; their lordships were enthusiastic about Hooley criticisms of *Royscot*: (1991) 107 L.Q.R. 547.
[11] (1936) 46 Yale L.J. 52, 573.

contract for if the courts in effect take away the profit to be made from breach of contract there will be little or no reason for the seller (other than malice) to refuse delivery to the buyer.

## (2) The reliance loss

A purchaser who hires a lorry from a third party in order to collect goods may find that the goods are unavailable; the cost of hiring the vehicle from the third party would also be a legitimate head of loss which the purchaser may seek to recover. It must be said that such loss – reliance loss – will most frequently be recovered in cases where the court cannot estimate expectation loss because of the impossibility of finding that the plaintiff has or was likely to suffer loss. The plaintiff may elect to recover reliance loss in cases where expectation loss has not occurred as a result of the plaintiff making a bad bargain. It may be that where promissory estoppel succeeds as a plea the courts may elect to award reliance loss rather than expectation loss; justice may require the promisee recovering only the value of what he or she has lost rather than that which was promised.[12]

## (3) Restitution loss

If P has paid £500 to a seller who refuses to deliver the goods as promised, P will be entitled to claim the return of the consideration paid to the seller. This is to be seen as necessary in order to prevent the unjust enrichment of the seller. Restitution loss differs from reliance loss in that reliance loss may result from transactions involving third parties. In general there is a considerable overlap between restitution and reliance loss.

## (4) Other heads of loss

Other factors may justify an award of damages. Consequential loss may result from the breach of contract. Suppose a case where non-acceptance of goods constitutes a breach of contract by the buyer; the seller is unable to arrange an immediate resale. The seller's loss if forced to make the sale for less than the agreed price will be recoverable if it is not too remote. While this illustration may in fact be also an illustration of "expectation loss" – the resale price will provide evidence of value at the date of breach – other cases of consequential loss cannot fall into this category. A splendid illustration of this point is provided by the facts of *Stoney v. Foley*.[13] Ten ewes, warranted sound were sold by the defendant to the plaintiff. A few days after the sale, scab developed on the sheep and the plaintiff's land was proclaimed unfit from February until June. Besides compensation for the loss of sheep the plaintiff recovered damages for being unable to let the land for that period.

The defendant may be liable to reimburse the plaintiff for "incidental" losses, for example, the expense involved in arranging to buy substitute goods

---

[12]    See s.90 the U.S. Restatement (2d.) Contracts and *Hoffman v. Red Owl Stores Inc.* 133 N.W. 2d. 267 (1965).

[13]    (1897) 3 I.L.T. 165.

when a defendant vendor refuses to perform the contract, or, in cases of non-acceptance, warehouse costs incurred prior to effecting a resale at a higher price than that fixed by the contract.[14]

### (5) The performance interest

Recent case law[15] and academic comment have drawn attention to the need for the recognition of a performance interest.[16] In many of these cases the courts are asked to compensate the plaintiff for the cost of remedying any defective performance by the defendant under the contract. This is often described as a "cost of cure" measure and it is to be distinguished from the diminished value of, property that the plaintiff experiences due to defective performance or the reliance loss occasioned by the breach, or the consequential loss that results from the breach. Performance loss is illustrated by Professor Coote's example of a contract to build a folly which the builder repudiates before commencement. The "economic" measure of loss might be the fall in value of the building site (which will be zero if work is not commenced) or the reduction in value that the site bears if the folly is incomplete. But, Coote argues, if the disappointed landowner is able to obtain substituted performance elsewhere "damages must be based on the cost of getting the work done or completed" even if the folly is an eyesore that has a neutral or even a negative financial implication for the landowner. Indeed, Coote argues forcefully that the protection and vindication of the performance interest should be seen as a "primary object" of the award of damages in contract.

## Punitive Damages

It is often said that there is no scope for an award of damages designed to punish a party who deliberately breaches a contract. Nevertheless if a cause of action arises both in contract and tort it is clear that punitive damages may be awarded by placing stress on the tortious aspect of the defendant's conduct. In *Drane v. Evangelou*[17] the English Court of Appeal awarded punitive damages against a landlord who was held liable in trespass for the unlawful eviction of tenants.

In *Garvey v. Ireland*[18] the plaintiff, a Garda Commissioner, was summarily dismissed from his post. Applying the classification advanced by Lord Devlin in *Rookes v. Barnard*[19] this action was held to be arbitrary and unconstitutional conduct on behalf of the Government which was seen as meriting the award of exemplary damages against the State. Decisions from other jurisdictions provide support for this approach; the Canadian provinces have all produced

---

14  *Baker Perkins Ltd. v. C.J. O'Dowd*, unreported, High Court, April 13, 1989.
15  *Ruxley Electronics Ltd. v. Forsyth* [1995] 3 All E.R. 268.
16  Coote [1997] C.L.J. 537; Friedmann (1995) 111 L.Q.R. 628.
17  [1978] 1 W.L.R. 459: *Whelan v. Madigan*, unreported, High Court, July 18, 1978.
18  Unreported, High Court, December 19, 1979. For other issues see [1981] I.R. 75.
19  [1964] A.C. 1129; *Bradford Metropolitan City Council v. Arora* [1991] 3 All E.R. 545.

decisions in which employees have recovered punitive damages for the manner in which they have been dismissed. These cases go further than *Garvey* for it is clear that punitive damages are available even against private sector employers; it is essential for the plaintiff to show that the contract "has been breached in a high-handed, shocking and arrogant fashion so as to demand condemnation by the Court as a deterrent"; *per* Linden J. in *Brown v. Waterloo Regional Board of Commissioners of Police*,[20] applied in *Pilato v. Hamilton Place Convention Centre*.[21] The Ontario Court of Appeal in *Brown* stressed the need for bad faith to be shown. In some instances the courts have taken the view that damages may be awarded to compensate the plaintiff for the distress and upset that can result from violent, aggressive or insensitive conduct by the party acting in breach of contract, and some judges distinguish clearly between damages which are intended to punish or mark the court's disapproval of the defendant's conduct on the one hand, and instances where the objective is to compensate the plaintiff. In this latter situation, often described as instances where aggravated damages are payable, the issue is regarded, increasingly, as an aspect of remoteness of damage. There are several Canadian cases that go further than this. While punitive damages are not generally available in breach of contract cases, there are decisions which indicate that where a contracting party acts with shocking disregard for the safety of others, for example, by letting a property to tenants while suppressing information that the water supply is unsafe to drink, punitive damages are available.[22]

The Law Reform Commission in a recent Consultation Paper, *Aggravated, Exemplary Restitutional Damages*[23] has indicated that in general the Commissioners do not welcome the use of exemplary damages in the context of contract claims.

## Unjust Enrichment

There is Irish support for the view that persons who deliberately break contracts because they calculate that they will make a profit from so doing, even after calculating damages payable for loss suffered by the victim, are to be deterred from considering this kind of conduct. In *Hickey & Co. Ltd. v. Roches Stores (Dublin) Ltd. (No. 1)*[24] the defendants broke a contract to allow the plaintiffs to sell fabric in their store, calculating that even after paying agreed damages they would profit from carrying on the business themselves. Finlay P. stated *obiter* that where a wrongdoer calculates that by breach of contract or through

---

[20] (1983) 103 D.L.R. (3d.) 748.

[21] (1984) 45 O.R. (2d.) 652.

[22] *MacDonald v. Sebastian* (1987) 43 D.L.R. (4th) 636; also where a party acts with cynical disregard for the rights of others, as in *D.K. Investments Ltd. v. S.W.S. Investments Ltd.* (1986) 6 B.C.L.R. (2d.) 291.

[23] April 1988, L.R.C.

[24] Unreported, High Court, Finlay P., July 14, 1976. See also *Hanley v. I.C.C. Finance* [1996] 1 I.L.R.M. 463.

tortious conduct he will profit thereby, such *mala fide* conduct should lead the courts to look at both the injury suffered by the victim and the profit or gain unjustly obtained by the wrongdoer. If the wrongdoer would still obtain a profit after quantifying the victim's loss, damages should be increased to deprive the wrongdoer of this profit. However in *Surrey County Council v. Bredeso Homes*[25] the Court of Appeal awarded only nominal damages for breach of contract when the defendants built five homes more than the planning permission obtained allowed for. The Court of Appeal found there was no authority at common law for a measure of damages that was not compensatory in nature.

While *Hickey & Co. Ltd. v. Roches Stores (Dublin) Ltd. (No. 1)* case may be out of step with the English rules on assessment of damages there is Canadian support in the Manitoba Court of Appeal case of *MacIver v. American Motors*.[26] Professor Jones has concluded that these cases are illustrative of a general trend against the view that assessing damages is a purely economic matter.[27] The Law Reform Commission, in the Consultation Paper on *Aggravated, Exemplary and Restitutional Damages*[28] has taken a very conservative position on unjust enrichment, taking the view that while restitutionary damages should be available at least in cases of deliberate wrongdoing and perhaps for all torts and equitable wrongs, such awards should not be available in cases of breach of contract.

## "Speculative" Damages

In many situations the courts are placed in the invidious position of having to calculate damages in relation to events that will happen at some time in the future, as in cases of anticipatory breach, or according to a formula that must depend on a hypothetical set of circumstances. In *Hickey & Co. Ltd. v. Roches Stores (Dublin) Ltd. (No. 2)*[29] a claim for loss of profits was sustained on the assumption that Hickeys would suffer loss of business even after the contract could have been lawfully terminated and that the repercussions would last (at a diminishing volume) for a further two years. Finlay P. in particular has shown a considerable degree of willingness to estimate loss of profits figures once it can be shown that loss of profits are certain to result; in a memorable passage in *Grafton Court Ltd. v. Wadson Sales*[30] the learned judge observed that a court "should be alert, energetic and if necessary ingenious to assess damages where it is satisfied that a significant injury has flowed from breach". In *Callinan v. Voluntary Health Insurance Board*[31] Keane J. at first instance declined to award damages in favour of the plaintiffs when certain payments were discontinued, causing contraction of the nursing services provided by the plaintiff

---

[25] [1993] 1 W.L.R. 1361; *Jaggard v. Sawyer* [1995] 1 W.L.R. 269.
[26] (1976) 70 D.L.R. (3d.) 473.
[27] (1983) 99 L.Q.R. 443.
[28] April 1998 L.R.C.
[29] [1980] I.L.R.M. 107.
[30] Unreported, High Court, February 17, 1975.
[31] Unreported, High Court, April 22, 1993.

nursing order. The Supreme Court[32] remitted the case back to the High Court, observing that it was clear that loss had been occasioned by the defendant's breach of contract. Blayney J. held that Keane J. had fallen into error when he took the view that "because the plaintiffs had not established the full extent of the loss they were claiming, they had not discharged the onus of proving that they had not suffered any damage. In my opinion this does not follow."

A court may also be persuaded to award damages if it can be shown that a particular event was almost certain to occur. In *McGrath v. Kiely*[33] the plaintiff who had been injured in a motor accident sued her doctor and solicitor, both of whom had negligently failed to bring to Counsel's attention the full extent of her injuries. She claimed that this failure adversely affected the damages recovered. Henchy J. formed the view that this injury would have resulted in additional damages of £100 being awarded. An even more extreme situation arises when a plaintiff claims loss of opportunity to earn a prize in a competition as the English case of *Chaplin v. Hicks*[34] shows. In the remarkable Irish case of *Hawkins v. Rogers*[35] the plaintiff purchased a racehorse "plus engagements", thereby entitling him to run the horse in a series of Irish "classic" races. The defendant however maliciously withdrew the horse from the races after the sale, thereby denying the plaintiff the opportunity to win prize money. Even though it was clearly impossible to determine the likelihood of the horse winning all or any of the races Dixon J. awarded damages "calculated" in part by reference to the horse's performance in later races. In contrast Pringle J. in *Afton v. Film Studios of Ireland*[36] refused to award damages for lost future profits because he was unable to hold that it was probable that a net profit would result from the venture.

The normal practice in cases where the expectation loss is so uncertain that damages cannot be recovered under this head is to award reliance loss; in *Hawkins v. Rogers* the court could have awarded the plaintiff the price paid plus any expenses incurred in maintaining the race horse had the plaintiff wished to treat the contract as discharged through breach. The plaintiff wished to retain the race horse however, so Dixon J. seems to have awarded damages simply to punish the defendant rather than compensate the plaintiff for ascertainable loss; Dixon J. felt that "the law might justly be accused of futility if the plaintiff were in such circumstances left without any legal remedy."

## Date of Assessing Loss

In cases where a contract has been broken, and the breach is treated as putting the contract to an end, the assumption is that the injured party will go into the

---

32 Unreported, Supreme Court, July 28, 1994.
33 [1965] I.R. 497.
34 [1911] 2 K.B. 786.
35 (1951) 85 I.L.T.R. 129.
36 Unreported, High Court, July 12, 1971.

market place and obtain identical goods or services, or sell identical goods or services, as the case may be. However, where the subject matter of the contract has shifted in value, it will be necessary to fix the dates upon which the goods or services are to be valued in order to assess the plaintiff's loss. The normal contractual measure is the difference between the contract price and the value of the goods at the time of due delivery, but in real property transactions the courts are increasingly permitting the plaintiff to submit that a different time be selected. Because the plaintiff may reasonably seek specific performance it may be that the plaintiff can obtain damages based upon the value of the property at the time when it was clear that specific performance was going to be unsuccessful, or even the date of judgment.[37] In accordance with this approach, should the vendor obtain a specific performance decree which cannot be enforced, it is possible to obtain damages based upon the valuation at the date of the order being aborted.[38] So, in the leading Irish case of *Vandeleur & Moore v. Dargan*,[39] the plaintiff had agreed to sell property for £320,000 to the defendant on a buoyant market. The market fell dramatically. Specific performance was ordered but could not be enforced. At the date the specific performance order was vacated, the value had fallen dramatically to £170,000. Damages were assessed at £150,000. The general rule, that damages in respect of services are to be calculated by reference to the cost of obtaining a replacement service, or another employer, can be found in *Hoenig v. Issacs*.[40] However, in *Corrigan v. Crofton & Crofton*[41] a contract for building work was completed negligently. In an action for breach of contract in respect of workmanship and materials, O'Hanlon J. held that damages could be calculated by reference to the date of judgment rather than an earlier date, the date when a schedule for remedial work was drawn up. The fact that completion of the work was delayed because of the plaintiff's impecuniosity, because it was a substantial job, and the defendants had denied liability, made it reasonable for the plaintiff to postpone the work until he knew the outcome of the legal action.

The measure of damages in relation to sale of goods actions is considered below.

## Relationship between the Heads of Loss

In principle the plaintiff should not be able to recover both wasted expenditure – reliance loss – and lost profits – expectation loss. If P has hired a lorry in order to collect goods which the seller now refuses to sell, P should not be able to recover the cost of hiring the lorry *and* profits lost because a resale of those

---

[37] *Malhotra v. Choudhury* [1980] Ch. 52.
[38] *Johnson v. Agnew* [1980] A.C. 367.
[39] [1981] I.L.R.M. 75.
[40] [1952] 2 All E.R. 176.
[41] [1985] I.L.R.M. 189, following *Dodd Properties (Kent) Ltd. v. Canterbury County Council* [1980] 1 All E.R. 928; *Perry v. Sidney Phillips & Son* [1982] 3 All E.R. 705. See also *James Stewart Ltd. v. Callaghan*, unreported, Supreme Court, July 28, 1982.

goods has now fallen through; had the seller not broken the contract the hire charges would have been necessary in order to realise the profits on resale.

Nevertheless the injured party may choose between the various heads of loss; see the English Court of Appeal decision in *Cullinane v. British Rema Manufacturing Co.*[42] followed by the Supreme Court in *Waterford Harbour Commissioners v. British Rail Board.*[43] In *Waterford* the defendants repudiated a statutory obligation to provide a shipping service between Waterford and Fishguard. The plaintiffs, in anticipation of the service continuing, spent £300,000 in building a new wharf, which, at the time of trial, did not produce any income because of the termination of the service. Henchy J., giving judgment for the majority on the question of quantum of damages, observed that the plaintiffs in this case could not sell the building because of its unique nature and situation. If this were possible, Henchy J. continued, the plaintiffs would have the choice of claiming damages either for their net capital loss after the sale or for loss of profit.

In England the plaintiff who opts for lost expenditure has been held able to recover for expenditure incurred before the contract was struck or before the contract became legally binding: see *Anglia Television v. Reed*[44] and *Lloyd v. Stanbury.*[45] The plaintiffs may on occasion seek to recover heads of damages that are mutually exclusive as in *Fitzpatrick v. Frank McGivern Ltd.*[46] The court must be vigilant in guarding against over-compensating the plaintiff in this manner. Thus in the *Waterford* case the Supreme Court by a majority were of the view that Costello J. at trial had in effect permitted recovery for net expenditure and loss of profits, reversing the decision on this point.

The decision in *Anglia Television v. Reed* has recently been qualified both in Canada and in England. The plaintiff cannot recover reliance loss if it is clear that the plaintiff had initially entered a bad bargain and it can be established that but for the breach of contract by the defendant the commercial venture would have proved an even greater financial disaster for the plaintiff. In *Bowley Logging Ltd. v. Domtar Ltd.*[47] the plaintiff employed the defendants to haul logs by trailer. The defendants failed to provide the agreed number of vehicles and were sued for breach of contract, the plaintiff (the liquidator of the company) seeking to recover all wasted expenditure. It was shown that the initial contract entered into by the plaintiff company was itself the cause of the company going into liquidation. They were selling logs for $7 a ton less than it cost to produce and, in a sense, the defendants' failure to provide the requisite number of trailers actually kept the losses down; the British Colombia Court of Appeal upheld the trial judges conclusion that damages were not

---

[42] [1954] 1 Q.B. 292. See however the formula developed in *T.C. Industrial Plant Pty. v. Robert's Queensland Pty.* (1963) 180 C.L.R. 130.
[43] Unreported, Supreme Court, February 18, 1981.
[44] [1972] 1 Q.B. 60; *Salvage Association v. Cap Financial Services* [1995] F.S.R. 654.
[45] [1971] 2 All E.R. 267.
[46] Unreported, High Court, February 10, 1977.
[47] [1978] 4 W.W.R. 105, affirmed (1982) 135 D.L.R. (3d.) 179.

available in this case. In *C.C.C. Films Ltd. v. Impact Quadrant Films Ltd.*,[48] Hutchison J. held that if the plaintiff seeks to recover damages for wasted expenditure, the onus is upon the defendant to prove that the expenditure would not have been recovered had the defendant performed his contract. Because the defendant could not show that the films, which the defendant had failed to deliver to the plaintiff would not have enabled the plaintiff to break even, the defendants were liable to compensate for wasted expenditure. In *Milburn Services Ltd. v. United Trading Group*[49] another case in which a wasted expenditure claim was made in relation to a loss-making project, the court observed that if the plaintiff could show he would have made less of a loss had the defendant performed the contract, the plaintiff is to be put in the position of having made that smaller loss.

## Quantification of Damages

Few problems arise where the plaintiff is seeking damages for reliance loss or restitution; money spent or the estimated value of services rendered will be the basis of the award. If the claim is for expectation loss the court may, in certain cases, have to consider whether the plaintiff should recover compensation for deterioration in the value of the property or the cost of remedying the defect. For example, a house that is insulated by poor quality or pungent cellulose foam may reduce the value by £2,000; it may cost £10,000 to pull down the walls and remove the offending substance. Which measure is to apply? In general the courts award the measure that seems most appropriate; cost of curing the defect applies in building contracts: *Kincora Builders v. Cronin*.[50] In the Republic the measure of damages recoverable against a tenant for non-repair is the fall in the value of the reversion that results: section 55 of the Landlord and Tenant Act 1931, considered extensively in *Groome v. Fodhla Printing Co.*[51] and *Gilligan v. Silke*.[52] *Gilligan v. Silke* was recently applied in *Trustees of St. Catherines Parish v. Alkin*.[53] In cases where the covenant is a covenant to repair and it is the landlord who is in breach, the Court of Appeal, in the leading case of *Hewitt v. Rowlands*,[54] has indicated that the measure is the diminution in market value of the premises created by the lack of repair. This may be an appropriate measure in commercial lettings, but in residential lettings the trend is towards the cost of cure and consequential loss,[55] such as damage to personal effects.[56] This issue

---

48  [1984] 3 All E.R. 298: see also *C. & P. Haulage v. Middleton* [1983] 3 All E.R. 94.
49  (1995) 52 Con. L.R. 130.
50  Unreported, High Court, March 5, 1973.
51  [1943] I.R. 380.
52  [1963] I.R. 1.
53  Unreported, High Court, Carroll J., March 4, 1982; *Fetherstonhaugh v. Smith*, unreported, High Court, February 12, 1979.
54  (1924) 93 L.J.K.B. 1080: but see *Olympia Productions v. Olympia Theatre*, unreported, High Court, February 25, 1980.
55  *Calabar Properties v. Stitcher* [1984] 1 W.L.R. 287.
56  *Siney v. Dublin Corporation* [1980] I.R. 400; *Burke and Others v. Dublin Corporation* [1990] 1 I.R. 181.

was graphically explored by the House of Lords in *Ruxley Electronics Ltd. v. Forsyth.*[57] The defendant engaged the plaintiffs to build a swimming pool to a depth of 7 foot 6 inches. On completion the pool depth varied from 6 foot to 6 foot 9 inches and he refused to pay, counterclaiming for cost of cure. At the trial the judge found that the pool was not reduced in value by the breach and awarded £2,500 damages for loss of amenity. On appeal, the Court of appeal increased damages to cost of cure at £21,560 although it was unlikely that Forsyth would demolish and rebuild. The House of Lords allowed the appeal by Ruxley, accepting that while in this kind of case cost of cure is the normal measure, the court is not constrained to order either cost of cure or the diminution in value measure. A median path, the lost amenity value, was a further option and the House of Lords opted to restore the trial judge's decision on this point.

When the issue of the appropriate measure of compensation arises within the context of a contract of insurance (typically a contract insuring a building against destruction by fire) an additional premium may normally be payable in order to obtain the cost of reinstatement rather than market value, but, in the absence of this additional payment, the insured it seems may recover reinstatement costs if there is an intention to rebuild: see *Murphy v. Wexford County Council,*[58] applied by the Supreme Court in *St. Alban's Investment Co. v. Sun Alliance.*[59]

## Sale of Goods

In cases where the seller fails to deliver goods, the buyer, it will be assumed, can go into the market to buy identical goods at the market price. Damages will be the amount by which the market price at the date of breach, that is, the time when delivery should have been made,[60] exceeds the contract price: section 51(3) of the Sale of Goods Act 1893. In *Cullen v. Horgan*[61] a wool merchant in Cahirciveen agreed on October 26, to sell and deliver wool to the plaintiffs in Dublin. No date was fixed for delivery. The defendant declined to answer the plaintiff's letters seeking delivery: meanwhile the market price of wool rose steadily until the following March. The plaintiff was held entitled to recover damages based on the difference between the contract price and the market price in the following January, the date by which delivery (in the view of the court) should have taken place. It should be noted that no evidence was introduced to show an available market in Cahirciveen at the date of breach. The court instead heard evidence of the market price in Dublin – some £100 more than the contract price, and after deducting transport costs of £50 saved, awarded £50 in damages.

---

[57] [1995] 3 All E.R. 268; Coote [1997] C.L.J. 537.
[58] [1921] 2 I.R. 230.
[59] [1984] I.L.R.M. 50. On the measure of damages in respect of fire loss due to non-repair of leasehold premises, see *Taylor v. Moremiles Tyre Services,* unreported, High Court, June 6, 1978.
[60] s.51(3) provides that where no time for delivery is fixed the relevant time is the time of refusal to deliver.
[61] [1925] 2 I.R. 1.

awarded £50 in damages.

The rule found in section 51(2), that the measure of damages is the estimated loss directly and naturally resulting, in the ordinary course of events, from the sellers breach of contract, is a restatement of the first limb in *Hadley v. Baxendale*. The measure of damages can be broadened so as to include consequential loss, such as loss of an exceptional profit made by agreeing a resale of the goods prior to the buyer taking delivery, at higher than market rates, but in order to do so the person suing for non-delivery must show that the seller had knowledge of these exceptional circumstances. In general, a resale is irrelevant in fixing market value[62] and the resale price will not be available to reduce damages (where the resale price is lower than the market price at the date of delivery) or increase damages (where the resale is at a price higher than the market price at the date of delivery). If there is no available market, however,[63] then a resale price will be utilised to fix market value.[64] If the buyer does not obtain the same goods because there is no available market, the buyer may purchase goods of a superior quality, if, for example, goods are needed urgently to complete a contract. The extra expense involved in such a case will be recoverable: *Blackburn Bobbin Co. v. Allen*.[65]

In cases of late delivery of goods the measure of loss is the fall in the value of goods from the agreed date until the date of actual delivery; this rule will also apply if an immediate resale was contemplated.[66] However, it does not follow that this measure will inevitably be employed, for in a case where a builder is deprived of materials which are delivered late but used by the builder additional costs rather than a shift in the value of the materials would appear to be the appropriate measure.[67]

If goods are sold in breach of the condition that the seller had the right to sell, section 53(2) provides that the correct measure of damages is the difference between the ordinary retail price and the contract price. In *O'Reilly v. Fineman*[68] the plaintiff buyer was prevented from obtaining a chesterfield which he had purchased in a sale for £21; the sofa had been initially priced at £24. £3 was awarded to the plaintiff in damages. This measure of compensation may include any improvements made to the goods by the dispossessed purchaser, such as repair or renovation of the property. The leading case is *Mason v. Burningham*.[69] The plaintiff purchased a typewriter for £20, and spent £11 to repair it. The typewriter had been stolen, and was repossessed. Damages of £31 were awarded.

Where the cause of action is breach of condition or breach of warranty, sections 53(2) and (3) apply. Section 53(2) again re-emphasises the first limb

---

62  *Williams Bros. v. Agius* [1914] A.C. 510.
63  For a definition of available market, see *Charter v. Sullivan* [1957] 2 Q.B. 117 at 128 *per* Jenkins L.J.
64  *Patrick v. Russo-British Grain Export Co.* [1927] 2 K.B. 535.
65  [1918] 1 K.B. 540.
66  *Heron II* [1969] 1 A.C. 350; *Victoria Laundry (Windsor) Ltd. v. Newman Industries Ltd.* [1949] 2 K.B. 528.
67  *Croudace Construction v. Cawoods Concrete Products* [1978] 2 Lloyd's Rep. 55.
68  (1942) Ir.Jur.Rep. 36; *Stock v. Urey* [1955] N.I. 71.
69  [1949] 2 K.B. 545.

in *Hadley v. Baxendale*, and section 53(3) indicates that the measure under section 53(2), in relation to quality, is, prima facie, the difference between the value of the goods at the time of delivery and their value if in accordance with the contract. This measure also applies to breach of fitness for purpose and description obligations. Again, sub-contracts are generally ignored.[70]

Where the loss is due to non-acceptance of goods by the buyer, the measure of damages found in section 50, in cases where there is an available market, is said in section 50(2) to be governed by the first limb in *Hadley v. Baxendale*. Section 50(3) states this to be the difference between the contract price and the market price at the date when the goods ought to have been accepted or, if no time was fixed, the date when the buyer refused to accept the goods.

In cases of so-called lost volume sales, that is where the seller is a dealer in goods who finds that a purchaser has not accepted the goods, the dealer is entitled to claim that a resale of the goods on the market does not prevent a claim for the lost profit, for the dealer has, at the end of the day, sold one less car, or caravan, or telephone than he would otherwise have sold. In *W.L. Thompson Ltd. v. Robinson (Gunmakers) Ltd.*[71] the defendant failed to take delivery of a standard Vanguard car from the plaintiff dealers. The plaintiffs returned the car to their suppliers, who did not charge for the lost sale. The price was fixed by the supplier and the profit on each for the dealer was £61. The defendant claimed that loss was non-existent because the plaintiff could either resell the vehicle or return it, which the plaintiff had done. Given that the demand for these vehicles was less than the supply available within the plaintiff's region, the prima facie rule in section 50(3) was inapplicable. There was no available market for these cars – they could not be readily re-sold – and the loss of profit was in this case a tangible loss. If, however, demand outstrips supply then it will be assumed that a re-sale will be effected and only nominal damages will be recoverable: *Charter v. Sullivan*.[72]

In hire-purchase and leasing contracts, where the goods are defective, the measure of damages is calculated by reference to the hire charges due under the contract, subject to a deduction for the hirers use of the goods.[73] However, the prima facie rules found in sections 50, 51 and 53, by mirroring the first limb of *Hadley v. Baxendale*, are similarly displaced by the second limb of *Hadley v. Baxendale*. Section 54 of the 1893 Act makes this clear by stating that other losses are recoverable if within the reasonable contemplation of the parties at the time of the contract. The leading case remains *Victoria Laundry (Windsor) Ltd. v. Newman Industries Ltd.*,[74] considered below.

---

[70] *Slater v. Hoyle & Smith Ltd.* [1920] 2 K.B. 11. But see *Bence Graphics International Ltd. v. Fasson U.K. Ltd.* [1997] 1 All E.R. 979.

[71] [1955] Ch. 177.

[72] [1957] 2 Q.B. 117; contrast second-hand vehicles: *Lazenby Garages Ltd. v. Wright* [1976] 2 All E.R. 770.

[73] *Charterhouse Credit Co. v. Tolly* [1963] 2 Q.B. 683; *U.C.B. Leasing v. Holtom* (1987) 137 N.L.J. 164.

[74] [1949] 2 K.B. 528.

## Remoteness of Damage

A party in breach is not liable to compensate for all loss resulting from the breach of a contract. In a contemporary context, Lord Reid, in the *Heron II*,[75] indicated that not every type of damage that is foreseeable will be recoverable in contract. The loss must be "of a kind which the defendant, when he made the contract, ought to have realised was not unlikely to result from the breach."[76] The rules determining the extent to which damages are recoverable are in the main set out in the leading case of *Hadley v. Baxendale*.[77] The plaintiffs owned a mill. A shaft broke and had to be despatched for replacement or repair, the defendants being employed to carry the shaft. It was returned at a date later than could have been expected, the defendants being less than diligent in transporting it. The plaintiff's mill was stopped for the entire period because they could not operate without the shaft. They sued the defendant carriers for loss of profits. Alderson B. observed:

> "[W]here two parties have made a contract which one of them has broken, the damages which the other party ought to receive in respect of such breach of contract should be such as may fairly and reasonably be considered either arising naturally, *i.e.* according to the usual course of things, from such breach of contract or such as may reasonably be supposed to have been in the contemplation of both parties, at the time they made the contract, as the probable result of the breach of it."[78]

Although it is not clear whether the rule in *Hadley v. Baxendale* consists of one rule with two limbs or is in fact two rules the point is largely irrelevant.[79] What is important is the fact that different factors are material to each of the separate rules or limbs. While *Hadley v. Baxendale* is the cornerstone of the law on contractual remoteness of damage, the clearest statement of principle is found in the judgment of Asquith L.J. in *Victoria Laundry (Windsor) Ltd. v. Newman Industries Ltd.*[80] The injured party is only entitled to recover that part of the loss which occurred, and, at the time of the contract, was reasonably foreseeable.[81] In turn, foreseeability depends on the knowledge possessed by the party in breach. Asquith L.J. indicated that for this purpose, knowledge possessed is of two kinds:

> "Everyone, as a reasonable person is taken to know the 'ordinary course of things' and consequently what loss is liable to result from a breach of

---

75 [1969] 1 A.C. 350.
76 *Ibid.* at 382–383.
77 (1854) 9 Ex. 341.
78 *Ibid.* at 354–355.
79 Ogus, *The Law of Damages*, (1973), pp. 72–73.
80 [1949] 2 K.B. 528.
81 The test of reasonable foreseeability was criticised by the House of Lords in the *Heron II* [1969] 1 A.C. 350 as likely to confuse the contract and tort remoteness principles: Lord Reid

contract in that ordinary course. This is the subject matter of the 'first rule' in *Hadley v. Baxendale*. But, to this knowledge, which a contract-breaker is assumed to possess whether he actually possessed it or not, there may have to be added in a particular case knowledge which he actually possesses of special circumstances outside the 'ordinary course of things,' of such a kind that a breach in those special circumstances would be liable to cause more loss. Such a case attracts the operation of the 'second rule' so as to make additional loss also recoverable."[82]

Asquith L.J. went on to stress that knowledge is the knowledge that would be attributed to a reasonable man.

Under the first limb it is clear that loss will be recoverable if it can be said to flow naturally from certain breaches of contract; a diseased animal may render the land upon which it grazes unsafe for some agricultural purposes: *Stoney v. Foley*.[83] Animal fodder laced with lead pellets will fail to meet the contract description and, in the ordinary course of things, injure animals that feed upon it: *Wilson v. Dunville*.[84] In that case the supplier pleaded that such loss was outside their reasonable contemplation. Palles C.B. pointed out that under the rule in *Hadley v. Baxendale* if the consequences of a breach of contract "result solely from the act in question, and an usual state of things, they are the ordinary and usual consequences of that act". The state of knowledge or expectation of the parties is irrelevant under the first limb. So, in *Stock v. Urey*[85] the defendant sold to the plaintiff a car registered in the Republic, the sale taking place in Northern Ireland. The car had in fact been smuggled into the North. The vehicle was seized by the United Kingdom customs authorities and the plaintiff was obliged to pay £68 to get it back. This constituted a breach of the implied condition and warranties under section 12 of the 1893 Sale of Goods Act. The court held that payment of this sum to the authorities was loss naturally resulting from breach of section 12 for which the defendant was liable.[86] Similarly, in *Lee and Donoghue v. Rowan*[87] a farmer was held able to recover the amount of money required to complete the construction of a drying shed from builders, who, in breach of contract, had refused to complete the work. Costello J. held this loss to be recoverable under the first limb.

If however loss does not arise in the ordinary course of things from the breach it must be shown that the defendant in particular was possessed of such knowledge that would enable an ordinary man, at the time of contracting, to foresee that extraordinary loss would ensue from the breach of contract. In

---

in particular favoured the view that the common knowledge and contemplation of the parties, rather than reasonable foreseeability, should determine remoteness of damage issues in contract.

[82] [1949] 2 K.B. 528 at 539–540.
[83] (1897) 31 I.L.T. 165.
[84] (1879) 6 L.R.(Ir.) 210.
[85] [1955] N.I. 71.
[86] Contrast *Maye v. Merriman*, unreported, High Court, February 13, 1980, discussed at (1981) 16 Ir.Jur. 28.
[87] Unreported, High Court, November 17, 1981.

*Waller v. The Great Western Railway (Ir.) Co.*[88] the defendant failed to supply horse boxes to transport the plaintiff's hunters to a sale in Dublin. The horses had to be ridden to the sale where they were sold at a lower price due to their deteriorated condition. The plaintiff indicated that the horses suffered on the journey because of an earlier change in diet; but for this change the journey would have been undemanding. Morris C.J. in his speech indicated that loss arising naturally would be the deterioration in the condition of the horses that were fit to make the trip, such loss being nominal. The second limb of *Hadley v. Baxendale* was not satisfied because the defendants were unaware of the extraordinarily delicate condition of the horses. Fitzgibbon L.J. observed that the only loss recoverable was the expense of using riders to transport the horses plus any fatigue and inconvenience resulting to both riders and horses. Similarly, in *Diamond v. Campbell-Jones*[89] the purchaser of a leasehold property in Mayfair sued the vendor for wrongful repudiation of the contract. He sought to obtain damages based on the profit he, as a dealer in property, would have made in converting the house into offices and maisonettes. Buckley L.J. held that the only damages recoverable were based on the ordinary measure of difference between contract price and market value at the date of repudiation: "special circumstances are necessary to justify imputing to a vendor of land a knowledge that the purchaser intends to use it in any particular manner."[90]

If we return to the facts of *Hadley v. Baxendale* we can also see that the first limb would not be satisfied for it was possible, for example, that a spare shaft was available to the plaintiff. Nor would the second limb be satisfied for the law report indicates that the defendants were unaware that the mill was stopped. The leading English cases provide very good illustrations of the limits of the "reasonable contemplation" test which is often said to form the basis of the second limb. In *Victoria Laundry (Windsor) Ltd. v. Newman Industries Ltd.*[91] the defendants delivered a boiler five months after the agreed date had expired. They knew the plaintiffs intended to use it immediately in their laundry business and were held liable for lost profits that would ordinarily result from being deprived of its use; the defendants were not liable for profits lost as a result of having to pass up exceptionally profitable government contracts, for in the absence of knowledge of the existence of these specific contracts they could not have reasonably contemplated their existence. In the *Heron II*[92] a shipowner who was transporting a cargo of sugar to the port of Basrah, aware that a market for sugar existed in that port, arrived in Basrah nine days late. The owner, who, unknown to the shipowner intended to sell immediately on arrival lost £4,000 by having to sell on a falling market. This loss was held recoverable. A reasonable man would, in the view of the House of Lords, have regarded an immediate sale as "not unlikely" or a "serious

---

[88] (1879) 4 L.R.(Ir.) 326.
[89] [1961] Ch. 22.
[90] *Ibid.* at 35–36.
[91] [1949] 2 K.B. 528.
[92] [1969] 1 A.C. 350; *Kpohraror v. Woolwich B.S.* [1996] 4 All E.R. 119.

possibility"; when this very real possibility was prevented by the delay, thereby occasioning loss, the owner was able to recover for loss of bargain. Similarly, in *Lee and Donoghue v. Rowan*[93] a farmer was obliged to plough under crops grown on his land when a drying shed, to be build under the terms of a contract, was not completed in time for the harvest. Costello J. held that while the builders knew that a failure to complete the shed would require the farmer to incur the cost of transporting his crops to some other farmer's drying sheds they could not have contemplated that a shortage of drying facilities would lead to the loss of the farmer's entire crop. The farmer was held to be able to recover the estimated cost of putting his crops into storage and the transport costs that would have been involved if storage could have been obtained. Nor can the purchaser of real property recover the cost of storing furniture when the vendor refuses to complete the sale unless knowledge can be attributed to the vendor.[94] A most useful illustration of both limbs in an everyday situation is afforded by the decision of the Court of Appeal in *Kemp v. Intasun Holidays Ltd.*[95] The plaintiff's wife booked a family package holiday in Spain. On arrival, their chosen hotel was full and they were billeted in the staff quarters of another hotel. The room was filthy and dusty, triggering off the plaintiff's asthma for several days. The plaintiff's wife on booking the holiday had not informed the travel company of his asthma condition. In the County Court, £400 was awarded for inconvenience and discomfort, loss of enjoyment and disappointment, and £800 for the consequences of the plaintiff's asthma attack. The Court of Appeal held that this second amount should not have been awarded. The condition, asthma, was not so common as to be within the reasonable contemplation of the tour company as a necessary or natural consequence and, in the absence of special knowledge of the plaintiff's condition, the second limb of *Hadley v. Baxendale* was not satisfied.

## "Type" of Loss and "Degree" of Loss

Once the species of loss is held to arise naturally it is unnecessary for the defendant to be able to reasonably contemplate the degree of loss that results. So, in *Parsons Ltd. v. Uttley Ingham*,[96] the plaintiff was able to recover for the loss of a herd of pigs that had been poisoned when the plaintiff fed mouldy pignuts to the animals, the condition being caused by a defect in the pig hopper supplied by the defendant. Even though the consequences of feeding these foodstuffs could not be foreseen – the strain and severity of infection was quite unprecedented – the Court of Appeal held that it was sufficient for the plaintiff to show that a natural consequence of defective feed being given to animals was illness. It did not matter, under the first limb, if the illness was of an

---

[93] Unreported, High Court, November 17, 1981.
[94] *Malone v. Malone*, unreported, High Court, June 9, 1982; *Pilkington v. Wood* [1953] Ch. 770.
[95] [1987] 2 F.T.L.R. 234.
[96] [1978] 1 All E.R. 525: *Wilson v. Dunville* (1879) 6 L.R.(Ir.) 210.

extreme kind unknown to veterinary science at that time. If however the loss arises under the second limb it may be possible to argue that where the degree of loss is outside the reasonable contemplation of the parties this may truncate the defendant's liability. In *Hickey (No. 2)*,[97] Finlay P. held that while the defendants could reasonably contemplate that loss as a result of inflation may occur they would not be able to anticipate that the effects and consequences of inflation would be felt for a period of six years; the defendants were therefore not liable to compensate the plaintiffs for this head of damage suffered. Similarly, in *Malone v. Malone*[98] the defendant agreed to sell a boarding house to the plaintiff but failed to complete, in breach of contract. The plaintiff had borrowed money to pay for the property, intending to meet the interest due on the loan from the profits made by the boarding house. Because the sale did not proceed these profits did not accrue and additional interest on the loan accumulated. Costello J. held that while the defendant could contemplate that the plaintiff would borrow funds to pay for the property it could not be contemplated, nor was the defendant aware, that the plaintiff was not in a position to pay interest to the bank if the defendant did not complete the sale. There are however contrasting English cases in which the impecunious plaintiff has been, on the facts, entitled to recover additional finance charges.[99]

## Cases in which *Hadley v. Baxendale* does not apply

While the test of reasonable contemplation seems well established, there are several situations where the test would appear to point to recovery of damages but, nevertheless, the courts are reluctant to apply the logic of the reasoning in *Hadley v. Baxendale*; often this can be seen as the result of historical or policy considerations. However, a discernable trend towards rationalisation of the law is evident in many of these special situations. A foremost illustration is provided by recent case law on the payment of interest, considered in detail below, but traditional views are still influential. The fact that a person may have to borrow monies due to breach by another contracting party, or be financially ruined, or lose out on a business opportunity does not in general give the plaintiff any prospect of compensation for such loss.[100]

Where the failure to pay a sum of money involves a breach of contract the measure of damages recoverable is limited to the sum in question plus interest: *Fletcher v. Tayleur*.[101] The common law judges departed from this rule in cases of a banker's refusal to honour a cheque drawn by a customer, the account

---

[97] [1980] I.L.R.M. 107.
[98] Unreported, High Court, June 9, 1982.
[99] *Wadsworth v. Lydall* [1981] 1 W.L.R. 598; *Bacon v. Cooper (Metals) Ltd.* [1982] 1 All E.R. 397. In Ireland see also *Brohan v. Crosspan Developments Ltd.*, unreported, High Court, February 26, 1985.
[100] See *Wallis v. Smith* (1882) 21 Ch.D. 243; there are signs that the position is not so fixed as it was: *Trans Trust S.P.R.L. v. Danubian Trading Co.* [1952] 2 Q.B. 297.
[101] (1855) 17 C.B. 21.

having sufficient funds to meet it. The resulting damage to the reputation and creditworthiness of the customer was thought worthy of compensation: *Rolin v. Steward.*[102] This principle was extended by the Court of Exchequer in Ireland against a mercantile agent who failed to pay a money order submitted to him for payment by a customer of the principal: *Boyd v. Fitt.*[103] If however the cheque is presented by the customer himself but the bank refuses to meet it this is outside the "commercial trader" exception established in *Rolin v. Steward*; even if third parties overhear the conversation between cashier and customer the sole recourse is an action in defamation: see Kennedy C.J. in *Kinlan v. Ulster Bank.*[104] These common law rules are unaffected by sections 57 and 89(1) of the Bills of Exchange Act 1882: see section 97(2). However, in a spirited attack upon this rule the Court of Appeal in *Kpohraror v. Woolwich Building Society*[105] has decided that credit ratings and credit reputation are important for all citizens and that the trader exception should go. Thus, general damages under the first limb of *Hadley v. Baxendale* should be available in all cases of wrongfully dishonoured cheques. However, liability for unforeseeable trading losses under the second limb was not established against the defendants even though the defendant's were aware that the plaintiff was a small trader.

A further exception is provided by *MacKenzie v. Corballis.*[106] The plaintiff was engaged as a servant in South Africa by the defendants who brought her back to Ireland, agreeing that upon leaving their employment the plaintiff would be paid her fare to return to South Africa. The defendants refused to pay the fare and the plaintiff was obliged to stay in Dublin pending the outcome of the litigation. She was held entitled to the fare and the cost of lodgings for this period. Andrews J. explained this case as coming within the second limb of *Hadley v. Baxendale*; the agreement "may reasonably be supposed to have brought it within the defendant's contemplation that the plaintiff might suffer damage through being detained by reason of not having any funds to return to South Africa."[107]

The general rule in *Fletcher v. Tayleur* was not framed by reference to *Hadley v. Baxendale* however; it was designed to prevent juries from awarding damages on an arbitrary basis; this view of the origins of the rule is supported by observations made in *Parker v. Dickie.*[108] The same institutional conflict – the judges devising a rule of remoteness that took this head of loss out of the reach of the jury – explains too the old common law rule denying damages for any distress, disappointment, frustration or loss of enjoyment resulting from a breach of contract. While there are old Irish cases that go the other way – in *French v. West Clare Railway Co.,*[109] for example, the plaintiff recovered £10 by way of damages for missing a concert because a train was delayed as a

---

[102] (1854) 14 C.B. 595.
[103] (1863) 14 Ir. C.L. Rep. 43.
[104] [1928] I.R. 171.
[105] [1996] 4 All E.R. 119.
[106] (1905) 39 I.L.T.R. 28.
[107] *Ibid.*
[108] (1879) 4 L.R.(Ir.) 244.
[109] (1897) 31 I.L.T. 140. The plaintiff later immortalised the railway company in song, "Are Ye Right there Michael".

result of the defendant's negligence – the rules laid down in *Hobbs* case[110] were accepted by the Supreme Court in *Kinlan v. Ulster Bank*.[111]

In England these older cases have been swept away in recent years. In *Jarvis v. Swans Tours*[112] the Court of Appeal compensated the plaintiff for a disappointing holiday that failed to meet up to the warranties given in the holiday brochure. This case has been followed in Ireland also. MacMahon J. in *Johnson v. Longleat Property*[113] indicated that where a builder fails to provide a house which meets the standards set out in the contract, damages for physical discomfort, loss of enjoyment and inconvenience will result: see also *Murphy v. Quality Homes*.[114] There have been several extempore Circuit Court and District Court decisions in which damages have been awarded against travel firms who have failed to provide satisfactory holidays and it is clear from newspaper accounts that compensation has included compensation for inconvenience and disruption, for example: *Hynes & Hynes v. Happy Holidays Ltd*.[115] In one recent Circuit Court case[116] damages of £10,235 were awarded in respect of the late cancellation of a luxury cruise which the plaintiffs were to enjoy as their honeymoon, the defendant substituting a much inferior package at a very late stage in the booking. While this award may seem high, the consideration paid for the cruise was around £13,000. At the other end of the scale, four women on a disastrous holiday weekend to Blackpool were awarded a cash refund of £168.[117] The most significant discussion of principle is found in the High Court of Australia case of *Baltic Shipping Co. v. Dixon*.[118] Damages for mental distress will not be automatically awarded to every plaintiff who can show that the breach of contract resulted in this head of loss. In *Kelly v. Crowley*[119] the plaintiff purchased licensed premises. His solicitor failed to investigate whether the premises had a satisfactory licence and was held in breach of contract. The plaintiff suffered mental distress when he discovered the licence was a hotel licence and not a public house licence. Murphy J. held "damage of that nature is not reasonably foreseeable. No doubt all commercial ventures carry a considerable stress . . . but I do not think it gives rise to any additional claim for damage." If the contract involves the provision of services of a recreational or social nature, then damages for distress and disappointment will be available. Several cases have arisen in the context of contracts to provide services at a wedding reception. If a hotel cancels a reception due to a double booking, transferring the reception to

---

[110] *Hobbs v. L.S.W.R.* (1875) L.R. 10 Q.B. 111.
[111] [1928] I.R. 171.
[112] [1973] 2 Q.B. 233: *Jacobs v. Thomson Travel* [1986] C.L.Y. 975.
[113] Unreported, High Court, May 19, 1976: noted in (1978) 13 Ir.Jur. 186.
[114] Unreported, High Court, June 22, 1976.
[115] *Irish Independent*, March 28, 1985.
[116] *Irish Times*, July 2, 1997.
[117] *Irish Times*, January 15, 1998.
[118] (1992) 176 C.L.R. 345.
[119] Unreported, High Court, March 5, 1985; *Hayes and Another v. James and Charles Dodd* [1990] 2 All E.R. 815; contrast *Lennon and Others v. Talbot (Ireland) Ltd*., unreported, High Court, December 20, 1985; *Knutt v. Bolton, The Independent*, May 8, 1995.

cramped accommodation with a cold buffet rather than the full meal contracted for, the guests having nowhere to dance, the father of the bride may recover damages for the very real inconvenience that will result.[120] If the band fails to show up[121] or the mobile disco fails to arrive,[122] leaving the guests to entertain themselves, the embarrassment, loss of status and aggravation that results can also be compensated. If the white Rolls Royce and the photographer, both to be provided by the defendant, fail to arrive and the resulting audiovisual and photographic record "rivals a low grade comedy film", in the words of the judge, very substantial damages may be awarded.[123] If the contract is intended to secure peace of mind but this does not result, then again damages can include anxiety and disappointment as heads of loss, as in *Heywood v. Wellers*[124] where the defendants failed to perform legal services intended to obtain an injunction to prevent a third party from molesting the plaintiff. However, if the contract is an ordinary conveyance of a dwelling house, damages for distress, annoyance and inconvenience will not be recoverable according to *Smyth v. Huey & Co.*,[125] *a fortiori* if the plaintiff is a company.[126]

In cases of wrongful dismissal the older Irish cases hold that damages cannot be recovered for the high-handed or arbitrary manner in which a servant[127] or an apprentice[128] is dismissed. While an oblique attack was mounted on this rule in England in *Cox v. Phillips Industries*[129] – a demotion and not a dismissal case – McWilliam J. in *Garvey v. Ireland*[130] accepted that the sole remedy a dismissed employee has (subject to he or she being employed by the State, in which event punitive damages may be awarded) is an action in defamation. In fact, the English position is now realigned with the traditional view after the decision of the Court of Appeal in *Bliss v. South East Thames Regional Health Authority*.[131] Dillon L.J. observed that until the House of Lords reconsiders the *Addis* case, the rule preventing damages for injured feelings in wrongful dismissal cases is too firmly fixed. *Cox v. Philips Industries* was overruled by a unanimous Court of Appeal. In contrast several Canadian decisions establish the proposition that, while damages are not to be awarded for the mental distress occasioned by a dismissal *per se*, damages may be awarded for mental distress caused by the employer's failure to give proper notice.[132] In *Malik v. Bank of Credit and Commerce International*[133] the plaintiffs were able to sidestep

---

120 *Hotson and Hotson v. Payne* [1988] C.L.Y. 1047.
121 *Dharni v. Dhami* [1989] C.L.Y. 409.
122 *Dunn v. Disc Jockey Unlimited Co.* (1978) 87 D.L.R. (3d.) 408.
123 See "£13,000 award for wedding day miss": *Irish Times*, March 2, 1995.
124 [1976] 1 All E.R. 300.
125 [1993] N.I. 236.
126 *Firststeel Cold Rolled Products v. Anaco Precision Pressings, The Times*, November 21, 1994.
127 *Breen v. Cooper* (1869) 3 I.R.C.L. 621.
128 *Parker v. Cathcart* (1866) 17 I.C.L.R. 778.
129 [1976] 3 All E.R. 161.
130 Unreported, High Court, December 19, 1979.
131 [1987] I.C.R. 700.
132 e.g. *Brown v. Waterloo Regional Board of Commissioners of Police* (1983) 103 D.L.R. (3d.) 748; *Fitzgibbon v. Westpres Publications Ltd.* (1983) 30 D.L.R. (4th) 366.
133 [1997] 3 All E.R. 1.

*Addis* by pleading that the defendant, their employer, had breached the implied duty of trust and confidence in operating its business dishonestly and corruptly, causing the plaintiffs difficulty in obtaining new employment when the defendant bank collapsed. These stigma damages were characterised as financial loss, not injured feelings, and thus, by distinguishing both the cause of action and the head of loss, the *Addis* case was removed from the equation. All *Addis* decides is that the "loss of reputation in that particular case could not be compensated because it was not caused by a breach of contract", *per* Lord Steyn.

## Contracts for the Sale of Land

Four rules of particular importance here are:

### (1) The rule in Bain v. Fothergill[134]

This rule, which developed as a result of the particular difficulties a vendor had in showing title to land, limited damages, in cases where the vendor, without deceit or wilful default, was unable to make a good title, to the sums paid by the purchaser including costs of preparing the conveyance. While the rule may have been valid at earlier periods of time it is unnecessary today. Nevertheless it has been accepted in *Kelly v. Duffy*[135] and *McDonnell v. McGuinness.*[136] The courts have refused to extend the rule into areas other than real property: *Lee & Co. (Dublin) Ltd. v. Egan Wholesale.*[137] Attempts to limit the scope of rule in property transactions are evident: see O'Higgins C.J.'s judgment in *Irish Leisure Industries Ltd. v. Gaiety Theatre Enterprises Ltd.*[138] and the English case of *Wroth v. Tyler.*[139] The vendor must show that everything possible was done to make a good title otherwise wilful default will be imputed: *Malhotra v. Choudhury.*[140] In *Ray v. Druce*[141] the defendant granted an option to purchase his land to the plaintiff. Some years earlier the defendant had conveyed some property to third parties. These conveyances were defective, wrongly indicating that part of the property conveyed included a portion of the land included in the later option agreement. The third parties, by litigation, prevented the defendant from making a good title when the plaintiff exercised the option. *Bain v. Fothergill* was applied because the vendor's difficulty in making good title was caused, not by the voluntary act of the defendant, but by the dispute between himself and the third parties, a dispute the plaintiff was aware of at the time the option was exercised.[142]

---

[134] (1874) L.R. 7 H.L. 158; the case of *Flureau v. Thornhill* (1776) 2 Wm. Bl. 1078 marks the origin of the rule and was applied in Ireland, *e.g. Buckley v. Dawson* (1854) 6 Ir.Jur.R. 374.
[135] [1922] 1 I.R. 82; O'Driscoll (1975) 10 Ir.Jur. 203.
[136] [1939] I.R. 223.
[137] Unreported, High Court, December 18, 1979.
[138] Unreported, Supreme Court, February 12, 1975.
[139] [1978] 3 W.L.R. 825.
[140] [1980] Ch. 52.
[141] [1985] Ch. 437.
[142] The rule in *Bain v. Fothergill* was abolished by the Law of Property (Miscellaneous Provisions) Act 1989. This Act applies in England and Wales.

## (2) Damages following breach of (or an award of an unenforceable decree of) specific performance

English authorities until recently held that a person who had elected to sue for and obtain a writ of specific performance was bound by this election; if the decree was unenforceable the holder could not collect damages in lieu of specific performance. This peculiar state of affairs was established in cases like *Horsler v. Zorro*.[143] The House of Lords have now overruled this line of authority in *Johnson v. Agnew*[144] and it is firmly established in Irish law that damages in such a situation are recoverable: McWilliam J. so held in *Murphy v. Quality Homes*[145] and *Vandeleur & Moore v. Dargan*.[146] In the more recent decision McWilliam J. expressly approved and applied rules 4 and 5 in Lord Wilberforce's speech in *Johnson v. Agnew*.

## (3) Deposit

Sums paid to the vendor of property by way of a deposit may serve the dual function of being part-payment and providing security against non-performance by either party. In general the purchaser who fails to complete is by this default prevented from recovering this sum, the courts holding the deposit to be liquidated damages. Nor will the doctrine of unconscionability and the equitable doctrines granting relief against forfeiture provide relief.[147]

## (4) Purchaser receives incorrect advice on the value of the property

If the purchaser of real property pays more for the property than it is really worth as the result of incorrect advice from a professional adviser – a solicitor, estate agent, valuer, surveyor or architect for example – the English case of *Ford v. White & Co.*[148] holds that the measure of compensation must be the difference between (1) the market value of the property at the date of the purchase; and (2) the price actually paid. This proposition was endorsed by Finlay P. in *Taylor v. Ryan & Jones*[149] as generally applicable although on the facts a slight modification was made. The decision in *Taylor v. Ryan & Jones* was applied by Murphy J. in *Kelly v. Crowley*.[150] In cases where a lender acts upon a negligent valuation, lending monies to purchasers who default on the loan, leaving the lender to try to resell property that is worth less than the sum advanced due to the collapse of the property market, the House of Lords has held that the measure of loss is the difference between the valuations made and the figure a careful valuer, using the information available at the time, would have come up with.[151]

---

143 [1975] Ch. 302; Oakley (1980) 39 C.L.J. 58.
144 [1980] A.C. 367.
145 Unreported, High Court, June 22, 1976.
146 [1981] I.L.R.M. 75.
147 Wylie, *Irish Conveyancing Law* (1996, 2nd ed.), Chap. 13.
148 [1964] 1 All E.R. 885.
149 Unreported, High Court, March 10, 1983; Clark, (1984) D.U.L.J. 279.
150 Unreported, High Court, March 5, 1985.
151 *South Australia Asset Management Corp. v. York Montagne Ltd.* [1996] 3 All E.R. 365.

## Mitigation of Damage

It is economically desirable that the resources "released" by the breach of contract be used by the innocent party to minimise the damage that results from breach. In *Bord Iascaigh Mhara v. Scallan*[152] the owners of a fishing vessel which had been abandoned by the hirer were held obliged to retake possession when the hirer wrongfully repudiated the contract. They could not sit by while the vessel was deteriorating and recover for physical damage that resulted. Further, had a prospective hirer come along they would have been obliged to hire it out to him if possible: see *M.C.B. (N.I.) Ltd. v. Phillips (Coleraine) Ltd.*[153] Similarly the buyer of goods which the seller refuses to deliver cannot sit by and watch the market rise, choosing to sue when the goods in question reach an optimum price. The court in *Cullen v. Horgan*[154] said that, in the case of non-delivery of goods, the buyer must at some reasonable point after breach regard the contract as at an end and seek to mitigate his loss by purchasing substitute goods elsewhere.

The duty to mitigate may even extend to requiring the injured party to contract with the party in breach. In *Payzu Ltd. v. Saunders*[155] the defendant had agreed to supply silk to the plaintiff on monthly credit terms but after some delays in payment, the defendant demanded payment on delivery: this was a breach of contract and constituted a repudiatory breach which the plaintiff accepted. However, the plaintiff was held not to be entitled to damages. The market had risen considerably and no alternative source of supply was available to the plaintiff. The plaintiff should have accepted the defendant's offer to supply the silk on cash terms. There are limits, however. If the plaintiff is offered re-employment by an employer who has previously dismissed the employee in a high-handed manner, or accused the employee of theft, a reasonable person would not require the employee to accept the offer of re-employment. Also in *Lennon and Others v. Talbot (Ireland) Ltd.*[156] the plaintiffs were motor dealers who sought damages from the defendant who had wrongfully terminated their dealerships and had appointed the Gowan Group, a large garage group, to be the sole distributor of Talbot cars in the Republic. The issue arose whether the plaintiffs should have limited their loss by ordering vehicles and parts from the Gowan Group. Keane J. indicated that where the terms presented in the revised offer are both prejudicial and substantially different to those in the contract which has been breached, *Payzu Ltd. v. Saunders* is not applicable.

A similar rule entitles the party in breach to plead that certain benefits which have accrued to the plaintiff should be taken into account in order to reduce the damages payable. Here the object is not to encourage the efficient use of resources but to prevent over-compensation of the plaintiff; a plaintiff should not be in a better position as a result of breach than would have been the case

---

[152] Unreported, High Court, May 8, 1973.
[153] Unreported, N.I. High Court, December 17, 1974.
[154] [1925] 2 I.R. 1.
[155] [1919] 2 K.B. 581; Bridge (1989) 105 L.Q.R. 398.
[156] Unreported, High Court, December 20, 1985.

had the contract been performed. In *O'Brien v. White Spunner*[157] the plaintiff was awarded a decree of specific performance entitling him to enforce a contract for the purchase of a house. The defendant vendors who had refused to complete were held liable to pay the rental value of the property from the agreed date for completion and the date of actual entry into possession. The amount of interest that had accrued to the plaintiff as a result of having the unpaid balance of the purchase price on deposit was offset against the plaintiff's damages however. In *Malone v. Malone*[158] damages were not awarded to compensate the purchaser of real property for additional interest charged against him by a bank in respect of a loan taken out to pay for the property; Costello J. held the plaintiff should have mitigated his loss by repaying the money to the bank. If the innocent party has a choice of two methods of mitigating damage, both of which are reasonable in the circumstances, it is not possible to say that the innocent party acts unreasonably because it transpires that the loss would have been less had the innocent party adopted the other method: *Gebruder Metelmann GmbH & Co. v. N.B.R. (London) Ltd.*[159] The guiding principle, as stated by Lord MacMillan in *Banco de Portugal v. Waterlow and Sons Ltd.*[160] was followed by Keane J. in *Lennon and Others v. Talbot Ireland Ltd.*:

> "Where the sufferer from breach of contract finds himself in consequence of that breach placed in a position of embarrassment, the measures which he may be driven to adopt in order to extricate himself ought not to be weighed in nice scales at the instance of the party whose breach of contract has occasioned the difficulty. It is often easy after an emergency has passed to criticise the steps which have been taken to meet it, but such criticism does not come well from those who have themselves created the emergency. The law is satisfied if the party placed in a difficult situation by reason of the breach of a duty owed to him has acted reasonably in the adoption of remedial measures, and he will not be held disentitled to recover the cost of such measures merely because the party in breach can suggest that other measures less burdensome to him might have been taken."[161]

In cases of anticipatory breach by the seller of goods, if the innocent party accepts the breach and terminates the contract, the duty to mitigate will lead to damages being assessed as at the date of the purchase. If the innocent party does not purchase, then damages will be based on the value on the date when the goods ought to have been delivered.[162] If the anticipatory breach is not accepted, mitigation does not arise until breach occurs.[163] In cases where the

---

[157] Unreported, High Court, November 23, 1979.
[158] Unreported, High Court, June 9, 1982.
[159] [1984] 1 Lloyd's Rep. 614.
[160] [1932] A.C. 452.
[161] [1932] A.C. 452 at 506.
[162] *Melachrino v. Nicholl and Knight* [1920] 1 K.B. 693.
[163] *White and Carter (Councils) Ltd. v. McGregor* [1962] A.C. 413.

seller of property seeks damages from a defaulting buyer, a resale at an increased price will result in nominal damages or damages for incidental expenses. In *Baker Perkins Ltd. v. C. J. O'Dowd*[164] the defendants refused to take delivery of bakery equipment ordered from the plaintiffs. The equipment was sold for £60,359 more than the price agreed with the defendant. The plaintiffs could recover warehousing charges incurred pending disposal by way of a resale, for such loss was contemplated by the parties arising out of the breach.

Where the injured party has received compensation from another source – an insurance policy or a gift from friends or relatives – the common law rules prohibit those advantages from reducing the damages payable to the defendant: *Bradburn v. Great Western Railway.*[165] In the Irish Republic the E.A.T. deduct employment benefits paid from any award of compensation for unfair dismissal or redundancy but not from wrongful dismissal claims under the Minimum Notice and Terms of Employment Act 1973. In Northern Ireland the leading case of *Hill v. Cunningham*[166] holds unemployment benefit deductible from damages for breach of contract, but Barrington J., in *Irish Leathers Ltd. v. Minister for Labour and Foley*,[167] has rejected this argument, preferring instead to deny a contract breaker the advantage of deducting social welfare payments from compensation payable to a worker following implementation of a redundancy agreement. Statute often provides that certain social welfare benefits are not deductible – see the Civil Liability (Amendent) Act 1964, section 2, which provides that state and other benefits payable upon the occurrence of a non-fatal injury are not deductible. However, section 75(1) of the Social Welfare Consolidation Act 1993 provides that occupational injuries benefits are deductible in part: an employee who recovers damages for breach of contract which has caused an occupational injury will find damages reduced by occupational injuries benefits for a period of five years after the cause of action arose. Section 237 of the Social Welfare (Consolidation) Act 1993 similarly requires the deduction of disability benefit, invalidity pension and pay related benefits, payable in respect of injuries received following the use of a motor vehicle when damages are awarded to the injured person, regardless of whether the cause of action is contract or tort. In *Dennehy v. Nordic Cold Storage Ltd.*[168] the defendant employer was held to be entitled to take advantage of any insurance payments made to the plaintiff on the foot of a private insurance contract that the defendant employer had taken out in respect of the employer's liability, section 2 of the 1964 Act not operating within that context. In *Greene v. Hughes Haulage Ltd.*[169] however, section 2 was held to come into play when the payment was the result of a contract of insurance effected by the plaintiff's employer, who paid the premiums. These insurance provisions were held to be

---

[164] Unreported, High Court, April 13, 1989: contrast *Hussey and Another v. Eels and Another* [1990] 2 W.L.R. 234.
[165] (1874) L.R. 16 Ex. 1.
[166] [1968] N.I. 58.
[167] Unreported, High Court, March 12, 1986.
[168] Unreported, High Court, May 8, 1991.
[169] *Irish Times Law Report*, September 29, 1997.

part of the plaintiff's remuneration package although in the nature of a disability payment calculated by reference to the plaintiff's salary levels. Other collateral benefits may not be used to offset damages on basic grounds of public policy.[170]

## Contributory Negligence

In England it has recently been decided that, save in cases where liability in contract and negligence are the same,[171] contributory negligence is not material in actions based on a breach of contract. Apportionment of liability under section 1(1) of the Law Reform (Contributory Negligence) Act 1945 is only possible in respect of tortious liability.

The provisions of the Civil Liability Act 1961 lead to a quite different conclusion in Ireland. Section 2 of the Act defines "wrong" so as to include "a tort, breach of contract or breach of trust". The Act is the basis upon which a defence of contributory negligence is made available to the defendant. In *Lyons v. Thomas*[172] the purchaser of real property sought damages for the deterioration in the condition of property between the date of the agreement and closing of the sale. While the vendor was clearly liable Murphy J. held that a deduction of 10 per cent should be made. The plaintiff was aware of the deterioration but failed to notify the vendor of this fact. In *O'Flynn v. Balkan Tours Ltd.* the level of assessment was 75 per cent.[173]

## Taxation

Although the *Gourley* principle was approved and applied by Kenny J. in *Glover v. BLN (No. 2)*,[174] and considered to be good law by the same judge in *Browne v. Mulligan*[175] and by Pringle J. in *Afton v. Film Studios of Ireland*,[176] its general applicability in the Republic remains uncertain outside cases of wrongful dismissal. Finlay P. in *Hickey No. 2*[177] was reluctant to apply *Gourley* in a loss of profits case, preferring instead to find that the damages themselves should in principle be subject to taxation; indeed the learned judge went further by holding "that the rule or principle followed by Mr. Justice Kenny in *Glover v. B.L.N. (No. 2)* applies only to damages for wrongful dismissal and breach of a contract of service and is so expressly to be confined."[178] The Supreme Court

---

[170] *McKenna v. Best Travel Ltd.*, unreported, High Court, December 17, 1996.
[171] *Forsikringsaktieselskapet Vesta v. Butcher* [1988] 2 All E.R. 43.
[172] [1986] I.R. 666.
[173] Unreported, Supreme Court, April 7, 1997, affirming High Court judgment of December 1, 1995.
[174] [1973] I.R. 432.
[175] Unreported, Supreme Court, November 23, 1977.
[176] Unreported, High Court, July 12, 1971.
[177] [1980] I.L.R.M. 107.
[178] *Ibid.* at 124.

have approved this approach in *Marah & Marah v. O'Mahony*.[179] However, it must be established that the damages recoverable by the plaintiff are exempt from tax and in two recent cases, *Allen v. O'Suilleabháin*[180] and *Sullivan v. Southern Health Board*,[181] the courts have been unwilling to impute a tax liability exemption for the damages in question in the absence of proof.

## Interest

Under the provisions of the Debtors (Ireland) Act 1840, it is possible for the courts to award interest upon judgment debts; section 26 of the Debtors (Ireland) Act 1840, as amended in the Republic by the Courts Act 1981, section 19(1), obliges the debtor to pay interest of 11 per cent from the time of entering up the judgment until satisfaction of the judgment. Section 20(1) of the 1981 Act gives the Minister for Justice the power to keep this rate in line with current interest rates. A recent statutory instrument reduces the interest rate to eight per cent.[182] Whether interest can be awarded to cover the period between breach of contract and the date of judgment is controlled by section 53 of the 1840 Act. The sum in question must be a liquidated or certain amount and the creditor must have served notice in writing of intention to claim interest at the current rate as from the date of demand. In the absence of such a notice damages cannot attract interest: *East Cork Foods v. O'Dwyer Steel Co.*,[183] as applied in *Incorporated Food Products Ltd. v. The Minister for Agriculture.*[184] The Courts Acts 1981 seems to have superseded section 53 of the 1840 Act by providing that where money, including damages, is payable as a result of the decree of the court, the judge may "if he thinks fit" award the rate of interest in force under section 26 of the 1840 Act as amended by the 1981 Act, "on the whole or any part of the sum in respect of the whole or any part of the period between the date when the cause of action accrued and the date of the judgment". This discretion to award interest on damages under section 22 must depend on the facts of each particular case and Finlay P. has stated that it does not follow that recovery of interest on arrears in regard to a liquidated demand will follow automatically: *Mellowhide Products Ltd. v. Barry Agencies Ltd.*[185]

The common law position in respect of the charging of interest, other than when following on a judgment given against a creditor, was extensively reviewed in *President of India v. La Pintada Compania Navigacion SA.*[186] The House of Lords considered whether it was possible for interest to be charged in cases where proceedings have commenced but the debtor pays before their con-

---

179 Unreported, High Court, November 1, 1985.
180 Unreported, High Court, July 28, 1995. See the Supreme Court judgment of March 11, 1997.
181 Unreported, Supreme Court, July 30, 1997.
182 Courts Act 1981 (Interest on Judgment Debts) Order, 1989 (S.I. No. 12 of 1989).
183 [1978] I.R. 103.
184 Unreported, High Court, June 6, 1984.
185 [1983] I.L.R.M. 152.
186 [1985] 1 A.C. 104; Mann (1985) 101 L.Q.R. 30.

clusion, or where the debtor pays late but before proceedings have commenced. While there are exceptional circumstances where interest is awarded in the field of admiralty law and equity, the common law position was established by the House of Lords in *London, Chatham and Dover Railway Co. v. South Eastern Railway Co.*[187] In the absence of agreement or statutory authority, a court has no power to award interest, simple or compound, by way of damages for late payment of a debt. The House of Lords, in *La Pintada*, reaffirmed this rule, with reluctance, and endorsed the decision of the Court of Appeal in *Wadsworth v. Lydall.*[188] In this case the Court of Appeal confined the rule in the *London, Chatham and Dover Railway* case to general damages. The plaintiff was allowed to recover two items of special damage, namely interest paid because of late completion of a contract of sale by the plaintiff to the defendant, and additional mortgage costs.

It is possible for the parties to agree to provide interest upon a certain event as a term of the agreement; this is particularly common in cases where a sale of land is not completed on time: *Lappen v. Purcell.*[189] A stipulated rate of interest of 20 per cent was upheld in *Treacy v. Dwyer Nolan Investments.*[190] The Prompt Payment of Accounts Act 1997 allows the supplier of goods or services to state bodies – identified in the Act to cover government departments, agencies, health boards and hospitals as well as universities, *inter alia* – to obtain interest on overdue accounts of just over 11 per cent per annum.[191]

## Damages in Foreign Currency

It is possible for an Irish arbitrator or Irish court to order payment of damages in a foreign currency.[192]

## Penalty Clauses and Liquidated Damages Clauses

The parties to a contract may agree that should one or indeed either of the parties fail to meet contractual obligations a fixed sum of money shall be payable as compensation to the injured party. Both the common law courts and the courts of equity viewed these covenants with suspicion, being of the view that a clause which could oblige a party to pay a measure of compensation

---

[187] [1893] A.C. 429, recently reaffirmed by the Supreme Court in *O'Donnell & Co. Ltd. v. Truck and Machinery Sales Ltd.*, unreported, April 1, 1998.

[188] [1981] 1 W.L.R. 598; *President of India v. Lips Maritime Corp.* [1987] 3 All E.R. 110 holds that demurrage, as a liability in damages, is outside this exception and there can be no liability for currency conversion loss arising out of late-payment.

[189] [1965] Ir.Jur.Rep. 1.

[190] Unreported, High Court, October 31, 1979; such clauses are standard in finance leases where the lessee is in default of payments.

[191] See the Annotation by Hoy in *Irish Current Law Statutes Annotated.*

[192] *Cremer (Peter) Gmbh v. Co-operative Molasses Traders Ltd.* [1985] I.L.R.M. 564.

grossly disproportionate to the injury produced by the breach, should not be enforceable. A fundamental distinction has been drawn in the modern cases. A clause will be valid if it is a genuine pre-estimate of the damage which will probably result from a breach of contract. Such a clause is called a liquidated damages clause. If the clause is designed to deter one party from breaking the contract by stipulating that breach will result in the payment of a fixed amount the courts will refuse to enforce the clause by holding it to be a penalty. The burden of showing that the sum is a penalty rather than liquidated damages is upon the defendant.

The case of *Toomey v. Murphy*[193] presents a simple illustration of a liquidated damages clause. The defendant agreed to complete construction work by an agreed date. If the work was then incomplete he agreed to pay "a penalty as liquidated damages" of £5 per week. The plaintiff sued for £160 being 32 weeks at £5 per week. The Queens Bench Division held the sum to be liquidated damages.

Whether the clause is a penalty or liquidated damages depends on the intention of the parties at the date of agreement; in this context the words used to describe the clause will provide some indication of their intention. In *Toomey v. Murphy* the words "penalty" and "liquidated damages" were used so the terminology was equivocal; if the parties describe the clause as a penalty this will provide evidence that the clause is to be held "*in terrorem*" over the head of one party. There are many cases in which a clause has been described as a penalty but has been held a valid liquidated damages clause, for example *Gerrard v. O'Reilly*.[194] The converse is also true.[195]

It is generally accepted that the best summary of the rules to be applied in testing whether a clause is valid or invalid is to be found in the speech of Lord Dunedin in *Dunlop Pneumatic Tyre Co. v. New Garage & Motor Co.*[196]:

> (a) The sum will be held to be a penalty if the sum stipulated for is extravagant and unconscionable in amount in comparison with the greatest loss that could conceivably be proved to have followed from the breach . . .

This is generally the most important test. In cases where there is only one obligation, the chance of this test being operative in a way which strikes down the clause are less pronounced than in cases of multiple obligations, for here the clause, if it strikes at a variety of possible breaches, in the same way, will probably be held to be a penalty. In *Irish Telephone Rentals Ltd. v. Irish Civil Service Building Society Ltd.*[197] Costello J. had to consider a clause which obliged a subscriber who repudiated a contract for the hire of telephone equipment to pay all accrued charges plus all remaining rentals due under the

---

[193] [1897] 2 I.R. 601; *French v. Macale* (1842) 4 Ir.Eq.Rep. 573.
[194] (1843) 2 Connor and Lawson 165; *Alder v. Moore* [1961] 2 Q.B. 57.
[195] (1829) 6 Bing. 141.
[196] [1915] A.C. 79 at 86–87.
[197] [1991] I.L.R.M. 880, following *Robophone Facilities Ltd. v. Blank* [1966] 1 W.L.R. 1428.

contract, a five per cent allowance being made for receiving rentals immediately and not over future years, and a 25 per cent discount being made because of the saving to the owner on maintenance costs. Costello J., after citing the above rule, concluded that the discounting process was not sufficient to prevent the acceleration clause from infringing the rule. Wages of maintenance staff and other costs were not included in the 25 per cent discount. The profit figure estimated by the plaintiffs, 71.25 per cent of the gross rent, seemed to be excessive, and because the exercise undertaken by the plaintiffs did not attempt, in any methodically consistent way, to identify actual loss, this standard provision was held to be a penalty. See also *Bradshaw v. Lemon*[198] where a sum payable upon non repair of premises was held a penalty because the loss that could result from breach would not in any case match the sum stipulated: the repairer could breach the contract in a variety of ways.

> (b)  The sum will be a penalty if the breach consists only in paying a sum of money, the sum stipulated being greater than the sum which ought to have been paid.

Thus if the clause obliges a person to pay £200 upon failure to pay a rental of £50 the clause will be penal: see the dictum of Lawson J. in *Wright v. Tracey.*[199] In the leading Irish case of *O'Donnell & Co. Ltd. v. Truck and Machinery Sales Ltd.*[200] the Supreme Court held that where the breach consists of a failure to pay a fixed sum, the damages payable will be that sum plus commercial rates of interest. Should the contract provide for payments in excess of this formula then the "agreed rate" will be regarded as a penalty and not a genuine pre-estimate of loss. An "acceleration clause" has been held not to infringe this rule. These clauses (which operate in contracts where a debtor repays sums of money in instalments) provide that upon failure to pay any of the instalments the whole balance will become immediately due. Even though the obligation to pay the entire sum will generally be more expensive to the party in breach the validity of such a clause was upheld in *Protector Loan Co. v. Grice,*[201] a decision of the English Court of Appeal: see a similar clause in *National Telephone Co. v. Griffen.*[202]

The acceleration clause will be carefully policed however. In *U.D.T. Ltd. v. Patterson*[203] the plaintiff advanced £900 to the defendant, repayable with interest by 36 equal monthly instalments. It was a term of the agreement that immediately upon default the whole amount would be due and payable. The defendant paid one instalment and then defaulted. The plaintiffs claimed £1,137.50 being the sum lent minus one instalment paid and interest over the period at 10 per cent per annum. McGonigal J. ruled the clause penal. It was noted that if the

---

[198]  [1929] N.I. 159.
[199]  (1873) I.R. 7 C.L. 134.
[200]  Unreported, Supreme Court, April 1, 1998.
[201]  (1880) 5 Q.B.D. 529.
[202]  [1906] 2 I.R. 115.
[203]  [1975] N.I. 142.

loan were repaid at an early date the contract provided that no interest would be payable for the period after repayment; in this instance the default clause did not provide for payment of interest calculated up to the date of repayment of the principal only. McGonigal J. distinguished *Grice's* case by holding:

> "The amount to be paid on default is a larger amount than the amount actually due if calculated on the basis of the balance still outstanding and interest to that date and a larger sum than the amount which would have to be paid if the borrower had elected to pay at that point of time during the currency of the loan."[204]

It may be that the party in default will seek to discharge the duty to show the clause is penal by giving the clause an extreme interpretation. Just such an attempt failed in the case of the *Angelic Star*.[205] The acceleration clause, found in a shipbuilding contract, required the purchaser in default of instalment payments, to pay immediately "the loan together with all other monies due". While Donaldson M.R. was prepared to accept that a clause in a long-term loan contract which provided that on any breach the capital sum and interest for the full term would be a penalty, this agreement did not have this effect. The words "together with all monies due" referred simply to all monies due at the time of the default. Conversely, in *Trustee Savings Bank Dublin v. Maughan*[206] Costello J. held that unless the alleged clause is a genuine pre-estimate, agreed between the parties, the clause will be liable to be considered a penalty clause.

(c)  There is a presumption that a clause is penal when a single lump sum is payable on the occurrence of one or more or all of several events, the events occasioning varying degrees of loss.

The unusual case of *Jobson v. Johnson*[207] is perhaps to be seen as illustrative. Here the defendant had purchased shares in a football club. The contract provided for a price of £351,688 payable by a down-payment of £40,000 and six equal half yearly payments of the balance. The contract provided that upon default, the buyer would be obliged to reconvey the shares for a fixed consideration of £40,000. The clause was penal because the repurchase was to be effected at £40,000 regardless of whether the defendant defaulted on the second or last instalment, for example. The clause also operated prejudicially by requiring the repurchase for less than £40,000 if the default of the purchaser occurred on the first of the six instalments.

*Re An Arranging Debtor*[208] presents an illustration of how this rule can be avoided. Patentees installed equipment into premises under a contract which obliged the hirers not to allow others to use, repair or purchase the machinery, £30

---

204  *Ibid.* at 145.
205  [1988] 1 Lloyd's Rep. 122.
206  Unreported, High Court, October 8, 1981.
207  [1989] 1 All E.R. 621.
208  (1916) 51 I.L.T.R. 68.

being payable if any of these events occurred. The clause was held not to be penal; the covenants were held to import obligations of equal, not varying, importance. This rule seems to best explain the case of *Schiesser International (Ireland) v. Gallagher.*[209] The defendant went to Germany to be trained as a textile cutter. He agreed that if he left the employment of the plaintiff within three years of his return to Ireland he would reimburse them for travelling expenses and training expenses incurred. The clause was struck down as a penalty. It was pointed out that if the plaintiff had left employment one day after his return from Germany or one day before expiry of the three-year period the same sum would be payable.

(d)  If the consequences of breach are difficult to estimate in financial terms this, far from being an obstacle to the validity of the clause, will point in favour of upholding it, the courts taking the view that it is better for the parties themselves to estimate the damages that will result.

While the best illustration of this rule is to be gleaned from contrasting the *Dunlop Pneumatic Tyre* case with *Ford Motor Co. v. Armstrong*[210] Irish students should note that this rule was used to "explain" the difficult case of *Smith v. Ryan*[211] by the majority in *Dickson v. Lough.*[212]

## Penalty Clauses in Agricultural Lettings

It is clear that the modern case law on penalty clauses has produced different results to those that could have been anticipated under the earlier rules; McGregor observes that the nineteenth century cases on penalties were often confused and difficult to reconcile and he concludes that, "perhaps today they are of real value only as illustrations of type-situations".[213] This is particularly true of clauses in agricultural leases in which a tenant was bound not to plough land or take away meadowing or grass (*Smith v. Ryan*)[214]; not to raise a stone weir (*Gerrard v. O'Reilly*)[215]; nor sublet premises (*Boyle v. McGovern*)[216] upon pain of having to pay double the rent due. In these early cases the sums were held not to be a penalty, either at common law (*Hubbard v. Grattan*)[217] or in equity (*Smith v. Ryan*). Since then the Irish courts have moved towards holding these clauses to be penalties by holding the leading case of *Smith v. Ryan* to depend on rule (d) above: see *Dickson v. Lough*[218] and the Northern Ireland case of *Bradshaw v. Lemon.*[219]

---

209   (1971) 106 I.L.T.R. 22.
210   (1915) 31 T.L.R. 267.
211   (1843) 9 I.L.R. 235.
212   (1886) 18 L.R.(Ir.) 518.
213   *McGregor on Damages* (15th ed.), s.439.
214   (1843) 9 I.L.R. 235.
215   (1843) 2 Connor and Lawson 165.
216   (1841) 6 Circuit Cases 308.
217   (1833) Alcock and Napier 389.
218   (1886) 18 L.R.(Ir.) 518.
219   [1929] N.I. 159; *McGregor on Damages*, s.477, says of the English cases that they "trail in a desultory way into the twentieth century: the result is always penalty."

# Sums Payable on Termination not Breach

It should be noted that in the *Schiesser* case the clause was designed to deter the defendant from lawfully terminating his employment rather than from breaking the contract. The clause then could not be an agreed damages clause in the orthodox sense unless the contract there was for a fixed period of at least three years; no such finding appears in the law report however. Nevertheless the rules applicable to penalties upon breach were held applicable.[220]

The applicability of these rules to hire-purchase contracts has caused great difficulties for the courts in Northern Ireland and England. It is an essential part of a hire-purchase contract that the hirer has a right to terminate the agreement; should the hirer so wish a minimum payment clause may be inserted into the contract obliging the hirer to compensate the owner for depreciation in the value of the goods by bringing payments up to a percentage of (or indeed the whole of) the hire-purchase price. In the Republic, section 5 of the Hire-Purchase Act 1946 obliges the hirer to pay any sum necessary to bring the sums paid up to 50 per cent of the hire-purchase price; any minimum payment clause which seeks to vary or increase this figure would appear to be void.

If however the hirer does not *terminate* but rather *breaks* the contract, typically by defaulting on a payment, it is a vexed question whether section 5 of the 1946 Act applies in the Republic so as to invalidate as a penalty any stipulation that the hirer pay a sum in excess of this figure.[221] While it is clear that section 5 of the 1946 Act makes it impossible to stipulate a "penalty" in excess of 50 per cent in cases of *termination* by the hirer, it is the author's view that section 15 of the 1946 Act makes it clear that a penalty clause obliging the hirer to pay a fixed percentage of the hire-purchase price following *breach* by the hirer remains perfectly valid. It is suggested that section 5 of the 1946 Act be amended to apply to all cases of termination.

If the concern of the Oireachtas is to provide a degree of consumer protection, then hire-purchase and leasing transactions must be scrutinised at some future date in order to counteract the effect of contractual terms which attempt to secure for the owner compensation for loss of future instalments, in the form of minimum percentage or acceleration clauses as well as the return of the contractual subject-matter. This is highlighted by attempts to evade a decision[222] of the Court of Appeal which held that any contractual term which seeks to allow the owner to claim damages for loss of future instalments following the owner's decision to terminate for breach will not be successful. Damages will be limited to instalments unpaid at the time of the owner's decision to rescind. It has been held, however, that if the contract contains a clause which makes prompt payment of the essence of the contract, then any

---

[220] *Schiesser International (Ireland) v. Gallagher* (1971) 106 I.L.T.R. 22; compare *Alder v. Moore* [1961] 2 Q.B. 57 and *Export Credits Guarantee Department v. Universal Oil Products Co.* [1983] 2 All E.R. 205 with *Schiesser.*

[221] The leading English case of *Bridge v. Campbell Discount Co.* [1962] A.C. 600 holds that at common law, those clauses are subject to the rules against penalties.

[222] *Financings Ltd. v. Baldock* [1963] 2 Q.B. 104.

breach will go to the root of the contract and entitle the owner to terminate at common law, independently of the terms of the contract.[223]

## Effects of the Penalty Clause

If the clause is held to be a penalty clause it is unenforceable. If the plaintiff can prove actual loss he will be limited to the amounts proved: *Schiesser*.[224] If the clause is a penalty, which, because of subsequent events, does not cover the loss suffered, it is said that the plaintiff can opt to rely on the clause or sue for the actual loss suffered: see *Wall v. Rederiaktiebolaget Lugudde*.[225] In cases where the actual loss exceeds the amount fixed by the unenforceable penalty clause, it may be that the amount recoverable will be set by the penalty clause and cannot be exceeded, but McGregor doubts this proposition[226] and, on principle, if the clause is unenforceable as a penalty it should not interfere with ordinary rules of assessment. Where the obligation struck down is not an obligation to pay money, but to perform some agreed act, such as transfer property,[227] the process of determining the remedies available to the injured party can be difficult indeed.

---

[223] *Lombard North Central plc v. Butterworth* [1987] 1 All E.R. 267.
[224] *Schiesser International (Ireland) v. Gallagher* (1971) 106 I.L.T.R. 22; *Irish Telephone Rentals Ltd. v. Irish Civil Service Building South* [1991] I.L.R.M. 880; *O'Donnell & Co. Ltd. v. Truck and Machinery Sales Ltd.*, unreported, Supreme Court, April 1, 1998.
[225] [1915] A.C. 79.
[226] (15th ed.) para. 449.
[227] *Jobson v. Johnson* [1989] 1 All E.R. 621.

# 20 Quasi-Contractual or Restitutionary Relief

## Introduction

Traditional legal scholarship has tended to regard the categories of tort and contract as the two primary sources of liability in private law. The impact of this bifurcation for legal theory has in England been profound. Apart from attempts by Lord Mansfield, primarily in *Moses v. McFerlan*,[1] to establish a third category, that of unjust enrichment – a category that would both cut across contract and tort and at the same time establish a third or quite self-contained area of private law within which the judiciary could operate – there was until recently a tendency to argue that restitutionary relief could only be available if the plaintiff's cause of action fell within contract, tort or possibly the equitable concept of the fiduciary relationship: see *McNeill v. Millen & Co.*[2] Both judicial and academic opinions have shifted from the position taken by the nineteenth century judges who repudiated *Moses v. McFerlan*, primarily because of the authoritativeness of the modern view that the old causes of action should not rule us from their graves, and also because it is realised that unjust enrichment – rather than implied contract for example – provides a more realistic and coherent basis for explaining the cases, particularly the mistake of fact cases. Judicial activism and academic scholarship – using *Moses v. McFerlan* as the starting point – has produced a very sophisticated set of principles and rules and the work of the American Law Institute has been very influential.[3]

In Ireland the courts have until very recently tended to resist the temptation to consider whether the principle of unjust enrichment forms an essential element in Irish law. While there are isolated cases in which the unjust enrichment doctrine has surfaced, witness *Hickey v. Roches Stores (No. 1)*,[4] there has been a tendency to decline to accept counsel's invitation to consider a broad application of *Moses v. McFerlan*: see Morris J. in *Leader v. Leader*.[5] There are, however, cases where the unjust result of not allowing an action for recovery to succeed has contributed to the reasoning, *e.g. Carse v. Taylor*,[6] without in any way suggesting that this forms the basis of a cause of action. Twentieth century Irish judges have considered either unjust enrichment or

---

[1]  (1760) 2 Burr. 1005; Birks (1984) 37 C.L.P. 1. See generally Birks, *Introduction to the Law of Restitution* (1989); Burrows, *The Law of Restitution* (1993).
[2]  [1907] 2 I.R. 328.
[3]  Perillo (1981) 81 Col.L.R. 37.
[4]  Unreported, High Court, July 14, 1976.
[5]  (1874) I.R. 6 C.L. 20.
[6]  (1858) 5 I.C.L.R. 451.

fault to be possible explanations for a successful action in restitution – witness Judge O'Briain in *O'Connor v. Listowell UDC*[7] and the Supreme Court in *Rogers v. Louth County Council.*[8] More recently, however, see *O'Callaghan v. Ballincollig Holidays.*[9]

The most significant Irish development on the jurisprudential basis upon which restitutionary relief is founded is the treatment of the topic by Keane J. in *Dublin Corporation v. Building and Allied Trade Union.*[10] Inspired perhaps by recent English case law that had rejected *Sinclair v. Brougham* but relying heavily on a creative interpretation of Irish case law, the learned judge declared, in the context of a claim for the return of compulsory purchase monies paid in order to allow the defendant to rebuild premises, such work not being done:

> "It is clear that, under our law, a person can in certain circumstances be obliged to effect restitution of money or other property to another where it would be unjust for him to retain the property. Moreover, as Henchy J. noted in *East Cork Foods Ltd. v. O'Dwyer Steel Co. Ltd.*, this principle no longer rests on the fiction of an implied promise to return the property which, in the days when the forms of action still ruled English law, led to its tortuous rationalisation as being "quasi-contractual" in nature.
>
> The modern authorities in this and other common law jurisdictions, of which *Murphy v. Attorney General* [1982] I.R. 241 is a leading Irish example have demonstrated that unjust enrichment exists as a distinctive legal concept, separate from both contract and tort, which in the words of Deane J. in the High Court of Australia in *Pavey & Matthews Pty. Ltd. v. Paul* (1987) 162 C.L.R. 221 at pp. 256–257:
>
>> '. . . explains why the law recognises, in a variety of distinct categories of cases, an obligation on the part of a defendant to make fair and just restitution for a benefit derived at the expense of a plaintiff and which assists in the determination, by the ordinary process of legal reasoning, of the question of whether the law should, in justice, recognise the obligation in a new or developing category of case.'
>
> The authorities also demonstrate that, while there is seldom any problem in ascertaining whether two essential preconditions for the application of the doctrine have been met – *i.e.* an enrichment of the defendant at the expense of the plaintiff – considerably more difficulty has been experienced in determining when the enrichment should be regarded as 'unjust' and whether there are any reasons why, even where it can be regarded as 'unjust', restitution should nevertheless be denied to the plaintiff.
>
> As to the first of these difficulties, the law, as it has developed, has avoided the dangers of 'palm tree justice' by identifying whether the

---

[7] [1957] Ir.Jur.Rep. 43.
[8] [1981] I.R. 265; [1981] I.L.R.M. 144.
[9] Unreported, High Court, March 31, 1993.
[10] [1996] 2 I.L.R.M. 547.

case belongs in a specific category which justifies so describing the enrichment: possible instances are money paid under duress or as a result of a mistake of fact or law or accompanied by a total failure of consideration. Whether the retention by the union of the entire compensation in the present case falls within such a category or not, however, it would in any event be necessary to consider whether restitution is precluded because of other factors."[11]

Thus, to sum up, Irish law recognises an independent cause of action in unjust enrichment. The "triggering" issue is whether the defendant has been enriched at the expense of the plaintiff. If so, the court proceeds to consider if such enrichment is unjust, by reference to determined categories into which the case at bar falls. The final issue is whether, notwithstanding the unjust enrichment, there are broader issues that point away from requiring the defendant to disgorge those ill-gotten gains.

For the sake of ease of exposition restitution will be broken into two parts: quasi-contractual claims on the one hand, and *quantum meruit* on the other.

## Quasi-Contracts – Typically Restitution of Moneys transferred by the Plaintiff

### *(1) Mistake of fact*

Earlier in this book,[12] through the leading Irish mistake cases, one central proposition was established to which we now return. Payments made on the basis of a mistaken belief are generally recoverable if the mistake is fundamental and relates to the terms of the contract. The general rule was stated thus by Parke B. in *Kelly v. Solari*[13]:

> "Where money is paid to another under the influence of a mistake, that is, upon the supposition that a specific fact is true which would entitle the other to the money, but which fact is untrue and the money would not have been paid if it had been known to the payer that the fact was untrue, an action will lie to recover it back."[14]

This dictum was endorsed in Ireland by Budd J. in *National Bank Ltd. v. O'Connor & Bowmaker Ireland Ltd.*[15] and it provides an important exception to the general rule that payments voluntarily made are irrecoverable. There are, however, some important restrictions on this restitutionary principle:

---

[11] [1996] 2 I.L.R.M. 547 at 557–558. The earlier Irish cases, both direct and oblique, are well collected and put into context in O'Dell, (1993) D.U.L.J. 27.
[12] Chap. 10.
[13] (1841) 9 M. & W. 54.
[14] *Ibid.* at 58; *Rover International Ltd. v. Cannon Film Sales (No. 3)* [1989] 3 All E.R. 423.
[15] (1966) 103 I.L.T.R. 73.

(i) The mistake must be a mistake of fact. If the mistake can be characterised as one of law then it may not be possible to order restitution. A mistake as to the interpretation of a Public General Act is a mistake of law: *O'Loghlen v. O'Callaghan*,[16] and *Jackson v. Stopford*;[17] as is a mistake based upon the mis-interpretation of delegated legislation: see *Holt v. Markham*.[18] The Supreme Court's decision in *Casey v. The Irish Sailors and Soldiers Land Trust*[19] is illustrative. A trust was established under statute to provide and administer a scheme for the provision of cottages for ex-servicemen. The trustees charged rent for the cottages provided but in *Leggett v. Irish Sailors and Soldiers Land Trust*[20] the Supreme Court held that the plaintiffs in that action should not have paid rent. Casey and others brought actions to recover the rent paid under their illegal tenancy agreement with the trustees. The Supreme Court, applying *Sharp Brothers & Knight v. Chant*,[21] affirmed that "the rule that money paid under a mistake of law cannot be recovered back is founded upon principles of conven-ience as well as justice. The rule has been so long and so firmly established that it cannot be called into question."[22]

Nevertheless there are ways of avoiding the full force of this arbitrary rule. In *Casey's* case counsel for the various plaintiffs argued that the statutory authority vested in the trustees created, *vis-à-vis* their tenants, a fiduciary relationship. The Supreme Court rejected this argument, holding that there existed only a statutory tenancy. The argument was made in order to avail of certain English cases which establish that restitution may be ordered even following a mistake of law when there has been a breach of trust by the defendant. The Privy Council, in *Kiriri Cotton Co. v. Dewani*[23] affirmed *Rogers v. Ingham*[24] in which James L.J. indicated that equity sometimes provided relief by way of restitution if the case involved something more than a mere mistake of law. Lord Denning in *Kiriri Cotton* indicated that if the obligation to observe the law is to be placed on the shoulders of one of the parties, as against the other, the parties to the contract are not *in pari delicto*. While in this case Lord Denning also stressed that the duty imposed by law should be imposed in order to protect the other person, this requirement, it is submitted, has been quietly dropped in later cases (*e.g. Shelley v. Paddock*[25]). As a result it can be confidently stated that where the parties are not equally situated and, in particular, when the payee has either a duty *vis-à-vis* the plaintiff or perhaps

---

[16] (1874) I.R. 8 C.L. 116.
[17] [1923] 2 I.R. 1.
[18] [1923] 1 K.B. 504.
[19] [1937] I.R. 208.
[20] Unreported, Supreme Court, 1923, cited in [1937] I.R. 208.
[21] [1917] 1 K.B. 770.
[22] [1937] I.R. 208 at 222, *per* Murnaghan J. However, if money is paid under *ultra vires* tax demands, a general restitutionary principle may operate: *Woolwich Building Society v. I.R.C.* [1993] A.C. 70.
[23] [1969] A.C. 192.
[24] (1876) 3 Ch.D. 351.
[25] [1980] 2 W.L.R. 647.

is simply in a better position to ascertain the true state of the law, or indeed is primarily responsible for making the error in interpretation (negligently or otherwise), then the payee may be obliged to make restitution. The Irish cases which adopt this approach, like *Kiriri Cotton* itself, do not actually require a fiduciary relationship to be shown. In *Dolan v. Neligan*[26] overpayments made by the plaintiff to the Revenue as a result of an incorrect interpretation of sections 30 and 31 of the Customs Consolidation Act 1876 were held to be recoverable within *Kiriri Cotton*. No fiduciary relationship existed between the payee and the plaintiff importer but Kenny J. in the High Court held that the defendant, a collector of customs, had been responsible for making the incorrect demand. While the Supreme Court in *Dolan v. Neligan* did not find it necessary to consider the decision in *Kiriri Cotton*, the dictum of Lord Denning was later endorsed in the Supreme Court in *Rogers v. Louth County Council*[27] An overpayment made by the plaintiff in order to redeem an annuity was held recoverable even though at the time of payment both parties believed the sum calculated was correctly estimated by the defendant council in accordance with guidelines provided by the Department of Local Government. The error only came to light, after the demand had been made, as a result of a Supreme Court decision on the correct interpretation of the relevant statutory provision, section 99 of the Housing Act 1966. These facts were held to be sufficient to bring the case within *Kiriri Cotton*: "the plaintiff's solicitor could not be expected to know the redemption price. He relied on the defendants to give him the correct figure."[28] Hamilton J. in the High Court in *Dublin Corporation v. Trinity College Dublin*[29] has also endorsed the view that *Kiriri Cotton* means that a mistake of law for which one person is "primarily responsible" can oblige that person to make restitution. Hamilton J.'s decision was later reversed by the Supreme Court but on another ground.

The distinction between mistakes of fact and law has been examined by the House of Lords in *Woolwich Building Society v. IRC*.[30] The majority of their Lordships House doubted the distinction, Lord Goff in particular observing that the distinction was unreliable and unprincipled. In *O'Rourke v. The Revenue Commissioners*[31] Keane J. cited the following extract from Lord Goff's judgments with approval:

"I would therefore hold that money paid by a citizen to a public authority in the form of taxes or other levies paid pursuant to an *ultra vires* demand by the authority is prima facie recoverable by the citizen as of right. As at present advised, I incline to the opinion that this principle should extend to embrace cases in which the tax or other levy

---

26 [1967] I.R. 247.
27 [1981] I.L.R.M. 144.
28 *Ibid. per* Kenny J. at 148.
29 [1985] I.L.R.M. 283.
30 [1993] A.C. 70.
31 Unreported, High Court, December 18, 1996.

has been wrongly exacted by the public authority, not because the demand was *ultra vires* but for other reasons, for example, because the authority has misconstrued a relevant statute or regulation. It is not, however, necessary to decide the point in the present case, and in any event cases of this kind are generally the subject of a statutory regime which legislates for the circumstances in which money so paid either must or may be repaid. Nor do I think it necessary to consider for the purposes of the present case to what extent the common law may provide the public authority with a defence to a claim for the repayment of money so paid: though for the reasons I have already given I do not consider the principle of recovery should be inapplicable simply because the citizen has paid the money under a mistake of law."

While *Kiriri Cotton* has produced a subtle change in the area of restitution there are other, perhaps more soundly based, exceptions to the general rule that a mistake of law cannot ground restitution of overpayments made. If there is a misrepresentation by the defendant there is a possibility of restitution by virtue of the misrepresentation. In *Carse v. Taylor*[32] the plaintiff paid money to the defendant on the basis of a statement that the defendant was the administrator of the deceased Mary Scott. The plaintiff made the payment fearing that civil execution was about to be levied against him. It later transpired that Mary Scott was not dead and the defendant was not able, in law, to be the administrator of a living person's estate. The defendant argued, distinguishing the annuity case of *Strickland v. Turner*,[33] that this was a mistake of law. The Irish Court of Queen's Bench held that the misrepresentation entitled the plaintiff to recover the payments made. This case would seem to come within the test propounded by Whiteside C.J. in *O'Loghlen v. O'Callaghan*[34] in which it was said that restitution of moneys overpaid may be ordered if "mala fides . . . fraud or imposition" is practised. An example of *mala fides* (suppression of facts which may have led the plaintiff to refuse to make the payment) is provided by *Leonard v. Leonard*.[35]

The other important exception to the position established by, *inter alia*, *Casey v. Irish Sailors and Soldiers Land Trusts Co.*[36] stems from a dictum of Lord Westbury in *Cooper v. Phibbs*[37] when he observed that the private right of ownership is a matter of fact even though it may also be the result of a matter of law: "If parties contract under a mutual mistake and misapprehension as to their relative and respective rights, the result is that the agreement is liable to be set aside as having proceeded upon a common mistake."[38] While this

---

[32]  (1858) 5 I.C.L.R. 451.
[33]  (1852) 7 Exch. 208.
[34]  (1874) I.R. 8 C.L. 116.
[35]  (1812) 2 Ball & B. 171.
[36]  [1937] I.R. 208.
[37]  (1867) L.R. 2 H.L. 149.
[38]  (1867) L.R. 2 H.L. 149 at 170.

dictum is clearly in step with the decision of the Irish Court of Chancery,[39] it provides difficulties in reconciling the cases. It is clear that whenever the boundary between fact and law becomes pertinent the courts endeavour to characterise the mistake as one of fact or title. In *Platt v. Casey's Drogheda Brewery*[40] overpayments made to debenture holders on the foot of a mistaken interpretation of their rights under statute were held to be recoverable as made on a mistake of fact, not law: *cf. National Pari Mutuel Association Ltd. v. R.*[41]

(ii) If the plaintiff overcomes the hurdle presented by the aphorism, "money paid under a mistake of fact may be recovered but money paid under a mistake of law cannot", described by Kenny J. in *Rogers v. Louth County Council* as "grossly inaccurate",[42] there are two other obstacles to recovery.

First, it is by no means clear whether the mistake of fact is operative if, when the payment was made, the person making the payment knew that he was not in law liable to make the payment to the payee. The distinction is illustrated by a simple example, taken from Cheshire, Fifoot and Firmston's *Law of Contract*.[43] A has given B a sum of money in the erroneous belief that B is pursuing a particular piece of research or has no means of subsistence. Can A sue B in quasi-contract when he discovers his error? There is a clear mistake of fact but the payment, according to at least one nineteenth century case,[44] is irrecoverable because the payment was made voluntarily without the belief that there existed a legal liability. More recent cases, however, adopt a more liberal approach[45] and it is now established that money mistakenly paid will be recoverable if paid in order to discharge a liability owed by the person making the payment. Thus, if a bank makes a payment to the defendant in circumstances where the payment was gratuitous (*i.e.* consideration is absent) recovery is still possible by the bank (see Budd J. in *National Bank Ltd. v. O'Connor & Bowmaker Ireland Ltd.*[46]) if the mistake is a "fundamental" one.

The second obstacle to recovery arises when the payment involves more than two parties. Despite some English authorities which favoured the view that the payment must be made to a person to whom the payer is obliged as against a third party, Budd J. in *National Bank Ltd. v. O'Connor & Bowmaker Ireland Ltd.* indicated that the mistake need not apply *inter partes*. Budd J. summarised his conclusions thus:

> "It is not easy to reconcile all the decisions with regard to the recovery of money paid under a mistake of fact. It is therefore difficult to arrive at a precise statement as to when in law money thus paid is recoverable. Reviewing the authorities cited and others it can however, I think, safely

---

[39] (1865) 17 Ir.Ch.R. 73.
[40] [1912] 1 I.R. 271.
[41] (1930) 47 T.L.R. 110.
[42] [1981] I.L.R.M. 144 at 148.
[43] (13th ed.), p. 673.
[44] *Aiken v. Short* (1856) 1 H. & N. 210 at 215, *per* Bramwell B.
[45] *Larner v. London County Council* [1949] 1 All E.R. 964.
[46] (1966) 103 I.L.T.R. 73.

be said that it can be so recovered in the following circumstances. First where it has been proved that it has been paid under a mistake of fact. It must be a fundamental mistake but no question really arises here as to that because such mistakes as arose were obviously of that nature in this case. It is of course necessary in order to establish a mistake of fact to show that the fact supposed to be true was untrue, and that the money would not have been paid if it was known that the fact was untrue. Secondly, it must be shown that the mistake was as to a fact, which, if true, would make the payer either liable or under a duty to pay the money. Having regard to the decision in *Waring and Gillow Ltd.* I am satisfied, however, that the mistake has not been shown to be a mistaken belief on the part of the payer that he was under a liability to pay the payee. It is sufficient if it be shown that the payer was under a mistaken belief that he was under an obligation to pay someone and that payment to the actual payee would be appropriate and would discharge the obligation.

There is then another matter to be considered. It is urged on the part of the defendant O'Connor that the mistake must be inter partes and there is a good deal to support this in the cases cited. But just what it means is difficult to say. I am not satisfied that it must necessarily exist as between payer and payee exclusively. There seems to be no logical reason why it should be so confined. There would seem no logical reason why a mistake between the payer and the person to whom the supposed obligation exists should not also involve a mistake as between payer and payee. In other words why a mistake between the payer and the other two parties should not be equally well a mistake inter partes as regards both.

Moreover the case of *Jones Ltd. v. Waring and Gillow Ltd.* indicates that where the supposed obligation is to pay someone and a person to whom such supposed obligation does not exist, but who it is supposed can give a discharge, is paid, the money is recoverable."[47]

The distinction between (operative) mistakes of fact and (inoperative) mistakes of law has been denounced by the English Law Commission. The different treatment given to mistakes of law and fact has been denounced as inconsistent and arbitrary and the law of restitution on this point is uncertain and complex. The Law Commission have provisionally recommended abolition of the rule precluding restitution when the mistake is one of law, recommending that recovery should be permitted in the same way as is currently allowed under a mistake of fact. However, a defence of change of position should accompany such a change, the defence of change of position to be developed by the courts.[48]

---

[47] (1966) 103 I.L.T.R. 73 at 96: *Jones Ltd. v. Waring and Gillow* [1926] A.C. 670.
[48] Law Com. No. 120, *Restitution of Payments Made Under a Mistake of Law* (1991).

## (2) Total failure of Consideration

Where one contracting party has not received any part of that contracted for, it is said that there is a total failure of consideration. In this context consideration takes on a narrower meaning than that utilised for the purpose of determining whether a contract has been formed. As Lord Simon put in the *Fibrosa* case:

> "In the law relating to the formation of contract, the promise to do a thing may often be the consideration, but when one is considering the law of failure of consideration and of the quasi-contractual right to recover money on that ground it is, generally speaking, not the promise which is referred to but the performance of the promise."[49]

So, if there is defective performance by one contracting party in circumstances entitling the other party to rescind the contract (breach of an express or implied condition for example), the injured party may pursue whatever contractual remedies are available or elect instead to claim restitution. If, however, there has not been a total failure of consideration the quasi-contractual remedy will not be available, and if the defendant has a valid defence in contract to the plaintiff's action (frustration, for example) the plaintiff may not have any financial remedy at all.

Examples of total failure of consideration can be found in several Irish cases. In *Hayes v. Stirling*[50] the plaintiff made a payment to the defendant, a putative director of a company to be formed in the future. The payment was made in order to secure shares in the company. The company was never established. The Court of Exchequer held the money recoverable on the basis of a consideration that had wholly failed. Similarly, in *P. v. P.*,[51] money was paid in consideration of marriage. The marriage was a nullity. The money paid was recoverable for total failure of consideration. The terms of the bargain, however, should be closely scrutinised for if it is clear that one person is taking the risk that the shared venture will not result in a tangible benefit accruing to that person then recovery in quasi-contract may not be possible. Witness cases where the buyer of real and personal property knows and accepts that there is a possibility that the property is not the seller's to dispose of: see *Griffin v. Caddell*[52] and section 12 of the Sale of Goods Act 1893, as amended by the 1980 Act.

If the plaintiff seeks restitution of money paid it will be fatal to the claim for the court to conclude that the plaintiff received any part of the promised consideration. *Hayes v. Stirling*[53] should be contrasted with *Lecky v. Walter*.[54] In the latter case the plaintiff purchased shares on the basis of a misrepresentation. The shares were virtually worthless. It was nevertheless impossible

---

[49] *Fibrosa Spolka Akcyjna v. Fairbairn Lawson Combe Barbour Ltd.* [1943] A.C. 32.

[50] (1863) Ir.C.L.R. 277.

[51] [1916] 2 I.R. 400.

[52] (1875) I.R. 9 C.L. 488.

[53] (1863) Ir.C.L.R. 277.

[54] [1914] I.R. 378.

to say the consideration had wholly failed. Similarly, in *Stapleton v. Prudential Assurance*[55] restitution of insurance premiums paid by the plaintiff on the foot of a voidable contract was denied because there was no failure of consideration; while no claim on the policy had been made, she was covered by the policy throughout the duration of the period in which the contract was valid.

In contrast, it does not follow that because the plaintiff received some tangible benefit a court will be constrained to hold that a total failure of consideration did not result. While the leading English case is *Rowland v. Divall*,[56] the Irish case of *Chartered Trust Ireland Ltd. v. Healy & Commins*[57] illustrates this point. Healy hired a truck on hire-purchase terms. The transaction was financed by the plaintiff finance company. It later transpired that the truck was illegally brought into the State and was not in fact the vehicle it was represented to be. Barron J. held the contract was null and void and awarded Healy the return of all moneys paid by way of hire-purchase instalments and all other payments made in pursuance of the agreement, following *United Dominions Trust (Ireland) v. Shannon Caravans Ltd.*[58] The fact that Healy had used the truck for over a year did not mean that he had received any part of the consideration; in contracts of sale, title to the property and in hire-purchase cases the option to purchase are seen as the consideration. Because the action is not brought for damages for breach of contract but in quasi-contract there is no allowance made for the benefits that have accrued under the contract. The view that appears to be gaining ground is that the fact that the plaintiff has received some benefit (*e.g.* payment of interest but not capital on a voidable loan) is not payment of consideration, but, even if it were, the fact that the plaintiff can restore the benefit conferred, will keep the plaintiff within this exception: contrast *Baltic Shipping Co. v. Dixon*[59] with *Goss v. Chilcott.*[60]

### (3) Money paid under a conditional contract

When a contract is conditional upon a stated event occurring and the event does not occur it is possible to maintain an action for the recovery of money paid in furtherance of the conditional contract, unless there is an express clause to the contrary. In *Lowis v. Wilson*[61] the plaintiff agreed to purchase the defendant's land "subject to contract". She declined to proceed with the sale and successfully maintained an action for the return of the deposit paid to the defendant on the ground that it was money paid without consideration.

---

[55] (1928) 62 I.L.T.R. 56.
[56] [1923] 2 K.B. 500; *Rover International Ltd. v. Cannon Film Sales Ltd.* [1989] 3 All E.R. 423.
[57] Unreported, High Court, December 10, 1985.
[58] [1976] I.R. 225.
[59] (1992) 176 C.L.R. 345.
[60] [1996] A.C. 788.
[61] [1949] I.R. 347.

## (4) Money paid or property transferred in consequence of a void contract

While it is clear that restitution of money paid under a void contract will be recoverable, either as being paid under a mistake of fact of a fundamental nature (see *National Bank Ltd. v. O'Connor & Bowmaker Ireland Ltd.*)[62] or because there is a total failure of consideration (see *Chartered Trust Ireland Ltd. v. Healy & Commins*)[63] there are difficulties when the contract is void because of some statutory provision; readers should refer to the discussion on the effects of section 1 of the Infants Relief Act 1874.[64]

## (5) Money paid or property transferred on the foot of an illegal contract

Return of money or property transferred under an illegal contract is recoverable if there can be some cause of action utilised which does not require disclosure of the illegal purpose contemplated by the illegal performance, but this method of avoiding the *in pari delicto* rule is not always likely to lead to success: *Taylor v. Chester*.[65] Where the source of the illegality is some compelling moral imperative, restitution will be denied. In *Brady v. Flood*[66] money paid to secure the discontinuance of criminal charges brought against the plaintiff's sons was held irrecoverable. Similarly, if the source of the illegality is a statutory provision the statute itself may declare whether there is to be restitution. If statute declares a money-lending transaction illegal it is unlikely that an action upon the contract or for restitution of the principal moneys advanced will succeed.[67]

The exceptions to the *in pari delicto* rule should also be remembered; if the parties are not *in pari delicto* or if one party has perpetrated a fraud on the other, as in *Shelley v. Paddock*[68] for example, or if there has been repentence before the illegal objective has been substantially performed, then there exists the possibility of restitution for the more deserving party to the illegal contract. In *Byrne v. Rudd*[69] the plaintiff entered into an illegal insurance contract following the fraudulent misrepresentations of an insurance agent. The insurance company were held not to be entitled to retain the premiums obtained from the plaintiff, for, in these circumstances, they were not to benefit from the fraud of a third party, *i.e.* the agent.

## (6) Restitution from a wrongdoer

Suppose the plaintiff pays money or transfers property to the defendant because the defendant has made an unwarranted demand which the plaintiff is in no

---

[62] (1966) 103 I.L.T.R. 103.
[63] Unreported, High Court, December 10, 1985.
[64] Chap. 16.
[65] (1869) L.R. 4 Q.B. 309.
[66] (1841) 6 Circuit Cases 309.
[67] *Irvine v. Teague* (1898) 32 I.L.T.R. 109; *Handelman v. Davis* (1937) 71 I.L.T.R. 268.
[68] [1980] 2 W.L.R. 647.
[69] [1920] 2 I.R. 12, applying *Hughes v. Liverpool Victoria Friendly Society* [1916] 2 K.B. 482.

position to resist. The emerging doctrine of economic duress suggests that the plaintiff can seek the return of his property or money even if the threat made, if carried out, would not be independently actionable: *Universe Tankships of Monrovia v. International Transport Workers Federation*.[70] The possibility of restitution by way of an action for money had and received has long existed in English law; witness the dictum of Willes J. in *Great Western Railway Co. v. Sutton*.

> "I have always understood that when a man pays more than he is bound to do by law for the performance of a duty which the law says is owed to him for nothing, or for less than he has paid, there is a compulsion or concession in respect of which he is entitled to recover the excess by *conditio indebiti*, or action for money had and received. This is every day's practice as to excess freight."[71]

This dictum, later restated by Reading C.J. in *Maskell v. Horner*,[72] was applied in the Irish case of *Great Southern and Western Railway Co. v. Robertson*.[73]

An action for money paid to the defendant's use was successful in *Midland Great Western Railway v. Benson*.[74] The defendant transferred a consignment of butter to Kelly via the plaintiff company. The defendant, being dissatisfied with the financial arrangements made between himself and Kelly, wrongfully secured the return of the butter before it reached Kelly. Kelly had paid £40 on account for the butter and upon the threat of legal action the plaintiff paid £40 to Kelly. Monahan C.J. in the Court of Common Pleas indicated that in these circumstances the law would imply that the defendant promised to repay the company that which they were bound to pay to Kelly, who could maintain an action against the company.

The *Benson* case leads us on to examine one further requirement, apart from the requirement that the plaintiff make the payment because of the existence of some element of practical compulsion. There should be an obligation in law upon the defendant to pay the money due. It is possible that the defendant may have promised to make restitution to the plaintiff, in which case an action will be brought upon the express promise[75] but an implied promise will not be imposed upon the defendant unless the defendant was bound to make the payment: *Brooks Wharf v. Goodman Brothers*[76] So in *Irish National Insurance Co. v. Scannell*[77] the defendant, a licensed auctioneer, and the plaintiff company executed a professional indemnity bond which obliged the company

---

[70] [1982] 2 W.L.R. 803.
[71] (1869) L.R. 4 H.L. 226 at p. 249.
[72] [1915] 3 K.B. 106.
[73] (1878) 2 L.R.(Ir.) 548. In a different context see *Hanley v. I.C.C. Finance Ltd.* [1996] 1 I.L.R.M. 463.
[74] (1875) Ir.C.L.Rep. 52.
[75] e.g. *Cook v. Wright* (1861) 1 B. & S. 559.
[76] [1937] 1 K.B. 534.
[77] [1959] Ir.Jur.R. 41.

to meet any claims brought against members of the Irish Auctioneers and Estate Agents Association, of which the defendant was a member. The company met certain lawful debts and liabilities incurred by Scannell. The plaintiff company was held to be able to recover these moneys as money paid for and on behalf of the defendant. In cases where there is a joint liability on both plaintiff and defendant, *e.g.* the plaintiff stands as surety for another, upon payment of the debt due to a third party the surety can sue his co-sureties, if any, for a contribution or seek reimbursement from the principal debtor: *Gore v. Gore*.[78] Where liability is imposed by a court upon one of several tortfeasors the tortfeasor held liable may also seek to obtain a contribution from the other tortfeasors: see the Civil Liability Act 1961, s.21, discussed in *East Cork Foods Ltd. v. Dwyer Steel Co.*[79]

### (7) Money paid by the plaintiff for the defendant's use

When payment has been made by the plaintiff in circumstances where the defendant has benefited therefrom – typically the plaintiff makes a payment and in so doing he discharges a legal liability imposed upon the defendant – there exists the possibility of recovery through an action for money paid by the plaintiff to the defendant's use. There are few cases, however, in which the plaintiff has been successful in such an action and it is generally accepted that at common law the plaintiff will generally be treated as having voluntarily paid the sums in circumstances where restitution will not be ordered.

If, however, the plaintiff has been obliged by force of circumstance to make the payment because failure to do so will seriously prejudice the plaintiff, restitution may be possible. In *Beresford v. Kennedy*[80] the defendants owned farmland in Waterford. The plaintiff, who farmed adjoining land, discovered that the poor-rate collector had seized some of his cattle which had strayed on to the Kennedys' land, the defendants having failed to pay the poor rate. The plaintiff paid the rates due in order to obtain the return of his stock and then sued the defendants for the sums paid, seeking to rely on the English case of *Exall v. Partridge*.[81] Andrews J. distinguished *Exall v. Partridge* on the ground that in that case Exall paid Partridge's landlord arrears of rent due from Partridge in order to prevent distress being levied on his carriage, which he had left on Partridge's premises. Andrews J. held that in the case before him Beresford's cattle were not lawfully on the defendants' land whereas Exall had lawfully bailed the carriage with Partridge. Andrews J. said: "there is no authority in the books to show that where property is unlawfully on defendants' premises, the wrongdoer can recover against the defendant."[82]

---

[78] [1901] 2 I.R. 269.
[79] [1978] I.R. 103.
[80] (1887) 21 I.L.T.R. 17.
[81] (1799) 8 Term Rep. 308.
[82] (1887) 21 I.L.T.R. 17 at 19. See also *Gormley v. Johnston* (1895) 29 I.L.T.R. 69.

## (8) Money had and received from a third party to the use of the plaintiff

There is authority[83] for the view that where money is received by the defendant for the use of the plaintiff, the payment being made by a third party with instructions to the defendant to pay the sum over to the plaintiff, the plaintiff can maintain an action in quasi-contract to secure payment. A quasi-contractual action is necessary here because the contract, if any exists, is between the defendant and the third party and, further, the plaintiff rarely provides consideration in these circumstances. Sometimes the doctrine of privity of contract intrudes into this area, witness the Irish cases of *Leader v. Leader*[84] and *Sweeney v. Moy*,[85] but because the claim is quasi-contractual the doctrine of privity of contract should not properly intrude.

Recent English case law extends this cause of action from cases where the defendant is obliged to administer a specific amount of money or a particular fund for the third party to cases where the defendant is simply under an obligation *vis-à-vis* the transferor to administer a monetary liability.[86] The action for money had and received, as a common law conception, was a personal claim. Until recently, in the absence of a constructive trust or a fiduciary relationship it was thought that only this common law action could be available to a plaintiff. However, in *Lipkin Gorman (a firm) v. Karpnale Ltd.*[87] and in *F.C. Jones & Sons v. Jones*[88] principles of tracing at common law have been utilised to allow the legal owner of property to trace his property into the property into which it has been transformed, and also allow the owner to obtain any profits that the wrongful use of his property has produced.

## Defences

Even if the defendant has been unjustly enriched a number of defences, or obstacles to restitution may exist. These include estoppel[89] and change of position[90] as well as the fact that there may be a bona fide purchaser for value involved. The fact that parliament has apparently not intervened on the issue and the broader public policy that a matter has been decided – *res judicata* – is at the heart of the decision of the Supreme Court in *Dublin Corporation v. Building and Allied Trade Unions* not to order the return of at least part of the monies paid, citing Henchy J. in *Murphy v. A.G.*[91]:

---

[83] *Stevens v. Hill* (1805) 5 Esp. 247.
[84] (1871) I.R. 6 C.L. 20; *Murnaghan v. McCreevy*, unreported, High Court, December 21, 1981.
[85] [1931] L.J.Ir. 42.
[86] *Shamia v. Joory* [1958] 1 Q.B. 448. The decision is criticised by both Goff and Jones, *The Law of Restitution* (4th ed.), Chap. 26, and in *Chitty on Contracts* (27th ed.), Chap. 29. Cheshire Fifoot and Furmston's, *Law of Contract* (13th ed.), p. 681 seems to support the result reached.
[87] [1991] 2 A.C. 548.
[88] [1996] 4 All E.R. 721.
[89] *Avon C.C. v. Howlett* [1983] 1 W.L.R. 605.
[90] *Lipkin Gorman (a firm) v. Karpnale Ltd.* [1991] 2 A.C. 548.
[91] [1982] I.R. 241 at 314. The *Dublin Corporation* case (above, p. 497) also suggests that the

"Over the centuries the law has come to recognise, in one degree or another, that factors such as prescription (negative or positive), waiver, estoppel, laches, a statute of limitation, *res judicata*, or other matters (most of which may be grouped under the heading of public policy) may debar a person from obtaining redress in the courts for injury, pecuniary or otherwise, which would be justiciable and redressable if such considerations had not intervened."

## *Quantum Meruit*

We now turn to examine the converse situation to that just considered; suppose the plaintiff has transferred property or performed some service for the defendant without a price having been paid or expressly agreed upon; can the plaintiff succeed in an action either for some consideration, in which case the claim is really contractual, or, otherwise, in quasi-contract for the value of the benefit conferred upon the defendant. Sometimes the generic term of *quantum meruit* is applied to both situations. When the claim is really contractual in nature the plaintiff often seeks to recover a price for goods delivered or property sold under the terms of an agreement which did not itself fix the amount. The measure of compensation is generally the amount the defendant would expect to pay in order to obtain the benefit which has been duly conferred; where this process is open to a court a reasonable price will be fixed, either by reference to general principles[92] or statute.[93] In *Fanning v. Wicklow County Council*[94] building work was completed in the mistaken belief that a contract had been negotiated. There was no contract because the price had not been agreed beforehand, as was the common intention of the parties. O'Hanlon J. held the builder entitled to recover the value of the work on a *quantum meruit*. In *Rover International Ltd. v. Cannon Film Sales (No. 3)*[95] both Kerr and Nicholls L.JJ. were of the view that where *quantum meruit* is sought in respect of work done under a supposedly valid contract, it was incorrect to assess the *quantum meruit* by placing a ceiling on the amount due by reference to a maximum amount set by the invalid contract. The appropriate measure is equitable restitution as between the parties, regardless of their respective positions if the contract had been valid.

The most enlightening series of Irish cases involve claims in *quantum meruit* brought by auctioneers and estate agents seeking reasonable remuneration for work completed. While we have considered the general position in relation to actions brought upon an implied contract,[96] two contrasting decisions indicate

---

courts are aware of the implications for the Exchequer on follow-up claims, as does *O'Rourke v. Revenue Commissioners* [1996] 2 I.R. 1.

[92] *e.g. Hillas v. Arcos* [1932] Comm.Cas. 23.
[93] *e.g.* Sale of Goods Act 1893, s.8.
[94] Unreported, High Court, April 30, 1984.
[95] [1989] 3 All E.R. 423.
[96] Chap. 6.

that quasi-contract may provide the auctioneer or estate agent with an alternative to the implied contract argument. In *Stokes & Quirke Ltd. v. Clohessy*[97] the plaintiff auctioneers were instructed by the defendant to find a buyer for his house. They introduced a buyer prepared to purchase at a satisfactory figure but the sale did not proceed when, prior to execution of the formal contract, the defendant received a higher offer from a third party. Nothing had been said about the plaintiff's commission. Their action in contract failed as did their action in *quantum meruit*. McLoughlin J. held it was not evident that the plaintiffs were to be paid simply upon introduction of someone willing to buy, even if the sale did not ultimately proceed. In contrast in *Henehan v. Courtney & Hanley*[98] an estate agent was held entitled to recover on a *quantum meruit* when instructed by an intending purchaser to find a farm for him. The estate agent did find a farm which was suitable and, more to the point, the purchase was closed. Even though nothing had been said about the commission Teevan J. quoted *Bateman on Auctions*:

> "It is the employment of a professional agent to perform duties of the kind usually undertaken by members of his profession which gives rise to an implied promise to pay him reasonable remuneration."

Therefore if one engages an architect to undertake planning work of a kind normally undertaken by members of the profession a *quantum meruit* will lie for reasonable remuneration.[99] Similarly, in *Chieb v. Carter*[100] the plaintiff had been appointed sole agent by the defendant to arrange the shipment of cattle from Ireland to Egypt, the plaintiff being required to liaise with the Egyptian authorities for an agreed commission. The sale did not proceed at the time anticipated, but the defendants later independently arranged for shipment without the assistance of the plaintiff, nevertheless building upon the work that the plaintiff had done as sole agent. The Supreme Court upheld the decision of the High Court, finding that the plaintiff's work and expenditure subsequently utilised by the defendants entitled him to payment *quantum meruit*.

When the claim is brought in quasi-contract the case often proceeds on the assumption that no valid contract subsists. For example, the contract may have been discharged by frustration and the plaintiff, who has nevertheless afterwards conferred a valuable benefit upon the defendant, may seek to recover the value of the benefit actually conferred, which may or may not be higher than any price fixed by the contract which has been discharged by operation of law: see *Davis Contractors v. Fareham UDC*.[101] However, the fact that the performance is rendered more expensive by virtue of circumstance or additional costs incurred is not generally sufficient to ground a *quantum meruit*, for the

---

[97] [1957] I.R. 84.
[98] (1966) 101 I.L.T.R. 25.
[99] *Devaney v. Reidy*, unreported, High Court, May 10, 1974; *McCarthy v. VHI*, unreported, High Court, July 24, 1984.
[100] Unreported, Supreme Court, June 3, 1987.
[101] [1956] A.C. 696.

courts are reluctant to allow contracting parties to seek to pick and choose which obligations they will observe and those for which they will seek relief via *quantum meruit*. For this reason, in *Travers Construction Ltd. v. Lismore Homes Ltd.*[102] Gannon J. held that, where a contract had been voluntarily terminated by the agreement of both parties, one party could not subsequently seek a *quantum meruit* remedy, for the rights of the parties had to be governed by their agreement.

It may also be possible to bring *quantum meruit* on the basis of a contract that has been wrongfully discharged by the defendant. The old Irish case of *Lawlor v. Alton*[103] indicates that where the plaintiff is wrongfully deprived of his employment but work has been carried out a remedy in damages may also be available.[104]

In contrast, where the contract is void there may be no alternative but to sue in quasi-contract. The principle stated in the leading English case of *Craven-Ellis v. Canons Ltd.*[105] is that recovery turns upon a rule of law imposed by virtue of the work done rather than an inference of fact arising from acceptance of services or goods. This case and the reasoning therein were expressly accepted by Judge O'Briain in *O'Connor v. Listowel UDC.*[106] The plaintiff had been appointed engineer and town surveyor by the defendant council but the appointment was invalid. The plaintiff, before the invalidity came to light, had rendered services for six months. It was held that the plaintiff was not entitled to recover in contract, for the transaction was invalid, but that he was entitled to a reasonable remuneration for such services requested and accepted by the defendants.

The law will not, however, impose the obligation to pay reasonable remuneration to the plaintiff when the plaintiff fails to complete an entire contract. In *Creagh v. Sheady*[107] a labourer left his employment before the agreed period of employment – it was an annual hiring – had run. He was held not entitled at common law to bring *quantum meruit*. Nor is a claim sustainable when the plaintiff has committed a civil wrong: *Beresford v. Kennedy*.[108] Where the contract is unenforceable, *e.g.* there is a failure to satisfy the writing requirements of the Statute of Frauds (Ireland) 1695, it is well established that an action in *quantum meruit* can be brought to recover the value of benefits conferred upon the defendant on the foot of the unenforceable contract.[109]

When negotiations which are intended to produce a contract are in train it is by no means unusual to find that the parties undertake preparatory work, or indeed commence to perform the contract, in the optimistic belief that the negotiations will be successful. If the negotiations break down it is clear that any benefits conferred by the plaintiff upon the defendant can be compensated for through *quantum meruit*. In *British Steel Corporation v. Cleveland Bridge*

---

102  Unreported, High Court, March 9, 1990.
103  (1873) I.R. 8 C.L. 160.
104  *De Barnardy v. Harding* (1853) 3 Exch. 822; *Brown v. Wood* (1854) 6 Ir.Jur. 221.
105  [1936] 2 K.B. 403.
106  [1957] Ir.Jur.R. 43.
107  [1955–56] Ir.Jur.R. 86; contrast *Brown v. Wood* (1854) 6 Ir.Jur. 221.
108  (1887) 21 I.L.T.R. 17.
109  *Deglman v. Guarantee Trust* [1954] 3 D.L.R. 785.

*& Engineering Co.*[110] the plaintiff delivered a quantity of steel nodes to the defendants, to be used in building a bridge. The steel was ordered on the foot of a "letter of intent" which indicated that while negotiations were still in progress the defendants would like performance to commence pending preparation and issue of a formal sub-contract. Both sides refused to accede to the other's terms *vis-à-vis* delivery and quality of the goods. Robert Goff J. held that there was no contract for there was a failure to agree on essential terms but, notwithstanding this: "the law simply imposes an obligation on the party who made the request to pay a reasonable sum for such work as has been done pursuant to that request, such an obligation sounding in quasi-contract, or as we now say, in restitution."

It is also established that a *quantum meruit* may entitle the plaintiff to recover for preparatory work so requested even if the defendant receives no benefit (unlike *British Steel* when some of the materials were actually delivered). The Irish case of *Folens & Co. v. Minister for Education*[111] provides an excellent illustration. The plaintiff entered into negotiations with the Department of Education with a view to publishing a children's encyclopedia in Irish for the Department. While negotiations progressed the plaintiff undertook preparatory work on the publication with the approval of the Department. The Department eventually decided not to proceed with the publication. The company sought to recover expenses incurred. While McWilliam J. found it impossible to hold that a concluded contract had resulted from the negotiations, relying on the leading English case of *Brewer Street Investments Ltd. v. Barclay's Woollen Co.*,[112] McWilliam J. found for the plaintiff company in quasi-contract:

> "I have no doubt that had the Department said: 'we want you to put this work in hand but we are only going to pay for it provided we eventually agree upon the terms of a contract between us,' the plaintiff would not have done the work at its own risk as to cost. On this basis, I am of opinion that the plaintiff is entitled to be paid for all the work which had been done with the approval or at the direction of the Department."[113]

Similarly, in *Premier Dairies v. Jameson*,[114] the *Brewer St.* case was again relied upon by McWilliam J. when he awarded quasi-contractual relief to the plaintiff when it became apparent that both parties to a contract mistakenly believed that a binding and enforceable contract had been concluded. It appears from the *Folens* decision that the court is not confined to assessing the costs incurred by the plaintiff alone; McWilliam J. also awarded the plaintiff company compensation for an element of lost profits. It is submitted that this was speculative on the facts before the court and to this extent the decision may be unsound.

---

[110] [1984] 1 All E.R. 504.
[111] [1984] I.L.R.M. 265.
[112] [1953] 3 W.L.R. 869.
[113] [1984] I.L.R.M. 265 at 276.
[114] Unreported, High Court, March 1, 1983.

# Index